Suggestions for Reading to a Group of Young Children (Figure 10.7), p. 320

Suggestions for Asking Open Questions and Making Statements That Build Inquiry (Figure 10.8), p. 322

Ways to Teach Math to Young Children, p. 324

Guidelines and Steps for Creating a Written Activity Plan, pp. 344–350

Guidelines and Steps in Planning an Integrated Study, pp. 350–363

Guidelines for Identifying Children with Special Needs, p. 371

Suggestions for Including a Child with Special Needs (Table 12.1), p. 374

Strategies for Working with Children with Special Needs

with Orthopedic Impairments, p. 378

with Vision Impairments, p. 379

with Hearing Impairments, p. 380

with Communication Disorders, pp. 380–381

with Cognitive Delays, pp. 381–382

with Learning Disabilities, p. 382

with ADHD, p. 383

with Emotional or Behavioral Disorders, p. 384

with Autism, p. 385

Strategies for Reporting Suspected Child Abuse, pp. 385–386

Understanding Warning Signs of Child Abuse or Neglect (Table 12.2), p. 386

Strategies for Working with Families of Children with Special Needs, p. 388

Awareness of Many Aspects of Cultural Differences, p. 399

Strategies for Making Families Feel Welcome, pp. 403–404

Strategies for Addressing Families' Questions and Concerns, pp. 407–409

Guidelines for Conducting Family Conferences, pp. 409–410

Strategies for Involving Families in Programs and Schools, pp. 410–413

Steps for Addressing an Ethical Dilemma, p. 423

Questions to Ask in Planning Your Career, p. 425

Strategies for Becoming a Professional, pp. 428–432

Sample Observation Forms

Example of a Running Record (Figure 5.3), p. 141

Examples of Anecdotal Records, p. 142

Anecdotal Record Form (Figure 5.4), p. 144

Example of a Time Sample (Figure 5.5), p. 146

Example of an Event Sample (Figure 5.6), p. 147

Example of a Checklist (Figure 5.7), p. 147

Example of a Rating Scale (Figure 5.8), p. 148

Social-Cognitive Play Scale (Figure 6.3), p. 183

Sociodramatic Play Checklist (Figure 6.4), p. 184

Environment Checklists (Appendix B)

Safety Checklist, pp. 456–458

Health Checklist, pp. 459–460

Infant-Toddler Learning Environment Checklist, pp. 461–468

Preschool/Primary Learning Environment Checklist, pp. 469–470

Classroom Areas/Centers Checklist, pp. 470–476

Curriculum Planning Tools and Examples

Basic Planned Curriculum Activities and Ways to Present Them (Figure 11.1), p. 342

Activity Plan Outlines (Figures 11.2 & 11.6), pp. 344, 351

Sample Activity Plan with Anecdotal Records (Figure 11.5), pp. 348–349

Questions to Ask About Selecting a Topic for Integrating Curriculum (Figure 11.7), p. 354

Outline for an Integrated Thematic Study (Figure 11.10), p. 359

Example of a Graphic Representation of Learning Activities in a Unit (Bird Sunburst, Figure 11.13), p. 362

Appendix A: The NAEYC Code of Ethical Conduct

Who Am I in the Lives of Children?

Who Am I in the Lives of Children?

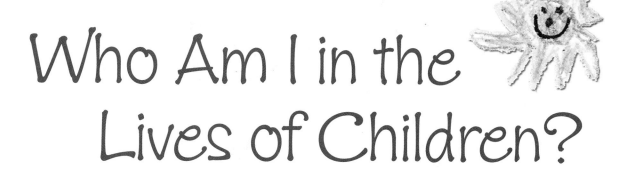

An Introduction to Early Childhood Education

Seventh Edition

Stephanie Feeney
University of Hawaii at Manoa

Doris Christensen
Honolulu Community College

Eva Moravcik
Honolulu Community College

PEARSON

Merrill
Prentice Hall

Upper Saddle River, New Jersey
Columbus, Ohio

Library of Congress Cataloging-in-Publication Data

Feeney, Stephanie.
   Who am I in the lives of children? : an introduction to early childhood education / Stephanie Feeney,
Doris Christensen, Eva Moravcik—7th ed.
      p. cm.
   Includes bibliographical references and index.
   ISBN 0-13-170996-8 (hardback : alk. paper)
   1. Education, Preschool—United States. 2. Preschool teaching—United States. 3. Child development—United States.
   4. Early childhood education—United States. I. Christensen, Doris. II. Moravcik, Eva. III. Title.

LB1140.23.F44 2006
372.21'0973—dc22

2004027734

Vice President and Executive Publisher: Jeffery W. Johnston
Publisher: Kevin M. Davis
Acquisitions Editor: Julie Peters
Editorial Assistant: Michelle Girgis
Production Editor: Linda Hillis Bayma
Production Coordination: Thistle Hill Publishing Services, LLC
Design Coordinator: Diane C. Lorenzo
Text Designer: Kristina Holmes
Photo Coordinator: Lori Whitley
Cover Designer: Kristina Holmes
Cover Image: Jeff Reese
Production Manager: Laura Messerly
Director of Marketing: Ann Castel Davis
Marketing Manager: Amy Judd
Marketing Coordinator: Brian Mounts

This book was set in Garamond by Carlisle Communications, Ltd. It was printed and bound by Courier Kendallville, Inc.
The cover was printed by The Lehigh Press, Inc.

Photo Credits: Jeff Reese, pp. ii, vi, x, 2, 5, 7, 13, 15, 23, 28, 31, 32, 33, 35, 36, 39, 44, 68, 71, 77, 86, 90, 93, 97, 101, 106, 113, 117, 126, 130, 135, 138, 145, 151, 155, 161, 168, 171, 174, 177, 181, 187, 190, 192, 200, 205, 209, 213, 216, 222, 225, 227, 236, 238, 239, 242, 245, 247, 251, 254, 256, 263, 271, 276, 279, 284, 289, 294, 296, 297, 298, 301, 303, 312, 316, 317, 324, 325, 332, 333, 339, 343, 344, 359, 360, 366, 369, 370, 371, 373, 378, 381, 383, 387, 392, 395, 396, 400, 404, 409, 414, 415, 418, 420, 421, 422, 423, 424, 428, 429, 431, 432; Kindergarten & Children's Aid Association of Hawaii, p. 54; Dennis MacDonald/PhotoEdit, p. 59; Library of Congress, pp. 60, 64; North Wind Picture Archives, p. 61; Provided by the authors, p. 65; Courtesy of the Library of Congress, p. 69; Corbis/Bettmann, p. 72; Hella Hammid, pp. 87, 122; Eva Moravcik, pp. 363, 364.

Pearson Education Ltd.
Pearson Education Singapore Pte. Ltd.
Pearson Education Canada, Ltd.
Pearson Education—Japan

Pearson Education Australia Pty. Limited
Pearson Education North Asia Ltd.
Pearson Educación de Mexico, S.A. de C.V.
Pearson Education Malaysia Pte. Ltd.

10 9 8 7 6 5 4 3 2
ISBN: 0-13-170996-8

Foreword

As a long time admirer of the authors and their writing, I am delighted to contribute a foreword to the seventh edition of this excellent book.

To those just beginning their journey to become early childhood educators, those reexamining their current role as teachers, and those seeking updated information on trends and developments in the early childhood field, this edition will serve as a valuable resource. However, *Who Am I in the Lives of Children?* is much more than a book to read and then put away on the shelf.

Rather, it is a book that compels interaction. Readers are encouraged to reflect on a series of important questions: how and by whom they have been influenced in their own growth and development; why it is important to understand the relationship between theory and practice, play and learning, care and education; what is involved in becoming a professional early childhood educator; how "big picture" issues of policy and legislation affect teacher compensation and individual classroom quality; what ethical issues they may face and how their core values will influence their actions; and, of course, the most important questions, who they are and who they want to be in the lives of children.

My decision to become a nursery school teacher (my parents thought I wanted to teach people how to grow fruit and vegetables) was influenced by my visit to an exposition in San Diego in the 1930s where for two days I observed three- and four-year-old children through a one-way vision glass. It was the first time I had ever been in a nursery school and I was fascinated with how active and verbal the children were; how engaged they were in play and routine activities; how well they related to one another; how friendly, interested, knowledgeable, supportive, and involved the teachers were.

When I was a beginning teacher, I found it easier to describe who I was as a person than who I was in the lives of children. It wasn't until I had more experience that I could begin to name my various roles—friend, model, educator, facilitator, stage setter, scene shifter, guide, comforter, dispenser of Band-Aids, lap provider, initiator, encourager, protector, catalyst, advocate, stable adult.

Though early childhood education has evolved dramatically in the seventy years since my first job in a parent cooperative nursery school, and change is continually taking place, the following description of a teacher's impact (taken from the cover of a 1970 NEA journal) is as true today as it was then . . . "They put bandages on my hurts—on my heart, on my mind, on my spirit. Those teachers cared about me . . . They gave me wings." The journey toward becoming someone who can give a child wings is continuous, but I believe when you begin knowing who you are in the life of a child, you begin knowing who you are in this journey. Reading and reflecting on what the authors have written has helped me in my own journey.

As early childhood educators, we may have diverse views, teaching styles, and sometimes beliefs and values, but on the whole we are more alike than different. We share a common goal, to create an environment that is safe and rich with opportunity; that nurtures enthusiasm for learning; that meets the fundamental needs for growth and development common to all children.

Kudos to the authors who, with increasing pressure on more direct instruction and emphasis on achievement, hold fast to their belief that a child-centered approach with children actively involved in the learning process is the best way for children to learn. As Rachel Carson wrote, "It is more important to pave the way for children to want to know than to put them on a diet of facts they are not ready to assimilate."

This edition of *Who Am I in the Lives of Children?* continues the work of the authors of making visible and transparent the values and principles that underlie excellent practice and will continue to give guidance and support to those in the life-long process of becoming early childhood educators.

—Docia Zavitkovsky

A Letter to Readers

Dear Reader:

Welcome to the seventh edition of *Who Am I in the Lives of Children?*, an introduction to the field of early childhood education. Our purpose in writing this book is to support you in becoming a professional who can enhance the development of young children in early childhood care and education settings.

It is not our intention for everyone to come to the same conclusions or to work with children in the same way. We feel strongly that in order for you to become a skilled early childhood professional you must develop your own style and philosophy and reflect on your values and actions. It would be impossible to include everything you might need to know in this book. Rather, we have tried to provide you with a lens through which to view the many choices you have to make in designing meaningful and appropriate learning experiences for young children.

ABOUT THE AUTHORS

When we read a book, we like to know about the authors—who they are and why they wrote the book. We want to share that kind of personal information with you. Among us we have filled the roles of preschool teacher, social worker, kindergarten teacher, center director, education coordinator, parent and child center program director, consultant, parent educator, CDA trainer, Head Start regional training officer, and college instructor. We have worked in parent cooperatives, child care centers, preschools, infant-toddler programs, Head Start programs, public schools, government agencies, and college settings. We have been child advocates and board members of our local and national early childhood organizations. Today the three of us are all college instructors in early childhood education. Stephanie teaches at the University of Hawaii at Manoa, and Doris and Eva teach at Honolulu Community College. Eva coordinates a small child development center as part of her responsibilities.

This book grows out of our experiences as children, as adults, as learners, and as teachers. Our early schooling included experiences in child-oriented nursery schools

much like those we describe in this book, as well as in large public schools, a small multinational school, and a one-room country school. Although our childhood experiences were different, our values are similar, and we have many of the same feelings and ideas about education. We have all long held a strong commitment to programs for children that are nurturing and humane and support all aspects of their development.

In 1979, the first edition of *Who Am I in the Lives of Children?* was published when Stephanie was a recently hired assistant professor and Doris and Eva were teaching assistants working with her. We began writing because we wanted an introductory text consistent with our belief that the personal and professional development of early childhood educators are inextricably linked, a text that emphasized the importance of reflection on values and educational choices. At that time our approach was very innovative—today it is more in the mainstream of early childhood teacher education. Because we wanted to speak to our readers in as direct a way as possible, we wrote in an informal and personal voice. Over the years many readers of the text have expressed their appreciation for this style of writing. In this edition we continue to strive to communicate clearly and directly. We also continue to emphasize the development of personal awareness and the ongoing process of reflection on values and choices.

This seventh edition, like the previous six, reflects a process of reading, reflection, and integration of new information and experiences. Eva's daily work with children, family, staff, and college students at Leeward Community College Children's Center continues to provide her with grounding in the reality of life in a program for young children. Doris's work on a grant to develop literacy training for teachers has provided new understanding of current approaches to literacy development. Stephanie has continued to be involved in work on professional ethics and state initiatives related to school readiness. Eva and Stephanie helped to develop the Hawaii Preschool Content Standards and designed and delivered training in using those standards.

We were joined in writing this edition by our friend and colleague, Sherry Nolte. Sherry teaches at Honolulu Community College with Eva and Doris. She brings extensive experience working in programs for military families, low-income children, and infants and toddlers. Sherry revised the chapters on child development, guidance, and caring for children. We are also joined in this edition by another longtime friend and colleague, Robyn Chun. Robyn has taught with us at the University of Hawaii at Manoa, at Honolulu Community College, and at the UH-Manoa Children's Center. Robyn is responsible for the *Instructor's Manual and Test Bank* and Companion Website for this edition. We also wish to express our appreciation to Steve Bobilin for filming and editing the curriculum DVD. We are delighted to have them join us in working on this edition.

ABOUT THE BOOK: A CHILD-CENTERED APPROACH

Since the first edition in 1979 and through five subsequent revisions, we have used *Who Am I in the Lives of Children?* in a variety of programs and in a number of different places. It has been used across the United States and in countries as diverse as Canada, Australia, Japan, Singapore, and China. Each edition has reflected developments in our field, the feedback of our students and colleagues, and our own growth as educators and child and family advocates.

The cornerstone of this book and our work with children is what we refer to as a *child-centered* approach to early childhood education. This approach has its roots in a long tradition of humanistic and progressive education and the unique history and philosophy of early childhood education. Our ideas have been profoundly shaped by educators, psychologists, and philosophers who have advocated child-centered educational practice, including Friedrich Fröebel, Maria Montessori, John Dewey, Lucy Sprague Mitchell, Arnold Gessell, Erik Erikson, Lev Vygotsky, Jean Piaget, Margaret Mahler, Abraham Maslow, Carl Rogers, Sylvia Ashton-Warner, Bruno Bettelheim, John Holt, A. S. Neill,

Barbara Biber, Howard Gardner, James L. Hymes, and Loris Malaguzzi.

Programs that evolve from the child-centered tradition are dedicated to the development of the whole child—physical, social, emotional, and intellectual. They are characterized by a deep respect for the individual and the recognition that individual differences need to be responded to in educational settings. They reflect the understanding that children learn best from direct experience and spontaneous play. Educators in these programs begin with children as they are and try to understand and help them grow in ways that are right for the individual rather than according to a predetermined plan. They look at children in terms of potential to be actualized and in the context of their culture and family.

ABOUT THE SEVENTH EDITION

We continue in this edition to strongly affirm our values and commitment to a respectful, culturally sensitive, child-centered, and family-friendly approach to working with young children. We strive to make the values and guiding principles of early education visible and affirm our commitment to them. Over the years it has become clear to us that this approach is broader than just a way of viewing early childhood education—it is an approach to working with people of all ages, to learning at all stages, and to life.

 We subscribe to a constructivist approach to early childhood learning experiences and have added more specific examples of how constructivism is translated into classroom practice. An example of an integrated curriculum in a constructivist early childhood program is featured in Chapter 11, "Curriculum Planning," along with a 23-minute DVD, "Birds: An Integrated Curriculum," showing this approach in action.

Since we last revised this book, state and national emphases on educational accountability and assessment have had a significant impact on the field of early care and childhood education. At this time they are of great concern to early childhood educators. In this edition we have tried to put these issues into perspective and explore some of the causes for these concerns.

Another change in the field since we wrote the last edition is increased attention to different kinds of educational standards: standards that relate to programs for children and standards for the training of teachers. Both types of standards are reflected in this edition. Curriculum content standards are described in Chapter 10, "The Curriculum." The relevant *NAEYC Standards for Early Childhood Professional Preparation* are included as a new Learning Outcomes section at the end of each chapter.

In Chapters 4 through 13, which concern the day-to-day work of being an early childhood educator, we have included more stories and given more examples of tools to use in your practice. We hope that they will be helpful to you as you begin your work as a teacher.

Professionalism and advocacy have grown more important for teachers of young children since we last revised this book. Chapter 14, "Making a Commitment to Being an Early Childhood Professional," is a much expanded chapter that will help you to think about these important topics.

OUR VISION FOR YOU

Many approaches can be taken in teaching others to work with young children. In this book we want to help you discover who you are as an educator and what you value for children instead of focusing exclusively on content and skills. Like creating a clay figure in which each part is drawn out of a central core, we strive to help your work to be an integral part of who you are. Without this foundation, it is difficult to know how to respond to a group of real children. A clay figurine constructed by sticking head, arms, and legs onto a ball often falls apart when exposed to the heat of the fire. Similarly, a teacher whose education consists of bits and pieces may fall apart when faced with the reality of the classroom.

You will play an important part in the lives of the children and families with whom you will work. We hope that *Who Am I in the Lives of Children?* will help you to become a competent, nurturing, and reflective early childhood educator and an active and committed advocate for young children.

S. F., D. C., and E. M.
Honolulu, Hawaii

Acknowledgments

We have been writing and revising *Who Am I in the Lives of Children?* since 1977, and during that period of time have been influenced and supported by many colleagues, friends, and students. Our list of individuals to acknowledge continues to grow, as does our gratitude.

We offer thanks to educators who have contributed to our thinking and practice since we launched this book: Georgia Acevedo, Steve Bobilin, Barbara Bowman, Elizabeth Brady, Sue Bredekamp, Liz Chun, Richard Cohen, Harriet Cuffaro, Carol Darcy, Jane Dickson-Iijima, Barbara Essman, Richard Feldman, Marjorie Fields, Nancy Freeman, Jim Greenman, Randy Hitz, Lilian Katz, Kenneth Kipnis, Elizabeth Jones, Gwen Morgan, Robert Peters, Rebecca Severeide, Karen VanderVen, and Docia Zavitkovsky. We remember with fondness Elizabeth Gilkeson and we honor the memory of Jean Fargo for helping us to realize that values must lie at the heart of the work of the early childhood educator.

We wish to thank the following people for their assistance with this and previous editions: Steve Bobilin, Linda Buck, Robyn Chun, Thomas Duke, Jonathan Gillentine, Diana Ginsburg, Paul Haygood, Christine Jackson, Linda McCormick, Sherry Nolte, Julie Powers, Larry Prochner, Jackie Rabang, Alan Reese, Kathleen Reinhardt, Cyndi Uyehara, and Teresa Vast.

Our students in the early childhood/elementary education program at the University of Hawaii at Manoa and the early childhood program at Honolulu Community College have given us insight, asked thought-provoking questions, and provided us with the viewpoint of the future educator.

Like you, we learn by doing. Our attitudes, values, knowledge, and skills have been developed as we have worked with the children, families, and staff at programs in Hawaii: the Leeward Community College Children's Center, University of Hawaii at Manoa Children's Center, the Early School, and St. Timothy's Children's Center.

We would also like to thank the reviewers of this edition for their insights and comments: Rosemarie Allen, Front Range Community College; Alicia Biggs, Community College of Denver; Judie Ericksau, Snow College; Nora Rucker, Oakton Community College; and Elsa Weber, Purdue University-Calumet.

The photographs that bring this book to life are the work of two talented photographers: the late Hella Hammid, whose work we have used since the second edition of the text, and Jeffrey Reese, who took new photographs for this and the previous two editions. Photos for this and previous editions were taken at John Adams Child Development Center, Beverly Hills Montessori School, the Clay Street Center, St. Thomas Parish Preschool, the University of Hawaii at Manoa Children's Center, Leeward Community College Children's Center, Keiki Hauoli Children's Center, Hanahauoli School, Promise Children's Center, Kaneohe Marine Base Child Development Center, and Rainbow School at Prince Kuhio Federal Building in Hawaii. The artwork that adds such vibrancy to this edition is the work of the children of Leeward Community College Children's Center. We appreciate the cooperation of the children, staff, and families of these schools.

Special thanks to our editor Julie Peters for all of her support and encouragement during this revision.

No book is written without affecting the lives of the friends and families of the authors. We especially want to thank our husbands, Don Mickey, Gregory Field, and Jeffrey Reese, who have encouraged us and supported our efforts with patience and good humor.

Using This Book

The way in which you will use this book will depend on where you are in your career, the course for which it is adopted, and your instructor or trainer. It is designed so that it can provide you with an introduction to early childhood education and can be read from beginning to end. Your instructor may decide, however, to teach the content in a different order. In many colleges it is used for more than one class: a foundation of early childhood education class and a class on examining early childhood practice. If you are an experienced practitioner, you may have selected it to provide an update and review.

THE CHAPTERS

Each chapter in this book is constructed to help you to gain awareness, acquire knowledge, or develop skills in an essential area of early childhood education. We envision the chapters as building blocks, with earlier chapters providing the foundation for those that follow.

The first chapters introduce some of the distinctive traditions and features of the field. Chapter 1, "The Teacher," explores the nature of the teacher of young children both as a person and as a professional. Chapter 2, "The Field of Early Childhood Education and Care," presents an overview of the programs and practices that you may encounter as you begin your career. Chapter 3, "History and Educational Models," describes the origins of early childhood education and care and some educational approaches and models that are influential today. Together these chapters provide the context for working with young children.

The next three chapters are written to help you understand and observe children. They focus on child development and play because understanding children is of central importance in early childhood education. These chapters form an essential foundation for practice. Chapter 4, "Understanding Development," provides an overview of the research and theory that are used to inform practice in early childhood education and care. Chapter 5, "Observation and Assessment," acquaints you with basic skills that you will use to learn about individuals and groups of children, assessment of how to support children's growth and development, and documenting children's learning to share with others.

Chapter 6, "Play," helps you understand this critical aspect of children's development and discusses how you can support productive play.

The knowledge and skills that you must have to create a good program for young children are the focus of the next chapters. They are based on the foundation laid down in the previous chapters. Chapter 7, "Caring for Children," explores the importance of meeting children's basic physical and psychological needs and the approaches to doing this. Chapter 8, "The Learning Environment," looks at how you can structure the use of space and provide the equipment and material necessary to support children's development. Chapter 9, "Guiding Young Children," helps you understand how to develop positive relationships with children to support their development in a group setting. Chapter 10, "The Curriculum," addresses aspects of the curriculum in early childhood programs in four broad areas of development: physical, creative, communication, and inquiry.

Chapter 11, "Curriculum Planning," gives a framework for thinking about and designing meaningful and appropriate learning experiences for young children. We have included comments in the margins of Chapter 11's pages to support your viewing of the DVD, "Birds: An Integrated Curriculum." A DVD accompanies every copy of this book.

Chapter 12, "Inclusion of Children with Special Needs," provides information and insight to help you to identify and work with those children whose needs are somewhat different and more complex than those of the mainstream. In it we give you a foundation for thinking about working with children with special needs.

Chapter 13, "Working with Families," provides an overview of your responsibilities to families and the importance of developing good relationships with them. It includes ideas for ways to involve families in your program.

In Chapter 14, "Making a Commitment to Being an Early Childhood Professional," we talk about the things you will do as you make the transition from your role as a student to that of professional. We help you reflect on the commitments you must make personally and professionally as you move into the next stage of your career. We also provide you with some resources you can use.

REFLECTION BOXES

In each chapter there are boxed reflections with questions for you to think about, write about, and talk about. We hope that you will engage with them as part of your learning process. Many students find that writing about these topics is a good way to focus their learning and clarify their thinking.

FEATURES TO SUPPORT YOUR LEARNING

Three features are included at the end of each chapter:

- *Learning Outcomes:* We had a purpose and specific learning outcomes in mind as we wrote each chapter of this book. These learning outcomes relate to the NAEYC standards for professional preparation.

- *To Learn More:* This section includes suggestions for projects to help you to learn more about the chapter's content.

- *For Your Portfolio:* This section suggests items that you might wish to put in a professional portfolio. Today, professionals in many fields create portfolios in which they document for employers and themselves their qualifications, skills, experiences, and unique qualities. Portfolios are "living documents" that will change as you grow, learn, and have new experiences. (Guidelines for starting a portfolio can be found in Chapter 1, pp. 20–21.)

In addition, in the back of the book is a bibliography that lists the books we have used and referred to in each chapter. These references may be helpful if you want to read more about a specific topic. We hope you will have the opportunity to read some of them as you develop into a committed early childhood educator.

THE COMPANION WEBSITE

The Companion Website for *Who Am I in the Lives of Children?* is designed to assist you as you reflect on and apply the content of the book. It includes additional ideas for your professional development, including links to related websites where you can learn more, and reflection questions that you can complete online to submit to your instructor. It also includes practice observation exercises and self-test questions (with feedback) for each chapter to help you to assess what you know and what you may need to work on in order to gain mastery. You will find the site at **www.prenhall.com/feeney**.

Discover the Companion Website Accompanying This Book

THE PRENTICE HALL COMPANION WEBSITE: A VIRTUAL LEARNING ENVIRONMENT

Technology is a constantly growing and changing aspect of our field that is creating a need for content and resources. To address this emerging need, Prentice Hall has developed an online learning environment for students and professors alike—Companion Websites—to support our textbooks.

In creating a Companion Website, our goal is to build on and enhance what the textbook already offers. For this reason, the content for each user-friendly website is organized by chapter and provides the professor and student with a variety of meaningful resources.

For the Professor—

Every Companion Website integrates **Syllabus Manager**™, an online syllabus creation and management utility.

- **Syllabus Manager**™ provides you, the instructor, with an easy, step-by-step process to create and revise syllabi, with direct links into Companion Website and other online content without having to learn HTML.
- Students may logon to your syllabus during any study session. All they need to know is the web address for the Companion Website and the password you've assigned to your syllabus.
- After you have created a syllabus using **Syllabus Manager**™, students may enter the syllabus for their course section from any point in the Companion Website.
- Clicking on a date, the student is shown the list of activities for the assignment. The activities for each assignment are linked directly to actual content, saving time for students.
- Adding assignments consists of clicking on the desired due date, then filling in the details of the assignment—name of the assignment, instructions, and whether it is a one-time or repeating assignment.
- In addition, links to other activities can be created easily. If the activity is online, a URL can be entered in the space provided, and it will be linked automatically in the final syllabus.
- Your completed syllabus is hosted on our servers, allowing convenient updates from any computer on the Internet. Changes you make to your syllabus are immediately available to your students at their next logon.

For the Student—

Companion Website features for students include:

- **Opening Thought**—Summarizes key ideas from the chapter.
- **Interactive Self-Quizzes**—in Multiple-Choice, True/False, and Essay formats; complete with hints and automatic grading that provide immediate feedback for students.

After students submit their answers for the interactive self-quizzes, the Companion Website **Results Reporter** computes a percentage grade, provides a graphic representation of how many questions were answered correctly and incorrectly, and gives a question-by-question analysis of the quiz. Students are given the option to send their quiz to up to four email addresses (professor, teaching assistant, study partner, etc.).

- **Web Destinations**—Provide links to Internet sites that relate to chapter content.
- **Message Board**—Virtual bulletin board to post or respond to questions or comments from a national audience.

To take advantage of the many available resources, please visit the *Who Am I in the Lives of Children?*, Seventh Edition, Companion Website at

www.prenhall.com/feeney

Educator Learning Center: An Invaluable Online Resource

Merrill Education and the Association for Supervision and Curriculum Development (ASCD) invite you to take advantage of a new online resource, one that provides access to the top research and proven strategies associated with ASCD and Merrill—the Educator Learning Center. At www.educatorlearningcenter.com you will find resources that will enhance your students' understanding of course topics and of current educational issues, in addition to being invaluable for further research.

HOW THE EDUCATOR LEARNING CENTER WILL HELP YOUR STUDENTS BECOME BETTER TEACHERS

With the combined resources of Merrill Education and ASCD, you and your students will find a wealth of tools and materials to better prepare them for the classroom.

Research

- More than 600 articles from the ASCD journal *Educational Leadership* discuss everyday issues faced by practicing teachers.
- A direct link on the site to Research Navigator™ gives students access to many of the leading education journals, as well as extensive content detailing the research process.
- Excerpts from Merrill Education texts give your students insights on important topics of instructional methods, diverse populations, assessment, classroom management, technology, and refining classroom practice.

Classroom Practice

- Hundreds of lesson plans and teaching strategies are categorized by content area and age range.
- Case studies and classroom video footage provide virtual field experience for student reflection.
- Computer simulations and other electronic tools keep your students abreast of today's classrooms and current technologies.

LOOK INTO THE VALUE OF EDUCATOR LEARNING CENTER YOURSELF

A four-month subscription to Educator Learning Center is $25 but is **FREE** when packaged with any Merrill Education text. In order for your students to have access to this site, you must use this special value-pack ISBN number **WHEN** placing your textbook order with the bookstore: 0-13-171228-4. Your students will then receive a copy of the text packaged with a free ASCD pincode. To preview the value of this website to you and your students, please go to www.educatorlearningcenter.com and click on "Demo."

Brief Contents

Chapter 1   The Teacher   2

Chapter 2   The Field of Early Childhood Education and Care   28

Chapter 3   History and Educational Models   54

Chapter 4   Understanding Development   90

Chapter 5   Observation and Assessment   130

Chapter 6   Play   166

Chapter 7   Caring for Children   190

Chapter 8   The Learning Environment   222

Chapter 9   Guiding Young Children   254

Chapter 10   The Curriculum   294

Chapter 11   Curriculum Planning   332

Chapter 12   Inclusion of Children with Special Needs   366

Chapter 13   Working with Families   392

Chapter 14   Making a Commitment to Being an Early Childhood Professional   418

Contents

Chapter 1 The Teacher   2

The Work We Do   3
 Many Tasks and Many People   4
  Working with Children   5
  Working with Families   5
  Being Part of a Team   6
The Teacher as a Person   6
 What Personal Qualities Make a Good Early
   Childhood Teacher?   7
 Personal Characteristics   8
  Temperament   8
  Multiple Intelligences   9
 Personal Values and Morality   10
 Attitudes Toward Diversity   11
 Self-Knowledge and the Ability to Reflect   12
The Teacher as a Professional   14
 The Knowledge Base and Training   15
  The Training and Certification You Will
    Need   15
 Professional Commitment and Behavior   15
  Legal Responsibilities   16
 Professional Values and Ethics   17
  Professional Values   19
  Professional Ethics   22
Final Thoughts   24
Learning Outcomes   25
To Learn More   25

Chapter 2 The Field of Early Childhood
            Education and Care   28

Programs for Children from Birth to
  Age 5   30
 Center-Based Programs   31
  Full-Day Programs   31
  Part-Day Programs   31
  Sponsorship and Funding   32
  The Trilemma   32
 Home-Based Programs   34
 Programs for Low-Income Children   35
  Head Start   35
  Early Head Start   36

  Research   36
  Head Start Legislation   37
 Programs for Children from Birth to Age 5
   with Special Needs   38
 Parent Education Programs   39
 Regulation of Programs for Children from
   Birth to Age 5   39
  Licensing   40
  Accreditation   40
  Teacher Education   41
Programs for Children Ages 5 Through 8   41
 The Purpose of Kindergarten   42
 The K-3 Curriculum   43
 Programs for Children Ages 5 Through 8 with
   Special Needs   43
 Home Schooling   43
 School-Age Child Care   44
 Teacher Education and Licensing   44
Issues Facing the Field Today   45
 Whose Responsibility Is Early Education and
   Care?   45
 The Movement Toward Greater
   Professionalism   47
 Standards, Assessment, and Accountability   47
  Standards   48
  The No Child Left Behind Act   48
  Readiness   49
Final Thoughts   51
Learning Outcomes   52
To Learn More   52
For Your Portfolio   53

Chapter 3 History and Educational
            Models   54

The Humanistic Tradition   55
The Origins of Early Childhood
  Education   56
 Ancient Greece and Rome   56
 The Medieval Era, the Renaissance, and the
   Reformation   57
 The Enlightenment   60
 The 19th Century   61

Educational Movements That Shaped the Field of Early Childhood Education   62
  Fröebel and the Kindergarten   62
    Kindergarten Education   64
    The Long-Term Impact of the Kindergarten   64
  The Nursery School   66
    Nursery School Education   66
    The Long-Term Impact of the Nursery School   66
    A Contemporary Example: The High/Scope Model   68
  Progressive Education   69
    Progressive Education Programs   70
    The Long-Term Impact of Progressive Education   70
    A Contemporary Example: The Developmental-Interaction Approach   71

Three European Approaches   74
  Waldorf Education   75
    Waldorf Education Programs   75
    The Long-Term Impact of Waldorf Education   76
  The Montessori Method   76
    Montessori Programs   77
    The Long-Term Impact of Montessori's Approach   78
  Reggio Emilia   78
    Reggio Emilia Programs   79
    The Long-Term Impact of Reggio Emilia   80
  Reflection on These Approaches   81

Child Care in the United States   81
  The Origins of Child Care in the United States   83
  Child Care in Times of National Emergency   84
  Child Care After World War II   85

Government Involvement in the Care and Education of Young Children   86
  Programs for Low-Income Children   86
  Programs for Children with Disabilities   87

Final Thoughts   88

Learning Outcomes   89

To Learn More   89

For Your Portfolio   89

Chapter 4 Understanding Development   90

The Study of Child Development   91
Principles of Child Development   92
The Child Develops as a Whole   92
Development Follows Predictable Patterns   93
Rates of Development Vary   93
Development Is Influenced by Maturation and Experience   94
Development Proceeds from Top Down and from Center Outward   95
Culture Affects Development   95

Understanding Child Development Informs Practice   96

Foundations of Development   96
  The Biological Basis of Development   97
    Inherited Characteristics   97
    Basic Needs   98
    Temperament   99
  The Impact of Environment   101
    The Critical Nature of Nurturing Relationships   101
    The Importance of Early Experiences   102
  Brain Development   103
    What Do We Know About Brain Development?   104
    Understanding of Brain Development Informs Practice   104

Development of the Whole Child: Theory into Practice   105
  Periods of Development   105
  Domains of Development   105
    Physical Development   106
    Cognitive Development   109
    Social Development   120
    Emotional Development   125

Final Thoughts   128

Learning Outcomes   128

To Learn More   129

For Your Portfolio   129

Chapter 5 Observation and Assessment   130

What Is Assessment?   132
  Purposes for Assessment   132

Observation   133
  The Observation Process   135
    Observing   135
    Recording   137
    Interpreting   137
  Narrative Observation Techniques   138
    Running Records   140

Anecdotal Records   141
Interpreting Narrative Observations   143
Using Narrative Observations   144
Structured Observation Techniques   145
Time Samples   145
Event Samples   146
Checklists and Rating Scales   147
Interviews   148
Electronic Observation Techniques   148
Photographs   149
Video and Audio Recording   149
Selecting an Observation Technique   150

Authentic Assessment   150
Portfolios   151
What Is a Portfolio?   151
Why Use Portfolios?   151
What Belongs in a Portfolio?   151
Organizing and Creating a Portfolio   152
Using Portfolios   153
Observation Systems   154
The High/Scope Child Observation Record   155
The Work Sampling System   155
The Creative Curriculum Developmental Continuum   155
The Ounce Scale   156

Formal Assessment   156
Kinds of Assessment Instruments   156
Screening Instruments   156
Developmental Assessments   157
Diagnostic Tests   158
Readiness and Achievement Tests   158
Issues in Standardized Testing   159

What Teachers Need to Know About Assessment   160
Confidentiality   161

Sharing Information with Families   162

Final Thoughts   162

Learning Outcomes   163

To Learn More   163

For your Portfolio   164

Chapter 6 Play   166

The Nature of Play   167
Characteristics of Play   168
Purpose of Play   169
Contemporary Theories of Play   170
Stages of Play   170
Parten: Stages of Social Play   171
Piaget and Smilansky: Cognitive Stages of Play   171
Understanding the Stages of Play   173
Dramatic and Sociodramatic Play   174

Diversity and Play   174
Culture, Social Class, and Play   175
Gender and Play   176

The Value of Play   176
The Value of Play in Physical Development   177
The Value of Play in Emotional Development   178
The Value of Play in Social Development   178
The Value of Play in Cognitive Development   179
The Value of Play in Integrating Development   179
The Value of Play in Integrating Curriculum   180

Supporting Development Through Play   180
Supportive Attitudes   180
Supportive Roles   181
Stage Manager   181
Observer   182
Protector and Mediator   184
Participant   185
Tutor   186

The Special Role of Outdoor Play   186
Violence and Children's Play   187
Gender-Stereotyped Play   188

Final Thoughts   188

Learning Outcomes   189

To Learn More   189

For Your Portfolio   189

Chapter 7 Caring for Children   190

Physical Safety and Health   191
A Safe Place   191
What Is Safe?   192
Developmental Differences and Safety   192
A Safe Environment   193
Equipment and Materials Safety   194
Vehicle and Trip Safety   195
What You Do to Ensure Safety   195
Helping Children Learn to Be Safe   196
Abuse Prevention   198
A Healthy Place   198
Preventing Communicable Illnesses and Conditions   199

Keeping the Environment Healthy 200
Helping Children Learn to Be Healthy 202

Psychological Safety and Health 204

Good Beginnings 205
The Transition from Home 205
First Days and First Weeks 206
A Good Day 208
Children's Needs and Developmental
Stage 208
The Physical Setting 209
The Program Day 210
Staff-Child Ratio and Group Size 211
The Time of Year 211
Classroom Routines 212
Arrival 212
Diapering, Toileting, and Toilet Learning 212
Mealtimes and Snacks 214
Cleanup 215
Rest Time 215
Departure 216
Good Endings 216
Changing Classes 216
When You Leave 217
The Next School 217

Final Thoughts 218

Learning Outcomes 219

To Learn More 219

For Your Portfolio 220

Chapter 8 The Learning Environment 222

Creating a Learning Environment 224

Self-Contained and Open-Design
Classrooms 225
Advantages and Disadvantages of Self-Contained
and Open-Design Classrooms 226

Principles for Designing Learning Environments 226

Arrange the Environment for Safety and
Health 226
Organize the Environment in Areas 227
Design Principles for Indoor Areas 227
Design Principles for Outdoor Areas 228
Design Principles for Storage 229
Design Principles for Equipment and
Materials 233
Pay Attention to Aesthetics 235
Reflect the Children 236
Avoid Being Cute 237

Creating Interest Areas 237

Blocks 237
A Unit Block Area 238
A Hollow Block Area 238
Dramatic Play Area 239
An Area for Toys and Games 240
Sensory Play 241
Art Area 242
Woodworking 243
Library 244
Writing Area 245
Computer Area 245
Discovery Centers 246
Science 247
Math 247
Social Studies 247
Outdoor Zones 247
Transition 247
Manipulative-Creative 248
Active Play 248
Natural Elements 248
Social-Dramatic 248

Special Considerations 248

Environments for Infants and Toddlers 248
Including Children with Special Needs
in Your Environment 249
Including Adults in Your Environment 250
Television and Video 250

Making the Environment Work 250

Final Thoughts 252

Learning Outcomes 252

To Learn More 253

For Your Portfolio 253

Chapter 9 Guiding Young Children 254

What Is Child Guidance? 255

Guidance Is About Relationships 256
Guidance Honors Differences 256
Guidance Honors Differences in Families 256
Guidance Honors Differences in Children 258
Guidance Is Different from Punishment 259
Goals for Guidance 259
Building Inner Control 260
Supporting a Sense of Self 260
Enhancing Self-Concept and Self-Esteem 262

Relationships Are Built Through Communication 263

Communication Strategies 263
Interactions with Children 264

Effective Listening   264
Responding Clearly and Authentically   266
Encouragement Versus Praise   267
Strategies to Enhance Communication with Infants and Toddlers   269
Cultural Differences in Communication   269
Barriers to Relationships   269
Avoiding Communication Barriers   270

Guiding Groups   271
Trust, Attachment, and Relationships   271
I-Messages   271
Dealing with Conflict   272
A Process for Peaceful Conflict Resolution   274
Learning to Treat Others with Respect and Fairness   274
Making the Environment and Schedule a Partner in Guidance   275
Managing the Classroom   275
Becoming Comfortable with Authority   276
Creating Appropriate Expectations   277
Problems with Rules   278
Redirection Instead of Distraction   279
Anticipating and Preventing Problems   279
Transitions   281
Managing Large Group Times   282

Dealing with Difficult Behaviors   284
Finding Your "Button Pushers"   284
The Child Is Different from the Behavior   284
Mistaken Behavior   285
Approaches for Dealing with Difficult Behaviors   285
Natural and Logical Consequences   286
A Time and Place to Calm Down   287
Reinforcement   287
Spanking Is Never a Choice   287
Challenging Behaviors   288

Child Guidance in an Increasingly Violent and Uncertain World   289

Final Thoughts   290

Learning Outcomes   291

To Learn More   291

For Your Portfolio   292

Chapter 10 The Curriculum   294

What Is Curriculum?   295
Where Does Curriculum Come From?   296
Curriculum in Early Childhood Education   297

The Physical Development Curriculum   301
Sensory Development   301
Large Muscle Development   302
Small Muscle Development   303

The Creative Arts Curriculum   306
Art   308
Music   311
Creative Movement   312
Aesthetics   314

The Communication Curriculum   314
Language   316
Literacy   317
Literature   319

The Inquiry Curriculum   321
Math   323
Science   325
Social Studies   327

Final Thoughts   329

Learning Outcomes   330

To Learn More   330

For Your Portfolio   331

Chapter 11 Curriculum Planning   332

Planning Considerations   333
Influences on Curriculum Choices   334
Values and Beliefs   334
Knowledge of Children   335
Family, Culture, and Community   336
What's Worth Knowing?   336
Organizing Curriculum   337
Learner-Centered Organization   337
Subject Area Organization   338
Integrated Organization   338
Presenting Curriculum   338
Planning for Play   339
Teacher-Child Activities   339
Small Group Activities   340
Large Group Activities   341
Selecting Activities   341

Kinds of Planning   341
Long-Term Plans   343
Weekly Plans   343
Activity or Lesson Plans   344
Rationale and Curriculum Area: Why This Activity?   345
Objectives: What Children Gain   345
Preparation: What You Need   347
Procedure: What You Do   347

Assessment and Documentation   347
Implementing an Activity Plan   349
Evaluation: What Worked and What Didn't Work   350
Writing Plans in the Real World   350
Planning an Integrated Study   350
Select a Topic of Study   353
Look at Your Purpose   355
Identify Major Understandings   356
Generate Ideas for Activities   357
Enrich the Environment   358
Make the Plan   358
Implement the Study   359
Evaluate the Integrated Study   363

Final Thoughts   364
Learning Outcomes   364
To Learn More   365
For Your Portfolio   365

Chapter 12   Inclusion of Children with Special Needs   366

People-First Language   367
The Law and Inclusive Education   368
Identifying a Child Who Has Special Needs   369
Including Children with Special Needs   371
Preparing for Inclusion   372
Program Modifications   375
Developmentally Appropriate Practice and Children with Disabilities   377
Collaboration   377
Strategies for Working with Young Children with Special Needs   378
Young Children with Orthopedic Impairments   378
Young Children with Sensory Impairments   379
Vision   379
Hearing   379
Young Children with Communication Disorders   380
Young Children with Cognitive Delays   381
Young Children with Learning Disabilities   382
Children with Attention Deficit/Hyperactivity Disorder   382
Young Children with Emotional or Behavioral Disorders   383
Young Children with Autism   384

Other Special Needs   385
Children Who Have Been Abused or Neglected   385
Children with Chronic Health Conditions   386
Children with Special Gifts and Talents   387
Working with Families of Children with Special Needs   388
Final Thoughts   389
Learning Outcomes   389
To Learn More   390
For Your Portfolio   390

Chapter 13   Working with Families   392

Preparing to Work with Families   394
Values and Attitudes Regarding Families   395
What Parenting Is Like   395
Supporting Diverse Families   397
Building Relationships   400
Communication Skills   400
How to Support Families in Times of Stress   401
Ethical and Legal Responsibilities   402
Including Families in the Early Childhood Program   403
Making Families Welcome   403
Sharing Information   404
Getting Started   404
Daily Communication   404
Addressing Questions and Concerns   407
Conducting Conferences   409
Involving Families in the Program   410
Providing Family Education   413
Working with Families of Children with Special Needs   415
Final Thoughts   416
Learning Outcomes   416
To Learn More   416
For Your Portfolio   417

Chapter 14   Making a Commitment to Being an Early Childhood Professional   418

Make a Commitment to Children   419
Develop a Philosophy   420
Know About Children and Best Practice   420

Understand and Use the Code of Ethical
  Conduct   421
Addressing an Ethical Dilemma   *422*

Make a Commitment to Yourself   **423**
Take Care of Yourself   424
Connect with Colleagues   424
Plan Your Career   425
Understand Your Development as a
  Teacher   426
Other Roles   427

Make a Commitment to Your Profession   **427**
Behave Like a "True Professional"   428
Continue to Learn and Grow   428
Join a Professional Organization   428
Advocate   429

Potholes, Wild Beasts, and Other Perils   431
Final Thoughts   **433**
Learning Outcomes   433
To Learn More   433
For Your Portfolio   434

Bibliography   **435**
Appendix A   *The NAEYC Code of Ethical
  Conduct*   *451*
Appendix B   *Environment Checklists*   *456*
Name Index   **477**
Subject Index   **481**

Note: Every effort has been made to provide accurate and current Internet information in this book. However, the Internet and information posted on it are constantly changing, so it is inevitable that some of the Internet addresses listed in this textbook will change.

Who Am I in the Lives of Children?

1

The Teacher

We teach who we are.

John Gardner

- -

*W*elcome to the field of early childhood education and care! You are embarking on the important career of educating and caring for young children. The kind of person you are and the kind of professional you will become will have a lasting impact on children, families, and society. The purpose of this book is to help you become an early childhood educator who can nourish the growth of children, support families, and work amicably with colleagues. In this chapter we encourage you to look at your personal qualities, attitudes, values, morality, skills, and professional roles and choices. These things will play an important role in the kind of person you will be in children's lives. In the process of learning about early childhood education and care, you will become an early childhood educator.

We begin this first chapter with some basic definitions. What is *early childhood?* What is *early childhood education and care?* What is an *early childhood educator?* These terms have evolved over time and continue to change in response to new developments in the field.

> **Reflect and write about your current ideas about early childhood teachers***
>
> What do you see in your mind when you think of an early childhood teacher? What do you see when you think of the children? What do you envision when you think of an early childhood classroom?

THE WORK WE DO

Working with young children is varied and challenging; it demands knowledge, skill, sensitivity, creativity, and hard work. If these challenges excite you, you have probably chosen the right field. Early childhood education and care is especially rewarding for those who enjoy the spontaneous teaching and learning opportunities that abound in daily life with young children. It will not be as gratifying for people who think that teaching is a matter of dispensing subject matter or for those who like everything to be tidy and predictable. Sometimes college students who begin their careers with visions of shaping young minds become discouraged when they discover how much of

---

*This is the first of many reflections that you will find in this book. Reflecting on the questions asked and writing down your ideas will help you become a good teacher of young children. Your instructor may assign reflections as a formal part of your class. If not, you may wish to get a notebook and briefly write down your ideas. They will form a valuable way to document your own growth as an early childhood educator.

their time is spent mixing paint, changing pants, arbitrating disputes, mopping floors, and wiping noses. But while working with young children is demanding and tiring, it can also be invigorating and gratifying.

Early childhood is generally defined as the period in the life span that includes birth through age 8. The field is most often referred to as "early childhood education and care," or "early care and education," to emphasize the dual focus on learning and care that distinguishes early childhood programs and educators from other educators and schools. "Care and education intersect in early childhood, so most settings provide care with an educational focus, and education with a nurturing aspect. The goal of both is to promote positive development" (VanderVen 1994, 86).

Early childhood programs provide education and care for children from birth through age 8 in schools, child care centers, and homes. These programs may be referred to as *early childhood programs, early childhood education, child development programs, children's centers, child care centers, preschools, kindergartens, primary schools* (including kindergarten through grade three), and *elementary schools*.

The terms *teacher, early childhood educator, early childhood professional, practitioner, caregiver,* and *provider* are all used to describe the people who are involved in the care and education of young children. *Teacher* usually refers to a person who has completed a course of specialized early childhood training and who works with children between the ages of 2 and 8 in a school or child care center, though it is also used for those who teach children younger than 2. *Caregiver* and *provider* are terms that are often used to refer to those who work with infants and toddlers or who work in home settings, though it is also used for those who work with preschoolers. We will use all of these terms but will use *early childhood educator* and *practitioner* interchangeably. In some editions of this book we have called this first chapter "The Teacher" while in other editions we have called it "The Early Childhood Educator." The change in terminology reflects the multifaceted nature of the field and the ongoing tension that exists because of this. What we call things is important because words create an image of who we are and what we do.

Programs, regardless of what they are called or where they are housed, provide both care and education. People who work with young children, regardless of their job title or the age of the children, strive to ensure children's well-being and help them learn.

In this edition we have opted to call this chapter "The Teacher" because we believe this best reflects you, a student reading this text, and your career aspirations, whether you are considering working with infants or 8-year-olds. It also is a term that the general public—people like your family and friends—will understand and have positive associations with. We hope to convey the importance and seriousness of your chosen profession to you; and we hope this will help you to convey it to others.

Many Tasks and Many People

You will perform many tasks as an early childhood educator. Most of them involve day-to-day interactions with children; others entail working with families, colleagues, and community agencies; still others involve the preparation and record keeping that are a part of your professional role. We have found that this wide range of tasks makes work with young children endlessly interesting and challenging.

If you embarked on a career in early childhood edcuation because you enjoy relating to young children, you may be surprised to find the extent to which early childhood professionals work with adults. You will interact with families and work with other staff members daily. You may also communicate with agencies concerned with children and families, and work with other professionals as you further your own professional development.

Early childhood programs resemble one another in the breadth of their responsibilities to children, in the attention to children's physical and psychological health and safety, in the organization of environments, and in the learning experiences that they provide. Because of these program similarities, every early childhood practitioner has some similar tasks.

As one of tomorrow's early childhood educators, we hope that you will make a commitment to high-quality programs for young children. You may also want to develop knowledge of broader societal issues and become an advocate for the rights and needs of young children.

Working with Children

The first and most important of your many tasks is working with children. Each day that you work with young children you will talk with them, play with them, care for their physical needs, teach them, and provide them with a sense of psychological comfort and security. The younger the children with whom you work, the more you will need to provide the same kind of nurturing provided by families. You will also observe and support children as they play, mediate relationships between children, model the way you want people to treat one another, and help children develop skills and learn about the world. In a single day you may function as a teacher, friend, secretary, parent, reference librarian, interior decorator, colleague, nurse, janitor, counselor, entertainer, and diplomat.

In early childhood care and education we regard all areas of development—social, emotional, intellectual, and physical—as important and interconnected. Because young children are vulnerable and dependent on adults for responsive care, you will be expected to nurture and support all these aspects of development. We call this attention to overall development *concern for "the whole child,"* an idea you will encounter over and over in the pages of this book. Responsive care and education that is mindful of the development of the whole child is known today as *developmentally appropriate practice* (sometimes shortened to DAP), and that is the term we will use in this book.

Your work with young children will begin before the first child arrives, and will continue each day after the last child has gone home. It starts when you create an environment for care and learning that is safe, healthy, and stimulating. The learning environment is the primary teaching tool of an early childhood educator. You will also design the daily schedule, plan learning experiences, and collect resources. This stage setting is an essential part of working with young children.

Working with Families

Young children cannot be separated from the context of their families, so relating to and working with parents and other family members is an important part of the role of the early childhood educator. Because early childhood programs often provide the first transition from home to the larger world, you play an important role in helping families and children learn to be apart from each other for a period of time each day. In fact, you may be the second professional outside the home (the first is usually the pediatrician) who has a relationship with the family and the child. Although a close relationship between home and the early childhood program is absolutely

essential in programs for infants, toddlers, and preschoolers, it is also an important component of good programs for older children.

Just as your work with children brings with it diverse roles and demands, your work with families involves a similar range of skills different from those you need in your work with children. You may find yourself being a consultant, a social worker, an advocate, a professor, a reporter, a librarian, a mediator, a translator, a social director, and a postal carrier. Work with families is discussed in Chapter 13.

Being Part of a Team

Another important feature of the role of the early childhood educator is working collaboratively with other adults. Working as part of a team involves collaborating with coworkers, supervising volunteers, interacting with program administrators, and working with a host of others from custodians to counselors. Many early childhood practitioners report that participating in a team gave them support, stimulation, and a sense of belonging. Team support can reduce stress, contribute to a pleasant work environment, minimize conflict, and increase motivation (Rodd 1994). The ability to work productively on a team is an important professional skill that must be learned.

In effective teams the members work together on behalf of the shared goal of providing a high-quality program for children and families. They support and respect one another despite differences. They acknowledge and make best use of one another's strengths and contributions. They understand their roles and fulfill their responsibilities. Perhaps most important, they communicate productively and resolve the conflicts that inevitably occur when people work together.

Being a part of a team is more than just turning up for work each day. It involves a special conceptualization of team roles and responsibilities. It means taking an active role in the work situation rather than being a passive follower of instructions and directions (Rodd 1994, 91).

THE TEACHER AS A PERSON

Each early childhood educator has a story.

> *Fred always enjoyed being with children. He took a child development class in high school and loved the time he spent with kids in a preschool. Like his older brother, Fred went into auto mechanics and became a certified mechanic. His family approved and he made good money. But Fred was dissatisfied; working as a mechanic was not fulfilling. After 3 years he decided to go back to school to train as an early childhood educator. He knows he won't make as much money but he knows this is what he wants to do.*

> *As a young mother Ann enrolled her son in the campus child care center while working on her B.A. She often stayed at the center and helped out. One day the staff asked her if she wanted to work part-time at the center. The next semester Ann changed her major to education. Today she is a kindergarten teacher.*

> *Ruth always knew she wanted to be a teacher. She enrolled in pre-ed classes as soon as she entered college. She worked in a child care program as a part-time aide while she was going to college. Ruth became a preschool teacher after she graduated and soon went on to graduate school. Today she is the education director for a small preschool.*

Where are you coming from and where will you go as an early childhood educator? Have you always known you wanted to be a teacher? Do you have training in another field? Are you a parent yourself?

Not everyone enters the education and care field with specialized training. People come to it in a variety of ways. It is estimated that only 25% of early childhood educators began their careers in the "traditional" manner by majoring in early childhood education before they began work in the field. Some were introduced to the field as parents, observing the benefits of a good program for their young child then going to school to get training in early care and education (about 25%). Others (about 50%) have come by a "serendipitous" route, discovering the field as a happy accident, often after receiving a degree in another field and later obtaining the necessary education to become an early childhood professional (Bredekamp 1992a).

We reflect two of these typical paths. Stephanie and Doris "worked their way up" to early childhood education. Stephanie studied anthropology and secondary social studies, and only after receiving her degrees and working as a social worker did she find her way to early childhood education. Doris got a degree in elementary education and then discovered the field of early childhood education when she helped start a small preschool program. Eva and Sherry completed early childhood training before they entered the field. Eva always knew she wanted to become a preschool or kindergarten teacher and entered college with that as her career goal. As an undergraduate majoring in sociology, Sherry took a child development class as an elective and switched her major to child development in order to work with young children.

> **Reflect on your path**
>
> How did you find your way to early childhood education? Did you plan to be an early childhood educator? Did you discover the field by happy accident? Did you come to early childhood education with your own children? How do you think the path that brought you to early childhood education might influence your perspective as a teacher?

Because who you are as a person is the foundation for the professional you will become, we begin by looking at the early childhood educator as a person and ask you to think about yourself. Then we look at what it means to be an early childhood professional. As you enter the field you bring with you the sum total of your experiences—your personality, gender, race, culture, family circumstances, values, beliefs, and life experiences. These aspects will blend over time with your professional training and experiences working with children and families to forge your identity as an early childhood educator.

What Personal Qualities Make a Good Early Childhood Teacher?

Are you intellectual and practical? Are you active and outgoing? Are you quiet and reserved? Are you creative and flamboyant? You can become a good teacher with any of these traits. Many kinds of individuals can work successfully with young children. There is no one right personality type, no single set of experiences or training that will impart the required traits, no one way of being a good teacher of young children. No single mold produces the good early childhood educator.

Though many people from many different backgrounds *can* be good early childhood educators, not everyone finds success and satisfaction in this field. What *does* make a good early childhood teacher? There are many opinions and beliefs and some research to help answer this question. Research suggests that some attributes are characteristic of successful early childhood educators. These attributes include a positive outlook, energy, physical strength, a sense of humor, flexibility, self-understanding, emotional stability, emotional warmth, and sensitivity (Feeney & Chun 1985).

Many early childhood scholars have written with passion about the characteristics that early childhood teachers need. In 1948 Barbara Biber wrote:

> A teacher needs to be a person so secure within herself that she can function with principles rather than prescriptions, that she can exert authority without requiring submission, that she can work experimentally but not at random and that she can admit mistakes without feeling humiliated. (Biber & Snyder 1948)

Other needed characteristics include good physical health, self-awareness, integrity (honesty and moral uprightness), theoretical grounding, general knowledge, trust in children, unconditional caring for children, intuition, detachment, laughter, and the ability to be a model for children (Cartwright 1999). Lilian Katz describes a number of *dispositions* (relatively stable habits of mind or tendencies to respond to one's experiences in certain ways) that she believes are crucial—such as curiosity, openness to new ideas, and so forth.

There is no end to the list of desirable teacher qualities. We agree with Biber and Cartwright and many others who have written movingly about the qualities of good early childhood teachers. We are firmly convinced that a deep appreciation for children and childhood lies at the core of the good early childhood teacher. We know that such appreciation paired with an inquiring mind and spirit lead to a sense of joy, hope, and commitment that can turn teaching young children from a career into a calling.

Personal Characteristics

Over the years we have asked beginning students in our college classes to think about the characteristics of the teachers they had as children whom they liked best and least. We always find that many of their memories are about the distinctive personal character or qualities of their former teachers. The teachers that they liked best were kind, fair, compassionate, warm, and listened to them. The teachers they liked least sometimes humiliated them and were uncaring, inconsistent, and inattentive. This has contributed to our belief that who a teacher is as a person has a strong and lasting impact and is the first thing that should be considered as you embark upon a teaching career.

Temperament

We have found the research of pediatricians Alexander Thomas and Stella Chess on the temperament of infants, adapted to adults by therapists Jayne Burks and Melvin Rubenstein (Burks & Rubenstein 1979) a good place for our college students to begin to look at their personal characteristics. Thomas and Chess refer to *temperament* as an individual's behavioral style and characteristic ways of responding. They found that newborns show definite differences in traits that tend to persist over time. Though modified through life experiences, the nine dimensions of temperament are helpful in explaining personality differences in adults as well as children. (See Chapter 4 to learn more about temperament in children.)

Figure 1.1 gives a brief description of the nine traits as they apply to adults, and a continuum accompanying each trait. We have used the continua in our teaching as a tool for personal reflection. Traits of temperament are neither good nor bad; they are simply part of you. However, some characteristics like positive mood, a high activity level, and ease in adapting will be helpful in working with young children.

Consider two teachers:

> *Ruby and Michelle teach together in a classroom of 3- and 4-year-olds. Ruby arrives at school an hour before the children and families arrive; she likes to be alone in the classroom to gather her thoughts and get materials ready. Michelle rushes in at the last minute with a bag of intriguing items she has gathered related to their curriculum on plants. A half-hour after the school has*

Figure 1.1 Thomas and Chess's Nine Dimensions of Temperament

---

1. ACTIVITY LEVEL—Level of physical and mental activity.
   very active _____|_____ very inactive/quiet

2. REGULARITY (Rhythmicity)—Preference for predictable routines or spontaneity.
   highly regular/predictable _____| highly irregular/unpredictable

3. DISTRACTIBILITY—Degree to which extraneous stimuli affect behavior; readiness to leave one activity for another.
   easily distracted _____| very focused despite distractions

4. APPROACH-WITHDRAWAL—Ways of responding to new situations.
   enjoys new experiences _____|_____ avoids new experiences

5. ADAPTABILITY—Ease of adjustment to new ideas or situations (after initial response).
   adapts very easily to change __|_____ has difficulty adapting

6. PHYSICAL SENSITIVITY (Threshold of Responsiveness)—Sensitivity to changes in the environment including noise, taste, smell, and temperature.
   very aware of changes __|_____ not too attuned to changes

7. INTENSITY OF REACTION—Energy level typical of response, both positive and negative.
   very high intensity ____|_____ very low intensity

8. PERSISTENCE/ATTENTION SPAN—The amount of time devoted to an activity, even when it is difficult, and the ability to continue working when distracted.
   not easily distracted _____|_____ very easily distracted

9. QUALITY OF MOOD—General optimism or pessimism; tendency to enjoy things uncritically or to be more selective about situations enjoyed.
   generally happy or optimistic _||_____ generally sad or pessimistic

---

Source: Based on J. Burks and M. Rubenstein, *Temperament Styles in Adult Interaction,* 1979.

opened Ruby is quietly reading to a few of the younger children including Joshua, who has been having a hard time separating from his mom. Michelle is leading the rest of the children on a hunt through the yard for flowers.

Ruby and Michelle display some quite different temperamental characteristics, particularly rhythmicity and intensity of reaction. Realizing that a child or a colleague has a temperament that is different from your own (as Ruby and Michelle find each other) can keep you from finding their behavior negative or difficult. To heighten your awareness of your own temperament you may wish to plot yourself on the continua in Figure 1.1.

Multiple Intelligences

Howard Gardner's conception of multiple intelligences (see Chapter 4) is another resource for you to use to understand yourself. Gardner describes intelligence as culturally defined based on what is needed and valued within a society. When you realize your unique talents and strengths (your intelligences) you are better able to maximize them. Figure 1.2 presents the eight categories identified by Gardner.

Understanding that people can be intelligent in different ways can also help you in your work with colleagues. If Ruby and Michelle, from the earlier example, are wise they will build on one another's strengths and learn from one another. Ruby with her strong interpersonal intelligence will become the expert on addressing children's social-emotional needs, and Michelle with her strong naturalist intelligence will become the expert on creating science curriculum. If they are not wise, they may come to resent each other for their differences.

Figure 1.2 • Gardner's Multiple Intelligences

- **Musical intelligence:** The ability to produce and respond to music. This might be you, if you are especially sensitive to the aural environment of the classroom and play instruments and sing easily as you work with children.

- **Bodily kinesthetic intelligence:** The ability to use the body to solve problems. This might be you, if you demonstrate good coordination and play actively with children.

- **Logical-mathematical intelligence:** The ability to understand the basic properties of numbers and principles of cause and effect. This might be you, if you love to invent challenges for yourself and children.

- **Linguistic intelligence:** The ability to use language to express ideas and learn new words or other languages. This might be you, if you are very articulate and enjoy word play, books, storytelling, and poetry.

- **Spatial intelligence:** The ability to be able to form a mental image of spatial layouts. This might be you, if you are sensitive to the physical arrangement of a room, are able to easily see how to rearrange the classroom, or especially enjoy working with children in blocks.

- **Interpersonal intelligence:** The ability to understand other people and work with them. This might be you, if you are attentive to relationships and demonstrate sociability and leadership.

- **Intrapersonal intelligence:** The ability to understand things about oneself. This might be you, if you have strong interests and goals, know yourself well, are focused inward, and demonstrate confidence.

- **Naturalist intelligence:** The ability to recognize plants and animals in the environment. This might be you, if you know all about the flora and fauna in your community and have an especially well developed science curriculum and science area in your classroom.

Source: Based on H. Gardner, *Frames of Mind,* 1983.

Reflect on your personal characteristics

Consider your temperamental characteristics using the temperament continua, and your "intelligences" using Gardner's model. What are you like? What are your preferences for activity and setting? What are you good at? What is harder for you? How might knowledge of these characteristics help you in relating to children, families, and colleagues?

Learning more about yourself can help you be more sensitive to and accepting of differences among people, more aware of the impact of your personality on others, and better able to consider the kinds of work settings in which you might function most effectively.

If you are interested in learning more about your personal qualities, abilities, and characteristic ways of responding, there are instruments, such as the Myers-Briggs Type Indicator (MBTI), which examine the way that people characteristically look at the world and make decisions. Other assessment instruments are available in most college counseling centers. You can also take the MBTI on the Internet, formally for a fee or informally in modified versions. One source for both is Personality Pathways (www.personalitypathways.com).

Personal Values and Morality

Values are principles or standards that a person believes to be important, desirable, or worthwhile and that are prized for themselves (for example truth, integrity, beauty, love, honesty, wisdom, loyalty, justice, respect for others). You absorb your values during a complex process that combines your family background and culture with your life experiences. In countless ways values underlie major and minor life decisions. The things you do each day, the foods you eat, the place you live, and the work and play you choose are all influenced by your values. Your professional values will grow out of these personal values. If you spend some time reflecting, you will be able to identify your personal values and see how they affect your life.

You may have chosen early childhood education because you value children. You may be motivated by religious values, a commitment to world peace, a concern for social justice, or the desire to help children have fulfilling lives and become productive members of society. Awareness of your personal values will help you to be clear about what you are trying to accomplish in your daily work.

It is sometimes surprising to discover that other people do not share values that you believed were universal—one of the reasons the first year in a new community or a new relationship and the first year of working in an early childhood program can be difficult. Awareness can help you to realize that values are very much a part of who you are and that the values you hold dear may not be held by everyone you encounter in your life and work.

Morality involves the ability to make choices among values and to make decisions about what is right and wrong. It can be defined as people's views of what is good, right, or proper; their beliefs about their obligations; and their ideas about how they should behave (Kidder 1995; Kipnis 1987). From an early age people also learn that moral issues are serious. They "concern our duties and obligations to one another" (Strike, Haller, & Soltis 1988, 3). We quickly learn, for example, how we *ought* to treat others and that adults expect even children to behave in these ways.

The roots of personal morality can be found in the early childhood years. You can probably identify the standards of behavior that were established by the adults you looked up to in your home, church or temple, and neighborhood. *Telling the truth, being fair, putting family first,* and *respecting differences* are all examples of some of the earliest lessons that many people learn from their families and religious leaders.

As you begin your preparation for becoming an early childhood educator, it is worthwhile to consider what values have brought you to this decision and how your values will influence the decisions you make about working with and for young children.

> **Reflect on your values and the moral messages you received as a child**
>
> Make a list of your values. How do you think you developed these values? Which values were directly taught in your home, church/temple, or neighborhood? Were there any that were taught in indirect ways? What everyday behaviors do you think of as moral or immoral? How do these reflect your childhood and upbringing?

Attitudes Toward Diversity

Closely related to people's values are their attitudes toward groups of people whose culture, religion, language, class, ethnicity, sexual orientation, appearance, or abilities are different from their own. Attitudes toward these and other kinds of differences grow from our values, the messages we get as children from the adults in our lives, and from our own experiences (or lack of them) with different kinds of people.

We all develop preferences and expectations about people. The inclination to favor or reject certain individuals or groups of people (*biases*) may be based simply on the human tendency to feel comfortable with those who are similar to us. Unlike other values and preferences, biases can lead to stereotypes and prejudices that have a negative impact and may lead to unfair or unjust treatment of individuals or groups of people. A *stereotype* is an oversimplified generalization about a particular group of people. It is an unjustified fixed mental picture that is not based on direct experience. *Prejudice* is "an opinion, or feeling formed without adequate prior knowledge, thought or reason. Prejudice is prejudgment for or against any person, group or sex" (Derman-Sparks 1989, 3). When less favored individuals observe your preferences, they may perceive themselves as less worthy. If you can recall the experience of having been rejected or negatively judged because of your family, race, ethnicity, culture, gender, religion, language, appearance, ability, status, or any other personal characteristic, you will be aware of the powerful effect of prejudice. We usually think of prejudice as negative feelings about a group, but it can also be harmful to be prejudiced in favor of one group of children or families.

Most of us fail to recognize our own biases, but we all have some. If we are aware of our biases we may deny them and feel embarrassed by them. This does not make them go away. They influence our relationships with children, families, and colleagues.

Working to identify your biases will help you to know when you may be having negative effects on children or their families. When you become aware of a bias, simple awareness may be enough to help you to be more accepting of diversity or to correct a tendency to overreact to a child or family. Indeed, many fine teachers actively work to dispel these feelings by identifying the things they like about the child or family member who triggers a negative reaction. When you focus on positives, you may be more easily able to develop a special affection for a child or adult whom you were once inclined to dislike. Your newfound appreciation of a child or family may help to transform your feelings about other members of that group.

It is also a good idea to ask yourself if there are any particular children or groups of children with whom you should not work. If you find that you have strong prejudices toward groups of children or families that you can't overcome, you may need to consider seriously whether you should become an early childhood educator.

We live in an increasingly diverse world. As an early childhood educator you are certain to have close contact with people who have different racial, economic, cultural, and linguistic backgrounds, sexual orientations, and lifestyles. This diversity offers both challenges and opportunities. Although you may have moments of discomfort and self-doubt, you also have the possibility of gaining new appreciation and insights as you learn to appreciate the range of human differences.

> **Reflect on your attitudes toward diversity**
>
> In what ways and in what circumstances have you experienced prejudice in your own life? How did it influence your view of yourself and other people?
>
> Are there people you tend to dislike or with whom you feel uncomfortable? What are the characteristics of these people? Do you tend to prefer children of one race, culture, economic background, sex, or style of behavior?
>
> When you consider working with diverse children, what opportunities interest you? What challenges worry you?

Self-Knowledge and the Ability to Reflect

You bring your whole history to your work with children and their families. Who you are as a person includes the characteristics you were born with, your personality, culture, life experiences, attitudes, and values. These things will have an impact on the early childhood professional you will become. You may not be fully aware of these aspects of yourself if you do not reflect on them. And you must come to understand yourself if you are to understand others. Self-knowledge and the ability to reflect on the impact of your personality and behavior on others are essential attributes of the good early childhood educator.

Cheryl grew up as an only child. Both of her parents were teachers and she always pretended to be teacher to her dolls and toy animals. Cheryl loved school but she was shy and did not make friends easily. She volunteered at a neighborhood preschool when she was in high school and discovered that she didn't feel shy with children. She decided to become a preschool teacher. She completed her degree in early childhood education and became a teacher in the preschool where she did a practicum placement. No one who meets her today can believe that she was ever shy and friendless.

Sue is a kindergarten teacher who grew up in the inner city. Her parents did not speak English. She has vivid memories of her first unhappy days in kindergarten. But Sue soon loved school. When she was 8, Sue's father died. Later her brother died of a drug overdose. There was never enough money, and there were many sad days in Sue's life. But she did well in school and earned a scholarship to go to the state college. Sue was the first person in her family to earn a degree. Sue loves her job and often talks about the ways in which she feels she is making a difference to children from families like hers.

Sarah is a preschool teacher who came from an abusive family. She left home before she was 16, but Sarah managed to go to school and earned an A.S. degree. She is now a teacher of 3-year-olds. She is fiercely protective of the children in her class and says most parents don't deserve to have children. She is negative about authority figures like her director and the preschool board. She is frequently absent and often comments on the poor quality of her program. Sarah complains that she is paid too little to put in extra hours to fix up the classroom or conference with parents.

As you enter the early childhood field, remember that you were once a child and that the ways you feel about yourself and others were profoundly influenced by your early experiences. Working with other people's children may generate long-forgotten feelings and attitudes. It is a good idea to reflect on your early experiences and how they might impact your relationships before they crop up in unexpected and destructive ways. If you had your basic needs met in childhood, you are most likely to see the world as a good and nurturing place and it may be easy for you to support the growth and development of children. If—like Cheryl, Sue, and Sarah—you encountered problems in growing up, you may need to spend some time working through these issues, either on your own or with a friend or counselor. All of us have both happy and unhappy memories of our early lives. Many fine early childhood educators, like Sue, dedicate themselves to giving children the positive early experiences that they missed. Some, like Sarah, are not able to overcome their early experiences without help.

Educators who have the capacity for caring, compassion, and nurturing know and accept themselves. Self-knowledge depends to a great extent on the ability to observe yourself in the same honest and nonjudgmental way that you observe children and to realistically appraise your areas of strength and those in which change is needed. Self-knowledge means recognizing that everyone experiences negative feelings and strong and unpleasant emotions such as anger and fear. These feelings need to be identified, accepted, and expressed in productive ways (for example, by creating paintings to depict feelings about an unhappy childhood) or they may become destructive.

> **Reflect on who you are and who you want to be in the lives of children**
>
> What events and experiences in your childhood most influence who you are today? What, if any, unhappy or difficult experiences have you had to work to overcome? What are the connections between your childhood experiences and your desire to teach young children? Who do you want to be in the lives of children?

The capacity for self-knowledge and acceptance is the cornerstone for the quality of compassion that is so important in a person who works with young children and their families. Arthur Jersild describes it this way:

To be compassionate, one must be able to accept the impact of any emotion, love or hate, joy, fear, or grief—tolerate it and harbor it long enough and with sufficient absorption to accept its meaning and to enter into a fellowship of feeling with the one who is moved by the emotion. This is the heroic feature of compassion in its fullest development: to be able to face the ravage of rage, the shattering impact of terror, the tenderest prompting of love, and then to embrace these in a larger context, which involves an acceptance of these feelings and an appreciation of what they mean to the one who experiences them. (Jersild 1955, 125–126)

Part of the process of professional development (and the major theme in this book) is to ask yourself: "Who am I in the lives of children? Who do I want to be?" No one is completely self-aware, mature, wise, compassionate, and insightful all the time. Everyone has tendencies to be hostile and defensive. It is important to learn to look at yourself as objectively as you can and to accept feedback from others as valuable information that can help you to grow instead of something to defend against or to use to berate yourself.

THE TEACHER AS A PROFESSIONAL

You are learning to be an early childhood educator, which means that you are planning to enter a *profession* and to become a *professional.* We hear these terms used every day but their meanings are not always clear. What is a profession? A basic definition of *profession* is that it is an occupation that provides an essential service to society. A profession has the following elements:

1. Prolonged training required for its members
2. A specialized body of knowledge shared by all of its members
3. A mission, commitment to a public good, and a set of shared values
4. Agreed-on standards in the form of a code of ethics that lays out members' moral obligations to society and ensures that they serve the public good
5. Autonomy and self-regulation (Feeney & Freeman 1999)

The status of profession is not formally granted. Rather, it is earned over time as an occupational group acquires more of the characteristics of a profession. A professional is an individual who has received training and who uses personal skills and abilities to realize the commitments of the profession.

Is early childhood education and care a profession? Are early childhood educators professionals? Members of our field perform the significant social function of promoting positive human development in children. We have distinctive values that involve recognizing and respecting the humanity and dignity of children and adults. We have a knowledge base and training based upon it. And we have a code of ethics and professional organizations. The field, in most nations, is a long way, however, from being well paid, autonomous, or self-regulated. Most private preschool programs in the United States are licensed by social welfare agencies, and public school policies are made not by educators but by members of boards of education. Salaries for teachers who work in programs for children younger than 5 are typically much lower than those of teachers who work in elementary and primary schools, with the average Head Start teacher salary at about $21,000, compared to the average public school teacher salary at about twice that much, $43,000 (Barnett, State Preschool Yearbook 2003, National Institute of Early Education Research).

At present, early childhood education can best be described as an occupation that is striving to become a profession. While our field does not have the years of graduate training, autonomy, prestige, or compensation associated with professions like law and medicine, we do make important contributions to society by nurturing young children during a critically important period in the life cycle. We are working to become a profession and to gain greater public recognition of the work we do.

As a professional you will need to learn the content and speak the language of your field. In the last few years a good deal of work has been done on defining the knowledge base of early care and education. Many states have described core knowledge for early childhood practitioners.

You will gain core knowledge through specialized training in early childhood education and care. Such training is essential to becoming a competent practitioner who can provide positive experiences for young children. Research tells us that formal education has a critical impact on the teacher's ability to provide good experiences for children (Kontos & Wilcox-Herzog 2001). Teaching experience alone or a degree in another field (even a related field like elementary education) cannot provide you with the necessary knowledge and skill.

In *Preparing Early Childhood Professionals: NAEYC's Standards for Programs* (Hyson 2003), the National Association for the Education of Young Children (NAEYC) has identified the standards for professional training in early childhood, describing what all graduates of early childhood training programs need to know and be able to do.

Figure 1.3 presents these standards. It should come as no surprise to you that the content they represent comprises most of the substance of this book.

The Training and Certification You Will Need

Training requirements vary depending on the age of the children, the agency that regulates the program, the state or country in which you live, and the particular program sponsorship. Requirements for working in programs for children under the age of 5 are usually quite different from those for programs for children aged 5 through 8. It is helpful for you to understand this distinction as you plan for your career.

There are many settings in which you can work with young children, and many different roles you can take. They require different kinds and levels of training and provide different working conditions and compensation. Tables 1.1 to 1.3 (see pp. 17–19) lay out the roles, responsibilities, and training required in different early childhood settings.

Two recent developments are having an impact on requirements for teachers in early childhood centers. Head Start, a federally funded program for low-income children, recently raised the requirements for teachers. As of fall 2003 all newly hired and half of all Head Start teachers must have an associate degree in early childhood education or a related field. By the year 2008 all newly hired and half of all Head Start teachers must have a bachelor's degree in early childhood education or a related field. The second development is the revision of standards for NAEYC accredited programs, which propose that teachers have at least a baccalaureate degree.

Professional Commitment and Behavior

Being a professional goes beyond an accumulation of methods, courses, and experiences. It involves *commitment, knowledge,* and the *willingness to continue to learn and grow.* You should keep a portfolio and update it regularly, as described in the box "Starting Your Professional Portfolio" on pages 20–21. Professional commitment and professionalism are essential attributes of the good early childhood educator.

Figure 1.3   **NAEYC's Standards for Programs**

Standard 1. Promoting Child Development and Learning
Use understanding of young children's characteristics and needs, and of multiple interacting influences on children's development and learning, to create environments that are healthy, respectful, supportive, and challenging for all children.

Standard 2. Building Family and Community Relationships
Know about, understand, and value the importance and complex characteristics of children's families and communities. Use this understanding to create respectful, reciprocal relationships that support and empower families, and to involve all families in their children's development and learning.

Standard 3. Observing, Documenting, and Assessing to Support Young Children and Families
Know about and understand the goals, benefits, and uses of assessment. Know about and use systematic observations, documentation, and other effective assessment strategies in a responsible way, in partnership with families and other professionals, to positively influence children's development.

Standard 4. Teaching and Learning
Integrate understanding of and relationships with children and families; their understanding of developmentally effective approaches to teaching and learning; and knowledge of academic disciplines to design, implement, and evaluate experiences that promote positive development and learning for all young children.

Sub-Standard 4a. Connecting with children and families
Know, understand, and use positive relationships and supportive interactions as the foundation for work with young children.

Sub-Standard 4b. Using developmentally effective approaches
Know, understand, and use a wide array of effective approaches, strategies, and tools to positively influence children's development and learning.

Sub-Standard 4c. Understanding content knowledge in early education
Understand the importance of each content area in young children's learning. Know the essential concepts, inquiry tools, and structure of content areas, including academic subjects, and identify resources to deepen their understanding.

Sub-Standard 4d. Building meaningful curriculum
Use own knowledge and other resources to design, implement, and evaluate meaningful, challenging curriculum that promotes comprehensive developmental and learning outcomes for all young children.

Standard 5. Becoming a Professional
Identify and conduct oneself as a member of the early childhood profession. Know and use ethical guidelines and other professional standards related to early childhood practice. Be a continuous, collaborative learner who demonstrates knowledgeable, reflective, and critical perspectives on work, making informed decisions that integrate knowledge from a variety of sources. Be an informed advocate for sound educational practices and policies.

Source: Adapted, with permission, from National Association for the Education of Young Children, Preparing Early Childhood Professionals: NAEYC's Standards for Programs, (Washington, DC: NAEYC, 2003), 29.

Professional behavior involves *being a good employee.* It means following through on commitments, being punctual, dressing appropriately, being aware of your responsibilities, taking your work seriously, applying the knowledge you have acquired to your work with children, and representing the program and field positively in the community. It also involves *behaving collegially,* keeping personal feelings and grievances out of the classroom, and knowing about the *ethical* responsibilities that are described in the section that follows.

Legal Responsibilities

Early childhood teachers have legal commitments. Like every citizen, we are required to follow the laws of our country and community. Additionally, early childhood edu-

Table 1.1 **Roles, Responsibilities, and Training Required in Homes**

Setting	Role	Responsibilities	Required Training
Homes	Family Child Care Provider	Provide care and education for small groups of children in their own homes Run own small business	Most states—no formal training is required Can receive a CDA* credential family child care and accreditation by the National Association for Family Day Care Must have some business skills as well as skill in working with children
	Nanny	Provide care and education in the child's home Employed by the family or families of the children Room and board may be a part of the compensation	Most states—no formal training is required Colleges and private agencies have nanny training programs that vary from 6 weeks to a year in length Training modeled on British nursery nurse training but American counterpart is generally less rigorous
	Home Visitor	Provide appropriate learning experiences to children with special needs or who are considered to be at risk in the child's home Model positive ways of interacting with and teaching young children to families Employed by an agency	Most states—no formal training is required Can receive a CDA credential for home visitors

* The CDA (Child Development Associate) is a nationally awarded early childhood credential. It requires 120 clock hours of approved training (from a community college, agency, or distance learning organization), a standard exam, and demonstrated competency in working with young children.

cators are "mandated reporters" of child abuse and neglect. This means that you have a legal and ethical responsibility to report suspected cases of child abuse and neglect, such as a child who comes to school with visible bruises that you suspect are the result of being hit by a parent or other family member.

One of the first things you will do in your first job is to find out the reporting procedures for your particular workplace. While you may fervently wish never to have to use this information, it is critical that you know what to do in order to fulfill your responsibilities to children.

Professional Values and Ethics

Personal values and morality cannot always guide professional behavior since not everyone has the same values and life experiences, or has learned the same moral lessons. Even those who have the same values and moral convictions may not apply them in the same way in their work with children. Early childhood educators need more than personal values and morality to guide their work. Personal attitudes, values, and morals need to be supplemented with professional values if the members of a profession are to be able to speak with one voice about their commitments.

Table 1.2 **Roles, Responsibilities, and Training Required in Centers**

Setting	Role	Responsibilities	Required Training
Centers (early childhood programs for children under the age of five and after-school programs for elementary school children as centers)	Teacher Aide/ Assistant	Help implement the program in an early childhood classroom Work with children under the supervision of a qualified early childhood educator	Orientation and on-the-job training
	School-Age Program Leader	Provide care and activities for elementary children during out-of-school time Responsible for safety and supervision of children May be responsible for program planning May interact informally with families Supervised by a site coordinator	High school graduate Orientation and on-the-job training
	Assistant Teacher/ Assistant Caregiver	Responsible for implementing program activities as part of teaching team Work with a supervising teacher or caregiver Provide care and education for a group of young children May help plan and implement activities, participate in assessing children, work with families, and have responsibility for a small group within a larger class	Some training in working with young children May require a CDA (infant and toddler, preschool, or bilingual) or a degree Usually less training or experience than the supervising teacher
	Teacher/Caregiver	Responsible for the care and education of a group of young children May be part of a teaching team and function as a team leader Plan and implement curriculum with other members of team	Specialized training to work with young children Most states require a college degree (sometimes in education, early childhood education, or child development) Some states accept a CDA
	Master, Lead, or Head Teacher	Responsible for one or more groups of young children Serve as team leader Usually perform some administrative duties Serve as mentors or trainers to other teachers	Same as teachers Employer may require specialized training Positions involving staff supervision or curriculum development may require ECE bachelor's or master's degree
	Director	Perform administrative duties May serve as mentors and trainers to teachers In small program may serve as teacher-director	2- or 4-year degree with specialized training in working with young children Additional training in program administration

Table 1.3 **Roles, Responsibilities, and Training Required in Elementary Schools**

Setting	Role	Responsibilities	Required Training
Elementary Schools	Educational Assistant	Supervise, teach, and tutor children in work under the supervision of a qualified teacher	Requirements for educational assistants vary from state to state; in some states 2 years of college is required
	Teacher	Responsible for the education and care of a class of young children Plan and implement the curriculum work with parents	Bachelor's degree and elementary teacher certification Specialized training may include training in early childhood A few states have early childhood certification that covers infancy through third grade Some offer a preschool-primary teaching credential that covers PS through third grade Some offer an early childhood or kindergarten endorsement in addition to elementary certification, or credential that covers K through sixth grade
	Resource Teacher or Specialist	Responsible for supplementing the education of groups of young children May provide special instruction to children May serve as trainers to other teachers	Degree and teaching credential plus training to prepare in subject area
	Principal or Headmaster	Responsible for the administration of a school Serve as leader for staff	Graduate degree in education Coursework in administration Special coursework in early childhood education usually not required

Professional Values

The values of a profession are not a matter of preference but are agreed-upon statements that members hold to be important. Professional values spell out the beliefs and commitments of a profession. The National Association for the Education of Young Children has developed a *Code of Ethical Conduct and Statement of Commitment* to guide its members in responsible professional practice (there are similar codes in other countries). The code identifies core values, presented in Figure 1.4, that express central beliefs, a commitment to society, and a common purpose. These core values make it possible to reach agreement on issues of professional ethics by moving from personal values to professional values that apply to all early childhood educators.

Most people who choose early childhood education as a career find themselves in agreement with the spirit of these core values. As you merge your personal values with the professional values of the field, you will join other early childhood practitioners in

Today in education, and in many other fields, one way to demonstrate your professionalism is through the creation of a professional portfolio. A professional portfolio documents your skills, knowledge, and training. In some colleges you will be asked to create a portfolio for the purpose of assessing whether you have accomplished the required performance outcomes for a class or program.

Regardless of whether or not you are required to create a professional portfolio, we recommend that you keep one as a convenient way to keep track of your accomplishments as well as a tool for recording your growth as an early childhood educator. At the end of each chapter we suggest additions to your professional portfolio that relate to the content of the chapter and will demonstrate your growth. Here are some ideas to begin:

Start Your Portfolio Select an open, flexible system that is easy to organize and modify (such as a three-ring binder) to hold your portfolio.

Introduce Yourself Use the reflections in this chapter to help you get started writing ideas you'd like to include in a brief *autobiography* that outlines the significant events in your life that led you to choose early childhood education and care as your career, a *personal mission statement* that explains your vision for yourself as an early childhood educator and your hopes and dreams as a professional, and a statement of *educational philosophy* describing what you value in the education and care of young children. Remember these will change as you progress from beginning student to beginning professional. Periodically go back to these to see how your ideas change and grow.

Collect Letters of Recommendation Letters of recommendation from people who know your work and your character are independent evidence of your ability. When an employer, supervisor, or college professor gives you a favorable evaluation or compliments you on your work it is a good moment to ask them to formalize their appreciation by writing you a letter for your portfolio.

Create a Resume A resume is a short outline of your qualifications and experience. It is useful to include an updated resume in your portfolio if you plan to use the portfolio as a part of your job application. It gives a prospective employer a quick way to see if you are suitable for a position. (www.write-a-resume.org)

Document Your Qualifications Make a section in your portfolio for degrees, certificates, personnel registry cards, and diplomas. Remember that training in other fields (for example, music, water safety) can be useful supplements to your formal training in working with young children.

Begin an Ongoing Training Record Over the course of your career you will have many opportunities for ongoing training. Your portfolio is an excellent place to keep track of this training and keep any certificates of attendance that you receive. For each training entry be sure to note the date of the training, the name of the trainer and sponsoring organization, and the number of hours of training. Remember to make a note of any ways in which you improve your practice as a result of the training.

Document Your Knowledge and Competence Use the statements of core knowledge and skills for your state, the CDA competency standards, or the NAEYC program standards as a

---

Figure 1.4 **Core Values in Early Childhood Education**

Standards of ethical behavior in early childhood education are based on commitment to core values that are deeply rooted in the history of our field. We have committed ourselves to:

- Appreciating childhood as a unique and valuable stage of the human life cycle
- Basing our work with children on knowledge of child development
- Appreciating and supporting the close ties between the child and family
- Recognizing that children are best understood in the context of family, culture, and society
- Respecting the dignity, worth, and uniqueness of each individual (child, family member, and colleague)
- Helping children and adults achieve their full potential in the context of relationships that are based on trust, respect, and positive regard

Source: NAEYC Code of Ethical Conduct and Statement of Commitment, 1998.

overkill better than not enough!

framework for the knowledge and competency sections of your portfolio. In each section provide examples of your knowledge or competency in this area. Document your work through photographs (for example, a photograph of a classroom environment that you arranged for children), written descriptions (for example, a description of a situation in which you successfully guided a child who was having difficulties), or actual work samples (for example, a lesson plan you have written, a paper that demonstrates your knowledge, or a newsletter you have written for families). Your portfolio should include only items that have a direct bearing on your professional abilities and growth. Items for the knowledge and competence section of your portfolio should have a brief explanatory statement that ties your work to the standard that is being illustrated, so that a reader will understand why they have been included.

Sample Portfolio Table of Contents

Introduction to a Teacher

Autobiography

Philosophy & mission —> *Paper due 11/30/06*

Letters of recommendation

Qualifications

Resume of education & experience

Personnel registry card

Degrees in early childhood education

First aid & CPR certification

NAEYC membership card

Ongoing Training Record

Certificates of attendance workshops and conferences, 2005–2006

Knowledge & Competence

Growth and development (for example, photograph of a toy you made for a particular age)

Professionalism (for example, a sample of a reflection you wrote after attending a workshop)

Diversity (for example, a plan for a child with disabilities)

Observation and assessment (for example, an observation you made and a plan based on it)

Health, safety, and nutrition (for example, a plan for teaching children about health)

Learning environments (for example, a sample floor plan for a classroom)

Relationships and guidance (for example, a reflection on a situation in which you guided a child)

Planning learning experiences (for example, a sample integrated study plan you created)

Working with families (for example, a newsletter or family conference outline you wrote)

Program management (for example, a sample of some ways that you maintain records)

Note: Your portfolio should not include brochures or handouts that you have gathered—only those you have produced yourself.

highlighted = already done

their commitment to supporting the positive growth and development of children and their families.

When Values Conflict. When you encounter conflicts in your work they often will involve personal or professional values. One kind of value conflict occurs within yourself. For example, you may face a value conflict regarding the needs and demands of your professional and personal life (such as when an important staff meeting is scheduled on your child's birthday). In your work with children you may value freedom of expression (for example, allowing children to engage in dramatic play about things that are important to them) versus the value of peace (forbidding war play because it brings violence into the classroom). Or you may face the predicament of having to choose between work that pays well and work you love. In these situations it will be helpful to analyze the conflict and decide which value is most important to you.

> **Reflect on your professional values**
>
> Brainstorm a list of values that you think that all early childhood educators should hold. Compare your list to the NAEYC core values found here. Think about why these lists are similar to or different from each other.

It is also important to be sure your actions are consistent with your values. Sometimes teachers are not aware of the ways in which their behavior may contradict their values. A teacher we know valued independence and child-initiated learning. But when she looked at her classroom she realized children were not allowed to choose their own materials from the open shelves.

At some point you will find yourself facing value conflicts with others. It helps to recognize that differences in values are a natural and healthy part of life in a diverse society. You can learn to address value conflicts thoughtfully, though it is not always easy to arrive at a solution. You may find yourself in a situation in which an administrator's actions (such as minimizing the risk of allegations of sexual abuse by forbidding staff to hug children) are in direct conflict with an important value (giving young children the affectionate physical contact they need). You may find yourself in conflict with colleagues whose values lead them to different ideas about what and how to teach.

You may also find yourself caught in a conflict between your beliefs and pressures from families who want you to teach and treat children in ways that violate these beliefs. You will almost certainly have to deal with parents who are anxious about their children's success in school and who want them to master academic content that you think is inappropriate.

When people from different backgrounds and with different values work together to care for children, different viewpoints inevitably arise. When you encounter a conflict, it is helpful to decide whether it is about values. If it involves an ethical responsibility or dilemma, guidance for addressing it can be found in the NAEYC Code of Ethical Conduct. Other conflicts are rooted in a difference of values that does not involve ethics.

Different and contradictory points of view regarding what is best practice in the care and education of young children are inevitable. Often they involve culture, such as whether to hold a crying child or give the child space and time to comfort him- or herself. Value conflicts can be best handled by suspending judgment (the inner voice that says "No! They're wrong! I'm right!") and listening carefully to the other person's viewpoint. Cultural differences need to be acknowledged and discussed. Together you can then seek a solution that is respectful to both parties. When competing views are based on strongly held value differences, especially those relating to culture, solutions may not be easily found and the individuals involved may have to agree to disagree.

Occasionally differences about teaching practices are so serious that you will find you do not want to continue to work in a program. For instance, one of our students chose to leave a good-paying job when her school adopted a curriculum that did not allow her to teach in ways that were consistent with what she valued. Coming to this conclusion can be painful, but it may be your only alternative if the value difference is too extreme. You may find that, like the student we just described, you are happier teaching in a setting that more closely reflects your values.

> **Reflect on a values conflict**
>
> Think about a time when you and another person had a disagreement based on values. What values did each of you hold? Were your values or the relationship changed by the conflict?

Professional Ethics

Ethics is the study of right and wrong, duties and obligations. Professional ethics address the moral commitments of a group, extending and enhancing the individual values and personal morality of practitioners through shared, critical reflection about right and wrong actions in the workplace. Standards of ethical conduct are not statements of taste or preference; they provide a shared common ground for professionals who strive to do the right thing.

The ethical commitments of a profession are contained in its code of ethics. An ethical code is different from program policies, regulations, or laws. It describes the aspirations of the field and the obligations of individual practitioners. It tells them how they should approach their work, and some things that they ought to do and ought not to do. A code of ethics helps professionals do what is right—not what is easiest, what will bring the most personal benefit, or what will make them most popular. When followed by the members of a profession, a code assures the public that practice is based on sound and agreed-upon standards and is in the best interest of society.

The NAEYC Code of Ethical Conduct. In 1978 Lilian Katz described some of the ethical problems that arise in early childhood programs and urged the early childhood field to develop a code of ethics. The most compelling reason for early childhood educators to have a code of ethics is that young children are vulnerable and lack the power to defend themselves. The adults who care for them are larger and stronger and control valuable resources that children want and need. Katz pointed out that the more powerless the client is with regard to the practitioner, the more important the practitioner's ethics become. Young children cannot defend themselves from teachers who are uncaring or abusive. For that reason it is extremely important that those who work in early childhood programs act fairly and responsibly on children's behalf.

Another reason that it is important for early childhood educators to have a code of ethics is that they serve a variety of client groups—children, families, employing agencies, and the community. Most early childhood educators would agree that their primary responsibility and loyalty is to children. But it can be hard to keep sight of this priority when parents, agencies, or administrators demand that their concerns be addressed first.

The Code of Ethical Conduct of the National Association for the Education of Young Children (NAEYC) was developed in the 1980s, adopted in 1989, and revised in 1998. It has been expanded to include a supplement for teacher educators (2003) and will eventually have a supplement for administrators. It is designed to help you answer the question "What should the good early childhood educator do?"

The code is organized into four sections describing professional responsibilities to children, families, colleagues, and community and society. The items in the code are designed to help practitioners make responsible ethical decisions. It includes *ideals* that describe exemplary practice and *principles* that describe practices that are required, prohibited, and permitted. (A copy of the code is found in Appendix A.)

Ethical Responsibilities. The code clearly identifies ethical responsibilities. The first, and most important, of these is to do no harm to children. Other responsibilities include being familiar with the knowledge base of early childhood education and basing what you do upon it; keeping personal information about children and families confidential; being familiar with laws and regulations that have an impact on children and programs; respecting families' culture, language, customs, and beliefs and their child-rearing values and their right to make decisions for their children; attempting to resolve concerns with coworkers and employers collegially; and assisting programs to provide a high quality of service.

Ethical responsibilities are clear-cut. They are those things that must or must not be done. For example, the code makes it clear that early childhood educators should never share confidential information about a child or family with a person who has no legitimate need for it. Facing a decision with an ethical component sometimes makes you realize that the "right" thing to do is not always the easiest or the most popular.

For example, even if you like a family, you must call child protective services when a child in your class explains that his bruises were caused when his father hit him. One of the most important aspects of the code is its affirmation of what is right.

Ethical Issues. When you encounter an issue or problem at work, one of the first things you will want to do is to determine whether it involves ethics. Ask yourself whether the problem or issue has to do with right and wrong, rights and responsibilities, and human welfare. Not all conflicts or concerns at work involve ethics. If the teacher next door fails to change the artwork on the bulletin board on a regular basis, she may not meet your standards or provide the best experiences for children or parents, she may even be lazy, but she is not unethical. Your choice of whether to accompany the rest of the school on a trip to the zoo when you are studying plants involves a choice but not an ethical choice. A conflict with a team member over whether to read children a story after lunch or after breakfast involves consideration but probably does not involve ethics.

If you are unsure, you will find it helpful to refer to the NAEYC Code of Ethical Conduct. If the conflict or concern is an ethical issue, you then need to determine whether the code clearly spells out what you must or must not do, whether it involves a responsibility, or if it is an ethical *dilemma.*

An ethical dilemma is a predicament encountered in your work, involving competing professional values and having more than one responsible solution. It might mean placing the needs of a child above those of his parent, or protecting the rights of the group even if doing so limits the options of an individual. Whatever choice you make in an ethical dilemma involves some benefits and some costs. We will discuss a reflective process for thinking about and resolving ethical dilemmas in the last chapter of this book.

The NAEYC Code of Ethical Conduct reflects the perspectives, needs, and values of American early childhood educators. If you live or work in a country other than the United States you may also have a code of ethics that reflects the local values and culture. You can find many of these on the Internet. The code developed for Australian early childhood educators can be found through the Web site of the Australian Early Childhood Association (www.aeca.org.au). The Canadian early childhood educator's code can be found through the Web site for the Canadian Child Care Federation (www.cccf-fcsge.ca). The ethical code of New Zealand early childhood educators can be found at the Web site of the New Zealand Teachers' Council (www.teacherscouncil.govt.nz).

> **Reflect on your experience with dilemmas**
>
> Have you ever been in a situation in which you were forced to choose between two alternatives, both of which were somewhat right and somewhat wrong? What were the choices? How did you decide what was the best alternative?

FINAL THOUGHTS

You are at the beginning of your career as an early childhood educator and have many joys and challenges ahead. You already know that you have work ahead of you in your college classes. There will be texts to read, papers to write, projects to create, programs to visit, and exams to study for. But you may not be thinking about the work you will have to do to become a teacher once your college work is over. Good teachers are life-long learners, by necessity and by disposition. If you aspire to be a good teacher, and we assume you do, you have lots of learning challenges and joys ahead as you become an early childhood educator.

LEARNING OUTCOMES

When you read this chapter, thoughtfully complete selected assignments from the "To Learn More" section, and prepare items from "Starting Your Professional Portfolio" (see box on pp. 20–21) you will be demonstrating your progress in meeting NAEYC **Standard 5: Becoming a Professional.**

Key elements:

- Identify and begin to conduct yourself as a member of the early childhood profession

- Know about and begin to use ethical guidelines found in the NAEYC Code of Ethical Conduct

- Demonstrate a disposition to be a continuous, collaborative learner

- Develop the ability to reflect critically on yourself as a person and a professional, and on the work you will do

- Have a disposition to actively advocate for children and families in personal and public arenas

TO LEARN MORE

Remember a Teacher: Write about a teacher you remember clearly from your own childhood. Describe:

- His or her personal qualities
- What you think your teacher valued and why
- His or her effect on children
- His or her effect in your life
- How you would like to be similar to or different from this teacher and why

Write a Newspaper Article About a Professional Early Childhood Educator: Interview an early childhood educator who has been working in the field for at least 5 years. Ask about the following:

- Basic information—job title, responsibilities, employer, training for the position
- Career path—education, experiences, and philosophy that led the individual to early childhood education and care
- Professional joys and issues
- Contributions—professional accomplishments, participation in the professional community
- Vision—what the person sees as the state of early childhood education and care and what the future holds for the field

Compare Two Programs: Observe two early childhood programs. Write a paper in which you compare the programs briefly and list what seem to be the primary values of each program. Explore the specific things you saw that led to your conclusions.

Write a Book Review: Read a book about an early childhood teacher using the books about teachers and teaching listed

below. Write a short review of the book as if you were writing for a newsletter or journal for teachers. Don't tell the whole story; give the highlights, share the personal meaning for you, and motivate your audience to read it for themselves.

Read a Book:

Ashton-Warner, Sylvia. 1963/1986. *Teacher.*

Axline, Virginia. 1971. *Dibs: In Search of Self: Personality Development in Play Therapy.*

Ayers, William. 1989. *The Good Preschool Teacher: Six Teachers Reflect on Their Lives.*

Glover, Mary Kenner. 1993. *Two Years: A Teacher's Memoir.*

Hillman, Carol B. 1986. *Teaching Four-Year-Olds: A Personal Journey.*

Kane, Pearl Rock. 1991. *My First Year as a Teacher.*

Kidder, Tracy. 1989. *Among Schoolchildren.*

Kohl, Herbert. 1968. *Thirty-six Children.*

Kuroyanagi, Tetsuko. 1982. *Totto Chan: The Little Girl in the Window.*

Marshall, Sybil. 1963. *Experiment in Education.*

Nieto, Sonia. 2003. *What Keeps Teachers Going?*

Pratt, Caroline. 1948/1970. *I Learn From Children.*

Rotzel, Grace. 1971. *School in Rose Valley.*

Van Cleave, Mary. 1994. *The Least of These: Stories of Schoolchildren.*

Weber, M. G. 1946/1970. *My Country School Diary.*

Other good choices might be one of the following by Vivian Paley: *White Teacher* (1979); *Wally's Stories—Conversations in the Kindergarten* (1981); *Boys and Girls—Superheroes in the Doll Corner* (1984); *Mollie Is Three—Growing up in*

School (1986); *Bad Guys Don't Have Birthdays—Fantasy Play at Four* (1988); *Boy Who Would Be a Helicopter* (1990); and *Kwanzaa and Me—A Teacher's Story* (1995).

Compare Fictionalized Accounts of Teachers' Stories: Watch film dramatizations of two or three teachers' stories (from the list below) and write a comparison of the characteristics of the values, temperaments, and intelligences of the different teachers. Describe which attributes of each teacher you would like to incorporate into your own developing teacher.

> *The Water Is Wide, Dead Poets Society, The King and I, Mr. Holland's Opus, The Sound of Music, Georgie Girl, Stand and Deliver, The Prime of Miss Jean Brodie*

Write an Autobiography: Briefly describe yourself using the characteristics of effective teachers described in this chapter, Thomas and Chess's Nine Dimensions of Temperament, and Gardner's Multiple Intelligences (you may wish to use your reflections from this chapter). Review the experiences and relationships in your life at home and in the world that led you to choose early childhood education as a career.

Write About Your Values: Discuss how they impact the way you work, or hope to work, with children. Discuss values you are acquiring as a professional. Where have they come from? What are your thoughts about the core values of the early childhood field as written in the NAEYC Code of Ethical Conduct? What do you see as you look ahead to becoming an early childhood educator (or as you continue your career)?

2

The Field of
Early Childhood
Education and Care

*E*arly childhood education and care touches the lives of nearly everyone in our society. Those who are most intimately affected by it are those children and families who participate and the professionals who work in the programs. It also impacts employers, teachers of children in later grades, and everyone else who deals with the children and families who are served, or not served, by early education and care programs. Families have immense challenges to meet, and they need help in the form of quality programs and supportive public policies if they are to do the important work of nurturing their children and preparing them to be successful learners. Nearly every issue confronting families of young children has become more pressing now that we have entered the new millennium. Increasing numbers of families of young children work and need child care, live in poverty, are without health insurance, are homeless, and experience violence in their communities. There is greater diversity culturally, linguistically, and in lifestyle choices; and there is also greater strife, less civility, and more uncertainty in our society. Early childhood educators will be called upon to work with children with a range of abilities, who come from different cultures, with a range of socioeconomic backgrounds, and whose families speak many languages. Those who work in this field need to understand and embrace this diversity and be prepared to focus on the best interests of young children in our rapidly changing, fast-paced and increasingly interconnected world.

Although early care and education programs cannot solve all of the social, economic, and political ills of our society, they can do much to give children a good beginning and to meet the needs of families whose members work or are in training. For programs and services to be beneficial they must be thoughtfully organized, responsive to the needs of children and families, and staffed by well trained and caring professionals.

In this chapter we lay out the broad outlines of the early childhood field as it exists in the United States today. As you become an early childhood educator, you will learn about and work in different kinds of programs for young children and you are very likely to encounter some of the issues that affect them. We recommend that you visit as many different settings as you can to get a direct experience of some of the kinds of programs we describe here. Your growing understanding of the complexity of the field of early childhood education and care and the important contributions it makes to our society will help you become a committed professional.

The many kinds of programs available to children today can be classified in a number of ways: by their purposes, the age of the children they serve, their location, the kinds of facilities in which they are housed, their hours of operation, sponsorship, funding, type of regulation, and educational philosophy.

The two principal purposes for early childhood programs are (1) to support children's learning and development, and (2) to provide care for children in families where adults are working or in training programs. As we pointed out in Chapter 1, care and education are inextricably linked, and child care programs, kindergartens, and primary classrooms are their major modes of delivery. Some early childhood programs have secondary purposes such as the education of parents and the provision of health, nutrition, and social services to children and families (Williams & Fromberg 1992). Another purpose—indigenous language revitalization—is found in community-based programs developed by groups of Native Americans and Native Hawaiians who want to pass their language and culture on to the next generation.

Early childhood programs can be found in centers (facilities dedicated to the care of children) or in homes. Center-based programs are located in churches or synagogues, community facilities such as the YWCA and YMCA, facilities built to house early childhood programs, public housing complexes, public schools, work sites, and recreational facilities. Home-based care may be in a family's own home or the home of a caregiver.

Sponsorship and funding of early childhood programs may be public (federal, state, or county) or private. The great majority of programs for children under age 5 are private and are paid for primarily by the families of the children who attend. Private programs may be not-for-profit, intended to provide a service to children and their families, or for-profit, designed as a service-oriented business. Some businesses offer or subsidize care for their employees' children because early education and care programs contribute to a reliable and productive workforce. Publicly funded preschool programs are most often provided for low-income children and those with disabilities, although the number of states that provide funding for programs for 4-year-olds (and sometimes even 3-year-olds) is growing.

The majority of children between the ages of 5 and 8 attend kindergarten through third grade in state-funded elementary schools. Some families choose and pay for private schools that may be religious or secular.

Following is a brief introduction to the most prevalent kinds of programs for young children today. The descriptions of these programs are organized by age groups to enable you to get a sense of what is available across the entire early childhood age spectrum. We will also discuss some vital issues facing educators who work in early education and care programs at the beginning of the 21st century.

PROGRAMS FOR CHILDREN FROM BIRTH TO AGE 5

Many kinds of education and care settings are available for children aged 5 and younger. They are designed to meet a wide variety of needs and circumstances. Full-day center-based care, family child care homes, and informal arrangements (care provided by relatives or friends, sometimes called "kith and kin" care) are most often used to meet the child care needs of working families. Since there is no one system for delivering and funding these programs, their availability and quality varies greatly from community to community. In our increasingly stressful society, family members may be working two or more jobs and may find it difficult to find the kind of care they need.

Other programs exist for the purposes of intervention and enrichment and may have as their primary aims supporting the development of the child, preserving a language or culture, providing education about parenting and child development to family members, or addressing other issues encountered by families, such as unemployment, potential child abuse, domestic violence, homelessness, and substance abuse. Private or public funds or a combination of the two may support these programs.

Child care is now a fact of life for a significant portion of children and families in our country. The most recent available data showed that 40% of preschoolers aged 5 or younger were cared for by their parents. The other 60% were in some form of regular nonparental care. Settings included center-based care, Head Start programs, relative care, and family child care (U.S. Department of Education 1998, 18).

Center-Based Programs care for full-day or p/t

Facilities that deliver education and care for young children are referred to as child care or day care centers. We prefer the term *child care* because, as someone once pointed out to us, programs care for children, not for days. (The term *day care* was originated to distinguish it from the historical practice of care that involved overnight boarding.) The majority of centers care for children for a full day, while members of their families are employed full-time or are in training to enter the workforce. Others are available only part of the day and focus on providing educational experiences of various kinds for children. All of these programs have a variety of kinds of sponsorship and funding sources.

In 2001, 56% of children ages 3 to 5 who had not yet entered kindergarten attended center-based early childhood care and education programs. Poor children were less likely to attend than those living in families at or above the poverty level (47%, compared with 59%) (Federal Interagency Forum on Child and Family Statistics 2001).

Full-Day Programs

Full-day programs for children under 5 have the challenge of providing a safe, nurturing setting and educational experiences for long hours each day. Until quite recently most programs served children between 2½ and 5 years of age. During the past 20 years the number of programs that care for infants and toddlers has increased rapidly. Center-based care for infants and toddlers was less prevalent than care for preschool children because many experts believed that it was best for very young children to be cared for at home and because the programs were costly. As more and more women entered the workforce, however, the demand for out-of-home care for infants and toddlers became more widespread. In order to meet children's needs and ensure their safety, experts believe that programs for infants should have a ratio of one caregiver to every three children. For this reason the cost of infant care is much higher than that for preschool care. The demand for care for infants and toddlers continues to exceed the supply (Children's Defense Fund 1999).

In some communities, programs in hotels and factories are open late hours or provide care for families who have extended work hours. Programs to serve sick children are also available in some places in response to the needs of working families. These programs, often housed in hospitals, are usually intended for children with mild, noncontagious illnesses.

Part-Day Programs

Part-day, center-based programs are often referred to as *preschools* to denote the educational orientation of the program (though this term is sometimes used to describe full-day programs as well). Part-day preschools are an outgrowth of the historical tradition of the *nursery school,* which focused on social-emotional development and provided play-oriented experiences for children 3 through 5 years of age. Most programs were half-day and followed a public school calendar. They were common when fewer women were in the workforce and there was less demand for full-day care.

Beginning in the late 1960s, nursery schools began to be called *preschools* as their programs were modified in recognition of the fact that important cognitive development occurs in the early years. Part-day programs have a variety of purposes and goals—some focus on overall development of the child, some are designed to promote academic skills, some to teach about language and culture, and others provide experiences designed to help low-income children to be successful in school. Some programs are committed to more than one of these purposes.

Parent cooperatives (called *co-ops*) are another type of part-day program. These programs, not prevalent today because so many women are in the workforce, are staffed by an early childhood educator who serves as teacher, director, and educational leader. Family members commit themselves to regular, active participation in the school. what ages?

Sponsorship and Funding

The great majority of child care centers in the United States today are privately sponsored, nonprofit, and funded by tuition paid by families. Many programs are housed in church facilities. Some are partly subsidized by the churches. Operating expenses for programs may also be sought from grants and fund-raising activities. Businesses—most often large corporations, but also hospitals, colleges, and government agencies—sometimes sponsor and subsidize child care programs for their employees. A small number of centers are found in colleges, universities, and high schools, where they are used as laboratory sites for students to learn about and gain experience in working with young children.

Some centers are set up as nationwide chains that attempt to make child care affordable and profitable by using standardized building plans, bulk purchase of equipment and supplies, and a uniform curriculum. These for-profit, franchised centers have become an increasingly common type of privately sponsored child care.

The Department of Defense provides the largest employer-sponsored child care program in the world. Federally sponsored programs serve more than 200,000 children (ages birth to 12) daily, with almost half of the care for infants and toddlers. Some 38% of those served are in child development centers (800 of them in more than 300 locations). Costs are shared between the government and the families served (Department of Defense 2004).

Other publicly funded programs include state and federally funded prekindergarten programs for low-income and disabled children and programs for children of teen parents.

The Trilemma

A well known set of issues related to programs for children younger than 5 is referred to as the *trilemma* of child care. The term *trilemma* refers to the interrelationship of (1) the need for quality programs to support children's development, (2) adequate compensation for staff, and (3) care that is affordable for families. This issue is sometimes referred to by the letters QCA—Quality, Compensation, and Affordability.

Quality. A number of large-scale studies have documented the positive long-term effects of high-quality early childhood programs on children and families (Barnett 1995; Gomby, Larner, Stevenson, Lewit, & Behrman 1995; Karoly et al. 1998; National

Institute of Child Health and Human Development 1999). Indicators of program quality used in these studies include low teacher-child ratios, small classes, strong parent involvement, well planned educational experiences, and teachers trained in early childhood education. All of the studies report that carefully targeted efforts produce social, emotional, and cognitive gains in children's development and a long-lasting impact on children's ability to succeed in school and to function as adults. Cognitive benefits are that children who attended high-quality programs score higher on assessments of school readiness and language development, show gains in IQ, and are less likely to be placed in special education or be retained in grade. Social outcomes include fewer behavioral problems and less contact with the criminal justice system. Other benefits include increases in parents' economic self-sufficiency, reduced rates of criminal activity, and improvements in children's health. The studies also suggest that programs must provide high-quality services if they are to generate long-term benefits (Barnett 1995; Cryer 2003).

The article "Defining and Assessing Early Childhood Program Quality" describes some core elements of quality related directly to the experience of children in education and care settings. These include:

- Safe care: Sufficient adult supervision and safe toys, equipment and furnishing
- Healthful care: A clean sanitary environment where children's physical needs are met
- Developmentally appropriate stimulation: The opportunity to learn through play and learn in a variety of areas of development
- Positive interactions with adults: The opportunity to trust, learn from, and enjoy the adults who care for them
- Encouragement of individual emotional growth: An environment in which adults encourage children to operate independently, cooperatively, securely, and competently
- Promotion of positive relationships: The opportunity for children to receive adult guidance and environmental support that helps them interact with their peers (Cryer 2003, 42)

National studies of program quality show that many programs are not delivering high-quality care. In their influential study, researchers from the National Institute of Child Health and Human Development (NICHD) found that most of the classrooms observed did not meet all standards. They also reported that children in classes meeting none of the recommendations achieved lower than average language comprehension scores in tests, while children in centers that met all guidelines had above average scores (1999).

Compensation. In privately supported center-based programs for children under age 5, teacher salaries are much lower than those for comparable positions in publicly supported programs because they are paid for from tuitions paid by families. Low teacher salaries, inadequate benefits, and lack of opportunity for advancement make it difficult to recruit and retain good people in these center-based programs. Other consequences of inadequate compensation are lower program quality and high staff turnover. The latter is especially unfortunate, because it undermines the stability of adult-child relationships and thus affects children's ability to form bonds with their teachers and benefit from program experiences. Children suffer because they do not have teachers who are adequately trained and because their young lives are disrupted each time a teacher leaves.

Compensation issues are also related to the fact that few men choose to enter the field, even though many would find it rewarding. They are discouraged by the low pay and, as well, by the common stereotype that caring for young children is women's work.

The first National Child Care Staffing Study conducted in the 1980s made the case that program quality is affected by the education of teaching staff and the adequacy of their wages. It also found that funding for child care had decreased in the previous decade, and that during the same period staff turnover had nearly tripled (Whitebook, Howes, & Phillips 1989). An update to the study published in 1998 found that wages for child care staff had remained mostly stagnant over the ensuing decade. Teaching staff continued to earn low wages (even in high-quality centers), though some improvements in health benefits were noted. Another finding was that child care centers continued to experience high turnover of teaching staff. In the sample of high-quality centers studied, the average turnover rate was 31% a year for all teaching staff. The study also found that more child care centers received public dollars in 1997 than in 1988, assisting more low-income families with child care costs. But the increases did not result in quality improvements, better wages, or lower staff turnover. A final and more encouraging finding was that programs accredited by NAEYC pay higher wages to staff, have lower teacher turnover, and have retained twice as many staff over the past decade (Whitebook, Howes, & Phillips 1998).

The 2004 yearly compendium of salary and benefit data published by the Center for the Early Childhood Workforce confirms that salaries remain low for both preschool teachers and child care workers and that turnover continues to rise. This document reports growing interest in raising the educational levels of teachers in early education and care programs and efforts (still mostly unsuccessful) to find a reliable stream of funding for preschool programs. It also discusses the use of scholarship programs as a mechanism for promoting recruitment and retention of teachers.

Affordability. A 2000 issue brief published by the Children's Defense Fund states:

> Every day, millions of American parents rely on child care to enable them to work and to provide the early education experiences needed to prepare their children for school. Good early care and education help foster each child's physical well-being and social development and give them opportunities to develop their early learning skills in a safe and secure environment. Yet finding and affording quality child care is a challenge for all families, particularly low-income working parents for whom the cost of quality child care is a real and daily barrier. (Schulman 2000, 1)

The brief goes on to say that center-based care for a 4-year-old averages $4,000 to $6,000 per year. This cost is hard for all families, especially those who have more than one child who needs care. In all but one state the annual cost of child care is more than the cost of public college tuition. Nonpoor families, on average, spend 7% of their income on child care. The burden is greatest on poor families who often have no choice but to place their children in lower cost, and often lower quality, care. "As a result, too many children are cared for in unstimulating or even unsafe settings. . . . It is particularly alarming given that children from low-income families are at greatest risk for school failure and are most in need of the strong start that high-quality care can provide" (Schulman 2000, 1).

Home-Based Programs

Home-based care is the least visible, yet most prevalent, form of privately sponsored child care in the United States. Throughout history, children have been cared for in their own homes and in the homes of relatives, friends, and paid caregivers. Home-based care can be provided either in family child care homes (usually three to eight children) and group child care homes (generally 12 to 15 children), in the homes of close relatives or family friends (informal or *kith and kin* care), or in a family's home by a trained or untrained caregiver. Some in-home caregivers receive training in working with children and become *nannies.* The most recent available informa-

tion indicates that approximately 40% of children who received child care were cared for in homes by non-relatives or by relatives (U.S. Department of Education, National Center for Education Statistics, 2000).

Home-based care is usually available from early morning to early evening and may be offered evenings and weekends to meet the needs of people who work unusual schedules. It can be less expensive than center-based care and is nearly always more flexible in scheduling and providing care for children who have mild illnesses. Home-based care is often chosen by families of infants and toddlers who prefer that their children be cared for in the small, intimate environment of a home. It is also an alternative to a child care center for preschool-age children.

In the past, the expense of in-home care was borne mostly by the families of the children served. Since the advent of welfare reform in the early 1990s government subsidies have been available for child care for women who were leaving welfare rolls to enter the labor force. The majority of these women choose *kith and kin care* (in-home care provided by friends and relatives). This kind of care is generally cheaper, more flexible, and more available in low-income neighborhoods than licensed care, especially for infants and toddlers. The provision of government subsidies led to questions about the quality and regulation of this kind of care. According to a recent study from the National Center for Children in Poverty (2001), these concerns are beginning to be addressed. By early 2001, 20 states had implemented programmatic strategies to improve kith and kin care, including home visiting, training, provision of safety kits and other resources, and distribution of newsletters.

The Department of Defense also offers the option of in-home care to military children in recognition of the fact that many families prefer to have their children cared for in more informal home settings (Department of Defense 2004).

Programs for Low-Income Children

Since the 1960s policy makers' concern with the effects of poverty on children's later school experience has led to government (first federal and more recently state) initiatives to provide a good school beginning for low-income children.

Head Start

Head Start, begun in 1965, is a federally funded program that grew out of the realization that many poor children did not have successful school experiences. Head Start was designed to provide these children with a good start in school. It is a *comprehensive* program because it provides a range of services for children with a focus on education, social-emotional development, physical and mental health, and nutrition. The program has a family focus that includes education about children's learning and child rearing and involvement of families in policy decisions.

For the first year, Head Start programs were offered in summer as part-day enrichment for 4- and 5-year-olds before they entered public school. The program was expanded to a full year when it became obvious that one summer was not enough time to provide children with the experiences they needed to help them succeed in school.

Head Start began as a part-day program because many of the participating families were on welfare and not working. When welfare reform, with its strong emphasis on employment, was initiated in 1996, Head Start began to provide more full-day programs in order to enable parents to pursue job training and employment opportunities.

In 2003 more than 900,000 children attended Head Start programs in their communities in all 50 states, the District of Columbia, Puerto Rico, and the U.S. territories (Head Start Bureau 2004). It is unfortunate that only three in five preschoolers eligible for Head Start were able to attend (Children's Defense Fund 2002).

Early Head Start

Over the years Head Start, which began as a program for 4- and 5-year-olds, has extended its services to younger and younger children. In recognition of research demonstrating the importance of development from birth to age 3 and the long-term

positive effects of high-quality early education and care, in 1994 Head Start established a new program, Early Head Start, for low-income pregnant women and families with infants and toddlers. The purposes of the Early Head Start program are to enhance children's development, to enable parents to be better caregivers and teachers to their children, and to help parents work toward economic independence. Services include quality early education and care; home visits, especially for families with infants; parent education, including parent-child activities; comprehensive health services; nutrition; and ongoing support for parents through case management and peer support groups.

In 2003, there were more than 650 programs to provide Early Head Start child development and family support services in all 50 states. These programs served nearly 62,000 children under the age of 3 (Head Start Bureau 2004). Currently fewer than 5% of eligible infants and toddlers are able to attend Early Head Start in spite of its potential benefits (State of Children in America's Union 2002).

Research

Longitudinal research on low-income and at-risk children who have participated in high-quality early childhood programs demonstrates that attendance has had a significant and lasting impact on cognitive development, social behavior, and health of its participants and has benefited their families as well. Moreover, it has been demonstrated that the cost is more than compensated for with savings in later remedial education programs and correctional institutions (Lazar & Darlington 1983; McKey 1985; Schweinhardt & Weikart 1997).

The Abecedarian Study, conducted by researchers at the Frank Porter Graham Child Development Center, showed long-lasting benefits for children who received high-quality early education and care. Many of the children were enrolled in a program from infancy through age 5. Quality components included good adult-child ratios, ongoing professional development and good salaries for staff, and individualized curriculum based on learning games. Researchers found significant differences in abilities and achievements between individuals who had attended the program and members of the control group. At age 21 those who had been enrolled in the program were more likely to score higher on IQ and reading and math tests, to be enrolled in or graduated from in a 4-year college, to have delayed parenthood, and to be gainfully employed (Frank Porter Graham Center 1999).

A national longitudinal study of the development of Head Start children, using a battery of instruments called FACES (Family and Child Experiences Survey), reported that children who attended Head Start showed significant gains in vocabulary, writing skills, and social skills, though few gains in aspects of early literacy, over the Head Start year. Head Start also had a positive impact on child health, readiness for school, and the children's families. The study found that Head Start parents reported reading to their young children three to five times a week (Administration for Children Youth and Families 2004).

Research has also been conducted on the kinds of educational experiences that are most effective for teaching low-income children. Studies have compared developmentally appropriate (DAP) programs with those that have an academic, skills-based focus. Results of the research are mixed with regard to academic achievement. A number of studies found that children in classrooms that were more developmentally appropriate showed less stress and anxiety than those in more academic settings (Burts et al. 1992; Stipek, Feiler, Ryan, Milburn, & Salmon 1998). A recent study (Van Horn & Ramey 2003) that compared former Head Start children with classmates in grades 1 through 3 found that developmentally appropriate practice accounted for little or no variation in children's academic performance. The authors of this study did not look at effects of different curriculum approaches on social and emotional development.

The research conducted to date raises questions about the impact of developmentally appropriate practice on cognitive development but makes the case that it has positive effects on children's social and emotional development. We believe that it is important to take into account the findings on social and emotional development and attitudes toward learning, since we know that these influences have a strong impact on children's later school experiences. We also believe that it is imperative for early childhood educators to find effective and appropriate ways to help children develop knowledge and skills that will help them succeed in school.

Head Start Legislation

In 1998, the Head Start Act was reauthorized by Congress to provide additional funding to enhance program quality and provide training and technical assistance. New funds for quality improvement were used to increase teacher pay and benefits, train teachers and other staff to meet Head Start's education performance standards, and extend the hours of service in response to the needs of families (Head Start Bureau 2004).

As we write in 2004, Congress is again considering reauthorization of the Head Start Act. Positive aspects of the proposed legislation are the emphasis on collaboration between federal and state early childhood initiatives, increasing qualifications for teachers, and continuation of standards-based reform. Concerns have been expressed that under this bill the provision of comprehensive services for children and families will be compromised or lost, that the requirement for teachers to earn advanced degrees will not be accompanied by funds to pay for their training, and that the required use of a standardized test that focuses on literacy and math will draw attention away from other important areas of children's development. Another reservation that has been expressed about the legislation is that the modest increase in funding is too little to sustain the program's success at a time of rising operating expenses (National Association for the Education of Young Children 2004; Raver & Zigler 2004).

Since the 1960s the millions of children who have attended Head Start programs have benefited from the provision of a high-quality, comprehensive program. Even though it has been expanded several times, Head Start has over the years served less than half of the eligible children.

In spite of limited access, Head Start has played a major role in focusing attention on the importance of early development. It has demonstrated the effectiveness of providing comprehensive services for young children and their families and has provided a model for other programs for low-income children. Head Start continues to receive public support and federal funding. Sadly, current legislative efforts appear to be backing away from the comprehensive, whole-child approach that has made such an important contribution to the lives of generations of poor children. The greater goals of providing a preschool experience for all low-income children and of diminishing the effects of poverty have not yet been realized and, sadly, are not among our nation's priorities at this time.

Programs for Children from Birth to Age 5 with Special Needs

In addition to the programs we have just described, there is in the United States a system of education and care programs for children who have disabilities. Programs and services for preschool children with disabilities are available in all states supported by a combination of federal and state funds. These programs are often, but not always, housed in public schools.

Passage of federal legislation—the Education for All Handicapped Children Act in 1975—marked the beginning of an alliance of families of children with special needs and professionals and other advocates in the field of special education. In 1990, this legislation was replaced by the Individuals with Disabilities Education Act (IDEA), which has guided implementation of childhood special education since that time. The purpose of IDEA is to ensure that all children with disabilities have access to a free, appropriate public education. Services are also mandated under the Americans with Disabilities Act (ADA), which requires access to public accommodations for all individuals regardless of disability. Such public accommodations include child care centers and family child care homes.

In order for children to be educated with their nondisabled peers, some communities have combined preschool special education classes with Head Start or community preschool classes. Head Start classrooms offer another source of opportunities for inclusion. In 2003, 12.5% of the Head Start enrollment consisted of children with disabilities (Head Start Bureau 2004). In some places private programs are subsidized to provide spaces in their programs for preschoolers with disabilities. Unfortunately there are still places where the only available option for children with disabilities is to attend self-contained special education preschool classes. These have been criticized because they do not allow children to interact with nondisabled peers. (We will explore this topic further in Chapter 12, "Inclusion of Children with Special Needs.")

Under Part H of IDEA, funds are available for infants and toddlers to receive early intervention services to minimize potential for developmental delays, to reduce the need for special education services when the child reaches school age, and to enhance the family's capacity to meet the child's special needs. Under this law children and families have the right to an individualized family service plan (IFSP), comparable to the individualized education plan (IEP) for older children. Ongoing research combined with an improved level of public awareness, and advocacy efforts by many parents and professionals has led to increased attention and funding for early intervention over the last decade.

When we look at who is eligible for special education services, it becomes clear that it is again the most disadvantaged children in society who need these programs. Disability appears to be directly related to poverty and the level of family education, and of course this impacts African-American and Hispanic children to a great degree. Nearly half of all students in special education are from low-income families in urban areas. And we know that poverty is associated with higher exposure to toxins, poor nutrition, less stimulating home and child care environments and lower birth weight. "Given the higher accumulation of risk factors in children by race/ethnicity groups, it is not surprising that race/ethnicity differences are evident in school readiness at the kindergarten level" (Turnbull, Turnbull, Shank, & Smith 2004, 13). We have come a long way as a nation in our commitment to children with disabilities. But it is hard not to think about how many children could avoid being identified as having special needs if their parents received adequate prenatal medical care and if they received high-quality early care and education programs from infancy.

Parent Education Programs

Many kinds of programs are available for parents of young children. They are based on the assumption that parents are children's first and most important teachers. These programs can take the form of parenting classes or meetings dealing with topics such as child development and child guidance, or they can involve parents in working with children in classrooms. Another type of program entails trained visitors who work with parents and children in their homes. Programs for infants and toddlers that combine parenting education with activities for children are becoming increasingly widespread due to increases in federal funding. Some programs provide literacy and job skills programs for the parents. Parent education, especially in combination with a high-quality program for children, appears to have a positive impact on children and their families (Barnett 1995).

The Even Start Family Literacy Program, begun in 1988, is intended to help break the cycle of poverty and illiteracy and improve the educational opportunities of low-income families by integrating early childhood education, adult literacy or adult basic education, and parenting education. This federally sponsored program seeks collaboration among existing community agencies, such as those that focus on adult literacy, social services, and early childhood education. The Even Start Program was reauthorized by the federal government in 2000 and 2001.

The large number of births to teenage parents has had major social and economic consequences for the teenagers themselves and for their children. Though the birthrate appears to be falling at this time, there are still an estimated 1 million teen pregnancies in the United States each year (Pregnancy Info 2004). Concern over this trend has led to the creation of new programs in schools and social service agencies. Parenting education programs for adolescents are being advocated as a necessary addition to the curriculum of intermediate and high schools. Some programs provide home visitors for teen parents and grandparents and their babies; others provide child care in public schools while the mothers complete their high school education.

Regulation of Programs for Children from Birth to Age 5

Because young children are so dependent and vulnerable, families and society want to be assured that the programs that serve them are committed to their welfare and will protect them from harm. The avenue used to ensure a minimal level of quality in programs for young children under 5 is licensing of programs. "Governments can regulate programs that are operated in the private market. Regulatory policy enables governments to protect the public and to set a floor of quality for programs in the private sector" (Morgan 2003, 65).

Licensing

Programs for infants, toddlers, and preschoolers are subject to government regulation based on standards developed in each state. All states license preschool programs. In some states all programs are required to be licensed, whereas in others certain categories of programs are exempt from licensing. Because early childhood programs have, until recently, been viewed as a social service for families, licensing is generally handled by departments of social welfare or human services. Historically, licensing focused on preschool programs, but it has come to include programs for infants and toddlers and before- and after-school care. Most states also have provisions for licensing or registering family child care and group child care homes, though these requirements are difficult to enforce because it is hard for the agency to find out who is offering care if they do not voluntarily seek licensing.

In states with minimal standards, licensing provides a "safety net" that ensures that the physical environment is safe and healthy and that enough adults are available to supervise children. In other states standards are higher and all aspects of development are required to be addressed in programs. State standards for licensing and for enforcing standards vary greatly and licensure in itself is no guarantee of quality. Unlike many other Western nations, the United States has no nationally mandated child care standards, even for federally funded child care programs.

The National Association for the Education of Young Children (NAEYC) 1997 position statement on licensing and public regulation of early childhood programs stresses children's right to care settings that protect them from harm and promote their healthy development. It offers principles for implementing an effective regulatory system—including the regulation of all programs with no exemptions or exceptions, licensing of all facilities including centers and family child care homes, and licensing standards that are clear and reasonable and reflect current research. The position statement also calls for regulations to be vigorously and equitably enforced, for licensing agencies to have sufficient staff and resources to do their job, for regulations to be coordinated to promote efficiency, and for incentives to encourage service beyond the bare minimum. Other recommendations are for strategies to be developed to raise public consciousness regarding the importance of high-quality programs and adequate regulation, and for states to invest sufficient levels of resources for licensing workers to protect children's healthy development and learning.

State or national programs that receive government funding may have standards that are different from or exceed state standards. Child care facilities run by branches of the armed services for the children of military personnel are subject to regulations that are higher than those for most states. All military programs are required to receive NAEYC accreditation to verify program quality. At present 99% of the programs are accredited. All family child care providers in military settings must go through licensure and they are encouraged to achieve accreditation (Department of Defense 2004).

Head Start programs are subject to state licensing requirements and must also follow national Head Start performance standards. These standards address four areas: child development and health services, family partnerships, community partnerships, and program design and management.

Accreditation

NAEYC accreditation is a process for recognizing early childhood programs that meet criteria for high quality. It is a private, voluntary system for group programs (child care centers, kindergarten and primary programs, and before- and after-school care programs) that met standards of excellence in serving young children. The accreditation system was developed with the goals of facilitating improvement in the quality of programs and evaluating program characteristics (Bredekamp & Willer 1996).

Although the program began as an NAEYC initiative, a separate unit, the National Academy of Early Childhood Programs, was created to award the accreditation. The process involves a program review, including a self-study that enables all program participants (parents, staff, and administration) to offer input. Programs for children younger than 5 must meet local licensing requirements before they can apply for accreditation.

Since it began in 1985, NAEYC accreditation has experienced tremendous growth. Today the system is recognized and respected. The standards have become benchmarks for the entire field and often influence licensing regulations and program funding. Substantial growth has raised the number of accredited centers—particularly in the military, Head Start programs, public school prekindergartens, and child care chains. NAEYC is now in the process of a major revision of the accreditation program that will involve more rigorous standards and require a higher level of compliance with the standards.

Current interest in accreditation as a way to improve program quality has led to the development of other accreditation systems for recognizing program excellence. The National Association for Family Day Care recognizes excellence in family child care; the National Early Childhood Program Accreditation Commission accredits private for-profit centers; and the National School Age Care Alliance accredits before- and after-school programs.

Teacher Education

The majority of training available for teachers who work in programs for children between birth and age 5 is found in community college programs. Teachers in preschool programs may have associate or bachelor's degrees in child development or early childhood education or even advanced degrees. Since the 1970s early childhood educators have had the option of working toward a national credential called the Child Development Associate (CDA). This credential, administered by the Council for Professional Recognition in Washington, DC, an agency affiliated with NAEYC, is awarded based on demonstration of knowledge in six areas. It was originally designed to recognize training received by Head Start teachers, and it now qualifies those who receive it for entry-level teaching positions.

In addition to licensing of centers, some states require a teaching certificate or license for teachers who work in early childhood programs with preschool children. Other states only license teachers who work in elementary (K-6) and preschool special education programs. NAEYC has developed guidelines for the preparation of teachers in 2- and 4-year teacher education programs. These guidelines are developed to assist states in designing their requirements for early childhood teacher preparation. Teacher qualifications for a variety of roles are described in Chapter 1.

> **Reflect and write about programs for children from birth to age 5**
>
> Think about a program for children under 5 that you know. What are its purposes? Who runs it? Who pays for it? Do you think it is a high-quality program? How can you tell? Would you enjoy working in it? Why?

PROGRAMS FOR CHILDREN AGES 5 THROUGH 8

The great majority of 5- to 8-year-old children, including those with disabilities, attend kindergarten and grades 1 to 3 in public or private schools. A small but growing number of children are educated at home by their families. In recent decades, before- and after-school programs for school-age children have become more widespread in response to the needs of working families. Some of these are administered by private agencies as part of the child care system and some are part of the public school system.

Traditionally, kindergarten has been a transition for 5-year-old children, between home or a preschool program and the more academically demanding first grade classroom. In the past most kindergarten programs were half-day, but the percentage of full-day kindergartens has greatly increased. The national study of kindergartens conducted reported by Wirt and colleagues (2004) states that enrollment of 4- to 6-year-olds in kindergarten increased in the period between 1977 and 2001. During this period, the percentage of children enrolled in full-day kindergarten also increased. By 1995 it was larger than the percentage of children enrolled in half-day kindergarten. These researchers also found that there were more full-day kindergartens in the South than in other areas of the country, and that there were more full-day programs in small towns and rural areas and in public schools with a high percentage of low-income children.

Kindergarten programs are most often a part of the public education system and supported by public funds. In many states kindergarten is offered, but attendance is not mandatory until children are in first grade. Privately operated kindergarten programs are often sponsored by private schools or religious organizations.

All children in the United States are required to attend school from age 6—in the public schools in their communities, in private schools, or in home schooling arrangements. Schools vary tremendously in the kinds of curriculum they provide for kindergarten and primary grades and the extent to which these programs are responsive to the developmental needs of young children.

The Purpose of Kindergarten

An issue that is likely to affect a new teacher of 5-year-olds is the lack of consensus regarding whether the purpose of kindergarten should be the development of the child or preparation for first grade. The kindergarten curriculum has been the subject of debate for many years and the debate continues today.

Many educators who were trained in early childhood education and child development believe that the focus of the kindergarten should be the developmental needs of children. Those who hold this view think that literacy will emerge as children have meaningful experiences with reading and writing. Teachers in this type of program provide an environment that is rich in print, with opportunities for oral language throughout the day, experiences with good children's literature, and instruction in the alphabet and phonemic awareness as they relate to topics that are interesting and meaningful to children. They also offer many opportunities for children to learn through play in a prepared learning environment.

The opposing viewpoint, more likely to be held by those trained in elementary education, is that the role of the kindergarten is to prepare 5-year-olds for the expectations of higher grades and for successful performance on standardized tests. Teachers in this type of program tend to focus on direct instruction in math and reading. They set aside time each day for formal instruction on the "basics." Their kindergartens often include drill on skills, phonics, basal readers, and worksheets.

For many years early childhood educators have hoped that the child-centered early childhood practices of the preschools would push their way up into the kindergarten and have feared that academic expectations from first grade would push their way down into the kindergarten. Kindergartens vary greatly from classroom to classroom and from school to school. You may see a range of practices, from informal programs stressing play, socialization, and hands-on learning to highly structured academic programs that are almost indistinguishable from upper-grade classrooms. In the past, reading was not formally taught until children entered first grade, though in recent years it has become a standard feature of most kindergartens.

The K–3 Curriculum

In the 1970s and early 1980s a wave of concern with the "basics" led to a strong emphasis on traditional academic instruction in the early grades. In the 1980s and early 1990s, traditional academic methods of teaching in the early grades began to be impacted by NAEYC's influential publication *Developmentally Appropriate Practice in Early Childhood Programs* (Bredekamp & Copple 1997), which focused on knowledge of growth and development and stressed the value of child-centered, hands-on approaches to learning. While curriculum based on developmentally appropriate practice (DAP) was popular for a time, the current emphasis on content and performance standards and school accountability has made it increasingly more challenging for teachers to implement this approach in most public and many private school classrooms. Current federal policies have led to a resurgence of programs that use direct instruction for math and reading in the early grades, especially in schools for low-income children who are believed to be at risk for school failure.

Today, the following issues regarding K–3 curriculum are being debated:

- The most desirable method for teaching reading to young children—phonics and direct instruction versus "whole language" or "balanced reading" (See Chapter 10, "The Curriculum," for more about these approaches.)
- The most effective teaching strategies for children who enter school speaking a home language other than English—initial instruction in the child's home language versus instruction in English from the beginning
- Whether kindergarten and primary grade programs should focus on academic preparation for later grades and scores on standardized tests or on meaningful, appropriate curriculum based on knowledge of young children's development

At the present time direct instruction in the kindergarten and primary grades is gaining prevalence over more child-centered approaches, especially in the teaching of reading.

Programs for Children Ages 5 Through 8 with Special Needs

The majority of 5- to 8-year-old children with disabilities are educated in public school classrooms. An increasing number of these children are being included in regular classrooms for all or part of the school day. Many school districts are implementing "full inclusion"—placement of children with special needs in regular education classrooms. Most educators believe that this practice is beneficial both for children who have disabilities and their peers who are not disabled. When children with special needs are included in regular classrooms it becomes imperative that school districts provide adequate support services for the teachers involved. If this is not done, inclusion adds another load to the already overburdened classroom teacher.

Home Schooling

Prior to the advent of universal public education in the United States, educating children at home was the only option for families who lived in isolated locations or could not afford to send their children to school. Today home schooling is a fast-growing form of education. An estimated 1.7 to 2.1 million children (grades K–12) were home schooled during 2002–2003 in the United States (National Home Education Research Institute 2004). Families vary in their reasons for home schooling. They may be concerned about the child's safety, want to keep a child away from bad influences, wish to convey a specific system of values, disapprove of the instructional methods used in local schools, or believe they can do a better job than a teacher who has to deal with a large group of children in a classroom.

Many states have established standards and requirements that families must meet in order to home school their children. These requirements vary greatly across the United States. Some states and school districts require a particular curriculum or adherence to an approved plan of instruction.

School-Age Child Care

In the past it was assumed that most children had a mother at home who would see them off to school in the morning and greet them when they returned home at mid-afternoon. The contemporary reality is that, in many families, all adults have work commitments and need care for their school-age children before and after school hours, during school holidays, and during the summer months when most schools are not in operation.

School-age child care may be provided by a number of programs and agencies including family child care homes, child care centers, municipal parks and recreation departments, YMCA and YWCA programs, elementary schools, and religious organizations. Most school-age child care is paid for by the families who use it; some is partially subsidized by a sponsoring organization or a state. In this area of education, as in the others we have discussed, the families most able to pay have care for their children and those with more limited resources do not.

Reflect and write about programs for 5- to 8-year-olds

Think about a kindergarten, primary grade, or after-school program that you know. Does the program focus on academic skills, or play and hands-on learning? Do you think the program provides a good experience for the children? Would you enjoy working in it? Why?

Teacher Education and Licensing

Public school systems use *licensure* (also called *certification*) of teachers rather than licensing of programs as the mechanism for ensuring that teachers are qualified to work with children. A bachelor's or master's degree in education or a set of courses that lead to licensure is required in all states. An agency, often the state department of education or a professional licensing board, establishes standards describing what teachers should know and be able to do in their work with children. University and other teacher preparation programs then design their curriculum to help students achieve these standards. The programs go through an accreditation process that assures the standard-setting agency that graduates will meet the standards and function effectively in classrooms.

Higher education programs that prepare people to work with children ages 5 through 8 (and sometimes younger) are housed in schools, colleges, or departments of education (SCDEs) and lead to a degree and licensure in elementary or early childhood education. Some states require early childhood teachers to complete a degree in early childhood education, others require a set of courses that lead to an early childhood endorsement on an elementary education license. Licensing requirements are developed by states based on their unique historical circumstances, so there is wide variation in the age range covered by teaching licenses and training programs. We are aware of states that license teachers to serve in programs for children from kindergarten to sixth grade, birth to kindergarten, birth to age 8, ages 3 to 5, and ages 3 to 8.

NAEYC has developed *Standards for Professional Preparation* for students enrolled in programs that lead to an initial teaching license and for advanced programs. This document lays out five standards that should form the foundation for all early childhood teacher education programs. (A section at the end of each chapter of this book indicates which standards the chapter content addresses.)

Colleges and universities may choose to apply for a national accreditation through NCATE, the National Council for Accreditation of Teacher Education. NCATE is a mechanism to help establish high-quality teacher preparation, providing a process for professional accreditation of colleges of education. It consists of a coalition of specialty professional associations of teachers, teacher educators, content specialists, and local and state policy makers. NAEYC is a member of NCATE, and as such it is responsible for reviewing the applications of early childhood teacher preparation programs in schools of education that are seeking national recognition through NCATE.

There is also a growing interest in national teacher standards. A National Board for Professional Teaching Standards (NBPTS) was created in 1987 in order to upgrade the nation's teaching force. The mission of the NBPTS is to establish rigorous standards for what accomplished teachers should know and be able to do. It operates a national voluntary system to assess and certify teachers who meet these standards, and it works to advance education reforms related to improving teacher standards. The NBPTS is dedicated to bringing respect and recognition to the work of teachers (National Board for Professional Teaching Standards 1994, 1). Many states and school districts provide incentives for teachers to seek National Board certification.

Issues Facing the Field Today

In this section we explore some of the current issues facing the field of early childhood education and care. You are very likely to encounter some of these issues as you embark on your career as a teacher of young children.

Whose Responsibility Is Early Education and Care?

In order to understand the most significant challenges that face educators who work with children under the age of 5 we need to address the question "Whose responsibility is it to meet the needs of young children and their families in our society?" In the United States, as in many other places in the world, this issue has been, and continues to be, the subject of great debate.

Public policy is government action that reflects the values and concerns of the citizens. Countries differ tremendously in their policies regarding the extent to which the needs of children and their families are met by government resources or by private means. Some countries have overall policy relating to children and families, while others, like the United States, have let policies develop in patchwork fashion based on emerging needs.

In the United States it has always been assumed that families would care for their own children. Government involvement was limited to the neediest: care for orphans, protection for abused children, and food and housing for the children of the poor. And while we have accepted in our society that it is every child's birthright to have free public education beginning at the age of 5 or 6, the years before 5, which we now know have significant impact on later development, still receive less attention and less funding than programs for children 5 and older. A serious gap separates what we know about development and what we do. Our current policies reflect the views that were held at the beginning of the 20th century, not what is known at the beginning of the 21st century. Because programs for young children have been seen as a family issue and not a societal issue, many people still believe that early care and education is a family matter. As a result the United States has a fragmented system (some call it a *nonsystem*) for coordinating and delivering early childhood programs and services.

In the past most people believed that preschool and kindergarten were not "real school"—but rather were only preparation for the serious learning that begins in the first grade. This attitude resulted in fewer programs and lower status and pay for teachers of young children. Even today, generally, the younger the children served, the lower the status and salary of the educator. Though early childhood education is taken more seriously today, the salaries of preschool teachers do not reflect this changing view.

Today we know that young children must receive adequate nurture and stimulation to give them a good beginning in life. If they are cared for outside of their homes, they need good quality early education and care programs. But only affluent families are able to afford the high-quality early childhood programs that all children need. Federal and state support for early childhood care and education is available for some poor families, but as we pointed out earlier in this chapter there are not nearly enough spaces in these programs for all of the eligible children. For many lower-middle and middle-class families, paying for child care is an overwhelming burden. The alternatives are not good. Either children receive no program at all, or they receive the least expensive (often unlicensed and unmonitored) care. When early childhood education and care costs are high, even middle-income parents are likely to turn to nonregulated sources that offer no assurance of quality.

It is informative to look at public policy relating to child care in other countries. According to the National Center for Educational Statistics, the United States ranked fifth in the percentage of children ages 3 to 5 enrolled in preprimary programs. The percentages were 100% in France, 98% in Italy, 83% in Japan, 72% in Germany, and 64% in the United States. In France, Italy, and Japan, systems are in place for delivering early education that is universally available and publicly supported and financed (U.S. Department of Education 2002).

Although early childhood education and care lacks adequate resources, there have been some promising developments in recent years. One positive sign is the growth of state-supported programs for 3- and 4-year-olds. Anne Mitchell (2001) found that at the beginning of 2001 only nine states were without any state-funded pre-K program and the governor of one of those states was proposing funding for these programs. Mitchell's study describes the growth of prekindergarten programs and the tremendous variability between the states in the kinds of programs that are funded, their sponsorship, and funding mechanisms.

The authors of *Early Childhood Education and Care in the USA* point to some other positive directions in the field. They note that policy makers are becoming more aware of early childhood issues and that there is more dialogue between policy makers and early childhood educators. New directions include greater understanding of the links between policy and program quality; more dialogue about what constitutes quality in programs, including the important role of teacher education and training; expanded state involvement in early childhood education; and growing recognition of the

Reflect on the responsibility for early education and care

Who do you think should be responsible for early care and education? Is it a family responsibility or a societal responsibility? Why? Would your family and friends agree with your view? What would be the view of most people in your community? What do you think policy makers could do to improve the situation?

need for a systemic approach to providing an infrastructure for the early childhood field at the local, state, and national levels. The authors also raise some vital questions: "Who will provide early childhood services? Who will teach and care for young children? Who will pay for early childhood services? And, who will govern early education and care?" (Clifford, Cochran, & Kagan 2003).

The Movement Toward Greater Professionalism

Awareness of the impact of high-quality education and care and its link to teacher preparation, combined with the other changes, have led to another positive development—the movement toward greater professionalism of the early childhood field.

One indicator of growing professionalism is the increase in membership in professional organizations like NAEYC. Membership in NAEYC, the largest organization of early childhood educators in the United States, has grown dramatically. In 2004 it had more than 100,000 members, with affiliate groups in every state.

Efforts have also been under way for a number of years to increase the professionalism of the early childhood field by establishing standards for competent practice and for educational qualifications. These initiatives include a model of professional development, program standards for 2-year and 4-year teacher education programs, national accreditation of high-quality early education and care programs, a Code of Ethical Conduct, and the creation by NAEYC of a National Institute for Early Childhood Professional Development.

Many states have been working to create career development systems to determine what early childhood educators need to know and be able to do in the diverse roles they hold. Most state systems include a career lattice (or ladder) with clearly articulated pathways between levels based on education and experience. States are also identifying standards for competent practice (sometimes called core knowledge, competencies, or knowledge, skills, and attitudes) in practitioners and trainers.

In the future we hope to see a coordinated professional development system that will ensure that individuals in the early childhood education and care workforce have access to training and career mobility. Such a system would help practitioners advance in their careers, and provide guidelines for compensation that link increased professional development and improved performance to increased compensation (Willer 1994).

Standards, Assessment, and Accountability

All education in the United States has been profoundly influenced by the movement for school reform that began two decades ago with the publication of a report called *Nation at Risk* (National Commission on Excellence in Education 1983). This report examined the state of American education and declared with a great urgency that a "rising tide of mediocrity" threatened the nation. The authors reported that test scores were falling, academic expectations were too low, and students educated in the United States were not competing favorably with their counterparts in other countries. Recommendations included the development of higher and measurable standards for academic performance and higher standards for teacher preparation.

In the years since *Nation at Risk* was released, accountability for school performance has become national priority. The federal government has become increasingly more involved in educational policy, which until the 1980s had been the realm of state and local governments. In 1989 the National Educational Goals Panel (NEGP), a bipartisan group of political leaders, took up the cause of educational reform and initiated the creation of eight national education goals. In 1994 the NEGP became a federal agency charged with monitoring and facilitating progress in reaching the eight goals (National

Education Goals Report 1997). This initiative, which ended in 2002, resulted in the development of current state systems for linking standards, assessment, and accountability.

Standards

The first task promoted by the National Education Goals Panel was the development of content standards that would help states and school districts ensure that worthwhile subject matter was being taught. Content standards address goals and objectives for each subject area for each grade. They were originally developed by professional associations (the National Council for the Social Studies, National Council for Teachers of Mathematics, International Reading Association, and others). States then developed their own content standards drawing on national standards but tailoring them to their own educational priorities. Performance (or achievement) standards and assessments, usually in the form of tests, were then developed to determine the extent to which children had mastered the prescribed content.

Standards are now a feature of every public school in the United States. Some educators believe that they lead to greater clarity about what should be taught and give useful information about whether it has been learned. Others feel that standards, when accompanied by testing, have narrowed the focus of education and diminished teacher spontaneity and creativity.

Preschools, too, have begun to experience the pressure for accountability. Elementary school administrators have become interested in how children's preschool experiences will help them meet kindergarten expectations. For this reason many states have developed preschool standards. Early learning standards (also called content standards) describe learning experiences that should be provided for young children in early care and education programs that will help prepare them for later school experiences. These standards can be used to assist preschool teachers and administrators in shaping a meaningful and well-rounded daily program for children. They include examples of what most children are able to do at a particular age when exposed to appropriate learning experiences.

NAEYC has recently developed a position statement to identify principles or criteria for developing, adopting, and using early learning standards. NAEYC states that "standards can help practitioners and policy makers create a clear focus on what is truly important in early education" (Hyson 2003, 66).

A survey of early learning standards (Kagan, Scott-Little, & Stebbins Frelow 2003) indicates that 39 states have or are in the process of developing early learning standards intended to improve instruction or increase children's readiness for school. The majority of these standards were developed for use by state-funded early childhood programs. States vary in the focus of the standards (some address only language and literacy; others address all domains of development) and in the extent to which their use is mandated.

In most states early learning standards have been connected to K-12 standards. In some places preschool standards have been "backmapped" (developed to correspond to each of the K-12 standards); in others the early learning standards are based on what their developers regard as appropriate content for preschool children. The resulting early education standards are then linked to the related K-12 standards.

Authors of the survey caution us, with regard to early learning standards, that early care and education professionals and policy makers must work together to ensure the effective development and use of standards so that they lead to positive outcomes for children and the field (Kagan et al. 2003, 58).

The No Child Left Behind Act

The federal No Child Left Behind (NCLB) Act of 2001 builds upon and expands previous work on school accountability. This legislation requires each state to measure every public school student's progress in reading and math, yearly, in grades 3 through 12. Assessments are required to be aligned with state academic content and achievement standards.

States are also required to plan annual, measurable objectives that each local school district and school must meet, and they are required to report their progress on an annual report card. When they do not show adequate progress, schools must use their federal funds to make improvements. In the event of a school's continued poor performance, parents have options including tutoring and moving a child to a school that is making satisfactory progress.

In order to receive federal funds for programs for low-income children, schools must use programs and practices that the U.S. Office of Education has determined to be effective based on a definition of "rigorous scientific research."

The NCLB bill began as a bipartisan effort. Its supporters claim that measuring children's progress will provide teachers with independent information about each child's strengths and weaknesses, that it will help principals improve programs, and that it will let parents know how their children are progressing. While the great majority of educators and policy makers agree with the need for accountability and support the goal of ensuring that all children are making adequate progress in school, many are now concerned that the provisions of this bill may have a negative impact on children, teachers, and schools (Graves 2002; Kohn 2000).

Concerns about NCLB are that it:

- Leads to downward extension of educational demands
- Leads to "teaching to the test" rather than allowing teachers to provide meaningful and appropriate learning experiences, especially for young children
- Results in a focus on teaching isolated facts rather than developing thinking skills
- Leads to lack of attention to and, hence, devaluing of the arts, social studies, physical education, and development of social skills
- Employs an unnecessarily narrow and rigid definition of "scientific research" that results in the adoption of skills-based, direct instruction programs and excludes other effective programs
- Results in teachers of poor children being required to employ federally prescribed programs and practices, while teachers in more affluent schools are able to use professional judgment in the selection of curriculum and instructional methods
- Has not provided enough resources to enable the states to implement its provisions
- Perpetuates the idea that the sole purpose for education is academic achievement as demonstrated by scores on standardized tests

Some critics even maintain the real problem with this legislation is that it diverts attention from inequities in race and class and lack of good beginnings for children that are the real cause of poor academic achievement. Charles Lawrence (2004) summed up this view in a recent lecture: "We leave these children behind long before they reach the classroom."

The current emphasis on evidence-based programs and high-stakes testing places a great deal of pressure on young children and their teachers. However, educational practice in the United States can be viewed as a pendulum that responds to social and political forces by swinging back and forth between emphasis on the needs and interests of children and emphasis on academic content and accountability. At this time the educational pendulum has swung sharply toward content and accountability. As in the past, policy makers, educators, and parents may begin to question whether the current emphasis on direct instruction and standardized testing is effective in meeting the needs of young children, and the pendulum may begin to swing back.

Readiness

When it was introduced in 1991, National Education Goal I stated that "all children in America will start school ready to learn" (National Education Goals Report 1997). In recognition of the fact that all children begin learning at birth, in many communities *ready to learn* was replaced with *ready to succeed in school.*

But what "ready to succeed in school" means has changed over the years. As the pressure for achievement on standardized tests grew, academic expectations were pushed down to the kindergarten. Five-year-olds were expected to learn to read and do paper-and-pencil tasks (things that until recently were not expected until the first grade). Teachers and administrators began to notice that some children were having a hard time meeting kindergarten expectations and were falling behind. Some school districts responded by raising the age of kindergarten entry because it was believed that older children would do better at meeting the new, higher academic expectations. In other places assessment tests were used to exclude children from entering kindergarten who were judged to be "unready." And more and more children began to be retained in kindergarten because they weren't ready for the more rigorous expectations of first grade.

Defining Readiness. As a result of these practices, educators began to raise the question "How should readiness be defined?" (Lewit & Baker 1995). How readiness is defined in large measure determines where the responsibility for improving readiness lies: with the child, the school, or the support provided to both. A readiness definition, then, has practical consequences. It affects decisions about assessment, about the direction and targets of community and state investments, and about how to gauge progress.

A general consensus on the broad components of readiness has emerged at the national level. The National Educational Goals Panel recommended three readiness components: (1) readiness in the child, (2) schools' readiness for children, and (3) family and community supports that contribute to children's readiness.

Many states have now turned their attention to more systematically defining each of these components, how they will be assessed, and how progress in each will be determined. Readiness initiatives in states include attention to providing high-quality preschool for more children (especially those at risk for school failure), educating families about things they can do at home to help their children to succeed in school, training teachers and principals in child development including realistic academic expectations for young children, and developing procedures that help children make a smooth transition from home or preschool to the kindergarten.

Age of School Entry. The issue of age of school entry is directly related to questions about "readiness." In the past when kindergarten was viewed as a time for children to get ready for the real work of first grade, no one questioned that a child would begin school when he or she reached the designated age for school entry. But as expectations for academic performance in kindergarten increased, parents and teachers became increasingly concerned about the "right" age for a child to enter kindergarten. Some research and observation suggest that the youngest children in a kindergarten class often have trouble keeping up with their peers. Two things have been done in response to this concern. In some cases children's entry to kindergarten is postponed for a year to allow them to mature (a practice referred to as *red-shirting*). This may be an acceptable option for families who can afford another year of tuition in preschool but does not serve the family who cannot afford to send their child to an early childhood program. The child who does not attend preschool or its equivalent enters school a year further behind. In some cases a child who cannot keep up with academic expectations is kept in kindergarten for an extra year.

Both of these practices may have harmful consequences. When schools emphasize academic skills in readiness decisions and keep younger children out of school, the average age of each cohort of students rises. This lead to rising expectations and the cycle starts again.

NAEYC's position statement on school readiness (National Association for the Education of Young Children 1993a)

Reflect on public school programs in your community

Think about an experience that you have had with standards, testing, readiness, or the age of kindergarten entry. What happened? What policies made this easy or hard for the child or family? What policies do you think would help children and families to deal with these issues?

states: "Schools must be able to respond to a diverse range of abilities within any group of children, and the curriculum in the early grades must provide meaningful contexts for children's learning rather than focusing primarily on isolated skills acquisition."

FINAL THOUGHTS

In the course of the last century, our understanding of childhood and the needs of young children was completely transformed. At the beginning of the 20th century, most people believed that young children were not ready to learn anything important until the age of 6, when they entered school. And until recently many people thought that anyone who worked with children under 6 was "only babysitting"—a phrase that you still hear occasionally today. As we enter the 21st century, growing understanding of the human brain in combination with research on the effects of high-quality child care have led to a new era of awareness about the importance of the early years. Research has shown that early experiences, including the quality of early childhood programs, have a tremendous impact on children's later development.

We recently heard Sue Bredekamp, a national leader in early education, base a comment on a famous quote from Charles Dickens. She pointed out that we are now experiencing both the best of times and the worst of times for early care and education (Bredekamp 2003). We agree! It is the best of times because the importance of the early years has been widely recognized and is receiving more attention than ever before. It is the worst of times because of the growing pressure to focus on academic skills and to make early education just like education for older children despite a large body of evidence that shows that young children learn in different ways than do older children.

At this time in our history there are many causes for concern among people who care about the welfare of young children and their families. The national emphasis on accountability is forcing educators to pay more attention to test scores than to the needs of young children. Budget deficits endanger adequate funding for schools in general and schools for low-income children in particular. There is a widening gap between the availability and quality of education for affluent and poor children. Many decisions that impact children have become tied to political positions rather than to what is in the best interests of our children and the nation.

There is also some cause for hope. There is a greater awareness of the importance of quality programs for young children; many states have initiatives for funding preschool programs; there is new concern with the development of infrastructure for policy, planning, and coordination of programs for young children; and more collaboration is occurring among organizations concerned with the well-being of children and families. Another bright spot is that early childhood education has wonderful "champions for children"—legislators, media personalities, program officers in foundations, scholars, benefactors, and practitioners—who are working to raise public awareness and to improve programs and services for young children. At this time in history many early childhood educators are especially appreciative of the work done by Marian Wright Edelman and the Children's Defense Fund (CDF) in their initiative to "Leave No Child Behind" (not be confused with the No Child Left Behind Act, which borrowed some wording but none of the spirit of the CDF initiative). Edelman has worked steadfastly for many years to raise awareness about the needs of young, low-income children and to garner support for programs and services that will help them to get a good start in life.

At the time of this writing we are concerned about the nation's lack of commitment to the needs of young children and about the possible effects of current federal initiatives. But we have been in this field for many years and know that trends change over time. We are saddened that the care and nurture of the young is still not an important priority in society. It does not receive the attention and financial support that is needed to ensure that every child has a good beginning in school and in life. Nor do we as a nation appear to be concerned about rights of children worldwide, as evidenced by the fact that we are one of only two countries that have not ratified the United Nations Convention on the Rights of the Child, which was adopted and opened for ratification in 1989.

Early childhood educators, more than any other group, have an obligation to consider children's developmental needs as part of the equation of what we do in schools and what we urge families to do with their children. Supporting children in becoming competent, thinking, caring, and fully functioning human beings involves much more than teaching them skills and facts and to become good test-takers. What we know for certain in this time of uncertainty is that knowledgeable and caring early childhood educators who are committed to the welfare of young children and their families have much to contribute and *can* make a difference.

Learning Outcomes

When you read this chapter, thoughtfully complete selected assignments from the "To Learn More" section, and prepare items from the "For Your Portfolio" section, you will be demonstrating your progress in meeting NAEYC **Standard 5: Becoming a Professional.**

Key element: Identify and begin to conduct yourself as a member of the early childhood profession.

To Learn More

Visit a Program: Observe and write a description of a program for young children in your community. Find out about its history, philosophy, sponsorship, tuition, staff-child ratios, teacher qualifications, and salaries. How is it regulated? Is it accredited? If so find out by whom and what the process was. How does it involve families? What are the major challenges it faces?

Survey Program Regulations: Survey your neighborhood and report on the kinds of programs that are available for children from birth to 8 years of age (preschools, child care, programs for low-income children, public and private school programs). Find out who is responsible for regulation of each kind of program. How do regulatory standards differ? Find out whether any programs in your community are accredited by NAEYC. Reflect and write about what you learned.

Research a Program: Research and report on one of the following topics:

- The history of Head Start and Head Start programs in your community (number of centers, number of children served, teacher qualifications, current status, and issues)
- Parent education programs in your community
- Requirements for home schooling in your community
- How early childhood education and care is administered in another country or in several countries

Research Training Opportunities: Research and report on training programs available for teachers of young children in your community and on typical salaries for teachers in different kinds of programs. What thoughts and issues are raised by your findings?

Research Policies: Research and write about what is being done in your state with regard to one or more of the following initiatives: state-funded programs for 3- and 4-year-olds, career development, infrastructure for coordination of early childhood programs and services, readiness, early learning standards.

FOR YOUR PORTFOLIO

Include one of the assignments from the "To Learn More" section as a demonstration of your understanding of the field of early childhood education and care.

3

History and Educational Models

What is past is prologue.

William Shakespeare

● ●

Knowledge of the history of early childhood education gives early childhood educators a sense of their roots in the past and an idea of how current approaches to working with children and families have grown out of previous thought and practice. Knowing about the history of the field can help you realize that much of what is called innovation in current practice has been thought about, written about, and experimented with before. Similarly, it makes it apparent that current philosophical debates are not new—they mirror issues that have been going on for a long time. This knowledge can give you a sense of connection to the past and to the field that you are entering. It can also give you a vantage point for looking at many of the things you will encounter as you begin to explore programs and work with young children.

Early childhood education is a fairly new field, although it has old roots and emerges from a long historical tradition. In this chapter we discuss some noteworthy people who applied themselves to understanding children and to making the world a better place for children to grow and learn, and we look at how their ideas continue to influence the field today. We examine three educational movements that profoundly influenced the nature of the early childhood education: the kindergarten, progressive education, and the nursery school. And we describe three approaches to early childhood education that had their origins in Europe, are still implemented, and continue to influence current practice. On these pages we concentrate on the evolution of some of the important ideas and trends that have contributed to the field today.

Every country has its own unique history of early education and care. We will look at how these have evolved in the Western world—largely from European roots. A comparative study of the history of early childhood education in different countries and cultures is outside of the scope of this book. It is always helpful to remember that what actually occurred in history is communicated in the voice of the person who wrote about it and from that person's viewpoint. It was recently pointed out to us that in the case of early childhood education, the women did most of the caring for children and the men did most of the writing about it. It may broaden your perspective as you read to think about who is not represented and whose voices are not heard and to think about how they might have told their story.

THE HUMANISTIC TRADITION

Early education as a specialized field in the United States and other Western countries is generally thought of as having begun in Europe in the early 19th century. However, many of the values and practices found in today's programs grow from beliefs about children and child rearing that have been passed down from generation to generation and from the ideas of religious leaders, philosophers, scholars, social reformers, and educators of the past.

Many of today's programs have their roots in what is sometimes called the *humanistic* approach to education—an approach that reflects concern for the values and potential of human beings. Those who contributed to this tradition were concerned with issues like respect for human dignity, the role of education in contributing to all aspects of children's development, the connection between mind and body, the importance of play in development, the value of observing children, support for individual freedom, and the important role of families in children's development. Some educational innovators believed in universal education rather than educational opportunity only for males and for the elite. Many of them saw childhood as a valuable time in its own right, not just as a preparation for adulthood. These ideas emerged in antiquity and have been generated in different periods in history, especially the 19th and 20th centuries and they continue to the present time.

Humanistic ideas were slow to be accepted, particularly during the lifetimes of the people we discuss here. Although their ideas were sometimes influential, they were often regarded as radical and treated with suspicion and hostility. At only a few times in history has the majority of practice in teaching young children been based on humanistic ideals. We can see today that the humanistic influence has been immense in the United States and in many other parts of the world.

In order to put our historical discussion into perspective, it helps to realize that today's concept of childhood is the product of centuries of social and economic change. In the past many different and conflicting ideas prevailed about the place of children in society and their appropriate education.

> **Reflect on why history is important**
>
> Think about ways that the history of your family, community, culture, or country has influenced your life. Reflect on why it is important to know about your own history and history in general.

THE ORIGINS OF EARLY CHILDHOOD EDUCATION

Some notable historical figures shaped the field of early childhood education. These philosophers, religious leaders, scholars, physicians, and educators were influential, though a number of them were concerned with education in general, rather than the education of young children in particular.

Ancient Greece and Rome

Our Western tradition of education can be traced back to ancient Greece. In ancient Mediterranean societies children younger than 7 tended to be cared for by their mothers and other members of their extended family. They were enjoyed, loved, and left to play or asked to do simple tasks near home. At about age 7 specific training for an occupation would begin in earnest. Such training differed widely between genders and among social classes.

In ancient Greece the ideal of a well-rounded education first came to be clearly expressed. The Greek word *paideia* (from which we get our words *pedagogy* and *encyclopedia* was used to express this cultural ideal. The Greeks believed that free human beings should strive for excellence in body, mind, and spirit.

The philosopher Plato (428–348 B.C.) founded a school in Athens in a grove of trees, called the Academy. This first academic believed that the early childhood years provided a splendid opportunity to shape the whole of the child's future social, cultural, and intellectual life. In *The Republic* (Plato's book on the ideal state), he said that state nurseries should be established to foster a spirit of community. He proposed that curriculum should include games, music, stories, and drama that would illustrate the values needed by all good citizens. Children's progress would be monitored to identify gifted children and provide them with an enriched program. Plato believed that children came into the world with all essential knowledge dormant within them. Education helped children to "remember" this knowledge and apply it to their daily lives.

Plato broke with the tradition of his own time by insisting on the education of girls and by criticizing the use of corporal punishment as a means of discipline. Plato's realization of the importance of early childhood in shaping future social and political views would come to influence many later thinkers including Jean Jacques Rousseau, Robert Owen, and John Dewey. Plato's view that knowledge of geometry and geometrical shapes was essential to understanding the order of the cosmos would later play a role in the spheres (balls) and the cylinder, rectangle, and square blocks created by Friedrich Fröebel for the first kindergartens.

Plato's pupil Aristotle (384–322 B.C.) also examined the nature and purpose of education. Whereas Plato was primarily interested in leading students and society to the contemplation of "the Good," "the True," and "the Beautiful," Aristotle was interested in the world visible to the senses and the logical organization of thought. He held that human beings could be defined as "rational animals." Aristotle valued the education of young children because he believed that good habits must be established early in life. Aristotle's most famous student was Alexander the Great, who spread Greek educational ideas throughout a vast empire that extended to India. Both Plato and Aristotle recognized the importance of beginning education with young children, believed in the potential excellence of human beings, emphasized the development of mind and body, and valued children's play.

After the collapse of Alexander's empire, the Romans came to dominate the entire Mediterranean and West European world. The Romans adapted much from the Greeks. By the 2nd century A.D. the Roman state subsidized an educational system for boys in cities throughout their empire.

In both Greece and Rome, play was considered a worthwhile activity. Structured physical play in the form of games and gymnastics began in childhood and continued to be important as recreation for adult men. The free play of young children was viewed as necessary and a way of learning. Plato believed that much could be learned about the character of a child by observing the child at play. He also suggested gathering together all of the village children between the ages of 3 and 6 for group play under adult supervision. In Rome similar views were held by Quintilian (A.D. 35–95), the foremost educator of his day. From observation he realized that children younger than 7 benefited little from the customary educational practices. Accordingly, he encouraged parents to allow young children to play. He suggested that it was important to pick good nurses and tutors, so that young children could learn good speech and correct behavior by imitation rather than intimidation.

While these Greek and Roman philosophers played a role in advocating some forms of early childhood education, it is worth noting that Greece and Rome as societies were not very humane. They practiced slavery and tolerated infanticide.

The Medieval Era, the Renaissance, and the Reformation

In the 4th century the Emperor Constantine became a Christian and began a series of reforms that put Christian leaders and their values in positions of moral and legal authority. Christians recalled how Jesus had once scolded his disciples for keeping the little children from coming to him. Although most Christians believed that children were born in sin, the ritual of baptism was believed to restore their original goodness. Christian emperors soon made all forms of infanticide illegal. Land and money was given by the Roman state to the church so that it could provide social services for the poor.

The Western empire collapsed in the late 5th century. The church under the leadership of the pope (the bishop of Rome) managed to convert the barbarian tribes that conquered the West. For the thousand years of the medieval era, the Catholic church struggled to carry the lamp of learning in an age of darkness.

Monks and nuns in monasteries labored to copy books that had survived the destruction of the ancient world and to pass on their knowledge to the young children given to them to be raised for religious life. These children, known as *oblates,* were the future of the monastery and their education was considered to be an important part of the community's activities. Boys and girls were educated separately but received the same education in grammar and the liberal arts. Monastic teachers (most of them former oblates) came to appreciate the psychology of young children to the extent that they abandoned corporal punishment in favor of gentler methods that would foster the love of learning and the desire for God. Singing, laughter, and play were part of the daily life of the monastery school. Exposure to the brightly colored illuminated manuscripts produced by the monastic script writers developed the child's sense of beauty. Many of these young people chose to remain in the monastery and become monks and nuns.

In the later Middle Ages new religious orders such as the Franciscan friars no longer lived in monasteries but went into communities to work among the poor. They often provided care and primary education to abandoned or orphaned children. St. Francis in the early 13th century emphasized devotion to the child Christ. Devotion to the childhood of Christ helped to inspire more love and concern for the children of the poor.

Among the noble families of the medieval era, boys were often sent away from home at an early age to learn as *pages* (child servants) in the households of other nobles. Girls remained at home longer and were taught to sing, play musical instruments, and weave tapestries. Some were taught to read and write by educated nuns in convent schools. Both boys and girls were expected to learn courtly manners by the example of adults.

Most people until the 1800s were peasants who worked land that belonged to the rich and powerful. Peasants and poor townsfolk needed the help of their young children. Boys and girls as young as 3 were expected to feed and tend animals and to work in kitchen gardens. Children in the towns were taught the basics of their parents' trade early and formally apprenticed to a craft at age 7.

During the Age of the Renaissance and Reformation in Europe (which began in Italy in the 1300s and moved westward until the early 1600s), cities continued to grow and became powerful centers for trade and for the arts. Attention turned from the church to the individual and the arts, stimulating a revival of the literature of the ancient Greeks and Romans (Gutek 1972). Renaissance men and women placed a high value on education. The invention of the printing press about 1485 helped make many books available so that knowledge was no longer the monopoly of the church. The ancient languages—Latin, Greek, and Hebrew—were held to be the key to all the lost knowledge of antiquity. In order to help young children make a good beginning in their study of Latin (the universal language of educated Europeans), men such as Sir Thomas More of England and his friend Desiderius Erasmus (1466–1536) encouraged parents and teachers to avoid using severe physical punishments as a way to motivate children. Both men believed that children would want to learn if an effort was made to make the subject matter enjoyable. Thomas More, for example, made targets shaped like the letters of the alphabet for his children to shoot at. His daughter Margaret later conversed with her father and Erasmus in both Latin and Greek. Erasmus was so impressed that he became an early advocate of the higher education of women.

Martin Luther

In 16th century Europe, religious reform was tied to new ideas about education. Martin Luther (1483–1546), a former monk whose biblical scholarship caused him to break with the Catholic church, began a movement of religious reform known as the Protestant Reformation. Luther was a strong advocate of universal education. He believed that boys and girls should be taught to read so that they could read the Bible for themselves. Luther believed that schools should develop the intellectual, religious, physical, emotional, and social qualities of children. An extensive school system was developed in Germany in response to Luther's views, but his goals of universal education did not become a reality until 19th century America.

During the 16th and 17th centuries, efforts by the Catholic church to respond to the Protestants led to a renewal of Catholic culture known to historians as the Counter-Reformation. This movement had an immense impact on the history of education in the early modern era, for it led to the creation of new religious societies dedicated to good works including the education of orphans and the children of the poor and non-Christian peoples in the New World. Both Protestant and Catholic schools in this period, however, tended to emphasize the sinful nature of the child. Christian missionary schools were all too often culturally insensitive to indigenous peoples they came to serve. The great exception to the severity of 17th century education was the gentle and learned Comenius.

Born and raised in what is now the Czech Republic, John Amos Comenius (1592–1670) was a bishop in the Protestant Moravian church. As a result of the Thirty Years' War, which began in Bohemia in 1618, Comenius and many other Protestants were forced to become lifelong refugees. In the hope that he could serve the Czech people in exile, Comenius began to write about education. He developed teaching methods that anticipated elements of modern early childhood education and produced some of the earliest materials for teaching children. His work was well received in Europe, where he consulted with governments and his books were widely translated. Like Luther, he believed in universal education. He saw all people as being equal before God and believed, therefore, that all individuals—rich or poor, common or noble, male or female—were entitled to the same education. Comenius believed that up to the age of 6 children should attend schools taught in their native languages, not in Latin. These schools prepared them for life and for further education that he envisaged as taking place in a series of ascending grades, where at each level the child would be exposed to an ever widening circle of knowledge. He hoped that by providing universal education he could bring about a world of peace and goodwill among those of differing faiths.

Long before the development of modern theories of child development, Comenius wrote about how young children learned. He closely observed them and recognized that the period from birth to age 6 was of the highest importance for human development. The "roots of all arts and sciences," he wrote, "though we seldom do anything about it, begin at this age" (Deasey 1978, 35). He believed that language was the foundation for later learning and designed programs for language and concept acquisition that were intended to begin in infancy and carry on through later childhood (Gutek 1972). Schooling for the youngest began in the maternal school, the "school of the mother's knee." The mother was to attend to her child's physical needs and encourage play. She might show the child a book designed by Comenius that had woodcuts illustrating words and concepts. *Orbus Pictus* is considered to be the first picture book; two pages are shown here.

Comenius observed that learning seems to occur spontaneously when children are allowed to play. He encouraged classroom use of puzzles, building materials, and other concrete objects as learning tools. Contemporary evolution of these practices can be seen in the ideas that children learn best when knowledge is personally relevant

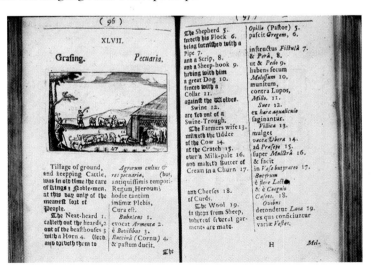

and that concrete experiences must precede abstract tasks. These ideas are important today in what we refer to as *developmentally appropriate* educational practice.

After the Reformation, basic schooling under civil or church auspices in reading, writing, and arithmetic was provided for the young before they commenced their training for specific vocations. Churches also founded charity schools for 5- through 11-year-old children to teach reading, writing, and arithmetic in local languages.

The Enlightenment

During the 18th century the scientific revolution led to a new emphasis on humankind's potential to understand the universe and transform society. Men and women of the Enlightenment tended to emphasize human reason and to doubt all traditional authorities. This period was characterized by a movement away from the influence of religion to a more humanistic (person-centered rather than religion-centered) view of life. The Enlightenment led to efforts to make education more practical and scientific.

John Locke (1632–1704)—academic, doctor, philosopher, and political theorist—was an influential thinker during the Enlightenment. He developed the theory, based on his medical knowledge, experience, and emerging philosophy of human understanding, that the child comes into the world with a mind like a blank slate (*tabula rasa*) and that knowledge is received through the senses and is converted to understanding by the application of reason. This view was in direct contradiction to the opinion, generally held during his time, that people entered the world with some aspects of their character already formed. Locke's belief in the importance of "nurture" over "nature" in determining the direction of human development led him to emphasize the influence of early training and education and to advocate for changes in parental care and education of children. He believed that infants should not be restricted by the common practice of swaddling them in tight strips of cloth, that young children should not be restrained from physical exploration, and that gentle forms of discipline rather than corporal punishment should be used. Locke believed that respectful, loving relationships are the best way for parents and teachers to inspire the child to imitate their examples and that learning should never become a task imposed on the child. Locke's ideas anticipated the modern notion of the role of education in the shaping of human potential (Cleverley & Phillips 1986; Weber 1984).

Jean Jacques Rousseau (1712–1778)—French philosopher, writer, and social theorist—eloquently challenged the prevalent view of his time that children came into the world with original sin and needed to establish habits of obedience, even if doing this required harsh treatment. He also challenged the view of the Enlightenment that emphasized the importance of reason over the emotions and civilization over nature. He disagreed with Locke's belief that one should always reason with children. Rousseau, pictured at left, did not believe that people were born evil, but rather that their inherent goodness was spoiled by civilization. In his famous novel *Emile,* Rousseau presented his view that innate goodness will flower when people are raised out of contact with corrupt society. Rousseau formulated a stage theory of development and believed that education should begin at birth and continue into adulthood. He advocated basing educational practice on knowledge of the nature of the child, whose ways of learning are different from those of adults. Educational practice, according to Rousseau, should be based on the understanding that children learn best from direct experience and exploration of the environment (ideas that are still held in early childhood education today). He envisioned children learning through their own natural, undirected play, free of adult interference and guidance. He encouraged parents and educators to express their confidence in the natural growth process by allowing for the interests and spontaneous activities of children. Given his progressive views, it comes as a shock to learn that Rousseau sent his own children to be raised in an orphanage. In spite of his human limitations, Rousseau's ideas—viewed as radical in his time and by many in ours—had tremendous impact on the educators who followed and anticipated later research on developmental stages.

The 19th Century

During the 19th century, national school systems were evolving in Europe and the beginning of public education was under way in the United States. New theories of education had widespread impact.

Early childhood education as a distinct discipline had its beginning with Johann Pestalozzi (1746–1827), a Swiss educator who had been influenced by the views of Rousseau and the Romantic movement. The Romantics looked to nature and the emotions, including those inspired by religion, rather than human reason alone. Pestalozzi experimented with Rousseau's ideas in the education of his own son. When his son still could not read at the age of 11, Pestalozzi concluded that Rousseau's ideas about teaching were not effective and went on to develop his own teaching methods. His ideas laid the foundation for the reform of 19th century education and had a strong impact on development of progressive education in the United States and Europe. Like Luther and Comenius before him, Pestalozzi, pictured at right, believed that all children had the right to education and the capacity to profit from it. He devoted his life to education, particularly for the orphaned and poor, and established several schools in which his ideas could be implemented. He believed that education could help to awaken the potential of each child and could thereby lead to social reform. He wrote that the first year of life was the most important in the child's development. He suggested that instruction be adapted to each child's interests, abilities, and stage of development. He rejected the practice of memorization and advocated sensory exploration and observation as the basis of learning. The learning experiences he designed were sequenced from concrete to abstract. He believed that children learned through self-discovery and could pace their own learning. Pestalozzi was also concerned with teaching human relationships. He wrote, "My one aim was to . . . awaken a feeling of brotherhood . . . make them affectionate, just and considerate" (Braun & Edwards 1972, 52).

Welsh industrialist and social reformer Robert Owen (1771–1858), disciple of Pestalozzi, became concerned with the condition of families who worked in the cotton mills during the Industrial Revolution. Owen worked for reforms in labor practices and the establishment of schools to improve the lives of factory children who, from the age of 6, were required to labor for long hours in the mills. He provided humane living conditions and abolished child labor in his textile factory in Wales.

Owen believed that the education of young children, combined with an environment that allowed people to live by the principle of mutual consideration, could transform the nature of people and society. His *infant school,* the first in England for children 3 to 10 years of age, offered a nurturing and emotionally secure setting. Owen did not believe in pressuring children to learn or in punishing them. Rather, he thought that the natural consequences of their actions would teach children right from wrong. Sensory learning, stories, singing, dance, nature study, and physical exercise were included in the school program.

Owen's ideas were considered extreme in his time, and his schools did not survive in England. Later in his life Owen moved to the United States where he thought he would find more support for his ideas about society and schooling. He was one of the founders of New Harmony, a utopian community in Indiana. Although the schools he created did not survive, many of the ideas that originated in them can still be found in today's early childhood programs. These include periods of time during which children choose their activities, emphasis on a caring and nonpunitive teacher, and the use of spontaneous play as a vehicle for learning.

Pestalozzi and Owen were directly involved in the education of young children, and both have had a strong influence on later educational practice. They were idealists, deeply humanitarian, and concerned with social reform as it affected the poor. Owen's concern for the education of his factory workers' children led to the creation in Britain of the Infant School Society (ISS) in 1825. This society later became a model for efforts to educate the children of working mothers in the United States.

Table 3.1 summarizes some of the important ideas presented by the educators and philosophers described in this section.

EDUCATIONAL MOVEMENTS THAT SHAPED THE FIELD OF EARLY CHILDHOOD EDUCATION

Some programs and ideas that originated at the beginning of the 20th century have had a profound and long-lasting impact on the field of early childhood education in the United States and in other places in the world. They include the kindergarten, created in Germany by Friedrich Fröebel; progressive education, which began in the United States and was based on the progressive political movement and the philosophy of John Dewey; and the nursery school, founded in England by Margaret and Rachel McMillan. Although these originated in different places and in response to different societal and educational needs, all three share the caring and respectful attitude toward children that characterized the reformers in the past whom we have just described. We will discuss two well known contemporary programs that emerged from these educational movements: the Developmental Interaction Approach, a direct outgrowth of progressive philosophy, and the High/Scope model, based on Piaget's theory of development that represents the tradition of the McMillan's nursery school.

Fröebel and the Kindergarten

Friedrich Wilhelm Fröebel (1782–1852) established the first kindergarten program in Germany in 1837. Fröebel's mother died before he was a year old and he suffered a lonely childhood as the only child of a Protestant minister. Before becoming interested in education he studied mathematics, philosophy, and sciences and was trained as an architect. After working in a number of different settings, he discovered that he had a talent for teaching and chose to develop his skills by studying with Pestalozzi and working in one of his schools. Fröebel found that he loved children and that they loved

Table 3.1 **Individuals and Ideas That Influenced Early Education and Care**

Time Period	Key Figures	Influential Ideas and Practices
Ancient Greece and Rome	Plato, Aristotle	Education should begin with the young child. Human beings are essentially good. Both boys and girls should be educated. Development of both mind and body are important. Play is a valuable tool for learning.
Reformation	Martin Luther	Education should be for all children. Individual literacy is important. All aspects of development are important.
	John Amos Comenius	Education should be for all children. Language development is important. Education should begin in infancy. Children learn through play. Children learn best from direct experience. Schooling should be conducted in the child's native language. The mother has a role in educating the young child. Knowledge should be personally relevant.
Age of Enlightenment	John Locke	Children learn through their senses. "Nurture" is more important than "nature." Respectful relationships are important. Children should be allowed freedom. Learning should not be imposed on children.
	Jean Jacques Rousseau	Human beings are essentially good. Children go through developmental stages. Learning should begin at birth and continue throughout life. Children's thinking is different from adult thinking. Education should be based on knowledge of the nature of the child. Children learn best from direct experience. Education should allow for play and the child's spontaneous interests.
The 19th Century	Johann Pestalozzi	Education should be for all children. Education can awaken children's potential. Education can lead to social reform. The first year of life is the most important in children's development. Instruction should be adapted to children's interests, abilities, and stage of development. Sensory exploration and observation are the basis for learning. Learning experiences should be designed sequentially so that they increase in level of complexity. Children can pace their own learning. Social relationships are important in children's learning.
	Robert Owen	Children should have choice in their educational experiences. Teachers should be caring and nonpunitive. Play is a valuable tool for learning.

him. After further study in science and linguistics, Fröebel (pictured at left) devoted his life to education. Fröebel's views on the importance of play, toys, and games in the intellectual, social, and spiritual development of young children were in part inspired by his study of Comenius (Deasey 1978, 32–46). He founded several innovative schools and directed an orphanage. Over the years he developed a philosophy of education and a program for 4- to 6-year-olds that he envisioned as a transition between home and school and between infancy and childhood. Because it was intended to be a place where children were nurtured and protected from outside influences, as plants might be in a garden, he called his school *kinder* ("child") *garten* ("garden"). This term is still used for all programs for young children in many parts of the world and for programs for 5-year-olds in the United States.

Like Comenius, Rousseau, and Pestalozzi, Fröebel believed that children were social beings, that activity was the basis for knowing, and that play was an essential part of the educational process. Fröebel, a deeply religious man, was particularly concerned with the education of children age 3 through 6 and with the mother's relationship to the infant and young child. He believed that the education of young children should differ in content and teaching methods from that of older children, and he wanted children to have the opportunity to develop those positive impulses that came from within.

Kindergarten Education

Fröebel described three forms of knowledge that he saw as the basis for all learning: Knowledge of *forms of life,* such as gardening, care of animals and domestic tasks; knowledge of *forms of mathematics,* such as geometric forms and their relationships with each other; and knowledge of *forms of beauty,* such as design with color and shape, harmonies and movement.

Children's play was guided by the teacher, who carefully presented special materials and activities designed by Fröebel to enhance sensory and spiritual development. The materials, called *gifts,* included yarn balls, blocks, wooden tablets, geometric shapes, and natural objects. Among the gifts were the first wooden blocks used as tools for children's learning. These objects were intended to encourage discovery and manipulation and to lead children to an appreciation for people's unity with God. Fröebel followed a long tradition of belief that each child was inherently good and born with innate knowledge that could be awakened by exposure to the fundamental principles of Creation. The outward symbols of Creation were the basic shapes of geometry. Fröebel's blocks and other gifts were designed to expose children to these shapes and allow for the exploration of their symbolic truths.

Handwork activities, called *occupations,* included molding, cutting, folding, bead stringing, and embroidery. They were intended to foster discovery, inventiveness, and skill. Songs and finger-plays (many written by Fröebel), stories, and games were selected to encourage learning the spiritual values underlying the program. Fröebel held that education must begin with the concrete and move to greater abstraction and that perceptual development precedes thinking skills.

The early kindergartens emphasized the importance of cleanliness and courtesy, the development of manual skills, physical activity, and preparation for later schooling. Kindergarten children were not made to sit still, memorize, and recite as older children were. The teacher's role was not that of taskmaster, but of affectionate leader.

The Long-Term Impact of the Kindergarten

Having conceived of the kindergarten as a nurturing place for the cultivation of children's natural goodness and an extension of the home, Fröebel proposed the idea of training young women as kindergarten teachers. Educators from Europe and the United States studied his methods and returned to their homes to begin kindergartens. Graduates of Fröebel's teacher training institute brought the ideals and practices of the kindergarten to the United States and many other countries.

The early American kindergartens (the first founded in Watertown, Wisconsin, in 1856 by Margarethe Meyer Schurz) were private ventures, often established in homes and taught in German by teachers who had studied with Fröebel (Beatty 1995, 53–54). Elizabeth Peabody founded the first English-speaking kindergarten in Boston in 1860. Later, after studying with Fröebel's disciples in Germany, she founded the first kindergarten teacher education program in the United States. She was influential in winning public support for kindergartens in the United States. The first publicly supported kindergarten was opened in St. Louis in 1873 and was followed by rapid expansion of kindergartens between 1860 and 1900.

Two aspects of the society of the late 1800s appear to have contributed to the rapid growth of the kindergarten. The first was the belief that because children were inherently good, they required a nurturing and benevolent environment in their early years. The second was a concern for the social problems created by the large influx of poor immigrants that gave rise to the field of philanthropic social work. Mission kindergartens for children of the poor were established by social workers with the expectation that if children were taught the appropriate values and behaviors, they and their families would be more successful in assimilating into American society.

Many of the first professional associations concerned with promoting early childhood education in the United States grew out of the kindergarten movement. These included the American Fröebel Union, established by Elizabeth Peabody in 1878; the International Kindergarten Union (IKU), begun in 1892 and merged with the National Council of Primary Education in 1930 to become the Association for Childhood Education International (ACEI), still an active organization today; and the National Kindergarten Association (NKA), founded in 1909 and active in working for universal acceptance of the kindergarten until it was phased out in 1976 (Williams 1993).

Fröebel was the father of the modern kindergarten. His ideas dominated the kindergarten movement in the United States until they were challenged by the progressive education movement at the beginning of the 20th century. The program that he created represented a radical departure from the schools of his day. Although the kindergarten allowed children to learn through play, it was far more structured than the individualized, free-play approach advocated by the progressives, and it little resembled what we consider to be developmentally appropriate practice today. It could, however, be considered as the beginning of early childhood education as it is practiced today in much of the world, and it was profoundly influential (Weber 1969; Williams 1993).

A period of ferment caused by conflicting philosophies began in the kindergarten movement in the 1890s and lasted for more than 20 years. Progressives, wanting the kindergarten to reflect their beliefs about education, challenged supporters of Fröebel's approach. By 1920, the progressive approach had achieved dominance. The reformed kindergarten curriculum reflected many of Fröebel's original ideas but added a new emphasis on free play, social interaction, art, music, nature study, and excursions. New unstructured materials, including large blocks and dollhouses, encouraged children's imaginative play. Books and songs reflected children's interests, rather than conveying a religious message, and activities were inspired by events in the children's daily lives.

As kindergartens gradually moved into public schools, they met with grudging acceptance. The rigid atmosphere of the traditional primary schools, with their emphasis on drill and practice of academic skills, was sharply contrasted to the more child-centered approach of kindergartens. However, the gap gradually narrowed. Many kindergarten activities found their way into the primary grades, even as primary activities filtered down into the kindergarten.

The Nursery School

Margaret McMillan (1860–1931) and her sister Rachel McMillan (1859–1917) were social reformers who spent their lives trying to address the problems of poverty brought about by the Industrial Revolution in England. The sisters were born in the United States to parents who were originally from Scotland. After the death of her husband, their mother Jane Cameron McMillan returned to Scotland when the sisters were still young children. As adults the sisters sought work in England. During the 1890s they began to visit the homes of the poor, which led them to lives of social activism with a focus on improving the welfare of the "slum child." They campaigned for school meals and opened Britain's first school health clinic.

In 1911 the sisters started the Open-Air Nursery School and Training Centre in London, attended by 30 children between the ages of 18 months and 7 years. This open-air, play-oriented nursery school was their response to health problems they witnessed in children of poor communities and was intended to be a model for other schools and a site for educating teachers. They called their new program a *nursery school* to show that they were concerned with care and nurture *and* learning. They recognized that many poor children in England needed both care and education in their first few years to give them a good foundation for later life. The nursery school had its foundation in the work of Darwin, Plato, Rousseau, Fröebel, and Owen. It was designed to identify and prevent health problems and to enhance children's physical and mental development before they entered formal schooling. The McMillan sisters were concerned with basing education on the child's "sense of wonder" and believed that teachers must know what attracts and engages children (Williams 1993). They also wanted to assist parents in interacting positively with their children.

Rachel was primarily in charge of the kindergarten until her death in 1917. Margaret continued to write books about education and to be involved in the school. In 1930, Margaret established the Rachel McMillan College to train nurses and teachers.

Nursery School Education
In providing for children's physical needs the McMillans strongly emphasized the value of active outdoor work and play. Health and nutrition, perceptual-motor skills, aesthetics, and the development of imagination were stressed. The teacher's role was both to nurture and to informally teach children. A planned learning environment that children could explore was an important mode of learning (McMillan 1919). The nursery school included materials for sensory development, creative expression, gardening, nature study, and sand play.

The Long-Term Impact of the Nursery School
The work of the McMillans, particularly that of Margaret who lived the longest, exerted a great influence on British, and later on American, early childhood education. At the same time that kindergartens were gaining hold in the United States, the nursery school movement began to appear as an effort to meet the needs of even younger children. Nursery schools in the United States were directly influenced by the English

nursery school, by Sigmund Freud's ideas about human development, and also by the philosophy of progressive education.

One of the first nursery schools in the United States was the City and Country School, established in New York City in 1913 by Caroline Pratt. In 1916, the Bureau of Educational Experiments opened its laboratory nursery school, under the direction of Harriet Johnson. In the 1920s, a number of other laboratory nursery schools were established in the United States, including one organized by Patty Smith Hill at Columbia University Teachers College in New York City, and the Ruggles Street Nursery School and Training Center directed by Abigail Eliot in Roxbury, Massachusetts.

Abigail Eliot studied with Margaret McMillan and observed her open-air nursery school for children in the slums of London. Early in 1922 Eliot returned to Boston and continued her education. In 1930 she was among the first women to receive a doctorate from Harvard University. The Ruggles Street Nursery School combined elements from Fröebel, Montessori, the McMillan sisters, and others. Eliot emphasized the use of scissors and paste, plasticene, hammer and nails, and several kinds of blocks (Paciorek & Munro 1999, 62).

Unlike most laboratory nursery schools, which served middle-class children, the Ruggles Street Nursery School followed the McMillans' example of providing a full-day program for children in a low-income neighborhood. While the McMillans concentrated on the physical health of the children, Eliot thought that more should be done to create a stimulating, child-centered environment. She also actively sought to involve parents in the school. Eliot found that most mothers were happy to attend meetings and help out when possible. Some of them went on to become teachers (Beatty 1995, 143–144).

Cooperative nursery schools, formed by educated middle-class parents, first began in 1915 and spread rapidly. Also founded during this period were prominent child-study institutions with laboratory schools: Yale University's Clinic of Child Development, the Iowa Child Welfare Research Station, and in Detroit the Merrill-Palmer Institute. Edna Noble White, who visited the McMillans' nursery school in England in 1921, established Merrill-Palmer Institute. White was interested in extending the mission of her school beyond the children by providing "motherhood training." Merrill-Palmer later became "world famous as a center for parental and pre-parental education" (Beatty, 153).

During the 1920s and 1930s, nursery schools were established in many college home economics departments to train future homemakers and to serve as centers for child development research. These programs were multidisciplinary in orientation because the early pioneers came from a number of fields, including nursing, social work, medicine, psychology, and education. The earliest nursery schools emphasized children's social, emotional, and physical development—hence the whole-child orientation described in this book. The intellect received less attention because of the common belief that significant cognitive development did not occur until children entered school at the age of 6. In the early nursery schools the emphasis was on social and emotional development. Children played freely indoors and outdoors in a learning environment that was designed for them.

In these early nursery schools and today's early childhood education and care programs, children are seen as always growing, experiencing, and learning through interactions with people and with the learning environment. The role of the school is to keep the paths of exploration open so children can develop in their own ways. The daily schedule is characterized by blocks of time in which children are free to choose activities and engage in them for long periods. The classroom is divided into activity areas, typically those for block construction, dramatic play, art, water play, sand play, science, math, and language and literacy. The role of the teacher is to create an environment that facilitates learning. Teachers support cognitive, language, and literacy development by giving children many things to explore, think about, discuss, and read about. They support social and emotional development by encouraging children to verbalize their feelings.

In response to new information about human intellectual development and the needs of poor children, the traditional nursery school has continued to evolve, especially in recognition of the important cognitive development that occurs in early childhood. What remains constant is the insistence that the child is a person whose development can benefit from play in a carefully designed environment under the guidance of a caring and sensitive teacher.

Concern with implementation and expansion of nursery school education led to the development of a professional organization for nursery educators. Patty Smith Hill, at Columbia University's Teachers College, founded the National Association for Nursery Education (NANE) in 1926. This organization has evolved into the largest and most influential organization for early childhood educators, the National Association for the Education of Young Children (NAEYC).

Today the terms *nursery school, preschool,* and *child development center* are used in the United States to describe programs that evolved from the legacy of the McMillan nursery school. More than 80 years later, programs such as Head Start and state-funded preschools for low-income children embody the purpose of the original nursery schools and the McMillan sisters' commitment to poor children.

A Contemporary Example: The High/Scope Model

The High/Scope model, a preschool program for low-income children developed by David Weikart and his colleagues in Ypsilanti, Michigan, addresses many of the concerns of the founders of the nursery school. High/Scope, which draws its theoretical

foundation from the work of Jean Piaget, was one of the first programs designed in the 1960s to ameliorate the effects of poverty on children's development. In the late 1960s the U.S. government authorized two studies in order to assess the impact of different educational approaches on the development and learning of low-income children. The first, *Planned Variation,* focused on Head Start programs. The second, *Follow Through,* looked at the effects of continuity in programming from preschool through third grade. Weikart and his colleagues at High/Scope built on their previous experience working with low-income, at-risk children and developed an educational model that was implemented as part of this study.

The High/Scope curriculum was based on key experiences related to the acquisition of mathematical concepts like classification, seriation, number, spatial relationships, and time. These key experiences provide the basis for planning and adapting the learning environment, making decisions about teacher-led group activities, and assessment of children's progress. Teachers use various strategies for facilitating children's learning experiences in relation to each key experience. The materials and what happens in learning centers primarily define the curriculum.

In a High/Scope classroom children are actively engaged in learning areas throughout the room. A variety of learning materials are available for building and construction, dramatic play, art, mathematics, reading and writing, music and movement, sensorial exploration, science, and motor development. The environment is consciously planned to enable children to actively manipulate and experiment with objects and then to represent what they have learned.

Attention is given to providing materials and activities that expose children to the key experiences. Throughout the classroom, teachers might foster seriation, for example, by providing three or four different sizes of the same materials and bringing relative sizes to children's attention during the play period. A pretend area might include several different sized spatulas. Where relationships are observable between materials, such as different sized pots and pans, they are displayed in gradually ascending order from smallest to biggest, so the relationships are evident to children.

During a typical day children engage in a three-step process called "plan-do-review." They talk about their plans before the work period and then meet to recall or represent them afterward. A typical morning begins with children gathering. Teachers work with all children to generate plans for the play period and to elaborate and rethink plans that appear unrealistic. As children carry out their plans during the work period, teachers observe, encourage, and extend children's ideas. After the play period ends, children once again gather to review their activities in a teacher-facilitated review time. Weikart and associates believe that the "plan-do-review" process makes children more conscious of their actions and fosters the connection between language and action. Representation of work is considered important and children's work is posted on classroom walls.

The role of the teacher is to carefully design the learning environment and support children in exploring and learning from it. A large number of publications are available that describe how to implement the High/Scope model. The developers have also been involved in an extensive network of in-service training that has led to this approach being widely disseminated in the United States and other countries.

Some Recommended Reading About High/Scope

High/Scope Education Research Foundation. 1989. *The High/Scope K–3 Curriculum: An Introduction.* Ypsilanti, MI: High/Scope Press.

Hohmann, M., & D. P. Weikart, 2002. *Educating Young Children: Active Learning Practices for Preschool and Child Care Programs* (2nd ed.). Ypsilanti, MI: High/Scope Press.

High/Scope Educational Research Foundation Web site (www.highscope.org).

Progressive Education

Progressive education was part of the progressive movement, begun in the late 19th century to seek social and political reforms for political corruption, poverty, and other problems that resulted from industrialization. Progressive theorists sought to use science and reason to better mankind. Progressive education evolved from a combination of the ideas of Rousseau, Pestalozzi, and Fröebel and from 19th century social reform movements (Williams 1993). The founders of the movement desired a "progressive" society in which people could develop their full potential. Their goal was to improve society through fundamental changes in the schools. They attempted to transform dreary educational environments that offered a skills-based curriculum learned by drill and recitation.

John Dewey (1859–1952), at right, though not the founder of the movement, became its most influential spokesperson. Dewey taught high school before studying for a doctorate in philosophy. He then taught at the University of Chicago where he was instrumental in setting up a laboratory school where innovative educational ideas could be tried. Later he moved to Columbia University in New York where he continued to write about education and philosophy for the rest of his career.

Dewey wanted schools to be places where children would grow physically, intellectually, and socially; where they would be challenged to think independently and investigate the world around them; and where school subjects would expand on children's natural curiosity. He believed that schools should reflect the life of the society and that education should be viewed as the life of the child in the present, not just as preparation for the future. He also believed that, in addition to their instructional role, schools should play a role in the acculturation of immigrants.

Progressive educators advocated techniques of instruction that were based on children's interest, involved hands-on activities, recognized individual differences, and were to the greatest extent possible initiated by the child, not the adult.

Progressive Education Programs

In Dewey's view, the school community offered children an opportunity to practice democratic ideals in a group situation and to learn through activities that were interesting and meaningful. Although early childhood programs at the University of Chicago laboratory school that he founded included some Fröebelian kindergarten materials, they were used in different ways. Dewey's approach emphasized greater freedom and spontaneity in play and involvement in the social life of the classroom instead of highly structured activities. An important instructional approach, still used today, was to have children in the elementary school work on collaborative projects related to their own interests.

Progressive education stressed observation of children's interests and needs. Educators were concerned with "teaching the whole child"—addressing physical, social, and emotional as well as intellectual development. Children learned through doing—through experiencing and experimenting with real materials and self-directed activities.

The role of the teacher was to provide a carefully prepared environment and curriculum that prepared children to be members of a democratic society. The curriculum included "real experiences" such carpentry, weaving, cooking, and the study of local geography. Teachers were expected to observe children and, based on their observations, ask questions and provide experiences designed to integrate different subject areas and help children expand their understanding of the world. The role of the teacher was to serve as a guide and observer, not instructor and disciplinarian.

The Long-Term Impact of Progressive Education

The ideas of progressive education combined with research in child development triggered a great deal of educational experimentation. A number of schools based on progressive ideas were established at the end of the 19th and beginning of the 20th centuries. These included the Laboratory School at the University of Chicago, which began in 1896 as a small experimental school; the Francis Parker School in Chicago in 1883; the Horace Mann School in New York City in 1887; and the Lincoln School at Teachers College, Columbia University in 1917.

Dewey's view that democracy could not flourish in a segregated society led to more democratic practices in schools. For example, in Hawaii a progressive educator was hired to transform kindergarten education from a racially and ethnically segregated system to one that was integrated to reflect the racial and cultural diversity of the state (Castle 1989).

The ideas of progressive education gained acceptance in American school systems during the first half of the 20th century and were influential in European schools as well. From its beginnings, however, progressive education had its critics. One of the major criticisms was that it did not emphasize systematic study of the academic disciplines. Eventually progressive education came under fire from those who felt that students were not gaining sufficient mastery of basic school subjects. The movement had become associated with permissiveness, rather than with its guiding principles that curriculum must challenge children intellectually and help them to develop self-direction and responsibility. The progressive influence on American education waned after World War II as more academic, skill-based teaching practices gained prevalence. The movement collapsed after the launch of the Russian satellite Sputnik in 1957.

Progressive education had a profound impact on American education, particularly on the kindergartens and nursery schools, which remain more closely allied ideologically with progressive philosophy than with more traditional academic approaches. A number of highly respected private schools continue to reflect the philosophy of progressive education, including the Bank Street Children's School and College, City and Country School in New York City; Shady Hill School in Cambridge, Massachusetts; and Hanahau'oli School in Honolulu. These programs are based on the progressive beliefs that curriculum should be integrated instead of based on distinct subject areas, that children should be active learners who have many opportunities to pursue their own interests, that schools should help children to gain understanding of their world, and that classrooms are places where children can live and learn democracy.

There was a resurgence of interest in progressive approaches to education when American educators visited England in the mid-1960s and 1970s to learn about state-supported schools for 5 to 8-year-olds (called *British infant schools*) that combined the ideas of progressive education with Swiss psychologist Jean Piaget's views of child development. In British infant schools young children learned from active involvement in tasks or projects.

Current interest in the Developmental Interaction Approach as developed and implemented at Bank Street College in New York City (which we describe in the section that follows), in the Reggio Emilia preschools in Italy (which we will discuss later in this chapter), and in the Project Approach developed by Lilian Katz and Sylvia Chard (which focuses on children's extended exploration of a topic) has its roots in progressive ideas and indicates that progressive education continues to have a strong impact on early childhood education today.

A Contemporary Example: The Developmental Interaction Approach

Many preschools and elementary schools today embody the philosophy of progressive education. A well known contemporary version was developed at Bank Street Children's School and College in New York City. The program developed at Bank Street has its roots in progressive education and also drew heavily from child development theory including the work of Anna Freud, Erik Erikson, Barbara Biber, and Jean Piaget. The founders of this approach emphasized the development of the "whole child," the interaction of different aspects of development, and the interaction of the child with other people and with the environment. In the 1970s the name of this method was changed from the Bank Street approach to the Developmental Interaction Approach (DIA) to call attention to its emphasis on interactions rather than its geography (Goffin & Wilson 2001, 67). The Developmental Interaction Approach was another of the models implemented and studied as part of the Planned Variation/Follow Through research.

In New York in 1916, Harriet Johnson, Caroline Pratt, and Lucy Sprague Mitchell, organized the Bureau of Educational Experiments (known today as the Bank Street College of Education) as an agency for research on child development. Mitchell, a friend of Dewey and strong advocate of progressive education, directed the Bank Street Children's School and was influential in its evolution into a teacher training institution. Mitchell (pictured at left) was deeply committed to young children's learning about their world through direct experience. Her book *Young Geographers* introduced the study of geography to young children through direct experiences in the community. This community study still characterizes the curriculum of Bank Street Children's School and the educational model based on its practices. Caroline Pratt's and Harriet Johnson's observations of preschool children at play led to the development of the wooden unit blocks, which continue to be standard equipment in early childhood programs today. Johnson's *The Art of Block Building* described her observations of nursery school children's stages of block building (Beatty 1995, 140–142).

This approach is based on the progressive principle that the classroom must allow children the social experience of living within a democratic community. Its creators believed that children needed to be actively involved in thinking and reasoning with real experiences that begin with direct experience in the community and extend outward to situations that are further removed.

A DIA classroom is viewed as a representation of society, with social studies and learning trips forming the core of the curriculum. Children explore topics they can experience directly in their communities such as the bakery, grocery store, harbor, and public works. Other subject areas are generally integrated into the exploration of social studies topics.

Play is an essential part of the curriculum, especially block building and dramatic play. These forms of play allow children to symbolically represent their growing knowledge of the world. They also provide teachers with insight into how children interpret their experience. If, for example, the children in a DIA classroom were studying the nearby harbor, they would first take a learning trip to the harbor and then follow up in the classroom with various ways of representing what they observed and learned. Follow-up activities involve reading books about harbors, writing, drawing, role-playing, and block building.

A DIA classroom is set up in centers where children can make choices about their own learning. Blocks and dramatic play areas are an important part of the classroom. While there are class meetings and group activities facilitated by a teacher, there is also much independent, productive play. The classroom contains books and artwork that children have created to express the learning gained on trips.

Educators who advocate this approach stress the importance of the child functioning as a member of the group. Teachers are expected to provide children with the experience of living within a democratic community, and to be sensitive interpreters and facilitators who respond to the needs and interests of each child. Emphasis is not on understanding "what or how" to teach, but on why each decision is made (Cuffaro 1995).

Reflect on your experience

Reflect on your experiences in preschool and kindergarten. How did the programs that you attended as a child, or that you observed or taught in, seem to reflect what is described about the history of these programs? Have you as a child or adult experienced a program that seemed to reflect the principles of progressive education? What was the program like? What were your reactions to it?

The whole-child and real world curriculum advocated by Bank Street College has had a strong impact of early childhood education in the United States for many years and remains a strong influence today. A number of the curriculum examples we use in this book reflect the developmental-interaction approach. It is also possible to observe it in action in the Bank Street Children's School, in the classrooms of teachers who were trained at Bank Street College, and in other schools that base their practice on the philosophy of progressive education.

Some Recommended Reading About the Developmental Interaction Approach

Cuffaro, Harriet K. 1995. *Experimenting With the World: John Dewey and the Early Childhood Classroom.* New York: Teachers College Press.

Mitchell, A., & J. David (eds.). 1992. *Explorations With Young Children: A Curriculum Guide From the Bank Street College of Education.* Mt. Rainier, MD: Gryphon House.

Nager, N., & E. Shapiro (eds.). 2000. *Revisiting Progressive Pedagogy: The Developmental Interaction Approach.* Albany, NY: SUNY Press.

Bank Street College of Education Web site (www.bankstreet.edu).

Table 3.2 summarizes some of the important ideas related to the three important educational movements we have just discussed.

Table 3.2 **Educational Movements That Shaped Early Childhood Education and Care**

Approach	Originator(s)	Goals	Significant Ideas	Influential Practices
The Kindergarten	Friedrich Fröebel (Germany)	To awaken the child's senses to the perfection of the God-given structure underlying all of nature To provide a common ground for all people and advance each individual and society into a realm of fundamental unity*	Activity is the basis for knowing. Play is an essential part of the educational process. The role of the teacher is to support the development of positive impulses in children. Teaching of young children should differ in content and process from teaching older children. The teacher is an affectionate leader.	The use of teaching materials and activities (called *gifts* and *occupations*) including clay work, paper cutting, block building, finger-plays, songs, drawing A preparation program specifically for teachers
Progressive Education	John Dewey, Lucy Sprague Mitchell, Harriet Johnson, Caroline Pratt (United States)	To improve society through schooling To help people to develop their full potential	Education is the life of the child in the present, not just preparation for the future.	Projects and active exploration as the core of the curriculum The community as a source of curriculum

(continued)

73

Table 3.2 Educational Movements That Shaped Early Childhood Education and Care (*Continued*)

Approach	Originator(s)	Goals	Significant Ideas	Influential Practices
Progressive Education (*continued*)		To prepare citizens to live in a democratic society	Cooperation and problem solving are important aspects of the curriculum. Curriculum is based on children's interests and needs. Children learn through doing. All aspects of development are important. The role of the teacher is to be a guide.	Unit blocks used to represent what is learned
The Nursery School	Margaret and Rachel McMillan (England)	To provide nurture (loving care) to children served To support the health, nourishment, and physical welfare of children To assist parents in improving their ways of working with children To provide a model for teachers of how to work with young children**	It is important to stimulate the child's sense of wonder and imagination. Play in a planned learning environment is an important vehicle for education. Outdoor work and play are important. Aesthetics are an important part of the curriculum. The teacher's role is to nurture and teach informally. Nursery school children should have trained and qualified teachers.	Sense training Outdoor activities including sandbox and gardening A focus on children's health, including personal hygiene and nutrition Creative expression activities

*Brosterman 1997, 12–13.
**Lascarides & Hinitz 2000, 121.

Three European Approaches

Three educational approaches that emerged in Europe in the 20th century are based on many of the same ideas and values that characterized the kindergarten, the nursery school, and progressive education. Each of these programs was developed by a brilliant and creative thinker and added significant new elements to what had gone before. The programs are the Waldorf education method conceived in Germany by Rudolf Steiner, the Montessori method developed in Italy by Dr. Maria Montessori, and the Reggio Emilia approach founded in Italy by Loris Malaguzzi. Many schools today directly implement or base their programs on these approaches and each of them has had an influence on educational thought and practice. Each of these programs has its own educational philosophy including ideas about nature of the child, curriculum content, teaching methods, design of the learning environment, and role of the teacher. As you visit classrooms you might hear someone say, "We base our program on Reggio," or "I work in a Montessori program," or "My child attends a Waldorf school." We hope that you will be able to visit and/or work with children in one or more of these programs to see them in action.

Waldorf Education

Rudolf Steiner (1861–1925) was a German philosopher, scientist, and educator whose method is known today as Waldorf education. As a young man Steiner studied mathematics, physics, and chemistry. He then went on to earn a doctorate in philosophy. He was interested in the intersection of science and spirituality. Steiner was a prolific thinker, lecturer, and writer and made many contributions to ideas about philosophy and the practice of education. He was the founder of a school of philosophy called *anthroposophy*, which explores the role of spirituality in contemporary society. He was deeply interested in the individual's search for self and the development of human potential.

After World War I, the owner of the Waldorf Astoria Cigarette factory in Germany invited Steiner to create a school to serve the workers' children. The first Waldorf school was opened in 1919 with the goal of educating people to build a free, just, and collaborative society.

Steiner believed that childhood is a phase of life important in its own right. His theory of human development is based on 7-year cycles that combine physical, mental, and spiritual development. Steiner's philosophy emphasized balanced development, imagination, and creative gifts. The schools he developed were designed to promote healthy, unhurried learning experiences for young children based on stages of development.

Waldorf Education Programs

Steiner's school stressed the development of the child's body, mind, and spirit. The focus was on educating the "whole" child because Steiner realized that the various academic, artistic, and handicraft subject areas would, over time, engender a balance of the human faculties of thinking, feeling, and will.

Steiner believed that in the first 7 years of life the most important development had to do with the child's body and will (propensity to activity), and that educational activities should, therefore, be practical, imitative, and hands-on in nature. The Steiner kindergarten program takes place in an ungraded setting for children 3 to 6 years of age. The curriculum consists of storytelling, puppetry, artistic activities (painting, drawing, modeling), imaginative play, and practical work (finger knitting, bread baking, gardening).

Steiner thought it was important for the young child to experience a feeling of warmth and security. Therefore, classroom environments for young children are like an extension of a home. Classrooms tend to feature soft colors, natural materials, and simple learning materials like homemade dolls that encourage imaginative use. In our visits to Waldorf schools we have been impressed with the beautifully appointed, aesthetically pleasing learning environments and were surprised (rather pleasantly) to find no plastic, academic materials or technology in the classrooms.

In the Waldorf educational system children are allowed to remain childlike in the early years. Steiner believed that there is a time for every aspect of development and that children under the age of 7 should not receive formal academic instruction. Children in Waldorf schools often do not learn to read and write until well after their counterparts in other school settings. They catch up with their peers in learning these subjects by second or third grade.

Teachers in Waldorf kindergartens stay with a group of children for 3 years. This allows teachers to create a community of learners and promote continuity of experience, and provides opportunities for older children to be role models for younger children, and to take on a nurturing role. The role of the teacher is to design the learning environment, to establish predictable routines, and to support and nurture the individual growth of each child. The focus is on self-discovery and sensory experience rather than direct instruction, with the goal of helping children develop a sense of responsibility and the ability to regulate their own behavior. The teacher is viewed as an important role model for children in a Waldorf school.

The Long-Term Impact of Waldorf Education

Waldorf schools are independent, self-governing schools (preschool through twelfth grade) that follow the ideas and theories of Rudolf Steiner. Currently there are approximately 800 Waldorf schools in more than 40 countries (including more than 150 in North America). There are 60 teacher training institutions worldwide. Waldorf education is attractive because of its views of development and profound respect for childhood. It is one of the fastest growing educational movements in the United States today (Williams & Johnson 2005).

Waldorf education has been criticized for having a spiritually based pedagogy (though it is not considered to be a religious school), for the lack of emphasis on skills development in the early grades, for lack of formalized assessment procedures, and for lack of attention to the role of technology in modern life. Some critics regard anthroposophy as a dangerous "pseudoscience." Others believe that the Eurocentric origin of some of the curriculum, the gnome- and giant-laden fairy tales, for example, are out of date and inappropriate in today's multicultural society.

There is also some discussion going on today about whether Waldorf education could be adopted in contemporary public schools. The questions are raised about whether it could work if parts of it were taken out of context and whether its spiritual underpinnings bring it into conflict with requirements for separation of church and state.

To Learn More About Waldorf Education

Oldfield, L. 2001. *Free to Learn: Introducing Steiner Waldorf Early Childhood Education.* Gloucestershire, UK: Hawthorn Press.

Steiner, R., & R. Trostli. 1998. *Rhythms of Learning: What Waldorf Education Offers Children, Parents and Teachers.* Great Barrington, MA: Anthroposophic Press (Steiner's lectures updated).

Association of Waldorf Schools of North America Web site (www.awsna.org).

Waldorf World Web site, Waldorf Education on the Web (www.waldorfworld.net).

The Montessori Method

Dr. Maria Montessori (1870–1952) overcame the opposition of her family and her society to become, in 1896, one of the first women in Italy to receive a medical degree. Early in her medical career she devised successful approaches for working with children who are mentally retarded, previously regarded as incapable of learning. In 1907 she founded the *Casa Dei Bambini* (Children's House) in Rome, where she explored the applicability of her educational methods to normal children. The program she designed was based on her observations of young children and how they learned. She reached the conclusion that intelligence was not fixed and could be stimulated or stifled by the child's experiences. Further, she believed that children learn best through their own direct sensory experience of the world. The foundation for her interest in education was her study of the writings of French physicians Seguin and Itard about their humane methods for educating children who are mentally retarded. Although Montessori's training was in medicine, the contributions she made to education have been her lasting legacy.

Montessori was interested in the first years of life and believed that children went through sensitive periods during which they had interest and capacity for the development of particular knowledge and/or skills. She believed that children had an inherent desire to explore and understand the world in which they lived. She saw these young explorers as self-motivated and able to seek out the kinds of experiences and knowledge most appropriate for their stage of development. Concerned with preserving the dignity of the child, she valued the development of independence and productivity.

Montessori Programs

Dr. Montessori's educational approach was distinguished by the design of a child-sized learning environment, carefully designed and sequenced learning materials, a series of learning experiences that actively involved the child, and a teacher role that involved observing and guiding rather than direct instruction.

In a Montessori classroom, children are grouped in mixed ages and abilities: 0–3, 3–6, and 6–12. Children learn from firsthand experience—by observing and by doing. Practical life experiences such as buttoning, zipping, cutting, and gardening enable children to care for themselves and the environment while building skills that will be useful throughout their lives. All learning in a Montessori classroom is cumulative. Each activity paves the way to future, more complex activities. Activities are organized primarily for individual work, rather than group interaction. Children move freely about the classroom and choose their own activities.

The classroom learning environment based on Montessori's principles is attractive and equipped with child-sized, movable furniture. Montessori stressed the importance of an orderly environment that helps children to focus on their learning and develop the ability to concentrate. Classrooms are equipped with didactic materials designed by Montessori to help children develop their senses and learn concepts. These carefully crafted materials are still the basis of the curriculum in a Montessori school. They are treated with care and respect and are displayed on open shelves so children can use them independently. The materials are graded in difficulty, sequenced from known to unknown and from concrete to abstract. Each concept to be taught is isolated from other concepts that might be confusing or distracting. For example, if the child is learning the concept of shape, the materials will be of uniform size and color so that the attribute of shape can be seen readily. Materials are also designed to have immediate, self-correcting feedback, so children know if they have successfully completed a task.

Purposeful activity is characteristic in a Montessori classroom. Children's work is taken seriously and is not considered play. Children can work on any material they understand at any time. Teachers do not make assignments or dictate what to study or read, nor do they set a limit as to how far a child follows an interest. Adults and children are expected to respect concentration and not interrupt someone who is busy at a task. Children are free to move around the room. A child can work at an activity for an unlimited time but is expected to master tasks in sequence.

In a Montessori program the role of the teacher is to observe and direct children's learning rather than to instruct; hence, a Montessori teacher is called a directress or director.

The Long-Term Impact of Montessori's Approach

Montessori's schools were successful in Italy and the Netherlands (where she had her headquarters for many years), and they eventually spread throughout the world. During World War II Montessori lived in India where she worked in classrooms and trained teachers in her approach. Although private Montessori schools have operated in the United States since 1915, it remains a separate movement that has not been widely implemented.

Historically, Montessori education was quite controversial in the United States, possibly because it differed from the mainstream of nursery education in the individualized nature of instruction. Most Montessori programs do not allow for a great deal of social interaction and classrooms have little or no provision for the development of creativity in the arts or in the use of didactic materials. Montessori schools are similar to nursery schools in that children are viewed as inquisitive, self-motivated learners, capable of selecting activities appropriate for their current needs and developmental stage. Montessori was an important educational innovator, and a number of her ideas—such as the provision of a child-size environment and the use of sensory materials—have found their way into most contemporary early childhood programs.

Montessori went beyond philosophy and guidance in the development of her method. She carefully prescribed the teaching techniques and materials for her schools. Montessori teachers are expected to have specialized Montessori training beyond a baccalaureate degree. During this training, teachers learn about the Montessori view of the child and learn how to use the specialized Montessori materials.

Two major professional associations are involved in the training of Montessori teachers and accreditation of schools and teachers. They are the original organization, Association Montessori Internationale (AMI), which has headquarters in the Netherlands, and the American Montessori Society (AMS), founded in 1956 to adapt Montessori methods to an American style of working with children. Today Montessori programs can be found in both private and public settings in the United States and in many other places throughout the world.

To Learn More About Montessori Education

Lillard, P. P. 1996. *Montessori Today: A Comprehensive Approach to Education From Birth to Adulthood.* New York: Shocken.

Montessori, M. 1965. *Dr. Montessori's Own Handbook.* New York: Schocken.

Montessori, M. 1967. *The Absorbent Mind.* New York: Holt, Rinehart & Winston.

American Montessori Society Web site (www.amshq.org).

Reggio Emilia

Since the 1980s educators from around the world have been visiting the publicly funded infant-toddler centers and preschools in the small northern Italian city of Reggio Emilia. American educators were excited and inspired by what they saw in Reggio and have brought home ideas that revitalize progressive educational concepts about working with young children.

After World War II, as part of its reconstruction, the city of Reggio Emilia developed an educational system for young children. The first school was built in 1948 by parents who hired an innovative educator named Loris Malaguzzi (1920–1994) as its director. By 1963, under Malaguzzi's leadership, the original schools had become a municipal system of early childhood programs. By the 1980s educators from all over the world were visiting Reggio Emilia to observe their preprimary schools.

The Reggio Emilia schools are characterized by a set of values and philosophical assumptions that are informed, in part, by constructivist theories and the progressive education movement, and by a deep commitment to honor the rights of children, parents, and teachers. Key concepts of this philosophy are (1) that the child is a strong and competent individual who has a right to receive the best education and care that a society can offer; (2) that education is based on relationships, especially the interrelationships among children, teachers, and parents; and (3) that education is based on the interaction of young children working and playing together in small groups.

Reggio Emilia Programs

In Reggio Emilia the school is seen as an amiable community in which teachers' dialogue with children, with each other, with the community, and with families is an essential part of the educational process. The curriculum is not established in advance, but emerges from children's intellectual curiosity, social interactions, and interests. Projects and curriculum goals are based on teachers' observations of children. The teachers consider themselves the children's partners in learning; together, they "co-construct" knowledge. The teachers enjoy discovering with the children.

The Reggio approach promotes the intellectual development of children through a systematic focus on symbolic representation. The focus of the curriculum is in-depth project work emerging from the interests of the children. The children are encouraged to represent their environment through many "natural languages," or modes of expression, often referred to as "The Hundred Languages of Children." These modes of expression may include drawing, painting, working in clay, sculpting, constructing, conversing, and dramatic play. Educators in Reggio believe that these languages must be cherished, nurtured, celebrated, and documented. They actively encourage children to explore the possibilities of working with a wide variety of materials.

Educators in Reggio Emilia often refer to the learning environment as the "third teacher," because children construct knowledge through their interactions with it. The goal is to provide an environment that promotes partnerships, social interaction, and constructive learning. Important elements of school design are the art studio called the *atelier* and a large central gathering area called the *piazza,* where children can gather and can play independently. The schools of Reggio Emilia have skylights and floor-to-ceiling windows, and the classrooms are flooded with natural light. Schools are designed with the idea of "transparency" so that they are filled with light and children can see from one area of the school to another. Mirrors and plants combine to create a bright and cheerful environment. High-quality art supplies, including paints and clay as well as recycled materials and natural objects, are beautifully arranged, often by color, on open shelves within the children's reach. Children's work is prominently displayed. The physical environment created at the Reggio Emilia schools honors the child's right to have a beautiful, functional space in which to work and play.

Teachers operate the schools on a day-to-day basis with support from a team of educational coordinators, or *pedagogistas,* who support the relationships among teachers, parents, and children by creating continual exchanges of information among and between them. These coordinators also interact with politicians and serve as advocates and lobbyists for children, parents, and teachers. Each school also has an art teacher, or *atelierista,* who helps teachers to support children in expressing their knowledge through symbolic representation. The atelierista works with small groups of children as they investigate and explore topics through a variety of media.

Teachers in Reggio programs are collaborators with community, children, and other teachers in the construction of curriculum. They regard themselves as researchers, who conduct systematic study in the classroom by collecting and preparing *documentation* of the children's work for the purpose of better understanding children, curriculum planning, teacher development, and connecting with families and communities. Photographs of the children working, and transcriptions of the children's questions and comments, are mounted and displayed with their actual work so that children and parents can examine them. Teachers also assemble portfolios of the children's work, listen to tape-recorded sessions with the children, and review videotape of the children working and playing.

The Long-Term Impact of Reggio Emilia

The early childhood programs of Reggio Emilia reflect a distinctive approach to working with children, families, and the community. This approach is entirely consistent with the social and political systems of the city of Reggio Emilia and its province, Emilia Romagna, which are among the most progressive and prosperous in Italy.

Many delegations of American educatiors have visited Reggio since the 1980s to learn about their educational system. American interest in the programs of Reggio raises interesting questions about whether educational practices from one country can retain their vitality when transplanted to another country that has a different history, traditions, and educational goals.

Leaders of the Reggio program caution against efforts to replicate it or to follow its provisions without question (in fact questioning, or *provocation,* is an essential component of the Reggio approach). They have avoided publishing curriculum or teacher manuals and insist that education in Reggio, as in every other community, must be constantly evolving and changing based on the unique characteristics of that community.

In spite of these cautions, American enthusiasm for Reggio is very great. When two of the authors of this book visited Reggio Emilia in 1996 we had rather mixed reactions. We were concerned that some American educators, in spite of warnings from Reggio staff, planned to replicate the program exactly. We were also struck by the homogeneity of the population of Reggio and saw no evidence of interest in the multicultural content that so enriches early childhood education in the United States. We admired the architecture of the schools, the exquisitely designed learning environments, the approach to documentation of children's learning, and educators' lively engagement with each other, with children, families, and the community. Our experience in Reggio reaffirmed our commitment to the progressive roots of American early childhood education and reminded us how important it is for educators to thoughtfully examine and discuss their practices.

The view that young children have the right to receive the best education that a society can offer is reflected in the policies of the municipal government of Reggio Emilia. This government commitment to the welfare of young children makes Reggio more than just another educational innovation. It is also a model of a society that cares for and nurtures the potential of young children. This dedication to the education of young children may be unprecedented in the world. We hope that this aspect of the Reggio Emilia approach will someday be emulated in the United States.

Some Recommended Reading About the Schools of Reggio Emilia

Cadwell, L. B. 2001. *Bringing Learning to Life: The Reggio Approach to Early Childhood Education.* New York: Teachers College Press.

Edwards, C., L. Gandini, & G. Forman (eds.). 1998. *The Hundred Languages of Children.* Norwood, NJ: Ablex.

Hendrick, J. (ed.). 1997. *First Steps Toward Teaching the Reggio Way.* Upper Saddle River, NJ: Merrill/Prentice Hall.

North American Reggio Emilia Alliance (NAREA) Web site (www.reggioalliance.org).

Reggio Children U.S.A., on the Web site of the Council for Professional Recognition (www.cdacouncil.org).

Reflection on These Approaches

Each of these approaches was created in western Europe as a response to unique historical circumstances, but each of them has qualities that has made it universally appealing and has led to current interest in it.

We included Waldorf schools in this edition of the text for the first time and decided to group the three European approaches together. As we did so, we were struck by the many similarities between them. Some of their common elements were discussed in a recent article by Carolyn Edwards who writes:

> All three approaches represent an explicit idealism and turn away from war and violence toward peace and reconstruction. They are built on coherent visions of how to improve human society by helping children realize their full potential as intelligent, creative, whole persons. In each approach, children are viewed as active authors of their development, strongly influenced by natural, dynamic, self-righting forces within themselves, opening the way toward growth and learning. Teachers depend for their work with children on carefully prepared, aesthetically pleasing environments that serve as a pedagogical tool and provide strong messages about the curriculum and about respect for children. Partnering with parents is highly valued in all three approaches and children are evaluated by means other than traditional tests and grades. (2002, 1)

We are not surprised that these approaches are gaining attention in the United States at this time. Each of them epitomizes the respect for and valuing of children, and childhood itself, that have characterized early childhood education for centuries, and each is, in many ways, consistent with our current conceptions of developmentally appropriate practice. These approaches may become increasingly attractive to teachers and families seeking an antidote to the diet of skill and drill being practiced in many schools today. Table 3.3 summarizes some important ideas related to the educational approaches described in this section.

Reflect on historical influences

Think about the three European programs described above. What appeals to you or makes sense to you about any or all of them? How are the programs you know similar to any of these? Have you had any experience of a Waldorf, Montessori, or Reggio Emila based program? What were your impressions of it? Was it a program that you would like to work in? Would you recommend it to a friend or send your own child to this kind of program?

CHILD CARE IN THE UNITED STATES

The history of the early education field is not just about those who developed educational programs; it is also about individuals who devoted themselves to helping families meet the needs of their young children. In addition to the history of educational thought there is another history—one that chronicles the efforts to provide care and education for working families who needed care for their children, and for children who were poor, handicapped, non-English-speaking or otherwise at risk for school failure.

Table 3.3 **Three Influential European Approaches**

Approach	Originator(s)	Goals	Significant Ideas	Distinctive Features
Waldorf Education	Rudolf Steiner (Germany)	To build a free, equal, and collaborative society To develop free human beings who have purpose and direction in their lives Balanced development of young children (mind, body, and spirit)	Childhood is an important phase of development in its own right. From birth to 7 years, children respond through movement and are sensitive to impressions from the environment. Emphasis is on development of inner strength. Teachers should protect the sensitivity of early childhood; warmth and security are important. Imitation and example are important strategies for supporting children's learning.	Warm, homelike, and aesthetic environment All natural raw materials for children to use in sensory and creative pursuits Storytelling, puppetry, artistic activities, imaginative play, and domestic activities Ritual and rhythms of life and seasons important Mixed age grouping (3 years with same teacher in preschool/kindergarten) The teacher as a warm, steady focal point for the program
The Montessori Method	Dr. Maria Montessori (Italy)	The psychological health of the child Development of independence and productivity Preserving the dignity of the child	Education begins at birth and first 6 years are critically important in development. Intelligence can be stimulated by experience. Children absorb sensory impressions from the environment and learn best through sensory exploration. There are sensitive periods for the development of skills. Children are intrinsically motivated and will seek out appropriate learning experiences. Learning is sequential.	Orderly, child-sized learning environment Materials arranged so children can choose activities based on level of complexity Self-correcting, sequenced educational materials designed to teach a single concept or skill Space delineated by mats or trays where children can work independently Mixed age grouping Teacher (directress) is observer and guide

(continued)

Table 3.3 **Three Influential European Approaches** *(Continued)*

Approach	Originator(s)	Goals	Significant Ideas	Distinctive Features
Reggio Emilia	Loris Malaguzzi (Italy)	For children and adults to learn through working collaboratively in a community Development of the child's potential Development of children's symbolic languages in the context of a project-oriented curriculum Making the young child visible to community and society	Respect for the child. View of the child as "strong, rich and competent." Systematic focus on symbolic representation. The learning environment is considered to be a teacher. Notion of teacher as learner, researcher, and co-collaborator with children and adults.	Light and transparency as features of an aesthetically pleasing learning environment A wide variety of creative and open-ended materials used as tools and resources In-depth project work based on children's interests Emphasis on using the arts for representing ideas with a trained artist (*atelierista*) as guide Documentation of children's work shown throughout the school

The Origins of Child Care in the United States

In colonial America, as in Europe, prior to the Industrial Revolution (which brought about the mass production of goods and moved the workplace from the home to the factory) most women were able to keep their children at home while they produced domestic goods and helped with farm work or the family's craft or trade. In some cases, children were sent to a "dame school" where an older woman would gather children from 2 to 6 years of age to teach them some reading, writing, and arithmetic (the "three R's").

The need for child care for poor families and widows greatly increased with the rise of industrial production and merchant capitalism in the late 18th century. While Americans came to idealize motherhood in the period after the Revolutionary War, changes in economic life made it impossible for many mothers to make a living at home. Many poor women were forced to choose between leaving their children at home alone or seeking alms from the community. As the number of poor increased, many communities no longer gave them money and food, but forced them to enter workhouses to earn their keep. Children were not allowed in the workhouses, so mothers were forced to give up their children to be raised as indentured servants (a form of time-limited slavery) for other families. Women who tried to keep their children found that the only work available was so poorly paid that they could not afford to hire anyone to care for their children. Some poor women pooled their resources to pay for care or had older children mind the younger ones. Others left their children to beg in the streets or even locked them indoors during the workday.

Quaker women in Philadelphia tried to help poor working women with child care by founding the Society for the Relief and Employment of the Poor. In 1798 this society built a house that provided religious education for children while their mothers worked at spinning in another portion of the house.

The Boston Infant School founded in 1828 is an early example of the positive influence of new ideas concerning child care and education in the United States. Robert Owen's concern for the education of his factory workers' children led to the creation in Britain of the Infant School Society (ISS) in 1825. Philanthropists in Boston who hoped to provide good care for the children of working mothers took this society as model. In the 1830s other infant schools were established in several U.S. cities. Two cities established separate infant schools for the children of African-Americans. Sadly, support for these schools was not sustained past 1850. By that time most middle-class Americans thought that young children should stay at home with their mothers. They failed to grasp the reasons that made working outside the home essential for so many women.

While the infant schools did not survive, the day nurseries of the mid-19th century served the most desperately needy of the great waves of immigrants arriving in the United States. The first of these was New York's Nursery for the Children of Poor Women, founded in 1854. Its mission was to provide care for the children of women temporarily forced to provide for their families (Michel 1999). The care provided in these privately run programs enabled immigrant parents employed in urban factories to keep their families together. Personnel in the day nurseries were largely untrained, worked long hours with high child-adult ratios, and provided minimal care for children. In the eyes of society, the great virtue of the day nursery was that the children served were given a reprieve from even more harmful environments. These programs were primarily concerned with the health of children and not with educational goals.

In 1878 Pauline Agassiz Shaw, a wealthy Boston woman influenced by the success of the middle-class American kindergarten movement, established a day nursery with educational programs for children of different ages (Michel 1999). Some day nurseries followed Shaw's trend in providing quite comprehensive services with long hours of operation, infant care, family education and training programs, and even counseling.

Unfortunately, most day nurseries did not provide services for both infants and 3- to 6-year-olds. An attempt to meet this need was made by Frances Willard of the Women's Christian Temperance Union in the 1880s. Willard's day nurseries were provided free of charge to poor mothers. The day nurseries were not open to all racial and ethnic groups and never to the children of unwed mothers. Such discrimination left many working mothers with no option but to send their children to orphanages or to unsatisfactory arrangements in the homes of strangers (Michel 1999).

The National Association of Colored Women (NACW) became active in the 1890s in establishing day nurseries for urban African-American children. Many African-American women had a history of domestic servitude, first as slaves before the Civil War and then as domestic servants. In most cases they had been required to care for white children while leaving their own babies to the care of only slightly older children. This history helped the founders of these day nurseries to understand mothers' need to work outside the home (Michel 1999).

The 19th century witnessed a number of experiments in child care, which enabled many women to avoid the worst extremes of poverty by working outside the home. Society's attitude was that child care was a stopgap measure that a decent mother would use only in the most dire circumstances. While mass public schooling was winning acceptance as a necessary condition for the rights of citizenship, the provision of care for young children remained mired in its association with social welfare (Michel 1999).

Child Care in Times of National Emergency

Child care in the United States has never been viewed as a basic service that government should help provide, except as a temporary response to families in need of aid or during times of national political or economic crisis. During the Depression in the

1930s, federal child care centers, called Emergency Nursery Schools, were established to provide relief work for teachers, custodians, cooks, nurses, and others who needed employment. These programs were terminated as the Depression ended.

Again, during World War II, the U.S. government became involved in the business of sponsoring child care. This time, the purpose was to meet the needs of the large numbers of women employed in defense plants. Under the Lanham Act (1942–1946), federally funded child care centers served children in 41 states.

Employer-sponsored child care, which was common in Europe, emerged as part of the response to the demand for workers during the war. Most notable were the two child care centers run from 1943 to 1945 by Kaiser shipyards in Portland, Oregon. The Kaiser centers were outstanding for their comprehensive, high-quality services made available to employees with children aged 18 months to 6 years.

The Kaiser company made a commitment to providing the best services possible to children and families. They hired Dr. Lois Meek Stolz, an early childhood expert who had been director of the Child Development Institute at Columbia University and was on the staff of Stanford University as director of the centers, and the highly respected early childhood educator James L. Hymes, Jr., graduate of the Child Development Institute, as the manager. Teachers trained in early childhood education were hired and the centers were especially designed by an architect to serve young children. The centers functioned 24 hours a day, all year long (except Christmas). They included an infirmary, provided hot meals for mothers to take home when they picked up their children, and offered other services that helped families combine work in the defense industry with caring for their children. During the short time they were in operation the Kaiser centers served almost 4,000 children (Hymes 1996). The centers were closed down after the war when workers were no longer needed, but their legacy remains and reminds us that we as a nation can provide high-quality, comprehensive programs for children and families if we choose to do so.

Government- and industry-sponsored child care were temporary measures, intended only to support the war effort. They were largely phased out as peace heralded a return to the image of the "traditional family" with mothers in the home, tending to their children. Of course, many mothers did not return home, but continued their employment. As child care facilities either closed or were reduced to prewar levels, these employed mothers had limited options for child care. A patchwork of private arrangements was the common solution. The California Children's Centers were among the few survivors of the Lanham Act programs. With state funding, they continue today to serve the children of employed parents and low-income, full-time students.

Child Care After World War II

The postwar attitude toward women's appropriate role as homemaker, combined with the belief that children of employed mothers suffered from a lack of maternal care, gave strength to the contention that child care was at best unnecessary and at worst harmful to children. Between 1950 and 1965, it received little attention or support. Meanwhile, family life in America started to undergo major changes. The extended family system began to disintegrate as family mobility increased and the divorce rate soared. More and more women entered the workforce either out of financial necessity or because of a desire to find meaningful work outside the home. Single parents, if employed, could no longer assume complete responsibility for their young children, but had to share this responsibility with other caregivers, usually nonrelatives.

Today's early childhood education and care programs grow out of the two historical streams we have just discussed: the nursery school, which focused on the health and development of the child, and the day nursery, which served families by providing care

for children while family members were at work. Today we have joined the terms *education* and *care* to define the early childhood field. This new terminology indicates that efforts are under way to bring these two strands together into a coherent system that will meet the needs of children *and* their families.

GOVERNMENT INVOLVEMENT IN THE CARE AND EDUCATION OF YOUNG CHILDREN

Federal involvement in promoting the health, education, and welfare of children began with the creation of the Children's Bureau in 1912. Its charge was to investigate child health and labor, and its role was mainly to make investigations and report the findings. Since that time, the federal government established a Department of Health, Education, and Welfare (HEW) in 1959 (now the Department of Health and Human Services). The Office of Child Development (now called the Administration for Children, Youth, and Families) was begun in 1969 as an agency of HEW. These agencies have been involved in providing welfare to families unable to care for their own children, health and nutrition programs, child abuse prevention, and educational programs for poor children. Sometimes they have supported care for children whose parents need to work outside the home.

Over the last several decades government has taken an increasing responsibility for providing legislation and funding to assist in the education of special populations of children. The 1960s and early 1970s were a period of national concern with social reform. During this period there was a swell of interest in early education as a public policy issue. Research in child development, combined with a desire to counteract the effects of poverty on young children, led to the creation of Head Start, a federally funded educational program for 4-year-olds. During the rest of the 1970s, attempts to pass federal child care legislation failed repeatedly because they were perceived as threatening the stability of the family. Direct federal support for early childhood programs for nondisabled children was limited to Head Start.

During the 1980s and 1990s a variety of federal legislation regarding early childhood education and care was introduced, but no major legislation was passed. Most of the bills that did pass took the form of tax credits that were most beneficial to middle-class families.

Programs for Low-Income Children

In the beginning of the 20th century, philanthropic kindergartens existed in many U.S. cities. Their purpose was to help children overcome the disadvantage of growing up in the slums by teaching them skills and middle-class values. When kindergartens became integrated into the free public school system, special attention to the educational needs of disadvantaged children was postponed until the 1960s.

During the 1960s, research by Jean Piaget, J. McVicker Hunt, and others began to dispel the widely accepted idea that intelligence was fixed and static and pointed to the importance of early experiences on later intellectual development. Researchers and educators suggested that planned intervention in the early years might enhance children's development, help them succeed in later schooling, and perhaps enable them to be more successful in their adult lives. Hence the notion that early childhood programs could help ameliorate the effects of poverty became influential once again.

Given the surge of concern about the quality of U.S. education in the 1950s and 1960s, the publicity given to this new child development research meshed with the political climate in paving the way for a whole new era in early childhood education. President Lyndon Johnson's concern with the plight of the underprivileged in America extended to an interest in the lost potential of those children disadvantaged by living in poverty. The Office of Economic Opportunity was formed, and the "War on Poverty" was launched.

In the early 1960s an interdisciplinary panel representing the fields of pediatrics, education, child development, and social services was formed and directed to develop a program to counter the effects of poverty on children. It was hoped that such a program would increase achievement and opportunities and give poor children a "head start." Project Head Start was unique in its focus on the total development of the child, its emphasis on strengthening the family, its involvement of the community, and its provision of comprehensive services. The Head Start program represented a new view of child development as a valuable end in itself and an unprecedented mobilization of resources on behalf of children.

Programs for Children with Disabilities

Since the 1960s, recognition has been growing concerning the needs and rights of children with disabilities. Legislation and funding that support programs for these children have increased dramatically over the last two decades. The care and education of children with special needs is a field with its own history and traditions. The development of special education programs has been affected by the same social and political influences that have affected other early childhood programs. Today's emphasis on bringing children with special needs into the mainstream of society through placement in regular education classrooms has resulted in the gradual merging of two distinct approaches to education—special education and early childhood education—into the new field of *early childhood special education.*

The challenge of providing education for all children, including those with disabilities, was first confronted in the early 1900s when compulsory school attendance laws were enacted. Public and private residential schools were established at that time for the severely handicapped.

From the 1920s to the 1960s, most children with disabilities were placed in special schools or segregated into classrooms in separate school buildings, far from regular classrooms and other activity centers. Usually only those children with mild disabilities who were considered "ready" for education were included in regular public school classes. Children with more severe or multiple handicaps were confined to institutions or residential schools.

The civil rights legislation of the early 1950s is often credited with providing the impetus to secure the rights of the handicapped in the United States. When the U.S. Supreme Court ruled, in the *Brown v. Board of Education* decision in 1954, that separate education for racial minorities could not be considered "equal," the groundwork was laid for the position that segregated schooling for any purpose was questionable.

In the mid-1960s, special education classes in the public schools became an issue of controversy. Some saw them as dumping grounds for problem children, including those who were culturally different, in which no real attempts were made to meet their social and educational needs. At this time, too, some educators began to question whether special education classes were the best approach. They suggested that children with disabilities of all kinds could learn better if they had daily contact with children in regular classroom settings. Adding to this ferment, parents who had banded together to lobby for special education legislation took their concerns to court. A number of significant court cases since the late 1960s affirmed the right of all children with disabilities, regardless of severity, to a public education (Noonan & McCormick 1993).

Preschool-aged children with disabilities were first served in demonstration programs in 1968 when Congress passed the Handicapped Children's Early Education Assistance Act. Then in 1972, Head Start was mandated to reserve 10% of its enrollment for children with disabilities as a prerequisite for continued federal funding.

In 1975, the passage of the Education for All Handicapped Children Act required that all children with disabilities be provided with free, appropriate public education. In most states, however, this legislation did not lead to the provision of free public programs for preschool-aged children with disabilities, even though small incentive grants were available for the development of these programs. Subsequent amendments to this law have redefined the population to be served, specifically referring to children from birth through age 8 and have provided financial assistance and technical assistance to school systems for programs for infants and toddlers with disabilities. These laws also emphasize the role of parents and families in making early intervention efforts work. Since the 1970s there has been a national commitment to, and funding at the federal and state levels, for programs for young children with disabilities.

FINAL THOUGHTS

You are entering a field with a long history and a tradition of concern with the needs of children and their families. The pioneers in the field were often ahead of their time in their recognition that education had to address the "whole child," not just the child's intellect, and in their treatment of children in ways that were respectful and based on current views of child development. Many of these innovators recognized the important role of play in learning and advocated for universal education. They recognized that the education of young children was a valuable strategy for overcoming the effects of an impoverished background. They were concerned with improving society and saw that the creation of a caring and humane world must begin with the children. These values of respect for children and their development and the vision of a better, more humane world have been at the center of early childhood education and care since its beginning and have shaped the nature of the field today. The influential programs for young children that we described in this chapter are part of this legacy.

Over the years slow progress has resulted in more humane and egalitarian treatment of young children. We have become more aware of children's needs and the importance of meeting them in their early years; we have learned more about how children grow and learn and how to provide educational experiences based on this knowledge; and we have learned more about the kind of support that families need in order to do the important work of giving their children a good beginning in life.

LEARNING OUTCOMES

When you read this chapter, thoughtfully complete selected assignments from the "To Learn More" section, and prepare items from the "For Your Portfolio" section, you will be demonstrating your progress in meeting NAEYC **Standard 5: Becoming a Professional.**

Key element: Identify and begin to conduct yourself as a member of the early childhood profession.

TO LEARN MORE

Explore an Educational Approach: Read more about one of the educational approaches described in this chapter. If possible visit a program that follows the approach. Reflect and write about what you see as the major features of the program and its benefits to children. Include your thoughts and reactions to what you experienced and learned and the implications for you as an early childhood educator.

Research an Historical Figure: Research one of the historical figures mentioned in this chapter. Write a paper explaining who the person was and how he or she influenced the field of early childhood education. Include your thoughts and reactions to what you learned and the implications for you as an early childhood educator.

Research an Unrepresented Group: Do some research on the history of early childhood education of a group whose history is not included here (Asians, Hispanics, or some other group). Include your thoughts and reactions to what you learned and the implications for you as an early childhood educator.

Research Early Care and Education in Another Country: Do some research on the history of early childhood education in another country that is of interest to you. Include your thoughts and reactions to what you learned and the implications for you as an early childhood educator.

Read a Biography: Read a biography of one of the historical figures mentioned in this chapter. Write a review of the book that includes your thoughts about what you learned and implications for you as an early childhood educator.

Read a Book: Read a book about one of the three European educational approaches discussed in this chapter (from the lists at the end of each corresponding section). Include your thoughts and reactions to what you learned and the implications for you as an early childhood educator.

Observe a Classroom: Visit a nursery school or a kindergarten based on the principles of progressive education. Observe classroom practices and analyze how what you observed reflects the history of early childhood education described in the chapter. Include your thoughts and reactions to what you learned and the implications for you as an early childhood educator.

Observe a Classroom: Visit a program that is based on one of the influential educational models described in this chapter: Waldorf, Montessori, Reggio Emilia, High/Scope, or the Developmental-Interaction Approach. Describe classroom practices and analyze how what you observed relates to what you learned about the educational approach in this chapter. Include your thoughts and reactions to what you learned and the implications for you as an early childhood educator.

FOR YOUR PORTFOLIO

Include one of the assignments in "To Learn More" that demonstrates your understanding of the history of early childhood education and care.

4

Understanding Development

In all the world there is no other child exactly like you. In the millions of years that have passed, there has never been a child like you.

Pablo Casals

• •

*"I'm studying early **childhood** education." "I'm a teacher of young **children.**" "I work at the **children's** center." "I teach **first grade.**"*

A fascination with children is a hallmark of the early childhood educator. At the heart of the core knowledge of early childhood education is knowledge about children. You are becoming a specialist in understanding the needs and development of young children. You are learning about them today, and you will continue to learn about them throughout your career. Knowledge of child development in combination with your own direct experience in early childhood programs will give you a basis for understanding children and providing good experiences for them.

Learning about children's growth and development, their families, and their society is an essential part of becoming a competent early childhood professional. You will take courses in behavioral sciences such as child development and child psychology, in social sciences such as sociology (the study of human society and institutions like the family and the school) and anthropology (the study of cultures and the ways people live), and in "hard" sciences such as biology and nutrition. As you work with children and their families you will draw upon this knowledge base as a foundation for professional decision-making.

THE STUDY OF CHILD DEVELOPMENT

Researchers in a variety of fields gather information about how children grow and learn, and create theories that attempt to explain what they have studied. A *theory* is an organized group of statements that describes, explains, and predicts behavior. A theory shows us the relationship of facts and ideas and enables us to understand the past and predict the future. Theories help us understand the world, but they do not represent a truth, which is static and unchanging. As we gain new knowledge, a theory may be changed or replaced by another theory that is simpler, more accurate, more comprehensive, or more useful.

Research is the process that scientists and other professionals use to build knowledge. Some research is designed to help people describe and understand characteristics of children and patterns of how they learn and grow. Other early childhood research examines how certain events and experiences impact on children's growth and learning. Research may be used to substantiate or refute theory, and new theory may grow from meaningful research.

Over the years both researchers and early childhood practitioners have developed theories about the development of children. These theories differ greatly in the aspects of development on which they focus, in their underlying assumptions, and in the subjects and methods used as a basis for their conclusions. No single theory explains all aspects of child development. Each is like a lens that focuses on some unique aspect of the whole. As you read about and study theory and research, keep in mind that they are always influenced by the particular beliefs and biases of individuals who developed them. Race, ethnicity, socioeconomic status, geographical location, professional orientation, and other influences will significantly impact the ways that research is designed, how results are interpreted, which theories are applied in the research design, and what conclusions or theories are created from the study.

Knowledge of theory can help you understand children and their behavior, but it is important to keep in mind that no single theory is the only "right" answer that ties up everything we know about children into one neat package. It is most often educators, not the theorists, who create and implement educational practices based on child development research. It is important, therefore, that you read theory critically and that you choose to apply only those aspects of theories that support your goals for the education of young children.

People have studied children for centuries and in the last 60 years have done so with greater focus and scientific rigor. Information from this research tells us what young children are like and how they learn and grow. It helps us to understand the ways that young children are different from older children and adults. Understanding gained from contemporary child development theory helps us to organize our observations of young children and to plan programs and experiences that meet their needs. Programs based on this kind of knowledge of children are called *developmentally appropriate*. As a teacher in a developmentally appropriate program, you will strive to make practices (what you do) a good fit for children you teach. You will do this by understanding and selecting practices that are appropriate to their stage of development, their individual characteristics, and their family and culture.

> **Reflect on your interest in child development**
>
> How did your interest in young children begin? What did you first notice about them? What interested you? Did the children seem to be like you were as a child? How were they different?

PRINCIPLES OF CHILD DEVELOPMENT

There are six underlying principles, or main beliefs, that serve as a framework for the study of contemporary child development.

The Child Develops as a Whole

In early childhood education we often refer to the development of the *whole child*. By this we mean that we consider all domains or areas of development as we look at how the child grows and learns.

> *Three-year-old Sterling is playing in the sand. As he digs and dumps, he demonstrates his physical ability. He cups his hand, stretches out his arm, scoops, and makes vrooming noises replicating the action of a backhoe. This shows his understanding of concepts and his cognitive skill. He engages socially as he calls to his friend and beckons him into the play. When Sterling notices you watching, he reveals his emotional state—his eyes gleam with satisfaction and he uses his language skills to tell you, "I'm a backhoe man."*

Children use their bodies to move and their senses to explore the world (physical development). They acquire and order information and learn to reason and problem-solve (cognitive development). They learn to relate to others and make moral decisions (social development). They learn to trust, to recognize and express their feelings, and to accept themselves (emotional development). And they learn to talk with others about what they are thinking, experiencing, perceiving, and doing (language development). Early childhood educators recognize the importance of each of these four areas in children's development and know that they are interconnected and influence one another. They believe that these areas cannot be addressed separately and that no one area is more important than another.

Development Follows Predictable Patterns

Children acquire skills and achieve milestones in a predictable sequence.

> *For the first time today Sidney, 28 months, picks up the scissors and holds them awkwardly in a hammer grip. He struggles to open and close the blades and ineffectively cuts small snips in the paper, giving up after a few tries. Kim, his teacher, goes to the cupboard and gets out an activity of cotton balls and tongs. She invites Sidney to try to pick up the cotton with the tongs and he experiences much greater success and uses a pincer grip. Over the next weeks Kim provides other tong activities and brings in a variety of paint sample cards that Sidney takes to enthusiastically cutting. Sidney is not yet a master cutter but each day he gains skill and confidence in using scissors.*

Development is sequential and cumulative. For example, before children can learn to skip, they must have mastered the large-muscle coordination required to hop and run. New experiences that do not build from previous experiences can be meaningless or overwhelming to a child, while experiences that are not challenging or interesting may provoke boredom and restlessness. J. McVicker Hunt (1961) described the concept of an *optimal match* between a child's present level of understanding or skill and the acquisition of new knowledge or skill. New experience needs to provide just the right amount of novelty or challenge in order to interest the child.

You support and encourage children's development by planning experiences that provide challenge and by avoiding experiences that children find extremely frustrating (because they are too difficult) or boring (because they are too easy). Such planning requires that you make use of knowledge of the sequence of children's normal development.

Rates of Development Vary

A child's age in years and months (chronological age) and the child's stage of development are only approximately related. The direction and sequence of development are similar for every child, but each individual develops at his or her own rate.

Ella was born 2 weeks after Shane. Both children started at the community college child development center when they were 6 months old. Shane's teeth emerged 3 months before Ella's and he accomplished each milestone of physical development well ahead of Ella. Ella was a vocally responsive baby and by her first birthday had a vocabulary of about 25 words and syllables that she used skillfully in her interactions with people. Shane was cheerfully wordless until well into the middle of his second year. Now that both children are 2½ they are both healthy, verbal, active toddlers.

Each infant enters the world with a unique biological endowment, and because the interplay of physical and environmental forces is different for every person, no two children (even identical twins in the same family) are exactly alike.

What a child can do and understand today is the basis of future development. As you study child development, you will gain knowledge of milestones (developmental achievements) that mark children's development. This understanding will help you to plan a program that takes into account the wide variety of abilities you are likely to encounter, even among children who are close in age. In order to have appropriate expectations, you need to observe and become acquainted with the competencies of each child in your group and add that information to what you know about child development.

Development Is Influenced by Maturation and Experience

Development results from changes in the child that reflect the interplay of maturation and experience.

Twenty-two-month-old Gabriella is taking apart a knobbed puzzle of farm animals. She has been dumping the pieces out of puzzles for several weeks now, then saying, "Help!" to her caregiver who patiently works with her to pick up the pieces and fit them back in the spaces. Day after day she repeats this activity. Today without assistance she manipulates each animal piece back in its space. "I did it!" she cheerfully announces.

Maturation is the unfolding of genetically determined potential that occurs as the child grows older. *Experience* is made up of a person's interactions with the environment, with people, and with things. During the early childhood years, children's bodies increase in size and mass and the child gradually develops increasingly more complex responses and skills. Although it is not clear whether such development can be enhanced through special training, it can be delayed by factors such as poor nutrition, serious illness, and the lack of opportunities to explore the world.

The same processes occur in cognitive development. For example, infants lack the concept of *object permanence,* the awareness that even when an object is not in sight it still exists. As the child matures, this concept develops, but no amount of training seems to significantly accelerate its acquisition. A lack of experience with objects that can be seen, handled, and then removed may, however, delay the development of this concept. Gabriella, in the preceding example, learned to do the puzzle both because she had many experiences with it and because she was physically and cognitively ready.

Early childhood educators understand that they must provide a safe, healthy, stimulating program and then trust the children to take what they need to grow and learn. As you develop skill in observing children, your increasing understanding of child development theory will provide you with the knowledge base you will need to provide appropriate environments and experiences. With time and practice you will then be able to patiently and attentively wait for development to unfold.

Development Proceeds from Top Down and from Center Outward

Physical development proceeds from the top downward (the *cephalocaudal pattern*), seen most clearly in the development of the fetus. In the early stages of fetal development, the head is half of total body length, whereas at birth the head is one-quarter the body length. This same top-down pattern is seen in motor development. Infants develop control of their heads before sitting and walking.

> *When Monica was 3 she loved to paint. Each time she went to the easel she covered her hands with paint and used them to swirl the colors around the paper. Now that Monica is 5 she draws detailed pictures of people, animals, houses, and objects using fine-tipped marking pens.*

Growth and maturation also proceed from center of the body and move toward the extremities (the *proximodistal pattern*). The large muscles closest to the center of the body grow and develop coordinated functions before the small muscles of the hands and fingers. This pattern is reflected in Monica's developing skills in painting and drawing, described in the preceding example. Younger children paint or draw using their whole arm in large circular motions. As they get older they are better able to control the brush or pen and use their wrists and fingers to make more precise movements.

As children grow and mature they become more capable of coordinating their movements. It is important to be aware of physical capabilities so that you provide children with the challenges that they need to grow but do not frustrate them by expecting them to perform tasks for which they are not yet ready.

Culture Affects Development

> *Leanne, a teacher in a program with a large Samoan population, brings out a long rope to mark off a playground area. Four-year-olds Mele, Sione, and Talisa pick it up and skillfully begin to jump rope. Leanne looks on in amazement and comments to Sione's father, who has just dropped him off, that she has never seen preschool children jump rope. Sione's father smiles proudly and tells her that he always knew that young children could jump rope but was amazed when Sione began to talk so much after being in school a few months. He tells her that he did not expect children to talk that much until about age 8.*

Children's development is influenced by the culture in which they live and grow. Values and beliefs of each culture determine many of the experiences and opportunities that are provided for children. Developmental expectations also have a cultural component. This point was vividly brought to our attention when we visited the program described in the preceding example. As teachers we would not have thought of presenting a jump rope activity to our preschoolers, just as the father would not have considered engaging his 4-year-old in conversation.

UNDERSTANDING CHILD DEVELOPMENT INFORMS PRACTICE

The knowledge that development is a process that follows a sequential order, combined with information about the characteristics of each stage, lets you know what can generally be expected of children. Your knowledge of individual children, their families, and their cultures helps you to modify these expectations so that they are appropriate for the individual. You can then plan experiences for them based on this knowledge. Awareness of the cumulative nature of development will help you recognize that children cannot be expected to have knowledge or skill for which their level of development and life experiences have not prepared them. Sensitivity to individuals will help you to provide appropriate experiences that match their emerging abilities and interests.

Your understanding of developmental characteristics and principles will guide many of the choices that you make as an early childhood teacher. Perhaps most importantly, it provides a lens through which you view every experience you provide. Seen in this way, each routine and activity, piece of equipment, and interaction has potential for many kinds of learning. You will ensure that children's needs are met so that nothing impedes their development, and you will offer them varied opportunities to explore the world. You will choose for balance, ensuring that each area of development is represented in the activities, materials, and time provided. You will choose with knowledge of the child's stage of development, providing appropriate challenges that do not frustrate. You will choose with awareness of diversity and with sensitivity to individual variation and preference so that experiences enhance and do not limit children. And over time you will gain the ability to articulate your reasons for making each choice.

Reflect on optimal match in your own education

Think of a time when a teacher gave you an experience that was challenging and interesting for you. What made the experience an "optimal match" for you at that time? How was it different from other kinds of learning experiences?

FOUNDATIONS OF DEVELOPMENT

We know that the foundation for healthy development is laid down prenatally. Research has reinforced our understanding of the strong relationship between the health and well-being of the mother and other family members during pregnancy and the later development of the infant, child, and adult. We also know that when infants and young children have their basic needs met, when they are nurtured by the adults in their environment, and when they have adequate opportunity to explore the world, they are most likely to grow and develop optimally.

The history of thought about human development has been characterized by shifts in belief about the relative impact of biological versus environmental forces on personality and behavior. Biological forces on development (sometimes referred to as *nature*) are genetic traits or inborn capacities and are expressed in the process of growth and maturation. Environmental forces (referred to as *nurture*) have to do with the kinds of interactions and experiences that enhance or restrict the development of biological potential. For example, every child is born with the capacity to learn any language but will only learn those that he or she hears spoken.

Historically people have engaged in heated debate (called the *nature-nurture controversy*) over whether the biological endowment or the environment was the primary force in shaping human behavior. Today we know that both biology and environment have powerful influences on each individual. The way that children interact with their environment and organize their understanding from these interactions is determined by their biological abilities, their current stage of development, and their past experiences and interactions.

The Biological Basis of Development

Jonah and Megan are twins born into a large and loving biracial family. Their grandparents, aunts, uncles, cousins, and friends all visit to see the babies, to see who they look like. Megan has her daddy's chin and her mommy's nose. Jonah has his mommy's eyes and daddy's nose. But somehow both babies look uncannily like baby photos of their dad. During the first week home their mom reports that Megan is a calmer, "sunnier" baby, and Jonah is a fussier and more sensitive baby. Megan nurses easily, Jonah is harder to console.

Infants are born into the world with a complex combination of traits that derive from genetic inheritance. Each baby has some characteristics and needs that are universal and others that are unique.

Inherited Characteristics

No one questions that biological factors play an important role in development. The hereditary basis of development includes physical characteristics such as eye, hair, and skin color. Other characteristics—height, weight, predisposition to some diseases, and temperament—are significantly determined by individuals' inheritance, but can be influenced by environmental factors as well. Studies of identical twins reared separately who select similar careers and lifestyles raise intriguing questions about the impact of heredity (Santrock 2005).

The study of human genetics is complex. Biologists continue to learn about the ways in which development is and is not influenced by heredity. During your lifetime you will witness many new discoveries and interpretations of the impact of genetics on an individual's characteristics.

Understanding of Inherited Characteristics Informs Practice. Although we do not know the extent to which genetics influence characteristics we do know that each young child comes with a unique genetic inheritance, and no two are alike. In quality early childhood programs children are not expected to be the same. Differences are respected and valued. Good programs offer a variety of learning activities to address children's interests and learning preferences. Schedules and routines are modified to meet the particular needs of the children enrolled. Quality early childhood programs welcome children with diverse characteristics and abilities. Adjustment to schedules, routines, and activities can allow typically developing children and those with special needs to grow and flourish in the same program.

Basic Needs

In their first weeks Jonah's and Megan's lives consist of a host of needs expressed and met. They nurse, they sleep, they are held and rocked, they are changed and bathed. Their mother nurses the babies, and her life is an almost constant pattern of feeding and caring for their needs. Jonah and Megan's dad delights in caring for the babies. He holds, rocks and sings, changes and bathes them.

An undeniable biological factor in development is physiological need. Every human being has basic physiological needs for air, water, food, and shelter. If these needs go unmet, the individual may not survive.

An additional prerequisite for an infant's healthy development is warm physical contact with a caregiver (which we will describe in greater detail on pages 101–102, in the section titled "The Critical Nature of Nurturing Relationships"). Research motivated by the high mortality rates of unhandled research animals established the significance of comforting tactile experiences in the early development of all species of mammals. Harry and Margaret Harlow's classic research showed that baby monkeys had a marked preference for contact with a terrycloth surrogate mother who provided contact comfort but no food, to a wire mother who had the advantage of providing milk but little else to recommend her in the eyes of the baby monkeys (Schickendanz, Schickendanz, Forsyth, & Forsyth 2001).

Similar needs in human infants have been shown in studies of institutionalized babies. A percentage of institutionalized human infants in these studies did not survive the first year of life when provided little or no consistent, close contact and where only the needs for nourishment and cleanliness were met. Those children who survived showed pervasive delay in all areas of development (Dennis, 1973). Conversely, in institutions where caregivers provided frequent comforting physical contact, the mortality rate decreased sharply and infants developed normally. Other research has demonstrated that children who suffer maternal deprivation in infancy often have problems in later development (Skeels 1966). Research and clinical observation reinforce our awareness of the importance of warm intimate contact between the primary caregiver and the infant, and how this connectedness (or failure to connect) can influence many aspects of later development.

Understanding of Basic Needs Informs Practice. Because young children are vulnerable and dependent on others, the first and most important task of any early childhood program is to ensure that children's basic needs are met. An emphasis on basic needs is one of the similar features in all high-quality early childhood programs. Though the relative emphasis varies depending on the age of the children, all early childhood educators understand and devote a considerable amount of attention and time to meeting children's basic needs. Because of this focus, we provide safe environments, nutritious and regular meals, and warm physical contact in all good programs for young children. Infants, toddlers, preschoolers and school age children thrive when programs are attentive to their needs both for appropriate physical activity and for rest.

Beyond Basic Needs. The importance of providing for basic needs has a psychological as well as a physical dimension. Abraham Maslow formulated a theory regarding the necessary conditions for the full development of human potential. Maslow suggested a hierarchy of basic and growth needs (Maslow 1968, 1970). At the base of the hierarchy are the physiological needs for air, water, food, and shelter. If these needs go unmet or are only partially met, individuals may not survive or may focus their thoughts and energy on meeting these needs. When basic physical needs are satisfied, security becomes a more pressing issue. When people are free from fear of hazards and threats in their enviornment and when they are surrounded by others who are caring and predictable, they feel secure and are then able to focus on giving and receiving love, the pursuit of an understanding of the world, and the self-knowledge that satisfies the highest human need—that of self-actualization. Maslow's model suggests that those individuals who are self-actualized are able to perceive reality clearly, are open to new experiences, and can make choices that support the growth of their own potential. They have the ability to be spontaneous and creative and to form and maintain positive relationships with others.

As an early childhood teacher, you will learn to be attentive to meeting the basic needs of the children in your care. Your understanding of their individual routines, needs, and preferences will help you provide a program that encourages the children to focus on learning and allows them to grow into individuals with a strong sense of self-direction.

> **Reflect on your own basic needs and self actualization**
>
> Think about a time when you were unhappy and under stress and another time when you were especially happy and productive. How well were your basic needs being met during these times? What made it possible for you to be happy and productive? What do these conclusions suggest for your work with young children?

Temperament

> *By the time Megan and Jonah are 10 weeks old they are clearly different individuals. Megan sleeps, eats, and eliminates on a predictable schedule. She is soothed by being rocked by her parents in a special baby swing outside in a tree. She stares contentedly at the patterns of a mobile or of leaves and rests quietly inside when she can hear the sound of people's voices. Jonah's sleeping, eating, and elimination are much less regular than Megan's. He is calmed by a mechanical swing that does not vary in span or pace. He nurses and rests better if he is away from the sounds of people.*

An aspect of development that has its basis in biology is called *temperament*. Temperament refers to an individual's behavioral style and characteristic ways of responding. Different researchers have constructed different models of temperament (Santrock 1998). The most widely used model, and the one we find most useful, was described by physicians Alexander Thomas and Stella Chess (1977, 1996). In a study that began in 1996 called *The New York Longitudinal Study* (Berk 1997), Thomas and Chess reported that babies are not all alike at birth (something that parents have always known) and that distinct and observable differences in temperament are evident among newborn infants in their first days and weeks of life. According to Thomas and Chess, babies can be seen to differ in nine personality characteristics, listed in Table 4.1.

The individual differences tend to cluster together in three basic types of temperament in children:

- The *Easy Child* (about 40%) quickly establishes regular routines in infancy, is generally cheerful, and adapts easily.
- The *Difficult Child* (about 10%) has irregular daily routines, is slow to accept new experiences, and tends to react negatively and intensely.
- The *Slow-to-Warm-Up Child* (about 15%) has a low activity level, has mild or low-key reactions to stimuli, is negative in mood, and adjusts slowly.

Another 35% of children did not match any of these clusters but seemed to have unique blends of temperamental traits. Megan, in the preceding examples, fits the profile of an "easy" child while Jonah has more of the characteristics of the "difficult" child.

The inherited nature of temperament is suggested by studies that show discernible differences in temperament among infants of different ethnic groups. Two-day-old

Table 4.1 **Thomas and Chess Temperament Dimensions**

- **Activity level:** The proportion of inactive periods to active ones
- **Rhythmicity:** The regularity of cycles of hunger, excretion, sleep, and wakefulness
- **Distractibility:** The degree to which new stimulation alters behavior
- **Approach/withdrawal:** The response to a new object or person
- **Adaptability:** The ease with which a child adapts to the environment
- **Attention span and persistence:** The amount of time devoted to an activity and the effect of distraction
- **Intensity of reaction:** The energy of response regardless of its quality or direction
- **Threshold of responsiveness:** The intensity of stimulation required to evoke a response
- **Quality of mood:** The amount of friendly, pleasant, joyful behavior as contrasted with unpleasant, unfriendly behavior

Source: From *Child Development* (4th ed., p. 410), by L. E. Berk, 2003, Needham Heights, MA: Allyn & Bacon.

Euro-American babies tend to be more active and changeable than Chinese-American and Chinese babies, who were calmer and more able to console themselves (Berk 2003, Santrock 2005).

The longitudinal (long-term) nature of the Thomas-Chess research shows that the characteristics are moderately stable across childhood but that environmental circumstances seem to modify them over time. Contemporary research (Rothbart, Ahadi, & Evans, 2000) suggests that early behaviors tend to change and reorganize themselves into more complex responses and that temperamental stability may develop with age. It appears that temperament becomes more fixed after 2 years of age and that it influences a child's predisposition to behave in certain ways. With repeated experiences, certain temperamental traits and patterns tend to become more stable.

Understanding of Temperament Informs Practice. We have found the idea of temperament valuable in helping us to understand the wide range of personalities in the young children we have taught. We have also found the idea of "goodness of fit" (Thomas & Chess 1977) extremely useful when considering the impact of temperament. *Goodness of fit* refers to the interaction between children's characteristics and those of the adults who live and work with them. Some adults and children seem to have temperaments that easily mesh, while others conflict. When caregivers are aware of and sensitive to children's temperament and help them to adapt to their environment, then difficult or slow-to-warm-up children have more positive experiences. Early childhood teachers who are respectful of temperamental difference will prepare routines and environments that support the needs of children with a range of temperamental characteristics. For example, teachers who recognize that some children have a very high activity level will arrange their schedules to ensure that these children have frequent opportunities for vigorous play, rather than expecting them to sit quietly for long periods of time.

Practitioners who apply Chess and Thomas's principles appropriately use this model to provide programs that value and nurture children as individuals. Insightful teachers use their knowledge about temperament as one lens for understanding what the child brings into the world at birth and how genetic inheritance interacts with the child's experiences. They respond flexibly to individual children and find ways to modify the environment and their own behavior to provide a good match for each child's temperament.

Max, at 17 years of age, is a relaxed young man, enthusiastic about his upcoming choices for college and happy in his relationships with friends and family. As an infant and a young child, Max wasn't so easygoing. His high energy level and his intense personality were often challenging for family members and teachers. Max's parents were careful to ensure that he had many opportunities to use his physical energy in acceptable ways. They worked closely with his preschool and elementary teachers to encourage them to simultaneously hold high expectations and provide avenues for success that fit well with Max's personality and learning style. Max's energy, drive, and enthusiasm were seen as assets by teachers and family members.

> **Reflect on a child you know**
>
> Think about a child you know well. Can you characterize him or her as easy, difficult, or slow-to-warm-up? How well do this child's characteristics fit with those of his or her parents or caregivers? How do you respond to the child's temperament? What could you do to support this child if you were his or her teacher or caregiver?

The Impact of Environment

Jonah and Megan's parents are able to give their babies attention, time, and a safe and healthy home. By the time the babies are 3 months old, Megan sleeps happily alone in the crib while Jonah sleeps better in the family bed. Both babies love to be sung to and read to. As sensitive and attentive parents, they have modified their lives in response to their children's needs. In addition, mom's Asian culture encourages the perspective that the child is the center of the home.

Each baby is born into a particular environment, society, culture, family, and set of circumstances. They are shaped by and will shape their environment in a reciprocal dance that begins the first day of life.

The Critical Nature of Nurturing Relationships

A prerequisite for healthy development is a warm, intimate, continuous relationship between the child and his or her primary caregivers. Care given in the context of a loving relationship is essential to normal physical, social, and emotional development and helps a child learn that the world is a safe and trustworthy place.

The observation that institutionalized infants often failed to develop normally (or even to survive) led to a concern with the social and emotional development of children who were cared for in child care centers rather than by their mothers. John Bowlby identified attachment to the mother as an essential prerequisite for normal social and emotional development (Bowlby 1951). Ongoing research and clinical observation support the premise that attachment is crucial for healthy social and emotional development. However, researchers have found that the precise form the attachment takes is not important as

long as it provides a secure base from which infants can begin to explore the world (Clarke-Stewart, Perlmutter, & Friedman 1988).

In recent years researchers and theorists have confirmed that the nature of early attachments has a profound effect on development. Mary Ainsworth (1979) found that the degree of attachment between mothers and their children differed a great deal from securely attached to those who had not attached at all. Her work confirmed the belief that children must be secure in their primary relationships before they are able to fully explore the world. Recent brain research suggests that a secure attachment to a nurturing caregiver has a protective biological function. Babies who receive sensitive and nurturing care are less likely than other children to respond to stresses by producing cortisol, a hormone that destroys brain cells (Shore 1997).

In the 1950s, Bowlby's work led to the conclusion that care outside of the home deprived children of this vital connection to their mothers and could result in serious psychological disorders and problems with interpersonal relationships. Research on nonparental infant care has recently been extended into exploration of the effects of child care on development. A summary of research on the effects of nonmaternal care on development led Jay Belsky to caution that care outside the home may lead to heightened insecurity and aggression in children (Belsky 1988). Belsky's work prompted debate regarding the pros and cons of group care for infants and pointed to the significance of the quality of the care for very young children and the importance of stability, acceptance, and emotional responsiveness in those who work with infants in group settings.

More recent studies suggest that out-of-home care in quality programs for infants does not undermine children's attachment to parents and that in some cases a secure attachment to a teacher may enhance an infant's parental bonds (McDevitt & Ormrod 2002.)

Researchers from the National Institute of Child Health and Human Development (NICHD), conducting a comprehensive study of early child care and its effects on children's development, have found that higher quality programs are positively related to better mother and child relationships. Children enrolled in these programs also tend to show fewer behavior problems, higher cognitive and language ability, and increased school readiness. More hours in child care were associated with less harmonious mother-child interactions, more problem behaviors at age 2, and a high probability of insecure attachment in infants whose mothers were identified as low in sensitivity. Center care was associated with better outcomes compared to other care settings of comparable quality. Instability of care (number of different care settings) was found to be associated with higher probability of insecure attachment in infancy if mothers were not providing sensitive and responsive care.

The Importance of Early Experiences

In order for infants and young children to develop normally they need an environment that provides them with novelty and stimulation and includes opportunities for sensory exploration. Interaction with people and objects in the course of play—the important work of infancy and childhood—has positive effects on subsequent development. For example, children who were given colorful objects to look at began reaching and grasping earlier than those who were not (Berk 1996).

Research has demonstrated that the experiences of the first 5 or 6 years of life have a critical impact on all areas of children's susbsequent development. Until the 1950s and 1960s, the prevalent view was that people matured in predictable ways according to a biologically predetermined plan. In *Intelligence and Experience* (1961), Hunt cited many research studies that demonstrated the powerful effects of early experience on children's development. This book contributed significantly to the current view of the importance of early experience.

Animals generally exhibit *critical periods,* times of sensitivity during which the normal development of an organ or structural system must take place. If it does not occur during this period, permanent damage may occur or development may be retarded. Human beings also have *critical* or *sensitive periods,* times during which the individual is especially responsive to particular types of environmental influences and experiences. Many sensitive periods occur prenatally when the growing embryo or fetus is particularly susceptible to teratogens (environmental agents that causes prenatal damage) and infectious diseases. Sensitive periods also occur during the early years for attachment, brain development, and language development (Berk 1996).

Recent study of human neurological development indicates that "windows of opportunity," times when an individual can most easily learn a particular skill or mental function, are longer than originally thought. McCall and Plemons (2001) point out that even with long windows of opportunity, developmentally appropriate experiences should be available from the time the window opens, even if it may be many years before the window closes.

> *Maureen is the first child in a family of six siblings. Both her parents used alcohol and drugs from the time that Maureen was very young and she assumed the role of the caregiver for her younger siblings. She experienced regular episodes of parental anger and neglect. However, she was very close to her maternal grandparents who visited her often and created special family events for her and for her siblings. As an adult, Maureen is a successful executive of a large corporation. She is well liked by employees, friends, and associates. She is a loving wife and enjoys a warm relationship with her two teenage children.*

Evidence shows us that human beings can be resilient and can overcome adverse circumstances encountered in early life. Studies suggest that inadequate nurture and stimulation in the early years does not necessarily cause irreversible deficiencies later in life (Kagan 1984). A longitudinal study on children from the Hawaiian island of Kauai identified characteristics of children who are resilient in the face of adversity (Werner, Bierman, & French 1971; Werner & Smith 1992). Resilient children show a combination of inherited characteristics, such as a positive disposition, and environmental factors, the most important of which is a long-term, trusting relationship with a caring adult. In the example above, Maureen's relationship with her grandparents and her positive personal characteristics contributed to her success both as a child and as an adult, despite many challenges within her family. Although repeated experiences of extreme and early deprivation cause serious damage to the developing child, these studies suggest that human beings can be remarkably resilient, and early deprivation does not necessarily result in lifelong problems.

The contemporary view is that resiliency is a dynamic process and that children can be taught to cope with some stress. As a teacher, you can be aware of the fact that resilient children understand cause and effect and see the world as a positive place where events have reason and meaning. You can use this information to create experiences that support these outcomes and encourage the children in your care to believe that they are competent people and that the world is an interesting place (Gonzalez-Mena & Eyer 2004).

Brain Development

During the last decade, there has been a growing body of research on the development of the brain. Once it was assumed that the structure of the brain was genetically determined and fixed at birth. Today we know that only the brain's main circuits are determined at birth. The brain of a newborn weighs only 25% of its adult weight. At birth the baby's brain has all the neurons (brain cells) that it will ever have. The brain does not grow more cells; instead each neuron expands in size and develops more connections (called *synapses*) making the brain more dense. Synaptic connections are what enable us to think and learn. The brain continues to grow and change significantly during the early years in response to experience.

What Do We Know About Brain Development?

Rima Shore in *Rethinking the Brain* (1997) has summarized five essential points from brain development research:

- *Human development hinges on a complex interplay between nature (genes) and nurture (experiences).* Brain function is dependent on signals that are sent quickly and efficiently through a network of brain cells and synapses (the connections between cells). As a child interacts with the environment new synapses are created until the child's brain reaches a maximal brain density at about 3 years. This density is maintained during the first decade of life, after which a "pruning" of excess synapses occurs. In this way the brain actually "creates" itself. The brain prunes those connections that are unused. Brain development, therefore, is a "use it or lose it" situation with early stimulation playing a critical role.

- *Early experiences have a decisive and long-lasting impact on the architecture of the brain, and directly affect the way the brain is wired, the ability to learn, and the capacity to regulate emotions.* The ways in which significant adults relate to children have a direct impact on the formation of neural pathways. In other words, a secure attachment to a nurturing, consistent, and stimulating caregiver has a protective function. It supports brain development and helps a child learn impulse control and ways to handle stress.

- *The human brain has a remarkable capacity to change, but timing is crucial. The brain and the capacity to learn are not fixed; they change in response to experience.* During certain "optimal periods" or "windows" the brain is particularly efficient at specific learning (e.g., language).

- *At certain times, negative experiences or the absence of appropriate stimulation are more likely to have serious and sustained effects.* The developing brain is vulnerable. Trauma and neglect can lead to a dramatic impairment of the brain's capacity. Excess cortisol, a hormone that increases when stress levels rise, can destroy brain cells and lessen brain density. Maternal depression, trauma or abuse, early exposure to substances such as cocaine, nicotine, and alcohol can all have harmful and long-lasting effects on brain development.

- *Evidence amassed over the last decade points to the wisdom and efficacy of prevention and early intervention.* Intensive, timely, and well designed intervention can create significant and long-lasting improvement for children who are at risk of impairment.

Understanding of Brain Development Informs Practice

Increased interest in the implications of brain development research has encouraged additional study and review by neuroscientists, psychologists, and linguists. Some researchers suggest that the information about brain development has been overapplied to policy decisions that affect funding for children's programs (Bruer & Greenough 2001). While there is debate as to the particulars of how the brain builds and destroys synapses as a result of experience, it remains clear that nurturing relationships and developmentally appropriate experiences support optimal development and learning for all young children.

Current studies confirm much of the earlier research and provide clear justification for many of the practices that have been traditional in high-quality early childhood programs. As an early childhood teacher, you will apply this knowledge when you:

- Provide safe, healthy, stimulating environments and good nutrition to children
- Develop warm and caring relationships with children and support strong attachment between children and their families
- Ensure that each small group of infants or young toddlers has a consistent primary caregiver
- Respond sensitively to children's verbal and nonverbal communication
- Recognize that children are unique from birth, with individual temperaments and rates of development
- Design activities, environments, and routines to allow children of diverse abilities, backgrounds, interests, and temperaments to experience consistent acceptance and success
- Surround children with child-directed and relevant person-to-person language (not the background chatter of television or video)
- Encourage exploration and play
- Involve families in the program in meaningful ways
- Limit television exposure (even "educational" TV) and encourage families to do the same

DEVELOPMENT OF THE WHOLE CHILD: THEORY INTO PRACTICE

Periods of Development

Children at different ages have different characteristics. Studies of development have identified typical behaviors and characteristics of children at each age. We have found it most helpful in our work to think of four distinct periods of early childhood:

- *Infants* range in age from birth through 15 to 18 months.
- *Toddlers* are 15 to 18 months through 30 to 35 months.
- *Preschoolers/kindergartners* range from 30 to 36 months to 6 years.
- *School-age children* are those whose ages are between 6 and 8.

Notice that we have indicated a range at the beginnings and ends of most periods. This range reminds us of the highly individual nature of development. Keeping this in mind, we know that there are certain characteristic milestones, developmental achievements, for each period. Typically developing children show considerable normal variation in achievement of a milestone. Children will achieve developmental milestones based on their own internal genetic clocks as well as the opportunities that they have for experience and practice.

> **Reflect on developmental norms**
>
> What do you know from your family or your memories about your own development? Was it considered "typical" or "normal"? Did your development cause concern for your family? What might you imagine that families feel when they suspect their child's development is not "normal"?

Domains of Development

In order to clarify and define children's development it is common for researchers and educators to talk about different aspects or "domains" of development. In the four sections that follow we will consider physical cognitive, social, and emotional development. This breakdown is useful because it offers us a way to think about development and provides a "shorthand" for communicating about it. These divisions are not universal—social and emotional development are sometimes paired and referred to as *psychosocial* or *socioemotional.* Development of language and literacy are sometimes considered separately from cognitive development. And, regardless of how they are categorized by educators and theorists, in a real child they are parts of a whole that interact with and influence one another.

Janine is 5 years old. From early infancy, she has experienced frequent middle ear infections, a physical condition that limits her ability to hear. Because of this, her speech and language development are not as advanced as those of many other 5-year-olds. She has fewer words than most and it is difficult to understand what she says. This has limited her play with other children. Her delayed language also means that sometimes she doesn't understand spoken information as quickly as other children do.

In this example, the physical condition of the ear infections influenced Janine's social, cognitive, and language development.

Physical Development

From birth to 8 years of age, children undergo dramatic changes in their bodies and physical capabilities. The helpless newborn who is under 2 feet in length and has minimal physical control grows to become a strong, coordinated 6-year-old who is at least two-thirds of his or her future adult height. A child's physical competence influences other aspects of his or her development, especially self-concept. Some physically competent children will advance more rapidly than others in the cognitive domain simply because they are likely to explore more aspects of the world at an earlier age and perhaps more extensively than less physically competent children. Physical development is orderly and is marked by an increase in control. Physical development milestones include increased size and altered body proportions; changes in sleeping, eating, and elimination patterns; and the development of large motor and small motor skills. Knowledge of physical development at different stages can help you to have realistic expectations and to design appropriate experiences for young children (see Table 4.2).

Maturational Theory and Its Relationship to Physical Development.
Arnold Gesell (1896–1961) and his associates, Frances L. Ilg and Louise B. Ames, pioneered the scientific study of child development in the 1930s. By gathering information on dozens of children at each age level, they identified growth and behavioral characteristics (developmental norms) of children from birth through adolescence. The resulting guidelines for what can be expected of children at various ages and stages of development serve as the basis for many developmental charts (like the ones included in this chapter) and screening instruments that are in use today (Gesell 1940; Gesell & Ilg 1974).

Gesell theorized that genetic inheritance and maturation determined a major portion of an individual's development, but environmental factors could influence it positively or negatively. This theory, sometimes known as *maturational theory,* suggests that children need protection from disease, injury, and environmental hazards with day-to-day care supplemented by periodic medical examinations to ensure that health is good and growth patterns are normal.

Table 4.2 **Milestones of Physical Development**

	Growth, Sleeping, Eating, and Elimination	Large Motor Development	Small Motor Development
Infants	• Very rapid growth • By 1 year most sleep through the night and take several naps • By 1 year have 12 teeth and eat three meals of solid food plus snacks	• By 1 month lifts own head • By 6 mos. rolls over • By 7 mos. sits alone • By end of the first year stands and may walk	• Reaches for objects • By 6 mos. transfers objects from hand to hand • By 9 mos. coordinates two hands and uses thumb and forefinger to grasp small items

Toddlers	• By 18 mos. may use a spoon part of the time
	• By 36 mos. most have 20 teeth
	• By 36 mos. most control elimination when awake and need diapers at night
	• Sleeps 12 or 13 hours each day
		• By 15 mos. walks
		• By age 2:
		  • Runs stiffly
		  • Climbs stairs one step at a time and climbs onto other surfaces
		  • Throws a ball with two hands
		• By age 3:
		  • Jumps
		  • Begins to ride a tricycle
			• Picks up small items and drops into containers
			• Uses hands to scribble and turn pages of a book
			• Hand preference emerges but is not stable
			• By 18 mos. stacks two or three items
			• By 24 mos. stacks six or more items

Preschool/ Kindergarten Children	• Growth slows
	• Appetite is smaller
	• Naps for an hour or two a day
	• At 3 may have daytime toileting accidents, but by 4 rare
		• Walks with arms swinging
		• Runs with a "true run" (both feet leave ground); by age 4 varies speed and direction, and stops when running
		• Jumps from floor, over an object, and forward
		• Rides a trike with accuracy and speed
		• Climbs quickly and smoothly with alternating steps
		• Throws a ball overhand with accuracy
			• By age 5:
			  • Manipulates zippers, snaps, and buttons
			  • Uses scissors to cut along a straight line
			  • Uses paintbrushes, pens, and pencils to make shapes, letters, and numerals

Primary Children	• Reaches 2/3 of adult height by age 6, face lengthens • Independent in self-care • Eating patterns closely resemble those of adults • Permanent teeth appear	• Adult walking patterns • Skips alternating feet • Mature running • Jumps high, long, and far • Jumps rope • Mature climbing • Steps forward when throwing • Plays games involving physical skills like batting and throwing	• Has coordination to write, draw, use tools, small toys, and play an instrument • Mature pencil grip develops by 8 years

Maturationist theory postulates that genetic differences determine the rate at which children attain the growth and maturation necessary for learning skills and concepts. Progress cannot be made until the prerequisite growth and maturation have occurred and attempts to hasten development are futile.

Gesell's work led to the concept of *readiness*, a period of development in which a specific skill or response is most likely to occur. The notion of readiness is one that influences our thinking in many areas of children's growth and learning. Decisions about when children should be expected to learn to use the toilet, read, or drive an automobile are influenced by our understanding of and beliefs about readiness.

Critics of maturational theory have challenged Gesell's methods of data collection and have suggested that the small size and limited diversity of the population studied restricts the applicability of the conclusions. Other reviews have cautioned that the maturationist approach can be taken to mean that environmental stimulation is not important.

Implications of Maturational Theory for Practice. Because physical development follows a predictable sequence you will be able to plan activities that allow children to practice the skills they are building and to move on to the appropriate next steps when they are ready. Children grow and thrive in environments that invite the practice of emerging skills but avoid rushing or pushing children to reach new milestones before they have fully mastered prerequisite ones. One of the wonders of development is that when children engage in appropriate activity at any one stage, they are naturally building the skills needed to successfully enter the next. For example, the infant lying on his or her stomach, kicking vigorously, is strengthening the lower back muscles needed to begin to sit up. Increasing mastery makes large muscle activity enjoyable to young children, and it is a feature of much of their play. They gradually go on to develop small muscle control. The arms, legs, and trunk must work in concert before a child can pump on a swing; writing skills cannot develop until a child has mastered the visual and fine motor skills (along with cognitive, language, and literacy skills) needed for this complex activity.

Information about developmental norms can help us to determine whether children are developing according to schedule and when we might be concerned with a child's overall progress or with a particular aspect of development. Developmental norms can guide our decisions about when children can realistically be expected to acquire abilities and to learn skills.

As a teacher of children, it will be imperative that you apply developmental norms with sensitivity to the specifics of the groups of children with whom you work. You will get to know the circumstances of the families of the children in your care. You will learn about the values that they hold for their children's achievements and you will understand how these influence the opportunities and experiences that they provide for their children's growth and development. Your thoughtful reflection on individuals will allow you to use information about developmental norms appropriately and effectively.

Dynamic Systems Theory. Some contemporary research suggests that motor development, as well as development in other domains, is more complex than maturationist theories imply. Thelen and Smith (1998) suggest that motor skills develop through a complex interaction among development of the nervous system, the infant's perceptions, opportunities within the environment, and the infant's motivation to reach a goal.

Four-month-old Cory looks intently at a brightly colored ball just beyond her reach. She stretches her arm outward, waves her hand, wiggles her torso, and through this combination of movements is able to just touch the ball. Over the next several weeks, she repeats this series of movements over and over, particularly when her caregiver places different brightly colored objects just barely out of her reach.

Cory is motivated to touch the objects. She has had practice reaching for objects in the past. She uses her past skills—her ability to see the attractive objects, her growing control over her arms and fingers, and her motivation to touch—and creates a new stretching and wiggling movement that allows her to touch the desired object. Through repeated practice, she fine-tunes these movements to allow her to reach her goal more efficiently. She is an active participant in the creation of new motor skills.

Unlike maturationist theories, which suggest that motor development is a passive process in which genes determine how skills develop over time, dynamic systems theory suggests that infants actively put together skills that allow them to achieve goals, and that these achievements are either limited or encouraged by the child's body and by the environment.

Implications of Dynamic Systems Theory for Practice. Dynamic systems theory, coupled with increasing understanding of brain development, supports our understanding of the importance of providing children with a range of interesting objects to handle, manipulate, and explore. It reminds us that motivation is a key element in mastery of skill. As a thoughtful teacher, you will observe children's movement carefully and learn about their interest and skill level. You will determine what they are motivated to do and learn, then add objects and experiences to their environment that will encourage them to use their bodies in increasingly complex and effective ways.

> **Reflect on physical development, motivation, and feelings of competence**
>
> Recall a time when you mastered a physical skill such as learning to play tennis or creating beaded jewelry. What motivated you to learn this skill? How did this achievement make you feel about yourself? How did your success with learning these skills influence later choices you have made? What conclusions can you draw from this about the importance of success in physical activity for young children?

Cognitive Development

While each typically developing child travels a similar and visible path to basic physical competence, the road traveled to the development of thinking and reasoning abilities and the acquisition of knowledge about the world is more difficult to discern.

At each stage or period of development, children differ in their mental abilities. Some differences are based on genetic differential in rates of acquisition of cognitive skills; other differences stem from the opportunities and experiences that are unique to each child. Knowledge of some of the hallmarks of cognitive development at different stages can help you to have realistic expectations and to design appropriate learning experiences for young children (see Table 4.3). Use this information with sensitivity to the diverse needs and differing abilities of the children in your care to ensure that the choices you make are thoughtfully mindful of each child's development.

Concept Development. All children develop *concepts* (mental images or word pictures) to help them make sense of experience. As children repeatedly experience the characteristics of an object, animal, person, or event they mentally combine and organize these characteristics to construct a concept.

> *One-year-old Chanelle is dropped off at her family child care home. As her mom exits through the front door, Chanelle cries and cries. She spots a ring of keys on a coffee table, picks them up and takes them to the door, holds them up to the doorknob, and looks expectantly at the door.*

Concepts are generalized as children recognize common attributes. An infant may have constructed the concept *door* based on many repeated experiences, including a slam, mother entering, going through a door, the door being opened with keys, and the barrier to what is desired. In the door example, Chanelle's initial concept of *door* may only have been the door of her bedroom. As she experiences other doors, the concept is expanded. Although the doors differ, the common characteristics are recognized and the concept is established.

Table 4.3 | **Milestones of Cognitive Development**

	Concept Development	Language Development
Infants	• Explores the world with the senses—by looking, mouthing, and grasping • Initial reflexive actions become purposeful by 4 months • As a newborn, scans faces • Shows preference for contrast in visual display during first 6 months • Begins to focus attention and make choices after many interactions with people and things • Imitates the behavior of others, such as waving good-bye • Shows awareness of cause and effect by repeating own actions for the effect • Develops object permanence (by 12 months): searches for objects and people and protests when they disappear, retrieves a toy that has rolled behind something else by removing the obstacle	• Cries, coos, and responds to human language from birth • Discriminates various speech sounds from as young as 1 month • Participates in a "dialogue" of sound and gesture • Beginning about 4 or 5 months, babbles strings of consonants and vowels, which finally shorten to one or two repetitions • By the first birthday speaks first word; initially words are "holophrases" in which a single word stands for a whole sentence (e.g., "dat" for "what is that?") • Actively engages in language games like pat-a-cake • Recognizes that actions, objects, and ideas are represented by words and understands multiword utterances (e.g., "kiss mommy")
Toddlers	• Relies on sensory information but increasingly able to recall and anticipate events • Play is largely physical, involving the manipulation and exploration of objects • Engages in "pretend" play • Distinguishes a few objects from many • Begins to understand aspects of space and time (the park is near, grandma's is far; we will go to the park tomorrow) • Overextends concepts, such as calling all animals dogs	• First words approximate adult sound patterns and are understood and used in context with family and other familiar caregivers • Uses words differently from adults, sometimes underextending (using a word less broadly) or overextending (using more broadly; e.g., calling all beverages milk) • Recognizes and repeats simple nursery rhymes • Recognizes and names a few colors
Preschool/ Kindergarten Children	• Has many ideas about how the social and physical world works • Able to form more complex mental symbols of events and objects • Can't easily distinguish between reality and fantasy until close to age 5 • Groups objects by shared characteristics such as color, size, shape, and function • By 4, matches one to one • Understands that numerals (one, two, etc.) refer to a specific amount but is unable to relate numerals to more than about 10 objects, and by age 5 can rote count to 20 • By age 5, understands the practical use of clocks and calendars and may associate specific events to times and days	• Understands relational language (in, on, under) • Uses language to represent ideas • Overgeneralizes grammatical rules as exceptions are learned • Has a vocabulary of more than 1,000 words by age 3 • By 5, vocabulary nears 10,000 words

(continued)

Table 4.3   Milestones of Cognitive Development (Continued)

	Concept Development	Language Development
Preschool/ Kindergarten Children *(continued)*	• Increasingly able to make and follow a plan and predict the outcomes of own actions • Represents ideas through art media and dramatic play • Play often symbolic and pretend in which objects can stand for something they are not	
Primary Children	• Uses symbols as tools for thinking and literacy • Develops conservation of quantity (see the description of Piaget's stages): initially judges quantity by appearance (e.g., a tall narrow glass has more than a short, wide glass even when someone demonstrates the amounts are the same); begins to realize quantities remain the same even though form may change • Becomes able to visualize how something will appear if it is viewed from another position in space • Able to sequence objects from short to tall and arrange colors from light to dark • Has a more elaborate understanding of time—that includes own past—and beginning understanding of history • Play includes games that are governed by rules • Has beginning understanding of societal concepts such as laws, rules, and justice	• By age 8 uses language that is essentially "adult" in fluency and in articulation • May make errors with difficult grammar such as ask/tell • Understands word jokes and riddles • Changes language patterns to be appropriate to individual listeners

A child's ability to understand and develop a concept depends on cognitive maturation and the availability of relevant experiences. Concepts differ in how difficult they are for children to understand and how relevant they are to each child's life and experiences. The likelihood that a concept will be understood is related to its degree of abstraction, complexity, and novelty.

Concepts can be thought of as existing on a continuum from concrete to abstract. The *concreteness* of a concept refers to whether it can be directly experienced or observed. Concrete concepts are accessible to children. They can be experienced through the senses—seen, heard, held, felt, touched, tasted. Concepts that depend on information outside of direct experience are abstract and cannot be completely understood by a young child regardless of how hard an adult may try to provide the experience through language, books, or pictures. Their abstract nature makes times, events, and places that cannot be directly experienced in some way—President's Day, a trip to the moon, World War II, and abstract concepts like social justice and liberty, for example—mostly meaningless to young children.

The *complexity* of a concept—the amount of information needed to define it—is the second quality that affects a young child's ability to comprehend it. Children acquire concepts of low complexity more quickly than those of high complexity. Some concepts are available to children through direct experience but involve many interrelated ideas. These concepts are unlikely to be understood because young children's capacity for creating and retaining connections between such ideas has not yet developed. The concept of *wind* is both relatively simple and concrete, defined primarily by one's experience of it against the skin and its ability to move objects. The concept of a *weather system,* however, is complex and requires the grasp of numerous other supporting concepts including evaporation, wind patterns, cloud formation, low- and high-pressure areas, and precipitation. Young children will not fully comprehend the phenomena of a weather system because understanding requires attending to a variety of attributes simultaneously. Providing children experiences with some of the components of weather will, however, lay a foundation for later understanding of this complex concept.

Even simple concepts that have no relationship to children's past experiences are difficult for them to understand. A child who lives in an urban setting and has had limited opportunities to travel may not easily understand the concept of a farm or its characteristics and purposes. We were reminded of this when one of us took a group of urban children on a field trip to a forest preserve. Despite discussion and description prior to the trip, none of the children were prepared for what it would be like to be in a forest, and after a few minutes of walking most were tearfully begging to return to the comfort of the bus before the wolf got them!

Language Development. Language development, like physical development, follows a predictable sequence that is related, but not tied to, chronological age. Although individuals vary in the speed of language acquisition and in how much they speak, the language-learning process is universal.

Before they speak, children make and respond to many sounds. Crying, gurgling, babbling, and cooing are important parts of the language-learning process. Important language abilities are established as caregivers respond to the sounds infants make. Numerous psychologists and linguists have theorized about how children learn language. Linguist Noam Chomsky (Bruner 1983) proposed that humans have an innate ability to process language, which he referred to as a *language acquisition device* (LAD) to explain why children are able to produce word forms and sentences they have never heard. Current theories of language development proposed by Jerome Bruner (1983) and Gordon Wells (1985) suggest that early social experiences form the basis for language development.

Adults act as informal guides who support and foster language learning through their interactions with children. Dialogues occur between adult and infant during feeding and changing, and there are games like peek-a-boo, naming objects and events as they occur, picturebook reading, and nonverbal play. By their first birthday children generally speak their first word and more words soon follow. Bruner suggests that caring adults provide a temporary framework or *scaffold* for language by assuming young children intend to communicate, by listening carefully, and by assisting only as much as needed. In early conversations caregivers provide some of the child's responses. As the child's ability to participate is demonstrated, the adult adjusts, gradually permitting the child to take over on his or her own.

As children learn language, they master a complex task that involves a system of speech sounds (phonology), grammatical forms and relationships (syntax), meaning (semantics), and socially based customs for language use (pragmatics). Exposure to everyday speech and a desire to interact socially contribute to children's construction of understanding of language principles. Experimentation with all of the language elements is essential. Overextensions of a particular word are common. For example, a toddler we know called the family cat *mao* and overextended the word to label the neighbor's dog, a furry toy, and the lady across the street who had three cats. Similarly, preschool-age children overgeneralize grammatical rules: "I holded the baby bunny." "I have two feets." These natural developments in children's language learning help us realize that children analyze and construct language rather than merely imitating or learning by rote. This process of exploration is not affected by instruction or correction, but by speaking and listening. By the age of 5 or 6 most children have mastered the basics in all these areas in their native tongue; they have "learned language."

Language is inextricably tied to culture. Cultures and individuals vary not only in the obvious differences of the language spoken, but in the ways that language is used. Some cultures and groups place a high value on spoken language; others value different means of communication. It is important to note that not all cultures equate language with intelligence or with sophisticated cognitive ability.

Theory Relating to Cognitive Development. The process by which the helpless newborn becomes a talkative, reasoning individual is amazing, immensely complex, and largely hidden. We cannot watch an idea grow or see a thought. Perhaps because of its veiled nature, many theories have been proposed to explain children's cognitive development. We present a brief overview of three theories that we find most useful (constructivist, sociocultural, and multiple intelligences) and discuss the ways that each can guide practice in early childhood programs. Each theory provides useful insight for working with children, but we believe that none is sufficient in itself to fully explain cognitive development.

Constructivist Theory

Micah (age 2½) and Sage (age 4) sit down at the table. Their teacher gives them each a ball of play dough. Sage breaks up her dough into three small balls. Micah looks over at Sage's dough and begins to wail, "I want plenty like Sage!"

Many early childhood educators today hold a *constructivist* view of the cognitive development of young children. The basic premise of this theory is that the child constructs understanding through interaction with the environment (people and things) over time. At every stage a person is engaged in the cumulative process of receiving, organizing, and interpreting new information.

The best known constructivist theory of cognitive development comes from Jean Piaget (1896–1980), a Swiss epistemologist (one who investigates the nature and origin of knowledge). Piaget's complex theory focuses primarily on the nature and development of logical thought and on the construction of understanding as an individual activity (Flavell, Miller, & Miller 2002; Ginsburg & Opper 1988; Piaget 1966).

Kinds of Knowledge. Piaget postulated that children acquire three kinds of knowledge as they grow: physical, social, and logico-mathematical.

Physical knowledge, the knowledge of external reality, is gained from doing things or acting on the physical world. For example, by holding and playing with a ball, children experience and learn about its properties—texture, shape, weight, squishiness, and tendency to roll away and bounce.

Social knowledge is learned from others. It includes language, social conventions or rules, symbols, values, rituals and myths, and ideas about right and wrong, acceptable and unacceptable. It is learned by observation, through being told, and by reading. For example, children learn that balls are used to play games, that different kinds of balls are used for different games, and different balls have different names.

Logico-mathematical knowledge is the understanding of logical relationships constructed as children observe, compare, think, and reason. When children categorize and order, and observe relationships between things, they are developing logico-mathematical knowledge. For example, children will observe the relationship between a tennis ball and a playground ball (similar shapes, roll and bounce, but different size, color, texture, and weight). Through the experience of many balls, a child develops the idea of *ball* as a single category based on shared characteristics. Logico-mathematical knowledge requires direct experience but is based on the internal process of reflecting on what is experienced.

Constructivist theory stresses that individuals *adapt* (make related changes) based on their interactions with the social and the physical environment. Piaget believed that knowledge is not given to a passive observer; rather, it must be discovered and constructed by the activity of the individual.

As a teacher who has learned about constructivist theory, you will understand that you cannot pour knowledge into children. You will not expect to "cover" an idea or concept in your teaching. You will develop strategies that assist you in selecting materials and experiences that encourage each individual child to build his or her own understanding of concepts and ideas.

Processes for Construction of Knowledge. Piaget theorized that by interacting with the environment, the child develops organized ways of making sense of experiences. Piaget referred to these organizing structures as *schemata* (sometimes called *schema* or *schemes*). Early schemata become the basis for more complex future mental frameworks. Infants use mostly behavioral or physical schemes such as sucking, looking, grasping, and shaking. Older children move from only physical or action-based schemes and develop mental schemes that allow representational thought and the ability to solve problems. Piaget identified two processes (*assimilation* and *accommodation*) that children use to organize their experience into structures for thinking and problem solving. These processes are summarized in Figure 4.1.

Piagetian Stages of Cognitive Development. Piaget theorized that children progress through a series of developmental stages that build from the interaction among three elements: existing mental structures, maturation, and experience. Stages occur in the same predictable sequence for everyone, although the exact age at which a child enters the next stage varies with the individual and the culture. The characteristics of the stages are summarized in Table 4.4.

Most children in early childhood education and care programs will be in the *sensorimotor* and the *preoperational* stages of cognitive development. As they enter the preoperational stage, children are beginning to use symbols (words) to represent experiences. According to Piaget they are still bound to their perceptions and see things only from their own viewpoint (egocentrism). The primary way they learn is through direct experiences that involve sensory exploration and manipulation. During this period children are likely to focus on only one characteristic of an object or experience at a time, so they are easily deceived by appearances. Micah, in the example at the beginning of this section, did not have the ability to "conserve" so he was fooled by the appearance of the dough. One of our favorite stories that illustrates this concept concerns a child on his first plane ride who turned to his mother after the plane had completed its ascent and asked, "When do we start getting smaller?"

Figure 4.1 Piaget's Model of Cognitive Change

Child's Experience	Cognitive Process/ Adaptation	Child's State of Cognition
Child has many experiences with dogs.	Child creates a mental schema, a "dog scheme" that include the information that dogs walk on 4 legs.	Equilibrium: *Definition: A balanced and comfortable state*
Child sees a goat for the first time and calls it "dog."	Assimilates: *Definition: Includes new information into existing schemes or behavior pattern, but does not change the existing mental structures or patterns* Child includes the goat into her existing "dog scheme."	Equilibrium: Child has successfully adapted to the new information by including it into an existing mental structure.
Child notices that goat has different characteristics from dogs. She has experiences with other 4-legged creatures.		Disequilibrium: *Definition: A state of imbalance where new information does not fit into existing mental structures*
She calls goats and sheep "maa."	Accommodates: *Definition: Creates a new scheme, or rearranges one or more existing ones, so that new information will fit accurately into the mental structures* Child makes a new mental structure for these 4-legged animals that do not bark or wag their tails.	Equilibrium: By creating a new scheme, the child has successfully adapted her mental structures to new information.

As children approach their seventh birthday, their thinking becomes more logical, flexible, and organized than it was during the preschool years. They are now able to mentally organize concepts and images. This allows them to solve more complex problems mentally without the need to physically manipulate objects. However, their understanding is still tied to concrete concepts, those they have experienced. Children in this cognitive stage, which Piaget referred to as *concrete operations,* are developing more accurate understanding of space. They can order objects in a more complex manner than younger children.

> *Jeremy, age 7, has gathered rocks and pebbles since he was a preschooler. During a family vacation to the mountains he collected a number of different rocks, which he carefully wrapped and brought home with him. He added these to his collection and now delights in sorting and organizing his growing collection in many ways. He has organized the rocks in increasingly complex ways: by color and hue, from smallest to largest, and by where he found them. With the help of his dad, Jeremy is using an elementary geology book and is beginning to sort his rocks using some geological terms.*

Piaget was also concerned with how language influenced the development of thinking. He observed that preschool children's speech was more often egocentric (talking aloud to oneself) rather than socialized speech (dialogue with others). He

Table 4.4 | **Piaget's Stages of Cognitive Development**

Stage	Developmental Hallmark	Characteristics
Sensorimotor Stage (birth to 2)	*Object permanence*—understanding that objects exist even after they are out of sight	• Changes from a reflexive organism to one capable of thought and language • Behavior primarily motor • Depends on physical manipulation to gain information about the world • Not able to form mental images for events that cannot be heard, felt, seen, smelled, or tasted • Learns to differentiate self from others • Learns to seek stimulation • Begins to develop the concept of causality
Preoperational Stage (between ages 2 and 7) *Preconceptual phase* **(between 2 and 4)** *Intuitive phase* **(between 4 and 7)**	*Conservation*—realization that the amount or quantity of a substance stays the same even when its shape or location changes	• *Egocentric*—unable to take the viewpoint of others • Evolves from one who relies on actions for understanding to one who is able to think conceptually • Learns labels for experience • Develops the ability to substitute a symbol (word, gesture, or object) for an object or an event that is not present • Thought based on how things appear rather than on logical reasoning • Tends to classify by a single salient feature • Moral feelings and moral reasoning begin during this stage
Concrete Operations Period (between ages 7 and 11)		• Develops the ability to apply logical thought to concrete problems • Formal thought processes more stable and reasonable • Still has to think things out in advance and try them out through direct manipulation
Formal Operations Period (between ages 11 and 15)		• Able to apply logic to all classes of problems • Develops basic principles of cause and effect and of scientific experimentation • Can weigh a situation mentally to deduce the relationships without having to try it out

suggested that egocentric speech is an accompaniment to activity that reflects thinking. That is, children become capable of acquiring and using language *only* as they develop concepts. In this view, experience is most important. Language is acquired in social contexts *after* concepts are in place. From this perspective, cognitive development creates language.

Implications of Constructivist Theory for Practice. Piaget's work has helped parents and professionals become aware that children's thinking is fundamentally different from that of adults and that it relies on experience. As children have direct, repeated sensory experiences they construct their own knowledge.

Piaget's work has helped educators understand that children's cognitive development proceeds through stages, just like their physical development. It is as foolish to attempt to rush a child into thinking like an adult as it would be to attempt to teach a crawling infant to high-jump. This understanding has helped educators create and refine the construct of *readiness*. Although cognitive development cannot be rushed, research suggests that it can be impaired. Children need intellectual stimulation to learn to think and reason (Healy 1990).

Piaget's insistence that young children are always trying to construct a more coherent understanding of their world through their experience has led many educators to the belief that educational practices should allow ample opportunity for children to explore, experiment, and manipulate materials. Piaget was adamant that we cannot directly instruct children in the concepts they need to move on to the next developmental stage. These concepts are acquired as a result of a complex interaction between experience, maturation, and adult mediation.

In settings using a direct instruction method teachers have often taught social knowledge ("this shape—8—is called *eight*"; "the earth goes around the sun") rather than providing experiences that allow children to construct it. Direct instruction advocates argue that constructivist learning approaches do not provide children with specific content or with the comprehensive information they need for in-depth knowledge and mastery. Constructivists counter that direct instruction methods discourage creative thinking and turn children into passive learners who are not skilled at thinking creatively.

Piaget's study of the development and structure of knowing and thinking created a new methodology for the study of cognitive development. The interest and debate that Piaget's work has generated attests to its significance. His studies have been replicated in many settings and his work extensively critiqued. His careful observations of the strategies that children use in their thinking and his description of the processes and stages of development have made an important contribution to our understanding of how young children learn and have generated much fruitful thought and research about cognitive development.

Sociocultural Theory

Skye, age 3, is building with blocks. She builds a low building with a roof. Her teacher, Val, sits down next to her and also constructs a building with a roof. Then Val says, "I think I need more space in my house." Val puts a unit block at each corner and places a roofboard on top to create a second story. Skye looks on with great interest and tries to add a second story to her house using three units and a half-unit block for the corners. Her top floor collapses. Val says to her, "Help me find four that are just the same size for the next floor."

A number of theorists have focused on the role played by adults in facilitating young children's development. They are taking a social-interactionist perspective, often called *sociocultural theory*. The ideas of Lev Semenovich Vygotsky (1896–1934), a Russian psychologist, have contributed to this interest in the social origins of language and thought. Vygotsky, like Piaget, believed that children are active in their own ongoing process of development. However, Vygotsky believed that the relationship with other people is the major process contributing to development. In his view, children develop in a specific social and cultural context, with early communicative interactions with adults becoming internalized to form the basis for speech and thinking.

Vygotsky distinguished between two types of development: natural, which is a result of maturation, and cultural, which involves language and reasoning ability and is culturally derived. Vygotsky described development as proceeding from the inter-psychic plane (between the child and other people) to the intra-psychic plane (within the child). Social experiences were seen as the foundation for human development. In Vygotsky's view the development of language is of primary importance because all human meaning is mediated by language. The development of language allows children to organize and integrate experience—or, in other words, to develop concepts. Like Piaget, Vygotsky observed the egocentric speech of childhood (which he called *external* speech); however, he interpreted it as the *means* by which children develop concepts and plan actions. In this view children use language to understand and organize their experiences. So, language is essential for thinking. Communication with others is vital because children develop language in relationships with more competent speakers (adults and older children).

If we accept Vygotsky's premise that knowledge is created through interaction with other people, it is not only important to look at the child, as Piaget did, but it is also important to focus on the relationship between the adult and child. Vygotsky believed that every function in development occurs first at the social level and then at the individual level. Children develop through what he referred to as the *zone of proximal development,* or the point at which a child cannot accomplish a task alone but can do it with support. In the same way that caring adults provide a scaffold for language they provide a scaffold for thinking. In *Thought and Language* Vygotsky wrote, "What the child can do in cooperation today he can do alone tomorrow" (Vygotsky 1962, 104).

In Vygotsky's view, children collaborate with others in co-constructing the structures of their minds. Sociocultural theory, as conceived by Vygotsky, regards knowledge as deeply social and emerging from the mind of the child and of other people and out of the materials provided by culture, society, and nature (Williams 1992). Current research in the areas of language and literacy development reflects this social interactionist focus by exploring the connection between thought and language and focusing attention on the importance of the adult-child relationship.

Implications of Sociocultural Theory for Practice. Vygotsky helps us to understand that adults play a vitally important role in young children's learning and development because they are actually helping them to construct meaning. Through conversation relevant to the particular child, adults help each child find a personal meaning in the activities offered. This work makes us aware of the importance of the child's social context for learning. The family and culture of the child must be a welcome part of the program.

Vygotsky's concept of a zone of proximal development is also immensely useful. The early childhood practitioner who understands this concept knows how to support a child in a task, as illustrated in the example at the beginning of the section. Classrooms that draw on sociocultural theory will include a variety of opportunities for *assisted discovery.* Teachers will guide children's learning using a variety of techniques such as verbal prompts, explanations, descriptions, and demonstrations. They will also encourage cooperative learning by arranging activities where small groups of children with varying skills work together to complete tasks (Berk 1999).

Multiple Intelligences Theory

> *Phyllis drives into a town she visited once briefly. The gas is low and she remembers that a gas station is located on the corner a few blocks away. She navigates to it without a wrong turn. The week after she returns home, Ann, a creative and talented colleague who has lived in Phyllis's neighborhood*

all her life, agrees to pick her up on the way to a meeting. Ann is 20 minutes late. When she arrives she apologizes, "I stopped at the store, and I didn't know how to get to your house from there."

Recent research in cognitive development and neuroscience has led to a theory of intelligence called *multiple intelligences theory,* constructed by psychologist Howard Gardner. This theory suggests that, instead of a single general intelligence, each person's intellectual capacity is actually made up of different faculties that can work individually or in concert with one another. Gardner has identified eight "intelligences" (Gardner 1983; 1991) and believes that more will be identified in the future (see Table 4.5). Ann and Phyllis in the preceding example vary in spatial intelligence.

Intelligence is culturally defined based on what is needed and valued within a society. Imagine for a moment how different cultures may view diverse types of intelligence. For example, ancient people from Polynesian cultures used the stars to navigate from place to place. They put a high value on spatial intelligence. Individuals from cultures that were dependent on hunting for food valued those who had the bodily kinesthetic intelligence needed to be successful hunters. People who possessed these needed abilities were valued and

> **Reflect on your areas of intelligence**
>
> Consider the eight areas of intelligence that Gardner describes. Which are your areas of strength? Which are your areas of weakness? What were your best learning experiences in school? What were your worst? How do these relate to multiple intelligence theory?

Table 4.5 Gardner's Multiple Intelligences

- **Musical intelligence:** The ability to produce and respond to music. It is seen in children who are especially sensitive to sound and who frequently play with instruments and music.

- **Bodily kinesthetic intelligence:** The ability to use the body to solve problems (e.g., in playing a game or dancing). Children who have high bodily kinesthetic intelligence demonstrate good coordination at a young age, demonstrate expressiveness with their bodies, and have a hard time sitting still.

- **Logical-mathematical intelligence:** The ability to understand the basic properties of numbers and principles of cause and effect. Children who love puzzles and show an early interest in numbers are demonstrating this intelligence.

- **Linguistic intelligence:** The ability to use language to express ideas and learn new words or other languages. Children who have strength in linguistic intelligence may play with and be capable with language from an early age, love reading and rhymes, be imaginative, and able to tell stories.

- **Spatial intelligence:** The ability to be able to form a mental image of spatial layouts. A young child with good spatial intelligence may be able to read maps and draw at a young age, construct imaginatively with blocks, and be sensitive to the physical arrangement of a room.

- **Interpersonal intelligence:** The ability to understand other people and work with them. A child who notices the relationships between others and demonstrates sociability and leadership is demonstrating interpersonal intelligence.

- **Intrapersonal intelligence:** The ability to understand things about oneself. A child with intrapersonal intelligence has strong interests and goals, knows him or herself well, is focused inward and demonstrates confidence.

- **Naturalist intelligence:** The most recently identified intelligence is the ability to recognize plants and animals in the environment. Children with this intelligence may want to collect animals and plants, long to be outdoors, and show a highly developed ability to discriminate between different animals and plants. They also have a highly developed ability to identify specific cars, planes, dinosaurs, etc.

children were taught these necessary skills. Euro-American societies have typically valued linguistic and logical-mathematical intelligences. Teachers have to a great extent taught for those who have these abilities.

Implications of Multiple Intelligences Theory for Practice. Although multiple intelligences theory is relatively new, it is already proving useful in the design of educational programs. It supports the viewpoint that individuals have unique talents and strengths that we should identify and maximize. It also reinforces the view that we should plan a variety of ways for children to experience and learn the same skills and concepts. It encourages us not to limit our definition of success to traditional academic outcomes. When we have identified children's strengths, then we can plan to provide multiple effective ways to teach concepts and nurture their potential.

This has particularly important ramifications for how learning is designed for children in elementary school and beyond. Educators who embrace the multiple intelligences constructs will ensure that primary-age children will continue to have learning opportunities that develop intelligence in all areas. Decisions regarding funding and curriculum for programs that focus on the arts and on physical education should include consideration of diverse intelligences.

Social Development

Social development in young children can be seen in their growing ability to relate to others and to become productive members of society. It includes how children learn expectations about behavior and their emerging skill in social relationships. Social development involves *social competence* (the ability to function in social groups), *social skills* (behaviors used in social situations), *social cognition* (understanding thoughts, intentions, and behaviors of self and others), *prosocial behavior* (the disposition to share, help, cooperate, empathize, comfort, reassure, defend, and encourage others), and the acquisition of *values and morality* (the development of standards for judging right and wrong, and the ability to consider the needs and welfare of others).

Milestones of Social Development. During the early years children experience tremendous growth in their ability to relate to others. Knowledge of typical behavior at each stage can help you to understand children's actions and provide experiences that will support positive social development (see Table 4.6).

Social development involves a spiraling increase of knowledge about self and others. It is influenced both by the kinds of experiences and relationships that children have with significant adults in their lives and by their level of cognitive development. Four aspects of cognition are particularly significant to social growth:

- Movement from being egocentric—seeing the world only from one's own perspective—to the growing ability to understand how other people think and feel
- Growth in the ability to understand cause and effect—to see the connection between one's actions and the consequences
- Change from thinking concretely (you are my friend when you are playing with me) to thinking more abstractly (you are my friend even when I don't see you every day, because we like to play together)
- Growth in cognitive complexity, such as the ability to understand multiple relationships (my mother is simultaneously a mother, aunt, wife, and daughter)

Understanding others is not merely a matter of learning more; it requires organizing what one knows into systems of meaning or belief. As they grow, children become able to develop abstractions—first from direct experience of observable phenomenon (some people are called boys and some are called girls; boys have short hair and girls have long hair) and then from intellectual reflection on experience (if you are a boy, you can't be a girl; boys grow up to be men).

Table 4.6 **Milestones of Social Development**

	Social Competence and Skills	Social Cognition	Prosocial Behavior, Values, and Morality
Infants	• Builds strong bonds with important adults and develops basic trust • Develops secure attachments to primary attachment figures • Becomes socially responsive; returns a smile by 6 months • Participates in interactive games such as peek-a-boo • Becomes more selective about who he or she responds to • Becomes aware of and then anxious around unfamiliar people • May show anxiety at separation from adults to whom infant is attached	• Understands that people are different from objects • Knows that others act with intention (i.e., to achieve a goal) • Becomes increasingly aware of other people's mental states; sees how an adult responds and then patterns responses in a similar fashion	• Responds to another's distress some of the time
Toddlers	• Actively seeks closeness with primary attachment figures • Uses principal attachment figures as a "home base" to provide security as child gradually ventures out into the world • Prefers to play alone (solitary play) or with the exclusive attention of favorite adults • Begins to enjoy nearby company of other children in play (parallel play)	• Begins to understand that personal actions influence the feelings and behaviors of others • Chooses behaviors to elicit responses from others (e.g., will run from adults to engage them in chasing games) • Can identify self as a boy or a girl	• May try to comfort someone in distress, hugging, patting, or bringing them a favorite toy or love object • Makes vocal exchanges in social play with turn-taking, social imitation, and conflicts over toys • In group settings, begins to develop genuine friendships
Preschool/ Kindergarten Children	• More flexible, able to separate from significant adults • At 3 years, enjoys adult company but begins to play with other children (associative play) • At 4 and 5 years, prefers peers	• Understands that others have thoughts, ideas, and memories • May mistakenly assume that what they know is the same as what others know • May begin to show gender-stereotyped beliefs and behaviors	• At 3 years expresses aggression physically, but by 5 uses more verbal aggression • Growing in the ability to recognize the needs and wishes of others • Prosocial behavior increases (e.g., offers to help others) • Is likely to obey in order to avoid consequences

(continued)

Table 4.6 **Milestones of Social Development** *(Continued)*

	Social Competence and Skills	Social Cognition	Prosocial Behavior, Values, and Morality
Preschool/ Kindergarten Children *(continued)*	• Is learning to cooperate, share belongings, and negotiate with other children • Has friendships that initially are quite transient, depending on proximity and shared activities		• At 4 years bases decisions on self-interest: "I should have it because I want it." • At 5 years is able to see the conflict between what they want and external rules • Makes moral judgments based on the amount of damage done rather than on intentions
Primary Children	• Seeks interactions with peers rather than adults • Friendships increasingly important and less transient • Continues to engage in sociodramatic play • Becomes interested in sports and games • More independent at work and play • Works cooperatively with peers, teachers, and parents • Develops negotiation skills	• Increased awareness of self • Tendency to be competitive and make comparisons between self and others • Understands gender constancy • Gender identity is firmly established • More attuned to the subtleties of behavior; understand that actions do not always indicate thoughts and feelings	• Peer group is a powerful force • When games with rules lead to conflict, expresses views of fairness • Respects authority because of the power of the authority figure • Has a strict view of equality; everyone gets the same amount when resources are distributed • Is able to take into account subjective factors such as motivation in moral reasoning

Theory Relating to Social Development. Constructivist theory, derived from the work of Jean Piaget, is helpful in explaining how social understanding comes about. Although much of the writing based on constructivist theory has focused on how children develop physical knowledge, Piaget suggested parallel structures and functions that help explain the child's construction of knowledge of the social world (Edwards 1986).

Constructivist theory is particularly helpful in evaluating the development of social cognition. During the early childhood years, children move from an egocentric perspective toward an appreciation of the thoughts and feelings of others. They become capable of understanding the relationship between their own behavior and the responses of other people. They become capable of envisioning relationships as persevering over time.

Constructivist theory also contributes to our understanding of children's moral development, their development of a set of standards about what is right and wrong. In the past, people believed that morality was learned from "teaching." But we know today that it is actively constructed by the individual. The development of morality is a complex process that grows out of children's early social experiences in combination with their emotional and cognitive growth.

Understanding of children's moral development has been the concern of a number of researchers, beginning with Jean Piaget. In his pioneering work, *The Moral Judgment of the Child* (1965/1932), Piaget proposed that children develop concepts about morality through an interactive constructive process. Piaget's research demonstrated that children reason about fairness and justice in their daily encounters with peers. His ideas form the basis for most current research on moral development.

> *Jerrick is the lunch helper. He is carefully carrying a pitcher of milk to the table. Another child runs up behind Jerrick and bumps him; the pitcher of milk spills. Taylor, another child in the group, observes the disaster and exclaims, "I'm gonna tell! Teacher, Jerrick spilled the milk."*

Piaget associated moral development with children's growing ability to interpret rules, and he described stages and a sequence of moral development. Children younger than 6 base their judgments about what constitutes naughty behavior on the amount of damage done and not on intention, because their focus is on concrete and observable outcomes. By middle childhood, children are able to take intentions into account and to base their judgments on them. According to Piaget, both the child's stage of cognitive development and previous social experiences are precursors to moral development.

Piaget's research demonstrated that children move from the view that rules are unchangeable and derived from higher authority to the more mature perspective that rules are made by people and can be changed. This maturation process translates into two kinds of morality. The first is the morality of obedience, or *heteronomy*, which involves being regulated by others and conforming to rules that are accepted without question. The second, the morality of *autonomy*, involves being guided by oneself and by principles of moral conduct. A number of scholars today study how children think about authority and fairness and how the development of morality can be supported by the adults in their lives (Damon 1988; Edwards 1986; Eisenberg 1992; Lickona, Geis, & Kohlberg 1976).

Laurence Kohlberg's work on moral reasoning elaborates and extends Piaget's work to focus on how people make moral decisions across the life span. Kohlberg described three levels of moral development that relate to the child's views of moral conventions; thus, the terms *preconventional, conventional,* and *postconventional* are used to describe them (Kohlberg 1981). People move from stage to stage as a result of their own reasoning power and see for themselves the contradictions in their own beliefs. A person must pass through each stage in order, and each is dependent on the preceding one (Figure 4.2).

Carole Gilligan and others have been critical of Kohlberg's work because the subjects were primarily male and because research was based on hypothetical and not on real-life situations. Gilligan's research led her to conclude that males are more oriented toward fairness and justice in their moral decision making, and females are more concerned with caring and responsibility (Gilligan 1982). Further research provides compelling evidence that both males and females include a caring and a justice orientation in their moral decision making (Smetana, Killen, & Turiel 1991; Walker 1995).

Reflect on social development

What are some of the ways that you have observed adults in early childhood settings supporting the development of social skills among children in their groups? In programs you have visited, what examples have you seen of adults modeling prosocial behavior? What examples have you seen of children demonstrating their understanding of the concepts of fairness and justice?

123

Figure 4.2   Kohlberg's Stages of Moral Development

Level One: *Preconventional Morality* (characteristic of children from 2 to 7)—moral decisions are based on self interest—on emotion and what the child likes. At this stage children have no personal commitment to rules that they perceive as external. They will do something because they want to, or not do it because they want to avoid being punished. By age 4 children begin to understand reciprocity—if I am nice to you, you might respond by being nice to me.

Level Two: *Conventional Morality* (characteristic of children between 7 and 12)—people choose to conform to and uphold the rules and conventions of society because they exist. They are concerned with group approval and consensus. Action is guided by concern with the general good and a desire to maintain the social order by doing one's duty.

Level Three: *Postconventional Morality* (adolescent and older, though not everyone reaches this stage)—people accept rules and laws that are agreed on in society and based on underlying moral principles. When the highest level is reached, individuals may make decisions based on conscience, which places universal morality above law or custom.

Source: L. Kohlberg, (Ed.), *The Philosophy of Moral Development: Moral Stages and the Idea of Justice.* (San Francisco: Harper & Row, 1981.)

Implications of Social Development for Practice. Getting along with others in a group is not an inborn trait but rather a slowly learned skill that occurs as a result of interactions between people. Young children are egocentric and slowly develop social and moral competence. Opportunities for social development permeate the early childhood program as children are given many opportunities to cooperate, share, be helpful, understand the viewpoint of others, and solve interpersonal problems. These behaviors are not taught in isolation but should be integrated into everything that children do in the classroom. Just as learning to read with skill requires significant opportunities for practice, learning to understand and get along with others requires repeated chances to learn, practice, and build skill.

There is a growing body of research that indicates children who have well developed social abilities tend to be more successful in kindergarten and elementary school. In a 2003 study of kindergarten teachers' views of children's readiness for school, researchers found that kindergarten teachers indicate that social skills such as communicating wants and thoughts, avoiding disruptive behavior, and following directions are more important for children's success in kindergarten than academic skills such as counting and labeling colors and shapes (Lin, Lawrence, & Gorrell 2003).

Social competence is enhanced when children feel a sense of security and control over their actions and their environment. Socially competent children are more apt to behave in positive ways. Adults assist children when they offer nurturing and caring guidance, help children recognize others' rights and feelings, and encourage them to understand the impact of their actions on others. Teachers promote the development of problem-solving skills and prosocial behaviors when they invite children to role-play interpersonal problems and when they model prosocial behaviors.

Moral development can be fostered when adult-child relationships are characterized by mutual respect: when children have opportunities to regulate their own behavior, to think independently and creatively (Kohlberg 1981). Direct teaching of morals and values as "rote learning" and social knowledge (teaching by telling) is generally an ineffective way to inculcate values and morals. Becoming a moral person is a process that has little to do with being able to recite the rules of morality. Demonstrating reflection on moral issues, using good children's literature to promote thinking and discussion of moral issues, and discussing moral intentionality with children are some ways you can guide children on the road to moral understanding.

Emotional Development

During the early childhood years, children develop as individuals who have characteristic moods, ways of expressing feelings, and perceptions of themselves. Emotional development involves the development of a sense of identity and self-esteem. It includes learning to regulate emotional states and to control impulses. Emotional development evolves from the child's inherited characteristics and, like other aspects of development, is influenced by experience and follows a sequence of growth (see Table 4.7).

Milestones of Emotional Development. Each stage in childhood has distinctive characteristics of emotional development that affect how children will react to the experiences they encounter. Knowledge of these stage-related characteristics can help you to interact with children in ways that support their healthy development. For example, the attachment to primary caregivers is critical and lays the foundation for the development of feelings of security. Knowing about this characteristic will ensure that you form consistent, warm bonds with infants in your care. Similarly, knowing that primary-age children define their self-worth by what they believe that they know and can do, you will provide activities for a first grade class to ensure that each child experiences a sense of mastery and accomplishment.

Table 4.7 **Milestones of Emotional Development**

Infants
- Signals needs with crying and gazing
- Establishes attachment to primary caregiver
- Expresses a wide range of emotions through body movements and facial expressions
- Cannot tolerate frustration or control impulses
- Develops stranger anxiety (wariness of unfamiliar people) between 6 and 9 months of age, which dissipates by 12 months
- Amiable from 1 year

Toddlers
- Vociferous and demanding at 2 years ("No!" "Me do it")
- Calmer and more sociable at 3 years
- Begins to assert self strongly
- Can seem stubbornly self-centered and resistant to change
- Has little control of impulses and is easily frustrated

Preschool/Kindergarten Children
- Beginning to be able to tolerate frustration
- Developing self-control and a sense of humor
- Tends to be curious and generally positive in disposition at 3
- Seems to display a different personality from minute to minute at 4
- Becomes more aware of the effects of behavior on others by 4 or 5

Primary Children
- Tends to be active, outgoing, and assertive
- Involved in mastering new skills and learning
- May show off accomplishments, and can become defensive and argumentative when challenged
- More independent, but may feel insecure
- May resist expressing needs for affection and approval
- Able to express and label a variety of emotions
- Able to recognize mixed emotions

Theory Relating to Emotional Development. Why do children act the way they do? Why are 2-year-olds so volatile and 3-year-olds so loving? Your mother, your neighbor, and your college professor all have explanations, so it's not surprising that theories of emotional development abound. You will study many of these theories when you take courses in child development or child psychology.

Psychosocial Theory. Primary among the contributors to our understanding of children's emotional development is psychoanalyst Erik Erikson, whose 1963 work, *Childhood and Society,* continues to be influential for educators today. Erikson described a series of stages of social and emotional development (Table 4.8). He believed that basic attitudes are formed as individuals pass through the stages, and that serious problems at any stage lead to difficulty in mastering the next stage. Each stage is characterized by a major task or challenge. In infancy, the major task is the development of basic trust; for the toddler, it is the development of autonomy; for the preschooler, the development of initiative; and for the school-age child, industriousness (Erikson 1963).

For each stage, Erikson described the potential for healthy development at one end of a continuum and the potential for development of negative and self-defeating attitudes at the other. He saw development as a product of the tension between the two extremes, with more positive than negative experiences necessary for healthy progress.

Erikson also noted that normal development must be viewed in relationship to life circumstances specific to each culture. He used an example of Yurok Indians who abruptly wean their infants at age 6 months. Erikson explained that while this might appear cruel, this practice taught children the self-restraint and self-discipline needed to survive in a tribe where food sources are often limited (Berk 1999).

> **Reflect on the role of trust**
>
> How do you feel when you are with people you trust? What can you do when you are with individuals you trust that you cannot do when you are with those you do not trust? What would your life be like if you did not trust people?

Implications of Psychosocial Theory for Practice. Insights from psychosocial theory have important implications for people who work with young children. Because crucial aspects of the child's development occur in the first 8 years, when a child is greatly dependent on adults, the relationships between children and significant adults in their lives are extremely important. Understanding that the young child is in the process of becoming a separate person can help knowledgeable caregivers to support children's conflicting needs for connectedness and independence.

Many practices found in high-quality early childhood programs support children in moving successfully through Erikson's developmental tasks. Low ratios of children to adults and the designation of a primary caregiver in programs for infants and toddlers are important because contact with a limited number of warm, caring, available people is a necessary condition for the development of the sense of trust. The provision of many opportunities for toddlers and young preschool-age children to make

Table 4.8   Erikson's Stages of Childhood Psychosocial Development

Trust vs. Mistrust (Infant): During the first stage of development infants learn, or fail to learn, that people can be depended on and that they can depend on themselves to elicit nurturing responses from others. The quality of care an infant receives, especially in the first year of life, is essential to the development of basic trust. Through the love, nurture, and acceptance received, the infant learns that the world is a good and safe place.

Autonomy vs. Shame and Doubt (Toddler): During the second stage of life, which begins at 12–15 months, children develop a basic sense of autonomy: self-control and independent action. During this period they are growing rapidly. They are learning to coordinate many new patterns of action and to assert themselves as human beings. Conflict during this period centers on toilet training. If parents are accepting and easygoing and if they recognize the child's developing need to assert independence, the child will move successfully through this stage. If adults are harsh and punitive and if the child is punished for assertive behavior, then shame and doubt may become stronger forces in the child's life.

Initiative vs. Guilt (Preschooler): This period is one of interest, active exploration, and readiness for learning. Children need to express their natural curiosity and creativity during this stage through opportunities to act on the environment. If explorations are regarded as naughtiness and if parents or teachers are overly concerned with preventing children from getting dirty or destroying things, a sense of initiative may not be developed and guilt may be the more prevalent attitude.

Industry vs. Inferiority (School Age): During this period, children are ready for the challenge of new and exciting ideas and of constructing things. They need opportunities for physical, intellectual, and social accomplishment. They need many and varied interactions with materials. Success and a feeling of "I can do it!" result in a sense of industry.

Source: From *Childhood and Society* (rev. ed.), by E. Erikson, 1963, New York: Norton.

choices about play activities, materials, playmates, and self-help routines encourages the development a sense of autonomy. Skilled toddler teachers accept the toddler's need to say no. They encourage toddlers to demonstrate increasing independence while remaining available to toddlers for physical and emotional support. During the preschool and early elementary years, teachers in high-quality programs provide adequate time and resources to encourage children to explore, to plan, and to carry out play episodes so that the sense of initiative can develop. And during the school-age years, providing opportunities for children to experience success in many kinds of creative projects helps develop the sense of industry.

As you develop proficiency in including these teaching skills in your repertoire of practices, be aware that not all cultures have the same priorities for emotional competence in young children. In many cultures, families place a high value on interdependence and support of the group. These families may not support developing autonomy and initiative in their young children and may prefer that you employ practices that focus less on building these skills and more on encouraging children to be supportive members of a group. Open and sensitive communication with families will help

Reflect on emotional development

Trust vs. mistrust: Which people and situations in your childhood made you feel secure and trusting? Which people and situations were untrustworthy?

Autonomy vs. shame and doubt: Which people and situations in your childhood made you feel independent? Which people and situations made you feel ashamed or dependent?

Initiative vs. guilt: Which people and situations in your childhood made you feel like learning and exploring? Which people and situations made you feel guilty for wanting to know more?

Industry vs. inferiority: Which people and situations in your childhood made you feel capable and excited about projects? Which people and situations made you feel inferior and incapable?

How did your feelings at each stage affect your learning?

you to determine their preferences and to select practices that meet the needs of the children in the context of their own family and culture.

FINAL THOUGHTS

We hope that this chapter has given you a greater appreciation for the ways that children grow and learn and how this knowledge can contribute to your skills as an early childhood educator. As you move ahead in your professional development, keep two things in mind. First, always keep learning about children. Don't think that the information you get when you are a college student is all you need. Knowledge about children, like the children themselves, is always growing and changing. New research is being conducted, old theories are being refined and new ones created. And more knowledge is available than any one person could read and absorb in a lifetime. Be aware of and keep an open mind about new information. Sometimes you will discover information that is immensely helpful. At other times a popular new theory will simply be a discredited old idea in a new guise. We find that a reflective, curious, and somewhat cautious approach serves children best.

Second, keep in mind that you are in the process of personal and professional development. As you study and as you work directly with young children, your understanding will grow. Your daily experiences and observations of children will combine with what you read to give you an ever deeper and richer understanding. Working with young children involves a constant and dynamic interplay of information derived from the work of others and information you develop yourself based on your own experience and observation. Keep watching and listening to children and know that your understanding will continue to grow and that you can rely on your own conclusions as well as those of the experts.

Reflect on how you will apply child development knowledge

How do you think that your knowledge of child development might influence what you do in the classroom? Think about a concept from one of the theories discussed in this text that helped you to understand something important about children. How will you use that knowledge in your work?

LEARNING OUTCOMES

When you read this chapter, thoughtfully complete selected assignments from the "To Learn More" section, and prepare items from the "For Your Portfolio" section, you will be demonstrating your progress in meeting NAEYC **Standard 1: Promoting Child Development and Learning.**
Key elements:

- Knowing and understanding young children's characteristics and needs

- Knowing and understanding the multiple influences on development and learning

- Using developmental knowledge to create healthy, respectful, supportive, and challenging learning environments

To Learn More

Observe a Young Child: For at least 2 hours, observe a child. Write notes on what you see and interpret and report on his or her behavior in terms of one of more of the theories of development presented in this chapter.

Read a Book: Read a book about one of the aspects of development described in this chapter. Reflect on the book and write about what you have learned and the implications for you as an early childhood educator. Some good choices include:

Damon, William. 1988. *The Moral Child.*

Eisenberg, Nancy. 1992. *The Caring Child.*

Erikson, Erik. 1963. *Childhood and Society.*

Gardner, Howard. 1983. *Frames of Mind.*

Healy, Jane. 1990. *Endangered Minds.*

Kurcinka, Mary. 1991. *Raising Your Spirited Child.*

Shore, Rima. 1997. *Rethinking the Brain.*

Stern, Daniel. 1990. *Diary of a Baby.*

Thomas, Alexander, and Stella Chess. 1977. *Temperament and Development.*

For Your Portfolio

Make a Chart of What You Do: List at least five characteristics in each area of development (social/emotional, physical, and cognitive) for one age group of children (infants, toddlers, preschoolers, kindergarten, or primary children). After each item list what you have done or said in your work or practicum to support children's development of this characteristic.

Create an Activity Plan for Different Ages: Plan and implement an activity for a preschooler. Indicate how you would modify it for a toddler or a school-age child. Document how the two children respond to the activity through photographs, work samples, or anecdotal records (see Chapter 11 for information on activity planning and Chapter 5 for information on writing anecdotal records and documentation).

Make a Poster for Parents: Illustrate the milestones of development for one age group of children (infants, toddlers, preschoolers, kindergarten, or primary children) in one area of development (social/emotional, physical, or cognitive). Post it in a classroom. Photograph it and write a paragraph about what you have done.

5

Observation and Assessment

Bring with you a heart that watches and receives.

William Wordsworth

Childhood should be a journey, not a race.

Anonymous

• •

*T*hose who are interested in learning about children study their growth, development, and learning. Methods of study range from informal observations conducted during the course of daily life in early childhood classrooms, to formal assessment using standardized instruments administered under controlled conditions.

Portfolios, work samples, anecdotal notes, screening, performance-based assessment, achievement tests, diagnostic tests, rating scales, developmental checklists—what are these things? As a teacher of young children, what are you supposed to do about them? Over the last several years, assessment has become the focus of intense interest and concern in the field of early childhood education. Even noneducators have heard a lot about assessment and testing on the news.

Until recently early childhood educators felt that carefully and sensitively observing children provided them with most of the information they needed to understand and evaluate children's development and learning and to communicate this information to families. Most did not spend a great deal of time on other kinds of assessment. In fact, in the first edition of this book, published in 1979, the name of this chapter was simply "Observation."

Why is assessment such a vital topic today? Why does early childhood assessment now entail more than observation? Part of the reason lies in the national concern with educational accountability that we described in Chapter 2. This concern has now filtered down to early childhood education. Some comes from families and policy makers who want to be reassured that children are learning and are able to be competitive with peers in other communities and countries. The significance of early experience in children's intellectual development has also led to the desire to find out more about what children are actually learning and, as part of the movement for greater professionalism, to develop standards by which achievement must be assessed.

In her article "Framing the Assessment Discussion," Jacqueline Jones summarizes the issue:

> It is reasonable to ask for evidence of how young children are developing and learning. It is also reasonable to ask if early childhood programs are providing the most appropriate and effective learning environments. As portfolios of children's work compete with percentile scores, the nature of the evidence used to answer questions about children's progress and program quality has become a matter of considerable debate and angst. (2004, 4)

The topic of assessment has become increasingly complex. While it still includes observation, it is now much more. And because it is part of early childhood programs and state and national policy, it is important for you to understand some basics about it. In this chapter we will look at the nature of assessment as it is practiced in early childhood programs today, how observation fits into the assessment picture, and the role of the teacher in the assessment process.

WHAT IS ASSESSMENT?

Assessment is a multipart process for the purpose of appraising young children's development and learning. It has three interconnected components (Jones 2004; McAfee & Leong 1997; McAfee, Leong, & Bodrova 2004; National Association for the Education of Young Children 1991; Wortham 2005). The first component is collecting and recording information about children's learning and development. This information may focus on what children know, what they can do, and how they relate to others. It can come from observation, conversation, interviews, portfolios, projects, tests, checklists, children's writing and drawing, written records, photography, and tape recordings.

The second component entails interpreting and evaluating the information gathered. In other words, using it to make some kind of decision or judgment—for example, whether the child is reaching developmental milestones, progressing adequately, meeting program standards. Assessment can also be used to determine whether a program is successful in meeting its objectives.

The third part of the assessment process has to do with how the information and interpretation are used. This may involve providing information to families, making choices about instructional practice, deciding whether a child needs a referral for special services, making a placement decision, or conducting program evaluation.

There are two broad approaches to looking at assessment. The first is called *authentic assessment* (also called classroom assessment, alternative assessment, or performance-based assessment). This type of assessment occurs in the ongoing life and daily activities of the early childhood classroom. It may involve multiple sources of information but the most important always comes from teachers' observations of children engaged in meaningful activities. Information is generally collected at different times of the day, in a variety of classroom activities (large group activities, listening to books, building with blocks, playing outdoors), using a variety of methods.

The second approach, known as *formal assessment*, is intended to provide a more objective view of children's development and learning. It employs instruments (a test or other tool) that in some way measures and quantifies children's development and learning. Formal assessment focuses on well defined target behaviors. It includes specified guidelines for administering the test so that it is given in the same way from one setting to another. Formal assessment often takes the form of tests that give information on children's achievement in a specific area of knowledge or skill.

Purposes for Assessment

There are a number of purposes for assessment in early childhood settings. All share the ultimate goal of helping us to better understand and thus better serve children. By keeping this goal clear and by understanding the other purposes for assessment, you may be better able to understand and use assessment to support children's learning while coping with demands for accountability.

One primary purpose for early childhood assessment is to learn about individual children's learning and development. Information about individual children may be used to monitor and document growth over time, to provide for children's individual needs, to determine children's achievement of learning goals, to report on children's growth and development to their families, and to identify children who may need to be referred for special services.

A second major purpose for early childhood assessment is to provide information to teachers to help them to guide and support children's learning. Information from assessment can assist you in designing learning environments and in planning appropriate curriculum and effective learning experiences. The more you know about the children in a group, the more effective you can be in planning curriculum that builds upon their strengths and provides experiences that support their continued development and learning.

A third purpose for which assessment is used is program evaluation—to determine whether your program is effective in meeting the needs of children and is accomplishing its goals. Information gathered for this purpose can be used to provide feedback on program quality that can be used as the basis for making improvements or for allocating resources.

A fourth purpose for assessment is to make decisions such as what classroom or group a child is placed in, whether a child will be admitted to a particular school, or whether a child is passed to the next grade. This is sometimes referred to as *high-stakes accountability*. Early childhood educators strenuously object to basing decisions that have a significant impact on a child's life on his or her score on one test.

Caregivers and classroom teachers have traditionally collected information that relates the first two of these purposes. They have used the information to guide decisions about designing of learning environments, modifying programs, planning curriculum, making educational decisions for individual children, and sharing with family members and others. Assessment for program evaluation and placement decisions is most often collected and utilized by administrators and policy makers.

OBSERVATION

You see, but you do not observe.

Arthur Conan Doyle

How did you discover that you wanted to work with young children? You probably came to this field because you found children intriguing. You may have seen things about them that your friends didn't notice. If so, you are already an amateur observer of children. Observation (systematically watching and noting what children do) is your most effective technique for understanding children. It is the foundation of all the ways that you will learn about them. Observation is the most important technique because many things that children cannot express through spoken words can be inferred by watching them in their natural settings.

> Paul is fragile-looking, curly-haired, just turned 3-years-old. He drags a laundry basket into the shade of a tree. He sits down in the basket and stretches his legs. "I fit! I'm 3!" he says, holding up three fingers. Paul rocks his body and the basket back and forth: "I'm rocking the cradle. I'm rocking the cradle." He rocks and rocks till the basket tips, and with a look of surprise he spills onto the ground. Paul stands up and smiles. He turns the basket over and hits it on the top several times, listening to the hollow drumming sounds that his thumping makes. Then he lifts up the basket and crawls underneath. He crouches under the basket, peering out through the holes and announces, "I'm going to hatch the cradle." He stands up wearing the basket like a turtle's shell, "I hatched!"

The ability to observe—to "read" and understand children—is one of the most important and satisfying skills that you can develop. It will help you to know and understand individuals, plan more effectively, and evaluate your teaching. More important, observation is the window that enables you to see into the world of the child. By observing Paul and his laundry basket with your heart and mind you learn many things. You learn that he is a child who, like many 3-year-olds, enjoys solitary play. You note that he uses and enjoys language that is slightly more sophisticated than other 3-year-olds. You learn that he knows some things about cradles, drums, and eggs, and that he has a concept of "three," "fit," and "hatch." You discover that he is able to use materials in innovative ways. You note that he has the control of the large muscles in his arms, legs, and torso that you would expect in 3-year-olds. And you see that he can handle simple problems independently. Based on this you might evaluate your own teaching (the rock-a-bye-baby activity seems to have taught a concept!) and plan new experiences for him (perhaps use more rhymes and language games with Paul since he seems to be attuned to words). You gain an empathy toward him that helps you to be his advocate and his friend. You develop insight into how Paul (and all 3-year-olds) feels about and understands the world—insight that you can share with other adults who did not have the opportunity to observe Paul.

Observation will provide you with information that will help you to respond effectively to the needs of a frightened or angry child, to intervene, to mediate recurring problems between two children, to know what a child is experiencing as a member of a family, and much more (see Figure 5.1). Observation lets you know what children are learning and experiencing each day and helps you to plan for tomorrow. It also helps you to identify a child who needs more stimulation, or who might be troubled, have special needs, or be abused or neglected and in need of help. Observation will help you to communicate about children with other adults who share a concern about their well-being.

Observation is the basis for decision-making in much of your work with young children and their families. It is used in some form in almost every chapter in this book. You will observe many different children and use what you see to help you understand child development theories about which you have learned. You will observe children's characteristics, abilities, and interests, and in response you will plan for their development. You will observe them as you teach and will modify your teaching and your plans in response to what you see. You will observe their interactions with others and modify your behavior to help them to build good relationships. You will observe them with their families and use this information to help them build strong bonds with the most important people in their lives. And when you observe that their needs are significantly different from those of other children, you will use your observations to help you communicate with others to determine whether or not they require special services.

Figure 5.1   **What You Gain from Observation**

Through observation you develop:

- Increased sensitivity to children in general—awareness of the range of development and a heightened awareness of the unique qualities of childhood and the world of children **to give you greater understanding of and empathy for children**

- In-depth understanding of individual children—how they think, feel, and view the world, and their interests, skills, characteristic responses, and areas of strength and weakness—to use in **planning curriculum that meets the child's needs** and in **communicating the child's progress** to others

- Understanding of social relationships—among children and between children and adults and **to enable you to better facilitate relationships** in the classroom

- Awareness of the way the environment is used by children, families, and staff **so that you can improve it**

- Increased ability to share meaningful aspects of children's development and the ability to make visible the power of children's learning **to help you to be a better advocate for children**

To observe is to take notice, to watch attentively, to focus on one particular part of a complex whole. It means perceiving both the total picture and the significant detail. Learning to observe involves more than casual looking, and it is not nearly as easy as one might think. To make useful observations of children, their significant relationships, and their environments requires training and practice. You must be clear about why you are observing and be willing to gather information and impressions with a receptive eye and mind.

The consistent practice of observation will help you develop *child-sense*—a feeling for how individual children and groups of children are feeling and functioning. This deep understanding is based on a great deal of experience in observing individuals and groups of children over time. Observing can generate a sense of connection and greater understanding, and hence empathy, caring, and concern.

To observe more objectively and separate out feelings and reactions from what is actually seen, it is useful to divide the observation process into three components:

1. Observing: Gathering information
2. Recording: Documenting what you have observed in a variety of ways
3. Interpreting: Reflecting on what your observations might mean

Observing

The first and most essential step in observing is to experience as completely as possible while attempting to suspend interpretation and evaluation. This process involves consciously focusing on watching and listening while quieting the inner voice that usually adds a running commentary of explanations and evaluations. This is sometimes called *childwatching* or *kidwatching* and it is different from everyday seeing and the purposeful classroom scanning teachers do to anticipate problems. It is most like the "fresh eyes" and heightened senses one brings to a new experience, such as you do when you travel.

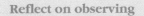

> **Reflect on observing**
>
> Remember a time when you observed something with fresh eyes (for example, a new home, a new city, or a new baby). What did you notice? How was this different from everyday looking? Look around at the place where you are right now and focus on the different colors and sounds in the environment. What do you notice? How is observation different when you focus? What might happen if you observed a child in this way?

An effective observer of young children has the ability to wait and see what is really happening instead of drawing conclusions based on hurriedly gathered impressions. Such "intensive waiting" (Nyberg 1971, 168) requires that you suspend expectations and that you be receptive to what is really happening:

behaviors, feelings, and patterns. It doesn't mean that you must become a machine, but it does require you to carefully separate what you see from what you might have wanted or feared to see.

To know what is actually taking place, you must avoid judgments and try to reduce the distortions that result from biases, defenses, or preconceptions. Objectivity is difficult in part because you are a participant in the life of the children, families, and settings that you observe, and you both influence the people and things in it and are influenced by them. It is also difficult because you have spent a lifetime learning to make judgments about the world.

Now you must learn to stop making those judgments. If you are aware of your impact on the situation and its impact on you, you can work toward becoming a more objective observer.

It is also helpful to be aware of your characteristics as an observer. When you realize what you tend to focus on, you can also get an idea of what you characteristically ignore. We have our college students observe a bowl of goldfish and describe what they see. Some notice the minute detail of fish anatomy like a biologist, some see the fish in relation to their environment, and some are aware of the interactions among the fish. They learn about what they tend to observe and they are surprised to find how different observations of the same fish can be. By doing these kinds of observation exercises you increase the range of things that you attend to and become a keener observer. Millie Almy says of keen observers:

> They study facial expression, note the steady and the shifting look, the tightly or loosely held jaw and lips, the grimaces and the smiles. They hear not only words but tones, pitch, strain, hesitation, and pauses. They note body posture, slumping shoulders and puppet-on-a-string gestures, as contrasted with flowing, graceful movements and accurate, efficient coordination. They see all the details in relation to the settings where the behavior takes place. The clenched hands and intent frown seen in the reading period are different from the freedom and *joie de vivre* of the playground. These finer details, this attention to its quality, provide clues to the meaning of behavior. (Almy & Genishi 1979, 39–40)

As Almy and Genishi suggest, a good observer goes far beyond the obvious. The more you know about children, the more differentiated and refined your observations become. You will learn to focus on features of a child's body, build, posture, tone of voice, appearance, ways of moving and manipulating objects, mood, interactions with others, and many other attributes. Keen observers know that children communicate a great deal through their bodies—facial expression; body tension; the language of hands, fingers, and eyebrows; the tilt of a head or shoulder—as much as through their spoken words and obvious actions.

As you observe you may become aware of your own biases. Are you drawn to children who are neat and tidy? Are you bored by children who are quiet and compliant? Do you have preferences for children of one race or one gender? As you practice observation you are likely to discover that there are things that you like about any child you observe. This is one of the important benefits of observing. It helps you to appreciate diverse children and thus makes you a better teacher.

Skillful early childhood educators observe all the time and adjust what they do in response to what they see.

> *Karen observed Arisa, a new 4-year-old, during her third morning in school. Arisa did not talk to anyone but her eyes followed Shan, another 4-year-old, as she played in the dramatic play area. With a sigh, Arisa lay down in the library corner and stared blankly into space. Karen invited Arisa to help her with a new cooperative puzzle activity. Yesterday Karen had observed Shan playing with this puzzle. Soon Shan and Arisa were playing happily together.*

Observing will give you helpful information about a child or a situation. Like Karen in the example above, you will sometimes use what you have observed immediately to respond to a child. However, few of us have good enough memories to remember all that we observe accurately, nor can we easily recall what we have observed when this information is needed. That is why early childhood educators also need to have skill in recording what they have observed.

Observing as a Student, Observing as a Teacher: Some Significant Differences

There are differences between observing as a student and observing as a teacher. As a student you are learning to *observe* and using observation to learn about children, programs, and teaching. You observe without having responsibility. Teachers observe to gain *information* about individuals, the effectiveness of instruction, and to give *direction* for future plans. They have responsibility for the well-being and education of the children while they are observing. As a student observer, keep in mind the following guidelines:

- Observe unobtrusively. Enter quietly, sit at children's eye level, close enough to see and hear but not so close that you distract the children with your presence.

- Don't get involved while observing unless it is necessary to protect a child. Briefly answer children's questions ("I am learning about what children do") and don't get involved in extended conversations.

- Take time just to watch; you will have other opportunities to get involved.

- Let the staff know you are practicing observation and will protect the confidentiality of children, families, professionals, and programs.

Recording

Recording what you have observed, then compiling and organizing what you have recorded, turns observation into a powerful tool to use on behalf of children. A number of techniques can be used to make an observation record.

All observation techniques have the common characteristic of beginning with a focus (a child, behavior, kind of learning, interaction, practice, or situation). *Narrative observation techniques* are open-ended and require writing. They can be time-consuming but can also provide rich detail and a vivid picture of children. *Structured observation techniques* are closed-ended and require little or no writing. They are quick and easy to use and can help you to understand patterns of behavior, but are usually quite narrowly focused and give relatively little detail. *Electronic observation techniques* (photographs, audio or video) can provide accurate and vivid representations but require skill and time to put together so that a concise and coherent depiction is made.

Interpreting

The third step in the observation process is to make an interpretation (sometimes called a *conclusion* or *inference*) based on what you have seen and heard. Although behavior is observable, the reasons for behavior are not visible and may only be inferred. You need to observe closely and then seek the relationship between the child's behavior that you have observed and its unobservable cause. You can never truly know why a child behaves as he or she does, but you will make decisions based on your understanding about children's behavior every day. It is important that you develop skill in making interpretations based on what you actually observe.

Understanding a child's behavior is difficult because many factors—stage of development, health, culture, and individual experience—combine in complex ways to determine how a child acts in a given situation. The same behavior can mean different things in different children. Edwin's downcast eyes may mean that he has been taught to show respect to adults by avoiding eye contact when spoken to, while the same behavior from Joanie may mean she is avoiding acknowledging what you are saying. Individual observers may interpret the same behavior or incident in dissimilar ways, depending on their knowledge and their own cultural and ethnic backgrounds. If your cultural and ethnic background is the same as Edwin's you are likely to understand his behavior, but if your background is more similar to Joanie's you might mistakenly assume he is trying to avoid hearing or acknowledging what you are saying.

It is best to be tentative in your interpretations. We have seen situations in which several individuals observed the same incident and made significantly different interpretations. For example, several of our college students noticed a little girl lying down in the shade of a play structure of a program they were visiting. One thought she was withdrawn and antisocial; another was convinced she was lonely, unhappy, and in need of comforting; and the third felt that she was just taking a few moments to relax. Obviously they needed more information about the child and the events that preceded their observation in order to make accurate and meaningful interpretations.

Narrative Observation Techniques

A narrative observation tells a story. It begins with a setting—where and when the observation occurs. It has characters—a child or children and the adults and materials with whom they interact. And it has action—the child's activities and interactions.

All early childhood professionals need to have well developed skill in writing narrative observations. They use this skill in communicating with parents and other professionals. The ability to write clear, concise, meaningful description, like the ability to teach, comes with lots of practice and lots of feedback. Good written observations use clear language and convey the uniqueness of children and their activity.

At first your writing may be awkward, and you may have difficulty deciding how much of what you observed to record. It also can be hard to clearly separate what you observed (objective description) from what you think about it (subjective interpretation). The three examples in Figure 5.2 demonstrate the range—one is too subjective and filled with personal opinions and interpretation, another is objective and vivid, and a third is lacking in detail.

A good description is specific. Broad general statements are not effective in capturing important qualities of the child or interaction. For example, the statement that "Sasha is playing with sand" does not tell the reader much. We have a better picture of the child and situation when the observer tells us, "Sasha fills the bucket with sand, slowly pokes three sticks in the top, and sings 'Happy Birthday to Sasha.'" Details such as when Sasha played in the sandbox, how long she worked, who she worked with, and how she worked increase the reader's ability to understand the child and the situation.

Remember that you are not only observing what you see but also what you observe using your other senses. The words children use, the sounds, smells, and temperature in the environment are all a part of what you observe. If these aspects are not included, you have only described a part of the picture and only told half the story.

The addition of expressive detail can communicate a great deal more. It takes practice to find a balance of vivid imagery and objectivity. The language used in recording should capture the subtleties and complexities of children's behavior. Carefully chosen words convey the essence of the person and situation and are an important part

Figure 5.2 **Three Contrasting Narrative Observations**

Subjective	Objective	Lacking in Detail
Sasha is a cute little 3-year-old girl with beautiful curly hair.	Sasha is a petite 3-year-old girl of African-American ancestry.	Sasha is a girl.
She is happy because she is playing pretend in the sand.	She is smiling as she sits in the sand, under the shade of the climbing structure, playing with a bucket and shovel.	She is in the sandbox.
Sasha is making birthday cakes in the sand. She is singing "Happy Birthday to Sasha," even though today is Carson's birthday. She wishes it was her birthday.	Sasha fills the bucket with sand, slowly pokes three sticks in the top, and sings "Happy Birthday to Sasha." She looks around the sandbox and smiles a wide smile as she sings.	Sasha is playing with sand.
Carson gets mad, he walks up to Sasha, and yells at her. He scares Sasha when he kicks over her birthday cake.	Carson, a classmate who turned 4 today, stomps up to Sasha and says, "Hey, it's not your birthday, it's my birthday!" Then he kicks over her bucket.	Carson walks up and yells at Sasha.
Sasha gets mad back and throws some sand at Carson.	Sasha's eyes widen and fill with tears. Then she picks up a handful of sand and throws it at Carson.	Sasha throws some sand at Carson.
Carson and Sasha don't know how to be nice to one another.	Carson yells "Teacher!" then he and Sasha both burst into tears.	Carson and Sasha cry.

of writing vivid descriptions; they enhance our ability to visualize the subject of the observation.

> *Sasha's eyes widen and fill with tears. Then she picks up a handful of sand and throws it at Carson.*

Notice how much more easily you can picture the scene, compared to "Sasha throws some sand at Carson."

In choosing modifiers, avoid words that have a strong emotional impact or bias built into them. Describe what the child *does*, instead of giving your views of what he or she *is, feels, wishes,* or *intends*, none of which you can see. Opinions of children such as *pretty, cute, bright, attractive, good, messy, slow, mean,* or *naughty* are to be avoided in written observations because they are value judgments. Describing a child in these terms tells more about the values of the observer than the nature of the child. Since the descriptions you write may be shared with others, you have the responsibility to convey useful information that is free from personal bias or unsubstantiated evaluations.

Running records and anecdotal records are the narrative observation methods traditionally used by early childhood educators. When you hear other early childhood educators talk about making observations, they are usually referring to these methods.

When you are learning to observe in a college class you may also be asked to write physical descriptions of children. This exercise is done to build your sensitivity to the unique qualities of individuals and to increase your ability to write vividly and objectively. In writing physical descriptions you will note basic physical attributes and write about them to help the reader to visualize the child: age, sex, size, build, facial features, coloring, and distinguishing markings. A plain physical description gives little sense of the distinctiveness of a child: "She is an Asian girl, 4 years of age, shorter than her peers. She has a slight build, oval face, and brown hair and eyes." You will convey a better picture of the child as a unique individual if you elaborate the basic physical description with some of the child's unique qualities: body stance, way of moving, facial expression, gestures, tone of voice. The following addition conveys a much more vivid sense of the child:

> She has black eyebrows and lashes, long black hair, almond-shaped eyes, a fair, smooth complexion, pouting lips, and a small upturned nose. She is slim and almost fragile looking, and strolls from activity to activity with small light steps, her head turning occasionally from side to side. Her arms hang slightly away from her body and swing with the rhythm of her stroll.

It is usually neither necessary nor desirable to describe specific details of children's clothing. They will be wearing something else the next time you observe!

Running Records

When you see a teacher or student teacher with a clipboard writing down everything a child says and does, they are writing a form of observation called a *running record*, sometimes called a *specimen record*. When you first learn to observe young children you will usually learn to write a running record.

Running records are written while you are watching. They are open-ended and detailed narrative accounts of behavior and events. When you sit down to write a running record you will observe a particular child engaged in a particular activity at a particular time. No other structure is placed on your task. You will observe and write down everything that the child says and does for the time you are observing. We often compare a running record to a video recording. You record what happens while it is happening, with as much fidelity as possible. Because it is written while it is happening, a running record is always written in the present tense. The critical skill you are developing is the ability to write vivid description quickly while avoiding interpretation and judgment. Learning to do this type of written observation well requires training and considerable practice.

When you are writing a running record you can do little else. For this reason running records are rarely used by practitioners who are "on the floor" and responsible for a group of children. As a student you will have opportunities to practice and master the skill of writing running records in order to develop sensitivity to and knowledge about children. As a practicing professional you may use this skill only when you need to do an in-depth study of a particular child and when you have assistance. For ordinary purposes you will select more efficient and less time-consuming methods.

The format used in Figure 5.3 is a standard way to write running records. During the actual observation, use the middle column to record what you see. As soon after observing as possible, write comments and note any feelings or other impressions in the right-hand column.

With this format you are able to review your description, add other comments, and decide whether you have enough information. If not, you can observe the child in other settings to see whether the behaviors are repeated and characteristic or simply the outcome of a particular situation.

Figure 5.3 **Example of a Running Record**

Child: John A.	Date: 10/10	Observer: Lisa L.
Time/Setting	**Observation**	**Comment**
10:30 art area New play dough set out on table. Each chair has a plastic placemat, ball of dough, apron hanging over back of chair. Teacher has told children new play dough available.	J. runs to table and sits down without putting on an apron. Starts to pinch the ball of dough apart. Teacher says, "Hey J., I think you forgot something." J. smiles, "Oh yeah." Stands up and takes yellow plastic apron and pulls it over head—wearing it backwards (long part behind). Teacher makes no comment. J. sits back down and picks up the dough.	Complies with reasonable requests
	J. rolls a teaspoon-sized "pinch" of dough into a ball. Eyes are fixed on the dough and his hands as he rolls. He rolls the dough with his right hand against the mat. He rolls and rolls the ball until it is a nearly perfect sphere. With a little smile, he picks it up and places it on the edge of his mat and glances up at other children.	Shows good fine motor coordination and persistence
10:35	J. continues pinching and rolling little balls of dough, placing them along the edge of the mat. His eyes stay fixed on the dough. J. glances up after completing each ball but does not interact with other children who are chattering to one another.	Doesn't seem too interested in the other children
10:45	When entire big ball of dough has been turned into little balls, J. stands up and walks to the collage shelf. He picks up container of straws and toothpicks and carries back to table.	Seems to have a plan
	J. pokes a toothpick into first ball of dough. Then he pokes another ball of dough onto the other end of the toothpick. He sticks a second toothpick into the second ball of dough and continues to link the balls with toothpicks.	Attempting to symbolize?
	He gets to the fourth ball of dough and it falls apart. J. says to the teacher, "Help me." Teacher says, "What are you trying to do?"	Uses adults as resources

Anecdotal Records

If observations are important but practitioners rarely write running records, you may be asking yourself what they do instead. The form of written observation most frequently used by practitioners is the *anecdotal record.* If a running record is the written equivalent of a video recording, an anecdotal record is the written equivalent of a photograph. Like a running record an anecdotal record is an open-ended, detailed narrative describing incidents, behaviors, and interactions. An anecdotal record, however, is brief and describes a single incident, the way a photograph captures a single moment (the word *anecdote* means a brief story). An anecdotal record is written after the fact. In other words, you write an anecdotal record after you notice something worthy of documenting. For this reason anecdotal records are written in the past tense.

Anecdotal records are helpful for teachers of young children, home visitors, and other early childhood practitioners who need to document events and changes in children. It is valuable to learn how to write them, and important to develop strategies to make them a part of your daily work with children.

What belongs in an anecdotal record? Like any other observation, an anecdotal record has a focus, is dated, includes the name of the child and the observer, and includes some context (place/time). And like any other observation, it should be as objective as possible and free of bias and judgment. Because anecdotal records are brief and are usually read by those who know the child already, it is unnecessary to give much background information. Tell what happened briefly but completely. We also suggest that you note why you wrote this observation. For example:

- *Behavior or interactions that seem typical for a child:*
  5/9—During activity time Shelly (age 3½) was building with blocks. She built a tall tower and placed little animals all over the roof. She said, "It's the animals' department." Shelly added a dollhouse child to the structure. In a high squeaky voice she had the dollhouse child talk to the animals, saying things like: "Mommy elephant don't step on your baby." "Don't worry I'll feed you." and "No, lion, don't bite the baby!"
  Comment: Able to take on roles in play. Interested in authority?

- *Behavior or interactions that seem atypical for a child:*
  10/15—At cleanup time Brooke (4 yrs.) threw all the dolls on the floor of the pretend area. When asked to pick them up she refused and left the home area. Teacher took Brooke by the hand to lead her back to the home area saying, "I'll help you pick them up." Brooke stopped and burst into sobs saying, "I hate you, I hate your face! You can't come to my birthday party!"
  Comment: Brooke is usually very cooperative. Unusual behavior—angry/unhappy and upset.

- *The achievement of a developmental milestone:*
  8/23—At 10:00 this morning Tevin (10 mos.) was on his hands and knees next to the coffee table. He sat back on his heels and reached up so that he was grasping the edge of the table. He pulled himself to a standing position. His eyes grew wide, he grinned and then his knees buckled and he sat down fast. He repeated this five or more times during the next half-hour.
  Comment: First time Tevin has pulled up at the center.

- *Incidents and interactions that convey the child's strengths, interests, and needs:*
  9/20—After lunch at his desk Ethan (5½ yrs.) drew a detailed picture of a car. The drawing included a tailpipe with exhaust, a spoiler, door handles, headlights, and tires with elaborate hubcaps. Ethan wrote RASG CR on his drawing.
  Comment: Shows understanding of and interest in cars. Uses inventive spelling.

- *Incidents and interactions that convey the nature of social relationships and emotional reactions:*
  11/14—During outside play this afternoon Bryan (4 yrs.) was riding on the rickshaw trike. He zoomed past Kengo (4 yrs.) who was shoveling sand into a bucket. He stopped and said to Kengo, "The garbage truck is collecting the garbage. You want to be a garbage man?" Kengo answered by picking up his bucket sitting on the rickshaw seat and yelling, "Let's go!" The two boys drove to one end of the yard where they filled the bucket with leaves, which they packed to the other end of the yard. They continued to play garbage man until Bryan's mom came, about 20 minutes.
  Comment: Cooperative friendships

- *Behavior or interactions relating to an area of special concern:*
  3/3—While working on an addition exercise Stanley (6 yrs.) put his head down on his desk. I asked, "What's up Stanley?" He said, "I'm just so dumb."
  Comment: This is the second or third time that Stanley has said this in the last 2 weeks—each time it was associated with seat work.

Anecdotal records can also be made with special emphasis on children about whom you have questions or concerns and those children who are "invisible"—so inconspicuous that they tend to be forgotten.

Making Anecdotal Record Writing a Part of Every Day. To help you to understand children and how they develop it is valuable to have anecdotal records you have written over time. To have these it is necessary to observe and write anecdotal records on a regular basis—if possible, every day.

With all the other things that you will have to do as a teacher, you may wonder how to find time to write anecdotal records. First of all you have to be committed to writing them. When you are, there are several strategies that will help you to actually write. Some teachers write them while they are supervising children, during children's nap time, or during their own break time. In some programs teachers are given dedicated time to write anecdotal records.

To make it possible to write anecdotal notes on a regular basis it is necessary to create a convenient and systematic way to write and keep them organized. We have used and seen a number of ways to make anecdotal record writing a part of everyday practice:

- *Clipboards posted throughout the classroom.* Clipboards with pencils attached are posted conveniently throughout the classroom with an anecdotal record sheet for each child on each clipboard. Teachers then can reach for the clipboard and make a few notes right after they have observed something of significance. In this method an anecdotal record form like the one shown in Figure 5.4 is helpful. The forms are filed weekly (or when they are filled up). A cover is used to ensure confidentiality.
- *Self-stick labels, index cards, or notebooks.* Teachers wear waiter's aprons with pockets, or fanny packs, and keep a pen and a stack of large self-stick labels, index cards, or a small notebook in the pocket. Anecdotal records are made with the child's name and the date. At the end of the day or week the teacher files the notes. They can be organized chronologically and/or by developmental domain. Some teachers later add selected sticky notes directly to the child's portfolio. (See the section on portfolios later in this chapter, on pages 151–154.)
- *Notebooks.* Each child has a notebook in which teachers write anecdotal records. Notebooks are kept in the classroom. Sometimes they are used as the basis of a portfolio and at other times they are kept where families can read them every day.

The anecdotal records you write in the course of your day may be just a few words or fragments of information with details that you fill in later (often referred to as *jottings*). Be sure to go back to any that are incomplete on the same day, or you will have lost the details that make records useful.

Anecdotal records, like all observations, are a part of your collection of information about each child. They need to be carefully monitored and filed with all other confidential records.

Interpreting Narrative Observations

Once you have written an observation of a child you may add your interpretations. Your interpretations, accompanied by the written description of what you observed, make it possible for others to read what you have written and decide whether they agree with your conclusions. Descriptions of the same child or incident written by different observers can be helpful because each of us tends to notice different things. It is eye-opening to have several individuals interpret the observations of a situation, because two people viewing or reading about a child or incident will often have different perceptions. It is also helpful to discuss your interpretations with someone else. Becoming aware of different perspectives can help you to realize how

Figure 5.4 **Anecdotal Record Form**

Observations of *Jenni*	
Physical Development Observer/Date: Comment on the observation:	Social Development Observer/Date: Comment on the observation:
Emotional Development Observer/Date: Comment on the observation:	Creativity Observer/Date: Comment on the observation:
Language/Literacy Development Observer/Date: Comment on the observation:	Discovery and Thinking Observer/Date: Comment on the observation:

difficult it is to interpret accurately. We encourage you to make liberal use of the words *might* and *seems to* in your written interpretations to underscore the tentative nature of conclusions about children's needs, feelings, and motivation.

Your written interpretations should be based on several observations. State your conclusions concisely, and cite the descriptive data on which they are based. A teacher who has made many observations of John (the child in our sample running record on page 141) might summarize with:

As can be seen in observations dated 11/6, 10/23, and 9/9, John finds inventive ways to use materials. Although he rarely interacts directly with the other children he frequently plays near them. John seems enthusiastic about engaging in classroom activities that allow for creative expression. He can stay with a creative task for a long time, as much as an hour. He cooperates with adults when reasonable requests are made.

Using Narrative Observations

There are several ways that you can use written observations to improve the quality of the educational experience you provide for children. They help you to understand and be more responsive to individuals and are the most useful kind of observation to use to guide you in planning curriculum and in assessing whether the curriculum is currently meeting children's needs. To use observations for curriculum planning, bring together observations and read through them to help you determine a child's strengths, interests, and needs. Plan activities that build on the strengths and interests and that provide opportunities to address the needs. Observations of all the children in the class can be used to inform the selection of a topic of study in an integrated curriculum.

Narrative observations form the basis of the *portfolio* (described later in this chapter). You will assemble the observations, organize them, and use them to present a coherent picture of the child in school.

Structured Observation Techniques

Narrative observation techniques help you to create a picture of a child over time. As you observe in many areas the picture grows. Sometimes, however, you may need or want to learn more about a child more quickly in order to make a referral or work on a particular problem. When this is the case some form of structured data-gathering may be useful or necessary. Structured observations can reveal trends and patterns in behavior. Designed well, they increase your objectivity and can correct for any misperceptions or biases.

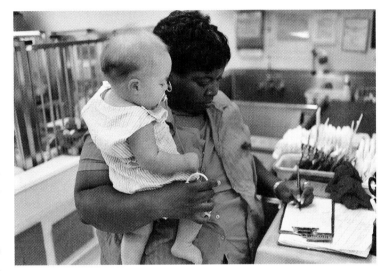

Time samples, event samples, chelcklists, rating scales, and interviews are some of the most commonly used structured methods of gathering information. They differ in the degree to which they are systematized, their most appropriate use, and their advantages and disadvantages. The particular method that you choose will depend on what you want to know and how you think you might best find it out. If you understand what information each provides and think carefully about the purpose of the observation, you will be able to select the approach that generates the information you need.

Time Samples

A time sample is a method for tracking behaviors that occur at regular intervals and in rapid succession (see Figure 5.5). It is not a record of everything that happens, but rather a system for collecting information on a predefined behavior or set of behaviors displayed by individual or groups. For example, you might use this technique to find out how often a particular behavior (trike riding, focused work, hitting, fantasy play, thumb sucking) is actually occurring.

A time sample uses a grid on which you tally the occurrence of particular behavior(s) during a short time period. A simple checklist or code will be devised to help you quickly record what type of behavior is occurring. For example, ✓ could stand for *a positive interaction* and x could stand for *a negative interaction*. A time sample must be conducted often enough to get a good idea of the frequency of the behavior—a minimum of three sample days are needed as the basis for any interpretation. You may want to then sample weeks or months later to determine whether change has occurred.

Time sampling is an efficient method of gathering information. It can be used for observing more than one child at a time. The information from a time sample can be used as a basis for drawing conclusions about the frequency and relative importance

Figure 5.5   **Example of Time Sample**

15 min. time sample	Michael	Teddy	Philip

Children: _Michael, Teddy, Philip_

Target: ✓ = engages in positive interaction   x = engages negative interactions
    0 = noninteraction   * = initiates interaction

Date: _3/3_

15 min. time sample	Michael	Teddy	Philip
0–3 min.	✓ * ✓	0 ✓	✓
3–6 min.	✓ x ✓	✓ * x	✓ ✓
6–9 min.	x * ✓ ✓ *	x ✓ *	0 ✓ *
9–12 min.	✓ * x	0	x* ✓
12–15 min.	✓ ✓ * x	x * ✓	x ✓ ✓ *

of particular behaviors. However, the behavior(s) being studied must occur frequently. Since information about the cause of behavior is not gathered, you cannot draw conclusions about the reasons a behavior occurs.

We once designed a time sample to test our belief that 4-year-old Michael was initiating an excessive number of conflicts with others. Several staff members felt that they spent a great deal of time each day intervening in the conflicts that he provoked. Another teacher had difficulty understanding our frustration because she perceived Michael as a very positive and cooperative person. The time sample was simple. We agreed to track how frequently Michael initiated interaction with two friends and whether it was positive or negative. The three 15-minute time samples uncovered that Michael had many more positive than negative interactions, as did his friends. We discovered, however, that Michael initiated interactions three times more frequently than his two playmates. This time sample helped explain our different perceptions and helped us to understand why we felt taxed by our frequent interventions. Our increased understanding helped us to become more trusting and to allow Michael more opportunity to handle interpersonal problems on his own.

Event Samples

An event sample is used to help you understand more about a behavior (see Figure 5.6). You watch for a particular behavior or interaction and then record what preceded the event, what happened during the event, and what happened after the event (called the *consequence*). The sample is made while it is occurring or immediately after. The purpose is to collect information about the relationship between the behavior and the context of the behavior so that you can understand the cause and possibly devise a way to alter the course of events.

Like a running record, an event sample relies on your skill in making detailed observations. For example, if you think a child has been engaging in a lot of aggressive behavior, you may want to note what precedes every aggressive act, exactly how the aggression occurs, and what teachers and other children as well as the child do after the aggressive behavior. You may discover that the behavior is only happening before lunch or nap, at the end of the day, is triggered by interaction with one child or group, or you may discover that there are unintended consequences that are encouraging the continuation of the aggression. Event sampling is not time-consuming, and it can provide useful information for figuring out the causes of behavior. It can be the basis for generating plans to help children and staff change their behavior.

Figure 5.6   **Example of an Event Sample**

Child's Name   _Mari_   Age   _4.5_   Date(s)   _September–October 05_

Date/Time	Preceding Event	Behavior	Consequence
9.24/7:48	M. was pouring juice at the snack table. She tipped over the paper cup and spilled a small amount.	M. set down the pitcher and struck out at a stack of paper cups, knocking them from the table.	Jim quickly grabbed M. in his arms and said, "It's OK, it was just a little spill."
9.26/8:07	M. entered the block area and began placing trucks from the shelf on the structure Pua and Jenny were building. Pua said, "You can't play."	M. ran from the block area past the art area on her way out the back door. On her way past the water-color table she made a wide sweep with her arm and knocked over a cup of water.	Ginger, who witnessed the block corner scene, followed her out. She took M. in her arms and told her, "I bet it made you mad when Pua told you that you could not build with them."
10.6/7:55	M. placed her blanket in her cubby on top of a plastic container. The blanket fell out as she turned to walk away.	M. shoved the blanket back into the cubby and pulled the entire contents of the cubby onto the floor and ran out the door to the gate.	Jim, who was greeting the children, followed M. out and said, "Please let me help you get your blanket in straight."
10.8/8:15	M. was playing with the tinker toys. Jenny joined her and accidentally bumped her construction and several pieces fell off.	M. screamed at Jenny and said she was stupid. With a single sweep of her arm M. knocked the pieces to the floor and threw herself on the rug.	Ginger gently rubbed M.'s back until she calmed.

Figure 5.7   **Example of a Checklist**

Child's Name _____   Age _____

Observer _____   Date _____

Instructions: Enter the date on which you first observe the listed behavior.

___ / ___ / ___   Scribbles

___ / ___ / ___   Paints with whole arm movement

___ / ___ / ___   Holds crayon with thumb and fingers

___ / ___ / ___   Paints with wrist action

___ / ___ / ___   Cuts with scissors

___ / ___ / ___   Holds cup with one hand

Checklists and Rating Scales

Checklists are lists of traits, behaviors, concepts, and skills on which an observer puts dates or check marks next to each item to indicate if or when it is observed (see Figure 5.7). They are a useful, relatively simple way to find out what skills and knowledge children demonstrate and what is working in the classroom. A checklist can also provide an informal profile of each child in a class if it is constructed to cover the different areas in the usual sequence of development. You can create your own checklists to help in documenting the progress of individual children. A customized checklist is actually a good strategy for reviewing the milestones of development. It also ensures that you have a systematic guide to observing and recording information about the aspects of development that you wish to emphasize in your program.

Figure 5.8 **Example of a Rating Scale**

Child's Name _____ Age _____

Observer _____ Date _____

Indicate the degree of success the child has with the following by marking the place on the scale that best represents the current level of functioning.

Scribbles:

easily _____ somewhat easily _____ with difficulty _____ not able to do

Paints with whole arm movement:

easily _____ somewhat easily _____ with difficulty _____ not able to do

Holds crayon with thumb and fingers:

easily _____ somewhat easily _____ with difficulty _____ not able to do

Paints with wrist action:

easily _____ somewhat easily _____ with difficulty _____ not able to do

Cuts with scissors:

easily _____ somewhat easily _____ with difficulty _____ not able to do

Holds cup with one hand:

easily _____ somewhat easily _____ with difficulty _____ not able to do

---

Rating scales are nearly identical to checklists in purpose and uses (see Figure 5.8). The only significant difference is that a rating scale provides a mechanism for indicating the degree to which a behavior or characteristic is present in a person or a situation.

Interviews

Informal conversations with children often provide you with insight into their ideas and learning. These can be documented in anecdotal records. When you ask a child to tell you about a block building or a painting, you are conducting an informal interview. Formally interviewing children is a planned technique for gathering information. Their answers can give you insight into language, social-emotional development, and understanding of concepts. An interview may be repeated after an interval of time to help you to understand a child's growth.

In a formal interview you select a focus (math concepts, feelings about friends, language development) and plan a series of questions and ask them of all the children. This allows you to compare children's responses and better understand how different children understand a concept. Children are usually interviewed individually and their answers recorded in writing or on audiotape.

Electronic Observation Techniques

As you can see from the turn-of-the-century photographs in Chapter 3, people have been taking photographs of children in school for as long as cameras have existed. Today, many devices are available (cameras, video and audio recorders, computers, scanners, printers) for you to use to record children's activities and work. Many teachers use them to support the process of documenting children's development.

Creating a photographic, video, or audio record of a child engaged in school serves much the same purpose as other forms of observation and requires the same level of understanding of its purpose. Just as written observations require skill and judgment, so, too, do electronic observations. Skill in managing technology is a new basic required of teachers of young children.

Photographs

As the saying goes, a picture is worth a thousand words. But is it? Photographs are valuable documentation[1] when they show something happening or provide a record of a child's work. They can quickly and accurately show something that is difficult to describe clearly—for example, a photograph of a child's elaborate block structure.

Photographs are not valuable when posed to be "cute" to adults without being genuine representations of what children can do. They are also not particularly useful as observation when they record an event that is exciting and fun but not especially meaningful in terms of children's development—for example, the entire class dressed up for Halloween, or 2-year-olds eating gooey cupcakes and getting icing on their faces. Exercise the same criteria for using photographs that you use for writing anecdotal observations. Photograph children engaged in something typical, something new (a milestone), or something that is of concern.

The term *annotated photograph* (McAfee et al. 2004) is used to describe a photograph that is accompanied by an anecdotal record. The annotation should include the child's name and the date of the photograph, the setting or context of the photograph (e.g., in the dramatic play area), an anecdote explaining what happened (e.g., what you observed when the photograph was taken), and what the photo tells about this child. Without annotation a photograph may not be enough to help another person understand its significance. It is valuable to take several pictures of a child engaged in an activity to show the process as the child engages in play or work to create a product.

Video and Audio Recording

Like photographs, video and audio recordings are valuable documentation when they show something happening or provide a record of a child's ability. They are particularly useful in documenting nuances of movement and language and for recording subtleties of interactions. They allow a number of observers to view/hear the same child engaged in the same activity. Since they capture everything, they are not subject to ability or the bias of the observer. You may notice detail in a recording that you would not have observed while writing an observation.

Video and audio recordings have some disadvantages, however. If they are not used regularly they can be distracting to children and the resulting recordings are not natural. Videotaping and editing requires technical skill. They are time-consuming since any type of recording creates an overwhelming amount of material from which you must cull the few significant minutes or seconds. Audio recording or videotaping in a typically noisy classroom environment can be frustrating to listen to, and children's language can be difficult to hear and understand.

In order to use video or audio recording effectively it is necessary to plan for it. Decide what type of activity or interaction you want to record. Give children plenty of time to get used to the camera or tape recorder. Try to record a few children in the classroom when the rest are outside. Ask volunteers or parents to help if you are trying to videotape yourself in teaching interactions. Finally, be sure to carefully select

---

[1] The term *documentation* in early childhood education today is used to describe tangible "evidence" collected by teachers. Teachers document children's learning and abilities, curriculum, and their own professional practice and growth.

only short relevant sections of tape to share with others. Editing in this way can make the resulting video or audio tapes useful as documentation.

Selecting an Observation Technique

Each of the techniques described in the preceding sections is particularly useful for one or more purposes. You are likely to use all of them at different times. Remembering what you are trying to accomplish can help you to select an observation technique. Figure 5.9 is designed to help you to do this.

AUTHENTIC ASSESSMENT

The different kinds of written narrative and structured observations described earlier in this chapter are part of *authentic assessment*. Authentic assessment, or *performance-based assessment,* is an evaluation of a child's development or performance in the context of everyday life.

The growing awareness of the issues and problems involved in standardized tests has prompted interest in the use of alternative ways to assess children's learning and development. In a natural or "authentic" approach the teacher observes and documents real-life examples in which the child demonstrates skills and knowledge. Photographs, videotapes and audio recordings, interviews with family members, and examples of children's work (called *work samples*) are also authentic evidence of a child's understanding and ability.

Authentic assessment is not a onetime event like a standardized test. Instead it is an ongoing process. It does not rely on the outside authority of a test but uses the input of teacher, parent, and child. Thus actual performance, rather than responses to artificial tasks on tests, is the measure by which children's knowledge and skill are assessed.

Reflect on authentic assessment

What are your skills and accomplishments? How could you demonstrate those abilities to someone else? How is this demonstration more "authentic" (real) than taking a test? Which is a better way to show what you know and can do?

Figure 5.9 **Selecting an Observation Method**

In order to:	Use:
Create a vivid record of a child's activity	Running record; videotape
Record a behavior or interaction or the achievement of a milestone	Anecdotal record; annotated photograph
Ascertain how often a type of behavior occurs	Time sample
Understand why or when a particular behavior occurs	Event sample
Gather information about children's play preferences, individual progress, how materials and equipment are being used	Checklist
Evaluate the extent to which a child has reached particular milestones	Rating scale
Compare how different children understand a specific concept	Interviews
Quickly and accurately document something that is difficult to describe	Annotated photographs; videotape
Document movement, language, or interactions (or related abilities, such as musical skill) in order to share them with others	Running record; videotape or audio recording

Because authentic assessment is much more varied, more complete, and more genuine than standardized testing, it is also more complex. It can be hard to organize and use. One of the most common ways to meaningfully organize the rich data that authentic assessment provides is in a *portfolio,* a term derived from the portfolios that artists and writers create to present their work to others. Just as an artist's portfolio gives a fuller understanding of the artist's abilities, so a child's portfolio gives a fuller understanding of who the child is and what the child knows and can do.

What Is a Portfolio?

A portfolio is a purposeful collection of evidence of a child's learning, collected over time, that demonstrates the child's efforts, progress, or achievement (McAfee et al. 2004, 52). It can take the form of a book, a box, a folder, a file, or digital computer documents (sometimes called an *electronic portfolio*). In a portfolio many kinds of evidence of a child's ability, growth, and development (observations, work samples, photographs, etc.) are systematically collected and organized.

In early childhood education and care settings, a child's portfolio documents the child's progress in all areas of development. In elementary school settings, it represents an innovative alternative to conventional evaluations of children's progress, which have typically included testing, report cards, and letter grades. In programs for younger children portfolios are a logical extension of the observational approaches that have traditionally been used to learn about individuals.

Why Use Portfolios?

Portfolios are a dynamic and flexible way to organize information about children. They focus on children's strengths, on what they can do. They provide a far more complete and real picture of a child than a checklist or a test.

Portfolios help teachers to look at children's work over time to gauge how they have developed—socially, emotionally, physically, and cognitively. They give a deeper understanding of a child so that you can select the appropriate next steps in support of the child's development. Portfolios also assist you as you share your understanding with families and other professionals, and represent the child's strengths and potential with the staff of the next program to which the child moves.

What Belongs in a Portfolio?

What you collect for each child's portfolio will depend on your purpose in creating portfolios and your program goals. While all portfolios document children's progress, you may be creating portfolios primarily to assess children for the purpose of guiding planning, or you may be creating portfolios as a way to share children's abilities, growth, and development with families and other professionals.

To make meaningful and useful decisions about what to collect for a child's portfolio, you must also identify goals and objectives for children, and decide what materials and information will indicate that these have been accomplished. For example, if you teach children in a program in which a primary goal is the enhancement of literacy

151

skills, portfolios should include documentation of a child's developing literacy awareness and skill. You might collect work samples in which a child has incorporated print or print-like marks, keep records of books read to or by the child, and write anecdotal records when the child makes use of written materials or uses pens or pencils to communicate. The following list summarizes items that can be included in a portfolio:

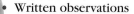

- Written observations
- Work samples including examples of the child's drawings and paintings, writing, journals, books or dictated stories, illustrations for stories, math work, maps made by the child, printouts of computer-generated work, key vocabulary word banks
- Photographs of the child at play, block structures and other constructions, group projects (e.g., murals), clay and dough objects
- Transcriptions of the child's discussions or his or her work
- Developmental checklists and rating scales
- Records of books read to or read by the child
- Audiotape samples of speech or musical production
- Videotapes of the child in action

What you collect for inclusion in portfolios will depend on the requirements of your setting and your reasons for documenting. In many programs a structure for portfolios is established. When your program has such a structure in place you may be asked to:

- Collect certain items at the same time from all children, such as a drawing from the first week of school and another from the last week of school—sometimes called *core items*
- Collect evidence of a child's ability in specific activities, such as a drawing, an observation of a social interaction, an observation or taped language sample, a photograph of a block building, or a writing sample
- Have children select examples of a favorite or "best" work to include in their portfolios

You are likely to collect more observations, work samples, and photographs than you will actually include in a portfolio. Each item included should be meaningful and informative—that is, it should tell something about the child's development, abilities, and learning. For example, if a child draws pictures of cars every day it is unnecessary to include five drawings of cars that are only minimally different. One representative drawing of a car will do. Since the purpose of a portfolio is to document the individual child's development, samples will not be the same for every child. School-age children can participate in selecting and explaining the work samples they include in their portfolios.

Reflect on documentation in real life

What mementos have you kept from your past? Why have you kept these things? How do you "document" your life and accomplishments? Is documenting your life and accomplishments important to you? Why?

Organizing and Creating a Portfolio

A folder full of random and disorganized "stuff" is not a portfolio. Your contribution to the portfolio is to collect, organize, and interpret the evidence that is presented.

Select an Organizational Structure. The first step is to select the categories into which you will organize the material you collect. A portfolio can be organized by domains of development—physical, social, emotional, and cognitive. Organization by developmental domain is often selected for portfolios for infant, toddler, and preschool-age children. It can serve primary-age children as well; however, primary grade teachers more often organize portfolios by subject or content areas such as social studies, science, literacy, and so on. Other teachers and published observation or portfolio systems use some variation on these two ways of organizing.

However you organize, it is important to include items that are an authentic representation of the child's understanding and skill in the categories you have determined to be important. Therefore, your curriculum must be rich enough to provide opportunities for children to produce concrete representations of their abilities. A collection of completed worksheets organized by subject areas is not adequate. Likewise, a large collection of a child's art productions might be useful to an adult who was interested in the developmental stages of art but would not give a complete picture of a child's abilities and interests.

Collect and Compile. Creating portfolios for a class of children is a lot of work! It is easier when you develop a system that makes the filing and retrieval of portfolio items simple. A large accordion folder that includes several file folders to organize different kinds of materials serves well as portfolio storage. Some people use file boxes, and others organize materials into notebooks that have folders and pocket sheets in which to store work samples. All of these systems work well for works in progress such as anecdotal records, checklists, and rating scales. Large items that must be stored elsewhere may be indexed in the system with a note about where they are stored. Some teachers construct cardboard or wooden files that are sized to fit the easel paintings so that everything can be stored together.

Collect samples of each child's work on a regular basis. Remember to collect items in every domain or learning area so that you can present a comprehensive picture of the child. It is frustrating to discover that you are missing critical observations, photographs, or work samples when you are ready to present the portfolio. Be sure to label, date, and annotate[2] all items before storing them. Figure 5.10 is a basic list of items that we ask our students to collect for a preschool child's portfolio.

The content that you assemble should be comprehensive, organized, and arranged chronologically so that it shows what the child can do and how he or she has grown and changed. While it is valuable for the portfolio to be professional, legible, and informative, it is not a scrapbook or a memory book. Time and money spent on backing photos with pretty paper, embellishing pages with stickers, or artfully cutting out heart-shaped frames is better spent on developing curriculum that will help the child.

Interpret and Describe. The next step in creating a portfolio is to reflect on what you have collected, analyze what it means, and finally write a description of the child's abilities and characteristics based on the evidence that you have collected. This description can be called an *individual profile,* a *developmental description,* or a *summary statement.*

The individual profile provides a picture of what makes this child unique. It should include a general description of the child's ability, interests, progress, and patterns of engaging in each of the areas of the portfolio. It should incorporate the teacher's appraisal of where the child is in terms of program goals and note any areas of concern to be monitored.

Portfolios are not static documents. They are typically updated at specific times. You might, for example, begin the portfolio at the start of the year, write an initial profile at midyear, continue to add items to the portfolio throughout the year, and review and update it the end of the year.

Using Portfolios

How do teachers use the picture of a child that the portfolio provides? One of the most valuable things you can do is to use it to share your understanding of the child with families and other professionals. The portfolio itself vividly depicts the child and his

[2] Like annotated photographs, annotated work samples and recordings should include the child's name and the date, the setting or context in which it was created, and an anecdote explaining what happened (e.g., when it was created), and what it tells about this child.

Figure 5.10 Sample Portfolio Contents for a Preschool Child

Background Information	
Child's date of birth	Date started school/class
Language(s) spoken in the home	Ethnic/racial/cultural identification

Evidence of Physical Development and Health: *Observations, photographs, work samples which show . . .*	
Size/weight compared to others of his/her age	Typical food intake/preferences
Toileting routines/accidents	Length of typical nap
Large motor activity	Fine motor activity
Sensory activity	Preferred hand and grip

Evidence of Personal/Social Development: *Observations, photographs, work samples, or recordings which show . . .*		
Self-regulation and self-help	Self-initiated activities	Friendships (also child-reports)
Making choices	Showing awareness of feelings	Interactions w/others
Separation from family	Cooperative behavior	Solving a social problem
Pretend play		Formal group activity

Evidence of Language and Cognitive Development: *Observations, photographs, work samples, or recordings which show . . .*		
Reading or writing	Dictated notes or stories	Writing samples (one per month)
Listening to or telling stories	Talking, or storytelling	Conversations with others

Evidence of Cognitive Development: *Observations, photographs, work samples, or recordings which show . . .*		
Noticing a natural phenomenon	Discovery or exploration	Sorting, counting, or classifying
Examples of maps or illustrations		Identifying a problem

Evidence of Creative Ability and Aesthetic Awareness: *Observations, photographs, work samples, or recordings which show . . .*		
Engaged in music	Painting (one per month)	Musical expression in song
Engaged in movement	Creative art or construction	Drawing (one per month)

or her work. It provides a focal point for a conference with the family or other professionals. The summary description that you wrote for the portfolio can be used as part of a narrative report given to families at a conference.

The portfolio can also be used to guide planning for the child and for the group. The individual profile that you created includes the child's abilities, strengths, interests, and challenges. These will help you to plan for this specific child. Taken together, the portfolios created for the group give you a picture of what curriculum might benefit the class as a whole.

Finally, the portfolio becomes a part of the documentation that moves with the child to the next class or into the archives of his or her family.

Observation Systems

It is relatively easy to complete a checklist on each child in a preschool group or give a standardized test to a group of first graders. It can be daunting to authentically assess a class of young children. Some programs devise structured ways for all the teachers to organize their assessments. A number of commercial systems also aid early child-hood educators in this task. These systems are valuable because they systematize and guide teacher observations with specific criteria and procedures.

The High/Scope Child Observation Record

The High/Scope *Child Observation Record* (COR) is an example of a system designed to help teachers and caregivers determine the developmental status of young children ages 2.2 to 6 years. It is an observational assessment that includes six categories: (1) Initiative, (2) Social Relations, (3) Creative Representation, (4) Music and Movement, (5) Language and Literacy, and (6) Logic and Mathematics. Activities that typically occur in a preschool day are used for assessment. The teacher or caregiver takes a series of brief notes over several months, and at the end of that time rates the child's behavior using a 30-item questionnaire. Scores must be interpreted by a test administrator, who is specially trained to evaluate the COR.

The Work Sampling System

The Work Sampling System (Meisels, Jablon, Dichtelmiller, Dorfman, & Marsden 1995) is a more comprehensive performance-based assessment system designed to be used from preschool through the primary years (ages 3 to 11). It consists of three components: (1) developmental guidelines and checklists, (2) portfolios, and (3) summary reports. The developmental guidelines and checklists are designed to assist teachers in observing and documenting individual children's growth and progress. They are structured around developmentally appropriate activities and are based on national, state, and local curriculum standards. Each checklist covers seven domains: (1) personal and social development, (2) language and literacy, (3) mathematical thinking, (4) scientific thinking, (5) social studies, (6) the arts, and (7) physical development. The checklists and guidelines create a profile of children's individualized progress. Portfolios provide documentation of each child's experiences and parallel classroom activities. Summary reports replace report cards as a means of communicating children's progress to families. They consist of performance and progress ratings in each domain, and teachers' reflections and comments about the child's development.

The Creative Curriculum Developmental Continuum

The Creative Curriculum Developmental Continuum is designed to accompany *The Creative Curriculum* (Dodge, Colker, & Heroman 2002). It is a preschool observational assessment system based on 50 skills related to preschool children's development (e.g., *Understands and follows directions*). The continuum uses a rating scale that includes examples of ways in which children might demonstrate the skills. These range from "fore-runner," behaviors that would typically be expected to occur prior to preschool (*Associates words with actions—says "throw" when sees a ball thrown*) to "mastery," behaviors that would typically occur when children have mastered the specific skill (*Follows directions with more than two steps—e.g., follows directions to put clay in container, wipe table, and wash hands when the activity is finished*).

155

The Creative Curriculum Developmental Continuum includes a form for reporting progress to families and a class summary worksheet to enable teachers to easily see the progress of the group. Since it is tied to a curriculum manual, it makes a clear connection between assessment and planning.

The Ounce Scale

The Ounce Scale (Marsden, Dombro, & Dichtelmiller 2003) is an infant/toddler observational assessment created to be used with children from birth to 3½ years. It includes three components: an observation record in which teachers record their observations; a family album in which families collect observations, photos, and mementos of their child's growth and development; and a rating scale used to evaluate children's growth and development at the end of eight age levels.

The Ounce Scale includes six areas of development: personal connections (trust), feelings about self, relationships with other children, understanding and communicating (language development), exploration and problem solving, and movement and coordination. Family involvement in the assessment is an integral part of the Ounce Scale. It is designed to be used in group programs, home visiting programs, and family support programs.

FORMAL ASSESSMENT

As you can see from the first part of this chapter, early childhood educators are committed to using observation and authentic assessment as their primary means for learning about and reporting children's development and learning. In this section we will tell you about some of the kinds of formal assessment instruments that are currently used in early childhood settings, discuss the appropriate function of each type, and explore some of issues associated with their use.

Kinds of Assessment Instruments

Some commonly used formal assessment tools are screening instruments, developmental assessments, diagnostic tests, academic readiness tests, and individual and group intelligence and achievement tests. Formal assessment instruments reflect the values of the people who created them—what they believe to be worthwhile for a child of a particular age to know, to do, or to have experienced. If you are ever called upon to select or use one of these assessment tools, you will want to determine whether it is a good fit for your purposes and the child or children whom you wish to learn about.

Screening Instruments

Screening instruments are designed to identify children who may need specialized services. They compare a child's development to that of other children of the same age. Screening is a relatively fast and efficient way to assess the developmental status of children. Every child is screened, in some way, beginning at birth. The newborn is observed for obvious defects. Simple screening such as observation and testing of heart rate, muscle tone, and respiration occur in the first few minutes after birth. As children grow and develop, they encounter other forms of screening in the course of regular medical care.

Another important kind of screening occurs in school settings to identify children who might have developmental delays or medical conditions requiring correction such as a vision or hearing impairment. Appropriate screening can bring about improvements in children's lives. Generations of children entering the Head Start program have been screened. Many with hearing losses, vision impairments, and other medical problems have been identified and given appropriate treatment. Children who are identified by the screening process as being at risk for learning problems can be evaluated and receive special services to help them do better in school.

Educational screening instruments are relatively short, have few items, address a number of developmental areas, and can be administered and interpreted by trained professionals or trained volunteers. Screening identifies children who need to be looked at more carefully. A child should *never* be labeled on the basis of screening, because screening *cannot* predict future success or failure, prescribe specific treatment or curriculum, or diagnose special conditions. It should not be used to determine individual development plans or as the basis for curriculum planning.

Screening services vary from community to community and from state to state. Many communities provide screening when children first enter kindergarten or first grade. Some have Childfind programs to make parents and other adults aware of the importance of early identification. As an early childhood educator you may participate in choosing or administering a screening instrument and be involved in follow-up. If formal screening is not available in your school or community, informal screening through sensitive observation can also identify children who need further assessment. No screening instrument is foolproof. Some children with developmental delays will remain undetected while others who have no serious delays will be identified as needing further evaluation. For this reason it is important that screening instruments be chosen carefully and that great care is taken in reporting results to families.

Good screening instruments are valid and reliable and focus on performance in a wide range of developmental areas (speech, understanding of language, large and small motor skills). They should also involve information from families who know the child best and have important information to contribute. Screening instruments are most likely to appropriately identify children if they use the language or dialect of the child's family. Children who are not tested in their first language will not be able to communicate their true abilities. Similarly, instruments should reflect the experiences and cultural background of the children.

Some screening instruments are specific to age and stage of development while others address a range of ages. Examples of screening instruments include the Bayley Scales of Infant Development and the Peabody Developmental Motor Scales. Multidomain developmental screening tests include all areas of development and are among the most commonly used. The Early Screening Inventory, the DIAL (Developmental Indicators for Assessment of Learning), and the Early Learning Accomplishment Profile are examples of these instruments.

Developmental Assessments

Developmental assessment includes checklists and rating scales that have been created for appraising children's skills and abilities. They are designed to help you learn about children's actual functioning in the classroom by identifying patterns of strengths and weaknesses in a number of developmental domains. They are criterion-referenced—that is, they reflect a child's degree of mastery over a skill or sequence of skills. Developmental assessments are not meant to label children; rather, they give you information so that you can design appropriate experiences for individual children and groups.

A developmental assessment is usually administered, interpreted, and used by program staff. It may take weeks or even months to completely administer a developmental assessment in a number of areas. In some programs it may be a process that continues throughout the school year. It may be administered early in the year to identify skills the child already has and then used as the basis for designing experiences and activities to help the child to move to the next step. The child may be assessed again later in the year.

157

Developmental assessments often include guidelines for lessons and materials that are designed to develop specific skills. Although these may provide good ideas, teachers should never teach assessment items in isolation or use them as the basis for curriculum. Examples of commonly used assessments include Learning Accomplishment Profile (LAP) and the Portage Guide to Early Education.

Developmental assessment may also serve a screening purpose, especially if no other screening has been done. Results can indicate that a child may have a problem. A general guideline is that if a 6-month lag is observed in language or a 1-year delay in any other area, the child should be carefully watched and receive additional support in the area of concern. If the delay is greater, the child may need a diagnostic evaluation.

Like screening instruments, developmental assessments only measure what can be observed and what their authors believe to be important. They may not assess what you or your colleagues value. If you decide to use a developmental assessment instrument, be aware of the limitations of the instrument and continue to use your own observations to create a more comprehensive picture of a child.

A developmental assessment instrument that is appropriate for a given program will have goals for children that are similar to or compatible with the goals of the program. Good instruments provide guidelines for use and can be easily administered and interpreted by staff—criteria for success are clearly spelled out. They can be used with the language or dialect of the program's population and can be adapted to reflect the culture and typical experiences of its children. Good assessments involve age-appropriate responses and timing (manipulative and verbal rather than written responses, and short testing periods followed by rest intervals).

Diagnostic Tests

Diagnostic tests are in-depth evaluations used to assess what children actually can do in specific areas of development. They are used to identify children with special needs, and serve as the basis for making decisions about instructional strategies and specialized placements. These tests vary from those designed to help understand a child's functioning in a single developmental domain to others that are more general. For example, a speech-language specialist might administer a diagnostic test to determine a child's receptive language capabilities, and a psychologist might administer a developmental inventory that assesses a half-dozen or more domains.

Diagnostic tests are often conducted as part of the comprehensive evaluation process carried out by an interdisciplinary team. The team may include a physician; psychologist; speech, hearing, and physical therapists; family members; and the classroom teacher. The team will evaluate whether a serious problem exists, what it seems to be (diagnosis), and the kind of strategies, placement, and services that would be most appropriate for the child (treatment).

The selection of diagnostic tests will be dependent on the purposes of the assessment. Some that are frequently used and that you may hear about are the Kaufman Assessment Battery for Children (KABC-II), the Peabody Picture Vocabulary Test (PPVT-III), the Stanford-Binet Intelligence Scale, and the Vineland Adaptive Behavior Scales.

Readiness and Achievement Tests

Readiness and achievement tests examine children (individually or in groups) to make judgments regarding their performance in comparison to some standard. They are standardized tests that are administered and scored using a prescribed procedure that is not a part of the regular program activity.

Readiness tests focus on existing levels of skills, performance, and knowledge. Their proper purpose is to facilitate program planning. Achievement tests measure what a child has actually learned, the extent to which he or she has acquired information or mastered identified skills that have been taught. Achievement tests determine the effectiveness of instruction.

Standardized tests have clearly defined purposes and have some distinguishing characteristics that set them apart from other approaches to learning about children. Each item on a standardized test has been carefully studied to establish the dependability of the test. Two kinds of data are used to establish dependability: *validity* or accuracy, the degree to which a test measures what it claims to measure, and *reliability* or consistency, how often identical results can be obtained with the same test. Standardized tests are either *norm-referenced* or *criterion-referenced*. Norm-referenced tests compare an individual child's performance on the test with that of an external norm, which was established by administering the test to a large sample of children (for example, the SAT test). Criterion-referenced tests relate the child's performance to a standard of achievement (for example, whether or not a child can skip) but do not compare the child to a reference group.

A standardized test should have a well defined purpose, a manual with information on standard procedures, data that confirms reliability and validity, and clear directions. Those who select the test need to have carefully considered the appropriateness of the purpose of the test for the children who will be tested. The language used in the test (both the particular language and the vocabulary level) should be comprehensible to the children being tested.

Readiness tests that are commonly used in early childhood programs include the Metropolitan Readiness Test, the Cognitive Skills Assessment Battery, and the Gesell Developmental Assessment. Achievement tests in use today include the Peabody Individual Achievement Test and the Boehm Test of Basic Concepts.

Issues in Standardized Testing

In recent years there has been a dramatic increase in the use of standardized tests for assessing young children. While these may be helpful in determining a child's readiness to benefit from a specific program or curriculum or to determine where children need additional instruction, they *should not* be used to reject, track, or retain children.

Those who advocate the use of tests maintain that having comparative data and a national frame of reference is helpful in assessing the effectiveness of instruction and in making decisions about school admissions and placements. They also claim that data on standardized tests are helpful in justifying programs and proving accountability to funding agencies.

When the primary purpose of assessment is to identify developmental problems or to gather information about children's progress in a systematic way, then standardized tests may be called for. Unfortunately, standardized testing is also being used to determine which children fit existing programs and to exclude those who do not "make the grade," rather than to make educational programs responsive to all children's needs and developmental stage.

Critics of standardized testing (Cryan 1986; Graves 2002; Kamii 1990; Kohn 2000; Wortham 1990) raise a number of issues and concerns. Some of the most frequently cited are:

- Test results may not be valid and reliable because it is so difficult to administer tests to young children. They may be beyond children's developmental capabilities, or their behavior may be unduly influenced by mood or by the test situation.
- Tests measure a narrow range of objectives, mostly cognitive and language abilities, and miss important objectives of early childhood education such as creativity, problem solving, and social and emotional development.

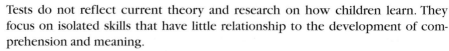

- Tests do not reflect current theory and research on how children learn. They focus on isolated skills that have little relationship to the development of comprehension and meaning.
- Many tests are culturally biased. Children who do not speak English as a first language and those from minority groups frequently not do as well on the tests.
- Tests are often inappropriately administered and interpreted because most early childhood professionals are not trained in the appropriate use and interpretation of standardized tests.
- Teachers who want children to do well on tests may introduce skills too early or alter their curriculum and "teach to the test," resulting in teaching methods and content that are inappropriate for young children.
- Tests are often used for purposes for which they were not intended. Test results are inappropriately used to keep children out of school, retain them in the same grade, place them in remedial classes, or make unwarranted placements in special education classrooms rather than for improving classroom practice.
- There has been too great an emphasis on standardized tests, rather than attempting to gather information from many sources.

The National Association for the Education of Young Children developed a position statement to address these issues and to help ensure that testing is used appropriately. Their position states:

> NAEYC believes that the most important consideration in evaluating and using standardized tests is the *utility criterion: The purpose of testing must be to improve services for children and to ensure that children benefit from their educational experiences. Decisions about testing and assessment instruments must be based on the usefulness of the assessment procedure for improving services to children and improving outcomes for children.* (1988, 44)

The NAEYC position statement on testing gives the following guidelines for decisions related to testing in early childhood settings:

- All standardized tests used in early childhood programs must be reliable and valid according to technical standards of test development.
- Decisions that have a major impact on children such as enrollment, retention, or assignment to remedial or special classes should be based on multiple sources of information and should never be based on a single test score.
- It is the professional responsibility of administrators and teachers to critically evaluate, carefully select, and use standardized tests only for the purposes for which they are intended and for which data exist to demonstrate the test's validity.
- It is the professional responsibility of administrators and teachers to be knowledgeable about testing and to interpret results accurately and cautiously to parents, school personnel, and the media. (1988, 44–45)[3]

Reflect on testing—

Think about the experiences you had as student (child or adult) with testing. How did you feel when you had to take a test? Did the test benefit you? Did it have any negative effects? Have you had any experiences with testing in early childhood programs? What did you notice? Why might it be important for you, as an early childhood educator, to know about tests?

WHAT TEACHERS NEED TO KNOW ABOUT ASSESSMENT

Teachers of young children need to be aware of different ways of gathering and using information, know the strengths and limitations of a range of assessment options, and remain sensitive and flexible in the ways they learn about children. No one technique

---

[3]*Source:* NAEYC Position Statement on Standardized of Young Children 3 Through 8 Years of Age, 1988. Used with permission.

or instrument will disclose everything that you need to know about a child. Understanding the uses, and abuses, of assessment can help you to become a better teacher and, when necessary, an advocate for children.

The first thing to think about in using any kind of observation or assessment is what effect it will have on children and their families. Ask yourself if the information you are collecting will lead to positive experiences for children and better teaching and learning. And be sure to keep in mind P-1.1 in the NAEYC Code of Ethical Conduct, which states: "Above all we will not harm children. We shall not participate in practices that are disrespectful, degrading, dangerous, exploitative, intimidating, emotionally damaging, or physically harmful to children" (Feeney & Kipnis 1998). The current enthusiasm for accountability has led to some testing that may have harmful effects on children. If you are concerned about a test you are being asked to administer, you might begin by learning something about it and the reason it was selected. If you don't think its use is warranted, you could explain your concerns and ask that the use of the test be reconsidered, or you might decide not to give the test. This is a

moral decision that may have serious consequences (we recently spoke with a teacher who was docked pay because she refused to give a test she felt was not consistent with good early childhood practice). We hope that these practices will be phased out and that this is not a decision you will ever have to face.

To guide your decisions, keep in mind the following principles of sound assessment practice:

- Learn to be a good observer and use observation as a primary source of information about children.
- Assess children in meaningful, and appropriate ways.
- Be clear about the purpose of the assessment and use the information collected only for this purpose.
- Be sure that an assessment is fair for all children.
- Check to be sure that an assessment instrument is valid and reliable.
- Be sure that an assessment instrument is age-appropriate in both content and the method of data collection.
- Be sure that an assessment instrument is culturally and linguistically appropriate (most assessments are, to some extent, a measure of language).
- Use family members as valued source of assessment information.
- Let families know the kinds of assessment you are using and why, and share what you learn about their child.
- Use multiple sources of information for making decisions about admission and placements.
- Protect confidentiality.

Confidentiality

When and how you share information that you have gained from observations and formal assessments with others, the degree to which you protect the information you collect, and the uses to which you put it are all important issues. When you do share such information it is important to consider your professional obligations to children, families, and society.

Written observations and assessments are confidential, and should be stored in such a way as to protect the privacy of children and families. Families have an undisputed right to access this information. And it is generally considered appropriate to share observations and assessment results with other teachers and administrators who work with the child. Who else has a "need to know"? Therapists, teachers in the next school, physicians, and others concerned with the child's welfare may have a genuine reason for being included. Generally, before sharing information you will get the written permission of the family. The Code of Ethical Conduct provides you with guidance. Everyone enjoys telling a funny or endearing story about a child with whom they have worked. However, it is never acceptable to gossip casually about your assessment of a child in a way that may be injurious to the child or in a way that the child can be identified by others. Even in your college observation papers, it is important to change the child's name or to use his or her initials to avoid breaching confidentiality.

SHARING INFORMATION WITH FAMILIES

Families want to understand their child's experiences in the early childhood program. They need to know how their child is growing and learning. Most programs have some system for sharing information with them. A conference with family members is the most prevalent way of sharing information and planning how to mutually support the child's development. Conferences enable families and staff to share and participate in a joint problem-solving process. They often culminate with a summary of the discussion and decisions of the conference and are followed up with a written report.

In some programs written progress reports are the primary way families receive information about their child's functioning. Written reporting methods that are frequently used include report cards and narrative summaries. Report cards are most commonly found in programs for primary-age children and are often criticized because they distill large quantities of information about a child into a single letter grade. In most early childhood programs some combination of conferences and written summaries are used to regularly report on a child's progress. And more and more the portfolio including its written summary statement, shared at a conference among parent, teacher, and child, is coming to be an accepted way of sharing information in programs for preschool and primary children.

FINAL THOUGHTS

You are becoming an early childhood educator, someone who understands children. Your ability to use the range of observation and assessment strategies discussed in this chapter will help you to better understand children and make sound educational decisions. Knowledge of both formal and authentic assessment techniques makes you a more competent professional and a more powerful advocate for children.

You will learn about children in many ways through reading, study, practice, and discussions with others. However, observing children clearly and objectively will teach you the most. The rewards of observing children are great. Like anything worth doing, developing observation skill takes time and work. We urge you to observe children consciously and frequently. And we encourage you to practice writing observations. As you hone these skills you will discover that you feel more joy and compassion in your work, teach with enhanced skill, and communicate with greater clarity.

LEARNING OUTCOMES

When you read this chapter, thoughtfully complete selected assignments from the "To Learn More" section, and prepare items from the "For Your Portfolio" section, you will be demonstrating your progress in meeting NAEYC **Standard 3: Observing, Documenting and Assessing to Support Young Children and Families.**

Key elements:

- Understanding the goals, benefits, and uses of assessment
- Knowing about and using observation, documentation, and other appropriate assessment tools and approaches
- Understanding and practicing responsible assessment
- Knowing about assessment partnerships with families and other professionals

TO LEARN MORE

Observe a Child: Select a young child you do not know in an early childhood program. Observe the child for a period of at least half an hour on three different occasions (engaged in outdoor play, an indoor work period, and one other time). Make notes on what you observe each time. Keep a running record of everything the child says and does while you are observing. When you are finished, rewrite your notes in the form of three narratives that include the following:

- A description of the physical attributes of the child and what makes him or her unique
- Where and when you observed, including the setting and the other people present during each observation
- A detailed account of all the things the child did and said during each observation

Summarize What You Observed: Write about what this child can do and what seems to be important for him or her right now. What did you observe that led you to these conclusions?

Reflect on the Child: Write about your interpretations. What do you think the child is thinking and feeling? What did you observe that led you to this conclusion?

Reflect on Your Own Learning and Reaction: Write a reflection on what you learned through these observations and what you think it means. Note any feelings or reactions you had to the child or the observation process. Why do you think you had these reactions? What did you discover about observation?

Use a Structured Observation Method: Use two or more of the structured observation methods described in the chapter to study a child you know. For example, you may wish to use a time sample of the kinds of play the child engages in. Observe the child at least three times on different days. Write about what happened and comment on:

- What you learned about the child
- What you didn't learn that you might want or need to know

- What might be done to support this child
- What the experience suggests about the possible advantages and/or disadvantages of using structured observation methods

Assess a Child: Use a standardized test instrument to assess a child you don't know. If the instrument has a large number of items, assess the child in one developmental area. Interview the child's teacher or parents and find out what they think the child can or cannot do in the areas you are assessing. Write about what happened and comment on:

- What you learned about the child
- What you didn't learn that you might want or need to know
- How consistent or inconsistent the assessment results were with the teacher's or parents' experiences of the child
- What the experience suggests about the possible advantages and/or disadvantages of using standardized assessment instruments

Create a Portrait of a Child (Case Study): Select a child to observe over at least an 8-week period as the subject of your portrait. Make observations of all aspects of the child's development on a regular basis. Write a narrative in which you summarize the observations. Describe what the child does without making judgments, assumptions, or interpretations of his/her interests or motivation. Refer to Chapter 4 for information about areas of development. Your portrait should include the following:

- *Physical description:* Include the child's age, gender, and a brief description of the child's physical appearance and characteristic facial and body expressions. Convey what the child is like, and how he/she is unique.
- *Physical development:* Observations of how the child responds to sensory experiences, skill in the use of hands and fingers, how the child uses his/her body in

physical activities. Comment on how the child compares to his/her peers in areas of physical development.

- *Social/emotional development:* Observe the child's relationship to children and adults, the extent to which the child is independent/dependent on others, how the child demonstrates self-control or lack of it, evidence of sharing, cooperation, and other prosocial behavior. Comment on emotions the child characteristically projects.

- *Cognitive development:* Observe the child's ways of interacting with the world and his or her approach to problem solving. Select other observations that indicate the child's stage of cognitive development and knowledge and understanding of the world.

- *Supplemental data:* Supplement your narrative observations with developmental checklists, work samples, and any other additional information (e.g., time samples) that you have collected.

- *Summary and conclusions:* Summarize what you have learned and share your thoughts about how the child is progressing developmentally and what the staff might do to continue to support his/her development. What did you learn about yourself and about children from this observation experience?

For Your Portfolio

Use a Written Observation: Include a copy of a written observation of a child (with the name changed or eliminated to preserve confidentiality). Describe how you use the information from this observation to meet this child's needs (e.g., by changing your way of interacting, adding an activity, modifying the environment).

Use Structured Observations: Include a copy of structured observations that you completed on a child (with the name changed or eliminated to preserve confidentiality). Explain how you might use the information from these observations

to better meet this child's needs (e.g., by changing your way of interacting, adding an activity, modifying the environment).

Create a Child's Portfolio: Create a portfolio for a child that includes observations in every developmental area, photographs, and work samples. Write a developmental summary based on these data. Share the portfolio with the child's family. Take a photograph of the portfolio itself for your own professional portfolio (with the name changed or eliminated to preserve confidentiality) and include a copy of the developmental summary.

6

Play

Play is a child's life and the means by which he comes to understand the world he lives in.

Susan Isaacs

Through play, children learn what no one can teach them.

Lawrence Frank

* * *

*D*o you remember the dizzy joy of rolling down a hill, the focused effort of building an elaborate structure with blocks, the exhausting satisfaction of learning to jump rope, or the prolonged concentration of pretending with friends? Whether rich or poor, in town or country, you played. Children all over the world play; they have always played.

Child development theory and the experience of practitioners tell us that children learn best through direct, hands-on experience. Play is the ultimate realization of the early childhood educator's maxim of "learning by doing." Since the field began, early childhood educators have sought to understand and support this most natural of activities. Today, as in the past, belief in the value of play is a distinguishing characteristic of early childhood education. It is a link to our past and a bond between early childhood professionals. As an early childhood educator you will learn about young children and their development. Similarly, you will become knowledgeable about play—what it is, how it develops, its function in growth and learning, its role in early childhood education and care, and the role of the early childhood educator in supporting children's play.

Play is the heart of the early childhood program, the center of the curriculum. Play is the way children develop and learn, the way they express their understanding of the world, and an important way for early childhood educators to achieve their curriculum and learning goals.

Children's play provides a window into their lives. Through your observations of children at play you can learn a great deal about what they understand and can do. You also come to appreciate and know what they are like as individuals—what their interests and unique characteristics are.

Play serves all aspects of development, provides an avenue for children to practice emerging skills, confirms emerging concepts, and enables you to assess the developmental status of children. Because of the impressive power of play to lead the development of social, emotional, and cognitive competence it is important that you have knowledge about how play has been viewed in the past, what is now known about it, and how this knowledge influences what you do as an early childhood educator.

THE NATURE OF PLAY

What is play? What is its significance? Why is play so compelling to children? Reflecting on the play of children and your own childhood play can help you to realize that many things can be play. As you observe a child at play, you may notice the characteristics of play. As you watch children of different ages, you will see that play changes as children grow. And as you observe boys and girls with different temperaments, experiences, and abilities, you will see some of the individual differences in children's play. The characteristics and stages of play described by theorists and researchers can help you to understand what you see.

Characteristics of Play

As the 4-year-olds gather, Sharis, the teacher, invites each child to select a center where they would like to begin the morning. Mitzu, Kekala, and Jeremy select the dramatic play area. Mitzu announces, "Let's play farm. I'm the lamb and Jeremy you be the farmer." Kekala protests, "You got to be the lamb last time. I get to be the lamb this time." Mitzu concedes and claims the role of the mommy lamb as she puts a blanket in the doll bed to serve as a bed for her baby lamb. Jeremy follows with a carton of eggs (large beads) and says, "I'm the mommy chicken and I'm making eggs." As he places the eggs in the doll bed, Mitzu pushes him away proclaiming that chickens use nests not beds. Sharis observes the interaction and responds by offering the hula skirt as nest material.

Ask adults how they can distinguish children at play and they will likely tell you "when they are having fun" or "when they are enjoying themselves" or even "when I can't get their attention." Although no single agreed-upon definition captures the essence of play, theorists, researchers, and educators have identified characteristics that distinguish play from other behaviors. These characteristics enable you to understand what play is and what it is not. It is important to be able to distinguish play from nonplay in order to make decisions and take actions that support and extend play and avoid interrupting or misguiding it.

- *Play is intrinsically motivated.* Play is its own reward. Children play because it is satisfying, not because it meets a basic need or receives an external reward. It is the motivation and not the activity that makes something play. Walking on a balance beam as you cross the playground is play; walking a balance beam as part of a gymnastics routine in an attempt to win a prize is most likely work. The pleasure and focus brought to play is a sign of this personal motivation.
- *Play is freely chosen.* Children choose play. The play opportunity beckons, and children decide to play. Adults may invite but never compel children to play. The moment compulsion enters and a task has been assigned it becomes work, not play.
- *Play is pleasurable, enjoyable, and engaging.* Pleasurable, focused pursuit of an activity is a hallmark of play in children and adults. Although play can be seriously pursued and can include challenges, fears, and frustrations, it is the quality of enjoyment that stands out when we think of play. Activity that is not enjoyable most of the time will not be chosen as play.
- *Play is process-oriented.* The activity, rather than the end product, motivates. Children are more involved in discovery and creation (the process) than the eventual outcome. Play can have a product or goal, but this will be spontaneously decided by the players as part of play, and may change as the play progresses.

- *Play is active.* It requires physical, verbal, or mental engagement with people, objects, or ideas. Although we clearly recognize the rough-and-tumble actions of the young child as play, quieter activities such as drawing, play dough, even daydreams can be play, for they are freely chosen, pursued for their own sake, process-oriented, pleasurable, and engage mental capacities.

- *Play is self-oriented rather than object-oriented.* In play the basic question is "What can I do with this object?" When confronted with a new or unusual object, the first order of business for most children is to find out the answer to the question "What is this object and what can *it* do?" Play theorists and researchers call this *exploration* and distinguish it from play (Bergen 1988; Johnson, Christie, & Yawkey 1999).

- *Play is often nonliteral.* It is pretend. Many activities are "playful," but it is nonliteral pretending that is the pinnacle of play. Children suspend and alter reality for make-believe. The external world is temporarily set aside for fuller exploration of internal imagining. The players are often heard saying things such as "Let's pretend . . . ," "I'll be the mommy and you be the baby," or (holding a block) "This can be the phone."

Children at play are powerful creators compelled by forces from within to create a world. Although the raw materials of their creations are their life experiences, the shape of their creations is their own. Play is simultaneously an attachment to and a detachment from the world at a time during which children can act autonomously and freely and experience themselves and the world with intensity.

Purpose of Play

Philosophers, theorists, educators, and psychologists have observed children at play for centuries and speculated about play's nature and purpose. Until recently, several "classical" theories were used to explain why children play.

During the 19th and early 20th centuries, a number of writers formulated explanations for the role of play in human development (Levy 1978). The surplus energy theory of play introduced by British philosopher Herbert Spencer suggested that the purpose of play was to help human beings use energy they no longer needed for basic survival. Adults have work to do, but children need to expend their energy in play. The relaxation or recreation theory of G. T. W. Patrick held that play was an essential mechanism to relieve the stresses of work. The recapitulation theory, credited to G. S. Hall, maintained that during childhood the history of evolution is relived. Play rids the human race of primitive and unnecessary instinctual traits carried over by heredity from past generations. Instinct theory, developed by German philosopher and writer Karl Groos, suggested that play was a natural instinct, necessary for children's growth and development. The practice theory suggested that play was practice for adulthood. Children at play practice the tasks and roles of adults (Levy 1978).

> **Reflect on your memories of play**
>
> When you were a child, how did you play? What made it play? As an adult what is your "play"? What are the characteristics of your play now?

When we observe a group of children, it is easy to see how these theories evolved. A group of energetic preschoolers cooped up on a rainy day certainly seem to have surplus energy. That same group, after an opportunity to run and yell outside, is much more relaxed when they come back in. A jungle gym full of climbing children is humorously reminiscent of our primate cousins and can seem to be replaying evolution. And it can be frighteningly apparent when we watch children playing house, school, or war that they are practicing adult roles.

Contemporary Theories of Play

Much is still to be learned, but recent theorists, researchers, and educators have expanded our understanding of why children play. Today we know that play is both a natural and instinctive activity that helps children to develop in all areas. Current theories of play strongly reflect the influence of Freud and Piaget.

Freud and his followers, particularly his daughter Anna Freud and Erik Erikson, felt that play provided a catharsis, an emotional cleansing, to help children deal with negative experiences. In play children feel more grown-up and powerful, exert some control over their environments, and can relieve anxiety created by real-life conflicts. Play therapy, psychotherapy for children, often uses play and play equipment and materials in the diagnosis and treatment of children who have psychological conflicts and problems (Hughes 1995). Play therapy strategies and techniques vary depending on the philosophical approach of the therapist.

Piaget and his followers believed that play both reflects and is the medium through which children develop cognitively (Athey 1984). Based on his observations Piaget described a set of stages in the development of children's play. Many of today's early childhood programs have a Piagetian orientation to play. Children are allowed time and materials to play and their teachers trust they will "construct" their own understanding.

Theorist Lev Vygotsky also believed that play served as a vehicle for cognitive development. Vygotsky saw the special role of play as a way to bridge between what children already understand and what they will soon be able to understand with assistance from other more experienced players or through independent replay. Vygotsky called this space between what the child understands and what she or he will soon understand the "zone of proximal development." In Vygotsky's view, play provides an "anchor" between real objects and the ability to symbolize (Monighan-Nourot 1992).

Theorists have consistently confirmed the role of play in development. Recent research has recognized the developmental importance of play in children learning to self-regulate or control their physical, emotional, social and cognitive behaviors (Bodrova & Leong 2003; Bronson 2000). Current theory and research confirm the pivotal role of play in children's learning of some of the competencies and skills that lead to their development of competence, mastery, and control of themselves and the world.

Stages of Play

As children grow and develop they engage in different and increasingly complex types or stages of play. The ability to understand and identify the various stages of play is a valuable tool in your work with children of all ages. If you know that two 5-year-olds can play happily together building a road with blocks and sharing a single vehicle, but anticipate that two toddlers will play separately and each need their own truck, you will be able to make more sensitive judgments of what behaviors are reasonable to expect from the children and you will know how to provide developmentally appropriate opportunities for the stage of play of each child in your setting.

Because the different play stages tend to parallel the stages of cognitive and social development, the play of individual children can serve as a valuable assessment of development (see Figure 6.1). However, the stages of play and the milestones of cognitive and social development are different in that the appearance or dominance of one stage of play does not signal the extinction of the previous play stage. For example, a child will continue to enjoy sensorimotor experiences typical of the practice play of an early stage (for example, playing with water and sand) even after cooperative play of older preschool-age children has become their dominant form of play. Indeed, we think of the companionable silence of sitting and reading a book near a friend as a grown-up version of the parallel play of the typical toddler.

Stages of play have been described by various developmental theorists from several perspectives. Parten studied the social dimensions of play and identified types that typified different age groups. Piaget and Smilansky focused on the cognitive aspects of play.

Parten: Stages of Social Play

In the early 1930s, M. B. Parten developed categories of play that described the nature of the relationships among the players. Her categories of play continue to be used by early childhood educators. Parten identified six stages of social play that can be viewed along a continuum from minimal to maximal social involvement. The first two (unoccupied behavior and onlooker) are periods of observation preceding the venture into a new situation. The four remaining stages each dominate a particular age (although they occur at other ages as well), with children tending toward more and more social play as they get older.

- *Solitary play* (dominates in infancy). During solitary play, children play alone and independently with objects. Other children playing nearby go unnoticed. Although solitary play is dominant in infancy and is more typical in younger children, older children also select and benefit from solitary play.
- *Parallel play* (typical of toddlers). In parallel play, children play side by side but still are engaged with their own play objects. Little interpersonal interaction occurs, but each may be aware of and pleased by the company of a nearby companion.
- *Associative play* (seen most in young preschool-age children). Parten identified two forms of group play. Associative play is the first. It involves pairs and groups of children playing in the same area and sharing materials. Interaction may be brisk, but true cooperation and negotiation are rare. Two children each building a zoo in the block area, sharing animal props and talking about their zoo, but *not* creating a joint zoo or negotiating what will happen at their zoo, are involved in associative play.
- *Cooperative play* (characteristic of older preschool and kindergarten/primary-age children). In the second and most social form of group play, children actively work together to create sustained play episodes with joint themes. They plan, negotiate, and share responsibility and leadership. For example, a group of children pretending to go on a picnic might cooperatively decide what food to take, who should attend the event, how to get there, who will drive, and what joys and catastrophes await them on their outing (Parten 1932).

Piaget and Smilansky: Cognitive Stages of Play

Unlike Parten, who was concerned with the social aspects of play, Jean Piaget looked at how play supports cognitive development. He developed a framework with three stages of play development that are parallel to his stages of cognitive development. In the late 1960s Sara Smilansky adapted Piaget's stages of play, based on her observations of young children from more diverse cultural and economic backgrounds (Smilansky & Shefatya 1990). She categorized play into four types, similar to those of Piaget, and

Figure 6.1 Stages of Play and Stages of Development

	Piaget's Stages of Cognitive Development	Erikson's Stages of Social-Emotional Development	Parten's Stages of Play	Piaget's Stages of Play	Smilansky's Stages of Play
Infants (birth through 15–18 months)	**Sensorimotor Stage** (Birth–2 years)	**Trust vs. Mistrust**	**Solitary play** Children play alone with toys, if other children are nearby, they go unnoticed.	**Practice play** Children explore the sensory qualities of objects and practice motor skills.	**Functional play** Children engage in sensory and motor exploration of toys, materials, and people in order to learn about them.
Toddlers (15–18 months through 30–35 months)	**Preoperational Stage** (2–7 years)	**Autonomy vs. Shame and Doubt**	**Parallel play** Children play side-by-side with little interaction, engaged with their own toys, aware of and pleased by the company of others.		**Constructive play** Children manipulate objects in order to create something.
Young Preschool Children (30 months–4 years)		**Initiative vs. Guilt**	**Associative play** Pairs and groups of children play together and share materials but cooperation and negotiation rare.	**Symbolic play** Children use objects, actions, and roles to represent reality and familiar or imagined situations.	**Dramatic play** Children pretend to be other than what they are and use actions, objects, or words to represent things or situations.
Older Preschool and Kindergarten Children (4–6 years)			**Cooperative play** Groups of children engage in sustained play episodes in which they plan, negotiate, and share responsibility and leadership.		
Primary School Children (6–8 years)	**Concrete Operational Stage** (7–11 years)	**Industry vs. Inferiority**		**Games with rules** In solitary or group play children recognize and follow rules that conform to the expectations and goals of the game.	**Games with rules** Children behave according to rules in order to sustain play.

added an additional type—constructive play. Piaget's and Smilansky's stages provide only slightly different ways of looking at similar play behaviors. Smilansky's work can be seen as building on Piaget's.

- *Practice play* (Piaget) or *functional play* (Smilansky) (infancy to 2 years of age). In practice or functional play, children explore the sensory qualities of objects and practice motor skills. This stage parallels Piaget's sensorimotor stage of development. Children who are engaged in functional play repeat actions over and over again, as if practicing them. Both a baby who repeatedly drops a toy over the side of the crib for you to pick up, or a toddler who dumps and refills a coffee can over and over, are engaged in practice play. These actions are viewed as explorations to learn about objects. Although practice or functional play is the common play of the first two years, it does not disappear. A preschooler repeatedly pouring water from one container to another and a teenager repeatedly combing his already perfect coiffure in front of the mirror are both involved in practice play.
- *Symbolic play* (2 to 7 years of age). In symbolic play, children use one object to represent another object and use make-believe actions and roles to represent familiar or imagined situations. Symbolic play emerges during the preoperational period as the child begins to be able to use mental symbols or imagery.

The different forms of symbolic play are further separated by Smilansky into two categories: *constructive play,* in which the child uses real objects to build a representation of something according to a plan (e.g., creating a birthday cake with play dough and wooden sticks), and *dramatic and sociodramatic play,* in which children create imaginary roles and interactions where they pretend to be someone or something (mommy, doctor, dog, etc.) and use actions, objects, or words to represent things or situations (a block for an iron, an arm movement for steering a truck, or "woof woof" for the bark of a dog).

- *Games with rules* (7 to 11 years). In games with rules, children recognize and follow preset rules in the interest of sustaining solitary or group play that conforms to the expectations and goals of the games. During the concrete operational period, children's play is typified by games with rules, though they can be introduced to and enjoyed by much younger children. The ability to agree upon and negotiate rules is viewed as growing from the cooperation and negotiation that developed in cooperative play. Chutes and Ladders, dominoes, kickball, jump rope, and perhaps even peek-a-boo are examples of games with rules (Piaget 1962).

Understanding the Stages of Play

Understanding the social and cognitive stages of play allows you to provide appropriate play experiences for children and helps you to appreciate children's play behavior. An awareness of Parten's stages makes it more likely that you will understand rather than be irritated by the infant whose solitary play takes the form of repeatedly banging a rattle on a tray and never seems to tire of dumping objects on the floor. You will appreciate the movement toward social competence represented by the toddler who engages in parallel play by carrying the basket of cubes to the block rug to build beside a friend. You will understand that 2-year-olds might enjoy a game, such as "ring-around-the-rosy," led by a teacher. You will realize that they are only just beginning to be involved in associative play on their own and would be unlikely to initiate such a group game. Likewise, you may be somewhat concerned about a 4-year-old who rarely engages in the associative or cooperative play typical of her age, such as building a tower in the block corner, and never uses materials to pretend. This child may require encouragement or play training from you, discussed later in this chapter. Knowledge of the stages of play enables you to plan a program appropriate for the children in your class and gives you some important clues to use in observing the developmental progress of each child.

In her work concerning the nature and importance of dramatic and sociodramatic play, Smilansky points out that dramatic play represents a different and potentially higher level of play behavior than any other play. "Dramatic and sociodramatic play differs from the three other types of play in that it is person-oriented and not material and/or object oriented" (Smilansky & Shefatya 1990, 3). *Dramatic play* is acting out human relationships using symbols (when I put on the big boots and hat I'm the daddy). It may be carried out in a solitary or parallel play style. *Sociodramatic play* involves the acting out of complex interactions in cooperation with others. A story line is created, roles assigned, and changes negotiated as the play proceeds (I put on the big boots and the hat, and you can be the little boy and get in the car and I'll drive you to the zoo). "Sociodramatic play allows the child to be an actor, observer and interactor simultaneously, using his abilities in a common enterprise with other children" (Smilansky & Shefatya 1990, 3).

Smilansky identified the important elements of dramatic and sociodramatic play:

- *Imitative role-play.* The child undertakes a make-believe role and expresses it in imitative action and/or verbalization. (Miriam shows that she's a puppy by getting down on all fours and barking to ask for supper.)
- *Make-believe with regard to objects.* Toys, nonstructured materials, movements, or verbal declarations are substituted for real objects. (Miriam uses a block as a pretend bone.)
- *Make-believe with regard to actions and situations.* Verbal descriptions are substituted for actions and situations. (Miriam acts out being scared of another child who she says is a mean lady who wants to steal puppies.)
- *Persistence.* The child continues playing in a specific episode for at least 10 minutes. (Even though activity time is over, Miriam continues in the role of puppy and comes to circle time on all fours. She barks for the first song.)
- *Interaction.* At least two players respond to each other in the context of a play episode. (Miriam and Rivera both are pets, but Rivera is a kitty. They play together and meow, hiss, whine, purr, and bark to one another.)
- *Verbal communication.* Some of the verbal interaction relates to the play episode. (Periodically Rivera gives Miriam directions on the next event in the play such as, "It's nighttime and the puppies and kitties have to go to sleep for 100 minutes.") (Smilansky & Shefatya 1990, 24)

These elements of play have been used as a basis for evaluating the play skills of individual children. When a particular play skill is not seen, play skill training can be used to teach it to the child. (See the sample sociodramatic play checklist in Figure 6.4 later in the chapter.)

DIVERSITY AND PLAY

Drew, a 4-year-old African-American child, enters the big playground running and calls to his friend Jason, "Come on!" They both scramble up the big climbing structure and slide down the fireman's pole then crawl into the tunnel made of tires. Yuki, whose family emigrated from Asia, sits in the shade of a tree. She has collected all the pebbles she can find and has lined them up from biggest to smallest. Their teacher, Vikki, noticing both children, is aware that the children are each playing their preferred ways.

Play researchers and practitioners have studied play in a variety of settings and found that cultural background, social class, and gender are factors, other than stage of development, that interact in dynamic ways to influence the types, amount, and quality of play that children engage in. In the preceding vignette the differences in play preferences and activity level could be attributed to cultural or gender differences or to a combination of both.

An understanding of the reasons for different play preferences, abilities, and styles among children will increase your sensitivity to individuals and help you be more supportive of the play of children.

Culture, Social Class, and Play

In Euro-American culture play is often seen as the means by which children learn about the physical and social world and develop language. In some cultures it is valued as entertainment, and in still others it may be seen as a needless distraction from work in which children are expected to participate. The value a culture places on play influences how much support the adults provide. Where play is assumed to contribute to learning, the adults are more likely to make available the materials, settings, and time for play. If it is seen as relief from boredom or a waste of time, children may be left on their own to improvise times, places, and materials for play. Whichever the case, children in all cultures play (Johnson et al. 1999).

Sociodramatic play is useful in the evaluation of a child's cognitive and social competence. However, children from different cultures may not respond to the play props found in the typical early childhood program designed for middle-class American children. When the play props relate more closely to their life experiences, their play is likely to become richer and more complex. For this reason it is important to provide play props and other materials that represent the cultural diversity of the children. For example, some cultural groups value the extended family, while the usual dramatic play area often represents the Euro-American nuclear family model. The addition of props that help represent the elders of the family might increase play in this area by children from Native-American, African-American, Mexican-American, and Asian-American families (Trawick-Smith 1994). Likewise, children whose home play settings have been the forest, the desert, or urban streets and yards may display more complex sociodramatic play in outdoor environments. You can support this play by providing props that travel beyond the dramatic play area of your classroom. The assembly of mobile prop kits (stored in boxes) that suggest gardening, farming, fishing, gas station, police officer, firefighter, and camping are a few of the possibilities (Johnson et al. 1999).

Cultures differ in the approach to relationships among people and these differences can affect the play abilities of children. A child whose cultural background emphasizes cooperation and inclusiveness may be intimidated by children who have been taught to be competitive and exclusive. As an educator you may need to assist such a child to learn how to enter a play situation dominated by children who may exclude others or not think to include them in their play.

Early research on play and development often identified play deficits and linked them to cultural background or the deprivations of poverty. More recent work by researchers and practitioners has uncovered bias in the prior work. When children of different cultural and social class backgrounds are observed at play in settings and with materials with which they are familiar, they too display rich, complex play behaviors.

175

Your job as an early childhood educator is to find ways to bridge the differences between your classroom and the home environments. You can do this by thinking beyond the dramatic play area and the usual middle-class, Euro-American-style housekeeping material found there. As you come to know the children in your group you can introduce play materials and props throughout your program that relate to their life experiences.

Gender and Play

Another characteristic of play has to do with differences between the play of girls and boys. Although the play of all children has many similarities, particularly during the first 3 years of life, differences exist in the play behavior and characteristics of boys and girls. It is difficult to determine the source of these characteristics. Evidence exists for a biological basis for more aggressive play in males, but the social environment also influences the expression of these characteristics (Schickedanz, Schickedanz, & Forsythe 1993). Some gender differences in play may be attributed to gender stereotyping. From birth, adults tend to describe girl babies as little, soft, and pretty and boy babies as big, strong, and active, even when identical in size and activity level. Toys, books, and media given to children tend to depict boys as more active, competent, and adventurous while girls are depicted in supporting roles and are shown to need help to overcome incompetence and fearfulness. Many gender-related play characteristics may be influenced by both environment and inheritance, but it is difficult to assign primary influence to one or the other.

Although the causes may remain a mystery, boys at all ages engage in active play of a rough-and-tumble nature, use the outdoors, and play in groups more than girls do. Girls begin to prefer same-sex playmates earlier than boys, but both do so between 2 and 5 years of age. By age 5, girls begin to be interested in cross-sex play, but boys tend to persist in their same-sex preference throughout the elementary years. The approach to materials and toys differs in both choice and uses. Girls generally prefer art materials, dolls, and small constructive toys and play with them in quieter ways. Boys generally prefer blocks and wheeled vehicles and play with them more noisily and repetitiously. Girls play with toys regardless of the gender category people ordinarily assign to the item; boys avoid "girls' toys." Boys appear to prefer larger groups of playmates from preschool age through the primary years, while girls show a marked preference for small groups (Johnson et al. 1999).

Although these gender differences have been noted generally, all of us know many individual children who do not conform to these stereotypical play behaviors. Averages or norms are not individuals—all girls are active at times, and all boys engage in quiet play at times. It is important to remember that girls and boys both explore, build, and pretend and need our support in fully realizing their play potential. The similarities are more important than the differences.

If you wanted to encourage Drew and Jason (described in the story at the beginning of this section) to engage in some art and literacy activities, an easel set up in a corner of the playground or a blanket beneath a tree stocked with books might attract them as a quiet break from more rambunctious play episodes. The same setup might entice Yuki and her friends to the playground, where they may discover some other more vigorous activities to enjoy.

THE VALUE OF PLAY

As an early childhood educator you will be confronted with frequent challenges to explain the value of play to families, educators of other age groups, and program administrators. This demand for explanations is reasonable in the current era in which the push for academic achievement continues to grow. You may occasionally hear the parental question "Why do they play all day? When are you going to start teaching them something?" Because play is so important for development it is important that you know how to explain its value even before you are asked to do so.

Children need to play. Play supports the development of the *whole child*—a person able to sense, move, think, relate to others, communicate, and create. It helps children to learn without direct instruction or time set aside for specific subject areas. The importance of play was recognized by the United Nations General Assembly in November 1989, which approved a convention on the rights of the child that asserts that every child of the world has the right to play and must have the opportunity to do so.

Early childhood professionals have long been able to justify play's value in supporting physical, social, and emotional development. In recent decades early childhood educators have met with ever-increasing pressure to justify play in terms of how it contributes to cognitive and language development. It is of particular interest that researchers have found positive relationships between the play abilities of children and their subsequent academic achievement and school adjustment. In their book *Facilitating Play: A Medium for Promoting Cognitive, Socio-Emotional, and Academic Development in Young Children* (1990), Sara Smilansky and Leah Shefatya describe many studies in which competence at sociodramatic play is highly correlated with cognitive, creative, and social abilities.

Play researchers continue to discover how play facilitates the development of children in all areas. As an early childhood educator whose program provides opportunities for children to play, you are likely to have many occasions in which you will need to understand and explain the role of play in children's development.

The Value of Play in Physical Development

From infancy on, children display an innate drive to gain control of their physical behavior as they strive to reach for and eventually grasp and manipulate objects of interest (Bodrova & Leong 2003; Bronson 2000). Children learn best when they have bodies that are strong, healthy, flexible, and coordinated and when all of their senses are operating. Play contributes to physical development and health throughout the early childhood years. Children at play develop physical competence efficiently and comprehensively. The vigorous activity of children's own spontaneous play builds the strength, stamina, and skills they need to succeed as learners.

Children have an innate drive to explore, discover, and master skills. The concentrated play of childhood leads naturally to the physical mastery that was probably essential to our survival as a species. Play is of prime importance in the development of *perceptual-motor coordination* (the ability to use sensory information to direct motor activity) and in the attainment and maintenance of the good health that is necessary if optimal development is to occur.

The Value of Play in Emotional Development

The control of emotions and the behaviors that accompany some emotional responses is central to ongoing development. Young infants have the challenge of learning how to control basic impulses and how to reduce or control the tension resulting from overstimulation (Bodrova & Leong 2003; Bronson 2000). Therapists and educators have long appreciated the rich emotional value of play. Freud and his followers identified play as a primary avenue in which children express and work through their fears, anxieties, and desires. Contemporary therapists still use play as the medium for helping children deal with the feelings associated with traumatic events and disturbing situations in their lives.

Children at play devise and confront challenges and anticipate changes. In the process they master their fears; resolve internal conflicts; act out anger, hostility, and frustration; and resolve personal problems for which the "real" world offers no apparent solutions. It is no wonder children are highly motivated to play all day.

Children at play feel they are in control of their world, practicing important skills that lead them to a sense of mastery over their environment and self. They discover the behaviors and the emotional expressiveness that suitably communicate their inner state and enable them to maintain the self-control that is necessary for a cooperative relationship with other players. For this reason those of us who work with young children value play for its role in healthy emotional development.

The Value of Play in Social Development

Emotional and behavioral self-regulation are closely related to the development of social competence. Children need to develop the ways of expressing emotions and working out behaviors that enable them to create positive relationships with other children (Bronson 2000).

From birth, children are enmeshed in a social environment. Survival depends on the care of adults from the moment of birth. Caregivers *play* with infants in a way that is unlike anything adults do in any other life situation. You will hear a grown-up addressing questions to the infant and then taking the infant's part to answer, "Now, don't you have about the most beautiful eyes in the whole world?" "Well, of course I do, I got them from my daddy." An ordinarily dignified adult will make undignified noises and facial expressions ("ZZZZZZZZZZZZZ Gotcha!") and respond with the greatest joy when the baby laughs aloud for the first time. Infant-adult play progresses to games like pat-a-cake and this-little-piggy.

All this social play leads to increased social interaction skills. Children learn how to initiate play with relatives, family friends, and peers. In early play encounters, children learn awareness of others, cooperation, turn-taking, and social language. They become aware of group membership, develop a social identity, and learn a lot about the rules and values governing the family, community, and culture. The play becomes increasingly complex and is sustained for greater periods of time. By the time children reach their second birthday, most are making attempts to portray social relationships through dramatic play. By age 4 or 5 most will have learned the things they need to know to enact complex social relationships with their peers in highly developed sociodramatic play. Soon after, they become able to play rule-governed games. Through this play, social concepts such as fairness, justice, and cooperation evolve and influence play behavior and other social relationships.

The social competence developed in sociodramatic play leads to the development of cooperative attitudes and behaviors. Most peers, families, and educators prize the sharing, helpful, and cooperative behaviors associated with high levels of social competence.

The Value of Play in Cognitive Development

A major task of the early childhood years is the development of the skills and strategies for learning and problem solving. In play children learn how to set goals, plan how to proceed, and create ways to organize their approach to cognitive tasks (Bronson 2000). Play is the primary medium through which young children make sense of their experiences and construct ideas about how the physical and social world works. The functional play that begins in infancy and persists through life is basic to the process of learning about the properties of objects and learning how things work.

Constructive play, typical of the toddler, is the mode we use throughout life for discovering and practicing how to use unfamiliar tools and materials (for example, learning to use a computer or a map).

The dramatic (pretend) play of preschool children has a critical role in the development of representational or symbolic thought and the eventual ability to think abstractly. In sociodramatic play children develop understanding of the world by reenacting with playmates experiences (e.g., a trip to the grocery store) they have had or observed. They alter their understanding based on the response and ideas of their friends ("I'm the store man and you have to give me 50 dollars for that orange. Oranges cost lots of money!") and then use the new meaning as they again experience the real world ("Mom, do we have enough money for oranges?"). This circular process is one in which information is constantly being gathered, organized, and used. It is one of the primary ways in which children construct their understanding of the world. We have found the following description of children's dramatic play to be useful in clarifying its significance:

> The familiarity of life's scripts is what makes the daily life of adults efficient. . . . We are free to think about other things. . . . We recognize this only when we find ourselves in an unfamiliar setting—driving a borrowed car, . . . placing a phone call in a foreign country. Young children . . . play in order to find their way around in what is for them the foreign country of adults, to master its daily scripts. (Jones & Reynolds 1992, 10)

Sociodramatic play is of particular interest to play researchers and practitioners because of its significance in cognitive development. A high level of competence in sociodramatic play has been found to be associated with cognitive maturity (Smilansky & Shefatya 1990).

The Value of Play in Integrating Development

Throughout this book, we refer to the development of the *whole child.* At play, more than at any other time, children engage all aspects of themselves and most fully express who they are, what they are able to do, and what they know and feel. Blocks, dramatic play props, construction toys, art materials, books, puzzles, climbing structures, sand, and water—equipment and materials found in almost every early childhood program—are rich in their potential for supporting all aspects of development.

Three or four children building a tower in a block area near a shelf stocked with several hundred blocks of 8 to 10 different shapes and sizes, a few vehicles, animal and human figures, have a full range of development and learning opportunities. They provide an example of how play supports development:

- *Physical development.* Coordination and strength are enhanced as blocks are lifted, carried, and stacked; small muscles are developed as children decorate the top of the building with a row of smaller blocks; and sensory awareness is gained as they handle the blocks, feel the texture, and note the grain of the wood.

- *Social development.* Cooperation and negotiation skills are practiced as they work out how to share materials so that they can also build a garage and create an office building; interpersonal sensitivity is used as they decide how to include a new child.

- *Emotional development.* A sense of competence is gained as the children create the building and garage based on a plan and accomplish the task in cooperation with friends.

- *Cognitive development.* Problem-solving skills are developed as the children solve the problems of balance and symmetry inherent in construction. And they plan and communicate as they build the agreed-upon structures.

Reflect on more memories of play

Reflect and write about a time when you developed or improved a skill or learned through play. Did the activity take energy and work? Was it still play?

The Value of Play in Integrating Curriculum

The preceding list contains only a few of the things a group of children might be learning and developing as they play together in the block area. Such a list could be developed for every spontaneous play experience in an early childhood program.

Spontaneous play in learning centers also integrates curriculum areas. In the block play example, the children created a building with an attached garage. What follows are a few examples of how you (and the children) might integrate curriculum based on the play experience.

You might introduce *social studies* concepts by suggesting to the children that they use what they know to create some ways for people to get to work at their office building. Children might then create roads and railways or build a bus by lining up a row of chairs. *Math* is occurring when one child comes up with the idea of setting out enough seats for all the players. Observing children riding the bus might lead you to introduce *music, creative drama,* and *movement* experiences by singing and miming "The Wheels on the Bus" with them as they ride. A child might initiate a *literacy* experience by asking you to help make a sign to label the parking garage. You might suggest that children use *art* materials to make road signs.

Every play activity contributes to the developing child. Just as "transportation to work" became the curriculum in this example, so could a curriculum focus—for example, on "community"—be introduced into the children's play opportunities. In the block area you might add street signs, trucks, cars, ambulances, planes, and other vehicles to suggest the building of a community's roads and streets. In the dramatic play area you might add cereal boxes, plastic food, a cash register, and a shopping basket to suggest the creation of a community grocery store.

SUPPORTING DEVELOPMENT THROUGH PLAY

As you learn about play you will come to understand it as a natural and compelling way for children to develop. You will then devise a variety of ways to support development through play. As an early childhood professional you have a significant role in children's play. By your attitudes and your actions you can support or discourage play. As you do so, you influence the nature of the play.

Supportive Attitudes

When you understand play's role in children's development and learning, you approach children at play with an attitude of respect and appreciation. You see play as your ally. When you understand that you have an important role to play in facilitating children's play, you approach it with an attitude of serious attention. You see the support of play as an important part of your job.

Some practitioners in early childhood education and care accept play as part of the "care" aspect of their work but fail to respect and trust it as a primary process in their "educator" role. These individuals may feel uncomfortable when children play in the educational part of the program and may try to intervene in play to make it seem more like "school." This lack of comfort with play indicates an incomplete understanding of play and its role in education and care.

Your view of play will be influenced by your professional setting and tasks. Those who work with infants and toddlers generally receive support and approval for giving play an important role in their programs. The same is true for many, though not all, who work with 3- to 5-year-olds. If you teach in an elementary school you may find that play is not understood or supported by your colleagues or the families of the children you teach. In this case, your appreciation for play must be coupled with information that supports its importance.

Supportive Roles

Seang and Jennifer are playing in the dramatic play area with the menus, dishes, and play food. Sharon, the teacher, enters, sits down and asks, "Is this the Fun Look Restaurant?" (naming a recently visited restaurant). "Can I have some noodles with black beans?" Seang looks quickly around the area then says to Sharon, "Can we get the restaurant stuff"? Sharon smiles and nods as she lifts the restaurant kit from the nearby storage cabinet.

Children play regardless of the circumstances. What you do before and during their play can make a vital difference in the quality of play and in what children gain in the process. Respect and appreciation for children's play brings with it the realization that in play children, not adults, are the stars. You can, however, fulfill many supporting roles that facilitate their play. Figure 6.2 graphically depicts how you can support children's play. Your role begins by setting the stage but continues throughout all the roles.

Stage Manager

The essential elements of play are *time, space, equipment,* and *materials.* Your first supporting role in children's play is providing these elements. Elizabeth Jones and Gretchen Reynolds (1992) refer to this important role as that of *stage manager.* Being a stage manager involves more than simply setting out materials for play. It includes selecting and organizing materials, space, and equipment so that they suggest play that is meaningful to the children. Children of all ages must have time to play. Early childhood educators who value play use time flexibly. They view children's play as more important than strict adherence to a schedule. You will learn more about creating an appropriate schedule and a stimulating play environment when you read Chapter 7, "Caring for Children," and Chapter 8, "The Learning Environment."

Figure 6.2 **Supporting Children's Play**

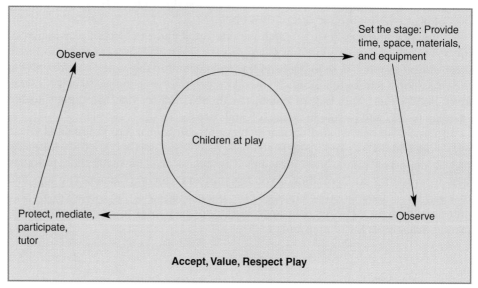

The artful arrangement of equipment and materials assists children in what Jones and Reynolds refer to as distinguishing figure-ground relationships—in other words, distinguishing what you are looking at from the background (Jones & Reynolds 1992). Too much equipment, or equipment that is disorganized, may be confusing and inhibit play. The cycle of setting up, playing, and reordering the environment is an ongoing process in early childhood settings. Early childhood educators participate in this process willingly and view it as critical to maintaining an environment that invites play.

Observer

Another important role you will have in children's play is that of observer. Thoughtful observation is the best tool that you have for coming to truly respect and appreciate play. When you observe carefully and assess what you see based on what you know about child development and play, you are better able to understand what is happening for children, what children might need, and how you can support them in play. This might involve offering a child a space to play near but not with other children when you have observed that the child still functions best in a parallel play mode. Or it could mean providing a length of cloth for a pretend cape when you observe a child dragging her blanket out of her cubby for this purpose.

Systematic observation can yield important insight about play. Several checklists or scales have been developed for looking at play behavior. These tools can be used to increase your understanding of play. Johnson, Christie, and Yawkey (1999), in their book *Play and Early Childhood Development,* describe several scales in detail and give instructions for using them to gain valuable information about the play of children. The social-cognitive play scale (see Figure 6.3) codes play on its social and cognitive dimensions and enables you to get a quick look at a child's stage of play development.

To develop a profile on the play behavior of each child in your class you use a sampling system over a period of several days. To begin you make a gridded sheet like the one in Figure 6.3 for each child in the class, shuffle the sheets so they will have a random order, start your sample with the top sheet, observe the child, and then place it on the bottom of the pile to be used for subsequent samples on the same day. Observe the

Figure 6.3 **Social-Cognitive Play Scale**

Name _____ Observation Dates _____

SOCIAL LEVEL

		Solitary	Parallel	Group
C O G N I T I V E L E V E L	Functional			
	Constructive			
	Dramatic			
	Games			

Source: Summarized from *Play and Early Childhood Development* (2nd ed.), by J. E. Johnson, J. F. Christie, & T. D. Yawkey, 1999, Glenview, IL: Scott, Foresman.

child for approximately 15 seconds, mark the play behavior on the sheet, then move on to the next child. You can sample three children each minute, so if you had a group of 15 you could take six samples of each child in a half-hour. After 4 or 5 days you would have enough material to see typical patterns of play behavior for each child. In a classroom of infants you would probably find more play occurrences marked in the solitary-functional grid. If you were to shadow an 8-year-old for a day many of the play behaviors would likely fall in the lower right-hand corner, indicating games played with groups of age-mates. Four- and 5-year-old children are going to be engaged in a good deal of group-oriented, dramatic play (Johnson et al. 1999). This information is useful to you in making decisions about what intervention might be needed to support the play of individual children.

In the example at the beginning of this section the teacher, Sharon, had observed that Seang did not often engage in sociodramatic play and intervened appropriately as stage manager, co-player, and tutor. Although the social-cognitive play scale may be used to see whether Seang is engaging in play at the social and cognitive level that you might expect, other instruments can be used to find out just which of the play elements (p. 174) she needs help with (Johnson et al. 1999; Smilansky & Shefatya 1990). The sociodramatic play checklist (Figure 6.4) may be used to determine which group-dramatic play skills each child is using and which are missing.

Figure 6.4 Sociodramatic Play Checklist

Instructions: Select children who have shown infrequent engagement in group-dramatic play on the social-cognitive play scale. Observe these children closely over several days in a variety of settings (indoors in the dramatic play area, blocks, etc., and outdoors). Check the appropriate column when you observe the play elements being used by the child. Refer to page 174 for a description of each of the elements.

Name	Imitative Role-Play	Make-Believe w/Objects	Make-Believe w/Actions	Persistence in Role-Playing	Interactions w/Others	Verbal Communication

Source: *Facilitating Play: A Medium for Promoting Cognitive, Socio-Emotional, and Academic Development in Young Children,* by S. Smilansky & L. Shefatya, 1990, Gaithersburg, MD: Psychosocial and Educational Publications.

Protector and Mediator

Children's play is most productive when they feel safe from harm and relatively free from interference. Because group play has the potential for disorder and disruption you will sometimes take the role of play protector and play mediator. As opposed to limit setter, disciplinarian, or rule enforcer, a *mediator* collaborates with children. As a mediator you help individuals to work out conflicts and concerns when a neutral third party is needed. A mediator does not intervene when the participants can handle a problem on their own. Children's conflicts in play can give you an opportunity to teach peaceful conflict resolution skills (see Chapter 9), which will assist children in handling problems on their own.

As a play *protector* you maintain the delicate balance between guidelines that support and sustain play and excessive control that interferes with or limits play. You encourage play but do not let it get dangerous or uncontrolled. The way you enter children's play to ensure safety and order needs to be sensitive and respectful of the

184

play ("Excuse me, birds, would you like me to help you move your nest here under the table? I'm afraid it might fall out of the tree and the eggs will crack."), rather than intrusive, thus interrupting the play ("Get down from the table. Tables are not for playing on; someone might get hurt.").

Dramatic play episodes that are prolonged and engrossing often attract latecomers who wish to join in. In this situation the play protector and mediator can observe carefully and assist shy or anxious children in entering the play. Delicacy is the order of the day. It is best if you can unobtrusively help the child find a role. For example, in a camp scene you might say, "Would you like to get wood for the campfire? I think I know where we can find some." If the entering child is disruptive you may help by setting the child a task that makes use of high energy in the scene, such as chopping the wood.

The hallmark of highly developed dramatic play is that the children use objects to represent things: A bowl becomes a hat, a plate becomes a steering wheel, a block becomes a telephone. Therefore play can be a disorderly process, as play materials for one type of activity are transformed in children's imaginative pretend. This tendency presents a dilemma. If you are overly concerned about the proper use of equipment, you may curtail play and important learning; if you provide no limits, the resulting disorder can be overwhelming for both you and the children. Deciding on the best course requires sensitivity and judgment. It can help to see the use to which children are putting materials; if they are being used in a way that is important to extending a play episode, don't discourage the activity. For example, in a classroom we know, when manipulative toys were consistently being used as "food" in the nearby dramatic play area the teachers moved the manipulative toy area and added materials to dramatic play to use as food.

Participant

The conventional wisdom in early childhood education was once that teachers should not become directly involved in the play of children. Play was seen as the arena in which children were to be left free to work out their inner conflicts and exercise power over their environment. It was regarded as the duty of an adult to keep out of the child's play world so as not to interfere with important psychological development. The only valid roles allocated to the adult were those of stage manager and observer. In recent decades, however, research has pointed to reasons for joining in children's play as a *participant.*

Why should adults play with children? When adults play with children they lend support to the amount and quality of the play. Your participation gives children a strong message that play is a valuable activity in its own right, so they play longer and learn new play behaviors from observing you. It also builds rapport with the children. As you learn more about their interests, needs, and characteristics you are better able to interact with them. When you participate, play lasts much longer, and it becomes more elaborate.

Of course, your participation must harmonize with the play of the children or else it will disrupt or end the play (Johnson et al. 1999). When you play with children, take your cues from the children and allow them to maintain control of the play. You limit your role to actions and comments that extend and enrich the play. When you join in, it is important that you do so in a way that supports ongoing play. Sometimes children offer a role to an adult. "Would you like a cup of coffee?" is an invitation to join a restaurant scene being enacted. If not invited, you might observe and then approach the player who seems to be taking leadership and ask to be seated as a customer and in this way gain entry into the play. As a customer you might inquire about the price of a cup of coffee, ask for cream to put in it, and praise the chef for the delicious pancakes she prepared. By asking questions, requesting service, and responding to things children have done, you introduce new elements into the play without taking over.

185

Sometimes teachers think they should intervene in children's play to teach concepts or vocabulary. We once observed a teacher stepping into a play scenario to comment on the colors and shapes of the food being consumed at a pretend picnic. Just as this interjection might interrupt the conversational flow at a real picnic, the interruption did not lead to a meaningful discussion of colors and shapes, and it stopped two players having a lively interchange on the merits of feeding hamburgers to the pretend dog. It is possible to help children to be aware of new ideas in play, but it takes skill to do so without manipulating and diverting the activity. For example, when joining the group at a pretend picnic it would be possible to comment, "Could you please pass me that red apple? It looks very tasty," rather than, "What color is this apple?"

Why play with children? Perhaps the best reason is because it is a way to share their world, to demonstrate your respect, and to renew your appreciation of the complexities and importance of children's play.

Tutor

Although children play naturally, not all children fully develop play skills. Children who have been deprived of opportunities to play, whose families do not value play, or who are traumatized by violence may need the help of a *tutor* in learning to play.

A study conducted by Smilansky (1968) in Israel found that children from low-income families in which parents lacked a high school education engaged less often in dramatic and sociodramatic play than did children from more affluent families. Since then other researchers have found the same pattern in other countries. Intervention strategies were designed to teach the play skills that a child lacked. In this play tutoring, you demonstrate or model a missing skill until the child begins to use the skill in spontaneous play situations. For example, if a child is dependent on realistic props you might offer substitution ideas—"Let's pretend that these jar lids are our plates" or "Let's pretend that the sand is salt"—until the child begins to do so independently. It is important to note that the goal of play tutoring is to teach play skills in the context of the spontaneous play episode. The adult does not change the content of the play by introducing new themes or taking a directing role. Play tutoring has proven effective in improving the dramatic and sociodramatic play skills of children, which in turn has brought about gains in cognitive and social development.

Other children also benefit from play tutoring. Just as some children lack play skills because they are deprived of a safe physical and emotional environment in which to play, other children do not develop play skills because they are deprived of time to play. They are compelled to conform to adult standards of behavior, to excel academically at an early age, and to master skills typically developed by older children. To them, play time is something they must "steal" from their busy schedule of dance lessons, soccer practice, birthday parties, and full-day school (Elkind 1981). Optimal development requires challenges, but it also requires relief from burdensome responsibility. Play may save these children from burnout at an early age.

> **Reflect on playing in school**
>
> Reflect and write about a time when you played in school. Where did you play? Who supported your play? How much time did you have for play? What do you think your teachers thought about your play? Why do you still remember this play today?

THE SPECIAL ROLE OF OUTDOOR PLAY

It is likely that some of your most poignant memories of play involve playing outdoors. Why? While all play is important there is something special about playing out-of-doors. Perhaps it is the freedom to run until you are exhausted, to yell as loud as you can, and to discover the limits of your physical abilities. Maybe it's the challenge of learning to use equipment like trikes, swings, and wagons, or the excitement of overcoming your fear at the top of a slide. Perhaps it is the opportunity to experience the adventure and unpredictability of nature. It might be feeling the joy of play that is not as bound by adult rules. Whatever the reason, outdoor play has a special role in programs for young children and deserves special consideration.

What is different about outdoor play? It is obvious that the outdoors affords children the opportunity for a wider range of large motor play than a classroom can. Similarly it is the place where children can engage in messy, sensory play with water, dirt, and sand without the mess-avoiding precautions of indoors. And it comes as no surprise to anyone that the outdoors is a much better place to explore and learn about the natural world and its animals, plants, and weather.

There are additional, less obvious, reasons that outdoor play is important. Young children's social development is enhanced when they play outside. Away from the density of play materials and the restrictions of the classroom, children out-of-doors have more space to develop friendships. They learn to be leaders, learn to be a part of a group, and they learn to be alone. Frost and Strickland (1985) report that children play differently outdoors than they do indoors. They engage in play that is more complex, filled with language, and less stereotyped by gender.

Children's lives and children's play in the 21st century are probably more restricted and controlled than they were when you were growing up. Because of this the children in your care may have few opportunities to play outdoors in their home lives. Knowing this, it is important for early childhood educators to advocate for young children, whatever their age and wherever they live, to have blocks of time each day to play outdoors.

Violence and Children's Play

Children's play reflects children's experience. The prevalence of violence in society and in television programming (much of which is aimed at an audience of children) makes it almost certain that in any group some children will introduce violence and war play into dramatic play. Although early childhood educators generally encourage children's spontaneous dramatic play, it is common for gun play to be forbidden. The proscription of gun and war play is a response to the fact that it tends to dominate otherwise peaceful classrooms. Additionally, in violent play children tend to imitate the stereotypic behavior of media characters and the violent story action of the programs. Imitation and repetition replace imagination and creativity (Carlsson-Paige & Levin 1987).

This dilemma requires a decision. Should you prohibit children's violent play, or allow children to play out any drama they choose? In deciding whether and how to intervene, it helps to understand some of the reasons that children are so attracted to violent play:

- Young children are fascinated by heroes, weapons, and machines. In a world where they are virtually powerless, young children are drawn to power.
- Violent play involves fast action and a thrilling chase. Adults find this exciting, and so do children.
- Today's toy weapons and accessories are much more realistic than were those in previous years. This realism is tantalizing and often creates a strong response in other children and adults.

- Intense interest may be evoked by sophisticated marketing aimed at children through television.
- Peer approval is important to young children in the preschool years. When one child has a highly prized toy, others want one.

Several strategies can be used in coping with violent play:

- Observe the violent play to help you understand what it means to the children.
- Participate in children's play by asking questions to increase empathy, such as, "How does the bad guy feel? Who does he play with when he goes home? What does he do on his birthday?" In doing so, it is possible to help children to think beyond stereotypes.
- Guide children in choosing times, places, and behaviors that do not interfere with the play of the group. For example, just as yelling and shouting disturbs others indoors, shooting and crashing is also disruptive. Ask children to think of where and when such play will not disturb other people.

In a society where violence is prevalent, we cannot eliminate children's fascination with violence. We can provide children with alternative models of human relationships and help them learn to be responsible and thoughtful members of their community.

Gender-Stereotyped Play

As noted earlier, some recognizable and persistent differences are present in the ways boys and girls play. Because these differences are in part a reflection of the stereotypes present in the environment, we can support all children engaging in a diverse range of play activities. We believe it is reasonable for early childhood educators to take steps to overcome and avoid gender stereotyping in the books and materials offered to girls and boys—to make certain that both males and females are depicted in a variety of family and occupational roles in books and posters.

Similarly, the environment can be arranged to encourage children to play with a wide range of materials. One way to encourage more diverse play for both boys and girls is by integrating block (particularly large block) and dramatic play areas. Another important way to overcome gender-stereotyped play is through your expectations and behavior. As you practice ball skills with girls and involve boys in domestic dramatic play episodes, you are taking small, important steps toward breaking down gender stereotypes that limit the choices of children in our culture.

> **Reflect on play you've observed**
>
> Think about a classroom you recently observed. How did the children play? How did the adults facilitate play? What seemed to be their attitudes toward play? Did you observe violent play or gender-stereotyped play? How did it make you feel? How did the adults respond? How did this affect children?

FINAL THOUGHTS

The full realization of the learning potential of play ensures that you will value it in its own right and make full use of it in your work with children. In this enthusiasm for play as a tool for promoting development, it is important not to lose sight of the exuberant, joyful, and nonsensical aspects of play. We urge you to value play. Treasure the creativity in fantasy and see worlds open up as children pretend. Appreciate the bravery, joy, and exhilaration as children take risks, laugh hysterically, run, fall, tumble, and roll without restraint. The uninhibited, imaginative quality of play distinguishes child from adult, play from nonplay. When we appreciate and understand the power of play for leading children to a full realization of their human potential, we realize that adult restraint on children's play can be harmful.

You may need to become an advocate for children and play. This role can be hard if other educators and children's families don't understand the value of play. We urge you to learn about play and help others to understand play's importance, not only in learning but as an inoculation against the stress and pressures that society imposes on children. The children in your care need the opportunity to play now. You can speak to protect, support, and ensure them this right. When you do, you give them a precious gift.

LEARNING OUTCOMES

When you read this chapter, thoughtfully complete selected assignments from the "To Learn More" section, and prepare items from the "For Your Portfolio" section, you will be demonstrating your progress in meeting NAEYC **Standard 1: Promoting Child Development and Learning** and **Standard 4: Teaching and Learning, Sub-standard 4b: Using Developmentally Effective Approaches.**

Key elements:

- Knowing and understanding young children's characteristics
- Using developmental knowledge to create healthy, respectful, supportive, and challenging learning environments
- Knowing, understanding, and using effective approaches, strategies, and tools for early education

TO LEARN MORE

Observe Two Groups of Children: Observe groups of children of two different ages, spending a half-day in each group. Compare them and report on the following:

- The types of play in which the children engage
- The stages of play shown by children
- What the adult's attitudes toward and beliefs about play seem to be
- What the adults do to facilitate play in their programs

Interview Two Educators: Ask the educators about how they view play and report on their responses regarding:

- The role of play in their classrooms and in the development of the children they teach
- What they do to support play in their program
- How they handle the issues of war play and gender-stereotyped play in their program

FOR YOUR PORTFOLIO

Write an Article: Write an article for a school or classroom newsletter addressed to a group of families who have questions about the role of play in the early childhood program. Explain your rationale for making play an important part of the child's early childhood education.

Create a Poster: Design a poster to educate others about the value of play. Choose a play material (for example, play dough), a type of play (for example, dramatic play), or a play experience (for example, jumping rope). Your goal is to help an av-

erage person (such as a parent) understand how this kind of play experience contributes to young children's development.

Support a Play Interaction: Describe a play interaction during which you played one or more of the supportive roles—stage manager, observer, protector/mediator, participant, or tutor. Describe how the children responded to you and how the play episode worked, how long it lasted, and what elements of play were used by the children.

7

Caring for Children

We must have . . . a place where children can have a whole group of adults they can trust.

Margaret Mead

● ●

*V*irtually all children in the United States receive some care and education outside of their homes. Early childhood programs are second homes for children. Whether in full-day child care, part-day preschool, kindergarten, or elementary school, all young children deserve to be in a good place—a place that allows them to feel safe and secure, and that encourages close and meaningful relationships with adults and other children.

A good place for children is flexible enough to be responsive to their needs and stable enough to provide security. The safety of the environment and the quality of relationships will make—or fail to make—the program a place where development and learning can occur.

PHYSICAL SAFETY AND HEALTH

Of the many important aspects of an early childhood teacher's job, maintaining safety and health comes first in the eyes of the world and the children's families. All states have regulations for safety and health that are a mandatory part of program licensing standards. Keeping children safe and healthy is, in large measure, a matter of common sense. Protect children from hazards. Supervise them well. Make sure they have clean air, food, water, and facilities needed for health. Teach them how to keep themselves safe and healthy.

Although these things may seem obvious and simple, they are complex and sometimes difficult to implement in a setting for a group of children. In fact, when programs are evaluated by measures such as the accreditation standards of the National Association for the Education of Young Children, health standards are among the most frequent areas where problems are encountered.

We recommend that you use a resource such as *Healthy Young Children* (Aronson 2002b) or *Caring for Our Children* (American Academy of Pediatrics, American Public Health Association, & National Resource Center for Health and Safety in Child Care 2002) to gain awareness of the broad scope of safety and health concerns in programs for young children. The *Caring for Our Children* standards are available online (http://nrc.uchsc.edu), at the Web site of the National Resource Center.

A Safe Place

A family that entrusts the care of their child to an early childhood program expects the program environment to be safe. They trust that staff are knowledgeable and skilled in selecting safe equipment, materials, and activities. Further, they assume that every precaution will be taken to prevent accidents and supervise children for safety.

A safe program for children has sound facilities and safe furnishings; equipment and materials do not present hazards. Staff follow regulations, policies, and procedures designed to protect children from harm and are trained in first aid and CPR. Plans are in place so that children are cared for and protected in the event of a disaster.

What Is Safe?

Decisions about safety are influenced by many factors including the age, experience, temperament, and skills of the children. The size of the group, the adult-child ratio, the purpose and policies of the program, the philosophy and beliefs of the staff, as well as particular circumstances, also determine safe practice. Adults differ greatly in their ideas of what constitutes an unsafe situation or practice. Many safety measures are absolutely necessary for the well-being of all young children; others are not as clear-cut. Educators must weigh possible risks against the potential for learning. The skill and joy gained by climbing a tree and sitting among its branches must be weighed against the damage that might occur if a child falls out of the tree.

Individuals have different opinions about some circumstances related to children's safety. For instance, some educators and family members advocate that potentially hazardous tools such as sharp knives and scissors be banned in early childhood programs, while others argue that learning the proper use of these tools is the best protection against possible injury. An inclined trike path or a demanding play structure may be considered a hazard by one teacher, while another views these as just-right challenges for a group of preschool-age children. Other decisions, such as covering electrical outlets, are less likely to be controversial.

When you make decisions about safety and risk, you will use your knowledge of children along with individual circumstances as guides for making appropriate choices for each situation.

Developmental Differences and Safety

Characteristic behaviors of each stage of development are often the ones that put children at risk. Infants and toddlers explore the world by putting things in their mouths—so choking and poisoning are common hazards. The inquisitive preschooler who is not yet able to read labels may ingest cleaning products that are mistaken for something tasty. In the midst of a competitive game, a school-age child may accidentally injure a playmate with a projectile toy.

Safety precautions change as children reach new developmental stages. For example, covering electric outlets is essential with mobile infants, toddlers, and preschoolers but is generally unnecessary with typically developing kindergarten and primary school children. Young children may be injured because of undeveloped physical skill, strength, and coordination. Their natural inclination to learn through exploration encourages risk-taking behavior. Three- and 4-year-olds are curious and active, so falls and scrapes are common during active exploratory play. Kindergarten and primary school children can do many things on their own and have well developed motor skills and infinite confidence in their own abilities, so injuries may occur during their exploration of materials and equipment. Children with special needs and developmental delays may explore and play in ways that are more typical of younger children.

As an early childhood teacher, you will need to evaluate the safety of the environment, keeping the needs, skills, and abilities of all children in mind.

A Safe Environment

A structurally sound building and playground are essential for early childhood programs. As you prepare and supervise learning environments, you will need to be attentive to particular features and constraints of the building and grounds, in order to ensure children's safety and well-being.

The Outdoor Environment. The outdoor environment can provide children with a range of learning opportunities. Opportunities to build motor skills, relate to peers, and learn to make decisions are all supported when children have appropriate outdoor learning spaces. Outdoor spaces offer chances for children to build skill and challenge themselves by experimenting and taking risks. Therefore outdoor environments need to provide protection, be free of hazards, and be outfitted with equipment that is safe and age- and stage-appropriate. Although you may have little control over the characteristics of the outdoor environment of your program, it is important that safety be a primary guide for your decisions regarding children's experiences while playing and learning outdoors.

Play yards for infants, toddlers, and preschool children must have secure fences with gates and childproof latches to ensure that children do not leave without supervision. Playgrounds for school-age children may use less structured boundaries such as plants and hedges to define outdoor play spaces. Plants in the outdoor area should be inspected and any that are poisonous should be removed. Many common plants are poisonous and if eaten will cause skin rashes or upset stomachs. Assume that plants are poisonous unless you know otherwise. Ask your local poison control center or cooperative extension service for information about poisonous plants and teach children to avoid putting any parts of a plant into their mouths without first asking an adult.

Playground equipment such as swings, slides, and climbers provides opportunities for engaging play and learning. It is important to be certain that such equipment meets current guidelines for safety and is appropriate for the skills of the children using it. Most playground equipment built prior to 1990 does not meet today's safety guidelines. Jungle gyms are often so high that serious injuries result when children fall. Many slides are constructed so that children's clothing can catch, causing strangulation. Some equipment, such as merry-go-rounds and seesaws contain mechanisms that can crush fingers. Such outdated equipment should be removed from young children's play spaces.

Falls are the number one cause of playground injury (Aronson 2002a). The risk of injury from falls is reduced when play structures are surrounded by railings and have the proper type, depth, and area-coverage of impact-absorbing materials beneath them. The U.S. Consumer Products Safety Commission's *Handbook for Public Playground Safety* (1997) and the *Accreditation Criteria and Procedures of the National Association for the Education of Young Children* (National Academy of Early Childhood Programs 1998) provide information about the various types of impact materials. Teachers must ensure that impact material is maintained properly. Sand and wood chips must be turned and raked regularly. When toys or other items are left in fall zones near climbing equipment they must be removed promptly. Be aware that grass, concrete, asphalt, soil, turf, and carpeting are unacceptable as impact material.

Outdoor play areas should be checked daily and dangerous substances such as broken glass and cigarette butts must be removed. Hazardous equipment, materials, or supplies such as yard tools and fertilizers should be locked away from children.

Regular use of a checklist such as the one included in Appendix B will help you ensure that your outdoor play areas are safe.

Outdoor play on hot and sunny days can put children at risk. Teachers should work with families to develop a policy that ensures that all children are shielded from strong sun by clothing or shade or have sunscreen applied before going outside. Be careful to check all equipment to ensure that it is not too hot for safe play. Children can be burned by slides and other equipment that have been heated by the sun. Look for ways to shade climbing equipment, or block access to it when it is too hot. Be sure that there are shady places for children to play outside and offer water frequently.

Even the safest playgrounds can't protect children from injury. Constant, attentive supervision by adults is necessary. We have visited schools where teachers spent much of the outdoor time talking with one another rather than engaging with the children. This puts children at risk and limits teachers' opportunities for enhancing learning. Early childhood staff members should develop a plan for outdoor supervision that will ensure that adults are close to play structures and alert to children's activity at all times. Outdoor safety rules that staff have jointly developed and agree to follow will help children learn to play safely while outside.

The Indoor Environment. Indoor environments need to be safe as well as attractive, appealing and functional. Like the outdoor environment, some aspects of the classroom environment may be beyond your control, but you should be aware of any risks inherent in your environment and do all that is possible to create an inside space that is safe for children's play and learning.

Floor coverings should be secured and nonskid to prevent falls. Glass windows and doors should be made of safety glass and have vision strips at both children's and adults' eye levels to protect against collisions.

Ensure that radiators and electrical outlets cannot be reached by children; strategically placed shelves or other furniture can prevent access to these hazards. Fans should be located well out of the possible reach of children and all electrical outlets should be covered with safety plugs when not in use. If space heaters are used, great care must be taken to ensure that they are placed in areas that are inaccessible to children and away from curtains or other flammable material. Water temperature in classroom taps should be kept below 120 degrees to eliminate the possibility of burns. Make certain that the fabrics in the classroom are flame resistant to reduce the risk of injury by fire.

Prevention of accidents includes removing or locking away hazardous tools and materials, including cleaning supplies and medications. Plastic bags can cause suffocation and should never be accessible to young children. Because young children, particularly infants and toddlers, explore objects with their mouths, you must be especially aware of potential choking risks. Balloons are a particular hazard for young children who are likely to put them into their mouths in an attempt to inflate them. Small toys, broken pieces of toys, and coins are also choking hazards. Latex or vinyl gloves should be kept out of children's reach. Classrooms should be checked daily to ensure that all items accessible to children are safe for them to use.

Childhood lead poisoning is a serious health problem. Buildings constructed after 1978 contain non-lead-based paint. If your classroom is in an older building, work with other staff and administrators to ensure that paint has been tested by a licensed inspector to determine whether or not lead is present. Follow local guidelines for removing lead-based paint from all surfaces.

Equipment and Materials Safety

A young toddler trying to board a tricycle designed for a large preschooler, a preschooler trying to reach a container of materials on the top shelf of an unstable cupboard, or a kindergartner scaling the front of a high television/VCR cart are all at risk for injury. To reduce injury it is important you make sure that equipment and furnishings are appropriately sized, stable, or securely anchored, and otherwise safe.

Toy safety information is available on labels and through consumer watch organizations. You increase safety when you pay attention to manufacturer labels regarding the intended age group for a toy and when you are attentive to consumer publications from government agencies and consumer groups that are concerned about child toy safety. Because new information about safety is always coming out, it is important to keep up to date. Periodicals such as *Child Health Alert* can provide you with this information.

Vehicle and Trip Safety

Learning trips extend children's learning opportunities beyond the program site and should be a regular part of the curriculum. Whether you travel by car to visit the seashore, take the city bus to a nearby shopping mall to see a performance, or walk outside the playground enclosure to explore puddles created by a recent rain, you need to take precautions for children's safety.

Safe learning trips require a low adult-child ratio and small group size. The age and characteristics of the children determine the ratio and group size required to ensure their safety. A walk that includes crossing a busy street with a group of six 8-year-olds and one teacher may be safe and reasonable. That same walk with six toddlers and one teacher would be unsafe.

All vehicles (including buggies and strollers) used to transport children should run well and have all of their safety features operational. Properly secured and fastened child safety seats and safety restraints should always be used when children are being transported by motor vehicle. Child safety seats should be appropriate for the children's size and meet the Federal Motor Vehicle Safety Standards. The use of child safety seats reduces risk of death by 71% for children younger than 1 year of age, and by 54% for children ages 1 to 4 (American Academy of Pediatrics et al. 2002). Determine drop-off and pick-up areas that minimize exposure to traffic.

Walking trips are a wonderful way of enriching the curriculum and helping children learn how to become safe as pedestrians. Ensure children's safety on walking trips by assessing all points along the route carefully before walking it with children. Determine potentially risky areas and develop a plan to ensure safe walking. Carefully prepare children before the walk to be certain that they know and are able to follow the safety rules for the trip.

For all trips, always take a well stocked first aid kit and emergency contact information for each child and adult. Develop an agreed-on plan for how to manage emergencies. Take a working cell phone or determine in advance the location of a nearby pay telephone—and be sure to have the appropriate coins!

What You Do to Ensure Safety

As an early childhood educator you must be aware of and committed to the safety of the children in your care. Safety requires constant attention to the condition of the environment and to how it is being used by children. It also requires attention to possible hazards and risky behavior. You will be expected to know about and maintain a safe environment for children. It is important to know that you may incur liability (that is, you may be sued and be required to make financial restitution) if a child is seriously injured as a result of your negligence. This can happen if you fail to supervise children or do not take reasonable steps to ensure their safety.

Supervise for Safety. A commitment to program safety means that you attentively supervise children at all times and are continually aware of potential dangers. Room arrangements and playground layouts need to be analyzed to make sure that staff can easily view all activity areas. Make sure that pathways and exits are clear and uncluttered and that exit gates and doorways are not blocked.

What is attentive supervision? It involves being aware of what children are doing at all times. It means knowing what constitutes a hazard. It also means knowing the children. When Courtney cautiously climbs to the top of the slide for the first time, she needs you to supervise by standing close for reassurance, available to offer a steadying hand if needed. Monica, on the other hand, may just need your watchful eye and the occasional gentle reminder to wait for the child in front of her.

Attentive supervision can also limit injuries that may occur as a result of child conflicts. When teachers are skilled at facilitating interpersonal problem solving among children, conflict-related injuries are largely prevented.

It is also critical to monitor who enters the program to prevent children from leaving with strangers or noncustodial adults. A system must be in place for ensuring that only authorized adults pick up children. In most programs for children under 5 and in some kindergartens, families must sign their children in and out.

Establish Systems to Ensure That Equipment and Facilities Are Safe.
Work with others on your teaching team to ensure that there is an established system for completing safety inspections on a regular basis and that hazards are noticed and removed or repaired promptly. Toys and materials should be checked at least weekly for splinters, loose parts, and sharp edges. Furnishings and equipment should be checked each month. Any time a hazard is noted, immediate action should be taken to protect children from risk. See Appendix B for recommended intervals for inspections and for sample checklists.

Prepare for Emergencies.
Advance preparation can limit the number or the seriousness of injuries that occur as a result of an emergency. Anticipate situations such as fires and accidents by knowing how to use fire extinguishers, maintaining current first aid and CPR training certifications, having a plan for what to do if someone needs emergency medical treatment, and practicing emergency evacuation with children. Day-to-day preparedness includes awareness of the availability and the location of first aid supplies (both on-site and during excursions), easy access to the telephone numbers for emergency medical services, and a plan for the supervision of children if staff must attend to an injury. Though the most frequent first aid you will use as you work with young children will involve soap, water, band-aids, and ice packs, every early childhood educator needs to have basic training for giving first aid and infant-child CPR. In most states such training is mandatory. Along with learning how to give mouth-to-mouth resuscitation and clear a blocked airway, you will learn how to handle a bee sting and to use universal precautions (wearing vinyl or latex gloves when handling blood and other body fluids).

Programs should have a carefully developed disaster plan to ensure that both staff and families know what to do in the event of a natural disaster such as a storm or earthquake or a national defense emergency. The staff of every program must be prepared to deal with disasters in a professional, expedient way. Effective evacuation and emergency management plans include prior agreements about the roles and responsibilities of every staff member. Be certain that your program has a comprehensive disaster plan in place and that you are familiar with this plan. Take time to share this information with families so they will know what will be done in these rare emergency situations. Bright Horizons (www.brighthorizons.com) offers sample disaster plans on its Web site that may be downloaded and modified to meet the needs of individual programs.

Helping Children Learn to Be Safe
All of us want to prevent children from being hurt. Traffic and water accidents, fire, accidental poisoning and abuse are common causes of injury and death in young children.

Because it is not possible for young children to protect themselves from the hazards of the natural and human environment, adults must provide this protection.

It is possible to help children begin to learn ways in which they can participate in their own protection. In order to help children learn to keep themselves safe, you need to learn to view the world through children's eyes. You will become skilled at providing information to children that they can understand and remember, and you will teach them safety skills that they can master quickly through practice. Children need information in new situations, such as on trips and when new equipment, materials, or experiences are introduced. You can help them to recognize hazards and activities that may be dangerous and teach them procedures for handling potential hazards. For example, we have discussed using a knife with 4, 5, and 6-year-olds in this way: "This is a knife. One side is sharp and the other side isn't. When you cut with a knife it's important to have the sharp side down and to make sure that your fingers aren't under the cutting blade. Hold onto the handle with one hand and use the other hand to push down—that way you won't accidentally get cut." Explanations for toddlers must be simple and accompanied with close supervision and physical protection: "The pot is hot. Let's just look until it cools down." (Place the pot out of reach and place your body between the pot and the toddlers.)

Children can also become familiar with the people and procedures to follow in disasters (such as fires and tornadoes). This can help to avert tragedies. For example, many children die in fires when they hide from firefighters whose protective gear looks threatening. Practice regular fire evacuation with children. Teach them to always come to an adult when they hear a siren or see something that may be dangerous.

It is tempting to teach safety as a series of warnings— don't play with matches, don't go near the water, don't run in the street, don't talk to strangers. Unfortunately, don'ts often don't work because taboos are alluring. (The story of Pandora's box is one of many myths based on the human desire to try what is forbidden.) Instead, you can help children learn things they can do and help them understand why they should do them. Affirming children's ability to take part in their own care and assuring them of your commitment to take care of them makes you partners in the effort to assure safety.

> **Reflect on childhood dangers**
>
> Remember a time in your childhood when you did something that was unsafe. Why did you do it? What happened? What would have helped you to have a good experience that was safe?

When children understand precautions, they are usually willing to cooperate. It is more effective to tell children what to do and why, rather than insisting that they stop something that is dangerous: "Please climb on the jungle gym instead of the table. The table could tip from your weight and you might fall."

Young children begin to be able to keep themselves safe when you help them learn to:

- Ingest only good foods and safe medicines that are given to them by trusted adults, and to avoid eating any other substances.
- Use a child car seat, or wear a seatbelt, whenever they are in a motor vehicle.
- Avoid street crossing unless they are with an adult; always use crosswalks, and obey traffic signals.
- Describe and practice safe ways to use materials and equipment—for example, "Walk when you carry scissors and make sure the tips point at the ground."
- Tell a grown-up about matches or lighters that they see.
- Stop-drop-and-roll if their clothing catches on fire; recognize and trust firefighters in firefighting gear.
- Practice safe ways to evacuate home and school buildings in cases of fire and other emergencies.

- Play in pools and other bodies of water only when they are with a supervising adult.
- Say "Stop" if someone wants to hurt or touch them in ways that feel bad, and tell a teacher or parent or other adult if someone has hurt them.

Young children learn about safety in the context of daily life. As you prepare for a field trip, children can help you to make up safety rules. The day before a fire drill you can talk about it and have children help to decide how to have a safe one. Safety concepts can be integrated into activities that you are already doing. For example:

- Sing a song such as Woody Guthrie's "Riding in My Car," and add a verse about wearing a seatbelt.
- Add a painted crosswalk to the trike path for practice.
- Include props and pictures of firefighters in full regalia in the dramatic play area.

You can also teach children about safety through planned curriculum on fire, home, and traffic safety or taking care of yourself. All of these can be appropriate and be integrated into the curriculum in preschools, kindergartens, and primary schools.

Abuse Prevention

All early childhood educators have a responsibility to protect the children in their care; this includes helping children avoid abuse. The heart of an effective child abuse prevention curriculum is you, a trained, skilled early childhood educator, who shows respect and appreciation for children. You help prevent abuse when you are respectful of and able to relate to the needs of children and families, and when you accept their feelings, ideals, choices, culture, and values. The quality of the relationships that you establish with families will enable them to feel that they can turn to you with questions and problems concerning their children.

It is essential for children to know that it is okay for them to resist physical intrusion and say, "No, I don't want you to do that to me!" to other children and to adults. It means that you must respect children's feelings and invite their cooperation rather than insisting on their compliance. You show respect for their bodies when you avoid using physical force (for example, picking children up and forcing them to be where they do not want to be) except in situations where a child's immediate safety is at stake.

It is impossible to "abuse-proof" very young children. No lesson, curriculum approach, or defensive strategy will guarantee children's safety. Although several popular approaches are specifically designed to prevent child abuse by focusing on the concept of private parts, or the idea of good touches, bad touches, or stranger danger, these tactics may mislead, alarm, or arouse the curiosity of children and tend to place responsibility on the relatively powerless child instead of on the adult. Adopting such a curriculum may lead to a false sense of security, thus endangering children.

Effective child abuse prevention is an ongoing part of children's learning rather than a onetime "inoculation." It uses the basic principles of early childhood education and development. Figure 7.1 gives you ideas for effective child abuse prevention.

A Healthy Place

A healthy place for children protects and enhances the health of each child. Early childhood practitioners create environments that foster children's health and well-being. In healthy environments, air temperature, light conditions, and noise are controlled and facilities, equipment, and supplies for maintaining health are available. Teachers work with administrators and health care professionals to develop and follow policies and procedures concerning health routines and health emergencies.

Figure 7.1 **Helping Children Avoid Abuse**

Provide choices: Offer children opportunities to make choices, including the choice to say no to an activity, food, or suggestion. This includes the right to reject physical contact. You offer choices by asking or alerting children before you touch or pick them up by saying things like "May I give you a hug?" "Would you like me to rub your back?" or "I'm going to pick you up and put you on the changing table," rather than doing so without warning.

Develop body awareness and appreciation: Provide many ways for children to appreciate their bodies through routines, games, songs, movement, and stories. Use correct names for body parts. When children are taught to value their bodies, they are less likely to passively allow themselves to be hurt.

Encourage children to express feelings, needs, and ideas: Help children understand feelings and encourage self-expression through words, stories, music, art, movement, and puppetry. Children who can express their ideas, needs, and feelings are better equipped to handle situations in which they are uncomfortable.

Integrate safety education: Integrate safety into topics and activities through discussion, role-playing, and dramatization so children learn things they can do to be safe in many contexts such as crossing the street, riding in cars, playing at the beach, shopping at the mall, answering the phone, being with a stranger, or with a friend.

Distinguish surprises from secrets: Explore differences between secrets and surprises to help children understand that surprises are things you are waiting to share to make someone happy (like a birthday present), and secrets are things that someone wants you to hide that feels dangerous, wrong, or scary.

Build positive self-esteem: Help children feel good about themselves—their characteristics, abilities, and potential. Recognizing and valuing differences and affirming individuality through song, celebration, and activities help children to feel that they are worthy of protection.

All young children need protections from health risks. Preventing health problems is an important task in early childhood education and care. Public health practitioners have noted the need for early childhood programs to follow basic health procedures in order to limit the spread of disease in child care settings.

Programs that serve infants and toddlers face some particular challenges. Children under the age of 3 are smaller and have less mature organs and body systems; they have less immunity, and are at greater health risk because they explore the world by touching and mouthing. Because they wear diapers, they are at additional risk for contracting one of the many diseases that can be spread through unsanitary diapering practices.

Preventing Communicable Illnesses and Conditions

Families and teachers are both concerned about infectious diseases. Both want to ensure that early childhood programs are doing all they can to prevent and control the spread of illness; learning to do this effectively will be an important part of your job. You control illness by eliminating pathogens (the bacteria, viruses, and parasites that cause disease) and by limiting the ways that pathogens can be transmitted. You also do things to improve overall health. Good nutrition, exercise, reduced stress, and good psychological health all improve resistance and decrease susceptibility to disease.

In early childhood programs people have close contact with one another. This increases opportunities for pathogens to be transmitted. Respiratory diseases such as colds and flu are spread when secretions from the mouth, nose, eyes, and lungs pass from one person to the other. This can happen through direct touching; sharing of toys, objects, and food; or contact with droplets in the air when individuals cough or sneeze. Diarrhea and other diseases of the intestinal tract are caused by viruses, bacteria, or parasites that are spread through contact with fecal matter. This may occur when handwashing practices are inadequate or diapering practices unsanitary. Hepatitis B and C and HIV/AIDS are serious infections that are spread when the blood of an infected person comes in contact with a mucous membrane (lining of the mouth, eyes, nose, rectum, or genitals) or with a cut or break in the skin of another individual.

Many serious diseases have been eliminated or controlled through childhood immunization. *Caring for Our Children* (American Academy of Pediatrics, American Public Health Association, & National Resource Center for Health and Safety in Child Care 2003) states that before a child is admitted to an early childhood program, families are required to submit a physician-prepared health assessment that documents the medical history of the child and includes the record of vaccinations.

Recognizing early signs of illness in children and having good policies and procedures for exclusion also help to prevent the spread of infection. *Model Child Care Health Policies* (Aronson 2002a) gives useful guidelines related to illness and health.

Keeping the Environment Healthy

A healthy environment is kept clean and sanitary through routines established and maintained by the adults in the setting. Children are protected from many pathogens when sanitary handwashing, diapering, and toileting practices are followed, when surfaces and toys are sanitized regularly, when personal possessions are kept clean, and when food storage and preparation are healthful.

Handwashing. The most effective and important measure for preventing the spread of disease is conscientious and thorough handwashing (Aronson 2002b). All early childhood practitioners, particularly those who work with infants and toddlers, need to wash their hands many times a day. By doing so, they limit the spread of disease and protect their own health. It is recommended that you wash your hands at the following times:

- When you first enter the classroom environment
- Before handling food
- Before and after feeding children
- Before and after changing diapers or assisting a child with toileting
- After using the toilet yourself
- Before and after giving a child medication
- After any contact with body fluids
- After handling pets
- After playing or cleaning up sand or water play areas
- After cleaning or handling garbage

To make handwashing effective in preventing disease, it is important to use running water and soap, rub hands together vigorously for at least 10 seconds, wash all over from fingertips to wrists, dry hands on a disposable paper towel, and turn off the faucet with a towel so as not to recontaminate hands. Children also must wash their hands and younger children must be assisted with handwashing. Take time to teach children effective handwashing routines and insist that hands be washed thoroughly and regularly.

Cleaning and Sanitizing. Regular cleaning and sanitizing of equipment and materials is another practice that effectively limits the spread of illness in early childhood programs. Whatever the age of children, regular cleaning and sanitation of all toys and equipment will limit disease transmission. The most common and least expensive sanitizing solution is a mixture of bleach and water: 1 tablespoon per quart, or ¼ cup per gallon. Spray this solution liberally on toys and equipment and leave it on for 2 minutes prior to wiping it off with a paper towel. Sanitizing solutions must be made fresh each day. Tables should be sanitized before and after meals. Toys, mats, and furniture should be sanitized whenever they are mouthed or contaminated by body fluids. Regular sanitation of all toys, furniture, and equipment is recommended. In programs for infants and toddlers, toys should be disinfected after each use, and furniture and equipment sanitation should be done daily.

When children bring personal items for use in the program such as bedding, clothing, and comfort objects, each child must have separate storage. It may be a cubby, a locker, or a tub or box, labeled with the child's name. Bedding, clothing, and soft toys should be washed at least weekly, either in program facilities or by families. Clothing or bedding that has come in contact with feces should be placed in tightly sealed plastic bags, labeled, and sent home with the appropriate family for laundering.

In programs that include toothbrushing, care must be taken that a procedure is developed to ensure that children brush teeth in a sanitary manner. Children must be taught how to brush teeth in a healthy and effective way and should be supervised during the toothbrushing. Toothbrushes require careful storage and sanitizing.

Sanitary Diapering and Toileting. Because diapering and toileting are some of the most prevalent ways of spreading communicable conditions, great care must be taken in managing them. In order to protect yourself from contact with possible pathogens in feces, wear disposable vinyl or latex gloves when diapering or assisting a child who has had a toilet accident.

Healthy diapering procedures can be more easily followed if the changing area is well set up and maintained. A diapering area needs a changing table with a washable mat. Procedures for sanitary diapering should be posted at adult eye-level and followed. Paper to cover the changing surface, plastic bags for soiled diapers, a lidded waste basket (preferably pedal operated), sanitizing solution, and each child's supplies need to be within easy reach. The sink used to wash hands after diapering needs to be separate from food preparation areas. To avoid the hazards of storing soiled diapers, most programs require families to provide disposable diapers and wipes. Diapering supplies, like other personal items, must be kept individually.

Toilet areas must be cleaned and sanitized daily and additional sanitizing may be necessary during the day. Toilet facilities should assist young children in being independent. To encourage both independence and sanitary use of toilets and sinks, it is best if they are child-sized. Otherwise stable stools will be needed to make them easily accessible. Use of potty chairs in group care settings is prohibited in most states because they are difficult to use and maintain in a sanitary fashion. Toilet tissue, running water, soap, and paper towels need to be within the reach of the children. Staff must carefully supervise toddlers' and preschoolers' use of the toilet. Older children will want privacy for toileting but may occasionally need assistance in the event of an accident.

Safe Food Preparation and Storage. Attention to food preparation—both what is prepared and how it is prepared—is important to children's health. In food preparation areas, surfaces and utensils must be kept clean and sanitized and all trash disposed of in tightly covered containers that are emptied daily. Perishable foods must be refrigerated at or below 40 degrees Fahrenheit and hot foods kept at 140 degrees until they are served. All who prepare and serve food are required to be free of communicable diseases and should use frequent and thorough handwashing to reduce the spread of pathogens.

The health checklist in Appendix B at the end of the book will help you to evaluate food preparation and storage practices in your own and other early childhood programs.

Health Training. Every early childhood educator needs to have basic training for maintaining a healthy environment, coping with minor health emergencies such as fevers and vomiting, recognizing when a child needs to be referred to a health practitioner, and knowing when a child should be isolated from others for health reasons. Some children will come to you with allergies, asthma, or other chronic health conditions that require management if they are to participate in your program. In some programs a nurse or health aide will attend to health-related matters; in others you will be responsible.

Helping Children Learn to Be Healthy

The early years are a critical time for developing good health habits. Awareness of and concern for health can be promoted as you help children learn to make wise nutrition and exercise choices and develop healthy habits such as handwashing and toothbrushing. Young children are intrigued with learning about themselves and their bodies. Early childhood is the time when the foundations of understanding health are formed and the underlying skills and dispositions for staying healthy are established. You have an opportunity to interest children in a topic that will be important to them throughout their lives.

Children can learn important things about good health habits in their early childhood programs in the context of daily routines and activities. As they experience classroom routines related to the provision of good health, and as you discuss these things with them, they begin to acquire some important understandings and skills. They can begin to understand human growth and development, body parts and functions, and the value of cleanliness, medical care, exercise, rest, and good nutrition. As they learn about these things they will come to appreciate their bodies and develop positive practices and habits.

Personal Care. Teaching children about health and self-care takes different forms for different ages of the children. When you allow infants and toddlers to control what is happening to them as much as possible and explain what you are doing and why, you help these young children become knowledgeable and competent.

As you engage in daily routines with children, you can model and discuss the reasons for what you are doing. Children will learn the following from repeated practice and discussion:

- Handwashing can keep you from getting sick.
- Toothbrushing and regular dental checkups help to keep your teeth strong and healthy.
- Rest helps your body to calm down and gives you energy for vigorous activity.
- Exercise helps your muscles grow and get stronger; it gives you energy and makes you feel and look good.

Exercise. Children who learn to enjoy an active lifestyle in the early years are more likely to maintain healthy activity levels as adults. Providing regular opportunities for active play is one important way that you can support this learning. When you create and expand safe and interesting areas for physical activity, both indoors and out, you are helping children enjoy the benefits of an active lifestyle. You can make small adaptations to your routines that will encourage activity. For example, you can take your group all around the playground before entering it; you can begin your group activity time with a game where everyone runs in place for several minutes; you can include movement games and exercises with and without music in your daily plans. Help children become aware of and appreciate the sense of well-being that active play provides and encourage families to provide active play opportunities at home.

Health as Curriculum.   When you discuss practices that build health and those things that are harmful, you are helping children develop concepts that will help them protect themselves from illness. As children mature, they can learn about how health practices like handwashing protect them. Primary-age children are interested in studying about bodies and can benefit from curriculum that builds on this interest. Educational materials, including informational books about health, are available for preschool and school-age children. Learning about heath and practicing health routines should be an integral part of the curriculum.

Young children are fascinated by their bodies. They only gradually learn to feel that physical functions are private or shameful. People who work with young children need to react to interest in body parts and functions in supportive ways. All body parts and physiological processes have names—shin, finger, knuckle, buttocks, knee, forehead, digestion, urination, saliva, and so on. The words are innocuous and easy to use. Children who learn accurate terminology in a low-intensity, supportive emotional climate are better equipped to understand and care for themselves. If all subjects can be discussed seriously, children are given an important message: Your body is okay; it is safe to talk with adults about it. Comfort with their bodies and the ability to talk about them give children the words to describe their physical needs, state of well-being, or symptoms of disease. We were delighted on a recent visit to a kindergarten classroom to find the children fully engaged in an exploration of digestion and elimination; one way they learned about these functions was by squeezing prepared oatmeal out of an intestine created from a stocking!

For primary school children health education is empowerment; it helps them feel responsible and is a first step on the road to being grown-up. They benefit from information that is presented in a straightforward, nonthreatening manner and from many opportunities for discussion. As they learn about caring for themselves they will share their ideas with you, and you may find that they have many misconceptions. Their eagerness to learn can provide valuable opportunities for you to support their ability to care for themselves.

Nutrition.   During the early childhood years, we can help children to understand that their health is affected by the food they eat and that they can make food choices that will help them to grow and be healthy. Children may learn to choose a healthier diet if we help them to appreciate the high-fiber, low-fat foods that have been demonstrated to contribute to good health. By expanding children's food horizons, we help them to discover new foods and to make wise food choices. Much of what adults experience as children's reluctance to try healthful foods may be the product of their own expectations and biases. Children usually enjoy fruits, vegetables, brown rice, and dishes like borscht, tofu with broccoli, and ratatouille if they participate in preparation and if they know that they will not be forced to eat.

Nutrition can be a part of everyday experience. You can teach nutrition by providing planned experiences that will help children to develop skills and understand concepts. Take advantage of daily meals and snacks and model behavior and attitudes that encourage health-supporting habits.

You can model appreciation for healthful foods and give children time and several opportunities to try any new or unusual food. When a new, healthy food appears in the school lunch, you can say something like, "We never had this for lunch before— I'm looking forward to trying it," rather than pushing the plate away and commenting negatively on the cook's choices. If children see adults enjoying healthy food and avoiding nonnutritious foods, they gain nutrition awareness. Poor habits can also be taught by modeling. For this reason you should restrict foods such as soft drinks, french fries, donuts, and candy bars in your own diet, saving them for times when you will not be with children. Better yet, learn to substitute foods that are better for your health and that will give you more sustained energy.

Good snacks for young children should consist of minimally processed foods that are low in fat, salt, and sugar. Fresh fruit or vegetables, whole grain bread or cereal, and milk or cheese are all components of healthful snacks for children. Because children's nutritional requirements are proportionately higher than or equal to adults but their calorie intake is smaller, young children's diets have less room for poor food choices. When children eat foods that have little nutritional value, they have to eat more calories to meet needs for other nutrients. With proportionately higher vitamin and mineral requirements and lower calories requirements, young children's diets are more likely to contain excessive calories or to be deficient in vitamins and minerals than the diet of an adult.

Helping children learn to make wise food choices is an important first step in combating the increasing frequency of obesity in young children. Obese children tend to remain overweight as adults, seriously compromising their health and well-being. You can help prevent childhood obesity by encouraging regular physical activity as well as by helping children to choose healthy foods and appropriate portion sizes. Teach children to appreciate food as part of a healthy lifestyle; never use food as a reward for positive behavior or withhold it as a punishment. Avoid asking children to eat all the food on their plates and instead teach them to pay attention to their body's signals of fullness and hunger.

Simple nutritious foods make rewarding "cooking" experiences for young children. For example, spreading cream cheese on a slice of celery is not usually thought of as a cooking activity, but it involves food preparation skills that young children need practice to master. Preschool-age children can learn to follow simple recipes. Primary children enjoy more complex cooking experiences that not only teach nutrition but other concepts as well. Many children who have resisted trying certain foods will do so when they have helped to prepare them. There are a number of excellent children's cookbooks that include healthy recipes, illustrated in a manner that makes it easy for children to follow them.

The times that children are actively involved with food and nutrition are good times to talk about nutrition. Children are interested in talking about where food comes from and how it helps their bodies to grow. They often echo the information that they have heard. For example, many children have been told that milk makes them strong or big. You can help to develop these concepts by adding short informative statements like, "Yes, milk has calcium in it. It helps your bones grow and be strong."

What we know about wise food selections for children is constantly changing. For example, in recent decades awareness has grown concerning the inability of many children to properly digest some foods, particularly milk or milk products. Many children experience severe allergic reactions to certain foods, particularly to eggs, wheat, seafood, milk and milk products, citrus fruits, berries, and various nuts and nut butters. As an early childhood professional it is essential that you are knowledgeable about food items that pose a threat to safety and health.

During the early childhood years you can help children understand that health and nutrition are important to them today and throughout their lives. This foundation can help them to respect their bodies, take responsibility for their health, and develop positive practices and habits.

PSYCHOLOGICAL SAFETY AND HEALTH

Psychological safety and health are essential for optimal development and learning. Children can tell when and where they are welcome. They know they are in a safe place when their needs are cared for and when adults show respect in the way they listen to and talk with them.

In psychologically safe and healthy programs, children do not fear rejection or humiliation. They are comfortable and feel secure. This sense of safety is dependent on warm, consistent adults who provide positive and respectful physical contact such as gentle carrying and rocking for an infant or toddler, or a friendly hand on the shoulder, a pat on the back, or an appreciative hug for an older child.

You contribute to psychological health by encouraging children and believing in their competence. You create environments in which it is safe to experiment and to make mistakes. You accept children as unique people with their own pace and unique needs.

In a caring place the routines of the day and the management of transitions are thoughtfully structured to make children feel psychologically secure. Thought is given to how to integrate new children into the environment in caring and nurturing ways and how to ease their transitions when a favorite caregiver or friend leaves the program or they must leave themselves.

Good Beginnings

Beginnings are times of change, excitement, and hope. They are also times of stress, fear, and anxiety. They are a time to say farewell to the security of the familiar and to go forward to meet new challenges. Life is composed of many beginnings; some are large and stressful, and others are small and easy to deal with. You can help guide children over the sometimes rocky paths of the transitions between home and classroom and the transitions within and between phases of the early childhood program.

The Transition from Home

All of us can recall the anxious feelings that we had when separating from the familiar: leaving our childhood homes, moving to a new city, starting a new job, becoming a parent. With a lifetime of experience behind us, we can still remember the stomach-clutching anxiety that accompanied those changes. When young children enter your program, they face an unfamiliar world. They are assaulted by sensations: new people, noises, objects, smells, and activities. They may have had little experience with being parted from their family members, with being among many children, or with making choices. This strangeness is made less traumatic when you and the family work together.

You can help children and their families to realize that the bonds that exist between them are strong enough to thrive despite separation. At the same time, you need to help children build relationships in the new setting. When children trust you and feel assured of their own competence, they become comfortable enough to benefit from their experiences in your program. They adapt more easily when they know that their family has confidence in the program and in you.

Young children make the transition from home best when the introduction is gradual and when they have an opportunity to integrate familiar aspects of their homes into their new lives in an early childhood program. One way to accomplish this integration is a home visit before the child's first day. Such a visit gives the child the opportunity to become acquainted with you from the security of their own home. During home visits, you build the base of later relationships with children and learn about their homes and families. Such visits are also opportunities for families to get to know and to develop confidence in you. Many families may find a home visit stressful. Care should be taken to make certain that a home visit is seen as one of several choices available to the family for helping their child make a smooth transition into the group setting.

Classroom visits by family members and children are a way to help both children and family members feel comfortable and competent in the new setting. All children entering a program for the first time benefit from experiencing their classroom in the company of a familiar adult. A visit orients the child to the setting, the staff, and the materials. In some programs, initial visits occur during the course of a regular day: The child and parent sit in on an hour or two of the program. In other places, a special orientation for several new children or individual family visits outside of regular program hours may precede the child's first day. Whatever its form, the initial visit helps prepare both child and family for the new experience. Visits similar to those just described are essential for infants, toddlers, preschoolers, and kindergarten children. A child entering a primary grade has had at least a full year of school. These children usually handle the transition to a new class or school with much greater ease. An orientation visit is still a valuable opportunity to get to know the teacher and the environment.

> ### Reflect on a separation
>
> Recall a change in your life that involved separation from friends and family or a familiar place. How did you feel? What strategies did you use to cope with this transition? How might you apply this experience to working with children who are undergoing separation?

First Days and First Weeks

Your goal for the first day is to begin to know the children and to help them to get to know you, one another, and the routines of the program. Because adjustment on the first day can be difficult, a family member is often asked to spend part or all of the day with the child. Some programs require someone familiar to stay for several days with the child. In general, toddlers and young preschoolers have a more difficult time making a transition to a new setting than do young infants or older children. The family of a toddler may spend a week gradually preparing to leave their child for a full day. A 4-year-old might pointedly ask a parent to go home at the end of the first hour. Each child responds in an individual way. We have worked with toddlers who had no difficulty saying good-bye to their parents after only minimal preparation and 4-year-olds who wept and clung each day for months. The temperament and experience of both the family members and child will interact with the kind of preparation that you provide to make each child's entrance into your program smooth. In our experience, the time and energy spent are well worth it.

Individual children react differently on their first day: Some want to touch and try everything, some are cautious observers, and others want to stay close to their family member or familiar person. All children carefully observe your behavior and the arrangement of the environment to understand what is expected of them and to find out how you will react. It is especially important to be aware of what you say and do those first days. You will want to be calm and caring, letting children know that you will help and protect them in this new, and possibly scary, place. Because so much is unknown, the environment, the activities, and the schedule of the first days should be simple to allow children to focus on a few new experiences at a time. This pace will allow them to understand what is happening without being overwhelmed or fearful of doing the wrong thing. Some suggestions for helping the first day to go smoothly can be found in Figure 7.2.

Almost all children experience anxiety the first time they are left at school. Some children overcome this anxiety easily; others express their anxiety through tears,

Figure 7.2 **Suggestions for the First Days**

CARING FOR CHILDREN

- Have the child begin with a short first day. Children who have little experience in group settings may have absorbed all they can in an hour.

- Encourage a parent or familiar caregiver to spend all or part of the first days with their child.

- Help families establish a "good-bye ritual." For example, a father may read one story, give two hugs and one kiss, then say good-bye and leave. This sequence can be repeated daily.

- Let families know that they are welcome to stay and participate, but when they say good-bye, it is easiest for children if they leave promptly. Remind them that they are encouraged to telephone to see how their child is doing.

- Greet children and their family members by name each day as they arrive, and say good-bye as they depart. Keep families informed of how their child is adjusting.

- Prepare a cubby, locker, or other space for each child before the first day. Label it with their name. Show them this safe place where they can store their belongings. Have an activity prepared that allows children to decorate their cubby or locker name label. If possible, make a photo of the child to include on the label.

- Show children the location of the toilet and the water fountain and how they work on the first day, and accompany them when they seem uncertain.

- Stay close to children who need extra reassurance. Infants, toddlers, and young preschoolers may need to be held; older preschoolers and kindergartners may need a hand to hold or may want to stay close to you until they feel more comfortable.

- Show clearly what you expect of children but do not be overly concerned if children cannot meet simple expectations.

- Encourage children to bring a special toy or comfort object to help provide a tangible bridge between home and school. Some children are comforted by a photograph of a family member.

- Allow children to borrow a book or toy from the classroom to provide a bridge when they return to their homes.

- Provide an interesting but limited number of age-appropriate materials.

- Provide soothing, open-ended materials like water, sand, and dough.

- Provide time for independent exploration of materials.

- Help preschoolers, kindergartners, and primary children to feel that they are a part of a group by introducing a short group activity such as a song or story. Sing name songs to help children get to know one another and to acknowledge each child.

- In the first weeks avoid abrupt or major changes and excitement (fire drills, films, trips, room rearrangement). Help children to know their environment by taking small excursions to important places: the parent room, the play yard, other classes, the library, the office, and the kitchen.

tantrums, or angry words; and still others become despondent and quietly wait while sucking thumbs or holding comfort objects. Some, not as visibly upset, may have toilet accidents, nightmares, or angrily reject their parents when it's time to go home. A few will appear fine for a few days or a week and then will react strongly as if it was the first day. Our interpretation of this delayed response is that, as the novelty of the new experience wears thin, the child realizes that going to school will henceforth be a perpetual part of life—one that involves little personal choice. If a reaction persists or is extreme, it may mean that the child needs a more gradual or a delayed entrance into the program.

Many toddlers and young preschoolers need the reassurance of physical contact with an adult during the first days and weeks. If you work in a program where many children enter at the same time, you may sometimes feel like a mother opossum moving about the classroom with the small bodies of children clinging to you. As they become comfortable, most children will find more interesting things to do. For many, a treasured blanket, stuffed animal, or piece of clothing (sometimes called a *transitional object*) is important in the separation process. These personal possessions are comforting reminders of home that help them to feel secure. It is important that children be allowed to keep them near. With time, comfort objects become less evident and may be needed only when a child is under stress or at nap times.

During the first days and weeks, children begin to adjust and learn to trust and feel competent. They become accustomed to the daily rhythm of activities linked by transitions, learn that they can care for many of their own needs, and discover that you will be there to help when needed. The most important tasks of this time are to develop trust, build relationships, and establish routines. These tasks are the curriculum. You will want to ensure that children experience frequent successes and that your expectations of them are realistic. It is a time when you learn what children can and cannot do.

As children become more comfortable, and as you become familiar with their individual skills, interests, and preferences, you can begin enriching the environment with materials, activities, and trips that might have been overwhelming at first. By understanding and supporting children as they go through the separation process during first days and weeks, you help prepare them to be active and competent learners.

Reflect on your first day of school

Remember your first day of school or your first day in a new school or class. What stands out in your memory? What was most reassuring? What was most distressing? Why? What did this experience teach you about what is important to do for children on first days? What do you want to make sure not to do? Why?

A Good Day

A typical day in any program for young children is an artful blend of routines and learning experiences linked by smooth transitions. We think of the daily ebb and flow of learning activities and routines as being part of a larger experience of living and learning with children.

A day for children in a good early childhood program has a relaxed pace. Children are not rushed from activity to activity. Children are offered lots of choices and large blocks of time (at least 1 hour long) in which to fully explore the activities chosen. Although many schedule differences depend on the age of the children and the characteristics of the program, great similarities are also present. Nine-month-old Camille delightedly crawling from shelf to shelf and exploring toys until she tires and crawls to her teacher for a cuddle and 7-year-old Harrison writing a story about tigers during learning center time over several days are both making choices and governing their own use of time.

The structure of the program day is influenced by the needs and developmental stage of the children and your observations of individuals, and by your values and the values and concerns of parents, community, and the school administration. It is also influenced by the physical setting, the length of the program day, and the time of year.

Both spontaneous and planned activities occur daily in every carefully prepared program for young children, though the amount of each varies. Your role is to build routines that allow for increasing independence and rituals that bring a sense of security for the children.

Children's Needs and Developmental Stage

Early childhood programs must include provisions for children's needs and take into account developmental differences. All children need time for rest, nourishment, and personal care. It is important to include periods of vigorous activity, quiet times, and daily times when choice is permitted to allow for individual interest and attention. The younger the children, the more flexible you will remain because younger children's needs vary greatly. At 10:00 in a group of toddlers we visited, Aimee was lying down and drinking a bottle, Ian was having a nap, Walden was looking at books, Nadine was cuddling on a teacher's lap, and Jonathan was using the toilet. A rigid schedule could not meet such diverse needs and would inevitably lead to frustration for adults and children. One particularly skilled infant teacher that we know creates a written individual schedule for each child and posts it in the classroom. This allows everyone in the care setting to be aware of each child's routine. By reviewing these schedules weekly, caregivers also take time to ensure that they are adapting their routines and expectations to meet the individual needs of each child.

As they mature, toddlers benefit from a schedule of daily routines with a predictable sequence that remains flexible. Structured group time activities for toddlers are likely to result in disaster as toddlers do not sit well together in a group. Wise toddler teachers notice times when one or two toddlers are interested in a book, puppet, or song and expand the interests of those children at those "teachable moments." The schedule for preschoolers is also organized around the predictable care routines of the day such as mealtimes and nap time. As children mature you can gradually forgo planned naps but many children will still require a period of rest if they are in a full-day program. More structured activities can be planned as children show longer attention spans. Preschoolers can begin to enjoy short group experiences, particularly if there are opportunities for them to actively participate. Kindergarten and primary-age children enjoy planned learning experiences and still need time for play and rest. Typical schedules for different age groups have the following characteristics:

- *Infants:* Each child regulates him or herself—meals, rests, toileting, active/quiet times.
- *Toddlers and young preschoolers:* Regular meals, snacks, and rest with toileting and active/quiet times occurring in response to children's needs and interests.
- *Older preschoolers, kindergartners:* Scheduled eating, rest, group, activity, and outdoor times with some flexibility based on children's needs on any given day. As children mature, closer adherence to plans for group and activity times is appropriate. A good way to start each day is with a group gathering to share news, sing a song, and map out the day's direction.
- *Primary children:* Similar to older preschoolers and kindergartners but with more structured group and activity times. A good way to finish each day is listening to a chapter from a book.

Your values and goals are among your most important considerations in planning your schedule. If you value creativity, independence, and the development of responsibility, you will allow large blocks of time (1 to 2 hours) during which children choose their own activities while you work with individuals and small groups.

The Physical Setting

The building in which you work will influence how you structure the day. If it houses only your program and has sufficient space for younger children to be separated from older ones, it is relatively easy to schedule the day to meet the basic needs of all age groups. Where space is limited or facilities are shared, you may need to work out ways to accommodate different groups of children. If the bathroom or playground is located at a distance from the classroom, you will have to take this into account in planning.

The Program Day

Children in a full-day early childhood program spend up to 60% of their waking hours out of their home. This time is a significant portion of a young child's life, and the program is like a second home. In full-day settings it is especially important to pay close attention to the quality of relationships, the design of the environment, and scheduling. For an example of scheduling, see Figure 7.3.

However long the day, early childhood programs must provide for the needs of children. A full-day program must provide lunch, a midday rest, and snack periods to avoid overstimulated, hungry children. Because their stomachs are relatively small, young children need to eat every 2 to 3 hours (Aronson 2002b) so schedules must be adjusted accordingly.

Children in full-day programs may stay 6 to 11 hours, but the staff in such programs generally remain for only 6 to 8 hours. The children may spend significant time with two separate groups of staff. The coordination of this transition must help children to maintain their sense of trust if they are to benefit from the experiences offered. One misperception is that anyone who cares for young children in the afternoon has a less important job than those who perform similar tasks in the morning. Children do not make this distinction. They learn and need nurturing throughout the day. Involving afternoon staff in planning and recognizing the vital tasks they accomplish is one way to maintain program quality throughout the day.

Programs will meet the needs of infants and toddlers most appropriately if they use a staffing plan based on a primary caregiving system. Programs using primary caregiving assign a small group of children (three to six, depending on age) to one

Figure 7.3 **A Daily Schedule for a Full-Day Preschool**

7:00–8:00	Arrival and child-chosen indoor activities
8:00–8:30	Breakfast—children may clean up their eating space and look at a book as they wait for the beginning of group meeting
8:30–8:45	Group meeting—staff and children gather to sing songs, discuss the events of the prior day, and share plans for the day
8:45–10:30	Learning center time—indoor activities are available and small groups may meet for part of the time for project work or teacher-led activities
10:30–11:30	Outdoor activity time
11:30–12:15	Lunch—handwashing, setting of tables, family-style service, and individual cleanup as each child finishes eating
12:15–12:30	Nap preparation—children toilet, wash hands, brush teeth, take out their mats or place nap bedding on cots, and settle down with a book while others prepare for nap
12:30–1:00	Book time—an adult reads several books aloud to children who wish to join the group while others continue to remain on their mats with their own book
1:00–2:30	Nap time—the lights are dimmed, soft instrumental music plays, and the staff are available to pat backs (from 2:00 on, snacks and quiet activities are available for children who wake up or who do not wish to rest longer)
2:30–4:30	Indoor/outdoor activities—children may select from a variety of activities indoors and outdoors with special activities and ongoing projects available
4:30–5:00	Closure—materials are put away, children wash up, settle down for songs, stories, and quiet activities as they wait for their families

main caregiver who is responsible for meeting the majority of the children's needs for nurturance and care. All caregivers on the team work closely together and assist with all children when necessary. The primary caregiver is able to develop a special bond with each child, get to know their communication styles, their preferences and interests, and their individual routines; other teachers know the children well enough to allow them to feel safe and comfortable when the primary caregiver is not present. A primary caregiving system also promotes close relationships with families since each teacher has only a small number of children and families for whom he or she is mainly responsible.

In part-day programs, it is likely that staff will remain consistent throughout the program day. Scheduled rest time is probably unnecessary, may meet with resistance, and is a waste of limited time. In a short program, a good blend of outdoor activity and indoor activities with a short snack break will provide for a pleasant, productive half-day experience.

Before- and after-school programs for kindergarten and primary children are designed to ensure children's well-being while parents are at work and to provide appropriate activities for children who have had a full day of school. There is growing recognition that children need high-quality care and education throughout the day, and after-school programs are much more than custodial care. However, children who are in structured school settings all day require a different, more relaxed program before and after school. Good after-school programs address children's needs with opportunities for play, socialization, and self-selected work. Although many see after-school programs as homework mills, and some homework can be incorporated, primary school children need the opportunity to play in the second half of their days away from home.

Staff-Child Ratio and Group Size

The number of staff members in relation to the number of children is an important factor in how you structure the day. In a program with a low staff-child ratio events, routines, and activities can be scheduled with more flexibility than if you work in a program with high adult-child ratios. With lower ratios you need not personally meet the needs of so many children and so are free to be more spontaneous and to plan for activities that have an unpredictable time frame or that require more intense adult-child interaction.

The size of the group will also influence the day. With smaller groups you can make spontaneous changes without disrupting others. You are able to give your full attention to individuals because fewer children require attention. Larger groups require more advance planning for the use of facilities, such as playgrounds, vans, and lunchrooms, and with them you must stick more closely to the schedule. Beyond a certain group size, no matter how low your ratios, you meet with inevitable problems. Large groups of young children are noisy, overstimulating, and stressful for the children and the staff.

The National Association for the Education of Young Children, which accredits early childhood programs, has set standards for adult-child ratios and group size in high-quality early childhood care and education programs. For a listing of those standards, see Table 7.1.

The Time of Year

A program day may differ from the beginning of the year to the end. During the first days and weeks, your program must allow time to help children become accustomed to routines and new activities. As the year progresses, children will have mastered routines and become accustomed to program expectations. They will have developed new skills and abilities. A clinging toddler may have become a bold explorer, an uncooperative preschooler may have become a group leader, and a shy first grader may have developed poise and confidence. Your schedule can be adjusted to recognize children's

Table 7.1   NAEYC Standards for Staff-Child Ratios and Group Size

Group Size:	6	8	10	12	14	16	18	20	22	24	30
Age of children:											
• Infants (birth to 12 months)	1:3	1:4									
• Toddlers (12 to 24 months)	1:3	1:4	1:5	1:4							
• 2-year-olds (24 to 30 months)		1:4	1:5	1:6							
• 2½-year-olds (30 to 36 months)			1:5	1:6	1:7						
• 3-year-olds					1:7	1:8	1:9	1:10			
• 4-year-olds						1:8	1:9	1:10			
• 5-year-olds						1:8	1:9	1:10			
• Kindergartners								1:10	1:11	1:12	
• 6- to 8-year-olds								1:10	1:11	1:12	1:15
• 9- to 12-year-olds										1:12	1:15

new competencies, cooperativeness, and skills. Group times may last longer as children come to enjoy group activities. Scheduled routines, such as toileting, may be omitted as children become independent and no longer require support and supervision.

Classroom Routines

Early childhood educators understand the importance of well executed daily routines for young children. They recognize that children must have their basic needs met in order to feel psychologically safe, secure, and accepted. Carefully designed routines support a primary goal of most early education and care programs: for young children to develop competence in independently meeting their physical and social needs. As an early childhood practitioner, you will want to give routines—the regular and more or less unvarying parts of classroom life—attention and thoughtful planning, just as you do the other aspects of the program. When daily routines are predictable, children know what to expect and have the resources they need for ordering and understanding their experiences. When you communicate your good reasons for establishing a routine and your commitment to having it work, children will usually cooperate and participate willingly. See the suggestions for routines in Figure 7.4.

Arrival

Arrival each day should be a friendly, predictable event. It is important to establish a routine in which every child is greeted. An arrival period during which you personally greet and talk briefly with families and children sets a relaxed tone. At this time, you can notice whether each child is in good health and appears ready to participate in the daily program. Arrival time may be one of the few regular contacts you will have with children's families, and it can be a good time for exchanging information. In some programs, one or two staff members greet families and help each child make the transition into the classroom.

Diapering, Toileting, and Toilet Learning

Diapering is an important part of routine caregiving for infants and toddlers. It is a time when children and caregivers can engage in one-to-one interactions that can be opportunities for both nurturing and teaching. Young children's emotional health, self-image, and ability to become independent are intimately tied to how they are treated during diapering and how they are helped to develop toilet skills. A positive, relaxed

Figure 7.4 **Suggestions for Routines**

- Give children several minutes' warning before a transition to the next part of the program day. Accommodate children who wish to finish an activity by extending activity time, providing additional time later, or by allowing them to return to the activity the next day.

- Be flexible about time while maintaining the usual sequence of events. Activity time might be lengthened if it doesn't mean skipping another important activity.

- Offer help when children request it or show unusual frustration, even if the task is one you know they ordinarily can do independently.

- Acknowledge cooperation by commenting on individual and group efforts rather than making negative comparisons. "Thanks for the help, Hur Youn!" not "I wish everyone cleaned tables as well as Hur Youn."

- Ignore noncooperation as much as possible, or give an alternative that is neither punishing nor rewarding. "If you are not helping, you may wait at that table." "Please come and stand by the door. I'm afraid someone will be hurt when you push in the bathroom."

- Maintain your communication style and tempo of movement during routines. It is disruptive if you suddenly start giving orders and rushing around.

- Avoid having children wait in lines or large groups with nothing to do.

- Give clearly stated reasons for routines. "We'll all clean up now so that we can sit down to lunch together."

- Offer choices only when there really is a choice. Avoid offering choices you are unwilling to allow. "It's time to go inside now," not "Would you like to go in?"

attitude toward diapering and toilet learning makes it a pleasant opportunity to interact with children.

Families vary in their beliefs about when toileting training should occur and how it should be accomplished. In some families early toilet learning is expected, while in others it is accepted if a child is still in diapers well into the third year of life. It is important that you discuss with families their expectations about when and how young children will learn to use the toilet and that you negotiate any differences in beliefs or practices in a respectful manner that honors both the needs of the family and of the early childhood program staff.

Children only gradually become self-reliant in using the toilet, but at no set age are all children ready to learn this skill. Between the ages of 2 and 3, young children generally are ready to begin to learn to use the toilet independently—but fears and reluctance to use the toilet at school are not uncommon and some children do not manage it until well into their third year. Children have an easier time using toilets when clothing is manageable and when fixtures are child-sized. Stable step stools that enable children to comfortably reach toilets and washbasins are essential if toilets and sinks are adult-sized. Children are more likely to become comfortable when you are patient and when attention is paid to making the bathroom a pleasant place. You will need to accompany reluctant or inexperienced children to the toilet to help and reassure them.

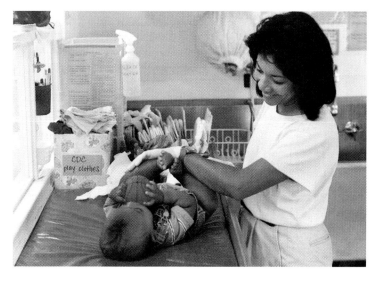

Even among children over 4, toilet mishaps are a normal part of life and may be a regular feature of the day. A child who is genuinely upset by an "accident" may need to be sheltered from public awareness and given help with cleanup. Other children may need only a small amount of direction and encouragement to take care of their own change of clothes. If your classroom of older children includes children with special needs who still wear diapers or have toilet accidents, you may need to take particular care to minimize potential humiliation and increase peer acceptance. A matter-of-fact attitude of acceptance on your part can make a great deal of difference.

Mealtimes and Snacks

Some of the most pleasant times in an early childhood program occur when adults and children sit down and eat together. Snacks and meals are pleasant when they are orderly enough to focus on eating and casual enough to be a social experience. Independence can be fostered as children participate in meal preparation and serving. For example, children can set the table, put their own cheese on a cracker, or pour their own juice. Children gain self-help skills when meals are served family style, passing bowls of food and small pitchers so that children can serve themselves. In some families and in some communities independence may not be a primary goal of mealtimes. In these settings children may be served by the adults rather than being expected to serve themselves.

Resistance to foods is common. You should neither force children to eat nor deny them the opportunity to eat. Food should never be withheld from children as punishment nor used as a reward. Young children become restless and irritable when they are expected to wait until everyone is served or while others finish. They may become anxious and unable to eat if they are hurried. Many problems can be avoided if you have a set routine for children who have finished eating before the rest of the group—for example, allowing them to leave the table to read a book or to play quietly with a game or toy.

In most programs children will have an opportunity to eat a morning breakfast or snack as well as a midday meal. In full-day programs they will also have an afternoon snack. Some full-day programs provide an additional snack toward the end of the day. This extra snack helps children and families to have more pleasant departure times without the "arsenic hour" syndrome of tired parents and hungry, whining children.

Not all families are able to feed their children nutritious foods. Therefore, it is important that meals and snacks meet children's daily nutritional requirements. The USDA food program guidelines are used as the standard for meals and snacks provided in many early childhood programs. To create appealing, nutritious, and culturally appropriate menus many programs use the services of a local nutrition specialist who is familiar with the food preferences of young children and their families. Guidelines are available from several sources for planning meals and snacks that meet the nutritional needs of infants, toddlers, preschoolers, and school-age children. In programs serving families from diverse cultural backgrounds, it is beneficial to have a committee of family members who are willing to review menus and give suggestions to ensure that the foods served are familiar and acceptable to the children. The traditional foods and food preparation methods of all cultural groups include foods that young children enjoy and thrive on. You can include such foods in your program menus and encourage family members from various traditions to share favorite recipes. If families provide children's food, you may need to give sensitive guidance concerning appropriate meals and snacks brought from home.

Reflect on routines

What routines do you have in your own life? How do you feel when the rhythm of daily routines is disrupted? What do you like about your routines?

What routines have you observed or implemented in programs for young children? When did these routines seem to harmonize with the activity of the classroom? When did they seem to be a disruption?

Cleanup

Cleanup prepares the classroom for the next activity and is a natural and necessary part of living with others. Children begin to understand that they are members of a community and that they need to share in the responsibility for maintaining cleanliness and order. All adults who work with young children find themselves doing a good deal of tidying of toys and equipment. As you straighten and reorder the environment you are helping children to see learning possibilities. In doing so, you also help children to understand the process of maintaining order.

Although cleanup is seldom a favorite activity, it need not be hard or unpleasant. Much of the drudgery that often surrounds cleanup comes from the attitude that is projected by staff. When you participate in cleanup with an attitude of expectant goodwill (I feel good about doing this and I expect that you share my feeling), children are generally also cheerful and cooperative. Often adults make cleanup the price that children must pay for the pleasure of play. Such an attitude discourages not only cleanup, but play itself. Children frequently resist cleanup when they are forced to straighten large messes without assistance. To a young child, a large mess may appear overwhelming and impossible to clean. Although it may seem easier to "do it yourself," it is important to persist in engaging children's participation. Your expectation and firm but gentle follow-through will help children become able and responsible members of a group.

Rest Time

Rest time can be a positive experience if children are tired, if the environment is made restful, and if children feel secure. If they are fearful of the setting, they will be unable to relax. Most children under the age of 5, and many 5-year-olds, sleep if the environment is soothing and comfortable. Every child in a preschool or kindergarten needs a mat or cot for sleeping. Infants need the protection of an individual crib or other sheltered sleeping space such as a mat surrounded by pillows. To create an atmosphere conducive to rest and sleep, dim lights, play quiet music, and allow children to cuddle personal comfort objects.

Infants and young toddlers signal their tiredness to caregivers who know them well through a variety of behaviors—some rub their eyes, others are "fussy" or clingy. Babies often fall asleep most easily if held close and rocked gently. Older toddlers and preschoolers may need a caring adult to rub their back or simply offer assurance by remaining nearby. At rest time focus on children, avoid speaking to others, and whisper when you must speak. When you are helping children to fall asleep it is important to be calm. Wait until most children are sleeping before you begin any other tasks. Children who nap will generally do so for at least 1 hour. When they are finished resting, children should be free to put away their mats and play quietly.

Children who do not sleep will respond to rest time positively if, after an initial rest, they are allowed to look at books and play quietly. Children who regularly do not sleep can rest away from others so their activity is not disturbing. Preschool children who are unable to sleep can rest but should not be required to lie down for more than an hour. The length of rest for nonsleeping children should be based on their needs and ability to relax. Five- to 8-year-olds also benefit from short quiet times in their day. In many programs this time is combined with an opportunity for reading.

The length of nap and rest periods should be based on children's needs. It may also provide a quiet period for teachers to collect themselves and do some planning or preparation, but it is not the primary purpose.

Each time a scheduled activity or routine ends, it is followed by a *transition*, a time of gathering children or of movement into a new activity. Transitions can be smooth and relaxed if they are well planned and if children are prepared for them. Suggestions for orchestrating smooth transitions can be found in Chapter 9.

Sometimes children must move to another area of the school as a group. The practice of lining up and walking silently can be difficult for young children (it is even challenging for adults!). In early childhood programs it is almost always unnecessary. To be a young child is to hop, skip, giggle, shout, jump, and run. You can encourage children to be safe by walking where running is hazardous, courteous by being quiet where others are working, secure by staying with the group, and attentive in a fire drill or emergency. Encouraging children to do all these things as necessary is reasonable and appropriate, but precision marching for an ordinary walk to the playground imposes an unnecessarily difficult task.

Experienced teachers design many creative ways for making transitions smooth, interesting learning experiences. You may wish to collect such ideas and invent your own.

Departure

The end of the program day should provide a smooth transition back into life at home. If all the children leave at the same time, departure can be structured to provide closure. You may read a story, go over events of the day, and plan for the next day. If children leave at different times throughout the afternoon, a staff member should be available to share information with families and say farewell as they leave.

Departure time can provide an opportunity to talk to families about children's experiences. Sharing this information helps families to know what kind of a day their child has had and to understand the behavior and needs the child may have when they get home. For example, a child who usually naps but does not one day may be unusually irritable, and a parent who knows the circumstances may respond with an early bedtime.

Sharing information about the child's day with families is essential in programs for infants and toddlers. Good infant-toddler programs have a systematic way of recording and sharing information about feeding, elimination, rest, and variations in the normal activity and behavior of the child, often a simple form kept on a clipboard in the classroom.

If closing staff are not the same as those who spend the day with children, some system for providing families with information is needed. We have seen teachers use mailboxes with handwritten notes, individual "sharing notebooks" with regular letters, and a daily bulletin of class events sent to each family with notes relevant to the individual child at the bottom of the page.

Good Endings

Just as beginnings and first days require thought and planning, so do endings require special care. All children enrolled in early childhood programs will experience times when they must change classes, teachers, or schools. The relationships that children build during their early childhood program experiences can be close, and it can be painful when they finish. For many children, it may be the first time that an important tie has ended.

Changing Classes

When children remain in a program for more than a year, they will usually experience at least one change of class or teacher. In programs that follow a 10-month or traditional public school calendar, the change will occur in the fall after a long summer vacation. In full-year programs, this change may occur when teachers feel that a child is ready for a new group or when space is needed in a group for younger children entering the program.

Although many children are ready and eager to move on to a new class, some are not. Making the transition to a new group requires the cooperation of both the staff and families. The change to a new class can arouse feelings of anxiety similar to those experienced during the initial days of school, and similar techniques can help make a bridge between the old and new class. This transition is easier when children know about their new class, when they can carry something familiar with them into the experience, and when the transition can be gradual. It also helps if children feel their parents and you have confidence in the new group and teacher.

Allow children in transition to make visits to their next class accompanied by you or a special friend. Let them visit for an activity that they especially enjoy, perhaps circle time one day and choice time another day, so that they can discover new materials, activities, and companions. On the official day of transition, have the child take responsibility for transferring personal belongings and setting up a new cubby or locker. Going back to the old room to share lunch or nap or simply to visit for a few minutes helps the child feel secure.

When You Leave

Like children, you will take vacations, become sick, and may eventually change jobs. These events sometimes take place in the middle of a school year. When you leave a group of children, either permanently or for an extended period of time, children experience feelings of loss. They may be sad that you are leaving and angry with you when you return. They may be fearful of the change and feel less secure until they build relationships with new staff. In programs for young children that have a team of staff in each class, the upsets of absences and departures are minimized. When children relate closely to two or more adults in the school, it is less traumatic when one of them must leave.

When you know that you or someone you work with will leave, it is important to consider the impact on children in planning and preparing for the transition. In one program we know, a staff member announced she would leave her job the same day that her teammate was going on a planned 6-week leave. The impact on children was serious. The 3- and 4-year-olds in the class were plagued by nightmares, bed-wetting, and fears about school. Another person we know learned that her husband was to be transferred and she would have to leave when her teammate had planned to move. They talked about the stress these changes would cause the children. They decided to have the staff member who was relocating leave the program 6 weeks early to give another person a chance to start so that both of the adults in the room would not leave at once. When you understand and take seriously your responsibility to children, you consider the impact of your personal decisions and adjust them to cause minimal distress.

Leave-taking is a natural part of relationships. Young children can accept these occasions more easily if adults do. When someone leaves, minimize changes in the environment and routines. Most importantly, help children understand that adults leave programs because of changes in their own lives and not in response to the behavior or actions of children or their families.

The Next School

Children in early childhood programs go on to other schools that can be significantly different from your program. One of your jobs is to prepare the children in your class for the transition to the next school.

Children may anticipate starting their new schools with both interest and concern. You can aid in the transition by helping to strengthen children's sense of themselves as competent, successful individuals. As you talk with them about the new school, acknowledge their growth and mention how the skills they have gained and the knowledge they have acquired will be useful in their new school. Say things like, "You know how to take care of your own lunch now, Tyrone. You're going to be able to handle it all by yourself in kindergarten."

Recent research has confirmed and early childhood teachers have long believed that children who experience successful adjustments from preschool to elementary school are more likely to succeed in school (Pianta & Cox 1999). You can help children, families, and other teachers if you take time to build relationships with the schools that children from your classroom are likely to attend. Learn all you can about their program and their expectations for children. Gather information about dates and application requirements and share this information with families. Encourage families to become familiar with their child's new school and if possible to arrange for a tour or visit prior to the child's first day. You help both child and family when you present a positive and enthusiastic perspective about the child's transition to a new school. Let families know that you are excited about their child's growth and progression to a new program and that you will welcome them and their child back for visits.

Early childhood programs should not be boot camps or training grounds for the next school! The time that children spend in early childhood programs should be spent on experiences that are appropriate for the early years. During the last few weeks before a transition to a new school, it may be beneficial to help children learn skills they will need. The more that you know about the schools in your community, the better able you will be to prepare children. If they will be expected to know about changing classes in response to a bell, standing in lines, getting their lunch from the cafeteria, doing work sheets, or raising hands, you can help children learn these skills in a short time. At the end of the program year, when they are more mature, children will be more able to learn them. We often practice these skills as large group dramatic play—"playing school."

> **Reflect on changing classes or changing schools**
>
> Remember changing to a new class or a new school. How did you feel? What did your teacher do? What made it easy or difficult? What does this experience suggest for you as an early childhood educator?

If your are in contact with the teachers in the next school, you may be able to get more specific information or even take the children to see their prospective school and meet the new teacher. Tell the children that they are practicing for their next school and role-play some of the routines that they will be expected to follow. Kindergarten and primary children often look forward to new events in their lives—new teachers, new classes, new challenges. Familiarity with the changes about to take place and time to talk about them and to consider their hopes and fears will fill endings with promise.

Everyone experiences some trepidation anticipating change. Whether the children are moving to a new class or a new program, or you or a colleague are leaving, you can work to turn endings into beginnings filled with enthusiasm and hope.

FINAL THOUGHTS

A good place for children, and a good place for adults, feels comfortable, feels like home. Safety and health, beginnings and endings, schedules and routines are the framework around which you will create a program for children. Alone they are not enough. Without them, your program will flounder. When the framework is sound, the experiences you provide are supported and your goals for children can be achieved. They are important foundations of your program day and of children's lives.

When children know that both you and the environment are trustworthy, they can direct their energy to exploring and experimenting in a setting designed to help them learn and develop. When you know that children are safe and healthy in the environment that you have designed, you are able to devote your energy to helping children to benefit from your program.

LEARNING OUTCOMES

When you read this chapter, thoughtfully complete selected assignments from the "To Learn More" section, and prepare items from the "For Your Portfolio" section, you will be demonstrating your progress in meeting NAEYC **Standard 1: Promoting Child Development and Learning.**
Key elements:

- Knowing and understanding young children's characteristics and needs

- Knowing and understanding the multiple influences on development and learning
- Using developmental knowledge to create healthy, respectful, supportive, and challenging learning environments.

TO LEARN MORE

Interview Practitioners About Health and Safety Issues: Interview two early childhood practitioners concerning health and safety. Ask them what issues they have dealt with. How did these issues become known? How did they deal with them? What community resources did they use? What did they learn? Report on what was said. Compare the two situations and suggest the implication for you as a future early childhood educator.

Use Health and Safety Checklists: Use the health and safety checklists found in Appendix B to evaluate an early childhood program. Report on what you found. Describe your thoughts about the safety and health of this program and the ways in which the staff could make it a safer and healthier place for children.

Keep a Separation Journal: Observe and keep a journal on a child during the first days and weeks of his or her school experience. Report on the child's responses to the school, the techniques used by the staff to support the child, and the family's reactions to the experience. Describe what you learned from your observation and its possible implications for you as an early childhood educator.

Observe a Classroom: Observe an early childhood classroom focusing on schedule, routines, and transitions. Describe them

and comment on their effectiveness. What changes would you suggest to better meet the needs of the children? Why? What are the implications of what you learned for you as a future early childhood educator?

Read a Book: Read one or more books about curriculum related to children's health and safety. Reflect on the book and decide on ways that you can use the information in your work with children. Some books to consider are:

Hendricks, Charlotte, and Connie Jo Smith. 1991. *Here We Go . . . Watch Me Grow!*

Johnson, Barbara, and Betty Plemons. 1994. *Cup Cooking.*

Katzen, Mollie, and Ann Henderson. 1994. *Pretend Soup and Other Real Recipes: A Cookbook for Preschoolers and Up.*

Rockwell, Robert E., Robert A. Williams, and Elizabeth Sherwood. 1992. *Everybody Has a Body: Science from Head to Toe.*

Smith, Connie Jo, Charlotte Hendricks, and Becky Bennett. 1997. *Growing, Growing Strong: A Whole Health Curriculum for Young Children.*

Veitch, Beverly, and Thelma Harms. 1981. *Cook and Learn: Pictorial Single Portion Recipes: A Child's Cookbook.*

FOR YOUR PORTFOLIO

Improve Classroom Health and Safety: Use the health and safety checklists to evaluate the early childhood program in which you work. Evaluate what you find and decide on some improvement(s) you wish to make to the health and safety of the program. Plan to document what you do (take photographs or make illustrations before and after the improvements). Write a paragraph explaining what you did and why. Place this documentation in your professional portfolio.

Plan and Implement Health and Safety Curriculum: Revisit the sections in the chapter titled "Helping Children Learn to Be Safe" and "Helping Children Learn to Be Healthy." Based on your observation and knowledge of the children in your classroom, select a safety or health concept or skill you feel is appropriate and important for them to learn. Plan an activity to help children learn about a health or safety concept or practice a skill. Implement the activity and document how it works. Place a description of the activity and your documentation of how it worked (photographs, a written analysis, etc.) in your professional portfolio.

Meet Children's Needs: After reading the chapter, reflect on how schedule, routines, and transitions are handled in your classroom. You may wish to include your coworkers in this reflection. Based on the ideas expressed in the chapter and your observations of the children in your classroom, generate ideas for what changes could be made to better meet the needs of the children. Briefly describe the proposed change and implement it. Observe and record the effect the change has on the children over several days, a week, then a month. Place the description of the change and your observations of its effect in your portfolio.

Build Your Recipe File: Review one or more of the children's cookbooks listed in the "Read a Book" section. Make a picture recipe that the children can follow, and then prepare the recipe with the children. Add the recipe to your file and place a copy of it along with a description and/or a photo of the children creating the recipe. Include discussion of what they learned from the activity.

8

The Learning Environment

3/13/06

A wonderful place to be a child is a place where a child can fall in love with the world.

Elizabeth Prescott

There is no behavior apart from environment.

Robert Sommer

● ●

The learning environment speaks to children. When they enter your program they will be able to tell whether it is a place for them and how you intend them to use it. A cozy corner with a rug, cushions, and books says, "Sit down here and look at books." A climbing structure with ladders, ramps, slides, nets, and a bridge suggests, "Climb up, go across any way you can think of, and come down a different way." An airy environment with light, color, warmth, and interesting materials to be explored sends a clear message: "We care—this is a place for children."

> *It is the first morning of a new school year. The teachers have carefully set up the indoor and outdoor environment. There are trikes to ride, easels with paint, tubs of water, sand, blocks, puzzles, building toys, picture books, a chameleon, pens and crayons, and a dramatic play area with dolls, clothes, and props including hats, shoes, fancy dresses, and lengths of cloth. Four-year-old Cordell and his mother enter the classroom and look around. Cordell makes a beeline for the dramatic play area, finds a construction hat, and puts it on. He slings a shiny beaded purse over his shoulder. He goes up to Kaito who is wearing a cowboy hat and says, "We're police guys, right?" He turns and smiles at his mom and then turns to play with his new friend.*

Environments with space to move, comfortable child-sized furnishings, inviting materials, and an arrangement that suggests how materials can be used provides a feeling of comfort and security. Materials and images that reflect children, their families, their cultures, and their community let children and their families know that they belong. Soft lighting, natural and man-made items of beauty, tell them that they are valued. Comfortable places for big and little people to sit tell them they are welcome. All of these create an atmosphere of warmth and informality that meets the social-emotional needs of young children and enables them to interact with people and materials in ways that support their development and learning.

A unique characteristic of the field of early childhood education and care is the careful attention that teachers pay to designing learning environments. As you read in Chapter 3, the philosophers and educators whose work forms the foundation of our field have long recognized the critical role of the environment in children's learning and development. When you look at a well designed environment for children you will see:

- Many opportunities for children to play, as suggested by Jan Amos Comenius
- Child-sized furniture and accessible and orderly shelves, as recommended by Maria Montessori
- Inviting hands-on materials like parquetry blocks and paper with scissors, based on the gifts and occupations of Frederich Fröebel

- Unit blocks designed by Caroline Pratt
- Daily opportunities for play outdoors with mud, sand, and water, as prescribed by Margaret and Rachel McMillan
- Natural play materials, as described by Rudolph Steiner

The learning environment that you establish should reflect your values for children as well as the values of the program and the children's families. It should confirm children's sense of identity, connection, and belonging. More than that, it should engage children in learning by awakening their senses, provoking curiosity and wonder, and stimulating their intellect.

Young children are learning all the time. The materials of their early childhood programs, as noted by Harriet Cuffaro (1995), can be viewed as the children's "textbooks." In the eyes of the educators of Reggio Emilia, the environment is the children's "third teacher" (Edwards, Gandini, & Forman 1998). The learning environment is both a powerful teaching tool and the outward and visible sign to families that you are caring for and providing appropriate experiences for their children.

Learning environments can meet the needs of children and support your educational values and developmental goals. The choices you make as you design the environment influence the quality of children's relationships with other people and learning materials. In making these choices, you need to ask yourself three very basic questions:

1. Is this environment appropriate for the age, stage, characteristics, community, and culture of these children? In other words is it safe, healthy, and reflective of who the children are?
2. Does it engage these children physically, socially, emotionally, and intellectually? Does it include elements that develop a sense of wonder?
3. Does this environment support relationships between all the people here—between children, between adults and children, and between adults?

CREATING A LEARNING ENVIRONMENT

Reflect on the environment of your first school

Remember your first school (or any school that was important to you during your childhood). What about the environment stands out in your memory: the classroom, the playground, the equipment and materials, storage and distribution of materials, the beauty of the setting? Was anything wonderful or magical for you? Why? How was the school similar to or different from your home? Did it reflect your culture and family in any way? What do you wish had been different? How do you think the environment affected your learning and relationships?

On your own or with a team of coworkers, you will have responsibility for organizing a learning environment. You will arrange the room and select equipment and materials to facilitate all areas of development. You will design a schedule that ensures that the children's basic needs are met and that they have enough time for activities that support learning and development. In fact, you are one of the most important aspects of the environment because you have control over, and responsibility for, all of the other parts—the time, space, equipment, and materials. Your knowledge of children will help you design a program that provides opportunities to move, interact, explore, represent, create, and manipulate.

Sally has been hired to teach a class of young 5-year-olds for a summer enrichment program in the basement of a neighborhood church. With little equipment or money she surveys the big room, which will be home to 15 children for the next 6 weeks. In one corner she has draped a carton of hymnals with a pretty tablecloth. On it she has placed a purple cup full of marking pens and a basket of recycled paper. In a corner marked off by a low pew she has created a dramatic play corner with "housekeeping" furniture that she made out of cardboard boxes, her childhood dolls, and dress-up clothes from the rummage sale bin. Dishpans with Legos, wooden beads, and blocks gleaned from her friends' closets fill a board-and-brick shelf next to a small carpet. Sheltered by the piano, a library corner has been created with a pile of pillows re-covered with remnant fabrics and a basket full of books from the public library. Tables and chairs from the Sunday school and a garage sale easel complete the classroom. The park across the street will provide the outside play area. There's water in a portable cooler and a bathroom a few steps away. It's not ideal, but Sally feels sure that she can provide a good experience for children in this learning environment.

The learning environment you create will be influenced by many things but first by the building and the grounds that surround it. You may find yourself working in a space that is "purpose-built" to be an early childhood program. However, early childhood programs are frequently housed in buildings created for other purposes. Although these settings may not be ideal, they can be workable and even charming. We have known and loved programs in converted homes, church sanctuaries, basements, apartment units, offices, and storefronts.

An appropriate environment for young children will be different for different ages, but some similarities cross the early childhood age span. All young children need a clearly defined "home" space for their group or class. They need secure, ongoing access to drinking water and toilets. They also need an outdoor play area with access to nature and space for active play that can be used year-round. Enough space indoors and outdoors is needed. A program also needs to provide access for individuals (children, family members, visitors, or staff) who use walkers or wheelchairs.

Self-Contained and Open-Design Classrooms

The design of a building suggests certain ways to use it as an early childhood program. One type of early childhood program building has self-contained classrooms and a shared playground. It is designed so that single classes work within four walls where most of the materials needed for learning will be found. Each group of children is intended to spend most of the time in "their" room with regular time alone or with other classes on the playground. Another type of building has an open design. These have been constructed so that many children (sometimes the entire population of a school) will be within one room most of the time. Teams are expected to arrange large interest centers throughout the room, usually with a large multifunction or large motor space in the middle. Adjacent outdoor space usually includes one or two large playgrounds.

Facilities need not be used as they were designed. A team of teachers can use self-contained classrooms, giving each room and yard area a particular function (e.g., one room may be the messy activity room with space for art and sensory activities and another for blocks and dramatic play; one playground may be used for trikes and another for climbing apparatus). Open rooms are often turned into self-contained "classrooms" using dividers, furniture, and taped lines to suggest walls. A large playground can be subdivided into different types of play zones.

Advantages and Disadvantages of Self-Contained and Open-Design Classrooms

Both self-contained and open-design classrooms offer advantages, and have drawbacks. Extremes are not optimal. We have seen children confined in classrooms that were little larger than closets and rooms housing more than 100 children where noise and confusion made conversation and concentration impossible.

Self-contained classrooms offer a homelike atmosphere, a feeling of security and belonging, and a pride of ownership in the classroom. This is good for all children and especially important for very young children. However, very small classrooms may not provide enough space for children to move or allow you to provide a rich variety of learning experiences at all times. Large open-design classrooms offer space for movement and allow you to make more, and more diverse, learning experiences available. They are inevitably noisier and less homey.

Smaller programs and smaller group size have a positive effect on children. It is possible to gain the advantages of a small program and small group in programs in self-contained classrooms; it is much more difficult to do so when a single large room holds many children. Large rooms with many children are less appropriate for most young children and inappropriate for infants and toddlers, who thrive in environments that are more sheltered from stimulation and that are more like homes.

> **Reflect on an early childhood classroom you have known**
>
> Think about an early childhood classroom you have observed. Was it a self-contained classroom or part of an open-design building? What advantages for children or teachers were evident to you in this kind of classroom? What were its drawbacks? If you were a teacher in this setting, how would you change the learning environment? Why?

PRINCIPLES FOR DESIGNING LEARNING ENVIRONMENTS

You will have many choices in designing an environment that supports children's learning and well-being. It will be a reflection of who you are and who the children are. Though your environment will be unique, it should follow some basic principles of learning environment design.

Arrange the Environment for Safety and Health

As we described in Chapter 7, every environment for young children must be safe and meet the health needs of their age and stage. Ensuring health and safety is the first principle of learning environment design. Your classroom and outdoor play area must be arranged so that they can be easily supervised, cleaned, and maintained. In a program for infants and toddlers this means an adult must be able to see all of the children, all of the time. Drinking water, diapering, sinks, and sleep areas must be accessible and supervised whenever they are in use.

In a program for preschoolers you have greater latitude. If there are no environmental hazards, a preschooler may be safely playing in one area while you work with other children a few feet away, supervising all the children by sight and sound. While standing you should be able to see the whole preschool room or yard and all the children in it. Water to drink, toilets and sinks, and quiet places for resting must be accessible and easy to supervise throughout the day.

School-age children can safely have more independence. It is desirable, especially for kindergartners, to have toilets and drinking water in the classroom or yard. However, first and second graders can, and often must, walk to nearby bathrooms, drinking fountains, playground, or classroom with minimal supervision.

Another principle for the design of both the indoor and outdoor early childhood learning environment is to organize it in areas, centers (terms we use interchangeably), or zones (which we usually use when talking about outdoor areas). The areas will vary with the age of the children and with the geographic locale of the program. For example, infants and toddlers need spaces in which to be changed and washed, to sleep, to eat, and to play. Preschoolers need areas for books, blocks, manipulative toys, sensory experiences, inquiry activities, art, dramatic play, and vigorous physical play. School-age children need spaces to work on their own and with others, to work on and display projects, for play, and for whole group meeting. Programs in geographic areas with extreme weather conditions need indoor areas for active play, while those in more mild climates can use the outdoors for a wide variety of activities.

Design Principles for Indoor Areas

There are several design principles to keep in mind as you arrange classroom areas or centers to ensure a smoothly functioning classroom. How you arrange each area, and how each relates to other areas, will determine how productively children will use the opportunities you offer them.

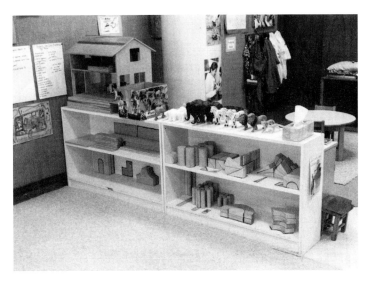

• *Begin by defining areas.* Common to the arrangement of a classroom in learning centers or areas is the idea of partial seclusion (that is shelter on two or three sides). Most areas are partially secluded from the rest of the classroom with shelves and dividers. A center that invites foot traffic on four sides is unlikely to be as successful as one that is protected on two or three sides. Art areas, eating areas, and areas for messy activities like water play should be near water and will be easier to clean if there is an uncarpeted floor. If children eat lunch in the classroom, the art center can double as the eating area. A library area requires good lighting. A science area may need an electric outlet for an aquarium. The tape player in a listening or music center will also need access to electricity. Blocks will be quieter on a carpeted surface, as long as the carpet has a very low nap.

• *Provide more space for areas for blocks, manipulative toys, and dramatic play.* Some areas will require more space than others. Children naturally tend to work together in groups when building with blocks, when engaging in dramatic play, and when constructing with manipulative toys. These areas need to be large enough to accommodate a group of children. Children tend to work independently when they read books, do puzzles, or write, so these areas can be smaller. A center with a table will naturally suggest how many children can play by the number of seats you have provided.

• *Separate noisy activities from quiet activities.* Young children are naturally talkative and noisy, a fact that you cannot, and should not, attempt to change. Carpeting and pillows will provide a comfortable place to relax and help to absorb noise. Some centers necessarily involve more noise than others (e.g., block building and dramatic play). If your classroom is spacious enough, these should be placed away from areas that involve quiet concentration (e.g., library, puzzles).

• *Provide space to be together and space to be alone.* There will be times, even in classrooms for infants and toddlers, that all of the children and teachers will gather together. For this reason every room needs a space large enough for the adults and children to sit comfortably together. This space may double as an area for large motor activities or block play. Quiet, comfortable space to be alone is also important. Children who spend long hours away from home need a place to be alone. By providing places where children can safely feel alone you will avoid having children create unsafe hiding places.

• *Avoid corridors and racetracks.* The space between centers must also be considered. Pathways give access to all the centers. Paths that are too long and narrow, or racetracks (circular paths around shelves or tables), will invite running. Work will be interrupted if paths lead through areas where children are working.

Design Principles for Outdoor Areas

Every program for young children needs an outdoor play area. When you recall your own childhood play experiences, you probably remember outdoor play. Inside play is restricted—*walk slowly, talk softly, don't break it, don't get it dirty.* But outside, the loud, active, enthusiastic play of children is safe, permitted, and encouraged.

Just as the buildings that house programs vary, so do outdoor space designs. Unfortunately, spacious yards carefully designed for young children are the exception rather than the rule. In a program located in the business district of a big city, play space may be a porch, a rooftop, or a paved parking lot. In a suburban or rural setting, it is likely to have a grassy yard with some play equipment. While almost every kind of learning activity can take place out of doors, one way of thinking about your outdoor environment is to think of it as having play zones with distinct purposes. Whether your outdoor space is a rooftop or a garden, there are principles for the design of the outdoor environment so that it meets children's needs.

• *Provide space and equipment for active play.* Every outdoor environment needs space—to run, jump, skip, and ride. Big areas, grassy if possible, are needed for children to safely run and play games. A place to climb up high and equipment for sliding and swinging (with safe surfacing underneath) allow children to see things from a different perspective and provide different kinds of sensation. Mud and sand in which to dig and water for pouring are soothing and provide important learning experiences. Riding toys, wagons, and carts to push require hard surfaces that lead somewhere. School-age children require greater variety and more challenge in their play yards than do younger children. They are able to go higher, jump farther, and learn new skills such as sliding down long poles, balancing along high balance beams, and turning on parallel bars. Primary children also will need additional movable equipment such as hoops, bats, and balls for organized games, and hard surfaces for rope jumping and ball bouncing. Storage shelves or sheds for toys, woodworking tools, easels, trikes, carts, and wagons should be located near the area where they will be used.

• *Make sure there are increasingly challenging experiences.* Children need challenge. Merely accomplishing something is not enough. Once a challenge has been met, a new one must be found. Once a child has learned to climb up and slide down a slide, a new way to slide will be sought. Every outdoor environment needs to have within it a variety of challenges. There should be some things that take time and persistence to master. If your outdoor environment does not have sufficient challenges, children will begin to invent their own. To make sure that these are safe you can add equipment and activities. For example, a row of tires half-buried in the sand can create a balancing challenge. A pathway of cones on the sidewalk is a challenge for the driver of a tricycle. Thinking of new ways to create challenge in the outdoor environment is one of your responsibilities. Whether the equipment is purchased or improvised, your outdoor environment requires thoughtful evaluation, planning, and change on a regular basis.

- *Provide access to nature.* In a society in which young children spend most of their time indoors, experience with the natural world is vital. An outdoor environment needs plants, dirt, trees, grass, and the creatures that inhabit them. When the outside play area is a rooftop or parking lot it is critical to make these include nature by adding potted plants, garden boxes, pets, and sand tables (to fill with sand, water, or dirt). Regular walks to parks can supplement but do not substitute for daily experience with nature in the playground.

- *Provide places to comfortably think, relax, and daydream.* In the outdoor environment, as in the indoor environment children need a place to escape the noise and activity of the group. A sturdy crate, a playhouse, a secluded nook under the play structure, or a quiet place under a hedge can provide this kind of opportunity. If the landscaping and permanent equipment don't provide these kinds of places you can add them temporarily with big cardboard appliance boxes.

- *Include many learning experiences outside.* Because children are learning all the time, not just when they are in the classroom, outdoor space and equipment should support a range of developmental goals: physical, social, cognitive, and creative. The playground can be used for an endless variety of learning activities. For instance, in places where the climate is mild most of the year it can be the primary location for sand and water play, pets, art activities, woodworking, block building, and even group times. As you design your outdoor environment you can keep this in mind. Animals, gardens, sandboxes, hollow blocks, dramatic play, and water play areas located outdoors can be the source of science, math, language development, and creative activities. Messy art materials such as clay and finger paint are especially well suited to outdoor use. Access to water is important near sand and water tables, art areas, gardens, and pets.

- *Provide ways for different kinds of activities to link.* While in the indoor environment much care is taken to separate and protect play areas, in the outdoor environment teachers look for ways to arrange play zones so that play in one area can naturally link to play in other zones. For example, children riding trikes can stop at a dramatic play zone to deliver a package or visit.

- *Create visual boundaries.* Visual boundaries help protect children's play, as well as their well-being. For example, children can be hurt by another child swinging, so a low border of tires or plants that identifies the swinging area protects all the children.

- *Bring indoor activities outside.* Even where it is sometimes cold, wet, or hot, there are times when indoor activities can and should be taken outside. Learning experiences take on new dimensions when they move outdoors. A story about trees, for example, read in the shade of an oak carries new meaning. Painting a picture with nature in view is different from painting in a classroom. Singing songs outside feels different from singing inside. Dressing up and pretending outside is more adventurous than doing so inside. We all enjoy a picnic now and again. Almost every activity that happens indoors can come outside at least once in awhile.

The floor plans in Figures 8.1, 8.2, and 8.3 illustrate the ways indoor environments for young children of different ages might be arranged.

Design Principles for Storage

Attention to storage can contribute to the smooth functioning of a program as well as to its aesthetic quality. Outdoors as well as indoors, storage should be organized and predictable. A thoughtfully organized environment helps children to understand and

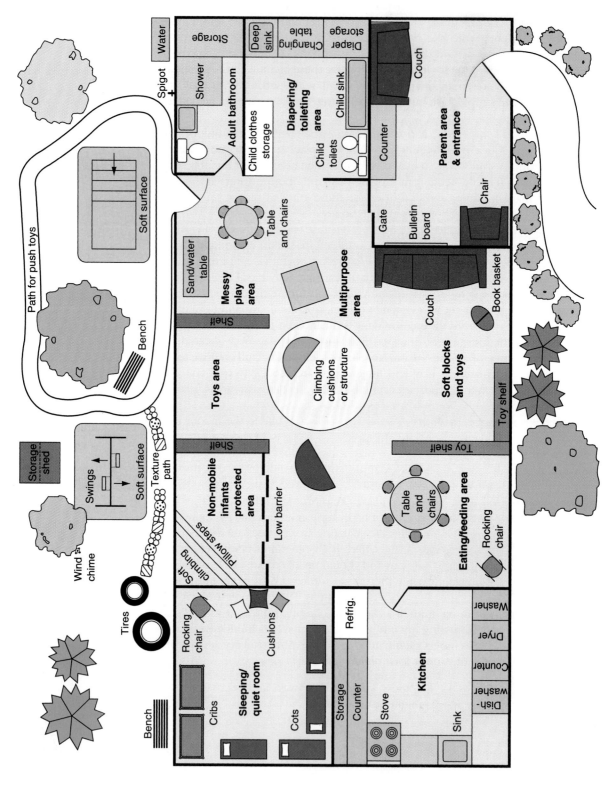

Figure 8.1   **Infant and Toddler Program Floor Plan**

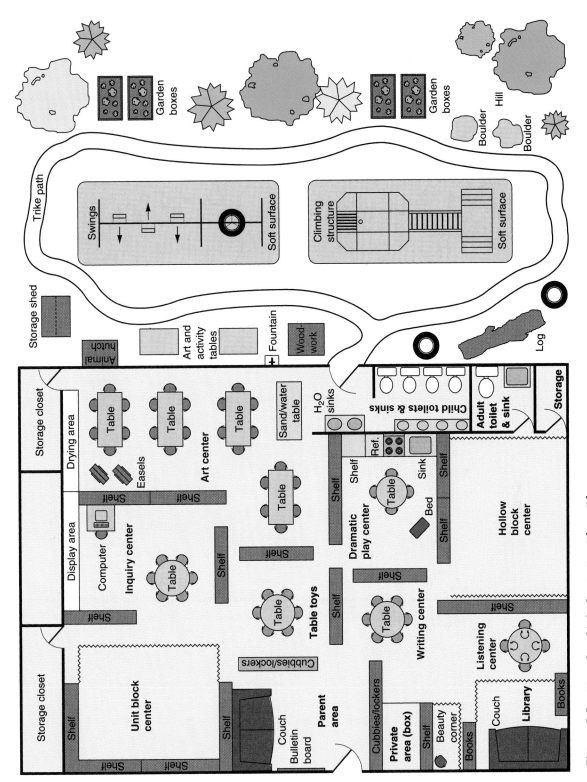

Figure 8.2 **Preschool/Kindergarten Floor Plan**

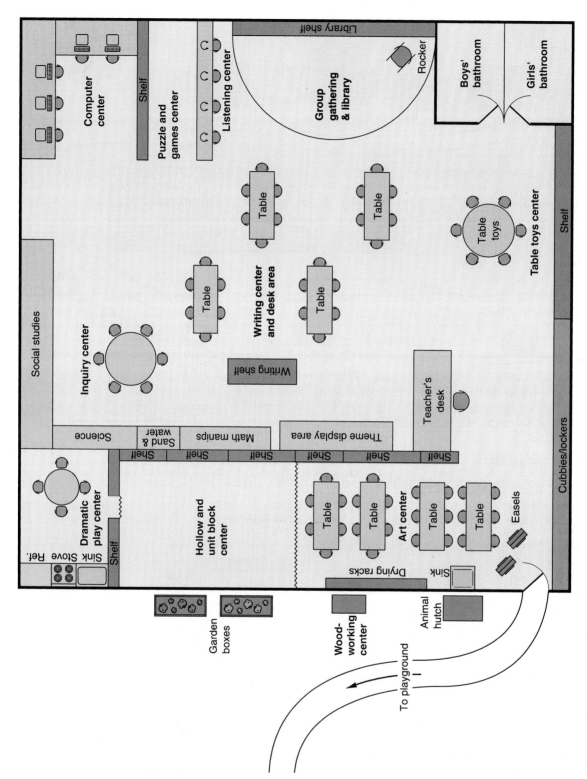

Figure 8.3   Primary Classroom Floor Plan

232

maintain order. Materials that are carefully and attractively arranged contribute to the design of a pleasant place in which to live and work.

- *Store materials for children's use on low, open shelves.* When children look at the environment they should be able to tell at a glance what materials are available to them. If materials are stored on low, open shelves, they tell children that they are available for their use.

- *Store restricted materials out of reach and out of sight.* Materials that are reserved for use by adults need to be stored so they are out of children's reach and view. Cleaning supplies, files, first aid equipment, and staff personal belongings need locked or high storage within the classroom or nearby areas.

- *Label shelves.* Children will be more self-sufficient if shelves and other storage areas are marked to indicate where to put things away. You can support their growing independence by creating systems that enable children to understand and participate in classroom organization. Materials can be stored in containers labeled with pictures of the contents. Some teachers code shelves and materials with self-adhesive colored dots to indicate the learning center in which they are stored (red dots for the manipulative toys, yellow dots for the writing area, and so on). Silhouettes of materials on shelves help children match an item to its proper place.

Design Principles for Equipment and Materials

Think of a plaything you loved when you were a child. Chances are good that you remember what it looked like, how it felt, what it did, and how you used it. You may even know where it is today. Good toys are attractive. They have sensory appeal and feel good to touch and hold. Because they are children's tools for learning, the materials in a classroom must be kept in good repair, work properly, and fit children's size, abilities, and interests. They must be nontoxic, clean, and free of hazards. They should be sturdy and not easily broken.

Equipment and materials suggest direction and provide raw material for children's exploration, development, and learning. Generally, *equipment* refers to furniture and other large and expensive items such as easels and climbing structures. The term *materials* usually refers to smaller, less expensive items such as puzzles, books, games, and toys. Consumables like paint, paper, glue, and tape are referred to as *supplies.*

- *Choose safe, good quality, sturdy equipment and materials and supplies.* Have you ever sat at a table that wobbled? Have you ever had a tool that broke when you tried to use it? It is frustrating, disappointing, and often unsafe to work with equipment and materials that are poorly made. Ensuring that the learning environment has safe, good-quality, sturdy equipment and materials is an important part of your job. Unless you are hired to open a new program with a lot of money to equip it, you are unlikely to have the opportunity to shop for the equipment and materials to set up your learning environment. Fortunately, selecting safe, good-quality, sturdy equipment and furnishings is not a matter of spending lots of money on lots of new things. It is more often a matter of discarding materials that are broken, damaged and unfixable; maintaining and fixing the equipment and materials you have; creatively recycling when appropriate; and purchasing materials that are of good quality that will last when you have money to spend.

- *Make sure furniture is appropriate for young children.* The furnishings in an early childhood program should support classroom activities and respond to the needs of children. We favor wood because of its beauty and sturdiness and because it is easy to maintain. Appropriate furniture for young children is stable, portable, and has rounded corners and edges. Infants need low, stable chairs that offer back and side support. Cube chairs that can double as stools for adults work well. Toddlers are better able to manage squat, four-legged stools than chairs, which tend to tip. Older children can be comfortable and can focus when seated at tables if their feet touch the floor and their elbows can rest on tabletops. Small tables where several children can sit provide greater flexibility than large tables and leave more space free for diverse activity than a room filled with desks for each child.

- *Provide individual storage for children.* Every child needs space for the storage of personal belongings. Cubby holes meet this need. Cubby holes can be manufactured or improvised using such materials as dishtubs, sweater boxes, cardboard boxes, or commercial 5-gallon ice cream tubs. Where children come to school in coats and boots, special hangers and storage shelves for these garments need to be provided.

- *Select low, open shelves.* Low, open shelves are good for storage of materials that children use independently. They allow children to make choices and make it easier for them to participate in cleanup. If shelves are on wheels they must be locked or on casters for safety. A shelf especially designed for books invites reading by displaying the books with their covers facing the children. It is relatively easy for young children to return the books to such a shelf, which helps to protect the books. Infant-toddler environments require lower shelves and appropriately sized, strong and safe furniture. Very young children are less likely to climb on shelves that they can see over. Additional furnishings should include a sturdy changing table at a comfortable height for adults (we prefer tables with stairs that roll in and out to encourage independence and save the backs of staff), a secure crib or sleeping space for each infant in the program, and comfortable adult chairs for holding and rocking children.

- *Include comfortable seating for grown-ups.* Since teachers and parents also spend time in the classroom it is important to have a comfortable chair for an adult and child to sit together. This contributes to the homelike feeling that is so important for young children in group settings.

- *Make sure there's enough to do.* As you set up an environment you will carefully choose the materials from which children will make selections. A few principles can help you to make wise choices. Every classroom should have enough materials for the number of children who play there to have several options. A classroom for 10 children might have 40 choices spread throughout eight centers, while a classroom for 20 children might have 70 choices. There is no precise formula—there should be enough choices in each area so that the number of children who play there can be actively engaged.

- *Avoid clutter.* Another principle is to avoid overcrowding the materials. Children should be able to easily see materials available to them and easily see where and how to put them away. Similar materials grouped together, stored in matching basins or baskets, demonstrate that you really care, and it helps others to care as well.

- *Introduce new materials.* While young children are natural players, they do not naturally know how to play with the wide array of materials that you have in your classroom. Whenever you welcome a new group of children to your classroom, or bring in a new material to your room, it is important to introduce materials to the children. This can be a ceremony. Materials have a longer and more productive life when their use and care is demonstrated and their initial use supervised. This does not mean that children's innovative use of materials should be discouraged, nor does it eliminate all problems. However it does minimize problems as children learn to treat play materials with respect.

- *Start simply.* It is tempting to put out the newest materials first, to give children what you enjoy most. However, children will benefit if you begin with simpler materials and gradually add more complexity as they gain familiarity and skill.

- *Rotate materials.* Regardless of whether you have a big classroom or a small one, it is valuable to rotate materials on the shelves. The same materials left out week after week will lose their allure. A toy that has been in the cupboard for a few weeks will be seen as more inviting and encourage more creative play.

- *Remove damaged materials.* It is a basic principle of good learning environment design to remove any broken toys, dolls with missing limbs, torn or scribbled-on books, tattered dress-up clothes, or puzzles and games with missing pieces. By leaving these in the classroom you give a message to children: *We don't respect the toys and you don't have to either—it's okay to break or damage play materials here.* Classrooms with damaged materials inevitably become home to even more damaged materials. They show children and parents that you don't care.

- *Model respect for materials.* When a book is torn, a puzzle piece is missing, or a block is scribbled on you can model respect for these resources by mending, refurbishing, or cleaning them. We like to do this with children, encouraging them to participate in the process (particularly, if the children were party to the damage). Using broken toys, puzzle pieces, or children's books as the raw materials of art projects is not recycling to a young child. Instead it sends an unclear message that appears to model abuse of materials and implies that it is acceptable to cut up books or glue puzzle pieces. Similarly, using a triangular block as a doorstop, or a hollow block as a stepstool in the bathroom suggests that you do not respect these play materials, and don't expect children to do so.

> **Reflect on a place you like to be**
>
> Think of a place that you like to be. What do you do there? What do you like about it? Why? How could you add some of these things to the learning environment you create for children?

Pay Attention to Aesthetics

An aspect of the learning environment that is often overlooked in the design and arrangement of classrooms and playgrounds is aesthetics. We believe that children's environments should be beautiful places. Attention to the aesthetic quality means looking for ways to make aspects of the classroom harmonious by paying attention to design, color, and texture in the selection and arrangement of furnishings, equipment and materials, and the decorative items.

In a center we often visit we are struck by the contrast between two classrooms. One is cluttered with many commercially produced materials on the walls, shelves stuffed with materials in storage, a high noise level, and the odor of an unclean rabbit cage. In contrast, a neighboring classroom is an oasis of pleasant sensory experience. The furnishings in each learning center are color-coordinated; large, well tended plants divide and define some learning centers; the carpets and window fabrics throughout the room complement each other in color and texture; art posters and children's art productions decorate the walls; instrumental music often plays softly; and a basket of herbs or blossoms scents the air.

Playgrounds become pleasant and sensorially rich places when a variety of ground surfaces are used; when careful attention is paid to the planting of trees, shrubs, flowers, herbs, and other plants; and when play structures and other permanent features are selected for both their function and attractiveness. We feel all children deserve to be surrounded by beauty in their early childhood programs and that such classrooms and playgrounds create an atmosphere that is more conducive to learning and development. Here are some specific suggestions for the aesthetic enhancement of environments for young children:

- *Color:* Bright colors will dominate a room and may detract from art and natural beauty present. If you have a choice, select soft light, neutral colors for walls and ceilings. Try to color-coordinate learning centers so that children begin to see them as wholes rather than as parts. Avoid having many different patterns in any one place because they can be distracting and overstimulating.
- *Furnishings:* Group similar furniture together and keep colors natural and neutral, to focus children's attention on the learning materials on the shelves. When you are

choosing furnishings, select wood rather than metal or plastic. If you must paint furniture, use one neutral color for everything so that you have greater flexibility in moving it from space to space. Have a cleaning day periodically; give children brushes and warm soapy water and let them scrub the furniture on a sunny, warm day.

- *Storage:* Rotate materials on shelves rather than crowding them together. Crowded shelves look unattractive and are hard for children to maintain. Use attractive storage containers (baskets and wooden bowls are appealing choices). If you use storage tubs use the same kind and color on one shelf. If you use cardboard boxes, cover them with plain-colored paper or paint them.
- *Decoration:* Mount and display children's artwork. Provide artwork by fine artists and avoid cartoons, advertisements, and garish, stereotyped, faded, or tattered posters. Make sure that much of the artwork (both by children and adult artists) is displayed at children's eye level. Use shelf tops as places for displaying sculpture, plants, and items of natural beauty like shells, stones, and fish tanks. Avoid storing teachers' materials on the tops of shelves. If no other choice is possible, create a teacher "cubby" using a covered box or storage tub.

- *Outdoors:* Design or arrange play structures as an extension of nature rather than an intrusion upon it. If possible use natural materials like wood and hemp rather than painted metal, plastic, or fiberglass. Provide adequate storage to help maintain materials. Involve children, parents, and other staff in keeping outdoor areas free of litter. Add small details like a garden or a rock arrangement to show that the outdoors is also a place that deserves attention and care. (Feeney & Moravcik, 1987)

Reflect the Children

We live in a diverse society and so early childhood learning environments need to reflect and honor that diversity. As you select materials that portray people (books, artwork, software, and dramatic play props) it is important that your choices reflect and affirm diversity (culture, gender, race, ability, language, and family lifestyle). They also need to reflect the specific culture and community of the children and families who attend your program. An early childhood program in rural South Carolina should look different from a program in Chicago, Alaska, or Delaware. You can reflect the children in your environment in several ways.

When children find photographs of themselves and their families in the classroom they know that it is a place that is for them. If you can, take pictures of the children and the families when they enter the school. Use these to mark cubbies, make books, and create games. Families can be invited to share a family photo and a picture of their child if you do not have resources for taking photos. When you are selecting dolls, books, puzzles, and posters be sure to look for those that resemble the children and their families.

Some of the ways that you can create a program with a sense of place is to include natural materials and art from your local environment and community. For example, in Hawaii, teachers often use lauhala baskets for storage, pandanus seeds as brushes, Aloha shirts and muumuus for dress-up clothes, and dry coconuts for pounding nails.

Some display the work of Hawaii artists depicting Hawaiian scenes on the walls. Similarly we have seen programs in Alaska where the dramatic play area was turned into a fishing camp.

Avoid Being Cute

For many years we have fought against the pervasive tendency to make environments for young children too cute. What is excessively cute? Children are endearing, attractive, and charming. They are also human beings who are individual, strong, and worthy of our respect. They have intense, real feelings and desires. Appropriate early childhood learning environments and materials are similarly endearing, attractive, and charming. They are also well made and real.

When a program environment is overly cute it suggests that, because children are younger and less accomplished than adults, they also feel less, are less individual, and are less worthy of respect. It is overly cute to have posters throughout the school with wide-eyed ladybugs that admonish children to be happy and well behaved, instead of books about insects and opportunities to observe them. It is excessively cute when the walls of a school are covered with pictures of cartoon characters instead of providing space on the walls to display children's work or the work of artists.

What's wrong with cute? Jim Greenman speaks against what he calls The Unbearable Lightness of Cuteness: "Cuteness robs wonder of its evocative power, pasteurizing awe and delight into one-dimensional chuckles and fuzzy glows" (Greenman 1998, p. 62). Overly cute materials are trivial. They suggest that the learning that occurs in early childhood programs is neither serious nor important.

CREATING INTEREST AREAS

When you arrange a learning environment into areas the equipment, furnishings, materials, and supplies available in each area must be adequate for the work and play meant to go on there. Each needs appropriate furnishings, necessary equipment, and sufficient supplies. The use of interest areas for distinct kinds of play is most common in programs for toddlers, preschoolers, and kindergarten-aged children, while in programs for primary school children more space for individual and group work usually supplants some of the play areas we describe.

Blocks

Since the time of Fröebel (and probably before) blocks have been used as toys for young children. There are many kinds of blocks available today including replicas of Fröebel's first "gift," the many relatives of small interlocking plastic Legos, and foam blocks for babies. However, when an early childhood educator says "blocks," he or she is referring to the hardwood *unit blocks* designed by Caroline Pratt and Harriet Johnson and their larger cousins, *hollow blocks.* Today a set of hardwood unit blocks is considered an essential part of a preschool or kindergarten learning environment. They can also be well used by 2-year-olds and primary school children.

Unit blocks and hollow blocks help develop motor coordination and strength, enhance imagination, and provide opportunities for children to work together. They provide learning experiences in measurement, ratio, and problem solving. Children building with blocks gain experience in abstract representation that contributes to the ability to read and write. Children also learn about mathematical relationships

237

when they experience that two blocks of one size are equivalent to the next larger size blocks. Hollow blocks allow children to build a world that they can physically enter. They inspire and contribute to rich dramatic play. All blocks serve as a vehicle through which children can express their growing understanding of the world.

A Unit Block Area

A unit block area begins with a set of hardwood unit blocks. A basic set includes at least 100 blocks and eight shapes, sometimes called a *nursery school set.* A larger set that includes approximately 400 blocks in 25 shapes is sometimes called a *classroom set.* Older children benefit from larger and more complex sets of blocks. Younger children may be overwhelmed by too many blocks as well as by the daunting cleanup task they present.

Blocks should be stored on low, open shelves. Storage shelves should be spacious enough so that each type of block has its own individual place. Store blocks so that those with similar qualities are stored near each other. Place them so that children can easily see how they differ (e.g., lengthwise for long blocks so that the differences in length are evident). Each shelf should be clearly marked with an outline to enable children to find the blocks they need for their constructions and put them back in the appropriate places (we recommend using solid colored contact paper to create the outline). Much of the benefit of block play is lost if they are stored without organization in a box or bin.

For blocks to be used well, children need adequate space and sufficient time for block play. A daily self-selected activity period that lasts for at least an hour provides time for children to benefit from blocks. The block area should be large enough so several children at a time can build. A smooth floor or low-pile carpet will enable children to build without structures tumbling down.

You can enhance and extend unit block play by adding toy vehicles, street signs, dollhouses, small human and animal figures, and other props. Provide special storage baskets and separate labeled space on the shelves for props. Posters, photographs, and books about buildings can be displayed in the block area. Older preschoolers and kindergarten children will use paper, pens, and tape for sign making and writing stories about their creations if you make them available.

A Hollow Block Area

Hollow blocks are much bigger than unit blocks—$11'' \times 11'' \times 5\frac{1}{2}''$ compared to $5\frac{1}{2}'' \times 2\frac{3}{4}'' \times \frac{3}{8}''$. Sets include short and long boards for making roofs and platforms. A hollow block area should have enough blocks for a child to build a structure that can be climbed on or entered (at least 15 big blocks). A larger collection promotes more extensive creative play. Because they are large and heavy, hollow blocks are not appropriate for toddlers, who should use big blocks made of plastic, foam, or cardboard.

Hollow blocks are expensive and require a good deal of space. When you set up a hollow block area, carpeting or other soft surfacing is essential to limit noise and to prevent damage to the blocks. Hollow blocks can be stored on shelves or can be stacked against a wall for storage. If you do not have indoor space for a hollow block area it can be set up on a porch or in the play yard if sheltered storage is available. They will be quickly damaged if they are unprotected from sun and rain.

We find that hollow blocks are used for more elaborate building and for more sociodramatic play if they are separated from unit blocks. If possible locate the hollow block area near the dramatic play area so that children can coordinate hollow block building with sociodramatic play. The firefighters in the hollow block area may be called to extinguish a fire in the home center; the carpenters in the hollow block area may build an addition or a garage onto the house. Good props for hollow blocks include hats, sheets, and lengths of colorful chiffon or gauze, which you can store in bins, boxes, or baskets nearby.

Dramatic Play Area

Dramatic play is one of the most important activities for young children. Children imitate the actions of the important grown-ups in their lives and thus enact how different roles might feel. When they take on roles and use materials to pretend, they learn to symbolize and practice the skills of daily living. Manipulating the physical environment (e.g., putting on clothes with buttons and zippers) and managing relationships are skills learned in part through dramatic play.

A dramatic play area requires sheltered space and simple child-sized furniture typically including a stove, a sink, and a table with chairs for two to four children. The addition of dress-up clothes motivates children to act out different roles. Dress-up clothes for both boys and girls should reflect different kinds of work and play, different cultures, and different ages. You may have to seek out props for the dramatic play area that reflect the families, cultures, and community of your children. Dolls representing a variety of racial backgrounds and common objects of daily life such as kitchenware, books, furnishings, and tools also form a part of the equipment of the dramatic play area. Open shelves with bins or baskets, or hooks on the wall, provide storage for dramatic play clothing and props. Arrange materials so they are easy to find. Make picture labels for storage shelves.

Dramatic play centers are frequently organized into a "home" area, emphasizing domestic activity. The home theme relates to the most common and powerful experiences in children's lives, but children find new ways to vary this theme. In one classroom we observed children become a family of spiders when they spread a crocheted shawl between chairs to become a giant web. Because of this, a dramatic play area is often called the Home Center, Housekeeping, or Dress-Up Corner (and in Great Britain, the "Wendy Corner," after Wendy in Peter Pan). Dramatic play areas can be changed to present other options: a post office, hospital, store, bus, farm, camp, or restaurant. For this reason when we talk to children about this part of the classroom we call it the *Pretend Area*. Simple sturdy furniture that can be reconfigured to create different scenarios furthers this broader vision of a dramatic play area.

Since it is impossible to have all the possible props available at all times, it is especially important to organize and rotate props in the dramatic play area. You can respond to children's dramatic play by adding appropriate materials when you observe a new interest developing or when you begin a new topic of study—for example, by contributing fire hats, a rain slicker, boots, and a length of hose when the children are pretending to be fire-fighters rescuing the baby or learning about their community. To prevent clutter, props can be stored in sturdy, attractive, lidded boxes organized by occupation, situation, or role.

In programs for toddlers' dramatic play, materials are simpler, fewer in number, and include duplicates. Furniture must be smaller without cupboard doors that pinch fingers. A good selection might contain hats, clothes with few fasteners, purses, dolls, lightweight aluminum pots, and wooden or plastic stirring spoons. Toddlers will incorporate manipulative toys in their first efforts at symbolic, dramatic play.

An Area for Toys and Games

Toys and games (sometimes called *manipulative toys,* or just *manipulatives*) such as puzzles, beads, Legos, Bristle Blocks, and pegboards give children practice in hand-eye coordination and help develop the small muscles of their fingers and hands. These experiences are important preparation for writing, and they expose children to such concepts as color, size, and shape, which help in the ability to recognize letters and words. In play with manipulative toys, children also have opportunities to cooperate, solve problems, and create.

For infants and toddlers, toys and games must be large, so they do not present a choking hazard, and sturdy enough to withstand frequent sanitizing. They can include homemade toys such as plastic bottles with clothespins to drop inside and commercially made equipment such as busy boxes. Duplicate toys placed side by side on the shelf will encourage parallel play and reduce conflicts. Infants and toddlers often interpret everyday objects as manipulative toys, so it is essential to keep unsafe or inappropriate items out of their reach.

Toys and games for primary children can be quite complex, like board games and jigsaw puzzles. Equipment for developing fine motor skills can be combined with cognitive tasks such as following pattern cards for geoboards, attribute blocks, and beads. Primary children also enjoy the challenge of duplicating the complex structures portrayed on the boxes and in the instruction pamphlets that often come with manipulative toys.

There are several distinct types of manipulative toys:

- Building toys such as Legos, parquetry blocks, Cuisenaire rods, hexagonal builders, and interlocking cubes: These are open-ended, have many pieces, and usually are used by more than one child at a time.
- Puzzles and fit-together toys like stacking cups: These are closed-ended, designed to be taken apart and put together in one or two ways, and are usually used by one child alone. It is especially critical to remove puzzles or fit-together toys when pieces are missing or damaged. A puzzle with even one piece missing is frustrating (as you may remember from the last time you did an incomplete 500-piece jigsaw puzzle). They also give children the message that it's okay to remove puzzle pieces.
- Collections of materials such as buttons, shells, bottle caps and lids, keys, or pebbles: Almost anything can be used as a collection. Safe recycled materials are very appropriate. These are open-ended materials that children can use for a wide variety of purposes including sorting (a cognitive task), creating designs (an aesthetic activity), or pretending. We encourage you to include collectibles that

reflect the children's cultures, community, and environment. If the toys and games area is located next to the dramatic play area children will often utilize collections in their dramatic play.

- Concept games including those that are manufactured (such as pegboards, lottos, geoboards, and board games) and those made by the teacher, often called *workjobs:* Concept games usually have simple rules. Older children will enjoy following the rules of the game while younger children are more likely to ignore the intended use and build or pretend with the game's pieces. Board games like checkers or Chutes and Ladders can be well used by children from age 5. We do not recommend battery-operated toys of any kind, even those that have an "educational" purpose, because these tend to prescribe and limit children's play.

If you have adequate space it is useful to have separate areas for the open-ended building toys that inspire noisier group play, and puzzles and games that require greater concentration and tend to be used by children alone or in pairs.

Because manipulative toys have many pieces that are easy to lose or mix up, storage in this area is especially important. An organized and clearly marked manipulative toy area invites children to play productively. An open shelf provides good storage. Children can use the materials on tables or on a carpet. Attractive place mats or small carpet pieces can define individual workspaces. Baskets, tubs, and boxes hold toys so that they are easy to find and put away. Make sure materials are not crowded and it is easy to see where each toy or game belongs. Arrange the materials on the shelf so as to offer a choice of materials at any one time.

Picture and word labels for the tubs and for the shelves help children to put things away and help them learn to make the association between the real objects and print. A puzzle rack makes it possible to store many puzzles in the classroom—although these make it hard for children to see the puzzles and can be hard for them to manage.

Sensory Play

Most early childhood classrooms have materials that clearly contribute to sensory development. Water, sand, mud, dough, and clay are traditionally used. Dry materials to pour and feel include rice, beans, macaroni, oatmeal, sawdust, and aquarium gravel. Mixtures like cornstarch and water, and "super sand" (coffee grounds, cornmeal, and salt), and "flubber" (white glue, liquid starch or borax, and water) are also used. Water, sand, and mud are often found out-of-doors but can also be provided indoors in sand and water tables or in basins on a table. If you have room in your classroom or playground, a special area can be provided for sensory play—otherwise these materials can be included in the art area. Set up the sensory area near a sink or on a porch so that spills can be cleaned up more easily.

Along with the sand/water table or basins you will need:

- Bowls, cups, and buckets
- Ladles, measuring cups, and pitchers to scoop and pour
- Funnels, tubing, whisks, and egg-beaters for liquids
- Aprons and plastic tablecloths or shower curtains to protect clothing and the floor

Natural materials such as sand and water suit a wide range of developmental stages and abilities. They provide children with rich sensory experiences and an opportunity to learn about mathematical concepts like volume and measurement. Observation of almost any child will tell you that these are satisfying play materials. They are open-ended and can be used in many ways. Children learn about the properties of substances through pouring, feeling, and mixing. They may be soothed by the responsiveness of the materials and can safely vent strong emotions in their play with them. Cooperative and imaginative play is fostered as children work together with them.

Natural materials are generally safe and are particularly satisfying for infants and toddlers. The younger the children, however, the more you will need to supervise. Because very young children are likely to put things in their mouths, you may wish to substitute dough for clay, and flour, cornmeal, oatmeal, or rice for sand.

Primary children tend to use sensory materials in more task-oriented ways. For example, they might compare and contrast different natural materials and record the differences. Water might be channeled with pipes and tubing, and the workings of a waterwheel or an aqueduct can be explored. Clay is likely to be used to construct objects that can be fired. Principles of claywork can be learned. Sand might be closely observed and different kinds of sand examined.

Another kind of sensory exploration that you may wish to add is a light table. These are used in the classrooms of Reggio Emilia. A light table has a translucent surface with fluorescent lightbulbs recessed underneath it. This provides a space for exploration of colored transparent materials, building with translucent manipulative toys, and exploring natural materials that are permeable to light. A light table can also be used for watercolor painting, tissue collage, and other art activities.

Art Area

In the art area, children can work with materials that are developmentally appropriate, functional, and satisfying to use. Art materials provide opportunities for creative expression, problem solving, and physical and sensory development. They may include crayons, scissors, tempera paint, watercolors, watercolor markers, nontoxic glue and paste, construction paper, food coloring, crewel needles, yarn, clay, clay boards, clay tools, fabric, small containers for water, and brushes.

An art area requires worktables and easels that are sized to the children (they should be able to reach the top of the easel) and cleanup facilities nearby. Old or secondhand furniture, smocks, and a good supply of plastic tablecloths minimize concerns about inevitable paint and glue spills. Additionally it will be helpful to have open shelves for supplies, closed storage for adults-only supplies, and open wide shelves children can reach for drying and storing work still in process.

In addition to furniture, an art center needs good tools and supplies including:

- Different kinds of paint (tempera, cake and liquid watercolors, and finger paint or finger paint base)
- Brushes in a variety of widths and lengths (from narrow for painting fine lines, to short-handled and chubby)—and other things to paint with, such as sponges, Q-tips, and feathers
- Lots of small containers to hold water and paint
- Paper in different sizes, weights, and colors (from tissue paper to cardboard)

- Things to draw with—crayons, markers, pencil crayons, chalk
- Clay and dough to mold and model with
- Scissors
- Place mats and trays to define spaces and limit mess
- Glue and paste, and spreaders to use with them
- Assorted materials to glue together (wood, paper, magazines, natural items like shells and leaves, recycled items like ribbon and cloth scraps)

Recycled materials can be used in art—old shirts for smocks, wrapping paper and ribbons, pretty cloth scraps, old magazines, or paper that is too old for the copy machine. However, it is important to buy good-quality basic supplies, especially brushes, paint, markers, crayons, and scissors.

Art materials need to be stored so that staff and children can easily find them and put them away. Children should be able to see what is available to them on low, marked shelves. Closed, well marked storage for materials that only adults may access is even more important. Paying attention to organizing this well and returning it to order each day will make your job easier and more pleasant.

For infants and toddlers, art is primarily a sensory experience. They explore the raw materials of the artist through all their senses. Appropriate materials for toddlers include large, stubby crayons and watercolor markers with big pieces of paper, easel painting and finger painting, paste and paper, and play dough. Young preschoolers explore and experiment with the materials and tools of art to discover what can be done with them.

Older preschoolers and kindergarten children begin to develop definite forms and shapes and use art materials to represent their feelings, experiences, and ideas, but not always in ways that can be recognized by an adult. By the primary school years, most children create recognizable representations that may include beginning ideas about perspective.

We suggest having a place in the art area where interesting objects (like a vase of flowers or a bowl with goldfish) can be placed temporarily to inspire observation and artistic endeavors, as you will see in the DVD "Birds: An Integrated Curriculum," that accompanies this text.

Watch the DVD to see how the art area is used as a site for enhancing a curriculum study.

Woodworking

In an environment with adequate space and staffing, woodworking can be a wonderful addition to a program for preschoolers or primary school children. Like blocks, it can contribute to the development of physical skills and problem-solving abilities. A woodworking area requires a specially built workbench. Make sure to have proper tools—not pretend, child-sized tools that are usually of poor quality and therefore hazardous. A list of equipment for woodworking in a preschool or primary classroom would include:

- A good workbench (including vise) and a platform for shorter children to stand on
- A sawing table that children can kneel on (NAEYC woodworking book has a plan for one you can build)
- C Clamps or a small bar clamp
- Teacher's safety glasses (not goggles)
- Two additional pairs of protective safety glasses (not goggles) for children (attach with an adjustable non-elastic glasses strap to make them fit snugly)
- Two lightweight hammers
- A regular adult hammer

- A hack saw and extra blades
- A small cross-cut saw
- Two bit braces for drilling and screwing in screws, and drill bits, auger bits, and Phillips bits
- A good flat-head screwdriver
- Two Phillips screwdrivers
- A rasp and file
- A 25″ tape measure
- A speed square (to make lines on wood)
- Various screws, nails, and glue
- Sandpaper
- Pencils
- Soft untreated wood such as pine or fir (never particle board because of hazardous chemicals)

Though young children love to do woodworking, teachers are often uncomfortable with having a woodworking area in their program. If you feel uncomfortable, gaining comfort yourself is a must. You might begin by learning about woodworking—by reading *Woodworking for Young Children* (Garner, Skeen, & Cartwright 1984), by taking a class, or by inviting someone who is familiar with woodworking materials into your program to teach you and the children how to use them. Like any other learning material, children will gain skills and use the materials more safely and productively if they have repeated opportunities to use them.

Library

The best way to help children learn the joy of reading and become motivated to read is to have good books available and to read to children often. Every classroom for young children should have a large selection of books. Children need many opportunities to look at books, to hear stories, and to see adults using and enjoying books.

Children feel invited to use well-cared-for, appropriate books displayed with the covers visible on an uncrowded bookshelf at their eye level. A book area that is comfortable, quiet, well lit, and stocked with a selection of quality children's books is an important part of a classroom. Locate the classroom library area in the best lit, quietest corner of the classroom and include soft pillows. An adult-sized chair or sofa will invite staff and parents to sit down and read to children. A library area can include decoration such as displays of book posters, alphabet posters, or laminated book covers. If there is room you can also include a listening center with books on tape and puppets, props, and flannelboard for storytelling.

Additionally, in programs for preschoolers and older children, books can be integrated throughout the classroom. For example, science books might be kept in the science area, picture dictionaries in the writing center, and the phone book, newspapers, and magazines might be located in the dramatic play area.

Children are drawn to the library area when it holds a supply of interesting and attractive books that are in good repair and that are changed on a regular basis. Your public library is an excellent source of books for the classroom. Books that are torn, have broken bindings, or are written on should be removed from the library area. When you carefully repair these in the presence of children (erasing pencil marks, covering ink or paint with white-out, taping torn pages, and repairing bindings with cloth tape) you teach an important lesson about caring for materials.

Infants also need, enjoy, and benefit from books but do not require a library area. In programs for infants, age-appropriate books can be provided in different places in the classroom. Small baskets provide accessible storage for sturdy, board books.

In a spacious classroom we like to combine the library with the writing center to create a literacy center. Besides books, storytelling, writing, and book-making materials, a literacy center can include literacy games.

Writing Area

Preschool, kindergarten, and primary classrooms need a writing center where children can explore, write messages and stories, and illustrate their writing. Children are encouraged to write to communicate when writing supplies are available and written words are available for them to look at and think about. In the writing center children can record, report, and create based on their abilities.

A writing center needs an open shelf for storage, a child-proportioned table, chairs, baskets or boxes to hold paper and writing materials, different types and sizes of paper and envelopes, note cards, paper notepads, pencils, erasers, markers of various widths, crayons, glue, staplers, string, and hole punches. Other useful materials include a children's dictionary, clipboards, chalkboards with chalk, carbon paper, word banks of words children like (see Chapter 10), a letter-stamp set for printing, and a set of wood or plastic letters (both uppercase and lowercase) for constructing words and sentences and for tracing.

Older children will enjoy keeping journals in the writing center. A computer with a simple word-processing program designed for children or a typewriter is also valuable in this area.

Computer Area

Technology is a part of our lives. We use technology when we drive a car, make toast, use a word-processing program, make a phone call, or hammer in a nail. We also use it in the classroom. As a teacher your responsibility with regard to technology is to provide children with appropriate learning experiences that contribute to their overall development. As in every aspect of the early childhood environment, you will provide children with technology that is appropriate to their stage of development. Young children are gaining technological skills in your environment when you help them learn to turn on the lights, flush the toilet, use scissors, and push the buttons on a blender or a tape recorder.

Today, every teacher needs to have skill in using the computer for creating things like letters and budgets, for accessing information on the World Wide Web, and for communicating with others. If you have space in your preschool or kindergarten classroom you can model doing this and also provide children with appropriate experiences with computers. Computers can supplement but cannot replace the traditional play materials and activities of the early childhood environment such as the art, dramatic play, blocks, and sensory materials. Because computers help people to communicate with one another it makes sense to place one in or near the writing center.

A computer area, to be successful, must have *hardware* (the computer, printer, keyboard, and other devices) able to run the more recent and developmentally appropriate *software* (the programs). The screen, keyboard, mouse, and other tools to operate the computer should be placed on a child-size table with several chairs so several children can work together.

While using a computer is often a solitary activity for adults, many children prefer to work with others as they explore and experiment with this tool. As a result of this preference they can develop skills in taking turns and working and solving problems cooperatively as they work on the computer. Young children learning to write are often much more fluent with the assistance of computers than without. We have seen creative writing and "publishing" occurring among primary school children that would not have been possible without the assistance of computers. Some children with disabilities may be able to be included in a regular classroom thanks to computer technology that allows them to communicate through the use of point-and-touch screens.

Although some computer programs for children are intriguing, many are simply electronic workbooks that provide drill and practice on isolated skills and concepts. Appropriate programs for young children help them to develop critical thinking skills and creativity. Any programs used in the preschool classroom should be appropriate for the children and consistent with your values. What makes software appropriate for young children?

- The concepts are developmentally appropriate—that is, relevant and concrete. For example, children learn how to create a picture, open a window, or initiate a train of interesting activity rather than learning to repeat a correct answer to a math problem.
- The programs are open-ended. They allow a great deal of child choice and child direction.
- The pace is set by the child, and not by the program.
- They have an intrinsically appealing process (such as exploring an environment) rather than an extrinsic reward (such as a smiling face for giving the correct answer to a problem).
- They invite collaborative decision-making and cooperation rather than competition.
- They provide models of prosocial behavior and are violence-free.

Computer technology changes at a rapid pace. The skills and programs that children learn to use today will be obsolete tomorrow. To make full and appropriate use of the current technologies you need to be knowledgeable about computer use and to learn how to use these emerging technologies to benefit children.

> ### Reflect on a classroom
>
> Think about an early childhood program you attended, observed, or worked in. Describe the arrangement of the classroom, the playground, the equipment and materials, space for children's belongings, storage and distribution of materials, and the aesthetics of the setting. What was included? What was omitted? How did the arrangement of the learning environment effect the experience of children?

Discovery Centers

In preschool, kindergarten, and primary classrooms discovery centers can include work areas for science, math, and social studies. These centers are laboratories for exploration and discoveries. Where did the new child come from? What does an earthworm need to survive? Who is taller, Kane or Yoon Ki? Children solve problems based on observations and research, using tools and books you provide in inquiry centers for science, math, or social studies. If you have space in your classroom, you can create activity centers devoted to each of these subjects. If not, you can join two or all three together.

Science

A discovery center is a home for science when you provide the tools of exploration and for ongoing projects such as aquariums and terrariums, animal families, and plants. You can also include science games, collections of objects and pictures, and science reference books. Sometimes sensory experiences such as water, sand, and light tables are placed in the science area. Arrange your science area in a place in the classroom that has access to electricity and water. Define the space with low, open shelves for storage and a low table or counter for investigation. Set tables for displays against a taller shelf or wall. Set up a shelf with tools for investigation: sorting trays, plastic tubs and pitchers, aquariums, insect and animal cages, airtight containers for storage, balances, scales, measuring cups and spoons, and magnifying glasses. Select materials for investigation, sorting, collections (like buttons or rocks), machinery to investigate and disassemble, information books, and photographs and posters that illustrate science concepts.

Math

A discovery center is a home for math when it contains materials—such as scales, balances, lotto, objects with different attributes, and matching games—that encourage children to experiment and think about math-related experiences. The processes of comparison, classification, and measurement, as opposed to rote counting and computation, are the bases of math in early childhood.

Materials such as attribute blocks, colored cubes, parquetry blocks, board games, and seriation materials like stacking cups are designed to enhance learning. Math manipulatives designed by Dr. Montessori teach young children math concepts through the exploration of carefully designed and artfully crafted materials. Additionally, many early childhood educators make use of simple materials such as button sorting, lotto games, and matching activities to foster math development. With all of these toys, children compare, classify, sort, seriate, measure, count, and create patterns.

Social Studies

A discovery center is a home for social studies when you include special displays and activities, bulletin boards, artifacts, learning games, maps and globes, and books that help children compare and contrast the attributes of the human and natural environments and how these affect people. Pictures, posters, and children's work relating to social studies can also be exhibited here. You might wish to use a single bulletin board or display area to attractively mount one type of work (for example, maps children have drawn) or set aside space for each child's work.

Outdoor Zones

Play areas or zones in the outdoor environment contribute to different kinds of play and learning. Active play areas are almost always found outdoors. Hollow blocks, sensory play, art, and woodworking are often found in both the indoor and outdoor environments. There is less consistency from program to program in what zones and activities are offered to children in the outdoor environment.

Transition

The transition zone is where children enter and exit the playground. This area should allow children to see what is available and make choices. This is sometimes where easels, trikes, and wagons are waiting. It may be the place where the sand and water table can be seen.

In a transition zone it is important to make sure that children coming and going can wait or gather if necessary. Benches, tires, steps, or the edge of a wall make good places to wait.

Manipulative-Creative

This zone is where table activities like art and woodworking take place outdoors. In some programs table games and books are brought into the manipulative-creative zone.

Active Play

Space for running, climbing, sliding, swinging, and experiencing different heights are important parts of the active play zone. Children engage in physically active play in large grassy areas, and on the climbing or "super structure." This structure is the current evolution of what used to be called the "jungle gym." These structures may be made of modularized segments that can be put together to meet the requirements of a particular center or school. They often include platforms, slides, tunnels, nets, and ramps. See Chapter 7 for a detailed discussion of playground safety. While teachers can usually do little to change play structures, they should be aware that these structures should be no more than twice the height of the tallest child in the group and that it should have more than one way up or down so children can change their minds if they decide that a challenge is too great for them. More challenging structures can be provided for primary-age children.

Natural Elements

Mud, sand, water, plants, logs, and smooth boulders are all valuable parts of the natural elements zone. These will naturally attract the animal life of your locale so it is a good place to put a bird feeder, or house a pet. A sandbox may be found in this area though it may also be included near the super structure, or adjacent to the social-dramatic zone where it may become an extension of the dramatic play.

Social-Dramatic

Children create their own opportunities for social and dramatic play in the outdoor environment whether or not there is equipment provided. Their play is richer when there are play houses, dress-up clothes and props, and "loose parts" like hollow blocks, sheets, small tires, planks, and other movable pieces that children can arrange. A social-dramatic area can be placed near a vehicle path to extend dramatic play with the use of trikes, carts, and wagons.

SPECIAL CONSIDERATIONS

Environments for Infants and Toddlers

Infants thrive in environments that, like homes, have fewer people and are sheltered from stimulation. Because more adults are needed, more space per child is required (typically 50 square feet per child). A classroom for infants has separate areas for routines and activities. Since children under 18 months do not eat or rest on strict or identical schedules, it is essential to have separate areas for sleeping that are quiet and shielded from stimulus and eating areas somewhat separate from play areas. Immobile babies need protected areas. Because diaper changing is a prominent feature of the daily program, a changing area with a sink and hot water must be close at hand and separate from eating and play areas. A stable, comfortable chair or couch is a must so adults can sit and hold children. It also contributes to a homelike atmosphere and provides good climbing experiences and excellent hand-holds for beginning standers and walkers. Since very young children are comforted by motion, a special rocker (designed so that fingers cannot be pinched) or other chair that allows motion is essential in rooms for infants and toddlers.

Play areas in programs for infants and toddlers must be flexible. (For an example of a program floor plan for infants and toddlers, refer to Figure 8.1.) They should include clean, carpeted surfaces for playing and crawling and different levels on which to crawl and climb. Several play spaces need to be available for mobile children so that different kinds of play can occur at once.

For toddlers the equipment and materials are best organized into large zones that combine the materials found in several different centers in preschool, kindergarten, and primary classrooms. For example, in a toddler room a messy play area may include art materials and sensory play materials such as sand and water (Lowman & Ruhmann 1998). Toddlers are climbers, so safe places to climb are a must, both indoors and out. It is essential to assume that anything that can be climbed will be climbed—therefore high and unstable shelves must be eliminated from toddler environments.

Just like preschoolers, infants and toddlers need time outdoors each day. They need safe, enclosed yards that are scrupulously maintained to minimize hazards. Infants need blankets for crawling on; low, portable, stable equipment to pull up and climb on; and small tubs where an inch or two of water can be safely explored. Light catchers and wind chimes hung in trees make pleasing additions to the infant yard.

Toddlers need opportunities for more vigorous play including push cars and outdoor equipment (climbers, water tables, play houses) scaled to their size. Play structures need to be low to the ground, stable, wide (to accommodate a child who needs time to climb up or down), and less steep than those for older children. They enjoy wide ramps and entrances and exits to be climbed into and out of. Infants and toddlers may make many false starts before they actually feel confident enough to slide down the slide or climb to the top; therefore, the equipment should have few irreversible choices (such as tall slides from which you can't back down). Push vehicles and pull toys that are stable and without joints that pinch, low belt swings, and swings with seatbelts are appropriate for younger children.

Toys and materials for infants and toddlers must be appropriate to their needs. This means that they must not be toxic, not present choking hazards, and have safe, smooth edges. They must be large enough to be easily grasped, light enough to be lifted, soft enough not to hurt, and strong enough to be dropped, stepped on, or thrown.

Including Children with Special Needs in Your Environment

If your group includes children with special needs you may need to make some adaptations in the arrangement of your environment. Sometimes such changes are obvious. Doors, pathways, centers, tables, climbing structures, and play materials must accommodate adaptive equipment such as wheelchairs and walkers. At other times adaptations may be subtler, such as creating additional alone spaces so a child with autism may have extra shelter from stimulation. Often small rearrangements of the furniture are enough to make your program a good place for all children.

It is important to adapt the outside environment, equipment, and activities so that children with physical challenges can also participate fully. Adaptations can be relatively simple. For example, creating conveyer-belt walkways across grass and sand (using recycled conveyer belts donated by airports or large stores) will extend the range of a child in a walker or wheelchair. A sling swing or hammock can be substituted for a child who does not have the upper body strength required to use a conventional swing. If your program receives government funding, it is required by law that children with disabilities be provided with the same access to playgrounds and equipment that is provided for nondisabled children.

Including Adults in Your Environment

Though your program is first and foremost a place for children, it is important not to forget adults when you design the environment. Create a place where you and other adults can sit comfortably. You may want to put this near the sign-in area or the library so parents feel invited to participate. Be sure to include an outdoor bench or chairs for family members who may be uncomfortable sitting on the ground. Because you too spend long hours away from home here, the environment contributes to whether you feel good about your work. Chapter 13 offers suggestions for a family area in the classroom. You will also need a place where you can keep your own things safely, keep confidential records, and prepare materials.

Television and Video

Most children will spend far more time in their lives watching television than they will in school. A debate is ongoing about the negative effects of television. A recent study published in the *Journal of Pediatrics* (Christakis, Zimmerman, DiGuiseppe, & McCarty 2004) recommends that children under the age of 2 not watch television because of its potentially damaging effects. The same study points to growing evidence suggesting that television viewing by preschoolers is linked to an increase in occurrence of attention deficit disorders. Whether programs created for children are thoughtfully produced or merely marketing devices for toys appears to be irrelevant. For this reason we believe that television should never be used in programs for infants and toddlers and should be used rarely, if at all, in classrooms for preschoolers.

Used carefully as a tool with appropriate content and active teacher involvement, TV and video programs may be acceptable for kindergarten and primary school children if:

- It is to be shown to children in short (under 15-minute) segments that you have previewed
- It contributes to educational goals
- You sit and watch with a small group of children and talk with them about what they have viewed
- It addresses children respectfully and is geared to their age

MAKING THE ENVIRONMENT WORK

Designing a learning environment is not a onetime event; it is an ongoing process. Children's needs change as they grow and learn. Any setting can be modified and improved. The perfect arrangement for this year's class of children may not work as well for a new group. Plan on regularly reevaluating and changing the environment as needed.

When you plan a learning environment, you need to consider what you want the space and the equipment to communicate to children and the kinds of experiences you want them to have. Keep in mind their age and experience. Make the environment as safe, aesthetic, and appropriate as you can. When problems arise—for example, if children consistently fail to get involved in activities—you may want to look first at the environment to see whether it is part of the cause of the problem. Robert Sommer, a psychologist who has studied the effect of environment on behavior, has said, "There is no behavior apart from environment, even in utero" (Sommer 1969, 19).

Before you finish arranging your classroom and outdoor space, and whenever you are about to change the environment, observe from the viewpoint of a child by sitting on the floor or the ground. From this perspective, observe from the entrance and each of the areas. Notice what you can see in each location, what is most attractive, and what is most distracting. This view may be quite different from what you perceive from your regular height and will help you to design an environment that works for children.

We have found it helpful to use specific dimensions or attributes described by Elizabeth Jones and Elizabeth Prescott in *Dimensions of Teaching-Learning Environments* (1984) as another kind of lens through which to observe and evaluate our environments. Here is a brief summary of these dimensions:

- *Hard-Soft:* Softness changes an environment, what happens in it, and how secure and comfortable people feel. Early childhood classrooms need to have soft furnishings, carpets, decorations, and lighting similar to homes. Hard environments, with indestructible materials like cement, unattractive colors, and harsh lighting are uncomfortable and indicate a lack of respect for children. Comfortable furniture, pillows, rugs, grass, sand, furry animals, soft toys, sling and tire swings, dough, finger paint, clay, mud, water, and warm physical contact soften environments.
- *Open-Closed* (the degree to which the environment and materials restrict): Open materials inspire innovation. Materials that are closed can be rewarding when they provide appropriate challenge. Overly difficult materials cause frustration. Younger or less experienced children require more open materials. Older, more experienced children need and enjoy open materials but also enjoy closed challenges. When children appear bored or frustrated the cause might be in the balance of open-closed experiences.
- *Low mobility-High mobility:* High mobility involves active motion. Low mobility involves sedentary activities. Both are important, both indoors and outdoors, throughout the day.
- *Simple-Complex:* Simple materials have one obvious use—they do not allow children to manipulate or improvise. They include trikes, slides, puzzles, and concept games such as Chutes and Ladders. Complex materials allow children to use two different play materials together, making play less predictable and more interesting. They hold children's attention for a longer period of time—for example, a sandbox with tools, blocks with props, collage with paint. *Super* materials offer an even larger number of possibilities and hold children's attention much longer. They include sand with tools and water, or dramatic play areas equipped with furnishings, clothes, and props. Classrooms for inexperienced or less mature children need to be simple to help them focus and make choices. Older children can handle more complexity, which can be added by materials or people.
- *Intrusion-Seclusion* (who and what crosses boundaries between spaces): Intrusion adds novelty and stimulation that enrich learning—visitors, trips, and other experiences with the world outside the classroom. Seclusion from stimulation

provides the opportunity to concentrate, think, and be alone. Tables or easels set up against walls provide partial seclusion; insulated spaces with protection on three sides allow privacy; hiding spaces, cozy closed places in crates, lofts, or under a table allow children to escape the stimulus of the classroom. When opportunities for seclusion do not exist, children often create their own seclusion by hiding or by withdrawing emotionally. (Jones & Prescott 1984)

Using a checklist like those in the Appendices, or the Harms-Clifford Early Childhood Environmental Rating Scale (1980), and reviewing accreditation guidelines designed by NAEYC can help you to take a systematic approach to the design of a learning environment.

FINAL THOUGHTS

What do you want your environment to say to children and their families? How can you make it say "Welcome! I care. This is a place for you"? The physical environment is an essential part of children's learning experience in an early childhood program. It communicates your caring and competence to their families. When you design a learning environment you are creating a tool that helps you do your job and you are creating your own work environment.

Your home changes as you change. It reflects your needs, tastes, activity, and lifestyle. It grows with you and your family. Creating an environment for children and making it work is also a process of growth. It allows you to use your knowledge of children's development, your sensitivity in observation, and your creativity. As you gain greater skill and information, and as you devote time, energy, and resources to the environment, it will better meet children's needs. This kind of creation is a challenging and satisfying aspect of the work of a teacher of young children.

LEARNING OUTCOMES

When you read this chapter, thoughtfully complete selected assignments from the "To Learn More" section, and prepare items from the "For Your Portfolio" section, you will be demonstrating your progress in meeting NAEYC **Standard 1: Promoting Child Development and Learning** and **Sub-standard 4b: Using Developmentally Effective Approaches.**

Key elements:

- Knowing and understanding young children's characteristics and needs
- Using developmental knowledge to create healthy, respectful, supportive, and challenging learning environments
- Knowing, understanding, and using effective approaches, strategies, and tools for early education

To Learn More

Take a Child's Eye View: Observe a classroom from a child's perspective by kneeling or sitting on a low chair. Observe from the entrance and the interest centers. Go back to each position and observe it again from your regular height. Reflect on how these are different and write about your experience. What did you learn about this classroom? What did you learn about the design of environments for children? What changes would you make in this classroom based on your experience?

Imagine a Dream Program: Pretend that you have the resources to create a perfect early childhood learning environment. Select the age and number of children for your class. Using the principles from this chapter to plan an ideal environment for them. Make a diagram of the indoor and outdoor space. Go through educational supply catalogs to select equipment and materials you would purchase, and plan the equipment and materials you would find or create. Present your program to your classmates or a colleague. You may wish to create a shoebox model. Describe your environment and explain your decisions in terms of children's needs and your

values and your goals. Explain how you will address the dimensions of teaching-learning environments in your environment.

Observe an Environment: Visit an early childhood program and observe the environment (classroom and outside play space) used by one class of children. Evaluate the environment using the Learning Environment Checklist in Appendix B. What is present and what is missing? Analyze the strength of the environment in supporting children's physical, creative, language, and cognitive development. Decide in what ways it is appropriate for the age and needs of the children. Share what you have observed and summarize your feelings about the environment. Sketch a floor plan of the environment. You may wish to include a few photographs. Discuss your thoughts about the environment and how you might change or modify it to better support children.

Compare Two Environments: Repeat the preceding assignment in another program or classroom for children of the same age. Compare and contrast the two.

For Your Portfolio

Improve an Environment: Sketch a floor plan and take photographs of an existing classroom environment in which you work or have a practicum assignment. Use the checklists located in the Appendices to evaluate the learning environment. Decide how you might rearrange, change, or modify the envi-

ronment to better support children's development. Implement some or all of the changes, take photographs and sketch a new floor plan to show the changes, and observe the effect on the children and program. Write about what happened, and place this documentation in your professional portfolio.

9

Guiding Young Children

Nothing I have ever learned of value was taught to me by an ogre.
Nothing do I regret more in my life than that my teachers were
not my friends. Nothing ever heightened my being or deepened my
learning more than being loved.

J. T. Dillon

Warm, positive relationships between children and teachers are the foundation for children's success in early education programs. As you develop caring and supporting relationships with children, you are providing the guidance that they need to become effective participants in the classroom as well as in the world. Building effective relationships with children and with their families is perhaps your most essential and rewarding task as an early childhood educator. The relationships you create will influence children's self-concepts, determine the quality of their experiences, influence their learning and relationships with others, and contribute to their deciding whether school is a safe and trustworthy place. They will make choices about their own actions based on the model you provide and the social climate you construct.

WHAT IS CHILD GUIDANCE?

The relationship between child and teacher is the most significant factor in children's perception of their early learning experiences. Although most young children enter early childhood programs with lively and inquisitive minds, only some come to feel good about themselves, to love learning, and to regard education as a rewarding experience. When you base what you do on genuine appreciation and respect for children and sound knowledge of development and early education, children are likely to retain the eagerness and curiosity with which they enter your program.

Good relationships between children and early childhood educators, like all good relationships, are characterized by honesty, empathy, respect, trust, and warmth. They are authentic and not forced or artificial. In good relationships children feel safe from fear of physical and psychological harm. No one can be productive when they feel threatened, anxious, or uncertain. Relationships and children's feelings about education, teachers, and learning can be irreparably damaged by tactics such as corporal punishment and humiliation.

The most effective early childhood educators we know genuinely like children and have clear, developmentally appropriate expectations of them. They enjoy and often share in young children's viewpoints and are playful. They gain children's willing cooperation without demanding unquestioning obedience. In fact, they welcome questions as signs of growth. They see children as partners, not adversaries, and view the process of helping children grow, through difficult as well as pleasant times, as central to their job.

In quality early childhood programs, practitioners guide young children based on core values (see Chapter 1) widely held by early childhood educators, knowledge of child

development, and an understanding of what families value and believe is important for their children. Early childhood teachers appreciate childhood behaviors and believe children have a right to be childlike. They try to understand how children's development affects their behavior and gear expectations to reflect how children grow and learn. They know that children learn through experiences appropriate to individual age, temperament, learning style, interest, culture, and family choice.

Early childhood practitioners share a fundamental belief that the quality of relationships is critical. Because of this belief, they are attentive to relationships with children, families, and staff, and they evaluate guidance strategies to see whether they are supportive of these relationships. They give time and attention to children's social and emotional growth and know it is foundational to the development of concepts and skills.

Early childhood educators also understand that children must construct knowledge, including social knowledge. Children learn about relationships through being part of a group and interacting with people and the environment. They learn through play and exploration. Children who are encouraged to make choices learn to take responsibility and to respect others. These opportunities demonstrate trust that every child can learn to be a cooperative, productive person.

Guidance Honors Differences

Because each child is unique, your relationship with each individual will be unique. You are also an individual, so you will have your own style of relating with and responding to young children and to their families.

Guidance Honors Differences in Families

Families have widely different beliefs and values about how children should behave. They most often choose guidance strategies based on what they have been taught by their parents and grandparents. Discipline and guidance practices are based on the values families have about what is important for children to learn and their beliefs about how individuals should behave toward other people.

The methods that families use to discipline their children reflect a variety of family and cultural circumstances. You will have children in your classroom whose families hold a wide range of divergent perspectives about child rearing and children's behavior. In some families and cultures, respect for authority is a foundational value. Families with this value expect children to do what they are told promptly, politely, and without questions. Obedience is expected; disobedience is often punished. Other families teach their children to question authority and to value individual decision-making. Children from these families may learn early that making choices and asking questions are behaviors to strive for.

Some children may be taught that conformity is important and that most decisions should be made based on what is best for the group, be it the family, the classroom or the society. Families who value the interdependence of group members may discourage independence and engage in practices that scold or punish children's autonomous actions. Children from these families may develop self-help and other skills later than children from families who place a high value on independence.

Early childhood teachers have values and beliefs about child rearing, too. You will bring with you into your classroom the values that your family and your culture have taught you about expectations for children's behaviors and about how to guide and influence that behavior. Your beliefs and practices will also be determined by what you are learning as a student of early childhood education and by the values of the field. There will be times when your personal beliefs, what you have been taught (or are learning) about child guidance, and the beliefs and values of children's families will be in conflict. In these instances it is important to remember that professional teachers learn skills for honoring the beliefs of the families of all children in their care. Children need to know that the values and practices of their families are respected in their classrooms. When teachers are insensitive to the differences in values between home and school, children may receive messages that indicate to them that their families' ways are "wrong" or "bad." Every child deserves to feel that what is learned at home is valued in school.

You can expect to have children in your classroom whose families have taught them behaviors that are different from the ones that are familiar to you.

Two-and-a-half year old Ajit has been enrolled in a full-day program for 4 months. Despite his teacher's warm overtures, he has not spoken directly to her. She has heard him speak to other children during play time. When his teacher looks at him, he looks away quickly and he resists her invitations to talk or play with her.

Because they are unfamiliar, these differences in behavior styles and ways of relating to others may make you feel uncomfortable, confused, or upset. As a teacher you may encounter differences such as these:

What families may do at home	How children may respond at school
Give directions Require unquestioning obedience	Confused when you ask them to make choices Unwilling to express personal wants Test limits often
Expect children to ask questions Encourage children to make independent decisions	Question adult decisions and reasons Take initiative; may seem to "get into everything"
Use discipline that is harsh and may include spanking or other kinds of physical punishment	Appear to ignore or disregard verbal requests
Have very few limits for or expectations of young children	Distressed when told "no" by adults
May see young children as "babies" and enjoy interacting with them in this manner	Stressed and upset when separating from family members

(continued)

What families may do at home	How children may respond at school
May see young children as "babies" and enjoy interacting with them in this manner *(continued)*	Limited self-help skills Resist or be upset when teachers expect them to feed, dress, and/or toilet independently
Expect independence	Difficulty sharing space, materials, or play activities
Express feelings openly and often	Yell, scream, throw a tantrum
Encourage self-restraint and control of expression	Appear shy, reticent, and quiet
Encourage strong sense of family pride, honor, and respect	Extremely fearful when they feel they may have misbehaved or disappointed an adult; have a high need for adult approval
Discourage children from calling attention to themselves; require children to demonstrate a humble or modest attitude	Reluctant to speak in group settings; uncomfortable when called on by the adult
Use language that may appear to "put children down" or avoid emphasizing their strengths and skills	Uncomfortable when praised or acknowledged

Use these examples along with the many others you will experience to begin to think about and expand your acceptance of differences. Engaging in dialogues with families about their child rearing beliefs and practices will help you continue to build relationships with each child that will provide the basis for appropriate guidance.

Guidance Honors Differences in Children

You will base your expectations for children's behavior and your choices of guidance practices on the age and developmental stage as well as on individual needs and circumstances of each child. Just as you would not expect a 1-year-old to ride a bicycle, you will not expect a 5-year-old to be able to sit at a desk engaged in a writing activity for an extended period of time. Learning to tell the difference between an unacceptable behavior and one that may be annoying but is to be expected at a particular age is an important skill to develop.

Behaviors That Are Typical and May Be Trying to Adults

Infants:
    Sob when parent is out of sight
    Refuse to communicate with unfamiliar adults

Toddlers:
    Joyfully empty containers
    Respond to most requests with a forceful "NO!"
    Treat all objects as "mine"

Preschoolers:
    Resist adult schedules; dawdle through routines
    May not always tell the truth
    Tell others, "You're not my friend" or "You can't play"

School-age:
    Become very competitive; love to be the winner
    Boss other children
    Say, "You can't make me" or "I hate you"

It is more consistent with the early childhood core values of respect, trust, and appreciation for childhood to choose strategies to guide behavior rather than techniques that are punitive. Young children are fragile and vulnerable. We know that early experiences have significant impact on their overall development. The choices that adults make about their relationships, and how they speak and act when they are with children, have a powerful and lifelong influence on the choices that children make about their own actions and how they feel about themselves and others. It is important that teachers take time to think carefully about how their guidance practices will affect children.

Guidance is a process designed to help children develop self-control—to understand and use constructive behaviors instead of misbehavior. *Guidance* can be defined as assisting or leading to reach a destination. Appropriate behavior resulting from guidance is the result of thought and internal control. Guidance occurs when adults and children have positive relationships.

Punishment can be defined as a rough or injurious penalty. It is designed to stop unwanted behavior by inflicting retribution that is painful or unpleasant. It does not teach alternatives or enhance understanding. "Good" behavior resulting from punishment is the outcome of fear. Punishment, by definition, is painful. Physically painful or corporal punishment is never acceptable in an early childhood program because it demonstrates that it is all right to hurt someone if you are big enough. Additionally, although children who have been physically punished may behave appropriately when an adult is watching them, at later times they tend to show increased aggressive behavior (Honig 1985).

> **Reflect on your family's expectations**
>
> Which children's behaviors were important in your family? How did your family want children to behave in public places such as church or a store? How did they expect children to act at gatherings with other adults? What did they expect from them at school? How did they let you know when they were pleased with what you did? How did they communicate disapproval or upset?

> **Reflect on guidance and punishment**
>
> How were conflicts and misbehavior dealt with in your school experiences? What techniques or strategies were used? Were they effective? What were your feelings about them? Recall an incident in which you were punished in school. What happened? How did you feel? What were the effects on you? What do you wish had happened? How did the teacher's ways of handling problems affect how you felt about your teachers, school, and learning?

Goals for Guidance

Skilled teachers reflect carefully on their goals for children. In consultation with families, they think about both their long- and short-term goals for children and they consciously choose relationship practices that are congruent with these goals. While individuals will have differences in the long-term goals they select, most will agree that the following can be included as appropriate goals for child guidance practices:

- To develop inner strength, self-confidence, and self-esteem
- To build self-control, inner discipline, and the ability to regulate behavior
- To develop skills for critical thinking and reasoning
- To develop skills for living in a community, including cooperation, responsibility, and empathy

It is important to keep in mind the fit between what you do and your long-term goals for children. Without this awareness you can accumulate a "grab bag" of techniques that "work" (that is, control immediate behavior problems) but fail to have long-term positive effects.

Short-term goals for child guidance are more immediate and less abstract. They often include objectives for controlling behavior and ensuring children's safety during day-to-day interactions and encounters. Short-term goals may include teaching children to behave in ways that:

- Ensure the safety of themselves and others
- Care about and respect the feelings and rights of others and of themselves
- Use toys, tools, and materials carefully

Teachers need to look carefully at both long-term and short-term goals when creating relationships and selecting guidance practices. Consider these examples:

Jeremy begins climbing on the upper railing of the slide. His teacher is worried that he may fall and hurt himself badly.

Marissa grabs a large block and is holding it in a threatening manner over the head of Kaleo.

Mei is merrily tossing the puzzle pieces into the aquarium.

In each instance, the teacher has an immediate goal to ensure the safety and well-being of other children and of the classroom materials. Thoughtful teachers know that behavior that threatens the children's safety or damages toys or materials must be stopped immediately. At the time of risk, they do not wait to allow the child to think critically or problem-solve independently. They will take action. Jeremy's teacher will require that he get down from the slide immediately. Marissa's teacher will prevent her from using the block to hit Kaleo. Mei's teacher will stop her from dropping the puzzle pieces into the aquarium. It is the *manner* the teacher uses, the words she chooses, the way she uses her voice and body and the subsequent actions that will determine what children learn from the experience.

> ### Reflect on your long-term goals for children
>
> What do you feel are the most important long-term goals for educators to have for the young children that they teach? Why did you choose these? How might they affect the types of guidance practices that you use? How are your goals related to the values that you identified in Chapter 1?

Building Inner Control

Learning self-control and self-discipline is an important goal of child guidance. Children aren't born knowing how to control their impulses or how to make acceptable choices of behaviors. These are skills that must be learned. In the past decade, there have been a number of studies designed to help us understand how children learn to regulate and control their own behavior. The increase in children's ability to self-regulate is one of the hallmarks of development during early childhood. During these years children develop important skills that allow them to control their own emotions and behaviors. Researchers have established the sequence of development of self-regulation and determined that it emerges as a result of both maturation and appropriate experiences that allow children to become increasingly able to take deliberate actions, plan ahead, and consciously control their responses (Bronson 2000). Bronson suggests that there are particular practices that teachers can use that support the development of self-regulation at each stage (see Figure 9.1).

> ### Reflect on self-control
>
> Think about a time when you felt very angry. How did you cope with that feeling? Did you use self-control? How did you learn to do this?

Children learn to control their emotions and their behavior when teachers and other important adults create environments that are warm and trustworthy and where responsible actions are expected, modeled, discussed, and valued. Emotional and social competence have been shown to be essential elements of children's readiness for elementary school and foundational for developing cognitive skills (Hyson 2002).

Supporting a Sense of Self

Another goal that is influenced by guidance practices is to help children develop strong, positive, and realistic self-concepts. *Self-concept* is the picture children have

Figure 9.1 **Supporting Self-Regulation**

	Milestones in the Development of Self-Control	Practices to Support Children's Development of Self-Regulation
Infants birth through 12 months	Not able to self-regulate Beginning control of motor abilities Begin to learn that self is separate from others Begin to anticipate events Begin to connect their motor actions with specific outcomes	Provide predictable schedules and routines based on individual needs Offer opportunities to interact with people and objects in their environment in ways that allow them to create interesting and pleasurable results
12–24 months	Begin to be able to start, stop, and/or maintain an action Begin to communicate and to understand the requests of others	Model actions that toddlers can repeat to successfully complete tasks independently Provide opportunities to make choices of play materials and experiences
Toddlers	Can remember what someone has done or said in the past Developing behaviors indicating autonomy Can carry out simple requests Can label their own actions and those of others	Give simple cause and effect reasons for desired behavior: "If you pour the milk on the table, you won't have any to drink" Use suggestions rather than commands Use language to describe actions and routines and to emphasize the relationships between actions and outcomes
Preschoolers	Can wait a bit for something they want Can sometimes control their emotions Can make choices between several options Understand cause and effect of physical and social events Are learning to understand that others have feelings different from their own Can follow increasingly complex directions Understand and follow clear rules Becoming consciously aware of their ability to control their actions and thoughts	Give simple responsibilities, such as opportunities to feed the classroom fish or set the table Provide choices of activities and playmates Provide materials and supplies that allow them to carry out a variety of plans and tasks successfully Model and describe appropriate ways to solve problems and deal with feelings Provide reasons for rules and limits Help children make connections between their behavior and the outcome it produces Encourage families to limit exposure to media violence Discuss strategies and assist them with making conscious choices Deemphasize or limit competition
School-age Children	Can use more complex strategies for solving problems Can consciously choose strategies to allow them to delay gratification Are beginning to compare themselves to others and use internal standards to judge behavior and achievements	Allow individual choices among appropriate learning activities Provide assistance that supports children's independent effort Expect, model, and teach respectful, responsible behavior Model and teach increasingly complex problem-solving strategies

Source: Adapted, with permission, from M. B. Bronson, "Research in Review. Recognizing and Supporting the Development of Self-Regulation in Young Children," *Young Children* 55 (March 2000): 32–37.

about themselves, based on their perceptions and on what others tell them. Self-concept includes perceptions of the physical self, social and cognitive qualities, and competence. It influences children's ability to develop meaningful relationships with people, ideas, and the physical world.

Children's self-concepts are greatly influenced by the "mirror" held up by significant people in their lives—family members, peers, and other adults. Self-concept begins to develop in the first days of life and continues to build and change. Families are children's first and most influential sources of information about who they are. It is from families that children begin to establish their identities as individuals of a gender, race, and culture.

Self-esteem, a child's internal appraisal of his or her own worth, is, like self-concept, initially based on the messages given by families and other important adults. As a result of their relationships with important adults, children learn whether or not they are valued and if their identity is desirable or undesirable. As children get older, peers become increasingly influential as well. Self-esteem is not the momentary pleasant feeling that some children have when an adult praises them or gives them a treat or a reward. Authentic self-esteem is built as children have many experiences that tell them they are valued and loved for who they are.

Helping children to develop strong and positive self-concepts is not the same as encouraging *narcissism*, which is excessive preoccupation with oneself to the exclusion of others. Instead, it means helping children appreciate who they are and what they can do and to accept what they are still learning to do.

As an early childhood educator, you will be a significant person who has the power to influence children's self-concept and who can help families view their children positively. Of course, for you to enhance the self-concept of children, you must yourself possess a positive self-concept. You need to appreciate your own strengths, acknowledge your weaknesses, and have an inner acceptance of who you are. If you are unable to accept yourself, you may have difficulty being truly accepting of children, however much you may think you like them.

Enhancing Self-Concept and Self-Esteem

Self-concept and self-esteem are affected by the experiences children have in their early childhood programs. Children come to accept and appreciate themselves in a positive social climate in which you help them to know that they are worthwhile and respected. You arrange environments to provide positive experiences and encourage independence and responsibility. You create routines to ensure each child feels safe, secure, and capable. You design curriculum in which every child has the opportunity to be challenged and successful. Most importantly, you relate to children, manage the group, and deal with interpersonal problems in ways that help children view themselves positively.

At different ages and stages, educators use different techniques to help children to develop positive self-concept. Infants and toddlers are developing their initial sense of self. As a caregiver for these very young children, your primary guidance task will be to help them to feel safe, secure, and lovable—the foundation of positive self-concept and self-esteem. Frequent, affectionate physical and verbal contact, responsiveness to each baby's needs, and the availability of attractive, appropriate materials help them feel valued. A comfortable environment with many safe "yes's" and few "no's," with enough toys, duplicates of favorite toys, available laps and hugs, and a positive view of their struggle to explore and do things for themselves help toddlers to feel good about themselves.

Preschoolers and school-age children are developing their sense of themselves in terms of their relationships with other people and the world. As you work with them, you will help them to see themselves as competent and worthwhile. Preschoolers come to have a positive self-concept when they are given lots of interesting things to do and many opportunities to do them. Their sense of self-worth is heightened when adults focus on their successes and forgive them for their mistakes. Lots of affectionate contact and adults who appreciate them, respect them, and provide clear limits complete the picture. Primary school children feel good about themselves as they take on more and more real and meaningful learning and work. They respond well to guidance from warm, consistent adults who appreciate their abilities.

Young children's sense of self is inextricably linked to their sense of family and culture. Teachers support self-esteem in all children when they learn about the types of behavior valued by each culture and when they understand that individual families assign meaning to particular behaviors. For example, many children whose families are from the People's Republic of China may be taught to avoid asserting themselves. These families may view quiet, reserved behavior as a sign of social maturity. Teachers who acknowledge and appreciate this behavior in these children are supporting their sense of self-worth (Marshall 2001).

Young children need educators who accept them as they are and who encourage them to value and positively evaluate themselves. It is not necessary to love all the children you work with all the time, nor is it realistic to expect to feel that way. It is essential, however, to communicate genuine respect and caring.

Three-year-old Becky started preschool unspeaking, thumb-sucking, and unwilling to engage with children or attempt simple activities. She responded to most activities with a defeated "I can't." Her teachers encouraged her, allowed her time, and made sure she had an opportunity to try activities. They noted what she could do well and sent other children to her as a resource. Becky gradually became more comfortable, gained friends, and spent less time sleepily sucking her thumb. By the end of the year she was a quiet but enthusiastic participant in the group.

RELATIONSHIPS ARE BUILT THROUGH COMMUNICATION

Early childhood educators who love their work genuinely enjoy relating to and communicating with children. Relating to and communicating with children requires some special techniques and an investment of time and attention. A key element of an effective classroom is the development of a positive social environment. By this we mean creating settings where children and adults use communication practices that allow them to understand and communicate with one another in supportive ways.

Communication Strategies

Along with a curriculum that includes learning about social skills and relationships with others, teachers create positive social environments through effective and persistent use of positive and effective communication strategies. Young children communicate through physical interaction as well as through words, so you must learn to consciously pay attention to facial expressions, sounds, body posture and tension, hugs, and touches. Children feel most comfortable communicating with adults who are physically on their level; therefore early childhood teachers spend a great deal of time stooping, squatting, and sitting on low chairs or on the floor. One of us whose knees are not as strong as they once were has taken to carrying a small chair around with her both indoors and outdoors. Having the chair nearby allows her to easily get to children's eye-level without having to stop conversations and look for a place to sit.

Respectful communication conveys to children that you value their feelings and thoughts and you trust their capacity to learn. Adults often speak to children in ways that are either condescending and insincere or brusque, bossy, and rude. You may have felt insulted when someone spoke to you "as if you were a child." When you talk to children "like people" you will find that you enhance communication and relationships, although it may feel awkward when you first try. Basic abilities that will help you to be effective in communicating with children include the ability to have genuine and positive interactions with them, a willingness to listen and perceive their meanings accurately, the capacity to respond clearly and authentically, an awareness of barriers to communication, and the desire to try to overcome these barriers. We have found the following strategies to be useful and meaningful.

Interactions with Children

Relationships are built on the small, shared individual experiences you have with children each day. Reading a story, having a conversation, feeding a guinea pig, watching the goldfish swim, digging in the sand, taking a walk around the yard to look for bugs, or singing a song together are the kinds of experiences that build relationships. Worthwhile relationships are built on shared interests and experiences. The workings of the plumbing, the quality of the easel paint, the traits of a favorite character from a story, home, family, the world, and thousands of other shared experiences make up the content of conversations you can have with children. Frequently adults make contact with children only to give directions, handle problems, pronounce facts, or teach skills and concepts. These aspects will be part of your day, but they are not the stuff of which genuine relationships are built.

Give children plenty of time and opportunity to talk. Adults often talk a great deal and leave little time for children's responses, perhaps because they feel it is a part of their role, because they are uncomfortable with silence, or because they are disinterested in what children have to say. Continual talking gives little opportunity or encouragement for children to express themselves.

Speak with children using a sincere and respectful pattern of speaking. Use a conversational tone and clear and straightforward speech pattern. "Cute," condescending, or artificially sweet ways of talking send the message to children that they are not worthy of sincerity and respect. Educators who have a genuine interest in children speak to them without such artificiality and never cut a conversation short because the subject matter isn't "nice."

Avoid using the same words and phrases over and over. Some examples that we hear often when we visit children's programs are: "use walking feet," "use helping hands," and the ever present "use your words." While we applaud that these requests are stated positively, we believe that many teachers become so accustomed to using these stock phrases that they forget to use authentic and real language to communicate. When children hear the same phrase repeatedly, it begins to fade into the background and fails to send true meaning. Instead, think of a number of different meaningful ways to phrase requests, such as: "tell him what you mean," "let her know what you need," or "you can talk instead of hitting." Taking time to use nonrepetitive language is one way to ensure that you are communicating with children in a meaningful manner.

Effective Listening

An essential skill for good communication is the ability to listen. Listening means paying attention to the message another person is communicating. Although it seems commonplace, listening requires concentration and effort. When we visit schools, we frequently hear teachers describe an upsetting relationship with a child by telling us, "she never listens."

> *Mitsu was sitting at the art table. "Look, teacher," she said, "look at my magic seeds!"*

Her teacher, Alyce, was nearby gathering materials. "That's nice, honey," she said to Mitsu.

"Teacher, my sister and I found these magic seeds and we're gonna use them to grow a whole big dinner," Mitsu explained. Still looking into the cupboard, Alyce murmured an "um-hum." Mitsu picked up a cup beside her and dumped its contents onto her paper, which was damp from using watercolors. Out came some sandy dirt along with a few small seeds. Mitsu rubbed the dirt around on her wet paper, trying to find all of the seeds.

Looking up, Alyce exclaimed, "Oh Mitsu, you've gotten your paper and the table all dirty. Please clean up and paint nicely!"

"But teacher," Mitsu said, looking very worried, "these are my magic seeds!"

"There's sand and dirt all over the art table," Alyce responded. "Please listen to what I'm telling you. You need to get that mess cleaned up so other children will be able to paint."

Who didn't listen? True listening is a most powerful tool for building relationships with children and creating a peaceful, productive classroom.

Listening means being obviously attentive to a child's meaning and feelings. You can demonstrate attentiveness and "listen" better if you look at a child, crouch or sit at his or her level, and give responsive verbal and nonverbal feedback that communicates that you really heard. Timing, the quality and register of your voice, facial expression, gestures, and body posture often convey more to a child than the words you use. Responding attentively with a nod, smile, or word of encouragement gives the child time to express ideas and feelings and gives you time to try to piece together words and body language. Statements like "I see," "Tell me more," "Yes," "Is there anything else you want to tell me?" and "Thank you for telling me" are encouraging responses. These general listening behaviors can be used in concert with the strategies discussed below to help you create an environment where all children and adults are learning to be skilled communicators.

Nonverbal Messages. Listening well requires that you pay careful attention not only to words, but to gestures, body stance, movement, and tone of voice. One message can be sent by a person's words while body and expression convey something else. Nonverbal messages are frequently your best source of information about children's thoughts and feelings. If you work with infants and young toddlers, they will be your main source. Even highly verbal preschoolers were nontalkers only a year or two ago. And despite their increasingly sophisticated language, primary children also speak with their bodies. Whatever age you work with, it is critical to listen with your eyes as well as your ears.

The more you know about a child (age, social and language habits, culture, family background, and experiences), the better you will be at really understanding the child. The combination of general knowledge plus attention to the immediate situation will enable you to understand the meaning behind words and behavior.

At the beginning of the school year, 3-year-old Noa's morning was punctuated by bouts of crying, "I want my Mommy!" As children left circle time to play, Noa's crying started again, and the cry for Mommy took on a new and more desperate tone accompanied by a dance-like motion. His observant teacher approached him, spoke with him quietly, and then led Noa to the bathroom.

This teacher's observations, her awareness of Noa's day at school, and her knowledge of 3-year-olds helped her to understand what the problem really was.

Active Listening. It is useful to think of words and body language as a code for feelings as well as thoughts. *Active listening* is a term we learned from Thomas Gordon in

265

his book *Teacher Effectiveness Training* (1974). It describes a process in which you listen and respond to the feeling as well as the content of a message. By asking a question or making a statement, you give the child the opportunity to clarify the meaning and express the feelings involved.

Here are two examples of situations where a child's words and actions had different meanings and the teacher used active listening:

> *Two-year-old Michelle, during the first month of school, was absentmindedly stacking blocks. Her teacher walked by, and Michelle said, "When my Mommy come?" Michelle's face and body slumped and her voice sounded worried and sad. The teacher responded, "It sounds like you wish you could see her right now." Michelle nodded and a tear spilled out. She whispered, "I miss Mommy."*

> *Four-year-old Chloe, during her fifth month of school, was intently building an elaborate block structure. The teacher walked by, and Chloe said, "When is my Daddy coming?" Chloe's body was tense, her eyes focused on her structure, and her voice was high pitched and anxious. The teacher responded, "Are you worried you'll have to stop before you're finished?" Chloe said, "Yeah, when I want to finish building, Daddy always wants to hurry up."*

Active listening is even appropriate with infants and young toddlers who have few words to communicate their feelings. For example:

> *Torin, a 12-month-old child who was familiar with his caregiver, reached for her new glasses. The child touched them, wrinkled his brow, and said, "Ga?" Torin's face and body were relaxed. The caregiver smiled, "You're touching my new glasses. I look different." The child smiled and touched the glasses again.*

> *Six-month-old Cameo reached for the glasses of her caregiver. She touched them, then grabbed on, pulled, and vocalized. The caregiver smiled, "Those are my glasses. They're nice to touch but I need them to see." Then she handed Cameo a rattle. "You can play with the sun rattle." Cameo gurgled and chewed contentedly on the rattle.*

The educators in these examples used knowledge of individuals as well as observation of nonverbal cues to make inferences regarding each child's feelings. Active listening helped them to understand what the child was trying to communicate and enabled them to support children in expressing their needs. Active listening is especially valuable because it demonstrates to children that you really pay attention to how they feel.

Active listening teaches children the very important lesson that all feelings are okay. It provides children with words to use to express feelings and models talking about feelings as a way to understand oneself and others. Children whose feelings are validated in this way come to feel good about who they are. Fred Rogers reminded us of the importance of honoring all children's feelings when he said, "Children can't be expected to leave the unhappy and angry parts of themselves at the door before coming in. We all need to feel that we can bring the whole of ourselves to the people who care about us" (Rogers 2003).

Responding Clearly and Authentically

In addition to listening carefully, good early childhood educators are skilled at responding to children's messages in ways that support children's sense of self and their learning about people and relationships.

Reflective and Responsive Statements. Reflective and responsive statements (Kostelnik, Whiren, Soderman, Stein, & Gregory 2003) are a deceptively simple and very powerful communication tool. "You are climbing so carefully up the slide." "You used all of the red paint to make your dragon painting." "You finished that math job very

Say What You See

R & R statements are . . .

- Nonjudgmental statements that describe what a child is doing or experiencing:
  "You're way up at the top of the climber."
  "You have been using lots of red paint."
  "You've been working on that puzzle for a long time."

- Statements that show interest in the child and her activity:
  "You've used a lot of Legos to make that building."
  "You seem to especially enjoy the Morris story."
  "You and Alex spent all of play time in the block corner this morning."

- Statements that help children understand what they are doing or feeling:
  "You're trying to figure out a way to balance a big block on top of a tiny one."
  "You're wondering how you can get a turn with the trike."
  "You wish your Mom could have stayed longer."

Statements that judge or evaluate are *not* R & R statements. Examples:
  "You're a great climber."
  "Your picture is pretty."
  "You are smart with puzzles."
  "What a good boy you are."

When you "say what you see"—that is, use R & R statements—children feel that their actions, speech, and ideas are valuable. Their emerging language skills are also supported.

quickly today." "You are waiting patiently for your turn on the tricycle." Simply put, "R & R statements" are words that tell children that you see and are paying attention to what they are doing (see Figure 9.2). When you use these statement frequently, children are aware that their actions and interests have value to you. Regular use of R & R statements also helps children to make sense of what they are doing and experiencing.

Encouragement Versus Praise

During a recent 1-hour visit to a classroom, one of us heard more than 30 instances where adults praised children. We heard phrases such as: "I like the way that Desiree is sitting so nicely at circle." "Good cleaning up, Bennie." "You're a great artist." "Good washing." "That's a beautiful drawing." "Great building, Danisha." And repeatedly: "Good job. Good job. Good job!"

Why were we concerned with this liberal use of praising statements? For many years educators were taught to use praise generously with children in their classrooms. Praise was viewed as a tool to make children feel good about themselves and motivate learning and good behavior. More recent research indicates that the consistent use of praise actually has the reverse effect, and that when children are praised repeatedly they may become anxious about their ability to perform and may be less likely to repeat positive actions (Hitz & Driscoll 1988; Kohn 2001).

Praise is often used by teachers not as a way to express genuine pleasure about a child's actions, but rather as a means to manipulate future behavior. In the example above, the teacher who commented on Desiree's "nice sitting" appeared more interested in using her words to encourage other children to come to circle than on giving Desiree any meaningful feedback about her behavior. In other instances, this type of praise is intended to encourage children to repeat a positive action in the future, not as a sincere acknowledgment of effort or skill. Used this way, praising statements become external rewards.

If a long-term goal is to help children build self-direction and inner control, then praise is not an effective practice. Praising teaches children to act to receive approval from adults, not because they feel an action is correct or worthy. In some cases, children become so dependent on external evaluation from adults that they can't determine what they like or value. We have known children who ask for adult approval constantly: "Do you like my picture?" "Am I climbing good?" "Am I a good helper, too?" These children were "praise junkies," dependent on praise as the only way to feel good about themselves.

Several studies have indicated that although praise may encourage children to continue an activity while an adult is watching, children are less likely to continue the activity when the adult leaves or to repeat the activity in the future. Rather than increasing children's commitment to positive behavior, praise encourages children to find ways to get future verbal "goodies" from important adults.

Less obvious, but equally important, is the fact that praise actually takes away from children a sense of pride and self-worth. Children who are praised excessively may lose their ability to evaluate their own progress or to feel intrinsic joy and delight. Praise is like the large pink icing rose in the center of the cake. It is appealing, and at first bite its sweetness tastes wonderful. A couple more bites still may taste good, but it quickly becomes overly sweet. It has only one simple flavor; we soon tire of it and if we eat very much at any one time, we may feel slightly ill. It may provide some quick energy but it provides no nourishment and doesn't support growth or health.

Encouragement, on the other hand, is like a warm soup. It has many complex flavors and eating it gives us nutrients we need to feel strong and to have sustained energy. While it may not have the initial appeal of the sweet icing, its long-term effects strengthen us and encourage our growth. For a comparison of encouragement versus praise, see Figure 9.3.

Figure 9.3   **Differences Between Encouragement and Praise**

Encouragement is . . .	Praise is . . .
Specific: *"Thank you. You helped pick up all the blocks and put them away where they belonged."*	**General:** *"That's beautiful."*
Descriptive and nonjudgmental: *"You did the pilot puzzle, it's a tricky one."*	**Making a judgment:** *"You're a great puzzle solver."*
About feelings and motivation: *"It's really satisfying when you finish a painting that you have worked on so hard, isn't it?"*	**About external products or rewards:** *"I'll put the best paintings on the bulletin board to show the parents."*
Thoughtful and individual: *"That was the first time you slid down the twisting slide by yourself."*	**The same for all and holds little meaning for the individual:** *"Good job."*
Encouragement focuses on . . .	**Praise focuses on . . .**
The process, experience, and effort: *"You really worked hard on scrubbing that table."*	**The person or outcome:** *"That's the best job of cleanup I ever saw."*
Growth of the individual: *"You wrote the names of everyone in our class. I remember when you could only write your name."*	**Comparison of children:** *"You're the best printer in our class."*
Self-evaluation: *"It looks like you feel proud of that picture."* *"How did you feel about finishing your science project?"*	**Judgment from others:** *"I love your picture!"*

Strategies to Enhance Communication with Infants and Toddlers

When you relate to infants and toddlers you communicate with your whole being—voice, body, and heart. A relationship with an infant involves being attentive and responsive by returning coos, smiles, and babbles. The best educators of infants relate to even the youngest child with the respect they would use with a friend. They always explain what they are doing before they move a child, and they give time and attention to each interaction—from play, to feeding, to diapering.

A good relationship with an infant involves really attending to the signals given. It is impossible to "spoil" an infant by responding to his or her needs (something some adults fear). By being responsive to nonverbal messages, you give the child exactly what is needed and build a positive relationship. This responsiveness does not mean jumping at every cry. Instead, by knowing the infant and his or her typical needs and behavior, you can acknowledge feelings and create routines and activities that meet the baby's needs.

Speak to infants and toddlers as you would speak to other people you know and care about. Although the conversation may be one-sided, the relationship is mutual. Just as with older children, you will build a relationship based on the things you do together instead of words. You will read nonverbal messages. You will also acknowledge, interpret, and provide a scaffold or bridge as sounds become talk. Not only does this verbal interaction build relationships, it is the way that human beings learn language.

Cultural Differences in Communication

Cultural differences exist in the manner and style in which individuals communicate with one another. Nonverbal behaviors such as eye contact, smiling, and touch can mean different things. In Euro-American cultures eye contact is usually interpreted as a cue that a person is listening attentively, while in many cultures it is interpreted as a sign of disrespect if a child makes direct eye contact with an adult. Likewise, you may assume that a smile indicates happiness, pleasure, and joy. However, the smile of a child from some backgrounds may be used to mask shame or anger. It is important that you learn about the communication styles of families whose children are in your care and learn to understand and respond appropriately to both their verbal and nonverbal communications.

Barriers to Relationships

Barriers to relationships include physical and psychological distractions, personal bias, and inappropriate or disrespectful ways of communicating. Distractions in the environment can create barriers. If it is too noisy, crowded, or uncomfortably hot or cold, it is difficult to focus on another person. If your thoughts are focused on situations not related to the children, your ability to focus on communicating clearly with them will be impaired. When you are aware of the things that get in the way of good relationships, you can work to avoid them.

Strong feelings about an individual's appearance, race, culture, or personality may also hinder relationships. As we discussed in Chapter 1, everyone has some biases, but these biases need not damage relationships. You can be aware of and thoughtful about your own strong feelings, with the goals of not allowing them to affect children and of becoming more accepting of others. Your example will help children and other staff members learn to be accepting as well.

Relationships can be damaged when you are unaware of the effect of your words and behavior. It is not respectful or appropriate to talk to others about children when they are present and can hear what is being said. It is also rude and unprofessional to

Roadblocks to Avoid in Communication

Jasmine is climbing on a piece of playground equipment and will not come inside at the end of an outdoor play period. She says, "I want to climb, I don't want to go inside."

Some roadblocks give orders, advice, or attempt to convince.

- Ordering, commanding, directing: "You have to come in right now."

- Warning, threatening: "If you don't come inside, you won't get a snack."

- Moralizing, preaching, giving "shoulds" and "oughts": "Nice girls come in with their friends."

- Advising, offering solutions or suggestions: "If you come inside you can play with your friends and have fun."

- Teaching, lecturing, giving logical arguments: "You're going to miss activity time and you'll be all alone with no one to play with."

Some roadblocks evaluate or interpret based on your values.

- Judging, criticizing, disagreeing, blaming: "Why are you so difficult?"

- Name calling, stereotyping, labeling: "Only babies want to play outside all the time."

- Interpreting, analyzing, diagnosing: "You must wish you had a friend."

- Praising, agreeing, giving positive evaluations: "You are such a good girl. I know you want to come in."

Some roadblocks avoid the problem.

- Reassuring, sympathizing, consoling, supporting: "Poor baby. I'm sorry you have to come in."

- Questioning, probing, interrogating: "Are you feeling sick?"

- Withdrawing, distracting, humoring, diverting: "Have you seen the new puzzles? You're really going to like them."

Source: Based on *Teacher Effectiveness Training*, by T. Gordon, 1974, New York: David McKay.

talk through a child for the benefit of the adults or other children who might be listening. Similarly, sarcasm and humor at children's expense while pretending to talk with them is disrespectful.

Avoiding Communication Barriers

Sometimes our actions and behaviors prevent communication with one another. When we fail to listen well or communicate thoughtfully, we may miss opportunities to relate meaningfully to children. Some responses don't acknowledge feelings and concerns. Gordon (1974) calls these responses *roadblocks*. Roadblocks tell the person you are communicating with that his or her ideas are unimportant, unacceptable, or irrelevant. Recognizing roadblocks and understanding how they stop communication helps you observe your own responses and learn new ways of listening and responding. The accompanying box, "Roadblocks to Avoid in Communication," gives examples.

As you read the roadblocks you may wonder "Why are these so bad?" or "What can I say that would not be a roadblock?" Even when offered with the best of intentions, as many roadblocks are, they ignore the child's feelings and concerns and reflect the adult's point of view, needs, and feelings. In contrast, the active listening response described earlier will help you understand the child's feelings and ideas without leaping to conclusions or solving the problem for the child. Such a response respects and acknowledges children and allows them to tell you what they are feeling. For example:

> **Child:** *"I want to climb. I don't want to go inside."*
>
> **Teacher:** *"You're enjoying climbing. You wish it wasn't time to go in."*

Reflect on your relationship with a teacher

Recall a teacher with whom you had a good relationship or a teacher with whom you had a bad relationship. What contributed to its being a good or bad relationship? How did the teacher communicate with you? How did the relationship affect how you felt about teachers, school, and learning?

The challenge is to be aware of the ways you talk and respond. Notice when children respond eagerly and contrast it with the times when a child withdraws or rebels. Be aware of the times when you feel threatened or "turned off" by other people and try to learn from these situations.

GUIDING GROUPS

Another aspect of child guidance you will encounter as a teacher of young children is to ensure that children can have a productive experience in a group. In addition to what we have already discussed about strategies for effective communication with individuals, you will need to create a positive social environment in the classroom, help children to get along with each other, and address the problems that inevitably arise among individuals in any group of young children.

Trust, Attachment, and Relationships

Trust is foundational to all social and emotional growth and health. Children create a sense of trust through their relationships with the important people in their lives. Recent work by Howes and Ritchie (2002) draws on premises of attachment theory (Bowlby 1982) and applies them to teacher-child relationships. These researchers stress that for children of all ages and life circumstances, a trusting relationship with the teacher is necessary in order for children to learn. Further, their research indicates that the quality of the attachment relationship between teachers and children significantly influences children's long- and short-term development. When children trust their teachers, they are able to use them as a resource that allows them to organize and structure their learning. Therefore, it is important that teachers pay significant attention to the quality of their relationships with each individual child. In classrooms where teachers create strong teacher-child relationships and support positive peer interactions, children are more likely to behave in socially acceptable ways. In classrooms with this focus, "classroom management" is about creating and maintaining positive relationships instead of finding ways to manage conflict and difficult behaviors (Howes & Ritchie 2002).

I-Messages

When you have a problem with a child's behavior you can give an *I-message*, a technique described by Gordon (1974) as a way to communicate your problems and feelings without blaming children. An I-message invites a child to participate in solving the problem rather than telling them what to do. When you give an I-message, you maintain your rights, get your point across, and avoid hurting children or your relationship with them. An effective I-message has three elements:

- It states the specific condition or behavior that is problematic.
- It states your feelings.
- It explains why you feel that way.

I-messages communicate that, even if you don't like a particular behavior or situation, you trust that the child is caring enough and capable of helping to solve the problem. Often the behavior will stop once the child knows that it causes a problem.

271

The order and wording of an I-message is not as critical as communicating the three pieces—behavior, feelings, and effect—and the implied invitation to the child to find a mutually acceptable solution. For example:

> *"It's hard for everyone to hear when there's so much noise. It makes me feel frustrated if I have to shout so you can hear the story. I'm feeling upset. There's too much noise for everyone to hear the story."*

This statement does not send a negative evaluation and it leaves the solution in the hands of the child. A more common response than the previous example might be to respond with a roadblock: "Stop talking! You're bothering everyone. You will have to leave if you can't be quiet." Such a you-message denies the child the opportunity to solve the problem. It focuses on the child's behavior in a blaming or evaluating manner, ignores the effect of the behavior on others, and imposes a solution on the child.

Even very young, preverbal children and second-language learners benefit from this approach. For example, a toddler with minimal language who pulls your hair can be told "Ouch!"—with an exaggerated sad expression. "It hurts when you pull my hair," followed by a gentle guiding of the hand in a patting motion and a smile: "I like it when you touch me gently."

When a toddler behaves in an unacceptable way or an infant's action must be stopped, teachers who understand development gently and clearly explain what must be done and why: "I can't let you pull my hair. That hurts me. Here, you can pull the raggedy doll." Do the children understand? Infants and toddlers, like the rest of us, understand kindness and respect; understanding the words will come later.

Older children will learn to use I-messages as a way to communicate with one another, when they hear this model used frequently. The use of I-messages is helpful in teaching children to resolve problems and conflicts with one another. Teachers who use R & R statements and active listening create a foundation for the use of I-messages because they have modeled describing situations and labeling feelings.

Dealing with Conflict

Problems and conflicts are an inevitable aspect of group life, both in and outside of early childhood programs. The way you deal with conflict provides an important model for young children. They can experience conflict as a part of life that, while not pleasant, is an opportunity for problem solving rather than something that is violently disrupting and harshly controlled.

How you feel about conflict is a reflection of your experiences, values, and culture. Reflecting on how you feel about and deal with conflict in your own life may be helpful in considering what you will model for children. Do you tend to avoid conflict? Do you try to impose a solution? Do you tend to let go of what you want or need so relationships will not be damaged or hoping that the problem will go away? Or do you work collaboratively to find mutually satisfactory solutions?

Conflict can be difficult to deal with because it is often accompanied by anger, a powerful emotion that can be hard to understand and express. Anger is a second-level reaction—a response to hurt, threat, frustration, or anxiety. Young children may not have words to express the feelings that lay behind their conflicts or may have been told not to express feelings. Before you can help children learn to resolve conflicts peacefully, you must help them to identify and acknowledge their feelings. The accompanying box, "Ways to Help Children Understand and Express Feelings," suggests some ways to help children understand and express feelings as a prelude to conflict resolution.

When disputes between young children occur, it is wise to watch first and refrain from intervening too soon. Children who are not hurting one another can try to work out their own solutions. Although it is tempting to step in to solve problems for them,

- Accept and name children's feelings for them: "You feel disappointed that Calder has the ball you wanted."

- Model expressing your own feelings: "When puzzles are tossed on the floor, I'm worried that the pieces will get lost."

- Invite children to talk to you and to one another about how they feel: "Your face looks sad. Would you like to tell me or Lizzy about how you are feeling?"

- Point out similarities and differences in feelings: "You both like to read stories. Briana likes to read by herself. Aaron wishes he had company."

- Provide opportunities for children to identify and express feelings through conversations, art, music movement, dramatic play, and writing: "Would you like to make a painting that shows how you felt after you watched the sad movie about the dog?"

- Rehearse expressing feelings through activities like role-playing: "Let's pretend that it is time to clean up and you aren't finished with your construction project. Show me what you could do."

this intervention does not help them learn to be problem solvers. If you find yourself struggling to allow children the time, space, and personal authority to resolve problems as independently as possible, it may help to recall: *"You can't teach children to think, by telling them what to do."*

With practice, children can learn to tell each other how they feel and what they want instead of striking out or running to an adult when a confrontation occurs. Even very young children benefit when teachers give names to what they are feeling. This helps them build vocabulary for expressing, explaining, and understanding their feelings as they get older.

Be sensitive to the fact that not all cultures value the open expression of feelings, and in some cultures it is considered rude to show feelings openly. If children are uncomfortable with labeling or discussing feelings, never insist that they do so. Engaging in discussion with families about their thoughts and preferences related to the expression of feelings and handling conflict can help you select strategies that meet the needs of all children in the group and still promote peaceful social environments.

When conflict threatens to cause serious harm, however, you must act. It is more effective to ask *what* can be done, so that children can return to their activities, than to ask *why* they came into conflict or who hit first. Causality is usually complex, and if you didn't see what happened before, during, and after the confrontation you are not likely to get an accurate picture of what occurred. In the long run it is more productive to help the children find a solution to their problem than for you to try to judge who's right and who's wrong.

Even very young children can be given time and opportunity to deal with conflict. We recently observed a teacher who simply put her arm between two toddlers who were hurting one another. She kept her arm there, saying little except, "You both want the white purse, but there's just one here," and "I can't let you hurt one another."

When children are "stuck" and cannot reach a solution on their own, a well timed word can sometimes help them resolve the conflict. The following suggestions can give you ideas of things to say when you are talking with children who are in conflict situations:

"Stop. I won't let you hurt Harrison. You can tell him that it makes you mad when he takes your truck. Ask him to give it back to you."

"I can see you're angry about what happened. What do you want to tell her?"

"Hitting hurts. Let's think of some other ways to handle this problem."

"That hurt Alethea's feelings and she's really sad now. Please stay with me—maybe we can help her feel better."

"There isn't room for five children in the tire swing. Would you like to choose who goes first? Shall I help?"

"What can we do to solve this problem so you can go back to building your tower?"

A Process for Peaceful Conflict Resolution

We want children to learn to be cooperative and to solve problems peacefully even when we are not present. By guiding children repeatedly through the process of peaceful conflict resolution, teaching negotiating skills, and offering encouragement, we can enable them to reach this goal. We do so by teaching children to use a process to solve problems and offering them support and guidance as they go through the steps.

- *Cool down.* Everyone involved may need a moment to take a deep breath and relax, particularly if the conflict has included children hurting one another. After encouraging children to take a deep breath, the adult helps them to complete the subsequent problem-solving steps.
- *Identify the problem.* Figure out what the problem is and what needs to be solved without making judgments: "Olivia and Stacy want to play in the home area. Jayson and Paul say 'No' because they're playing Power Rangers."
- *Describe the underlying feelings, worries, concerns, and values.* These must be acknowledged before solutions can be generated: "Olivia and Stacey are worried they might not get a turn if they don't play now. Jayson and Paul like playing here too. They're afraid they won't get to play Power Rangers if you join them."
- *Brainstorm solutions.* Ask the children what they can think of to solve this problem: "Olivia thought of two plans: Jayson and Paul can play Power Rangers outside, or she and Stacey can be Power Rangers, too. Paul thought of two plans, also. He thinks that Olivia and Stacey can play in the block area and play in the home area tomorrow, or they can play in the home area in 10 minutes."
- *Choose one and try it:* "What do you want to try? What do you think might work for all of you?" or "Okay, Olivia and Stacey will try playing Power Rangers in the home area for 10 minutes with Jayson and Paul. Then they will play another game."
- *Follow up.* If necessary, encourage and support children as they try the solution. At a later time, such as when the children are gathered at the snack table or at a group time or class meeting, invite children to reflect on what could be done to prevent problems in the future or how their solutions worked: "What do you think we could do so that this problem doesn't happen again? How did it work out when all of you played Power Rangers?"

We find that young children are interested in this process, and with patient facilitation from trusted adults they will learn to use it with skill. When we have consistently involved children in handling problems with us, we have found that they also start to do it quite effectively in their own problems with peers. In addition to being consistent to our goal of developing the cooperation skills children need to live effectively in a community, teaching children this skill relieves the teacher of the onerous role of being the "classroom police."

Learning to Treat Others with Respect and Fairness

Children can learn to treat others with respect and fairness when teachers strive to teach these beliefs and values. Adults can help children to negotiate conflicts in a just and fair manner and discuss these concepts in ways that children can understand.

Many teachers use frequent (weekly, daily, or sometimes several times each day) class meetings as a means of creating a positive social environment in the classroom. These can be a powerful tool for teaching children important skills as members of a community. When meetings are structured so that everyone is encouraged to talk and share feelings honestly but with kindness, children learn the skills they need as communicators, negotiators, and problem-solvers. Class meetings help teachers create a social environment where children feel emotionally safe and as a result are able to concentrate and learn (Gartrell 2004; Vance & Weaver 2002). This method of social problem solving is congruent with those used by Native-American, Native-Hawaiian, and other cultural groups. Some classrooms in Hawaii include a *ho'oponopono*, a time and place for individuals to gather to talk through differences. Including such tools strengthens the sense of community and trust that children experience.

Carefully chosen children's literature can also contribute to the positive social climate of the classroom and can promote comprehension of fairness, justice, and equality. Children can be encouraged to discuss and dramatize their understanding of these social concepts.

Making the Environment and Schedule a Partner in Guidance

Physical environments send strong messages to children about how they are expected to act and whether they are welcome and accepted. The guidelines for arranging the environment and schedule provided in Chapters 7 and 8 can help you set up physical spaces that invite children to work and play together in harmonious ways. When you notice that children are having difficulties in the classroom, it is useful to look first at the environment and schedule to determine whether either one is the source of the problems.

For example, in a preschool class we know, the block center was in the middle of the room. To get to any other area, children had to walk through the block center, often bumping into structures. Children whose buildings were knocked down responded by using blocks as defensive weapons, and children who walked through the block area regularly picked up blocks as props for other centers and deposited them far away. Creating a more sheltered block area reduced these problems. In a toddler program we recently observed, staff provided few duplicate materials and toddlers were often in conflict over toys. Replacing highly prized single toys with two to four similar toys minimized conflicts. In a primary program, children's behavior improved noticeably after the schedule was changed from two consecutive and lengthy seated activity periods to a routine where quiet seatwork was interspersed with time outside and in learning centers.

Managing the Classroom

Guiding a group of young children, sometimes called *classroom management*, is an art that requires knowledge, skill, sensitivity, and self-confidence. Like any art it is one that you will acquire through training and experience, and it becomes easier with practice. As your skill increases and you become comfortable using some of the tools discussed in this chapter, you will find that you will need to devote less of your time to "managing" and will be able to spend more of your time building relationships and creating learning opportunities. A disposition that enjoys children will serve you well! And it is useful to learn about and understand some particular attitudes and practices that can assist you in keeping groups running in a smooth and amicable manner.

Becoming Comfortable with Authority

By virtue of your role as an educator, society confers on you a certain authority: the rights to exercise power, make decisions, take action, give commands, and expect obedience. The most obvious source of this authority is adulthood. You are larger, stronger, and older, so most children acknowledge your right to give direction. Although authority is conferred by society as a part of your role, it is strengthened by your education, knowledge, skill, experience, and commitment.

Most of us have encountered teachers, bosses, family members, or others in authority who were harsh, punitive, or unfair. We have also experienced people in authority who were unclear and inconsistent, who thus abdicated authority and left us without a sense of what was acceptable. Neither of these uses of authority is beneficial. Instead, early childhood educators strive to use authority humanely, fairly, and with clarity. We call this use of authority "authoritative" to distinguish it from unfair or unkind "authoritarian" uses of power.

> **Reflect on teacher authority**
>
> Think about a teacher you liked and a teacher you didn't like. How did each exercise authority or power? Did he or she win your respect and gain your cooperation? If so, how? If not, why not? How did this influence what you learned and who you are today?

In his first weeks as a practicum student in a 4-year-old class, Mark actively engaged in play with the children. On the playground, he took the role of the chasing monster resulting in many giggles and calls of "catch me, catch me, Mr. Mark." His tickles and jokes and high-fives were enthusiastically welcomed by the children and he became their favorite play partner. In sharing his experiences in his college seminar, Mark expressed frustration. While the children were delighted to play with him, they ignored his requests and seemed to completely disregard him as an authority figure.

Becoming comfortable with authority is one of the first issues that any prospective educator faces. Our college students often struggle with authority as they learn to work with children. The way they approach authority involves their values and expectations. Some try to deny their authority. Like Mark, they behave as if they were one of the kids and become confused and frustrated when children do not respect them or cooperate with them. Others expect children to grant them authority simply because they are the "teacher." They make demands without first building a respectful relationship and are surprised when children are rebellious and resistant.

Authority that is authentic and lasting is based on mutual respect; it is used wisely and with compassion. There is no single right way to exercise authority and no one way that is appropriate for each age and individual. Some early childhood practitioners invite children's cooperation with a shared joke and a smile, and children seem delighted to join them. Others clearly and calmly state appropriate expectations in a friendly, no-nonsense voice and gain willing compliance. Still others almost silently step in to redirect children with a word or gesture and like magic prevent a blow, encourage a friendship, or assist in a routine. Each of these approaches is grounded in respect, clarity, knowledge of children, and positive relationships. As you develop skill using the strategies we have discussed in this chapter and as you become comfortable with your role as a teacher, you will find your own unique ways to guide groups effectively.

Your first experiences in trying to manage a group of children are likely to be somewhat challenging. Children will test you to find out what they can expect from you so they can feel secure. Experienced teachers are usually clearer about their expectations of children and communicate these expectations with kind authority from the beginning in words, body language, and behavior. Children quickly become "well behaved" with them. Less experienced individuals often hesitate and send mixed messages. Children respond with more testing. When you are clear about your expectations and communicate them with authority, your work becomes much easier. Authority comes with time, practice, and patience.

Creating Appropriate Expectations

Clearly stated expectations for behavior enable people to exist together in harmony. Some people try to achieve this by creating and enforcing a set of rules that define what is expected in every situation. A *rule* is a regulation, usually stated as behavior that is required or prohibited. The word *rule* suggests something that is inflexible. Rules are usually made by adults and adults are expected to enforce them. They are typically applied in precisely the same manner to all children, regardless of situation or circumstance. ("That's the rule!") Rules imply that there will be a punishment to those who break them. These circumstances create situations where children are in conflict with adults and struggles for power and control are inevitable.

We prefer the use of the terms *limits* and *guidelines*, which imply flexibility and cooperation more consistent with our values and beliefs. Limits provide boundaries that allow for personal choice within the confines of safety. Baby gates at open doorways, locks on cabinets containing cleaning products, and fences around playgrounds are examples of physical limits that help keep children safe. Adults also create guidelines for children's behavior. Whether you call them rules or guidelines (and we will use both terms), it is important that they be clear, fair, and used with sensitivity. When children know what they are, they are free to make choices about what to do and how to behave in a variety of situations.

Guidelines protect rights and property, make the program predictable, and help children to respect and get along with others. When fairly and consistently applied, they help children feel safe and comfortable. We were helped to understand this when we were given the example of limits being similar to the guardrails on a massive suspension bridge. While you may never actually need them to keep you from driving off into the water, without them it would be a frightening experience to cross the bridge (Gonzalez-Mena 2001). Guidelines for young children need to be simple enough so they can be easily understood, few enough to remember, and general enough to apply to a wide variety of situations.

A few general guidelines that address important principles are better than a laundry list of rules that address every conceivable situation. Good guidelines help young children to know what to do rather than what *not* to do. They are reasonable in terms of the developmental level of children. For example, it is unreasonable to require young school-age children not to move or talk, to insist that preschoolers keep their clothes clean, or to require toddlers not to put toys in their mouths. Whatever the age, however, it is appropriate to have the following guidelines:

- Take care of yourself.
- Take care of others.
- Take care of toys, books, tools and the environment.

These three guidelines are stated by early childhood educators in different ways—for example, "Treat yourself gently, treat one another gently, treat our school gently," or "Be safe, be kind, be thoughtful." The adults and children together can then decide what constitutes safe, kind, thoughtful care for people and the environment they share.

Guidelines are like an invisible fence around children ensuring their safety and the well-being of their environment. Because they cannot see these limits, you can expect that children will test to learn whether or not they are there and how firm they are. When you explain them clearly and enforce them firmly but with kindness, most children will gradually feel safe within them and their need to test them will dissipate.

Older preschool and primary children can participate in creating and modifying agreements about behavior. A good way to start this process is to ask the children, "What do we all need to agree to do so that everyone feels safe, happy, and can learn in school?" Agreements created by the group are not permanent; instead, the group considers them and changes them in response to changing situations. As they do so, they are likely to develop greater commitment to following agreements as well as an understanding of the principles of group living. This can be done quite successfully in class meetings.

You will need to communicate your expectations with clarity and simplicity. Problems often arise when children lack information or understanding. Children are likely to respect guidelines when they understand the reasons for them and when the behavior required is within their ability. Following are some examples of guidelines and their reasons:

> *Guideline*: Treat one another gently.
>
> *Reason*: No one can work and play if they are afraid of getting hurt.
>
> *Guideline*: Use toys, books, and games carefully.
>
> *Reason*: Toys, books, and games can get lost or damaged. Then we would not have them to use anymore.
>
> *Guideline*: Put toys, books, and games away when you are done.
>
> *Reason*: When they are not put away it's difficult to find them.

Problems with Rules

Problems with rules in early childhood programs occur either when there are too many, or when they are vague, unclear, or inconsistently enforced. Too many rules make it difficult for children to remember them. Adults then spend much of their time enforcing rules or else enforce them sporadically without clarity about what is important. When rules are ambiguous, children fail to understand and follow their direction and limits. Such a rule as "Blocks are for playing" fails to address the issue of using blocks as weapons or missiles and hence can be misunderstood. A clearer guideline would be "Use blocks only for building."

It is critical that all the adults who work with a group of children agree upon rules and limits. Problems occur when children see a lack of consistency among adults. For example, in a school we know adults did not agree on ways to use outdoor equipment. Children were told they must follow the rules of the teacher on duty. This gave little information to children who engaged in a range of unsafe behavior regardless of who was on duty, perhaps in an effort to try to figure out what was acceptable.

If you find that you have a deep philosophical disagreement with the other program staff about rules and guidance techniques, you face a professional dilemma. If these differences cannot be resolved in a manner that is consistent with your values, you may decide to leave the program rather than violating what you believe is right. For example, in a school we know 3-year-olds who did not follow the rule of sitting quietly with legs crossed at circle times were punished with long time-outs. A former student of ours was hired in the program and thought she could make changes. She left when it became clear she could not.

Redirection Instead of Distraction

When children are behaving in ways that are unsafe or that cause damage to the environment, you can redirect their energy and attention to an activity similar to the one that is unacceptable.

> *Eighteen-month-old Kawailani stands at the sink, pouring water from a cup onto the floor. Her teacher says, "You are really enjoying pouring that water. Someone might slip when water is on the floor—let's get out the water table and do some pouring there."*

In this example, Kawailani's teacher respects her interest in pouring. She offers her a similar activity that will allow her to continue her interest in a way that is safe. Children who are running in a block area can be directed to a movement activity; shouting can be refocused by playing a game with voice sounds including whispers and songs. This technique is much more respectful than distracting a child by offering an activity that has no relationship to what the child is interested in. Distraction tells children that their interests are not worthy or valued; redirection respects children's focus and energy while helping them to engage in an activity that is acceptable and appropriate to a particular circumstance.

Anticipating and Preventing Problems

Before your first day working with children, you can do important things to ensure that problems will be minimized. You can make sure children have appropriate and interesting things to do, sufficient time to engage in activities, and experiences that require no more adult supervision than you have available. An orderly environment with well defined space, appropriate materials, and a schedule geared to the needs of children with well organized routines and transitions will contribute greatly to order and calm and help to minimize conflicts. When you provide these things, children are likely to enjoy their day and play productively.

Some particular skills help you to minimize disruption from the minor problems that occur in every classroom. Researchers have identified the following teacher behaviors in classrooms where children are productively engaged and disruption is minimal (Kounin 1970):

1. *With-it-ness*: Being aware of what is going on throughout the classroom and dealing with inappropriate behavior quickly and effectively.
2. *Overlappingness*: Dealing with a number of events at the same time.
3. *Flow or momentum*: Keeping activities moving in a smooth flow without digressions and distractions.
4. *Group focus*: Awareness of the group at all times, alerting the group before changes, and keeping all children involved rather than losing track of the group while focused on individual children.

In practical terms this means being highly attentive to everything that is happening in your classroom. For example, in a typical preschool or kindergarten class you might need to attend to all of the following situations at once:

Yoon Ki and Michael are building a large block structure and wearing the construction hats they use for playing police, which often leads to rough and tumble play.

Teale and Harrison are painting at the easel, giggling with one another as they look at one another's work while Harrison holds up a wet paintbrush and drips purple paint on the floor.

Sarah, Tyrone, Billy, and Yukiko are listening to a story read by Tyrone's mom in the library corner.

Kellen, Max, and Nermeen are in the dramatic play area, dressed up in finery, feeding the dolls when Kellen announces, "No boys!"

John and Tiffany are staring intently at Squeakers, the mouse, while Tiffany pokes a piece of tinker toy in at Squeakers.

Anna, Mishka, and Sasha are at the writing center calling you enthusiastically to come write their words.

As the teacher in this classroom, you would need to make on-the-spot decisions in response to what children need, what will help individuals, and what is needed for the class as a whole. You would have to continue to attend to the rest of the group after you have made your decision, and you would need to have an interesting alternative ready for each group of children as they were ready for a change. The box "Suggestions for Group Management" lists some techniques that we have found helpful over the years in managing a group of young children.

Suggestions for Group Management

- Position yourself so you can see what is happening throughout the room.
- Get children's attention by moving close to them, crouching down, and speaking directly to them. Avoid shouting across the room or yard.
- Use children's names positively and frequently so that they don't fear something negative when you address them by name.
- Indicate what to do rather than what not to do when correcting behavior. Children often feel rebellious and challenged when told what not to do. Thus:

For	Substitute
"Don't run with the scissors."	"Please walk when you carry scissors so no one will get hurt."
"Don't get paint on your clothes."	"Wear a smock so you won't get paint on your clothes."
"Don't tear the book."	"Turn the pages carefully."

"Don't poke the guinea pig."	"Use very gentle pats and quiet voices so you don't scare the guinea pig."

- When a child doesn't respond appropriately to requests such as the preceding ones, provide two acceptable choices. Choices help children to feel powerful and in control.

  "Please walk when you carry scissors so no one will get hurt. I'd be happy to carry the scissors while you go outside to run."

  "Wear a smock so you won't get paint on your clothes. You may use pens or crayons if you don't want to cover up your new overalls today."

  "Turn the book's pages carefully—you can use newspaper if you'd like to tear."

- Avoid giving children choices that you are unwilling or unable to allow. "Would you like to give me the knife?" is not appropriate when you mean, "I must have the knife right now, it is dangerous."

Reading time is over for the kindergarten class. Mrs. Lester has asked the children to put away their books and line up quietly in the area in front of the door so they can go outside. She gathers her materials from the circle area, then goes to the table where the children used clay earlier and begins wiping the table, telling the children to get ready to go outside in just a few minutes. As she is cleaning, the children are becoming increasingly restless. Jackson grabs Becky's ponytail and tugs on it as she steps on his toes trying to cut into the line. Sasha is shouting at Jerome who is insisting that it is his turn, not hers, to be the line leader. Liane and Sarah are singing loudly and beginning to do a vigorous dance. Liane's elbow accidentally pokes Jacob's eye and he shouts at her to "Cut that out now, you dummy!" Genee, who has been struggling with her sweater, starts to cry when a sleeve rips. As the commotion level rises, Mrs. Lester raises her voice and says loudly. "I said to wait quietly in the line by the door! If you can't line up quietly, you will miss recess."

It is all too easy for situations like the one above to occur when transition times are not planned with thought and care.

Transitions are times when children are asked to move between types of activities and sometimes from one location to another. Children move from meals to center time, from centers to group activities, from group time to outside, and so on. At these times, it is easy for children to lose self-control. Teachers are often busy and distracted. Aggressive and destructive behaviors often escalate at these times. However, with advance planning, transitions need not be times of peril. The following strategies can help you to orchestrate peaceful classroom transitions.

- *Let children know before a transition will occur.* Young children do not understand time well and have difficulty predicting when one event will end and another begin. It helps them to take control of their own actions if they know when a change is coming. For younger children, a reminder just a few minutes before a transition is helpful. It is best if the reminder is made in terms of something concrete that the child can understand: "You have time to ride the tricycle around the path two more times before we go inside." Telling very young children that a transition will occur in 5 minutes is less helpful. It alerts them that the change is coming, but since 5 minutes is a very abstract concept, it is not especially useful in helping them to plan their remaining time in an activity.

   Older preschoolers and primary-age children are developing a sense of time. They appreciate a longer advance reminder and can understand when you tell them that they have 10 minutes before a change is coming. This allows them to have time to organize how they will complete an activity, game, or project.

- *Use music, movement, and/or fantasy.* It's much easier to help children move from a classroom to a playground when they fly like birds or swim like dolphins than when they must walk quietly in a straight line. Singing as you pick up blocks makes the activity more fun and encourages participation.

- *Keep the transition as short as possible.* Children are not good at waiting. Once you begin the movement from one activity to the next, do it as quickly and with as much focus as possible. In the example at the beginning of this section, Mrs. Lester's class would have handled the transition much more easily had she been present to assist them and then taken them outside as soon as all were assembled. When children are asked to wait, upsets are likely to occur.

- *Plan for children who struggle with transition.* Almost every class has children who have difficulty with transition. You'll learn quickly who these children are. You can help them by assigning them a role during the transitions and when possible remaining near them until they are reengaged in the next activity. The accompanying box, "Some Ideas for Transitions Between Activities," offers more suggestions.

We recently visited a classroom and heard a teacher saying, "Duncan, we'll be going outside soon and I would really appreciate it if you could remind me to take the hoops out today. They're kind of large so it would be great if you could carry them with me." We had seen Duncan struggle during transitions on previous days, but with this guidance, he moved from indoors to out with success and pride.

Managing Large Group Times

Additional skills are needed when you lead a large group (often at a daily event called "circle time," "morning circle," "morning meeting," or "group time"). Group times work best when they have a wide appeal, allow children to be active, and are relatively short (10–15 minutes for younger preschoolers). As children grow older, their ability to participate for longer periods of time increases (up to a half-hour for primary children). Structured group activities are not appropriate for infants and toddlers although a group may gather spontaneously if you do something interesting, such as playing a guitar, reading a story, or bringing in a puppy to visit. Toddler and 2-year-old teachers will have much more effective group experiences if they are prepared for interesting spur-of-the-moment gatherings rather than spending time herding resistant toddlers to a group area and insisting that they sit down.

Group times should be purposeful. Some good reasons to bring together a group of young children include helping them to develop a group identity or learn group roles and behavior, presenting activities such as singing and creative movement that are enjoyable in a group, introducing new activities, and ensuring that all the children have the same information. Advance planning and a few key skills will help you to make group times enjoyable for the children and you.

Group times work when children are comfortable (which means not too hungry, tired, or crowded) and when group size and teacher-child ratios are appropriate to age and abilities. Consider children's development and interests in selecting group activities that match their ability to participate. For example, a typical group of 3-year-olds will be more interested in moving and making noises like animals than in animal habitats and eating patterns. A group of 7-year-olds might be exactly the opposite.

Some Ideas for Transitions Between Activities

- **Clues**: Give a clue about the child's family, vacation, pet, or home: "A child whose mom is named Donna and whose dad is named Skip can go."

- **Riddles**: Ask a riddle about something related to the curriculum theme: "What grows in the ground, gives shade to sit in, makes a good place to climb, and is a place for birds to build their nests? The correct guesser can go."

- **Create a verse**: Sing "Old MacDonald" (or a similar endless song). Ask children to think of a verse, and they can go when their verse has been sung.

- **Props**: At activity time bring items from the various centers for each child. As you bring out the item ask a child to describe it, name its place, and take it there to play.

- **Friends**: Select a child to pick a friend with whom to leave the group.

- **Games**: For example, the Lost-and-Found game. Choose a child. Say, "Police Officer Maya, there's a lost child who's wearing blue shorts and a Batman T-shirt. Can you help me find him?" When Maya finds the child, she leaves and the found child becomes the police officer.

- **Name songs**: Sing a name song like "Get on Board Everybody" or "Hello" and have children leave when their name is sung.

Appropriate group activities for preschool and primary children have the following characteristics:

- They encourage participation.
- They include physical activity.
- They include something to look at or explore with other senses.
- They contain an element of novelty.

Singing songs, doing finger-plays, reading stories, presenting flannelboard stories or puppets engaging in creative movement activities, writing group stories, playing group games, and discussing something that is of interest are all potentially good activities for group time.

When leading a large group, you are the center of the learning experience and the children respond to your direction. Your sensitivity to their mood and energy and your ability to respond to it will determine whether the children stay involved and are cooperative. A large group will fail if it requires too much waiting or if children lack interest. When you reach the limits of children's interest you need to say, "That's all for today." Do so cheerfully and without blaming children or showing disappointment. Learning to read and respond to a group takes time, experience, and self-confidence.

Young children who are not ready for group experiences will tell you by wiggling, getting up, lying down, or walking away. When they do, they are giving you valuable feedback—something (the activity or the timing) is not appropriate to the needs of the group. Sometimes one or two children have difficulty while the rest enjoy group time. If so, have a simple alternative available for these children. Both you and the children will have a better time if expectations are appropriate and clear and if alternatives are available for children who aren't ready.

When group time works it can seem like magic—and like all magic, it is based on carefully practiced illusions. Here are some suggestions to make group times successful:

Group Time Magic

- *Have a good attitude.* If you present a group activity as something that is fun and desirable and you expect everyone to cooperate, the children are likely to believe you're right.
- *Be positive.* Focus on things children do right—don't focus on the negative.
- *Be prepared.* Plan the place, the activities, and the time to minimize distractions. Always have a backup activity to do if something doesn't appear to be working.
- *Be dramatic.* Use your voice for effect (change volume and pitch to catch interest). Use your face to communicate—eyes, eyebrows, and mouth can express feelings and ideas without words. Some practitioners even dress to focus children. A teacher we know has a collection of interesting T-shirts and earrings that she wears to go with the day's activity.
- *Direct attention.* Direct children's attention to what's happening by keeping the activities moving without long pauses, include lots of movement, and do different things.
- *Be flexible.* Make changes in response to what children do. Cut out an activity, add movement, or insert a song or finger-play as you notice children's responses.
- *Use the unexpected.* See the classroom from a child's point of view; anticipate what's going to interest children and incorporate it into what you are doing. If a firetruck drives by or a visitor walks in, make this a part of the group activity.
- *Quit while you're ahead.* Group times often fall apart when they go on too long. Instead of doing an interesting activity over again, save it for tomorrow.

DEALING WITH DIFFICULT BEHAVIORS

All teachers encounter children who have behaviors that they find difficult to handle. Some behaviors harm the child or others. They are called *challenging behaviors*. Many nonharmful behaviors are hard to deal with and are annoying, irritating, or disruptive. There is a great deal of difference among teachers regarding the behaviors that are difficult for them to deal with. One teacher becomes very upset when children spit. Another may deal with spitting easily but be unnerved when children swear. The difference in your acceptance of children's behavior comes from your own upbringing, and your beliefs about how children should behave.

Finding Your "Button Pushers"

It's helpful to identify those behaviors that you find particularly upsetting before you have to deal with them regularly. We call this "finding your button pushers." *Button pushers* are actions that cause you to become angry or upset very quickly. Many children seem skilled in identifying those buttons and pushing them. It gives children a sense of power when their actions create an immediate and strong response in adults. If you know which behaviors cause you to have a strong reaction, you can plan a calm response. Such a response lacks drama, is thoughtful, and is much less interesting for children than an angry response. Because of this they may be less motivated to repeat the behavior.

The Child Is Different from the Behavior

There are several points to keep in mind when dealing with upsetting or challenging child behaviors. First, always remember that it is the behavior, not the child, that is troublesome. When children's behavior is upsetting, it is easy to confuse *what* the child does with *who* the child is. It's tempting sometimes to think of Keiko as an annoying child, Jillette as the naughty one, Jake as cooperative, Aaron as a good boy. Some teachers begin to think of the child as characterized by the behavior. Roy is a biter. Yun Mi is a talker. Children are better served if we avoid these labels. Keiko's behavior has been upsetting. Roy is a child who has been biting lately. Even positive labels like "good girl"

put adults in the role of judges and may not have positive results. Children are helped to make appropriate choices about behaviors when their teachers view them as good, worthy, helpful, and lovable children who may sometimes make mistakes and have difficulty choosing appropriate behavior.

Another thing to remember is that all behavior has a reason. Even though we may not be conscious of it, there is a reason for everything we do. Your job is to be a detective and find out how an annoying, upsetting, or challenging behavior is serving a particular child. Once you understand the purpose, it is easier to help the child find a more appropriate, less disturbing way to get his or her needs met.

Dan Gartrell (1995, 2001, 2002) suggests that it is helpful for teachers to think about unacceptable behavior as *mistaken behavior* instead of the more familiar term, *misbehavior*. He explains that misbehavior implies that children are intentionally behaving in ways that are wrong and that they must, therefore, be punished for their "bad" actions. Teachers who think of misbehavior in this way may then label children as naughty, bad, or mean and punish them in an attempt to get them to end the misbehavior.

Mistaken behavior, on the other hand, suggests that children are learning to behave acceptably and therefore are subject to making mistakes. This perspective is more congruent with the principles of child guidance that we have discussed in this chapter. Teachers who adopt this viewpoint assume the role of one who guides children and helps them learn, rather than one who judges, scolds and criticizes.

> *Mikayla and Cherise are in the dramatic play area. Mikayla puts on a lacy tutu and turns to sit on a small sofa next to Cherise. Cherise sees the skirt and shrieks, "That is mine!" She begins tugging on the tutu as Mikayla holds it tightly around her. Mikayla stands and starts to try to move away and as she does, Cherise reaches over and slaps her face.*

The girls' teacher chose to view Cherise's behavior as "mistaken." She knows that it is hard to learn ways to get what you want. While she does not condone or accept behavior that hurts others, she does not judge children who haven't yet learned more cooperative ways as "bad." As she moves to assist the girls, she asks herself, "What can Cherise and Mikayla learn from this experience?"

> *Walking quickly to the dramatic play area, the teacher stoops and places an arm around each girl. She asks Mikayla, who is crying, to show her where it hurts. She asks both children to tell her what has happened. She empathizes with each, telling Mikayla that she knows it must have hurt when she was hit and that she obviously felt upset when Cherise tried to take the tutu. She is also empathetic to Cherise, letting her know she understands that she was using the tutu earlier and that she did not want Mikayla to take it. She says, "Cherise, I can see that you really want to use that tutu. You were trying to let Mikayla know that you did not want her to have a turn. Mikayla is crying now because her face is hurting where you hit it."*

She includes both girls when she asks, "What do you think you can do now?" After the negotiations are concluded, the teacher ensures that both Cherise and Mikayla are reengaged in an activity before moving to other responsibilities.

Understanding behavior as "mistaken" encourages this type of child-centered approach. It is based on the problem-solving model we discussed earlier in this chapter and has the following characteristics of effective guidance:

It avoids judging, labeling or victimizing either child.

It does not require a forced apology, but invites the child who offended to make amends if she so chooses.

It takes a learning-focused approach; the situation is viewed as an opportunity for each child to learn behaviors that work well in relationships with others.

Approaches for Dealing with Difficult Behaviors

There are several guidance methods that teachers may use that can be effective in dealing with mistaken behavior.

Natural and Logical Consequences

Children are served when they have experiences that respectfully help them to make connections between their own behavior and the outcomes that it produces. The use of *natural* and *logical* (or "related") *consequences* can help children make this association. Sometimes known as the *democratic approach* to guidance, this practice is based on the work of Alfred Adler, as interpreted and applied to classrooms by Rudolf Dreikurs (1969). Dreikurs noted that children become discouraged and disrupt the group when they do not know how to be positive and cooperative members of the class. The democratic approach can help children understand the mistaken strategies that they have adopted and allow them to redirect their behavior more positively.

Some consequences are the natural result of a child's actions and require no intervention on the part of an adult. For example, if a child pours his yellow paint down the drain, the natural consequence is that the paint is gone. Natural consequences allow a child to learn from experience. The teacher's task is to allow the child to experience the result of his or her action. No scolding or reprimanding is needed. This approach is appropriate when the consequence does not endanger a child and when it does not unfairly penalize another person or the group. Natural consequences seem simple, but they require restraint. It can be hard to see a child naturally disappointed, uncomfortable, or unhappy. It also can be difficult to refrain from voicing a smug "I told you so" when a child experiences natural consequences that you foretold. We find that reflective listening is a good response in these kinds of situations. For example, to a toddler who has dumped her juice onto the table: "You wish you had more juice but it's all gone." Or to a 5-year-old who has thrown the balls over the fence: "You would really like it if we had more balls to play with."

Some negative behaviors do not lead to any natural or acceptably safe consequences. In this situation you may choose to create logical or related consequences. With older preschoolers and primary-age children you can do this effectively as a group process. For example, in an after-school group the children got tired of not being able to find pieces of board games because they were often not put away. They decided the consequence for leaving a game out would be no games for the rest of the week. By confronting the direct consequences of their behavior, children learned the laws of living as a member of a group.

Younger children can benefit from situations where teachers use simple but directly related consequences such as, "Since you are breaking crayons, you will need to leave the art area and find another place to play." If a child hurts someone else the logical consequence might be to lose the opportunity to play with that child or in that area. In following through on a consequence, you would be calm and simply say, "You may not be in the block area with Yusuke now. You hurt him. You can come back when you are ready to play without hurting." Logical consequences must be reasonable, fair, and clearly related to behavior: "You threw the books off the shelf. When you are calm you can put them back on the shelf." Such consequences are consistent with the values of justice and responsibility.

For many years, teachers were taught that time-out was a logical consequence that could be used to help children learn appropriate behaviors. The premise of this technique was that children could learn that if they could not behave in socially approved ways, the logical result was that they would have to be separated from the group. Many child development experts have refuted this position and suggested that time-out, as it is frequently used in early childhood classrooms, is not a child-centered guidance technique but rather one that punishes children who have not yet learned how to behave acceptably in group situations. Katz (1984) has argued that time-out confuses young children because they cannot understand the relationship between the behaviors that happen during a conflict or other mistaken behavior and the forced removal to the chair.

A Time and Place to Calm Down

Providing a safe space away from others for a child to regain composure can be helpful. This island for calm reflection can be an effective and humane way to help children gain self-control. It is particularly effective when teachers help children learn to take themselves there when they are upset or need a quiet place. The key elements are that it is not punitive and that it is self-regulated—the child determines when to return to the group. Allowing the child to be in control expresses your trust in the child and teaches self-control. You can offer the child some criteria to determine readiness: "When your body is relaxed and you can keep your hands from hitting other people then you will be ready to come back." Contrast this with the teacher who says, "Sit in the time-out chair and think about what you did until I tell you to get up." This becomes a punishment, and fails to achieve the goal of helping children to become self-regulated group members.

Reinforcement

Reinforcement techniques developed by B. F. Skinner have been applied to the classroom by some theorists and educators. This approach is known as *behaviorism*. Behaviorists believe children misbehave because they have been taught to do so by improper rewards, or *reinforcement*. To change or *extinguish* old behaviors, new ones must be taught and rewarded.

All early childhood educators use behaviorist principles some of the time. When you smile at a shy child who attempts a new activity, you are providing reinforcement. When you ignore a child whose demanding behavior is disruptive, you are avoiding reinforcing it. The phrase "catch them being good" is a simple way of suggesting that you encourage, reward, or provide social reinforcement to children for desired behavior.

Systematic reinforcement can be effective, but it is also highly manipulative and counter to values of respect and freedom of choice. We do not believe that systematic reinforcement is appropriate for typically developing young children who are engaged in normal interactions. They will respond to approaches more consistent with the core values and goals of early childhood education.

In some elementary schools, Lee Canter's Assertive Discipline (1988), based on behaviorist principles, is in use. Teachers who use this method record children's unacceptable behavior on the chalkboard, using a system of check marks. Consequences for each check mark are predetermined. Early childhood educators (Gartrell 1987a, 1987b; Hitz 1988) have serious reservations about this approach. They question the equity of a system in which every infraction of rules is treated in exactly the same way in spite of intent, severity, and consequences. This method does not actively involve children in becoming responsible for their own actions.

Spanking Is Never a Choice

Neither spanking nor any other type of physical punishment is ever appropriate to use in early childhood programs. Not only are such practices illegal in most states, but they also have harmful effects on children and are in direct opposition to the long-term goals of teaching children to be self-directed, cooperative individuals who can resolve conflicts peacefully. When children are spanked they learn that it is acceptable to hurt others who are younger, smaller, or more vulnerable. They learn that hands are more powerful than words. Because children imitate the important adults in their lives, children who have been spanked are much more likely to deal with problems in an aggressive manner than those who have consistently experienced other forms of discipline.

Challenging Behaviors

Some children exhibit behavior that prevents them from being able to function in a group or that threatens their chance for learning and growth. Generally, the term *challenging behavior* refers to behaviors that are aggressive or antisocial. Kaiser and Rasminsky (1999, 2003) identify challenging behaviors as those that:

> Interfere with children's learning, development, and success at play
>
> Are harmful to the child, to other children, or to adults
>
> Put a child at high risk for later social problems or school failure

These behaviors are challenging for the children themselves, who are unable to be successful in a group and who probably feel helpless to control their behavior. They are also challenging for the adults who deal with these children daily and may feel helpless and overwhelmed by such behaviors.

It is important to remember that many young children engage in challenging behaviors at some time in their lives, and that in most instances consistent use of the positive guidance techniques discussed in this chapter will help them to learn more acceptable behavior. In some cases, however, challenging behavior indicates persistent difficulties that may require particular intervention strategies.

Causes of challenging behaviors are complex and still forcefully debated by researchers. Children whose mothers had complications or who used drugs and alcohol during pregnancy have a higher biological risk for developing challenging behaviors than other children. Children with developmental delays and attention deficit disorders may also be at risk. Environmental factors that increase children's risk of developing challenging behavior include poverty; exposure to violence; frequent exposure to harsh, inconsistent, and coercive discipline; family interactions that model antisocial dispute resolution; viewing violent television; and low-quality child care (Kaiser & Rasminsky 1999).

Children who use aggressive behavior need to know that you will not allow them to hurt themselves or other people, nor will you let anyone hurt them. As children learn that their feelings will be respected, their needs met, and that they will be protected from retaliation, they may turn less to destructive behavior. A child who is lashing out can sometimes stop this behavior given time and space to calm down. If the child presents a danger to self or others, you sometimes may need to use physical restraint, which can be done gently and firmly. Hold the child from behind so that you can contain flailing arms and legs. Speak calmly and let the child know that as soon as he or she regains self-control you will let him or her go. If your environment contains safe open space away from others, you might wish to take an out-of-control child to a space where the angry feelings can be worked out in vigorous physical activity that does not harm anyone. Violent outbursts are usually short-lived, especially if you help children learn to control themselves—and if you believe that they can.

In addition to helping a child negotiate problems, you can provide alternatives to disruptive behavior. Alternatives are especially important if the behaviors have been found useful in other settings or have been used to fulfill basic emotional needs. Children may need time, courage, and your persistent encouragement to change from old reliable behaviors to new untested ones, even when the old behaviors no longer work.

The techniques you have been studying will help you guide children with challenging behavior but you may find yourself more challenged in trying to apply them. Change does not happen overnight, and you may find that you need support as you help these children to become functional members of the group. In addition to being clear, consistent, and following the other strategies previously mentioned, we find it helpful when we:

- Identify things we genuinely like about the child, and tell team members and the child
- Identify for the child what he or she is doing right
- Let the child know we are committed to helping him or her make it in the classroom and that we believe it will happen
- Have sincere, positive physical contact with the child every day
- Notice our own aggravation and find ways to release it away from children
- Find a coworker to talk to during the days when the child's behavior is giving difficulty

If you are unable to find positive qualities to like, in spite of your best efforts, it's a good idea to find another adult who can give the child genuine appreciation. If the child must stay in your class it is essential that you make sure you are just in your treatment of him or her, whatever your own feelings.

You may also encounter children who need more intensive supervision and help than you are able to provide in a regular classroom. When a child is unable to function in your program in spite of your best efforts over a significant amount of time, you will need to work with the family and get outside help. State offices of child development, special education services in public schools, and state departments of mental health are possible sources of assistance. Together you can then plan for appropriate intervention, or possibly make a referral to a setting that can better meet the needs of this child. Remember that it is never helpful or productive to blame either the child or the parents for the challenging behavior. All children deserve opportunities to learn the skills they need to function in our society.

CHILD GUIDANCE IN AN INCREASINGLY VIOLENT AND UNCERTAIN WORLD

Children growing up in the world of the 21st century are exposed to violence in their lives. All children are affected by the violence that increasingly pervades our society, and as a result children's development and emotional health are in jeopardy. Research tells us that the younger the child, the greater the threat to healthy development from exposure to violence (National Association for the Education of Young Children 1993).

A fundamental "irreducible" need of every young child is the need for physical protection and safety (Brazelton & Greenspan 2000). Exposure to violent situations, both directly and through television and other media, compromises children's ability to feel safe and increases their risk of social and emotional developmental delay. As teachers of young children, it is your responsibility to do all that you can to ensure that children experience a sense of safety and protection from violence. Here are some strategies for helping children and families cope:

- Use the problem solving and conflict resolution strategies that we have discussed in this chapter and share them with families.

- Redirect play that focuses on repetitive violence recreated from television characters and encourage children to play in more imaginative and creative ways.
- Actively teach peace on a daily basis and include experiences that help children learn to be contributing members of a community.
- Encourage families to limit television viewing and to carefully supervise what young children watch. Research suggests that exposure to media violence leads children to see violence as a normal response to stress and as an acceptable means for resolving conflict. Children who are frequent viewers of violence on television are less likely to show empathy toward the pain and suffering of others and more likely to behave aggressively (National Association for the Education of Young Children 1993).

The powerful effects of the September 11, 2001, tragedies have taught us important lessons about helping children to cope in times of disaster and uncertainty. While the immediate pain and fear of these events has subsided, the power of this disaster continues to affect the lives of adults and children. Current political realities mean that young children may be consistently exposed to television images and talk of war and terrorism. It is helpful to remind families that the pictures of destruction that children view on television are real to them. Explaining that media images of explosions and torture are happening far away will not be enough to ease the anxiety that many children feel. Limiting children's exposure to television coverage of war and other violent events is one of the most effective ways of ensuring their sense of safety in troubling times.

When you know that children are experiencing upset as a result of trauma or disaster, here are some ways to help (Greenman 2001):

- Provide normal, predictable routines.
- Create lots of time for affectionate interactions that are appropriate for the individual child: hugs, laps, sitting together with a book, or an affectionate pat or touch are helpful.
- Provide verbal reassurance that you and they will be okay.
- Give them opportunities to express themselves with art materials such as clay or paint, as well as in conversation.
- Accept play that re-creates their concerns and fears.
- Listen carefully to their thoughts and ideas; answer their questions in simple ways.
- Gently and thoughtfully correct erroneous ideas that people who are different present a risk.
- Provide a curriculum and daily experiences that value differences.

FINAL THOUGHTS

Building relationships with children and guiding them toward positive behaviors is among the most important of your responsibilities as an early childhood teacher. As you make decisions about the approaches you will use to build relationships and guide children, we urge you to give thoughtful consideration to your values, the ways you use authority, and your long-term goals for children. We encourage you to be mindful of supporting children's self-concepts and aware of cultural and individual differences. We hope that you will continue to develop skills in relating to and communicating with children, anticipating and preventing problems, managing a group, and guiding children's behavior.

Working with young children is a voyage of discovery. The ways you relate to and guide children will determine whether or not it is a peaceful voyage taken with friends.

LEARNING OUTCOMES

When you read this chapter, thoughtfully complete selected assignments from the "To Learn More" section, and prepare items from the "For Your Portfolio" section, you will be demonstrating your progress in meeting NAEYC **Standard 4: Teaching and Learning,** and **Sub-standard 4b: Using Developmentally Effective Approaches**.

Key elements:

- Knowing and understanding young children's characteristics and needs
- Using developmental knowledge to create healthy, respectful, supportive, and challenging learning environments
- Knowing, understanding, and using effective approaches, strategies, and tools for early education

TO LEARN MORE

Observe an Early Childhood Educator: Visit someone who has been working with young children for several years. Observe him or her working with children for at least 2 hours. Notice this teacher's ways of communicating and relating in the following situations: with one child at play, with a child during a routine, mediating or preventing a dispute, and leading a group activity. Be aware of what the teacher and children say and do; how she or he listens, responds, and communicates problems; and any barriers or roadblocks to communication. Write about what you saw and comment on the goals and values that this practitioner might hold. Describe how he or she appeared to influence children's self-concepts, relationships, and feelings about school and learning.

Interview an Early Childhood Educator: Talk to an educator who has been working with young children for several years. Ask about the guidance strategies used most often, where they were learned, and why they were chosen. Ask which guidance problems are encountered most frequently, and which resources are used most often when a difficult problem occurs. Find out what this teacher thinks is the most important thing to know about guiding young children. Write about what you learned and comment on how this educator might influence children's self-concepts, relationships, and feelings about school and learning.

Compare Two Early Childhood Educators: Observe and/or interview two early childhood educators using the preceding suggestions and compare the strategies, goals, values, and impact of each educator. Write about what you learned and describe your impressions of which seems to best meet the needs of children.

Create a Child Guidance File: Gather articles about children's behavior and ways to build positive relationships with young children. Include articles that you could share with families. Organize them into a file for easy reference.

Read a Book: Read a book about one of the aspects of child guidance described in this chapter. Reflect on the book and write about what you have learned and its implications for your own child guidance practices. Some suggested books are:

Brazelton, T. Berry, and Stanley I. Greenspan. 2000. *The Irreducible Needs of Children: What Every Child Must Have to Grow, Learn, and Flourish*.

Gartrell, Dan. 2004. *The Power of Guidance: Teaching Social-Emotional Skills in Early Childhood Classrooms*.

Greenman, Jim. 2001. *What Happened to the World? Helping Children Cope in Turbulent Times*.

Howes, Carollee, and Sharon Ritchie. 2002. *A Matter of Trust: Connecting Teachers and Learners in the Early Childhood Classroom*.

Hyson, Marilou. 2004. *The Emotional Development of Young Children: Building an Emotion-Centered Curriculum*.

Kaiser, Barbara, and Judy Sklar Rasminsky. 2003. *Challenging Behavior in Young Children: Understanding, Preventing, and Responding Effectively*.

Wolfgang, Charles H. 2004. *Child Guidance Through Play: Teaching Positive Social Behaviors*.

FOR YOUR PORTFOLIO

Practice Problem Solving: In your work or practicum setting, find opportunities to facilitate problem solving between two children involved in a conflict over play materials (a trike, a pen, etc.). As soon as possible, after each event spend a few minutes making an anecdotal record of it—how the children behaved, what you said and did, how the children responded, how the problem was resolved (or not), how you did as the facilitator, how you felt about the role you played. After recording this information over several weeks, read over your notes to evaluate your progress. Observe and write down the effect it has had on your skill as a facilitator and on the behavior of the children. Keep these notes in your portfolio.

Create a Guidance Philosophy: Write one or two paragraphs that describe your beliefs about relating to and guiding young children. Include discussion of your long-term goals for children, how you respond to what diverse families value for their children, and the communication and guidance practices you use or plan to use.

10

The Curriculum

The universe is the child's curriculum.

Maria Montessori

All genuine education comes about through experience. . . but not all experiences are genuinely or equally educative.

John Dewey

• •

*I*n the preceding four chapters we introduced some important aspects of your work with young children: creating a safe and nurturing place for learning, supporting play, and relating to children. Another critical part of your work is the ability to plan and implement learning experiences, or *curriculum*—in other words, to teach.

Another word for the art and science of teaching is *pedagogy*. Because of the broad scope of their responsibilities, early childhood educators, particularly those who teach children younger than 5, must pay attention to all aspects of children's needs. This responsibility can be so demanding that early childhood teachers sometimes fail to attend seriously to pedagogy, to being professionals who teach. Yet nothing so clearly distinguishes you as a professional early childhood educator as your knowledge of what young children can learn in the early years and your ability to help them learn in ways that preserve their zest for school and learning.

Developing the necessary skills and knowledge to teach young children is complex. Good teachers continue to learn more about it throughout their careers. This chapter and the one that follows give you an introduction to the content of the early childhood curriculum and how teachers plan for learning. In this chapter we focus on the content of curriculum but do not attempt to include all of the content you will teach. Instead we give a framework so that you can think about curriculum and how children might best learn it. We cannot do more here than give you a taste of early childhood curriculum, but we hope you enjoy that taste and are inspired to learn more. In each curriculum content section we provide a list of easy-to-find books that you may wish to read to learn more about the topic.

WHAT IS CURRICULUM?

Different early childhood educators signify distinct, but related, ideas when they speak of curriculum. Some mean something very broad: everything the child experiences both in and out of school, called the *umbrella curriculum* (Colbert 2003). Others have in mind a curriculum approach or model like those you learned about in Chapter 3 (e.g., the *Reggio Emilia approach* or the *High/Scope model*). Still others mean a document or kit that is published and designed by a curriculum specialist, that addresses the whole early education program (e.g., the *Creative Curriculum*) or a particular content area (e.g., the *PEEK kit* for language curriculum, or the *Second Step* curriculum for social development). This is sometimes called *packaged* or

commercial curriculum. Another common definition, and the one we will use in this chapter, is the intentional learning experiences designed by a teacher, or team of teachers, in response to what they know and observe about children. We call this the *planned curriculum.*

Where Does Curriculum Come From?

Curriculum is based on a vision of society, values, a philosophy, a particular view of learners and teachers, and the ways educators translate this vision into learning experiences. It can originate from three broad sources: (1) beliefs about what is worth knowing, (2) knowledge of learners and their development, and (3) knowledge of subject matter (Armstrong 1989).

Curriculum in an early childhood program is significantly different from curriculum for older children because early childhood educators believe that all areas of children's development are important. They believe that planned learning experiences need to engage children and be responsive to individual interests, needs, and learning styles. They understand the critical connection between children's learning, family, and culture. They know that teachers play a role in designing environments and experiences and in scaffolding children's learning. They understand how play, child choice, and cooperative relationships are an important part of the serious business of learning. These understandings and beliefs are the underpinning of what is called *developmentally appropriate curriculum.*

Curriculum is also a product of its time. Educational values and practices are influenced by social and political forces. For example, in the early years of the 20th century when many immigrants were arriving in the United States, a strong curricular emphasis was placed on the acquisition of American language, culture, and values. In the years following World War II, curriculum reflected the value that society placed on nuclear families. Today's curriculum mirrors the cultural diversity that is prevalent and more valued today than in the past. It echoes our society's increasing concerns with violence, values, and the acquisition of basic content, especially literacy. Tomorrow's curriculum will address these and new concerns in ways that we cannot anticipate today.

As we discussed in Chapter 3, there is an "educational pendulum" that swings between emphasis on the nature and interests of the learner and emphasis on the subject matter to be taught. Each swing reflects a reaction of people to perceptions of the shortcomings of the current educational approach.

The swinging pendulum of popular opinion has some important implications for you as a beginning early childhood educator. One implication is that you must be aware that there will be ongoing shifts in accepted views of education during your career. For example, during the last years of the 20th century early childhood educators' views of "developmentally appropriate practice" had an impact on education, with a movement to focus school programs on the needs and interests of children. And predictably, in the early years of the 21st century, the pendulum has swung the other way, to shift focus back toward content standards, accountability, test scores, and less child-sensitive practice. If you find yourself disagreeing with today's outlook on education you are likely to find yourself agreeing with the views that will be favored in another 5 or 10 years (and vice versa, of course).

Knowledge is powerful. When you know about arts, sciences, and humanities and you understand how young children learn, then you are able to make more informed assessments of new views of early childhood curriculum. We urge you to keep an open mind so that you can learn, but to have a healthy sense of skepticism. You can rely on the combination of what research tells us about how children learn and your own observations. Your own stance will then be firm enough to withstand the inevitable shifts of popular opinion.

The second implication of the swinging pendulum of society's views on curriculum is the realization that early childhood education stands somewhat apart from vacillating popular opinion. As you learned in Chapter 3, respect for the individual, a belief in the value of play, and a vision of education as helping children to become self-directed and creative are consistent beliefs that have guided early childhood educators over time. You can hear this view in the words of the historical founders of our field:

> *The proper education of the young does not consist in stuffing their heads with a mass of words, sentences, and ideas dragged together out of various authors, but in opening up their understanding to the outer world, so that a living stream may flow from their own minds, just as leaves, flowers, and fruit spring from the bud on a tree.*
>
> John Amos Comenius, *Didactica Magna (The Great Didactic)*

> *Play is the highest expression of human development in childhood for it alone is the free expression of what is in a child's soul.*
>
> Friedrich Fröebel, *The Education of Man,* 1885

> *While devoted deeply to the growth of ideas and concepts, you have similarly consistently shown that education must plan equally for physical, social, and emotional growth.*
>
> James Hymes, speech to NANE, 1947

Our goal is to help you learn to design curriculum that reflects these views. As you develop your own educational philosophy we hope that you will see yourself as part of a long line of educators who put respect for children first.

Reflect on the curriculum of the schools you attended

What was taught in the schools of your childhood? What do you remember most about the curriculum? When were you motivated to learn more? Do any of these experiences influence you today? What are the implications of these experiences for you, as an early childhood educator?

Curriculum in Early Childhood Education

Young children are learning all the time and from all their experiences, both in and out of school. Early childhood educators need to ask themselves, "How, when, and in what ways do I want to participate in this natural process?" Because children are so interested in the world around them, the choices about the curriculum you provide in an early childhood program are almost infinite. Nevertheless, your choices must be thoughtful and appropriate for the children with whom you work.

What do early childhood educators teach? Every functioning adult knows more about the world than a young child. You have physical skills; you know how to take care

of yourself and relate to others; you can read, write, and compute; you know things about science and nature, the structure of society, and the arts. You know how to find out the answers to questions. These things will help you to teach but you need to know more than these basics to be an early childhood educator. You need to be educated. All early childhood college programs require that you study arts, sciences, and humanities because you need this broad education to effectively teach young children. You also need to know about children and how they learn so that you can design and implement meaningful and appropriate learning experiences. You need to understand curriculum content. States and national organizations of specialists in curriculum content areas have

created "content standards." These provide guidelines for selecting curriculum. Standards are almost universally available for teachers in K-12 programs and are starting to be available for teachers in programs for 4-year-olds. As you learned in Chapter 2, content standards can be controversial. However, they can provide you with important information to help you in the complex task of designing curriculum.

Because all aspects of development are interdependent, curriculum areas are not distinct entities but natural parts of the life of the child.

> *The 4-year-old class took a trip to the zoo yesterday. Today Kurt, Shauna, Max, and Kauri go to the block area. Their teacher suggests that they might build the zoo. Then they create enclosures around the animals and make a path on which several dollhouse people are placed. Shauna picks up a zebra and puts it in with the lions and Kauri says, "NO! The lions will bite the zebras!" The two argue about the placement of the zebras. The teacher asks the children to think of some ways to put the lions and the zebras together so the zebras won't get hurt. The girls build a nearby enclosure for zebras. Kurt and Max create a wall of blocks that encircles the entire block area. Another child stumbles over it. Max and Kurt yell and the teacher asks, "What could you do so people would know that they should be more careful?" Max goes to the writing center and makes a sign that says ZOO! STP! He tapes it to the wall and the teacher suggests that he tell the other children about the sign and what it means.*

These children were engaged in a planned inquiry activity designed to help them build an awareness of a social studies concept. But they were also engaged in a satisfying creative endeavor during which they were building motor coordination, using language, developing social problem-solving abilities, and gaining literacy skills.

> *On a hot, sunny day on the toddler playground, Georgia, the teacher, brings a bucket full of crushed ice and dumps it in the water table. Immediately Sango, Noah, and two other children rush to the table. Noah plunges his hands into the mountain of ice. His eyes widen. Georgia, who is crouched near the children says, "It's really cold!" As the group plays, Sango stands*

hesitantly a foot away. Georgia says, "You can touch it, Sango." Noah finds a cup that Georgia has placed nearby and scoops the ice and dumps it into a pail also conveniently set nearby. He scoops and scoops till the pail is full. Sango picks up a tiny scrap of ice and holds it in her hands. In a few seconds it is nothing but a drop of water. Sango looks at Georgia, who says, "What happened to the ice?" Sango says, "Wada." "Your ice melted into water," Georgia expands. Meanwhile Noah is placing little hills of ice on the sidewalk that quickly melt away.

Just like the 4-year-olds, these toddlers were engaged in a planned discovery activity. They were using their senses, building physical coordination, and learning concepts about the world. Their learning was skillfully guided by a teacher who knows about how toddlers learn. In addition, they were developing language, confidence, and a sense of self-reliance.

It is morning work time in the kindergarten class. Five children are working on their hundredth day collections (making trays with 100 things on them). Four more are constructing a block model of the path from their classroom to the cafeteria. Two sit on pillows in the library corner, reading books. Two more are finishing their morning journal assignment. One is painting using watercolors. Kit and Sierra are examining Checkers, a tortoise that was recently added to the classroom discovery center. They are looking at a book on tortoises. They ask Ms. Narvaez their teacher, "Can Checkers eat hamburger?" She says, "That's a good question. I see you have the tortoise book. What did you find out?" The children continue searching with some guidance. When the book fails to answer the question, the teacher asks them to write their question on a chart hanging in the discovery area. The class will try to find out the answer in some other way.

The skillful design of curriculum includes ensuring that in addition to planned activities there will be time, space, and interesting things to explore. Ms. Narvaez clearly knows that children of all ages can be self-directed learners. She has structured the environment, the time, the relationships, and the planned learning experiences to help these 5- and 6-year-olds to develop knowledge and skills in math, science, social studies, language, literacy, and art. Perhaps more important, she is helping them to become active, collaborative learners with a disposition to inquire.

Curriculum includes opportunities for learning that you will provide as choices in your program. It also includes the guided activities that you will implement with individual children and the whole group to help them learn. The planned curriculum can address domains of development (see Chapter 4) and it can be designed to help children develop understanding and skill in one or more subject areas (e.g., math, literature, art). Each subject area in the early childhood curriculum can contribute to all domains of the child's development but can be seen as primarily emphasizing one or two areas, as shown in Figure 10.1. In this chapter we will talk about subject areas in clusters that relate to each domain of development.

Each curriculum area is a specialty in itself that takes study to thoroughly master. You may have an area that is your forte, in which you have particular talent or skill, and other areas in which you feel less sure teaching. This should not stop you from bravely going forward and planning and teaching every curriculum area because each has value for children. Each early childhood teacher is, of necessity, a "general practitioner" in the art and science of teaching. You can use your skill in one area to teach your areas of weakness. An excellent storyteller with a math phobia, for example, might teach children, and overcome his or her own fears, by finding ways to incorporate math in storytelling!

For a list of books on general curriculum topics, see Table 10.1.

Figure 10.1 Curriculum Contribution to Child Development Domains

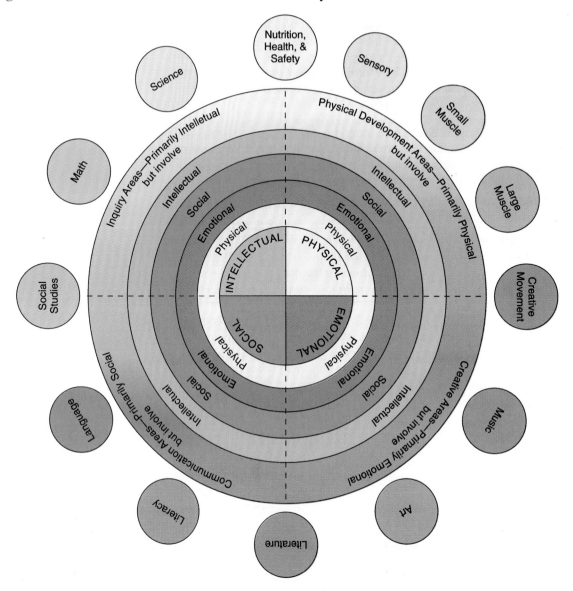

Table 10.1 **General Curriculum Books**

Developmentally Appropriate Practice in Early Childhood Programs (rev. ed.), by Sue Bredekamp & Carol Copple (eds.), NAEYC

Explorations with Young Children, by Ann Mitchell & Judy David (eds.), Gryphon House

Reaching Potentials: Transforming Early Childhood Curriculum and Assessment (vol. 2), by Sue Bredekamp & Teresa Rosegrant, NAEYC

The Creative Curriculum for Preschool (4th ed.), and *The Creative Curriculum for Infants and Toddlers,* by Diane Dodge et al., Teaching Strategies

THE PHYSICAL DEVELOPMENT CURRICULUM

. . . and look at your body, what a wonder it is!

Pablo Casals

The body is a young child's connection to the world. Sensory and motor development are prerequisite to many areas of competence. To learn to read and write, children must first develop the ability to make fine visual and auditory discriminations. To play an instrument or use a computer requires fine motor skill that emerges from practice in the control of the muscles of the fingers and hands. To make a discovery may require legs that have strength and stamina, eyes that see, and fingers that respond. To appreciate the order and beauty of the world, children must have the ability to perceive it.

The ways in which you provide support will have distinctive qualities and challenges depending on the age of the children, the place where you work, and the culture and values of the families.

Sensory Development

Learning depends on sensory input—hearing, smelling, seeing, touching, moving, and tasting. We are not born with the ability to fully discriminate sensations but must learn to distinguish them. If a child's ability to receive and use sensory input is impeded, normal development may be retarded. For this reason, all early childhood programs should include a strong sensory component.

The senses themselves give you a framework for thinking about sensory curriculum. The sense we most commonly associate with learning is *sight*, and like other senses it requires opportunities for practice. The auditory sense, *hearing*, involves learning to screen and attend—to exclude irrelevant sounds and pay attention to what is meaningful. The *kinesthetic* sense is an internal awareness of movement and position, which children develop as they learn to crawl, walk, jump, climb, and balance. The sense of *touch* is a primary mode of learning as well as a dominant aspect of our lives. All children need positive, appropriate human touch. We make many decisions based on our sense of *smell*. The sense of *taste* gives us information about what is safe and good to eat and what is not.

To support the development of the senses, make sure that you regularly provide experiences that use and develop each one. However, it is important to realize that senses are integrated, not isolated.

The "Elephant Groovers" (a group of 3-year-olds) are involved in making banana pancakes. Sheyden touches the flour and salt as he pours it in. Torie smells the banana as she peels it. Emily experiences resistance when she stirs the batter. Keila comments on the bubbles she sees forming as air is beaten in. Their teacher, Jackie, says, "Listen to the sizzle as batter is poured in the pan." And all of the Elephant Groovers eat the finished product with gusto, commenting on its warmth and delicious taste.

Which sense was being developed? To separate these individual sensations would be difficult and unnecessary. The children learned from the entire experience.

Figure 10.2 Sensory Materials to Explore and Pour in the Sand and Water Table

- Sand—dry or wet
- Water—plain or with added color, aroma, soap
- Ice—blocks, crushed, with salt
- Mud
- Whipped soap or shaving cream
- Aquarium gravel (inappropriate for infants and toddlers)
- Bird seed
- Recycled dried coffee grounds
- Cornstarch and water
- Flour, rice, or beans*

Other activities with a strong sensory component:

- Fingerpainting
- Collage
- Play dough
- Claywork
- Using musical instruments
- Cooking
- Tasting—compare different varieties of one thing such as cheese, apples, bread, vegetables
- Gardening
- Almost any field trips but especially to natural environments (e.g., a field, the beach, forest)

*The use of food as a sensory exploration material is controversial. It is accepted practice in some programs and with some families. It is highly offensive to others. It is inappropriate in any program in which families struggle financially to put food on the table or where any family feels it violates their values.

Children are developing their senses as they paint; manipulate clay and dough; play in sand, water, and mud; feel the shape, weight, and texture of blocks; observe fish in the aquarium; feel the rabbit's fur and its heart beating; listen to stories; move to music; sort objects by shape, color, and size; and cook, taste, and discuss what they have made. You can provide space and materials that can be fully explored without fear of mess and help them focus on sensory experiences (see Figure 10.2). For example, you might help children to notice the sensory qualities of the pancake batter by saying things like, "How does it sound when we pour it in the pan?" "What do you notice when you mash the banana?" "What does the taste remind you of?"

Large Muscle Development

Movement is central to the lives of young children. The large muscle or gross motor curriculum—the part of the program concerned with the development of arms, legs, and torso—helps children gain and maintain physical skills and abilities as they work and play. It is also an intrinsic part of every other domain of development. Children must learn to move and must also move in order to learn.

Physical activity is essential for lifelong health. Attention span and concentration increase as children use their bodies in challenging physical movement. Exercise helps to release tension and promotes relaxation. Children's early physical development experiences influence how competent they feel and whether they will enjoy physical activity throughout their lives. Large muscle curriculum activities help children develop greater strength and endurance, retain flexibility, and develop coordination and agility.

There are predictable patterns in children's development of large muscle skill. Physical suppleness lessens with age as the muscle system becomes less elastic. An infant easily brings toes to mouth, but this flexibility wanes as children get older. Older children generally are stronger and have greater endurance. Coordination—the ability to move body parts in relation to one another—grows with experience. Agility—the ability to move with control and precision—develops as children gain flexibility, strength, coordination, and a well-developed

Reflect on your school experiences with physical education

Remember a time when you were a child in a physical education class in school. Why do you remember this experience? How did the teacher encourage or discourage you? What physical activity do you do as an adult? Did your childhood experience influence this in any way?

kinesthetic sense. As children gain speed, grace, and precision they feel a sense of mastery. Much of the pleasure children find in large muscle play stems from the enjoyment of growing agility.

It used to be considered sufficient physical development curriculum to send young children outside to play and occasionally organize a game of Duck, Duck, Goose. Today we know we can do much more to help young children become physically fit and competent individuals who have a positive attitude toward physical activity. Children need time for large motor play several times a day. They need optimal challenge—equipment, materials, and activities that provide the right degree of difficulty—to develop the skill that is just within their reach. Eliminating recess, as is being done in some elementary schools to create more time for "work," deprives children of needed opportunities for physical

activity. In a nation in which obesity and inactivity are epidemic, even among children, this trend is foolish.

Many children develop physical competence from their self-directed play, but others need encouragement and support. All direct physical training and intervention needs to be carried out in pleasurable play situations so that the child's attitude will be positive and physical activity will be gratifying. Children may be discouraged if you are overly concerned about safety. If children are willing to attempt using a piece of equipment, they can usually manage it if you are prepared to provide careful supervision and occasional assistance and instruction.

Teaching young children to develop large muscle skills does not mean physical education as you remember it. Instead, children need teachers who know to place a toy just out of reach when they are learning to crawl; hold their hands as they struggle to take their first steps; sing as they play ring-around-the-rosy; follow as they play Follow the Leader; explain the rules of Red Rover; toss a ball as they learn to bat; and share their triumph as they learn to climb a rope.

By encouraging and playing *with* children, you support their activity and provide a model of an adult who is physically active—a powerful demonstration that being active is natural and pleasurable. Adult-led activities like creative movement, simple yoga, group games, and exercises provide focused practice in developing physical competencies. All children, not just those who are physically competent, will participate if you minimize competition and win-lose situations in games and other physical activities. Cooperative games that do not focus on winners and losers are particularly appropriate for young children and encourage children who are reluctant to participate for fear of losing. (See Figure 10.3.)

Small Muscle Development

Learning to coordinate the hands and fingers begins when babies in their cribs reach out to feel, grasp, and manipulate. Those initial impulses will eventually lead to the competent use of tools such as spoons, crayons, hammers, and keyboards. Small muscle

Figure 10.3   **Some Cooperative Games to Play with Young Children**

These games promote the idea that when everyone works together, everyone wins

Animal Families	It's feeding time on the farm, and the animals need to find their families for supper. Whisper the name of an animal (duck, cow, sheep, pig) in each child's ear. When you say "Animals find your families," children make their animal's sound and try to find their families by the sounds they make. When families are found, do it again or go on to a new activity. Have older children close their eyes or wear blindfolds, and locate their family through sound only.
Bean Bag Freeze	To the beat of a drum, children walk around the room balancing bean bags on their heads. If a bean bag falls off, the child must freeze until another child can carefully crouch down, pick up the bean bag, and return it. The child who was frozen has to stay frozen. When everyone is frozen, the game is over.
Big Turtle	A group of children get on their hands and knees and a teacher places a "shell" on their backs. The shell can be a gym mat, a blanket, or sleeping mat. The big turtle attempts to move around without losing its shell. An obstacle course can be made for the turtle.
The Big Wind Blows	Using a parachute, the group holds the edges and lifts the parachute up to billow. They chant, "Blow, blow, the big wind blows. Who oh who does the big wind blow." The teacher calls out categories, such as "Everybody wearing red." Those children run underneath the parachute and across to find a place to hold on the other side.
Cooperative Duck Duck Goose	In this version no one ends up in the center of the circle. Instead, two children are tappers, and if the chaser catches a tapper he or she joins the tappers.
Cooperative Musical Chairs	No one is eliminated. Each person finds a chair when the music stops for as long as interest holds.
Balloons in the Air	Give pairs of children a balloon. Have partners try to keep their balloon in the air by hitting it, blowing it, or catching it in a big scarf or piece of cloth that both hold.
Person to Person	Have the children walk around in the circle in a random fashion. Play the drum to a walking beat. With a hard beat say, "Person to person" and ask the children to find a partner near them. Then say the name of a body part such as "Knee to knee." Children touch knees. When the beat starts again they continue walking until the teacher calls out again.

Source: Adapted from T. Orlick, *The Second Cooperative Sports and Games Book*, New York: Pantheon, 1982 and J. Sobel, *Everybody Wins: 393 Noncompetitive Games for Young Children*, New York: Walker, 1984.

(or fine motor) curriculum involves activities that build control, agility, strength, and coordination of the hands, fingers, wrists, and arms.

Time, practice, and many experiences are required to develop competence. These skills involve sensory and muscular interplay—hand-eye coordination and coordination of the two hands. Children growing up with normal abilities and opportunities to use their hands develop the strength, coordination, and agility required to do most small muscle activities.

The small muscle curriculum is a part of many other curriculum areas. Many activities require the controlled use of hands and fingers. It can be helpful to think about some categories of activities and skills to plan specifically for small muscle development.

To support fine motor development you need to understand development, observe children, and be sensitive to individual differences. You can then interpret each child's level of development and provide materials and activities that present optimal challenge (many of these are described in Chapter 8). It is essential that children have materials and adequate time to practice using their small muscles. Some homemade and "found" toys and tools that can help infants and toddlers develop small motor skills include:

- Soft balls and pom-poms, and lightweight buckets and pails to fill and dump
- Oatmeal containers with holes cut in the lid and items to drop in
- Toilet paper rolls for children to string on tubing
- Boxes and lids
- Turkey basters and water
- Tongs and cotton balls
- Mailing tubes and small cars
- Paint brushes and water
- Plastic bottle caps to sort, stack, and explore
- Plastic hammers, golf tees, and Styrofoam blocks

For preschoolers and primary school children, you can use things like:

- Keys and locks
- Small boxes that nest inside one another
- Beads and laces
- Tweezers and tongs with beads, shells, or other small objects
- Crewel needles and yarn with plastic "fabric" to sew
- Woodworking tools and scrap wood
- Eyedroppers, jars of colored water, and an ice-cube tray
- Jars and lids (use plastic with preschoolers)

If a child becomes frustrated or bored with a small muscle activity you can support his or her continued involvement by offering assistance, encouragement, or a greater challenge. For example, if a child is having trouble cutting, you might say, "I see that paper is hard to cut. Would you like to use construction paper? Maybe it won't flop so much." You might also be sure to stock the shelf with a variety of different weights of paper and see whether more functional scissors are needed.

It is important to design experiences that will build prerequisite skills for more challenging small motor tasks such as cutting. The child who hasn't yet mastered scissors needs plenty of grasping, tension/release, coordination, and strength-building experiences. Providing dough and clay to build strength and tools such as tongs, hole punches, tweezers, and staplers that require similar motor action will contribute to this emerging skill. You may sometimes need to demonstrate and instruct to help children learn complex fine motor skills.

Table 10.2   Books on Physical Development Curriculum

Active for Life: Developmentally Appropriate Movement Programs for Young Children, by Stephen W. Sanders, NAEYC

The Outside Play and Learning Book: Activities for Young Children, by Karen Miller, Gryphon House

Mud, Sand, and Water (rev. ed.), by Dorothy M. Hill, NAEYC

Follow Me Too: A Handbook of Movement Activities for Three- to Five-Year-Olds, by Marianne Torbert & Lynne B. Schneider, NAEYC

A professional library of books to provide you with information and curriculum ideas will be invaluable. Table 10.2 provides you with a handful of useful books for learning about the physical development curriculum.

THE CREATIVE ARTS CURRICULUM

> *If you walk, you can dance. If you talk, you can sing.*
>
> African proverb

The arts are vital in the development of children who can feel as well as think and who are sensitive and creative. Art, music, and creative movement help children to recognize and express their feelings, communicate ideas in new forms, and develop their senses. Creativity, or originality, is not restricted to artists or to people who have great talent or high intelligence. All people are creative when they put together what they know and produce an idea, process, or product that is new *to them*. Creativity also occurs in activities such as building with blocks and dramatic play, though the creativity of play leaves no lasting product.

Through arts experiences, children come to:

- Feel good about themselves as individuals
- Develop the ability to observe and respond sensitively
- Develop skill and creativity in art, music, and movement
- Develop beginning understanding of the arts disciplines
- Become appreciative of music, art, and dance from their own and other cultures, times, and places
- Construct understanding and communicate what they know

Understanding how young children develop helps you to provide a climate that supports creativity, imagination, and self-expression. Satisfying and successful experiences with the arts occur when you understand what you can reasonably expect of children and when you provide activities that match their needs and abilities. When children's unique expressions are acknowledged, they become aware of their value as individuals, and their self-concept is enhanced.

> *Two-year-old Sienna comes to the children's center with her mom for the first time. She is attracted to the easel and the brilliant colors of paint. Sienna takes a brush full of magenta and paints a large blotch of color. A brush full of deep blue follows, then one of yellow and another of black. The dripping colors glisten wet and intense on the paper. Sienna steps back, turns, then grins at her mom.*

For very young children, like Sienna, the most important aspects of the arts are the development of awareness, new skills, and feelings of self-worth. Your role is to provide an environment, materials, experiences, and relationships that support creative development and aesthetic appreciation. A classroom that provides for all of these needs has a creative climate—an atmosphere where creative expression is nurtured and where creativity can flourish.

It is not necessary for you to be an artist, dancer, or musician yourself to teach the arts to young children. It is necessary, however, to believe that experiences with and participation in art are valuable. Because creative expression is an outgrowth of life, another aspect of your role is to provide experiences that heighten awareness and provide inspiration.

Creative expression is also stimulated by exposure to the arts. When children have opportunities to view artwork in public places, listen to music, and attend dance and drama productions, they begin to understand the potential of the arts.

Through their artwork, children can disclose private thoughts, feelings, and ways of perceiving. They can only risk this expression if they feel safe, valued, and encouraged. You support children's creativity by accepting *all* of their feelings, ideas, and creative expression, whether or not they are "nice" or "pretty" by adult standards. Things that move children and adults are not always the most pleasant aspects of their lives. Nevertheless, if they have the power to evoke strong feelings, they are important parts of life and a part of their expression in art, music, and movement. For an example, see Figure 10.4.

> **Reflect on your experiences with the arts in school**
>
> Remember an experience with the arts that you had in school. How did your teacher support or discourage your creativity and individuality? How did this influence your feelings about yourself as an artist, musician, or dancer?

Figure 10.4   **"My Mommy Is Mad at Me" (drawing by a 4-year-old)**

Art

Art is a way to express feelings and understanding; it provides opportunities for exploration and manipulation. It is a medium of learning and a medium of communication. The primary purpose of an early childhood art program is to enhance artistic and creative development. Its sensory and physical nature makes art especially appropriate for very young children and is their primary motivation for involvement in art. As they mature, children use art to express ideas, but they continue to enjoy the satisfaction of "messing about" with materials. For very young children, *process* is the whole of the art experience and *product* is not important. (Toddlers are unconcerned with their artwork after they are done.) As children grow older, they use art as a process both to construct understanding, create meaning, and to express what they know. They also may begin to be more self-critical of the quality of their creations and want to destroy work that does not meet their standards and share the work that does with others.

As children use art media they reap other educational benefits. They develop motor control and perceptual discrimination. They use language and learn new vocabulary. They learn about materials and develop problem-solving strategies. Developing aesthetic awareness and appreciation are important benefits of art experiences.

The work of John Dewey and the example of the preprimary schools of Reggio Emilia help us to understand that art is also a primary way to construct and communicate understanding.

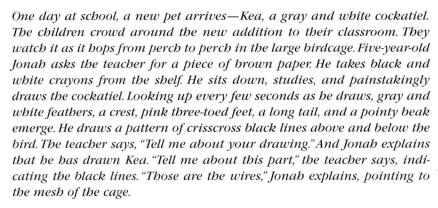

Watch how Jonah draws Kea in the accompanying DVD.

One day at school, a new pet arrives—Kea, a gray and white cockatiel. The children crowd around the new addition to their classroom. They watch it as it hops from perch to perch in the large birdcage. Five-year-old Jonah asks the teacher for a piece of brown paper. He takes black and white crayons from the shelf. He sits down, studies, and painstakingly draws the cockatiel. Looking up every few seconds as he draws, gray and white feathers, a crest, pink three-toed feet, a long tail, and a pointy beak emerge. He draws a pattern of crisscross black lines above and below the bird. The teacher says, "Tell me about your drawing." And Jonah explains that he has drawn Kea. "Tell me about this part," the teacher says, indicating the black lines. "Those are the wires," Jonah explains, pointing to the mesh of the cage.

You can see Jonah's drawing of a cockatiel in Figure 10.5.

Figure 10.5 **Jonah's Drawing of a Cockatiel**

There are two views of art curriculum in early childhood education, the first and most familiar is *studio art*, sometimes called *child-centered*, in which children explore and create using different art media and processes. The focus in this approach is on allowing the natural creativity of young children to unfold with the goal of providing an outlet for feelings and self-expression. The second view is called *discipline-based art education* (DBAE) or *subject-matter-centered*, in which children encounter, discuss, appreciate, and think about the subject of art. In discipline-based art experiences, children come to understand and appreciate the ways that art is created. They are exposed to artists from their own and other cultures and times. Both of these approaches have value and can be used in programs for young children.

Art for young children includes five basic processes: *drawing* (sometimes referred to as graphic art); *painting; print-making* (making an image by stamping or burnishing); *collage and construction* (creating a work of art by affixing flat materials to a flat surface or three-dimensional materials to one another); and *modeling and sculpting* (fashioning three-dimensional art out of a soft malleable material like clay or by carving a moderately hard material like soap or plaster with a safe tool). Table 10.3 presents the elements of art.

Young children do not automatically become artists simply because art media are available. They pass recognizable landmarks on the path to artistic maturity but need time, space, materials, and the support of adults in order to become artistically competent. Much of the creative process of art for young children is exploration rather than an attempt to represent something. Realizing this distinction can help you appreciate children's early artwork. Your most critical task is to understand and value the art of young children. It has worth in and of itself, not for what it may become when children get older and gain skill, but for what it is now.

The way you talk to young children can support their artistic development. As they work it is best, at first, to offer only minimal input. Avoid asking *what* they have created. They may have had nothing particular in mind and the question implies that

Table 10.3 **The Elements of Art**

Art Element	Some Aspects to Talk About with Children
Line	Quality: straight, curved, heavy, light, wide, thin, wandering, wiggling, jagged, broken, zigzag, long, short
	Direction of the line: up and down, diagonal, side-to-side
	Relationship: crossed, separate, parallel
Color	Name or hue: pure (primary colors—red, yellow, blue), mixed (secondary colors—orange, green, purple) (tertiary colors—for example—magenta, turquoise, chartreuse)
	Temperature: cool (blue end of the spectrum), warm (red end of the spectrum)
	Intensity/saturation: bright, dull
	Value: light, dark
Shape	Open/closed; irregular/regular (rectangle, circle, triangle, trapezoid, hexagon, octagon, oval, square, etc.); filled/empty; connected/overlapping/enclosed
Space	Center, top, bottom, side, corner, inside, outside, near, far, crowded, full, sparse, empty, balanced/unbalanced, included/excluded
Design	Organization, repetition, texture, concept, variation, symmetry, balance, alternation

they should have. Instead ask them if they wish to tell you about what they have done and accept it if they do not. You can comment on:

Effort—"You worked on your clay for a long time today."

Innovation—"When you used the side of the crayon, it made a different kind of mark than drawing with the tip."

Technique—"There are lots and lots of dots on your painting."

You can also comment on children's use of art elements:

Color—"The green looks really vibrant next to the red."

Line—"You used thick and thin lines in your painting."

Shape—"What a lot of circular objects you chose for your collage."

Space—"Your box collage is almost as tall as the top of the shelf."

Design—"The top of your paper has lots of little prints and the bottom has lots of big prints."

Some children may not seem interested in art. A long period of disinterest or observation may precede participation. Some children may simply be more interested in different activities or alternative ways of being creative. They may not want to attempt art activities because they already feel they cannot measure up to their teacher's or parents' expectations. Easily accessible, plentiful supplies, and acceptance will encourage these children to explore.

Today we know that children's artistic development is closely related to the culture in which they live. The work of young children in Asia and in the preprimary programs of Reggio Emilia, Italy, show a high level of aesthetic sensitivity and skill in artistic production. Studying the way art is taught in other cultures is leading to a growing understanding that teachers can support young children's aesthetic and artistic abilities in child-sensitive ways by providing frequent opportunities to be involved in art; giving careful thought and attention to the quality, organization, and presentation of art materials; providing appropriate tasks and challenges; talking with children about their intent and efforts; instructing children in technique; providing lots of time to explore and revisit methods; and respectfully and beautifully displaying children's work. The children's art that you see in this book (e.g., see Figure 10.6) are examples of work produced by children who were given this kind of support, and whose work was truly valued and respected by their sensitive teachers.

Figure 10.6 **Tissue Paper Collage: A Cardinal**

Creative expression should be a reflection of the child's ideas and abilities—not patterns from a teacher's magazine or book. Prepared patterns to be copied by children and coloring books have nothing to do with the development of creativity or self-expression—in fact they can be destructive to children's feelings of competence and self-worth. These activities take up valuable time that children should be using to develop other skills, awareness, and ideas. They are not a part of good early childhood programs.

Music

Music is pervasive. In the heart of a city we experience the "song" of traffic, footsteps, and voices. In the solitude of the country we listen to the harmony of birds, wind, and water. Even before we are born we experience the music of a heartbeat. Music has been called a universal language. It can make us happy or sad, calm or excited—and can evoke feelings of patriotism, sanctity, love, and empathy.

Whatever their age, all young children need music. The most important reasons to provide music to children are that it provides a powerful and direct link to emotions; that listening to and making music brings pleasure; and because sharing music with others is an important way to be a part of your culture. Music can also be a path to many other kinds of learning. It can be a vehicle for developing problem-solving skills ("How could we make motion for a mouse?"), and language ("The song says that Aiken Drum played upon a ladle—have you ever seen a ladle?"), and even for remembering facts that might not otherwise be easy to recall (singing the ABC song to remember whether Q comes before R). There is even some evidence that listening to music has a positive impact on learning (Campbell 2000). Table 10.4 presents the elements of music.

Music curriculum involves the processes of musicianship. *Singing* offers opportunities for children to experience music and to develop many musical skills. Children have an easier time learning songs that are relatively short and simple and have a distinct rhythm. All early childhood educators need a repertoire of singable songs with different moods, subjects, tempos, and styles.

Playing instruments helps young children to acquire musical skills. Simple rhythm instruments provide excellent first experiences.

Table 10.4 **The Elements of Music**

Music Element	Some Aspects to Help Children Notice
Rhythm (characteristics of music that relate to movement and time)	Beat: the musical pulse Melodic rhythm: the rhythm of the melody or words Tempo: the speed of the music Rests: the silences in music
Tone (characteristics of the notes)	Pitch: high or low Melody or tune: the arrangement of notes in a singable sequence Tone color or timbre: the characteristic sound of an instrument Dynamics: loudness or softness
Form (structure of a piece of music)	Phrase: short but complete musical ideas in a piece of music Repetition: when identical phrases recur in a piece of music Variation: when similar phrases occur in a piece of music Contrast: when very different phrases occur in a piece of music

Composing and *improvising* are the creative use of musical skills. Young children who have had many musical experiences spontaneously improvise songs to accompany their play. You help children to improvise when you ask them to think of new words for a song. Composing requires creating and preserving a new composition with a tape recorder or musical notation.

Listening to and *appreciating* music made by others is an important part of music education. Recordings can provide experiences with diverse styles of music and music from different cultures. When you play instruments and sing in the classroom or have musicians visit you help children to understand that recorded music is made by real people.

Performing by singing, moving to music, or playing instruments for others is another musical skill. Because the goal of music education is to help children to become comfortable with musical expression, performance is the least important part of the music curriculum for young children. Though it can be exciting, motivating, and enjoyable for older children it is never appropriate in early childhood education if an emphasis on precision in performance results in anxiety or stress in children.

When you share music with young children be enthusiastic! Show you like music by clapping, tapping your feet, and dancing as you sing or listen to music. Include diverse styles of music from many cultures. Sing with children every day, throughout the day—individually in spontaneous activities, during transitions, and during planned group times. Choose simple songs with singable melodies and lyrics. Sing in a comfortable range for children (approximately middle C to E an octave above). Vary the lyrics of songs to sing about the children and their activities and interests. During group music times, sit with children on the floor or on a low stool or chair. Add movement to music to establish and retain interest. Regularly use simple rhythm instruments in guided activity. Take good care of these instruments and avoid leaving them out to be damaged or turned into noisemakers. Learn to play a simple chorded instrument (e.g., guitar, autoharp, ukulele, omnichord) to accompany music activities.

A creative climate for music, where musical expression is nurtured and creativity flourishes, means that music is frequently present. When music making is a part of classroom, home, and community, children become spontaneous music makers. You can help children to be comfortable with music by bringing it informally into the classroom and by formal planned music experiences during a special time each day.

Creative Movement

Another way to express ideas and feelings is through creative movement. When is movement creative? When ideas and feelings are expressed in imaginative ways, through movement. It is different from, and not a substitute for, games or large muscle activities on the playground. It differs from dance, which is more formal.

In creative movement, children interpret and follow suggestions and are encouraged to find their own personal, creative, and innovative ways of moving. They express ideas with their bodies and develop a repertoire of movement possibilities. Creative movement offers challenges and new ways to use and practice developing physical skills. Table 10.5 presents the elements of creative movement.

Table 10.5 **The Elements of Creative Movement**

Movement Element	Aspects of the Element	Examples of Using the Element
Body awareness (awareness and control of body)	Location: where you are in space	"Look at who's in front of you, who's behind you, what's above you."
	Locomotor movement (actions): the ways you can move from one place to another	"Walk, jump, hop, run, skip."
	Nonlocomotor movement: the ways you can move while staying in one place	"Keep your feet planted on the ground and make your arms stretch."
	Body isolation: moving part of the body without moving the rest	"Wave good-bye with your elbow."
Space (how area is used)	Personal space (occupied just by you) vs. general space (used by the whole group)	"Imagine yourself inside a bubble."
	Level: high/low/middle	"Make your head float to the sky."
	Boundaries: inside/outside	"Put one body part inside the hoop."
Time (tempo or speed)	Slow or fast	"Flap your eagle wings slowly, then soar across the sky."
	Steady or changing	"March, march, march to the drumbeat."
Force (energy)	Heavy or light	"Tromp like an elephant across the room." "Float like a butterfly."
	Relaxed or tense	"Pretend your legs are made of boards and can't bend."
	Smooth or jerky	"Walk like a machine."

Successful creative movement activities take thoughtful planning. Basic rules for safety need to be established (no pushing or bumping, and so on) and an attitude of respect for individual interpretations and skill levels. We find it useful to have a written plan to use as a "map" to guide us as we lead children in creative movement activities.

With a group of very young children, creative movement might be as simple as jumping and stopping to the beat of a drum. As children become more experienced they can be given more complex movement tasks, such as moving a single body part in isolation ("Say hello to someone with your foot!") or representing something ("As I play my drum, slowly grow toward the sun and blossom like a flower."). Older children enjoy choreographing a song or story.

As children develop confidence and movement skills, they will become able to express creative ideas with little direction. In the beginning, however, you will need to provide guidance. Most children are delighted to participate in creative movement, but a few will hesitate. Children should never be forced to participate in a creative movement activity or ridiculed or criticized for the way they move. Here are some suggestions for creative movement with young children:

- When you first begin, establish a signal like a hard drumbeat to tell the children to freeze. Practice stopping to this signal as a game until they understand it as an integral part of every movement activity.
- Provide a role for children who are not yet comfortable enough to participate— for example: "Your job is to be the audience. You can clap when we are all done."
- Alternate vigorous and quiet activities, and begin activities sitting down or standing still before inviting children to move freely around the room.

- When you have reached a planned or natural ending place, finish the activity while it is still going well.
- End sessions in a way that provides a transition to the next activity:"Tiptoe to the playground when I touch you on the shoulder."

Aesthetics

Every human being has the potential to develop sensitivity to beauty and the heritage of the arts. You can help young children develop this potential. *Aesthetics* refers to the love of beauty, to the cultural criteria for judging beauty, and to individual taste. Malcolm Ross says:

> Aesthetic perception involves the capacity to respond to the uniqueness, the singular quality of things—to value individual integrity and to reject the cliché and the stereotype. (Ross 1981, 158)

You can support aesthetic development. Posters, books, postcards, and calendars of the work of fine artists (available in museum and gallery shops) can be a part of your environment. Beautiful music can be played for activities and routines. For preschoolers and older children you can make games in which children sort and classify artwork by subject matter, technique, color, or personal preference. When introducing children to art, it is important to guide them in a way that helps the art to be more personal and meaningful. For example, you might ask children to talk about what they see in the different parts of the picture and what the artist might have been thinking and feeling when she or he created the work. Areas that feature flowers, art prints, sculpture, and beautiful natural objects can create an island of calm and heighten aesthetic awareness. Beautifully illustrated children's literature can be used to discuss aesthetic impact and preferences in art. Chapter 8 provides ideas for the aesthetic enhancement of the classroom environment.

Experiences in the natural world nourish the aesthetic sense. Help children to reflect on colors, patterns, and textures found in nature. Trips to works of art in your community (e.g., to see a sculpture that adorns a public building) and to galleries, studios, and performances make worthwhile activities for young children. Children need exposure to beauty and time to reflect with a caring and thoughtful adult. The way that children are introduced to aesthetic experiences is important, and the early years may be the optimal time to lay the foundation for a lifetime of pleasure and enjoyment.

You have many gifts to give children. Being able to create and appreciate art, music, and dance and to express ideas and feelings through the arts is a gift. As you nurture children's innate responsiveness and develop their natural expressiveness, you help them to be sensitive, creative individuals who can give the gift of creative expression and appreciation back to others. Table 10.6 lists some books that can help you learn more about the creative curriculum.

THE COMMUNICATION CURRICULUM

Talking with one another is loving one another.

African proverb

To understand the world and function in it, we need to be able to communicate with others. Learning language is one of the characteristics that unites people and one of our most important challenges. *Language* (both talking and listening) is of primary importance in the communication curriculum. *Literacy* (the developmental process of

Table 10.6 Books on Creative Arts and Aesthetic Curriculum

Art

The Colors of Learning: Integrating the Visual Arts into the Early Childhood Curriculum,
by Rosemary Althouse, Margaret H. Johnson, & Sharon T. Mitchell, NAEYC

Don't Move the Muffin Tins: A Hands-Off Guide to Art for the Young Child,
by Bev Bos, Turn the Page Press

The Art of Teaching Art to Children: In School and at Home,
by Nancy Beal, Farrar, Straus & Giroux

Art: Basic for Young Children,
by Lila Lasky, NAEYC

Experience and Art: Teaching Children to Paint (2nd ed.),
by Nancy Smith, Carolee Fucigna, Margaret
Kennedy, & Lois Lord, Teachers College Press

Music

Music: A Way of Life for the Young Child,
by Linda Carol Edwards, Kathleen M. Bayless, & Marjorie E. Ramsey,
Pearson Education

Music in Our Lives: The Early Years
by Dorothy T. McDonald, NAEYC

Creative Movement

Hello Toes: Movement Games for Children, Ages 1–5,
by Anne Lief Barlin & Nurit Kalev, Princeton Book Company Publishers

Feeling Strong, Feeling Free: Movement Exploration for Young Children,
by Molly Sullivan, NAEYC

Aesthetics

Designs for Living and Learning: Transforming Early Childhood Environments,
by Deb Curtis & Margie Carter, Redleaf Press

---

learning to write and read) is the tool that extends language over distance and time. *Literature* is the art form that uses language. All are dependent upon language.

The goal of the communication curriculum is to help children become enthusiastic, competent users of spoken and written language. Your job is to provide relationships that are filled with language in all its forms. As you speak to children honestly and respectfully and listen to them attentively, you will encourage language use. As you use language to mediate problems, communicate information, and share feelings and ideas, you will demonstrate the usefulness and value of oral language. As you sing songs, tell jokes, recite rhymes and poems, and play verbal games with children, you help them find joy in talking. In a similar way the value of written language is demonstrated to children as you write a note, a grocery list, or a thank-you letter, or read a recipe, story, poem, or book. And as you introduce children to many wonderful children's books you will give them a gift and an appreciation that they will carry throughout their lives.

Reflect on communicating as a child

Remember yourself as a young child. Was it easy for you to talk to other people or did you feel shy or uncomfortable? When, where, and with whom did you feel most comfortable expressing yourself? Why? How did your family or teachers support you or discourage you from communicating?

Learning to understand and use language is one of the most significant accomplishments of early childhood. Almost all children acquire language at about the same age

and in about the same way, whatever their language or culture without any formal teaching. It is a skill that appears to be "caught, not taught." As they forge their language, children develop an inseparable part of themselves, as well as a tool for communication, self-expression, and learning.

Both developmental stage and the desire to communicate influence language learning. Children learn the complex structure, rules, and meanings of language and develop the ability to create speech through processes that are still not completely understood. Young children learn customs for language in their homes and communities. They learn to select speech for the setting and people: in the classroom, on the playground, to a friend, parent, or teacher. Very early they learn to include nonverbal features (gestures, facial expressions, intonation) in speaking. They come to understand the expectations and signals for turn-taking in conversations. These unspoken ways of communicating are highly dependent on culture. In a culturally diverse society young children in a group will have different nonverbal customs, such as whether to make eye contact during conversations with adults. Part of your role requires sensitivity to and respect for these kinds of communication differences. Hesitant or shy children, those who have less home language experience, or those who speak a different language at home than at school may require a longer time to become full participants in the language life of the classroom. It is important to be sensitive to these differences and give these children time and lots of opportunities to speak.

In early childhood programs language is taught in both incidental and planned activities. It is primarily taught through language-rich relationships. When you have conversations with young children you are teaching language. When you play with children, listen to their ideas, lead games, sing songs, tell stories, and recite poems, you are teaching language. Language learning is also part of structured group activities such as discussions that are included in most programs for preschool, kindergarten, and primary school children.

You will not actually instruct children in a subject called "language" (a discipline studied by linguists and other scholars). Instead you will help children develop language by encouraging them in using it. Children need a chance to express their ideas, to tell about the things they know and that are important to them. This helps them to learn to talk and to make sense of their experiences.

Children acquire and build language in relationships in *conversations*. What is a conversation? It is an exchange of ideas, a dialogue. Because there are more children and fewer adults, there are fewer opportunities for conversation in early childhood programs than in most homes. In language-rich homes, conversations are complex and are related to the child's life. By contrast, conversations in most schools tend to be brief, less complex, and more adult-oriented. It is important to know *how* to have conversations with children, and to *do so* regularly with every child. A conversation with a young child, like any other, involves mutual interests and requires you have a topic and take turns. It is different because of experience, size, status, and skills. It is an art that you will develop with experience. When you have a conversation with a young child, it will help to remember these suggestions:

- *Crouch or sit at the child's eye level.* This minimizes both the physical and social differences between an adult and child.
- *Show attention physically* as well as verbally with eye contact, smiles, nods, a gentle hand on a shoulder or back.
- *Read nonverbal communication.* Notice and put into words what the child is feeling and thinking: "You're really happy." or "That's very exciting." or "It's a little scary."
- *Respect the child's language.* Don't correct the child's speech or ideas. Don't hurry or interrupt. If you don't understand say: "Show me." "Tell me more about that."
- *Listen.* Focus on what the child says. Remember this is about the child, not about you. Ask clarifying questions. Help the child to extend: "What did your mom do when the eggs all spilled on the floor?"
- *Select what to say carefully.* Make it brief and to the point—a child cannot concentrate for as long as an adult. Use a vocabulary that is simple but with a few words that are new and interesting.
- *Participate.* Otherwise it's not a conversation. But it's also not a quiz or a lecture. Questions can be conversation stoppers. Say simple things like, "I like to do that too." or "I didn't know that."

As you plan for language, remember that all children (unless handicapped in some way) have language facility you can nurture. Talk to them. Listen to them. Trust them. They need and want to communicate.

Literacy

Reading and writing are facets of communication, tools to unlock ideas, and adventures. *Literacy* is the interconnected processes of reading and writing. *Emergent literacy* is the evolving process by which children become literate. The period of emergent literacy can be called the span "between birth and the time when children read and write in conventional ways" (Teale & Sulzby 1986, 1).

Children who live in a print-filled world have early awareness of written language and develop concepts about it from an early age. Learning about reading and writing does not wait for children to be declared officially "ready." The foundations for making sense of written language start long before they receive formal teaching.

Unfortunately many children do not learn to read with comfort and fluency. The Children's Defense Fund reports that 40% of the nation's fourth graders could not read at a basic level and a child who cannot read well by the end of third grade will be seriously disadvantaged throughout schooling (Children's Defense Fund 1999, 75).

Early childhood experiences are critical. By providing children with high-quality language and literacy experiences before first grade we are helping to prevent later reading problems.

The stages of emergent literacy, like the stages of language development, are predictable and individual. The phrase *literacy begins at birth* illuminates the idea that experiences in infancy with language, books, and reading are important parts of the process of becoming literate. Each child learns to read and write as an individual, putting together ideas in ways that make sense. The curriculum for literacy must be similarly individualized.

Your approach to teaching literacy will vary with children's developmental needs, family, and interests. There are several "predictors" that have been identified as increasing the likelihood of children becoming successful readers. Experience with language and background knowledge of the world are important components of a literacy curriculum. There is strong evidence to suggest that children who have lots of real-world experiences coupled with rich and varied language are more likely to become readers (Bowman 2003). Experiences with functional print—when you visibly use reading and writing as a tool and a pleasure—is another important predictor of literacy success.

> *When a child has the chance to hear one good story after another, day after day he is being taught to read. When a child hears good adult language, and when he has the fullest, freest chance to use his own language, he is being taught to read.*
>
> James Hymes

Phonological awareness (the realization that the sounds of words can be manipulated), alphabetic knowledge (familiarity with the shapes and sounds of letters and awareness that there is a relationship between letters and sounds), concepts of print (understanding that print is permanent—it always says the same thing), and book knowledge (how to use books) are other predictors of success (Neuman, Copple, & Bredekamp 1999).

Children show their developing awareness of written language in many different ways. Some begin to take an interest in favorite storybooks as they read along, point to the print, or retell the story. Others recognize or discuss the meanings of the signs or labels all around them—traffic signs, logos for products on packages, and in television advertising. Children's first interest is often in their own names, which they recognize and wish to write, or they may print their initial. Familiar books may be "read" to a group by a child who pretends to be the "teacher."

All of these provide you with evidence that print has been noticed and is being explored. To support children in becoming literate requires a watchful eye and sensitive ear. Whatever the age of children you work with, it is also important that you visibly enjoy reading and writing yourself. Write and read in front of children often and comment on your use of books and writing as resources: "I wonder what ingredients we'll need for the lasagna. I'm going to look it up here in my cookbook. Oh, mozzarella cheese. I'd better write that down on our shopping list." Share your writing with children so they will begin to understand adult purposes for writing. Here are some suggestions for helping children develop concepts about print:

- Comment on print, point out words or punctuation, and parts of the book.
- Do silly things like turn the book upside down and talk about why it can't be read like that.
- Label shelves and containers, puzzles and games, charts and posters.
- Have classroom signs that are permanent (The Block Area) and signs that are temporary (Bailey's Blocks, Please Don't Knock Them Down).

- Encourage children to write or dictate stories that they can illustrate and bind for the classroom library.
- Provide time and acceptance of "free" writing, including scribble writing and pretend writing.
- Keep favorite books in the classroom over time and reread favorite stories.
- Read so the child can see the print.
- Read individually to children and let the child turn the page as you read.
- Write and read purposefully in front of children as often as possible, for authentic reasons: to find something out, to communicate with others, to create reminders.

What constitutes a high-quality literacy environment for young children? Every classroom needs many appealing books. Every child needs to be read to. Planned and spontaneous reading aloud to individuals, a small group, and the whole class is an essential part of every early childhood teacher's day. A program for even the youngest children should have books and words throughout. Your appreciation of children's literature and your visible enjoyment of it will demonstrate that reading is a worthwhile experience.

Literature

Children who love books come to love reading. Children who have many positive experiences with literature come to love books. Literature is not merely the carrot with which we motivate children to read; in a real way, it is the most important reason for learning to read. Through good literature, children experience both language and art and learn about the world and relationships. It can provide information and motivate exploration, creativity, a concern for others, and a love of reading.

Young children are not able to purchase books or use the library on their own, so it is up to adults to present a range of quality literature from which children can make choices. As children's literature has become an accepted product it has also become a vehicle for marketing. Most grocery stores, variety stores, and even bookstores have a shelf of children's books that accompany television shows and movies. These are advertisements, not literature, and do not belong in early childhood programs.

Every classroom needs a variety of different kinds of books that change regularly. Part of what creates active, eager readers is the sense of adventure that accompanies making a choice and opening a new book. All books for young children must respect childhood and children's lives.

Fiction, which includes fantasy, folklore, and realistic fiction, should create memorable, believable characters and the illusion of reality in time and place (even in a fantasy). The plot should encourage children to understand reasons behind events. The point of a good story need not be heavy-handed; stories that preach or devalue their experience will not appeal to children. *Fantasy* has its own logic and rules that remain true for the story. *Folklore* touches on themes and questions that have universal appeal and universal similarity—magic, good and evil, joy and sorrow, the origins of the world, and the people and animals that inhabit it. *Realistic fiction* should have an affectionate, unsentimental voice. To make all children feel included and support children's appreciation of the common humanity they share with others, provide books that include a range of diverse characters.

Informational books can broaden children's understanding. To be appealing without being inaccurate is the great challenge of informational books for young children. To teach they must be factual. To enhance interest they must be well paced and skillful in their presentation. Illustrations help to convey more than the words alone can.

Mood and concept books sensitize children to ideas, feelings, and awareness. They include wordless books and books that use organizing concepts such as the alphabet.

These books encourage children to think and use language. Concept books are most valuable when they provide a sense of joy and wonder in the world and are not used to drill children.

Collections of *rhymes* and *poetry* belong in every program. Nursery rhymes and poetry present mood and melody in language in a natural and unforced manner. They help to enhance children's understanding of the world and develop their sensitivity to language. This heightened awareness of the sounds of language is an important precursor of literacy.

A literature-rich classroom has an extensive collection of high-quality books that fill the room. Books are presented in ways that connect (e.g., a set of books on friendship might be presented together). Time and space for children to interact with books is built into the environment and schedule. Daily story reading is a prominent part of the day in a literature-rich classroom. Good children's literature:

- Shows respect for the reader (is not condescending; does not stereotype by gender, race, culture, etc.)
- Has integrity (honesty and truthfulness within the context of the story)
- Uses aesthetic language
- Helps the reader to understand and feel more deeply
- Teaches by example; does not preach or moralize
- Has illustrations that enhance and enlarge the text in a medium that is appropriate to the book
- Has illustrations that are executed with care and craftsmanship

It is important to learn to read to children with skill and responsiveness and to design experiences to expand on literature. If you work with children younger than 3 it is best to read stories to individuals or in twos or threes. This is also usually the most comfortable when you first begin to read stories, even to older children. Reading a story to a group requires skill you will develop only through practice (see Figure 10.7).

Although children's literature can be expanded into many other areas of classroom life, it is important not to turn literature into reading texts or use it as a basis for worksheets and tests. When children's literature is "basalized" in this way, children's inherent love of books is in danger of being squelched. Table 10.7 lists some books that will help you learn about the communication curriculum.

Figure 10.7 **Suggestions for Reading to a Group of Young Children**

- Practice if you are new to reading to a group, or a book is new to you.
- Sit on a low stool or chair so children can easily see the book.
- Make sure all the children are settled, comfortable, and can see before you begin.
- With children under 4, or those with disabilities, have an alternative if they cannot stay attentive.
- Before you start, focus children's attention—for example, by saying a finger-play, looking at the cover of the book, reading the title and author's name.
- Read in a natural tone of voice and match tempo, volume, pauses, and facial expression to the story.
- Don't interrupt the story with lots of questions.
- Read body language to see if children are interested and attentive. If not, focus attention with a comment or question to help children think (e.g., "I wonder what he will do now"). Stop before interest is lost so they are eager for more next time.

Table 10.7 **Books on Communication Curriculum**

Language

Language in Early Childhood Education,
by C. G. Cazden, NAEYC

Spotlight on Young Children and Language,
by Derry G. Koralek, NAEYC

Learning Language and Loving It,
by Elaine Weitzman & Janice Greenberg, NAEYC

Literacy

The Living Classroom: Writing, Reading, and Beyond,
by David Armington, NAEYC

Let's Begin Reading Right: A Developmental Approach to Emergent Literacy,
by Marjorie V. Fields, Lois Groth, & Katherine L. Spangler, Merrill/Prentice Hall

Much More than the ABC's,
by Judith Schickedanz, NAEYC

Learning to Read and Write,
by Susan B. Neuman, Carol Copple, & Sue Bredekamp, NAEYC

Literature

Young Children and Picture Books,
by Mary Renck Jalongo, NAEYC

THE INQUIRY CURRICULUM

It is little short of a miracle that modern methods of instruction have not already completely strangled the holy curiosity of inquiry, because what this delicate little plant needs most, apart from initial stimulation, is freedom, without that it is surely destroyed.

Albert Einstein

Young children have a compelling curiosity to figure out why and how the world works. They learn by doing. From their earliest months they observe phenomena, discover relationships, search for answers, and communicate their discoveries. They construct understanding as they explore, experiment, and act upon their environment. Children *inquire* (seek information), construct understanding, and develop concepts as they play and participate in all curriculum activities. However, experiences in mathematics, science, and social studies are uniquely suited to the development of thinking and problem solving and are the areas of the curriculum in which inquiry is a primary emphasis.

If you remember math, science, and social studies education as memorizing facts to recall for a test you may question whether these subjects are appropriate for young children. If so, you will be pleased to know that learning "facts" is not the purpose of the inquiry curriculum in early childhood education. Instead the goals are to support children's natural curiosity and inherent sense of wonder, to help them to learn to think flexibly, to inquire and solve problems, and to construct understanding of the world.

The natural consequence of this purpose is that giving children information is not your primary role in the inquiry curriculum (indeed, it is not your primary role in early childhood education). Instead you help children construct understanding by providing the necessary raw materials: time, space, equipment, and experiences. You encourage and support them in discovering for themselves.

Inquiry does not mean learning right answers. It means to ask, to discover, to think, to take risks, to make mistakes, and to learn from them. Facts pronounced by adults deprive children of the opportunity to learn through inquiry and develop higher level thinking skills. Children need to understand that it is desirable to think creatively about problems, acceptable not to have an answer, and okay to give the "wrong" answers.

The processes a child uses to learn about the world and construct concepts are called *inquiry processes*. Inquiry for a young child involves the organization of experiences through exploration. An inquiring child uses the senses to gain information that will contribute to the development of concepts. Curriculum specialists identify between 10 and 15 distinct inquiry processes; the following are those that best apply to young children:

- *Exploring:* Using the senses to observe, investigate, and manipulate
- *Identifying:* Naming and describing what is experienced
- *Classifying:* Grouping objects or experiences by their common characteristics
- *Comparing and contrasting:* Observing similarities and differences between objects or experiences
- *Hypothesizing:* Using the data from experiences to make guesses (hypotheses) about what might happen
- *Generalizing:* Applying previous experience to new events

Supportive comments about children's discoveries and explorations encourage further inquiry and model an inquiring mind. They help children to form concepts but do not hand them preformed ideas.

Children are encouraged to think when they are asked *open-ended questions*. Open questions can be answered in a number of different ways and have more than one correct answer (see Figure 10.8). *Closed questions* have only one correct or acceptable answer—for example, "What color is it?" Even though closed questions do not stimulate inquiry, they can help you to learn whether children have acquired a concept or piece of information. For this reason, in most classrooms, educators use a mixture of open and closed questions.

Figure 10.8   **Suggestions for Asking Open Questions and Making Statements That Build Inquiry**

> Open questions can be answered in a number of different ways and have more than one correct answer. If you wish to stimulate children to inquire, you will ask many open-ended questions and allow children time to think and answer.
>
> Ask questions and make statements that help children to:
>
> - *Reason:* "What do you suppose?" "How do you know?" "What would happen if?" "How could we find out?"
> - *Notice details:* "What do you see (hear, feel, smell)?" "I wonder why clouds are moving so quickly?" "The baskets all nest together, the little ones inside the big ones." "I can feel the rabbit's heart is beating quickly and hard."
> - *Make comparisons:* "How are they the same (different)?" "Look how different each shell is."
> - *Come to conclusions:* "What would happen if . . . ?" "Why do you suppose that's happening?"

Mathematics is a way to structure experience to form ideas about the quantitative, logical, and spatial relationships between things, people, and events. Young children are natural mathematicians who are genuinely curious and unafraid of mathematical processes. During the early childhood years, young children come to think of themselves as part of a community of people who use numbers to order and communicate about their world. In the same way that young children will pretend to write and read, they will label distance and ages with numbers: "My doll is tenteen." "It's thirty-fifty miles."

The conceptual underpinnings of adult skills are based on many years of concrete experiences that may not seem to relate to mathematics. Concepts such as more and fewer, far and near, similar and different, short and tall, now and later, first and last, and over and under precede later mastery of complex mathematical concepts. Young children develop concepts that provide the foundation that help them to make sense of the physical and social world and to master abstract mathematical concepts later in their school careers (see Table 10.8). These form the math curriculum for young children.

Table 10.8 **Math Concepts Learned by Young Children**

Classification	Sorting or grouping by shared characteristics (e.g., putting all the beads in a basket and all the buttons in a box)
Seriation	Sequencing based on a difference in the degree of some quality such as size, weight, texture, or shading (e.g., arranging balls from smallest to largest)
Pattern and algebraic thinking	Ordering based on repetition (e.g., creating a bead necklace with alternating colors, or singing the chorus after every verse of a song)
Measurement	Comparing size, volume, weight, or quantity to a standard (e.g., finding out how many blocks cover the table top, or comparing the heights of friends)
Number and operations	Quantity and order
One-to-one correspondence	Matching objects one for one
Quantity or cardinal number	The amount or number of different objects
Order or ordinal number	The order of objects first, second, third
Numerals	The symbols that stand for certain quantities or order (i.e., 1-2-3)
Time	The *sequence* and *duration* of events (e.g., outdoor play lasting a long time in comparison to storytime)
Geometry and spatial sense	Properties of objects and the way objects relate to one another based on position, direction, arrangement, and distance (e.g., the long blocks go on the *bottom* shelf and the short on the shelf *above*; a tricycle goes *forward* and then *backward*; a child kicks a ball to a child who is *near*)
Shape	Regularity and irregularity; whether open or closed; how appearance changes based on position; and how shapes can be manipulated while retaining their characteristics
Display and analysis of data	The collection, organization, and representation of information (e.g., a chart comparing who has a cat and who does not have a cat—you are collecting, organizing, and representing data; a graph of how many pockets are in our clothes)

As you plan for math experiences it is important to be aware of when and how mathematics is meaningful to children. A child who is comparing and arranging the dishes in the dramatic play area and setting the table for the other children is using ideas of classification and quantity. Based on your observations of children you can add additional activities and ask stimulating questions that will provide more opportunities for them to learn.

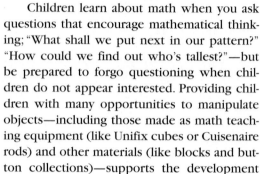

Children learn about math when you ask questions that encourage mathematical thinking; "What shall we put next in our pattern?" "How could we find out who's tallest?"—but be prepared to forgo questioning when children do not appear interested. Providing children with many opportunities to manipulate objects—including those made as math teaching equipment (like Unifix cubes or Cuisenaire rods) and other materials (like blocks and button collections)—supports the development of math concepts. Children learn about math as they handle the routines of the day. When each child has one cracker and rests on one mat, one-to-one correspondence is experienced. As they learn the sequence of the daily schedule, learn to pour half a glass of milk, or cut their apples in two parts, they are using math.

Because many teachers have "math anxiety," they are afraid to provide meaningful math experiences to young children. If you have math anxiety it may help if you consider all the ways you use ideas of pattern, measurement, reasoning, estimation, classification, and order in your life. As you do so, you may come to know that you are probably much better at math than you think. You *can* teach math. In fact, here are six ideas for ways to teach math in the early childhood classroom without even knowing it:

1. Sing songs with mathematical ideas—like "Eency Weency Spider" (geometry and spatial awareness) "Old MacDonald Had a Farm" (pattern) "Five Little Monkeys Jumping on the Bed" (number and operations), and so forth.

2. Read books that showcase math—like *The Doorbell Rang* by Pat Hutchins, and *Ten, Nine, Eight* by Molly Bang (number and operations), *Guess How Much I Love You* by Sam McBratney (measurement); *The Secret Birthday Message* by Eric Carle (space), *The Three Bears* by Paul Galdone (seriation), *The Very Hungry Caterpillar* by Eric Carle (pattern, number, and operations), and *Bread Bread Bread* by Ann Morris (displaying and analyzing data).

3. Build with blocks with children and use words like half-unit, unit, quadruple-unit, big, little, tall, short, wide (geometry and spatial awareness, number and operations, seriation, pattern, measurement).

4. Play with sand and water—provide scoops and containers of different sizes (number and operations, geometry and spatial awareness, measurement).

5. Cook good things to eat—follow recipes that are written out and visible to children (number and operations, measurement, time, geometry and spatial awareness, seriation).

6. Have routines—have children set the table (number and operations), clean up (classification, geometry, and spatial awareness), take roll (number and operations), feed pets (measurement), vote for activities/names (number and operations, displaying and analyzing data).

Young children are natural scientists. Their play is full of scientific exploration. It is true for an infant who is learning about physiology as she first discovers her toes and physics as she drops a bottle from a highchair. It is also true for a third grader who is carefully observing and drawing a wildflower.

For some adults science involves a collection of facts and concepts learned by rote from a teacher or a textbook. For others it is specific information that must be communicated to children. Some teachers believe that since young children don't learn in this way, "playing around" is sufficient science curriculum in the early years. We know today that science education for young children must not only be "hands-on" but must also be "minds-on"—in other words, mindful and intentional. Scientists—and educators who have maintained their own playfulness and enthusiasm for science—view it as a process of exploration and experimentation through which they find out about the world. It is this view that we want to share with children.

Science is a large field, encompassing many aspects of life. What do you teach young children about science? The most important thing you do is to build children's ability and disposition to inquire. The first of the National Science Education Standards for young children is that all children *should develop abilities to do scientific inquiry*. To do scientific inquiry children need to be able to:

- Ask questions about objects, organisms, and events in the environment
- Plan and conduct a simple investigation
- Employ simple equipment and tools to gather data and extend the senses
- Use data to construct a reasonable explanation
- Communicate investigations and explanations (National Research Council 1996)

You may find it useful to think about three broad categories: life science, earth and space science, and physical science.

Life science (the study of living things—plants and animals) is inherently interesting to children. Where did the butterfly come from? How did the bean grow into a plant? How did the bulging mother mouse get the babies inside her? Why does a dog have four legs and a spider eight? Life science involves the structures, origins, growth, and reproduction of plants and animals. Interest in their own growth can lead children to explore and learn about physiology. Children's fascination with their own bodies and with animals can be the springboard to further discovery.

Earth and space science (the study of the earth, sky, and oceans) involves children as they observe, explore, and wonder about the common features of the earth, sky, and oceans. Basic concepts of earth science are experienced and explored by young children in daily activity. As they walk over hills, look at layers of rock formations, or pound sandstone into bits, they are experiencing geology. When they observe the moon hanging in the sky above the playground in the morning, they are observing astronomical phenomena. When they guess that dark clouds hold rain, they are making meteorological predictions. Young children's concepts of earth science are limited to what they can see and experience. Children will be curious about these phenomena, and in school can have a place to talk, write, and read about them.

Physical science (the study of matter, form, and change) is learned about when children explore and observe the properties of substances—reactions to temperature and force and interactions. When children explore objects and act to create or alter speed, leverage, and balance, they are experiencing physics. When they act to make substances change by combining, heating, or cooling, they experience chemistry. An unbalanced pile of blocks collapsing, play dough disintegrating in the water play table, or an ice cube melting in the sun are children's first science experiments. Physical science activities are uniquely appropriate to young children because they involve action and observation of everyday things that are first experienced in play and daily life.

The National Committee on Science Education of the National Research Council has developed K–4 Science Standards. These were drawn on in the development of Hawaii's Preschool Content Standards six standards for science. We include them in Table 10.9 to provide you with some ideas about how science can be incorporated in an early childhood program.

Table 10.9 Hawaii State Preschool Content Standards for Science

Content Standards	Performance Indicators (some things a child does to demonstrate competency)
SCIENCE	
Standard 1: Increase sensory awareness.	• Explore and experiment using various sensory media in play (water, sand, paint, mud, rice). • Begin to identify and discriminate among sensory stimuli (tastes, sounds, textures, etc.).
Standard 2: Engage in scientific inquiry.	• Show curiosity and inquiry in play through exploration of objects and materials (rolling a toy car down a ramp made out of blocks, mixing all the colors of the paint together). • Ask scientific questions (Why does the spider make a web? Where did the rainbow go?) • Use materials appropriate for problem solving and exploration of the physical world, including equipment like magnifying glasses and scales. • Engage in discussions and/or document in drawing/writing what is learned through exploration and experimentation.
Standard 3: Explore physical properties of the world.	• Describe, compare and categorize objects based on their physical properties (These rocks have sparkles and these rocks don't.) • Explore and begin to identify changes that occur in natural and man-made materials over time (Ask, What happened to the puddle? Notice that the carved pumpkin decomposes over time). • Experiment with the effect of his/her own actions on objects (see if it's easier to pull the wagon with one or two children inside, drop toys into water to see if they float).
Standard 4: Explore characteristics of living things.	• Explore the nature of life through observation of and interaction with a variety of plants and animals. • Notice similarities, differences, and categories of plants and animals, as well as appearances, behaviors, and habitats (act out the behaviors of different animals in dramatic play). • Notice and ask questions about growth and change in plants and animals (changes in the garden, life cycle of classroom pets, caterpillar changing to a butterfly).
Standard 5: Learn about earth and sky.	• Investigate the properties of rocks, dirt, and water. • Talk about and/or draw their observations of the characteristics and movement of sun, moon, stars, and clouds. • Observe and discuss changes in the environment including weather and seasonal changes. • Notice and describe environmental changes such as erosion, tides, volcanic eruptions, and earthquakes.
Standard 6: Have a variety of educational experiences that involve technology.	• Pretend to use everyday technology in play (pretend to use a computer, use a block as a phone, bake mud cakes in a toy oven). • Use real technology with guidance (computer, tape player, telephone, blender).

Source: Hawaii Preschool Content Standards. Readiness Task Force, Good Beginnings Alliance, Honolulu, HI. Used with permission.

Your main role in science education is the preservation and encouragement of the natural curiosity of children. To maintain children's attitude of playfulness toward science you need to view their questions as an opportunity to model the attitudes of the scientist curiosity, questioning, openness to exploration, and problem solving.

In planned or spontaneous science activities, you can guide children's curiosity and help turn a pleasant experience into one that has deeper learning. For example, a small group of children looking at a squirmy family of baby mice will be delighted by their tiny size and their mother's care. They may not spontaneously realize that the babies are seeking milk, that their eyes are closed, or that these babies are like many other babies, including human infants, in some ways. You can encourage thinking and concept development by asking children questions like "Why do you suppose the baby mice were squirming?" "What do you think will happen if their mother goes and runs on the wheel?" and "What do the babies remind you of?" Part of your role is to find resources (books, people, or media) to expand their knowledge. As you model an inquiring and respectful attitude toward the world, you help children to think like scientists. Science is everyday, accessible, infinitely interesting, and definitely worth knowing.

Social Studies

Social studies concerns relationships among people and between people and the world in which they live. It is an umbrella term that includes many fields. In an early childhood program it can include aspects of psychology (emotions and behavior), sociology (society, its development and organization), cultural anthropology (the way people live in different cultures), economics (how people consume, produce, and deliver goods and services), political science (how people are governed and use power to make and enforce decisions), geography (the earth, its features, and the effects of human activity), and history (the events that make up the past).

You may remember school social studies as dull and unrelated to the real world, requiring memorization of dates, names, and places. You may have other memories of interesting and exciting social studies experiences taught in pleasant and memorable ways such as taking trips or cooking food from another culture.

Today, a good deal of interest surrounds teaching young children the social, political, and economic concepts that have an impact on people's lives, including such topics as racial and cultural differences, recognizing bias and prejudice and resisting stereotyping, understanding rules and laws, cooperation and conflict resolution, understanding feelings, awareness of aging, caretaking and compassion, developing positive self-concept, awareness of how we get goods and services, and learning about disabilities.

Children learn about power and rules by the way we treat them. They learn about acceptance and bias from us. You can help children by providing a model of a strong, competent, compassionate, active person. Your own feelings about age, race, class, handicapping conditions, and sex roles will communicate to children—so it is important to give positive, affirming, antibias messages. You can make sure that books, puzzles, pictures, and other educational materials present a similarly nonbiased view.

It is important to learn to talk thoughtfully and openly to children when social and political subjects come up and to think ahead about some of the things that you might say to help extend their understanding of things that concern them. A 4-year-old in a group that one of us taught brought a newspaper photograph to school that showed a starving child. His concern led to interest by the group and then to a study of a geographic area and a political situation that we would never have chosen based on their development. It led to worthwhile, if sobering, learning.

The National Center for the Social Studies has identified 10 themes that belong in education for children from kindergarten on. In Hawaii the national standards have been used in creation of *Preschool Content Standards for Social Studies*. These seven standards include performance indicators that show what children do to demonstrate competency. We include them here, in Table 10.10, to provide you with some ideas for how social studies can be included in programs for young children.

Table 10.10 **Hawaii State Preschool Content Standards for Social Studies**

Content Standards	Performance Indicators (some things a child does to demonstrate competency)
Standard 1: Learn about themselves and other people	Identify similarities and differences among people—such as height, hair color, eye color, skin color, language, etc. Take on a variety of roles in dramatic play ("I'm the big brother, you're the mom."). Draw or paint pictures of themselves and others with distinguishable characteristics ("I painted Emma with long hair and Micah with short hair."). Discuss how they and their families are similar to or different from those of classmates ("We don't have a baby in our family.").
Standard 2: Appreciate their own and other cultures	Participate in discussions of family rituals and traditions related to culture ("I call my grandma Ojiisan, you call yours Tutu."). Talk about stories set in different cultural contexts (discuss the ways the mother in *Mama Do You Love Me?* is similar to and different from the child's own mother). Identify their family's cultural identification in the context of classroom activities and discussions ("We make mochi at New Year because we're Japanese.").
Standard 3: Become aware of how things, people, and places change over time	Relate personal life to the process of change while talking about day-to-day events ("I used to drink from a bottle and now I use a cup. I used to crawl but now I can walk and run."). Notice/talk about similarities/differences between people *He's a grandpa, he has white hair* Talk about yesterday, today, tomorrow (going to the beach last weekend, an upcoming birthday party). Guess how events today or in the recent past will affect the near future *It rained hard so there will be puddles.*
Standard 4: Explore how people depend upon one another for the things (goods) and the help (services) they need	Identify jobs at school and home ("My daddy cooks dinner and my mom washes the dishes." "Everybody has to help clean up." "Today's my day to be the light switcher."). Contribute to discussions about things that everyone needs (food, water, shelter, clothing). Show awareness that people work to provide the things others need (pretend to be the doctor or firefighter in dramatic play; represent jobs in drawings). Talk about ways that people get the things they need (buy things, grow food, make clothes). Demonstrate awareness of money and how it is used (play store and use slips of paper to pretend to buy things; talk about needing money to buy something).
Standard 5: Understand what people need to do to work and live together in groups	Demonstrate awareness that everyone deserves to learn, be safe, respected, and listened to (waits his/her turn, protects other children, discusses what might be fair treatment). Participate in creating/following rules to ensure that everyone is safe, respected, listened to. Recognize the role of authority (leaders) and what leaders do (follows directions, talks about the role of the teacher, director). Participate in group decision making (voting for the name of the class rabbit).
Standard 6: Develop geographic awareness	Describe and/or draw aspects of the environment. Use blocks, clay, or other materials to re-create aspects of the environment. Create a simple map of the home, classroom, school, or neighborhood.
Standard 7: Develop awareness of the natural environment and how it can be protected	Become aware of characteristics of the place they live and of other places. Use blocks, clay, or other materials to re-create aspects of the environment. Talk about how people can take care of or harm the environment. Participate in efforts to protect the environment (e.g., pick up trash, save paper to be recycled).

Source: Hawaii Preschool Content Standards. School Readiness Task Force, Good Beginnings Alliance, Honolulu, HI. Used with permission.

Table 10.11   **Books on Inquiry Curriculum**

Math

Mathematics in the Early Years,
and
The Young Child and Mathematics,
by Juanita V. Copley, NAEYC

Spotlight on Young Children and Math,
by Derry G. Koralek, NAEYC

Science

Discovering Nature with Young Children,
by Ingrid Chalufour & Karen Worth, NAEYC or Redleaf Press

Science with Young Children (rev. ed.),
by Bess-Gene Holt, NAEYC

Science Experiences for the Early Childhood Years: An Integrated Approach,
by Jean D. Harlan & Mary S. Rivkin, Merrill/Prentice Hall

Spotlight on Young Children and Science,
by Derry G. Koralek & Laura J. Colker, NAEYC

Active Experiences for Active Children: Science,
by Carol Seefeldt & Alice Galper, Merrill/Prentice Hall

Worms, Shadows, and Whirlpools: Science in the Early Childhood Classroom,
by Karen Worth & Sharon Grollman, NAEYC

Social Studies

Explorations with Young Children,
by Anne Mitchell & Judy David, NAEYC

Active Experiences for Active Children: Social Studies,
by Carol Seefeldt & Alice Galper, NAEYC

Alike and Different: Exploring Our Humanity with Young Children,
by Bonnie Neugebauer, NAEYC

It takes thoughtful planning to weave social studies topics into meaningful learning experiences for young children. Social studies makes an excellent tool for organizing and integrating curriculum, since its basic strategies include field trips, examining and discussing artifacts, mapping activities, collecting and organizing data on a graph, food preparation, visits from resource people, teacher-made games, literature, dances, and art activities. Follow-up activities can occur in every area of the curriculum. Children gain deeper understanding when they re-create and reexperience concepts in block building, dramatic play, art, journal writing, and books, songs, and games. Table 10.11 lists some books that will help you learn more about the inquiry curriculum.

Final Thoughts

Young children learn by doing, observing, and interacting. They construct and order knowledge through play. You will guide children on this voyage of discovery and help them to understand the world in which they live. As you do so, you support their natural curiosity, develop their love of learning, and help them to be the thinkers and problem-solvers of the future.

There are many ways to organize curriculum to ensure that you provide a full range of appropriate activities for the children in your program. No single "right way" prescribes how to think about or teach a particular subject to young children (though some ways are "wrong" because they do not reflect what we know about how children learn).

As you learn to be an early childhood educator you will have opportunities to learn much more about curriculum. In creating this chapter we wanted to give you an overview of the kinds of learning experiences that are developmentally appropriate and meaningful to young children—a framework onto which you could add the practical details you will need to actually teach. We hope that it will prove useful to you.

Learning Outcomes

When you read this chapter, thoughtfully complete selected assignments from the "To Learn More" section, and prepare items from the "For Your Portfolio" section, you will be demonstrating your progress in meeting NAEYC **Standard 4: Teaching and Learning.**
Key elements:

- Knowing, understanding, and using positive relationships and supportive interactions

- Knowing, understanding, and using effective approaches, strategies, and tools for early education
- Knowing and understanding the importance, central concepts, inquiry tools, and structures of content areas or academic disciplines
- Using your own knowledge and other resources to design, implement, and evaluate meaningful, challenging curriculum to promote positive outcomes

To Learn More

Observe a Program: For a morning, observe a program and see how the staff structures the environment and program to support children's development in one of the curriculum areas: physical development, creative arts, communication, or inquiry. Look at the plans and see how the planning reflects what you observed. Interview a teacher to learn how he or she thinks about this area of curriculum.

Observe a Child: For a morning observe a child in a classroom, with a focus on the child's activity in one of the curriculum areas. Notice how the child engages with the experiences offered and how he or she constructs his or her own opportunities for learning. Notice the extent to which the child's learning experiences and the planned curriculum seem to match. Observe to see how staff support the child's learning in this area.

Observe a "Master Teacher": Spend a morning with an early childhood educator who is experienced and has a curriculum leadership role in a program. (This teacher may be called the "lead," "head," or "mentor" teacher.) Then interview

the educator about how he or she plans for and provides curriculum.

Observe an Activity: Observe a teacher teaching a planned activity. Using this chapter identify the curriculum content area and the specific learning that occurs. Interview the teacher to find out the objectives for the activity. Reflect on any differences between what you saw and the focus of the plan.

Compare Two Programs: Observe two early childhood programs in one of the curriculum areas. Compare the ways that the two address the area—their similarities and differences. Reflect on which program seems to best support children's learning and why. What implications does this comparison have for your future work with young children?

Compare Two Ages: Observe two classrooms, one preschool and one for infants and toddlers or primary school children. Report on how each enhances children's development in one of the areas of development. Talk to the staff about how they make their curriculum choices in this area. Notice how development influences curriculum choices.

FOR YOUR PORTFOLIO

Design a Learning Center: Design and draw a floor plan for an ideal learning center for one of the curriculum areas. Share your plan with an early childhood educator, discussing what you included and why. Ask for and consider the educator's feedback and suggestions. Set up the center and let children use it. For your portfolio, include the floor plan, photographs of children using the center, and a reflection on what you learned by doing this project.

Plan an Activity: Write and implement an activity plan in one of the subject areas, using the activity planning format described in the next chapter (Figure 11.2). Reflect on how children responded and how you felt about what you did. What worked? What might you do differently next time? How might you expand on this experience for children? For your portfo-

lio include the plan, a work sample or photograph, and a reflection on what you learned about yourself, children, planning, and teaching.

Create a Learning Material: Design and make a learning material to support the development of a particular child or group of children in one of the subject areas. Introduce it to the child or children and observe how it is used. Reflect on how the children responded and how you felt about what you did. What worked? What might you do differently next time? How might you expand on this experience for children? For your portfolio include a photograph of a child using the material and a reflection on what you learned about yourself, children, learning materials, and teaching.

11

Curriculum Planning

Awareness of alternatives and the bases of choices distinguishes the
competent teacher from the merely intuitive one.

Elizabeth Brady

Worthwhile curriculum contributes to all aspects of development and provides opportunities for children to learn about the world. As an early childhood teacher one of your tasks is to involve the children with whom you work in a variety of challenging and intellectually engaging experiences that will result in their constructing an understanding of the world, developing the skills they need, and acquiring attitudes that will lead them to become caring and productive human beings.

Curriculum—the intentional learning experiences designed by a teacher, or team of teachers, in response to what they know and observe about children—includes three interconnected elements: the nature of the learner (*who*), the content or subject matter (*what*), and the process or kinds of planned learning opportunities (*how*). In meaningful curriculum, the learner, content, and process are linked. In Chapter 4 we took an in-depth look at the *who*. In Chapter 10 we looked at the *what*, the content of the early childhood curriculum. Selection and organization of this content—*how* curriculum is planned and implemented in early childhood programs—is explored in this chapter.

Planning Considerations

What is a plan? In everyday life, simply having a predetermined idea of what you are going to do is a plan ("I plan to be home by 8:30"). But in working with young children, a plan means a written blueprint for teaching. Whether you are drafting an integrated study or outlining a specific activity, every educational plan includes some essential elements: purpose, content, methods, and assessment.

Every plan has an educational *purpose*, something you are trying to accomplish. Statements of purpose can be called *goals* or *objectives*. Although you may see these words used interchangeably, a distinction can be made between them. Goals are broad statements of desired ends

As you view the DVD, "Birds: An Integrated Curriculum," notice the many strategies that the teachers are using to deliver the curriculum.

toward which teaching is directed (e.g., a goal of the preschool curriculum is to help children become creative thinkers). More specific and immediate intended outcomes of curriculum activities are called *objectives* (e.g., at the end of this activity children will have greater ability to express ideas using clay).

Many strategies or *methods* can be used to deliver curriculum *content*. One of the pleasures of teaching young children is that there are many ways to teach. For example, to teach children that all birds have feathers and lay eggs, you might take a trip to the zoo to see different kinds of birds, cook dishes made with eggs, read books about birds, sing a song about birds that fly home to their nest, paint using feathers, play a game matching feathers from different birds, set up a bird feeder in the yard, or hatch eggs in an incubator. One of the challenges of teaching young children is selecting methods that both engage children and help them learn things that are meaningful about the world.

How do you know whether you have accomplished your purpose—whether children have really learned what you intended to teach? *Assessment* of what children have learned is a part of planned curriculum. In early childhood settings, this is most often done by observing children and making anecdotal records and by collecting work samples that document the children's acquisition of concepts and skills. In Chapter 5 we described the process of observation and uses of portfolios. You will use these methods to assess what children have learned.

Purpose, content, methods, and assessment interact with one another. To achieve a particular purpose (e.g., to learn about the characteristics of birds), you select the content and methods (observing and drawing a bird). The methods will determine how you assess (collect the children's drawings). What you assess depends on your purpose (do the drawings include characteristics of birds such as beaks, wings, feathers, legs, and feet?).

> ### Reflect on something you planned
>
> Think back to a time when you planned something in your life—a trip, a party, a project. Reflect on what you did and how you went about organizing the event or activity. What did you do? How did you know that you had succeeded? How did planning or lack of planning impact how it turned out?

Influences on Curriculum Choices

As you plan curriculum for children you will choose the content to be taught, how to organize it, and how to present it to children. These decisions will be based on your values and beliefs about children and education (and those of the program in which you teach); your knowledge of children and their families, culture, and community; and your assessment of whether the content is worthwhile for young children to learn.

Values and Beliefs

Your choices about teaching are the way you touch the future. Barbara Biber of Bank Street College pointed out that programs for young children are a powerful force in influencing the intellect, and more:

> . . . not only the excellence of intellect but in shaping the feelings, the attitudes, the values, the sense of self and the dreaming of what is to be, the images of good and evil in the world about and the visions of what the life . . . might be. (Biber 1969, 8)

What you teach and how you teach reflects your values for society. The children you teach today are potential doctors, politicians, artists, teachers, parents—people who will make decisions that will affect the lives of others (including your own). What do you want the people of the future to be like? What knowledge and skills will the children you teach need to be productive citizens in society as it exists now, and as it will exist tomorrow? Your answers to these questions will help you to determine your *aims* as an educator. Aims are inspirational ideals based on philosophy and values that frame the program as a whole (e.g., an aim of my program is to help create a society of participatory citizens).

What do you believe about how children learn and what they should be learning? Do you believe children are self-motivated and self-directed learners who will naturally choose what they need to learn? Do you believe that selecting what children will be taught is the responsibility of adults who have more experience and knowledge? Your beliefs about children's motivation and ability to choose worthwhile learning will have an influence on what you teach.

Reflect on the role of education in shaping the future

Think about what you want the world to be like in the future. What will people need to be like in order for the world you envision to exist? What do children need to learn and experience in school in order to become these people?

Teachers' beliefs about how children learn and what they should be learning fall along a continuum that ranges from the belief that children are capable of making choices that will help them acquire needed knowledge and skills (i.e., the process of learning is more important than the specific content) to a belief that young children will not naturally learn without direction (i.e., the content—the acquisition of specific knowledge and skills—is more important than the process). Most teachers' beliefs fall somewhere in the middle. If you have read the preceding 10 chapters of this book you are already aware that we, the authors, believe that all areas of children's development are important; that we trust children to create many opportunities for their own learning; and that we believe play, child-choice, and cooperative relationships are essential parts of the child's educational experience. We value the individuality and dignity of children and families, and appreciate that they are part of a culture and community. We also believe that adults have a responsibility to select rich and diverse educational experiences for children. Our beliefs fall in the middle of the continuum, somewhat nearer to the process end. In this chapter we will describe a way of planning curriculum that is consistent with this philosophy.

Values and beliefs are not restricted to individuals. Programs are founded on values and a view of children and learning, usually stated in the program's philosophy and mission statement. The views of the program in which you work will also influence your curriculum choices. Many early childhood programs are based on a view of children as capable learners and have a mission to foster the development of the whole child and create lifelong learners. Others are designed to impart the values of a religious or cultural group. Some are founded on the belief that children acquire knowledge through direct teaching and value the acquisition of academic skills and knowledge.

Knowledge of Children

Early childhood education program practice is based on knowledge of children. This knowledge enables educators to plan for children at the appropriate level for their age and for their individual needs, backgrounds, and interests. We call this *developmentally appropriate practice* (DAP).

According to NAEYC's influential document *Developmentally Appropriate Practice in Early Childhood Programs* (Bredekamp & Copple 1997), developmental appropriateness reflects knowledge of three dimensions:

- Child development and learning
- The strengths, interests, and needs of each individual child
- The social and cultural contexts in which children live

Knowledge of *child development and learning* provides a framework from which you will prepare the learning environment and plan appropriate experiences that are likely to benefit all the children of a particular age and stage of development. Knowing *the strengths, interests, and needs of each individual child* allows you to adapt and be responsive to each child's individual pattern and timing of

What do you notice about how different ages of children engaged with the curriculum?

growth as well as his or her unique personality and learning style. Both the curriculum and adults' interactions with children should be responsive to individual differences in interest, style, and ability. Knowledge of *the social and cultural context in which children live* helps you to ensure that planned learning experiences are meaningful, relevant, and respectful for children and their families (Bredekamp & Copple 1997).

Just as educational experiences for individual children within a group will differ, planning for the range of age groups is markedly different. The younger the children, the more child-centered and family-sensitive the program must be.

For infants and young toddlers, you develop very broad goals that are applicable to all children in this stage of development. Their basic needs are intense and must be met quickly. They need warm physical contact with a few affectionate adults. They are developing a sense of themselves. They are growing and developing new skills with amazing rapidity. They are imbedded in families with individual child-rearing practices that must be taken into consideration. The curriculum for infants and toddlers consists of opportunities for spontaneous exploration, with individualized activities for particular children. Planning will be flexible and done on a short-term basis.

Curriculum will be more elaborate for preschoolers. Planning for preschoolers should take into consideration their predictable characteristics. They learn by doing, by actively exploring. They are beginning to use language effectively. They enjoy playing with one another but have some difficulty working as a group. They eagerly seek new stimulation and have a low tolerance for inactivity. They benefit from planned learning experiences based on carefully chosen topics that supplement their play and exploration. Teachers need to plan for short-term activities, and also further in advance, to make sure that more complex activities (such as trips and projects) can occur.

For primary-age children, curriculum can be more subject-related, project-oriented, and structured. School-age children, like preschoolers, still learn best by active, hands-on experiences but they are able to think more abstractly than preschoolers. They represent ideas symbolically and are increasingly able to read and write about what they are learning. Curriculum in primary school can take advantage of these abilities by pairing experiences in which children learn about the world with many opportunities to represent what they have learned.

Family, Culture, and Community

Young children live in families. Their families, though individual themselves, reflect the characteristics and values of their culture and community. As you plan curriculum you might want to ask yourself: What do these families believe is important for children to learn? Are there subjects or activities with which the families or members of the community might be uncomfortable? How can the families and their cultures and this community serve as resources for curriculum?

Events in the families and community and locale will influence your curriculum. Think about what curriculum you might plan if several families in your class are having new babies; if a cultural celebration is taking place in your community; if the city is installing wheelchair access ramps at the street corner by your school; or if heavy rains caused a flood. Skillful teachers use the life of the families and the community as opportunities for discovery. They know that real events like these lead to powerful learning.

What's Worth Knowing?

What is worth knowing when you are a young child? Curriculum has little value if the content isn't worthwhile to the learner. Children want to know many things about the world in which they live. They want to know about themselves, about how to get along with others and care for their own needs, about their families and communities, and about the natural and physical aspects of their world. You can see this as you observe a 1-year-old's fascination with water, a 2-year-old's triumphant "Me do it!", a 4-year-old's passion for firefighters, or a 6-year-old's absorption in horses.

When we ask our students to reflect on what they wanted to know when they were young children, their memories are rich and sometimes surprising. They wanted to know about birth and death; the moon and the stars; the nature of God and the nature of sand; divorce and conflict; power and authority; the workings of the plumbing and the workings of the mind; the structure of their bodies and the structure of a worm. With few exceptions, they sought the answers outside of school.

> **Reflect on something you wanted to know when you were a child**
>
> Remember a time when you were a child and you really wanted to know something. What did you want to know about? Why was it important to you? What did you do to find out? What did you learn? How was this similar to or different from what you did in school?

Children want and need to know complex things about complex topics. But schools often limit curriculum for young children to simple facts to recite: shapes and colors, the alphabet and numbers. We maintain that for curriculum to be *of worth* to young children it must be based on the genuine investigation of a topic that has intellectual meaning—in other words, something that is real, that requires genuine investigation and thought. In this chapter we will give you an example of one such investigation: a study of birds.

What academic skills do you see children acquiring as they study the topic of birds?

What about shapes, colors, numbers, the alphabet, and so on? There is certainly value in knowing these things. And it is our responsibility to help children learn them. But they can be learned as children pursue tasks and learn about things that are interesting and meaningful to them rather than as isolated fragments divorced from sense. In isolation, they have little significance or relevance to children's lives.

As we have described in Chapter 2 and Chapter 10, "content standards" are becoming more and more influential in the design of curriculum. When they are written with knowledge of young children and how they learn, they provide useful guidelines for selecting curriculum. They can provide you with important information to help you in the complex task of designing curriculum. However, they should not be a substitute for thoughtfully considering what knowledge and skills are "worth knowing" for your group of children.

Organizing Curriculum

Curriculum can be organized in different ways. How you choose to organize the curriculum reflects your values and beliefs. The organizational approaches most often used are *learner-centered, subject-centered*, and *integrated*.

Learner-Centered Organization

When the organization of the curriculum is based on the developmental stage, needs, and interests of children, it is called learner-centered. In a learner-centered curriculum design, teachers provide few preplanned activities and instead ensure that children have large blocks of time to play and explore in a planned environment. Advocates of this approach believe that all learning experiences should be based on children's interests. They feel that imposing activities on children that originate from outside sources is counterproductive because children will fail to engage with the content. Planned activities emerge from observations of children and are based on their interests. For this reason it is often called *emergent curriculum*.

A learner-centered organization is appropriate in early childhood classrooms and is the best way to plan for infants, toddlers, and young preschoolers. It can also be used with older preschoolers, kindergartners, and primary-age children. But because it is limited by what children bring to the educational experience, it may not be sufficient to provide intellectual challenge and stimulation as children get older.

Subject Area Organization

Organization by subject areas (e.g., math, science, social studies, reading) reflects the view that education is primarily about the attainment of knowledge. Teaching is generally organized into blocks of time (e.g., reading 9:00 to 9:45, math 10:00 to 10:30). Sometimes two or more disciplines—for example, math and science—are combined for instruction.

Although organization by subjects assures that all the areas of content that are valued are given attention, it does not help children understand relationships that exist between subjects. It also fails to take into account children's different interests and different strengths. Although this approach is often used in classrooms for older children, adolescents, and adults, it is not appropriate for young children who best learn and understand when information is presented in more holistic ways—involving senses, body, and mind all together.

Integrated Organization

Integrated organization refers to curriculum in which a topic of study provides a focus for the curriculum. The topic serves as an umbrella under which different developmental and subject areas are integrated. In an integrated study, children investigate a topic in depth over a period of time. The topic forms the hub for curriculum in many different subject areas. Children's interests or the teacher's ideas about what children would enjoy or benefit from can be sources of the topic. *Unit planning, thematic planning, integrated study*, and *project approach* are all forms of integrated organization. They are similar to one another but each has a somewhat different emphasis.

Advocates of this approach believe that integrated organization is appropriate and effective, especially for children 4 years and older. It reflects that children learn holistically. It is mindful of the idea of multiple intelligences—that is, that individuals learn best through their particular strengths or intelligences (see Chapter 4). Good integrated curriculum provides many different avenues for learning about and exploring a topic. A study can be tailored to fit the learning styles of a group of children and of individual children in the group.

An integrated study of a topic simultaneously contributes to children's growing awareness, skill, and understanding in many areas. It provides opportunities for children to learn by doing and have many direct experiences with the world. Used well and thoughtfully, it helps children to understand that learning is connected to life. For these reasons we think that integrated planning is the most effective way to plan curriculum for older preschool, kindergarten, or primary school children. In our experience it also makes teaching more interesting, exciting, and satisfying.

Presenting Curriculum

Young children are learning all the time, from all of their experiences. Much of what they learn comes through the routines, relationships, and incidental encounters that they have with people, places, and objects. They learn through their own self-directed play. For infants and young toddlers these are the primary ways that they learn. Routines, learning environments, and relationships are the curriculum. These unplanned activities are the foundation of curriculum for all young children. Whatever the planned curriculum, when you ask a young child you are likely to discover that it is the life of the classroom that is most important. When we talk with young children about their school experiences we often discover that the quality of the snack, the length of the outdoor time, the "mean-ness" or "nice-ness" of the teacher, and the availability of toys are more pressing concerns than the quality of the learning experiences.

Routines, relationships, and spontaneous play remain important curriculum activities throughout the early childhood years. As children get older, however, teachers can begin to plan a variety of activities to present curriculum content. They can plan to teach through play in a planned learning environment. They also plan to teach concepts and develop skills and attitudes in planned activities led by a teacher. You will choose how to present specific curriculum content based on your knowledge of children and on your goals and objectives.

Planning for Play

Chapter 6, "Play," and Chapter 8, "The Learning Environment," provide information on how play and a planned learning environment contribute to children's development. Through their exploration and self-initiated play activities, children construct knowledge and develop skills and interests. The power of play is that it helps children develop skills and knowledge of many kinds simultaneously. At the same time they enjoy themselves and become motivated to keep exploring and learning.

Play is a powerful learning medium and the tools and "textbooks" of play include toys, blocks, paint, crayons, sand, water, clay, and wood. Dramatic play, blocks, manipulative toys, sensory materials, art materials, and outdoor play are the cornerstones of the early childhood curriculum.

Young children need many opportunities for play each day. How and when do you "plan for play"? Play is the most appropriate learning medium when you want children to explore and discover for themselves. When you purposefully provide play opportunities that support the curriculum you have chosen, you are planning for play. For example, to support a child's fine motor development you might plan for play opportunities with clay, dough, or stringing beads. To support the development of the understanding of concepts of volume and measurement you might plan for open-ended play activities with water, sand, and containers of different sizes. If you are planning play opportunities while using an integrated curriculum study you might plan to add dramatic play props related to the topic. For example, in the study of birds that we use as an example in this chapter, teachers added puppets, toy birds, and cloth hoods colored and shaped like the crests of birds to the dramatic play and block areas to encourage children to reenact their developing understanding of birds.

How do you see children using play to demonstrate their developing understanding of birds?

Teacher-Child Activities

Do you remember learning to drive a car? It's unlikely that you would have developed driving skill by playing with a car. You also probably would not have learned if you had attended a lecture class on driving. Instead, you learned when you were ready and interested with the guidance from someone more competent than yourself. We call activities that you plan to teach to individual children one-on-one *teacher-child activities*. As we described in Chapter 4, new abilities are first developed in collaboration with an adult or more competent peer in what Vygotsky called the *zone of proximal development* or ZPD (Berk & Winsler 1995).

When you want to help a child acquire a specific concept or skill in his or her zone of proximal development, it is often useful to plan a guided activity in which you work with that child. Teacher-child activities permit you to concentrate on a particular

In what ways do you observe teachers guiding children's learning? What kinds of questions do you see them asking?

child's learning process and participate in a learning dialogue. They allow you to observe and assess a child's knowledge and skill and modify what you do based on the child's response. Teacher-child activities can also be planned to support the development of skills, concepts, and attitudes that you want all the children to develop or the development of the major understandings of a topic of study in an integrated curriculum. For example, in the study of birds that we will describe later in this chapter, the teachers prepared several *workjobs*[1] that were introduced to children individually: One involved counting birds in fine art postcards; another involved matching photographs of different birds that inhabited the playground; and another involved sequencing the stages of a bird's development from hatching to fledgling.

Group size, teacher-child ratio, and the way you organize both time and the environment will influence the extent to which you can engage in teacher-child activities with children. The smaller the group and the more that time and environment support self-selected independent activities, the more you will be able to engage in teacher-child activities. Engaging learning centers and large blocks of time for children to work with one another are crucial if you are to have the opportunity for teacher-child activities.

Small Group Activities

When you work with a few children at a time it is called a *small group*. How many children constitute a small group? This varies with the age of the children. For toddlers a small group is 2 to 4 children. With preschoolers a small group may be 5 to 10 children, though fewer is better, especially for 3-year-olds. And with kindergarten and primary school children 8 to 12 children is a small group—though again, fewer is better.

Small group activities enable you to present concepts, facilitate an exchange of ideas between children, and have meaningful personal contact with each child. It is probably the most effective teaching strategy for preschool and primary children. This approach reduces waiting time and allows for activities that involve turn-taking, manipulation of materials, and quite a lot of teacher assistance.

In a small group activity you are able to attend to the way children respond and can evaluate and modify what you do. When you have children with diverse developmental needs (as you do in a mixed-age classroom) you can tailor the length of the small group time and the kind of activity to match the children in the group. For example, we recently planned a process for naming small groups in a class of children aged 2½ through 5. The younger children spent a 10-minute group time thinking of and naming their group (the Flowers). The older ones spent three 15-minute group times on subsequent days brainstorming, negotiating, and voting for their small group name (the Cloud-Airplanes).

If an adult needs to discuss the activity with the children while it is happening, then a small group is the best choice. Activities such as "I Spy," discussion, acting out stories, creative movement activities, cooking projects, and walks work best in small groups.

Small groups that meet together on a regular basis develop an identity of their own. When the children select a name for the group, they further cement feelings of belonging and responsibility. These kinds of regular small group meetings help children to develop some important skills including the ability to listen and talk in a group, solve problems and make decisions democratically, take leader and follower roles, and accept responsibility for the outcomes of their decisions.

---

[1] Workjobs is the name given by Mary Baratta-Lorton to simple teacher-made games that help children to learn concepts and develop skills.

Large Group Activities

Although they are often used in early childhood programs, large group activities are generally the least effective for teaching and the hardest for teachers to do well. A large group may include the whole class.

Whole class, large group activities can be valuable when they allow children to share a common experience and build a sense of community. They are appropriate only when children can all be active (e.g., by singing a song or engaging in creative movement). They are not appropriate if the activity requires you to attend to individual responses (e.g., show and tell) or if you want children to take turns (e.g., in cooking). With older preschool, kindergarten, and primary school children they are also effective for group games like dodge ball. In general, the younger the children the less you plan experiences with a large group.

Selecting Activities

There are many hundreds of different activities that make up curriculum in early childhood programs. You will select those that best meet your purpose, and those that you can present effectively in your program with your children and the resources available to you. Figure 11.1 lays out some basic activities in each broad curriculum area and suggests the modes (play, teacher-child, small group, large group) that can be effective for teaching.

Which of the curriculum activities listed in Figure 11.1 do you observe being implemented in the video?

The relative balance of child-initiated exploration of the planned learning environment and teacher-guided experiences will vary based on the age and characteristics of the children as well as on the philosophy and characteristics of the program. Both processes have advantages and disadvantages and are most appropriate for different kinds of content. For example, it is unlikely that a 5-year-old would spontaneously learn to read a clock or tie shoelaces without help from a teacher. Similarly, it is unlikely that any amount of planned activity would teach that same 5-year-old to climb a rope although she might learn to do so in focused, self-initiated play.

Infants, toddlers, and young preschoolers can learn little through direct instruction. Both you and the child will feel frustrated if you try. But as children get older they will gradually become more able to learn through direct teaching when they are interested and motivated. Every educator will seek an optimal balance between child-chosen and adult-directed activity. As you plan you need to ask yourself which approach best meets the developmental characteristics of the children and your educational purposes. The answers to these questions will help you find the right balance for your group.

We know that young children learn at varying rates, that they are active learners, that they learn through play, and that they need many opportunities to practice skills as they are acquired (Bredekamp & Copple 1997). They learn through active engagement and concrete experiences. Because we know these things, we also know that young children do not benefit from abstract methods of teaching such as worksheets, lectures, and drill on isolated skills. These methods do not build understanding and, because they are often aversive, can lead to negative feelings toward schooling. They do not belong in early childhood programs.

> **Reflect on presenting curriculum**
>
> Think of an early childhood program that you know. What did you see children doing as they were learning? How could you tell the children were learning? During what kinds of activities did you sense the children were most engaged?

KINDS OF PLANNING

All educators plan. You will choose what you will plan, how you will plan, in what detail, and how far in advance. When early childhood educators use the word *plan* they mean different things. Sometimes it refers to a detailed written outline for a specific

Figure 11.1 Basic Planned Curriculum Activities* and Typical Ways to Present Them

	Play	Teacher-Child	Small Group	Large Group
Language and Literacy	books			
		storytelling		
		discussions		
		guessing games		
	book making			
			story acting	
			story writing	
	puppets			
			language experience charts	
		word games		
	dramatic play			
Music and Creative Movement		singing		
			singing games	
			performing	
		listening to and moving to music		
		using musical instruments		
		composing and improvising songs		
			creative movement	
Art	drawing			
	painting			
	collage			
	construction			
			print making	
	play dough and clay		play dough and clay	
			murals	
		looking at and discussing works of art		
Physical Development	sensory table activities			
	puzzles and workjobs			
	manipulative toys			
			cooking	
		gardening		
		woodworking		
			tasting activities	
	wheeled vehicles			
	climbing			
			active games	
Inquiry	workjobs and other learning games			
	dramatic play			
			cooking	
	observation of phenomena and exploration of materials			
			learning trips	
			visits from resource people	
	block play			
		woodworking		
	manipulative toys			
	patterning toys (beads, parquetry, etc.)			

*Many of these activities occur spontaneously in play but cannot be planned for.

learning activity, called an *activity plan* or *lesson plan*. At other times it means a list of activities to be done at different times over a week or day. It can also mean a plan for several weeks of activities, in many different content areas, based on a topic, called an *integrated plan*. Most early childhood educators have very general plans for a long period (a year or a few months) and more detailed weekly or daily plans. They write activity plans for activities that need careful sequencing, or when they wish to share them with others. Elementary and special educators call these lesson plans and may write one for every lesson they teach.

Long-Term Plans

General plans for a long period (a year or a few months)—long-term plans—give a sense of direction. They are useful for thinking through how you will plan for the predictable events that occur during a month, semester, or year. For example, you may know that you want to plan a trip to the woods to see the fall colors or to a nearby farm where children have the opportunity to pick their own fruit. You may need to plan for school events like an annual holiday party or an open house. You will want to mindfully plan the children's transition to the next school or class. Long-term plans help you make decisions about ordering materials and organizing trips. They allow you to prepare children by letting them know what to expect. They are useful to share with

families so they will have advance notice of events that call for their participation. It is best if long-term plans are quite general and flexible (e.g., "We will go on four bus trips: one in September, November, March, and April"; not "We will go to the zoo in September, the farm in November, the aquarium in March, and the fire station in April"). If you find out that your advance planning was inappropriate or if you discover unanticipated interests or resources, you may be able to change them.

Weekly Plans

Unless you teach infants and very young toddlers, you will also sketch out planned activities each week for each day. Teachers vary in how much detail they plan. Many write a weekly calendar to share with others and keep track of what happens next. Others write more detailed plans with purpose statements and objectives for each activity in a day or week. Many teachers plan activities for specific children in their group, particularly if the group includes children with special needs.

The schedule of regular daily activities such as story time, circle, and outdoor time, and special events such as cooking and field trips, can provide the structure for daily and weekly plans. As you plan, you will consider the skills and concepts that you want children to develop throughout the days and week ahead. You will think about ways to include learning centers such as art, science, math, blocks, and dramatic play. You will also consider what will most benefit specific children.

The detailed written design for a single curriculum event is usually called an *activity plan* in preschools and a *lesson plan* in elementary schools and special education settings. Activity plans specify objectives, list needed materials, describe teaching procedures, and outline ways to evaluate success in achieving the objectives. They

should be easy to follow, specific, complete, and helpful. You can think of an activity plan as a recipe. It tells you each essential step but assumes that you know the basics.

Carefully thinking through the purpose and sequence of an activity helps to ensure success. When your planning is good you will express yourself clearly to children and feel more comfortable in teaching. Because this process is so valuable you will practice writing many detailed activity plans during your preparation to become an early childhood educator. We give our students a basic activity plan outline (see Figure 11.2) to use in planning activities.

Figure 11.2 **Activity Plan Outline**

Activity Name and Brief Description	
Curriculum Area	
Who It's For	(age and number of children)
Rationale	(why have you chosen this activity for these children at this time?)
Objectives	(experiences, skills, knowledge, or attitudes you want children to gain) By participating in this activity the children will . . .
Big Ideas	(major understandings if this is part of an integrated study)
Preparation	(what you need—materials, equipment, space, time required)
Procedure	(what you do to teach)
	Introduction: (how you will get children interested and help them know what to do)
	Teaching Steps: (what you will do and say, step-by-step, to teach children the content during the activity)
	Closure: (what you will do or say to summarize the activity and help children make a transition to another activity)
How to Assess	(what children will say or do that shows the objectives were met)
How to Document	(what to collect to show children's learning: observations, work samples, photographs, etc.)
Evaluation	(what worked, what didn't work, what you might do differently next time)

Rationale and Curriculum Area: Why This Activity?

The first step in the creation of a written activity plan is to decide what you want to accomplish and choose an activity that will fulfill your purpose. We ask our college students to answer the question, "Why have you chosen this activity for this child/ these children, at this time?" This question helps you make sure that what you are doing has some meaningful connection to the children.

Be sure to identify the primary curriculum area that the activity addresses. Although young children learn in integrated ways, identifying the curriculum area is helpful for a number of reasons. When you are clear about which area of development and learning you are primarily addressing, you are more likely to accomplish your purpose. For example, children engaged in a finger painting activity are developing sensory awareness (physical development), learning about color mixing (science), expressing feelings and ideas through art media (art), and providing a stimulus for conversation (language). If your purpose is helping children express feelings and ideas through art media, you will want to preserve their efforts and you will be sure to have good quality paint and paper. You will target many of your comments and teaching to help children be aware of how their work expresses a feeling or idea ("Your swirls of gray remind me of a stormy cloud."). If your purpose is enhancing children's sensory awareness, you might use colored shaving cream on a tray that can be easily hosed off and which leaves no lasting documentation of the feelings and ideas expressed. Again, your comments and teaching will be targeted: "How does the paint feel against your fingers? Is it slick or sticky? Sniff it. What does it remind you of?".

Since adults often cannot perceive the educational content of the play activities that form such a large part of the early childhood curriculum, an important part of your professional role is clearly articulating the area of learning and the educational purpose of every activity that you do with children (whether or not you have written a plan for it). Being able to do so distinguishes you as a professional and a teacher.

Objectives: What Children Gain

Every written activity has specific objectives: the attitudes, skills, knowledge, and experiences you want to help children acquire. It is rare for a single activity to "teach" a skill, understanding, or attitude for all time. Instead think of objectives as drops of rain contributing to filling a lake.

A plan's objectives describe its intended outcomes in terms of the experiences, attitudes, skills, or knowledge that you want children to acquire. For example, for a music activity you might write the following objectives:

By participating in this activity, children will:

- Learn new vocabulary to name musical instruments (maracas, rainstick, guiro)
- Develop skill in playing maracas, rainsticks, and guiros with care and with attention to the rhythm and tempo of a song
- Develop beginning appreciation for music from an unfamiliar culture

Objectives may include involvement, awareness, and appreciation as well as concepts, understandings, and skills to be acquired. The objectives should match the overall purpose and rationale. They should be reasonable for the scope of the activity. It is reasonable for a music activity to help children begin to develop appreciation for music from an unfamiliar culture. It is not reasonable to expect that same music activity to help children to be accepting of people who are different from themselves.

What do you think the teacher's objectives were in the activity on comparing birds? In the activity on cracking eggs?

Objectives can be thought of as progressing from simple to complex (see Figure 11.3). Simple objectives involve recalling and identifying. More complex objectives involve making connections, understanding relationships, solving problems by combining what is known and evaluating (Bloom 1964). As you write objectives it is useful to consider whether your objectives and your activities are helping children to acquire more complex skills. For example, in the objectives for the music activity described above, the first objective (learning the names of instruments) is a simple objective—recall; the second objective involves application (playing instruments); and the third (appreciating diverse music) is more complex and involves evaluation. If your plan is a part of an integrated study you will note which of the major understandings the activity will help children to know.

When you first begin to write plans you may find that writing objectives is not easy. There are many things to consider. Our college students find it helpful to look at a number of beginnings to objectives (see Figure 11.4) to get started.

Objectives that precisely describe a behavior are called *behavioral objectives*. They describe specific behaviors, the conditions under which they take place, and the criteria for success ("when presented with five sheets of paper with lines drawn down the center, the child will cut at least one sheet of paper along the line"). Behavioral objectives are often used in special education. Behavioral objectives leave little room for individual choice, require all children to be at the same place at the end of a lesson, and do not allow for spontaneity or creativity. They are not consistent with the belief that children must construct knowledge from their own active involvement with materials and experiences (Lawton 1988). Since they sometimes

Figure 11.3 **Bloom's Taxonomy of Educational Objectives**

	Level	What It Is
Least complex ← Most complex	Recall	The ability to repeat or recognize a concept or skill
	Comprehension	Understanding and the ability to explain what is known
	Application	The ability to use what is known
	Analysis	The ability to make connections, see patterns, or understand interrelationships
	Synthesis	The ability to integrate and recombine
	Evaluation	The ability to assess, critique, or appraise based on specific criteria

Source: Summarized from Bloom, Mesia, & Krathwohl (1964).

Figure 11.4 **Examples of Beginnings for Objectives**

Knowledge	Skill	Attitude	Experience
Learn about . . .	Practice . . .	Develop awareness of . . .	Try . . .
Gain understanding of . . .	Develop skill in . . .	Enjoy . . .	Hear . . .
Describe . . .	Begin to be able to . . .	Develop a dispostion to . . .	See . . .
Recognize . . .	Demonstrate . . .	Be sensitive to . . .	Taste . . .
Sort . . .	Show . . .	Be respectful of . . .	Feel . . .
Identify . . .	Differentiate . . .	Appreciate . . .	Smell . . .

focus on trivial though achievable goals, they can lead teachers to emphasize less important aspects of activities and lose track of important learning that isn't observable or measurable.

Preparation: What You Need

The next step in writing a plan is to begin to think through what you will need for your activity. Often the difference between an effective planning success and a failure is having the right materials, equipment, space, and time. Make a list of the materials that you need to prepare, borrow, or buy so that you have them ahead of time. Think about the space and equipment you need, the best time in the schedule for the activity, and how much time to allow. Think about what else is needed. Does anyone need to be called or alerted? Do you need to cut paper or cover the table with newspaper? Plan for it.

As you think through the steps of the activity and write down the procedures, you may discover that there are additional things you need. You will go back and add these to the *Preparation* section of your activity plan.

Procedure: What You Do

Teaching procedures spell out what you will do and say, and in what order. They are the heart of an activity plan. The steps of a teaching plan always include at least three parts—an introduction, teaching steps, and closure.

The *introduction* describes how you will get children's attention, engage their interest, and let them know what to do. For many activities the introduction can be very simple ("I brought a new game to share with you today. It's this box. I put something soft inside. You get to put your hand in here and guess what it is.").

Think through what children need to understand and be able to do in order to participate in the activity. You may need to introduce an unfamiliar word or concept, or teach a skill. If the activity involves an item that is novel or highly attractive to the children, plan a way for them to get acquainted with it before you begin teaching ("Each person will get a turn to pat the puppet before I tell you the puppet story."). Skilled teachers know that it is important to give children lots of time for a new experience. In fact, simply introducing an item may be an entire activity. One of the most common mistakes of novice teachers is to introduce many intriguing and exciting objects at one time ("Here are three new puppets, a cape to wear, and a magic wand to use in our story."). They are then surprised when children focus on the "things" rather than the content they were planning to teach.

Teaching steps describe what you will do and say to accomplish your objectives. The steps should match the objectives you wrote and should be appropriate to the age and stage of development of the children. The amount of detail can vary. You need at least an outline of the basic steps, simply described with enough information that you (or a colleague) will be able to use the plan again at a later date. Beginning teachers, and anyone planning an activity that is particularly complex, should map out what to say and questions to ask to support the objectives.

The *closure* of an activity sums up the learning in some way that makes sense for children. It may be a statement you make ("You really knew a lot about birds.") or it may be a way for children to show something that they know and make a *transition* ("Think of a bird and fly like your bird to the playground."). A well-thought-out closure and a smooth transition help you to focus children on what they know and are able to do.

Assessment and Documentation

What children do and say during and following an activity gives evidence of what they have learned. The last part of a written activity focuses on what to look for in children to indicate that they have gained the knowledge, skill, or attitudes that were described in the objectives, and ideas for effective ways to document children's learning.

In our music activity example, we look for whether children are attentive to the music and ask questions about it, or ask to have it repeated; whether they move to the music played; whether they play the instruments in ways that are appropriately gentle yet vigorous enough to make sound and rhythmic enough to keep time; and whether they began to recognize and use the names of the instruments. This growth could be documented through anecdotal records (see Chapter 5), through video or audio recordings, or even through children's drawings and journals. We like to use an anecdotal record form like the sample included in Figure 11.5—completed for our bird study example—to record children's responses.

Figure 11.5   **Sample Activity Plan with Anecdotal Records**

Activity Name and Brief Description	*The Names of the Birds Workjob* (children match photographs with names of birds to photographs of the birds and to the printed names of the birds)
Curriculum Area	Literacy
Who It's For	The Scary Monster Group (nine 4–5 yr. olds)
Rationale	The children are highly aware of the different birds in the yard and what they are called. Megan, Jonah, Janae, and Edwin are particularly intrigued by letters and words.
Objectives	By participating in this activity the children will develop . . . • understanding that print has meaning that is consistent • awareness that words can be written down • ability to make discriminations between different letters and begin to connect sounds to letters • vocabulary for birds (beak, bulbul, cardinal, crest, dove, egret, finch, golden, heron, java, mannikin, mejiro, northern, plover, saffron, sparrow, tail, talons, vented, waxbill, whiskered, wings)
Big Ideas	1) There are lots of different birds with many colors, sizes, and shapes. 2) All birds have feathers.
Preparation (What You Need)	*Time:* Introduce at small group and make available at activity time 10:15–11:15 *Materials:* Workjob in a box *Space:* Game shelf and table with chairs *How to prepare:* Download photographs of birds from the Internet. Make all the pictures the same size (about 2.5″ × 2.5″). Print two copies of each one with the name of the bird underneath. Also, print the birds' name separately. Cut out and laminate all the pieces. Modify a box (or find one) so it has three sections, one for each of the three sets: pictures and words, pictures only, and words only. Decorate the box with pictures of birds and the title of the workjob. Cover with clear contact paper.
Procedure (What You Do)	*Introduction:* At small group time show the children the game. Spread out several sets of the cards. Pick up one card with familiar bird pictured. Invite the children to look at it and name the bird. Tell them the name of the bird is written underneath the picture. (Children may want to name all the birds.) Explain: *There is a matching picture for this bird.* Ask: *Can you find it?* When they have found a matching picture (or several, depending on interest), say: *There's something even trickier with this game. There's a word that matches without a picture. Can you find it?* Once the word has been found explain that the game will be available for them to play with during activity time. Note: *You can play this on your own, with a friend, or with a teacher.* *Teaching Steps:* As children play the game observe and help as needed. • Extend the learning by saying things like: *That one says RED CRESTED CARDINAL. Can you find another bird with RED in its name?* Or: *That one is a Mmmmmmmejiro—I wonder what its name starts with.* • Encourage children who are more able to help those who have difficulty: *I saw Megan find the Northern Cardinal's name. Ask her if she can help you.* • When a child is having difficulty, suggest that the child just match the pictures. If a child is having an easy time, invite them to match the word to the word. *Closure:* Based on the children's ability with the game, play a putting-away version of it, saying something like: *You tell me one to put away and then I'll tell you one to put away.* Comment on the skill and competence of the child: *Wow, you know which one is the Northern Cardinal. I wonder if I'll be able to get the next one.* Or: *You know 10 different birds!*

Figure 11.5 **Sample Activity Plan with Anecdotal Records** (*Continued*)

How to Assess	Look and listen for children examining the words and making matches.
	Look and listen for children saying the name of the bird and looking for initial consonants.
	Listen for children using bird names and related vocabulary.
	Listen for children commenting on the colors and characteristics of the pictured birds.
How to Document	Write anecdotal records to document the individual children's responses to the game and literacy abilities.
Evaluation	TOO MANY PICTURES, TOO SMALL. Limit the number when introducing game. Add a set of pet bird pictures.

Anecdotal Records

Activity: *The Names of the Birds Workjob*

Child: Megan

Megan played the game first. She matched all of the pictures, then she matched about half of the words. When Janae came to play she commented: *I know how to do this I don't need any help.*

Child: Keila

Keila didn't seem to be very interested in the game. She stopped by to look at it and matched the cardinal pictures, but left shortly and did not put the pieces away.

Child: Jonah

Jonah wanted a teacher to play the game with him. When the teacher had "difficulty" finding a piece he laughed aloud and found it, saying: *I am very good at this.*

Child: Edwin

Edwin took out each different set (pictures and words, pictures only, words only) and lined them up. Then he matched all of them. He did not interact with any other child during the activity.

Child: Janae

Janae did about half the game matching pictures and words. She asked: *Why isn't the northern cardinal called a red cardinal?* Janae worked with Megan.

Child: Brandy

Brandy smiled a lot during the introduction to the activity and made several relevant comments (noting that the egret does not come to the bird feeder and that there were two kinds of sparrows). She did not try the game.

Implementing an Activity Plan

A good plan helps you teach in the same way that a good recipe helps you cook. However, children are not as predictable as flour and salt. The most beautifully planned activity can fail miserably if you are not responsive to the children. If you went to a lot of trouble to write an activity plan you may feel committed to using it just the way it's written. Just as a cook must adjust to the tastes of the diners, the characteristics of the ingredients, and the equipment, a teacher must adjust to the children and the circumstances. Experienced teachers know that they will need to make modifications in response to children's interests and needs. Their teaching resembles a dance in which the children are their partners. They observe and respond to the children—and the children respond to them.

Inexperienced teachers often find it difficult to be flexible in implementing a plan. For example, we recently observed a student attempt to lead a group of 4-year-olds in a movement activity (walking as a group like a centipede with many legs). The children all had many things to say about centipedes and did not attend to the well planned activity. The novice teacher became flustered by the children's inattention to her activity and was unable to incorporate their ideas into it or guide the discussion into the activity. With more confidence and attention to the children, the discussion could have led to the activity instead of away from it.

Evaluation: What Worked and What Didn't Work

Whether you plan an activity with children or an afternoon at the beach, you evaluate your plan. Did it go well? Could I have done it better? Should I do it again? Did I accomplish what I intended? After you have written and implemented a plan, take a few moments to reflect on what you did and how children responded. Taking time to reflect ensures that the learning experience you planned for children also becomes a learning experience for you. Evaluating your planning and implementation is different from assessing whether the children acquired the knowledge, skills, and attitudes you laid out in the objectives.

Sometimes an apparent planning disaster may be the result of overstimulating materials, timing mistakes (not allowing enough time for children to explore materials, or asking children to wait and listen when they need to move and do), poor room arrangement, insufficient opportunities for needed physical activity, or an activity that is too challenging or not challenging enough for the children. Modified and tried again, the plan may prove sound. But if you never think about what went wrong you will never be able to figure out what went wrong and make those modifications.

It may actually be even harder to evaluate a success. Were the children engaged in the activity because the materials were interesting, because you were responsive to the children, or because Jon was absent today? Evaluate your successes as well as your failures.

To help you remember, it is worthwhile to make a note of anything you would add or do differently on the plan. Reflecting in this way is usually a requirement for students but it is good practice for all teachers. Then when you go back to your plans, you will remember what happened last time. Reflecting and evaluating closes the planning circle.

Writing Plans in the Real World

When you become a teacher, will you write plans for every activity? It would be impossible and a little silly to spend many hours writing plans for everything you do with children. Written activity plans are useful and may be necessary when clarity and sequence are crucial or where procedure or content is complex or unfamiliar. An activity such as reading a simple, familiar story will be included in a weekly plan but generally does not call for a detailed written activity plan. Locating the book, reviewing it, and spending a few moments thinking about questions to ask and how to structure discussion may be enough preparation. However, you should be *able* to write a clear plan for even a simple activity.

> **Reflect on planning for children**
>
> Think about a time when you planned an activity to do with children. What happened? How did having a plan help you? What happened that surprised you? Would you use your plan again? What would you do differently?

As you gain experience, you may want to use an abbreviated format when you write activity plans (see Figure 11.6). We like to keep these so that they can be easily retrieved and used again on 5-by-8-inch cards that can be stored in notebooks, file boxes, or on metal rings. Digital storage, on computer disk, is useful because material can be easily revised. Since technology changes you may find that your digital version of a plan is unreadable in a few years, so it is wise to always keep a hard copy of your plans.

Experienced teachers almost always plan for each week by writing down activity titles, when they will be implemented, and noting what will be needed. They identify objectives for the activities, though not all teachers write these down. These few notes may guide them through most activities.

Planning an Integrated Study

As we have said, we believe integrated planning is the most effective way to plan curriculum for older preschool, kindergarten, or primary school children as well as an

Figure 11.6 **Short Activity Plan Outline**

CURRICULUM PLANNING

Activity Name and Curriculum Area:

Objective(s):

What You Need:

What You Do:

interesting, exciting, and satisfying experience for teachers. In a well-chosen and well-designed integrated study, children have real experiences with the topic. These real experiences are the foundation of the plan. Children then read about, reflect on, represent, and re-create the real experiences through dramatic play, block building, discussions, writing, drawing, art, music, movement, measuring, graphing, and mapping. Through their investigation of a topic, children develop skills in sensing and moving, thinking and problem solving, communicating, creating, and working and playing with others.

An effective integrated study starts with the investigation of something that is real and important to young children. It needs to be based on experiences and ideas that are interesting and complex enough to engage both children and adults since it will last several weeks to several months. It is created in a dynamic process that involves initial planning, providing experiences, observing children, and then planning additional opportunities for learning. When you are planning such a study it is important to stay open to possibilities that emerge from children's ideas and interests. A kindergarten teacher we know once planned an integrated study of gardening for her class. A swarm of bees settled in the children's play structure causing much fear. After thoughtful deliberation the teacher abandoned her gardening plan and embarked on a study of bees. The children's fear of the bees gave way to fascination as they learned about the social structure of the hive and the production of honey and watched a beekeeper relocate the hive to a site farther removed from the classroom.

Though integrated planning is widely accepted among early childhood educators it has sometimes come under fire. These criticisms are typically aimed at the *way* in which the integrated curriculum is planned and implemented. Specifically, integrated curriculum is criticized when it is short-lived (a week or two for a plan) so children can't explore a topic in depth, when it is planned far in advance and repeated each year and is not meaningful; when the topic cannot be experienced in real ways (e.g., pirates, outer space, dinosaurs); when the topic is "cute" but not actually worthy of serious study (e.g., Mickey Mouse's birthday, teddy bears' picnic); when it is used in a shallow way without developing understanding (e.g., playing with plastic bugs and making ants on a log without looking at what insects are like and their role in the environment); when children do not have open-ended materials to reconstruct or represent their understanding; or when it is used inflexibly and teachers go on with the plan despite children's changing interests. This kind of superficial planning is often associated with the words *unit* and *theme,* and for this reason we now avoid using those terms.

Children's Center Weekly Plans

Week of: April 19

Curriculum Focus: Birds

Big Ideas: Birds move their bodies in different ways—some fly, some hop, some walk, and some swim.

	Monday	Tuesday	Wednesday	Thursday	Friday
8:50 Story	One Crow	What Makes a Bird a Bird	Do Like a Duck Does		Tough Boris
9:00–10:00 Outdoor Special Activities	**Parachute Play** • to develop physical coordination • to engage in social cooperation • to understand cause and effect	**Waffle Blocks** • to learn to work together cooperatively • to build large motor coordination	**Woodworking** • to develop and use measurement concepts • to develop concepts of shape and space *Also: Shaving Cream Finger Painting*	**Field Trip!**	**Bubbles in the Water Table** • to develop sensory awareness • to engage in social interactions • to understand cause and effect
10:00–10:20 Scary Monsters Group	**Sculpting Lesson/Demonstration—Birds** • to develop creative skills • to explore bird shapes and body parts	**Sculpting Lesson/Demonstration—Birds** • to develop creative skills • to explore bird shapes and body parts	**Discussing Trip** • to prepare for our field trip to Waimea Valley • to remind children of safety rules • to build understanding of place • to develop the ability to hypothesize	**To Nature Park**	**Trip Book** • to express understanding about birds • to engage in literacy activities
10:00–10:10 Elephant Groovers Group	**Bird Movement** • to develop the ability to create and express through movement • to express understanding about birds • to increase coordination	**Bird Movement** • to develop the ability to create and express through movement • to express understanding about birds • to increase coordination	**Discussing Trip** • to prepare for our field trip to Waimea Valley • to remind children of safety rules • to develop awareness of place	Come to school wearing: • real shoes • bug repellant, if desired	**Trip Book** • to express understanding about birds • to increase awareness of writing as communication
10:20–11:30 Indoor Special Activities	**Clay with Sculpting Tools** • to develop the ability to create and express in a variety of art media • to use art elements of shape and design	**Clay with Sculpting Tools** • to develop the ability to create and express in a variety of art media • to use art elements of color and design	**Feather Collage** (also clay for two) • to develop the ability to create and express in a variety of art media • to use art elements of color and design	**Be here by 8:00**	**Play Dough Collage in Plastic Lids** • to develop the ability to create and express in a variety of art media • to use art elements of color and design
11:30 Lunch Circle (large group)	**Creative Movement** • to develop the ability to create and express through movement • to develop vocabulary • to increase coordination	**Creative Movement** • to develop the ability to create and express through movement • to develop vocabulary • to increase coordination	**Bird Songs** • to develop the ability to create and express through music • to develop vocabulary	**We will be back by 1:30**	**Baby Chicks Are Crying** • to develop the ability to create and express through music • to develop vocabulary

Ongoing activities available all week:

Outside Lanai: Sensory Table, Outdoor Table Activities, Easels, Hollow Blocks and Crates

Yard: Play Structure, Sand Play, Trikes

Inside: Unit Block Area, Pretend Play Area, Puzzles/Toys/Light Table Area, Library and Writing Center, Science and Workjobs Area

Good integrated planning helps children investigate meaningful ideas. It is appropriate to the individuals and group, flexible, and meaningful. In Chapter 3 you read about two program approaches (Bank Street and Reggio Emilia) that are based on integrated curriculum.

Select a Topic of Study

The first step in integrated planning is the choice of a topic of study. Meaningful thematic curriculum based on a well chosen topic helps children make connections. Children's lives and their environment—their families, cultures, community, or elements of the local environment—are good sources. Exploration of these kinds of topics can contribute to children's awareness and understanding of the world and themselves as well as heightening their sense of uniqueness and pride in their families and community. While these larger goals are being realized, children are exploring, experimenting, discussing experiences, building with blocks, manipulating materials, writing, and cooking.

Is one topic any better or worse than any other topic for the purpose of integrating curriculum? The best topics for an integrated curriculum study engage children. When you have chosen well there is an almost magical quality. Children are focused, energized, and intensely engaged in the business of learning. In order for this to happen, the topic must meet several criteria.

First, it must be *of interest* to children, teachers, and families. For example, when the teacher as well as several mothers of children in a 4-year-old class became pregnant, a curriculum study of babies and birth was a natural focus. The teacher brought in many books, made a sequencing game of fetal development, helped the children compose a simple lullaby, had babies and puppies visit, and took the children on a trip to the local hospital to view the nursery. The children built the hospital in the block area, created a nursery in the dramatic play area, and painted and drew many pictures and wrote many stories about babies. All the children—not just the new big brothers and sisters—learned a great deal about how babies develop and the ways that families care for infants. They were simultaneously developing fine motor and hand-eye coordination; understanding of letters and numbers; discrimination of size, shape, and color; and a myriad of other skills and understandings.

Do you think birds is a good subject for an integrated curriculum study for this group of children? What do you see that supports your conclusion?

Next, a topic of study must be *appropriate* for the group of children for whom it is planned—it should reflect the way they learn, their abilities, and their issues of concern. The first question you should ask yourself in selecting a theme is: Can I give children direct experience of this topic? If direct experience is not accessible, the theme—no matter how interesting—will not help young children gain genuine understanding. This is especially important for younger children.

In addition, you should make sure that the topic of study you choose is right for the children's age and stage of development: *simple* enough to be understood but *complex* and interesting enough to be explored in some depth. It should involve concepts and skills that provide the right level of challenge. We call this the "three bears" principle (not too easy, not too hard, just "right").

Many topics can be used for successful integration of subject areas. We have seen teachers of preschoolers plan successful integrated studies of topics such as water, food, trees, animals, insects, family, self, celebration, rain, gardens, and farms. We have seen teachers of older children use these same topics with more depth, and also more complex topics such as life cycles, the ocean, harbors, grocery stores, hospitals, and bakeries. Figure 11.7 provides you with some criteria to help you to choose wisely.

When you have selected a topic, write down the reasons for your choice. These reasons are your statement of *rationale*. Having a brief written statement of rationale will help you in explaining your curriculum to others and will help you in documenting your work. As mentioned earlier in this chapter, the topic that we will use as

Figure 11.7 **Some Questions to Ask About Selecting a Topic for Integrating Curriculum**

Is this topic . . .
- Interesting to children and teachers?
- Meaningful and relevant to these children at this time?
- Worthwhile—important to know about if you are a young child?
- Appropriate—can it be experienced by children in real ways (can it be visited, viewed, touched, smelled, manipulated)? Are the central concepts understandable to young children?
- Consistent with the philosophy and goals of the program and the values of the families and community?
- Substantial enough to allow for an in-depth study?
- Flexible enough to allow for a variety of interests and abilities?
- The right size—not too big to be understood, and not so small as to be trivial (what we call the "three bears" principle)?

Does this topic . . .
- Include ideas that can be taught through direct experiences?
- Help children to acquire greater understanding and appreciation of themselves, others, or the world?
- Integrate experience and subject matter?
- Contribute to many aspects of development?
- Generate a variety of activities and learning in all areas of development and in a broad range of subject areas?
- Encourage children to generalize and think more abstractly?
- Seem to be realistic in terms of resources available?
- Allow for and encourage family input and participation?

an example of integrated curriculum is a study of birds. The teachers of the 3- and 4-year-olds at the Leeward Community College Children's Center, along with Eva and her college students, selected this topic because:

- They had observed children's interest in the abundant bird life that visited the school playground and the surrounding community.
- A nest of baby birds had fallen into their yard and the class was caring for them.
- They had pet chickens, which were an ongoing source of interest to the children.
- The staff themselves were interested in birds, and both teachers had pet birds.
- Four families in the class raised birds or had birds as pets.

The topic of birds was clearly interesting, was appropriate for the community and families, and came with abundant resources. It also met all the other criteria that are described in Figure 11.7. The statement of rationale for the study was as follows:

In considering what is important for the 3- to 5-year-olds in our class to learn, we selected the topic Birds. *We made this choice because we observed children's interest in the many birds in our environment; there are many resources available in our community to support a study of birds; and it will serve to further our goals of helping children to become active, creative learners who appreciate and respect their environment and other people.*

Not all topics are effective for generating meaningful learning experiences. A topic can give a surface appearance of connecting ideas but do nothing to enhance children's understanding. We once observed 3-year-olds "studying" the letter M by making _magazine_ collages and _muffins_ and by coloring a picture of a _monkey_. When we asked the children what they had been learning, they responded that they had been gluing paper, cooking, and coloring. Their teacher corrected them, saying that they had been studying M. This approach failed to integrate children's learning because it focused on an abstract symbol that was not of real interest to an inquisitive group of 3-year-olds.

Similarly, just because children "like" or are fascinated by something does not necessarily make it a good topic. For example, after viewing a movie about pirates, children may seem to like and be interested in pirates. The reality of pirates at any time in history is quite chilling and has little to do with the swashbuckling fiction seen in movies and on television. It would be impossible to provide curriculum on pirates that had integrity (honesty) and that was appropriate to young children.

A good topic allows children to develop real understanding and mastery. A child might delight in red flowers, and enjoy mixing red and yellow while finger painting, but this does not make "red" a good topic of study. However, it might lead you to design an integrated thematic plan around the topic of flowers or rainbows. Remember not to confuse a subject area (e.g., math), an important way of learning (e.g., reading books), or an attribute that is related to many different topics (e.g., color) with a topic to be studied.

Often holidays are used as the basis for integrated curriculum. Some holidays have an impact on children's lives and can be studied in terms of culture, the joys of family celebrations, and their impact on children. Others have little or no appropriate content for young children. Even meaningful holidays used as topics are made trivial and inappropriate if they are reduced to look-alike crafts and commercial symbols. The study of religious holidays in public schools has come to have little meaning because the religious content has had to be excised based on the necessity of separating church and state.

An integrated study should be a source of genuine learning and not a way to sugarcoat inappropriate activities. Worksheets covered with dinosaurs or bees used as part of a "theme" are not even distantly related to meaningful learning or good integrated planning. When we encounter colleagues who dismiss thematic planning or unit planning as superficial or inappropriate, we know that this is the kind of plan they are thinking of.

> **Reflect on an integrated study in your childhood**
>
> Remember a time when your teachers planned an integrated study for your class. What did you learn about? What do you remember most about the study? How was it different from other ways of learning? What did you enjoy? Is there anything you wish your teachers had done differently?

Look at Your Purpose

Why have you selected a study? What is your purpose? The goals (broad statements of desired ends toward which teaching is directed) of all curriculum for young children include helping them to acquire knowledge, skills, and positive attitudes toward themselves, learning, and other people. The acquisition of "dispositions," what Lilian Katz calls "habits of mind" (Katz 1993), is another integrated curriculum goal. As you consider the topic you have chosen you will identify goals for your study. For instance, consider these goals for a curriculum study of birds:

To help children to develop:

- Increased knowledge of birds, their characteristics, and habits
- A disposition to be curious and inquiring about the birds in their environment
- An attitude of respect for, and disposition to be kind and humane to, birds and other living creatures
- Skills in language, literacy, inquiry, physical coordination, and creative expression

In what ways do you see the goals of the bird study being accomplished?

Identify Major Understandings

Once you have selected a topic and spelled out the goals of the study you will gather resources, read and reflect, then identify the *major understandings* (which we also call *big ideas*) that you wish children to acquire. Major understandings are the important concepts, related to the topic, that the activities in an integrated study are designed to help children acquire. They give direction to the study and help you to be clear about what you are intending to teach.

By taking some time to read about and reflect on the topic and identify the major understandings, you will have a guide to make sure your activity choices will help children to gain knowledge. This is a critical part of the planning process. Teachers often assume that since they are older and more experienced than children that they do not need to learn anything about a topic in order to teach. Background reading is often overlooked in the excitement of generating lots of activities. While you do not need to know everything about a topic in order to plan, it is necessary to learn something, particularly if the topic is outside your area of expertise. Children deserve to have accurate information given to them. Even if the topic is something "simple" such as studying "me" you will need to gather information on the children and their families.

We often use a process with students and staff to identify the major understandings for an integrated study. For example, the teachers and students at the LCC Children's Center, after researching birds on the Web and reading informational books about birds (including Mae Garelick's *What Makes a Bird a Bird*, the National Audubon Society's *First Field Guide to Birds*, the Hawaii Audubon Society's *Hawaii's Birds*, and the Dorling Kindersley *Introduction to Birds*), wrote down all the words they could think of about birds on slips of paper. Their work looked something like this:

> *aviaries, baby birds, bird feeders, by the freeway, cardinals, chickens, cliffs, colors, conures, crowing, ducks, egg farm, eggs, egrets, endangered birds, farms, feathers, flying, frittatas, guano, Hawaii birds, homes, hopping, incubator, mainland birds, migrating, mynah birds, nene goose, nests, omelets, parakeets, parrots, peacocks, pets, playground, seabirds, singing, state bird, swans, swimming, talking, Thanksgiving turkey, trees, walking*

They then sorted the words into four to six piles and assigned a category to each pile. The papers were sorted several different ways and the content was considered. These were the results:

- Different kinds of birds: *chickens, egrets, parakeets, parrots, conures, peacocks, endangered birds, ducks, swans, mainland birds, Hawaii birds, cardinals, nene goose, mynah birds, crowing, singing*
- Special things about birds: *flying, feathers, eggs, colors, nests, baby birds, incubators*
- Where birds live: *sea birds, cliffs, homes, aviaries, trees, farms, playground, by the freeway*
- How birds move: *flying, hopping, swimming, walking, migrating*
- Birds in our lives: *pets, Thanksgiving turkey, feathers, guano, chicken manure, omelets, bird feeders, egg farm, state bird*

They then thought about what they wanted children to know about each category and wrote a statement of major understandings:

Major understandings for a curriculum study of birds:

- There are lots of different birds with many colors, sizes, and shapes.
- All birds have feathers and lay eggs to create baby birds.
- Birds move in different ways—most fly, some hop, some walk, some swim.

- Birds are part of people's lives—some can be pets, some give us food and feathers, some help the plants to grow.
- Birds live in different places where they can find food, be safe, and raise their young.

We write "big ideas" in simple language such as a child might use or understand. The point of this activity is not to think of words that are *taught*—instead, they should help you to help children to *construct* these understandings for themselves.

Generate Ideas for Activities

The next step is to generate ideas for activities that help children to develop the major understandings that you have identified. For many years we have used a system called *mind-mapping* to begin our planning. In a mind-map you place a topic in a circle in the center of a piece of chart paper, off of which numerous lines are drawn to map ideas related to the topic. You will see similar charts referred to as *webs* or *curriculum maps*. The process of mind-mapping or webbing is useful because it allows you to add ideas as they arise without being concerned about their order or initial organization. When the map is completed you can examine each item to see how it fits in the whole plan.

In our own planning we begin by selecting trips and resource visitors because these may determine the direction of the plan and other activities that we will use. If trips require reservations it is also the time to make contact and set up the trip(s), making sure to plan an initial trip early in the study. Ideas for other activities that support the major understandings are then webbed. This is also a time to make a list of some of the new vocabulary, especially "rare words" that will be introduced and used during the study. Make sure to identify some activities that help children to acquire each of the understandings (see Figure 11.8).

Figure 11.8 **Initial Curriculum Activity Brainstorming Web**

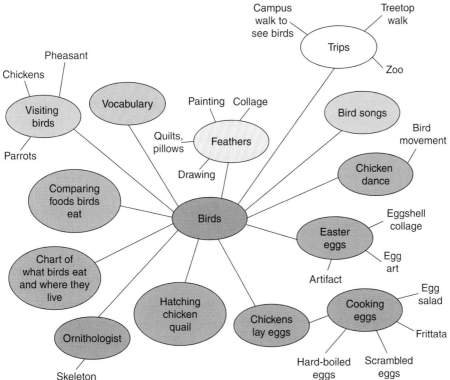

The value of different activities should be assessed with consideration of the goals, the extent to which the activities support the major understandings, and the resources and time required. If you find that there is a big idea for which you can think of no age-appropriate activities or if you think of good activities that do not seem to fit within your big ideas, it means you need to go back and reconsider the big ideas.

The activities that you will initially web are just the beginning. As you explore the topic with children you will plan additional activities, while activities you generated at the beginning may seem less feasible or appropriate as you get involved in the study. Your initial web is just the starting place.

Enrich the Environment

Following the initial planning process, you will begin to gather and create the resources you need to teach. This is the time when you will reassess the pictures, puppets, dramatic play and block props, games, puzzles and toys that are available and select some that will help children make connections to the topic. You will make a trip to the library to gather good children's literature on the topic. Be sure to ask a librarian to help you to find good resources. Tell families about the study and invite them to participate by sharing the resources that they have. Your local museum or art gallery may have prints, posters, or artifacts that can be borrowed to enrich the environment. Schedule trips and resource people and begin to plot activities for the first weekly plans.

How do you see the study of birds reflected in the learning environment of the classroom?

A good curriculum study is present in almost every classroom center. For example, in the bird curriculum the teachers at the LCC Children's Center added the items in Figure 11.9 to the environment.

Make the Plan

Once you have goals, major understandings, and a list of ideas you have generated, you are ready to organize them for teaching. Plan how you will introduce the topic to children and families. Plan ways to bring real experience into the study right away (a trip;

Figure 11.9 **Environment Additions for a Curriculum on Birds**

Blocks	**Dramatic Play**	**Library**
Bird figures (wooden and plastic)	Bird hoods	Storybooks on birds (see book list)
Stuffed bird toys (shared with dramatic play)	Bird puppets	Informational books for children on birds and eggs
Art prints of birds in a nest	Stuffed bird toys (shared with blocks)	Nature guides on birds
Wooden flying goose mobile	Mobile with origami cranes	Poster: bird book
	Plastic eggs	Pillows with bird print fabric
	Art prints of birds	
Science Center	**Manipulative Toys, Puzzles, and Games**	**Writing Center**
Egg poster	Bird puzzles	Birdcage with visiting birds to observe and draw
Egg and feather artifacts and magnifying glass	Workjobs: *1,2,3 Birds* art postcard game; words for birds; egg counting game; egg-to-fledgling seriation game	Art prints of birds
Bird nests		
Brooder house for baby chicks		
Art Area	**Display**	**Outdoors**
Feathers for painting and collage	Bird art and artifacts shelf for displaying objects brought by families and staff, including bird figurines, ostrich egg, feather hatbands, feather fans, painted eggs, and stone eggs	Cards for identifying birds
Eggshells for collage		Bird feeders
Bird visitors for life drawing and collage		Birdhouse
Art prints including birds		Chickens
		Binoculars

a visit from a resource person; making or cooking something; bringing in real animals, plants, or other artifacts). Think about which will make good beginning or introductory activities, which will help children build understanding to use in the middle of the study, and which will help children express and generalize their understanding at the end. Plan ways to involve families in these activities.

Because creating an integrated study plan is a big job, it's a good idea to begin to write a simple guide to refer to as you work. The outline for an integrated study plan in Figure 11.10 suggests some things to include. Remember that you will continue to observe children and plan for each week and day as you go along. The children's responses, teacher's new insights, families' input, and the serendipitous opportunities that you discover will be added to the integrated plan. You will not finish writing your integrated plan until close to the end.

Implement the Study

Once the initial plans are in place and you have started to make your environment reflect the topic, you will start to implement activities. The first activities to implement are those that provide an introduction to the topic. Introductory activities give children

Figure 11.10 **Outline for an Integrated Thematic Study**

1. **Theme:** the topic or focus of the study

2. **Children:** age and characteristics for whom you are planning

3. **Rationale:** why this topic was chosen for these children at this time

4. **Goals:** 3–6 broad statements of desired ends—the attitudes, skills, abilities, and experiences that children are intended to gain by participating in this study

5. **Major understandings:** 4–6 important ideas you intend children to construct by participating in this study, worded as children might understand them, not as objectives

*6. **Resources:** books, articles, and other resources that you used to guide your development of the study

7. **Environment additions:** a list of materials to add to each learning center to support awareness of the theme and the development of the big ideas; be sure to include ideas for blocks, dramatic play, manipulative toys, puzzles and games, art, writing center, library, science area, and outdoors

8. **Trips:** a list of learning trips to give children real experience related to the theme

9. **Activities:**
   a. Introductory activities: how you will introduce the study to children, including the activities that will build *awareness* of the topic
   b. Activities to build *understanding:* a list of activities to encourage exploration, support the development of the major understanding, and build skills
   c. Culminating activities: activities to help children *express* and *generalize* what they have learned, including how you will bring closure to the study

10. **Assessment:** activities and work that will demonstrate children's understanding of the big ideas and ideas for documentation through observation, photography, or the collection of work samples

*Items 6–10 will not be completed until you near the end of the study.

awareness of the topic, through real experience and books. They provide the input that children must have in order to construct understanding of the content.

Some teachers begin the curriculum by interviewing the children, asking them questions such as: What do you know about the topic? What would you like to learn? This activity is also often used as a culminating activity for an integrated study (called K/W/L, which stands for "What do you KNOW? What do you WANT to learn? What have you LEARNED?").

Teachers in elementary schools often use this process to guide the design of a study. While it is a good starting place for planning it must be supplemented with observation of children, reflection, and research. As you can see from the example in Figure 11.11, preschoolers are more able to identify what they know than to identify questions for investigation. Inquiry questions will emerge as they investigate a topic.

In preschool we usually select a more hands-on introduction to a topic. At the LCC Children's Center, teachers introduced the study of birds by bringing pet birds into the classroom and by asking the children what they knew about birds and what they wanted to learn about birds. They took a walk to look for birds in the trees and lawns around the school. During the first weeks they enriched the environment with fine art prints that included birds, puzzles, and workjobs featuring birds, bird toys and puppets for the dramatic play and block areas, and many books about birds. They constructed and put up bird feeders in the yard and added bird feeding (wild and pet) to the jobs that children did each day. During the third week they went on a trip to the local zoo, which had an extensive bird collection.

Figure 11.11   **Example of a K/W/L Chart Made with 4- and 5-Year-Olds**

What do you KNOW about birds?	**What do you WANT to learn about birds?**	**What have you LEARNED about birds?**
Humming birds fly really fast and eat from flowers.	How do peacocks eat?	Peacocks can fly up into the trees.
Some birds have sharp claws that scratch your arm.	What do peacocks look like?	Hornbills eat mice.
Birds peck branches.	How do birds lay eggs? How do eggs become baby birds?	Chickens eat chicken scratch and bread.
Birds drink water.		Baby birds have pink skin.
Birds use their beaks to eat. Cardinals use the tips of their beaks to eat.		Birds have sharp claws to hold onto branches.
Lovebirds sometimes bite you.		Peacocks make their tails big.
A little bird is called a chick.		Some birds can swim.
Baby birds can't fly but they can when they're older.		Baby birds have to peck on the eggs to get out.
Mama birds and daddy birds make nests with hay and sticks—they sit on the eggs to keep them warm.		Big birds have big nests and little birds have little nests.
Some birds chase tractors—they like the bugs.		Cardinals eat papayas.
		Baby birds get real hungry. Their mamas bring them food.
		Some people have pet birds.

Figure 11.12   **A 5-Year-Old's Theory of How a Mother Bird Lays Eggs**

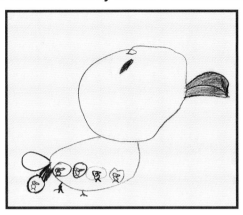

After the initial input, activities to help children build and demonstrate their understanding are implemented. Blocks, art media, dramatic play, music, and book making are all excellent ways for children to construct their understanding and to demonstrate what they are learning. This is a good time for children to have input and discuss their ideas about the topic.

While you are implementing the middle section of the plan it is important to remain open to changes in children's interests and to fortuitous events. For example, the interest that the children showed in birds laying eggs and nesting (see the child's drawing in Figure 11.12, and the photo of block nests on p. 363) convinced the teachers to begin a project incubating and raising quails.

Early in the study the teachers invited families to participate. Over the 3-month course of the study, families brought in pet birds, sewed bird hoods for dramatic play, went on trips to the zoo and a nature preserve, donated a pet cockatiel, made bird feeders with the children, came in to read stories, and loaned artifacts from their cultures, including Japanese origami cranes, Samoan fans, Hawaiian feather leis, and a Chinese platter depicting a peacock.

An integrated study has a life span of its own. You may find that children's interest in the topic deepens, as we saw in the study of birds that we are using as an example. The initial plan for 8 weeks of study extended to end of the school year—3 months. You may find that the study links to another topic, as we saw when a study of water led to a study of the ocean.

Eventually you will draw your study to a close. When you are ready to move on to a new topic it is important to plan closure for the children, families, and the teaching team. A class book or newsletter explaining what was learned, a documentation panel, a scrapbook or video that visibly shows the outcome of the study, or a social event during which children's work and learning are shared with others are good ways to both assess the study and bring it to an end. The study of birds was brought to an end by inviting families to the school for an evening walk to see the birds settling down for the evening, followed by a potluck and a sing-along of all the songs learned about birds during the study. During the evening children's work and documentation panels of the study were displayed and video of the children engaged in the many activities were shown.

For our own documentation when we are teaching children we create a sunburst, a graphic expansion of the original mind-map to show everything that was planned during the unit (see Figure 11.13). We make it an assignment for students in our college classes. Students then share these with one another as valuable resources for their future teaching.

361

Figure 11.13 **Bird Sunburst**

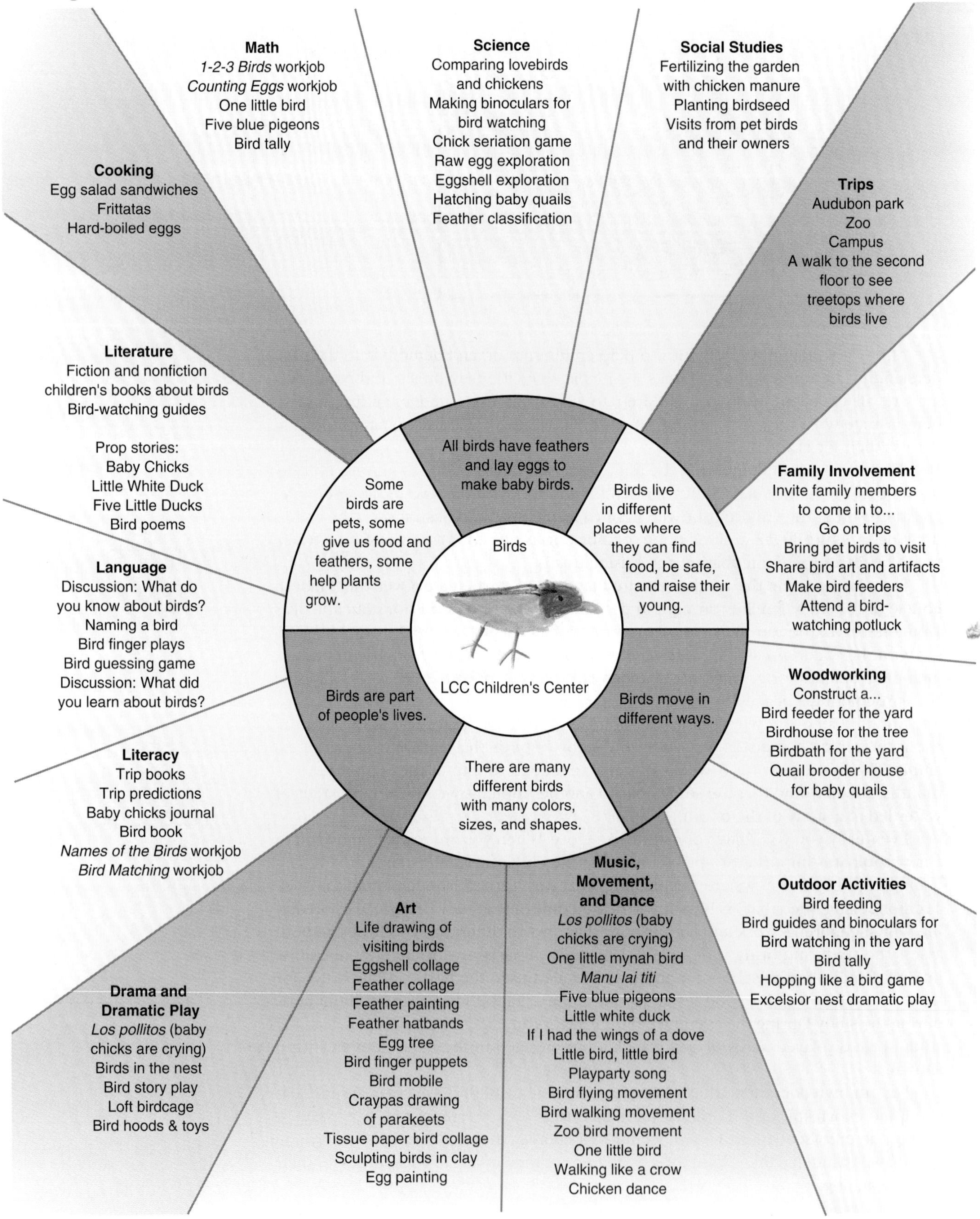

Math
1-2-3 Birds workjob
Counting Eggs workjob
One little bird
Five blue pigeons
Bird tally

Science
Comparing lovebirds
and chickens
Making binoculars for
bird watching
Chick seriation game
Raw egg exploration
Eggshell exploration
Hatching baby quails
Feather classification

Social Studies
Fertilizing the garden
with chicken manure
Planting birdseed
Visits from pet birds
and their owners

Cooking
Egg salad sandwiches
Frittatas
Hard-boiled eggs

Trips
Audubon park
Zoo
Campus
A walk to the second
floor to see
treetops where
birds live

Literature
Fiction and nonfiction
children's books about birds
Bird-watching guides

Prop stories:
Baby Chicks
Little White Duck
Five Little Ducks
Bird poems

Language
Discussion: What do
you know about birds?
Naming a bird
Bird finger plays
Bird guessing game
Discussion: What did
you learn about birds?

Literacy
Trip books
Trip predictions
Baby chicks journal
Bird book
Names of the Birds workjob
Bird Matching workjob

Family Involvement
Invite family members
to come in to...
Go on trips
Bring pet birds to visit
Share bird art and artifacts
Make bird feeders
Attend a bird-
watching potluck

Woodworking
Construct a...
Bird feeder for the yard
Birdhouse for the tree
Birdbath for the yard
Quail brooder house
for baby quails

Outdoor Activities
Bird feeding
Bird guides and binoculars for
Bird watching in the yard
Bird tally
Hopping like a bird game
Excelsior nest dramatic play

**Drama and
Dramatic Play**
Los pollitos (baby
chicks are crying)
Birds in the nest
Bird story play
Loft birdcage
Bird hoods & toys

Art
Life drawing of
visiting birds
Eggshell collage
Feather collage
Feather painting
Feather hatbands
Egg tree
Bird finger puppets
Bird mobile
Craypas drawing
of parakeets
Tissue paper bird collage
Sculpting birds in clay
Egg painting

**Music,
Movement,
and Dance**
Los pollitos (baby
chicks are crying)
One little mynah bird
Manu lai titi
Five blue pigeons
Little white duck
If I had the wings of a dove
Little bird, little bird
Playparty song
Bird flying movement
Bird walking movement
Zoo bird movement
One little bird
Walking like a crow
Chicken dance

Center circle labels:
All birds have feathers and lay eggs to make baby birds.

Birds live in different places where they can find food, be safe, and raise their young.

Some birds are pets, some give us food and feathers, some help plants grow.

Birds
LCC Children's Center

Birds are part of people's lives.

Birds move in different ways.

There are many different birds with many colors, sizes, and shapes.

Evaluate the Integrated Study

As you implement, remember to assess children's learning and evaluate the study. To evaluate whether children have acquired the major understandings you have targeted, you can observe their play as it pertains to the study or have children discuss the topic, dictate stories, or write in their journals. Children who make representational drawings may spontaneously, or upon request, draw pictures that demonstrate their understanding. For example, during the study of birds the 3- to 5-year-old children were provided with many different kinds of art media. Their drawings and collages provide visible proof of the internalization of concepts relating to birds (see Figure 11.14).

Photographs and video of the children engaged in learning activities also make valuable documentation of the learning that is occurring. Photographs, work samples, and observations can be put together into curriculum documentation panels. They are a valuable way to document children's learning and make children's learning visible to families and community members. An example can be found in the photo on page 364.

When you are finished teaching put the plans and materials you have created especially for this study in a resource box so you can easily store and retrieve them. Cardboard banker's boxes or lidded plastic storage boxes work well for this purpose. It may be some time before you use the resource box again, but when you do the materials will be there. You will make changes based on new ideas, interests, and materials, but you will not have to start over again from scratch.

How does the study of birds support children in all areas of development? What curriculum areas are children engaging with as they study birds?

What appeals to you about the approach to curriculum planning shown in the DVD? What concerns do you have about it?

Figure 11.14 **Children's Artwork Demonstrating Their Understanding of Birds**

Final Thoughts

The curriculum you plan should reflect your vision for children, for society, and for the future. It should be intellectually engaging for children and for teachers. The choices you make as you select what you will teach and how you will teach it impact children's lives, your own life, and possibly the larger world. If you take this responsibility seriously you will be thoughtful and thorough in your planning and use this important part of your work as a way to support all areas of children's development, increase their understanding of the world, build their love of learning, and help them to be the curious, creative active problem solvers that the world needs.

Learning Outcomes

When you read this chapter, thoughtfully complete selected assignments from the "To Learn More" section, and prepare items from the "For Your Portfolio" section, you will be demonstrating your progress in meeting NAEYC **Standard 4: Teaching and Learning**. Key elements:

- Knowing, understanding, and using positive relationships and supportive interactions

- Knowing, understanding, and using effective approaches, strategies, and tools for early education

- Knowing and understanding the importance, central concepts, inquiry tools, and structures of content areas or academic disciplines

- Using your own knowledge and other resources to design, implement, and evaluate meaningful, challenging curriculum to promote positive outcomes

To Learn More

Plan an Activity: Use the Activity Plan Outline found in Figure 11.2 to plan an activity and implement it with children. Assess whether you were successful in accomplishing your goals. Reflect and write about what contributed to the success or failure of the activity.

Research and Begin to Write a Plan for an Integrated Study: On your own or with a partner select an appropriate topic for an integrated study with young children. Research the topic and begin to write the plan using the outline in Figure 11.10. Write the goals and big ideas, brainstorm activities, gather and make materials, and implement all or part of the plan in a program with children. Assess whether you were successful in accomplishing your goals. Reflect and write about what you learned.

Observe a Classroom: Observe a classroom in which teacher-directed and child-chosen activities are planned. Notice how children respond to both kinds of learning. Reflect and write about what you think the goals and objectives of the activities might be, how the activities contribute to accomplishing the goals, and whether the activities are successful in accomplishing the teacher's purpose.

Interview a Teacher: Interview a teacher about his or her program goals and their influence on curriculum planning. Ask about how these goals are modified or influenced by the community, the interests of children, the concerns of parents, the school administration, and educational trends. Ask them to describe some ways that their goals impact the day-to-day curriculum. Reflect and write about how this affects children's experiences.

Interview Two Teachers: Interview two teachers about the kinds of planning that they do regularly, how much time it takes, how important it is in program success, and so on. Compare their responses. Reflect and write about what you learned.

For Your Portfolio

Write Your Philosophy (viewpoint) on Curriculum and Curriculum Planning: Identify your curriculum aims and values by asking yourself: As an educator, what am I trying to accomplish—for children and for society? What does that mean for the content of the curriculum I want to teach and how I want to present it? Write a one-page statement of philosophy to put in your portfolio.

Document Your Competence in Planning an Activity: Write a plan for an activity for children using the planning format found in this chapter. Implement your plan with children. Write anecdotal records on children's responses and reflect on what happened and what you learned, and evaluate your work. Put the plan and records in your portfolio to document your competence as a planner.

Document Your Competence in Integrated Planning: Develop and implement an integrated plan using the guidelines found in this chapter. Create a sunburst for the plan. Document children's learning by collecting work samples, writing anecdotal records, and taking photographs. Put the sunburst and a select sampling of the documentation in your portfolio to demonstrate your competence in integrated planning.

12

Inclusion of Children with Special Needs

Do what you can with what you have.

Theodore Roosevelt

*T*here are many kinds of special needs. An individualized approach to teaching is required for every young child—the child who is unusually active, the quiet child, the highly intelligent child, the child who learns with difficulty, the child who can't slow down and focus, the child who is emotionally troubled, the child from a minority culture, a child who speaks another language, the child who learns like a 3-year-old but has the feelings of a 6-year-old (or vice versa), the child who wears glasses, the child who has asthma, the child who is afraid of fire engines, the child from a single-parent family, the child who stutters, and all the others. In every early childhood program, you will find as many distinctive needs as there are children, and every child requires attention to his or her individual characteristics and needs.

But some children have needs that are exceptional. Some of them will have been evaluated and determined to have disabilities, and some have yet to be evaluated but still need some special attention. Working with them effectively will draw on the knowledge and developing skills that we have addressed in the previous chapters of this book—the ability to reflect on your own feelings and reactions, knowledge of child development, skill in guiding behavior, and knowledge of how to design a learning environment and plan curriculum. In addition to these basics, you need some specialized information and skill to work with children who have disabilities. You will also benefit from help from knowledgeable professionals who work in your community in the field of special education.

Most children with identified disabilities are served in special education programs in public schools. But other children in other programs also have special needs. You may find yourself working with children who have been abused or neglected, who are exceptionally intelligent or talented, or who have chronic health problems. These children often are not identified but you will need to be aware of, and responsive to, their needs as well.

> **Reflect on your own abilities and challenges**
>
> Think about your own abilities and challenges (the things that were hardest for you when you were a child). How have they affected your life? How did they influence your childhood experiences? What do you wish your teachers had known? What are the implications of these experiences for your work with young children?

PEOPLE-FIRST LANGUAGE

Although there are many kinds of special needs, in this chapter we will focus on children who have disabilities (and are regarded as *exceptional*). These children do not reach or are seriously delayed in reaching developmental milestones (described in

Chapter 4), or have conditions that make it impossible for them to learn and function as well as a typically developing child. According to McCormick:

> An *exceptional child* is one who is different enough from the "standard" or "average" child to require special methods, materials, services and possibly equipment in order to attain desired learning objectives. They may differ in the rate at which they learn (compared to age-peers) *or* they may learn in different ways. Many terms have been used to describe children who have challenges—*handicapped, disabled, special-needs, exceptional,* and others. Today professionals use the term *children with special needs* to describe such children. (McCormick 1994, 95)

Accepted terminology for describing exceptional children has changed over the years as educators have attempted to show the commonalities among all children rather than emphasize their differences. The accepted view today is that individuals with disabilities are *people* first and *people with disabilities* second. This view shapes the language we use. It is preferable to say "children with disabilities" rather than "disabled" or "handicapped children." The language emphasizes that it is important to see the whole child, including areas of strength and abilities. It avoids talking about children in ways that demean or stereotype them. A good guideline is to speak of the child first and his disability second (e.g., "a child with Down syndrome," rather than "a retarded child"). Refer to a child by his or her name and mention the disability *only* when that information is relevant in a particular situation. When we use "people-first" language ("the child with _____"), we are saying that the child is more important than the disability. The people-first language we just described helps us to focus on the whole child.

THE LAW AND INCLUSIVE EDUCATION

In Chapter 2 we pointed out that until quite recently children with disabilities were segregated—first in institutions, then in separate schools, and later in classrooms that served only children who had been diagnosed as having disabilities. Over the years it became clear that these settings did little, if anything, to prepare children to become functioning members of society. It was also apparent that a disproportionate number of the children in these settings were African-American, Hispanic, from non-English-speaking backgrounds, or from poor and single-parent families. In recent years there has been great progress in providing opportunities and access to full social participation to individuals with disabilities. This movement for equal rights for the disabled has had an impact on early childhood education. There is strong support today for including children with special needs in regular education classrooms.

Advocates for equal rights for the disabled worked diligently for the passage of the landmark Education for All Handicapped Children Act in 1975. In 1990, provisions of the law were strengthened and it was replaced by the Individuals with Disabilities Education Act (IDEA), which has guided the provision of special education since that time. Under this act state and local school systems are required to provide free and appropriate public education, including special education and related services, for all disabled children ages 3 to 21 with identified disabilities.[1]

Part A of IDEA sets out the intent of the law. Part B provides for special education services for children ages 3 to 21 whose needs cannot be satisfied in general education. In order to be eligible for special education the child must be determined to have

---

[1] *Special education* is specially designed instruction, available at no cost to parents or guardians, to meet the needs of the child with a disability. Related services include transportation and other support services that can assist the child with a disability to benefit from educational experiences. These may include speech and hearing services, psychological services, physical and occupational therapy, recreation, counseling, and medical assistance.

a disability, and the disability must cause the child to need specially designed instruction. Specific categories of disability are included in IDEA. The categories that are most likely to affect young children are discussed later in this chapter, in the section titled "Strategies for Working with Young Children with Special Needs." Part C of the law makes federal funds available for states to implement early intervention services for eligible infants and toddlers and their families. Children under age 3 may receive these

services if they have delays in one or more areas of development, or have a diagnosed physical or mental condition that has a high probability of resulting in a developmental delay. These services should be provided in natural environments (where the child might spend time if he or she did not have a disability) to the maximum extent appropriate to the child. Natural environments may include homes and community programs like child care centers.

Two important principles are set forth in IDEA. The first, the principle of *appropriate education,* calls for schools to provide individually tailored education for each child based on assessment of his or her needs. Every child served has the right to education that is appropriate to his or her level of development, abilities, and needs. The required plan for children ages 3 to 21 is called an *individualized education plan* (IEP) and describes services that the child must receive with a focus on educational outcomes. The plan for birth to age 2 is called an *individualized family services plan* (IFSP) and describes the services that both the infant and the family should receive. The second principle, *least restrictive environment,* calls for children with disabilities to be educated with their peers who do not have disabilities to the maximum extent appropriate (this is now called the *inclusion* principle). This law reflects a strong commitment to educating each child in the school and classroom that the child would attend if he or she did not have a disability.

The federal government provides financial support to states for special education. It is costly because of the low teacher-child ratios and the wide range of services provided. States must agree to comply with the provisions of IDEA or they are not eligible to receive federal funds.

Another important piece of legislation that has implications for early childhood education is the Americans with Disabilities Act (ADA), passed in 1990. The goal of ADA is to make reasonable accommodations for individuals with disabilities in order to integrate them to the greatest extent possible into society. One provision of this law is that people with disabilities are entitled to equal rights and protections in public accommodations such as early childhood programs. Each child must be evaluated on an individual basis to determine if a program can reasonably accommodate his or her needs. This means that a program cannot decline to serve a child who has a disability unless it can demonstrate that it is not able to do so.

IDENTIFYING A CHILD WHO HAS SPECIAL NEEDS

Research has shown repeatedly that the early years of life are critical for learning and growth. This is the period of maximum opportunity to promote children's cognitive, speech and language, physical, social, and emotional development. If their special needs are recognized and met during these years, children with disabilities will have

369

a much better chance of succeeding and becoming independent adults. (Hull, Goldhaber, & Capone 2002, 162)

As a classroom teacher you will be in the unique position of getting to know every child in a group in the natural context of daily activities. Because of this you may be the first person to recognize that a child may have a condition that requires additional support. Knowledge of child development and your observational skills will prepare you to identify a child who is different in significant ways from other children in your group.

Such early identification coupled with appropriate intervention (education and services) can sometimes help avoid developmental problems that will be more difficult to remediate when the child gets older. For example, a teacher we know observed that a child in her class often seemed to drift off in daydreams and was not making progress comparable to that of the other children. She decided that the problem needed to be explored. A full evaluation led to the conclusion that the child suffered from a form of epilepsy. The daydreaming episodes were actually *petit mal* seizures, and her developmental lags were caused by this undiagnosed condition. Medical intervention was needed.

In order to get help in a timely fashion, early childhood educators need to observe children carefully and know the signs of physical, emotional, or mental disabilities. Remember, however, that although you should be alert to physical and behavioral characteristics that suggest the need for evaluation, it is not your role to diagnose a disability.

> *Fifteen eager 4-year-olds are eating their morning snack. It is now the middle of the school year, and they have all learned how to cooperate to make snack time pleasant. Except Jeremy. He cruises the edges of the room, stopping briefly to dump a puzzle from a shelf and run his hands through the pieces, only to be distracted by the morning's paintings drying nearby. As he passes a table of children, his attention is again deflected. He tries to squeeze his body onto a chair occupied by another child.*

Jeremy's behavior consistently precipitates conflicts with children and adults. He is unable to engage for any length of time in meaningful activity. Many young children are easily distractible at age 4 but if you were Jeremy's teacher you might think that his behavior was extreme. The first thing you might do under these circumstances would be to try to understand what is causing his behavior. Then you might try modifying your learning environment, schedule, and curriculum to better meet his needs. If none of these things proved to be helpful, you might conclude that Jeremy needed additional help to cope with the demands of a preschool classroom. At that point you might initiate steps to have him evaluated and to find help for him, so he can learn to function in more positive ways.

If you were working in a setting with typically developing children, a situation similar to this one might be your first encounter with a child with special needs—a child whose condition has not been formally identified and who is not yet receiving any assistance. The behavior of a child like Jeremy may perplex you. Your observations can cue you to a possible problem and the need for some extra help to assess and serve the child. Many developmental or psychological issues are first detected when a child enters an early childhood program. You have an opportunity to identify and help these children, who may benefit greatly from a careful evaluation and special services.

What steps do you take when you believe a child in your care has a condition that may require special attention? Start by observing the child in a variety of situations. Note the child's strengths and the ways he or she is functioning appropriately and similarly to other children. Then pinpoint the ways in which his or her behavior and skills seem atypical or cause concern. Make written anecdotal records, being careful to make objective statements about what you observe the child doing. In what situations is the child unable to participate like the other children? Does the child's way of responding meet developmental expectations? Is there a cultural or language difference that might be related? Once you have documented the child's behavior and reviewed your observations, you can decide whether the second step—getting help—is necessary.

You might want to share your observations and concerns with a coworker, director, or supervisor. As you do this, be careful not to come to conclusions too quickly or stigmatize the child in any way. Colleagues can often offer insights from a more objective point of view that will help you to sort out your thoughts and feelings. You might want to ask one of them to make an independent observation of the child. Sometimes adult expectations for children's behavior are "developmentally inappropriate." For example, we have known teachers who were surprised when they encountered a 2-year-old who didn't talk in school, or a 5-year-old who did not follow directions well. But both of these examples reflect individual differences that were the result of the child's life experiences and not disabilities. When we have inappropriate expectations, the resulting problems are ones that we have created for the children and ourselves.

If you are convinced that the child truly does have a problem (like Jeremy's inability to focus and to get along with other children) that calls for attention you will talk with your program administrator and contact the family to get an evaluation and appropriate assistance for the child. As this process is going on you will do everything you can to meet the child's needs in your classroom.

While you are responsible for helping the child and family, you are not alone and need not assume total responsibility. Enlist the support of your colleagues and program administrator. Use resources available in your community. Both public and private agencies provide screening, evaluation, and consultation for children with special needs. A nearby preschool or elementary school may be able to provide such services, or help may be available through a state or county department of health, human services, or education. Private agencies such as the Association for Children and Adults with Learning Disabilities or children's hospitals may also be able to provide assistance.

INCLUDING CHILDREN WITH SPECIAL NEEDS

Whether you teach in an infant-toddler program, preschool, kindergarten, or elementary school, you may have children with identified special needs in your class. This is called *inclusion.* We, the authors, advocate for inclusion, for "open door environments in which all children experience a sense of pride, belonging, and competency" (Hull et al. 2002, 2).

Inclusion is not about a place, an instructional strategy, or a curriculum. It is about children belonging, being valued and having choices. It is about accepting and appreciating human diversity. And it is about providing the necessary support to children, teachers, schools, and families so that *all* children and their families can participate in the programs of their choice (Allen & Schwartz 1996). In the past the terms *mainstreaming* and *integration* have also been used for the educational practice of providing education for children with disabilities in regular education programs.

The practice of inclusion is based on the belief that it is good for all children to have a range of abilities together in the classroom.

- *Children with special needs benefit.* They gain friendships and observe and learn from their peers who are typically developing. They learn to cope with everyday expectations and problems, and they practice new skills in the real world of the classroom.
- *The other children in a group benefit.* They learn that people who appear different are like them in many ways, can be their friends, and are worthwhile individuals. They witness perseverance and the value of struggling to accomplish something. They have the opportunity to be a coach, a helper, or a teacher to another child. Early childhood educators report time and again that the caring relationships developed among the children are an overwhelmingly positive outcome of inclusion.
- *Teachers benefit.* They broaden their professional understanding and gain a sense of satisfaction as the child with special needs learns and functions in the classroom. It also gives them a valuable opportunity to teach some things they could not teach if the special needs child was not a part of the group.
- *Families benefit.* They feel their child is accepted and they feel part of a community of families and children.

Since it is increasingly common for children with a range of disabilities to be included in regular classrooms you are likely to have many opportunities in your career to work with children who have special needs. In publicly funded programs such as Head Start, public school, or a state-funded preschool program, you will be *mandated* (required by law) to serve these children. If you teach in a publicly funded program, children with special needs are likely to be included in your classroom on a regular basis. This is the spirit and the letter of the IDEA law: to enable children with special needs to attend school with their typically developing peers. In states where there are no state-funded programs for children under 5, you may occasionally be asked to include a child with identified special needs in your class.

Your first reaction to learning that there will be a child with a disability in your class may be negative. You didn't choose to be a special education teacher and you may be afraid that you are not prepared. We think you will be pleasantly surprised to find that a child with special needs isn't that much different from others you have known and worked with. Your training in early childhood education will have prepared you to view each child as an individual and to focus on children's skills, interests, and needs. You have learned to be aware of your own feelings, reactions, and biases and to monitor them so that they do not have negative effects on children.

Reflect on your experiences with people with disabilities

Recall a relationship or an interaction that you have had as an adult with a child or adult with a disability. How did you feel? Did this change your ideas about disabled people? How?

Preparing for Inclusion

Since it is increasingly common for children with a range of disabilities (from mild to severe) to be included in regular classrooms, it is likely that you will have many opportunities in your career to work with children who have special challenges. The most important thing you can do is to welcome a child into your classroom, help him or her to feel like a part of the group, and support the child in having a positive school experience. As we have said before, inclusion is consistent with what early childhood educators are already doing in a classroom to welcome, support, and nurture the development of children with diverse abilities. It is not that different to add a child with disabilities. You will not need to become an expert on the causes, symptoms, and nature of a disability to be an effective inclusion teacher. You will need to find out whether you will need special training or skills, such as using sign language or responding to a seizure, and in the case of severe disabilities it is important to seek out experts, including the child's parents, to help you understand the situation.

You will want to consider some things you can do to help the group understand and accept the new child. Think about the words you will use if children ask questions or need information about the child. A simple explanation of the disability with some examples to which they can relate a personal experience is probably the best method. You might say about a child with an expressive language problem, for example, "Mark has trouble saying what he wants to say sometimes. Do you ever want to tell someone something and the words come out all mixed up?"

Answer children's questions as honestly and directly as you can. Help them understand any differences they notice. You could say, "Rose wears a hearing aid so that she can hear us when we talk to her." If they seem interested you might bring in some hearing aids for children to try and to learn about how they work.

You may need to assure other children that a disability isn't "catching." Some children (especially those of elementary age) may initially laugh at or ridicule any child who is different. Remember that this response is fueled by their embarrassment. It provides you with an opportunity to talk about the wide range of differences among people and the value of helpful and respectful relationships. Your warm, accepting attitude will provide a powerful model for the development of these relationships.

Seeing each child as a unique individual is the first step in getting to know any child, including the one with special needs. In *Children with Special Needs: Lessons for Early Childhood Professionals,* Marjorie Kostelnik and her coauthors recommend that when a child with special needs is first enrolled in your class, you gather information about the child based on your observations and what you learn about her or him from others. They suggest that you find out:

- How the child reacts to sensations
- How the child processes information (his or her preferred way to learn)
- How the child approaches problems, makes plans, and takes action
- The child's level of emotional, social, and intellectual functioning
- How the child communicates with others
- How the child typically interacts with peers and adults
- What the family is like and their typical routines (Kostelnik, Onaga, Rohde, & Whiren 2002, 4)

As you observe, you will find out about the child's likes and dislikes, abilities, interests, and areas in which he or she needs assistance. Remember that knowledge about a disability may help you deal with your anxiety, but it will not help you to know the child. No two children with the same disability are alike. A disability or special need is only one characteristic of a person. When a child who wears a brace on her leg works a puzzle or paints at an easel, your first response will be to her competence in completing the puzzle or the colors of her painting. When she is on the playground and cannot run or climb like the other children, you may need to help in an activity or help her find alternative activities.

Your best source of information about any child will be his or her family. Pediatricians, therapists, special education teachers, workshops, and classes are other sources of information to help you understand and work with a child who has special needs. When you know the child with special needs as a person you will be much more able to relate to him or her and design appropriate educational experiences.

As much as possible you will want to treat a child with special needs just as you do any other child in your group. Be sure to give the child every opportunity to participate in the daily events of your classroom and to develop a sense of competence (see Table 12.1). Avoid overprotecting—this will make the child appear different. Other children may become overprotective or may exclude the child.

You will help the children in your class understand that no one can do everything and that every one of us has strengths and weaknesses. You can also help them find specific ways to include a child with a disability in their play. For example, you might show them how to help a child with impaired vision feel the shape of a block structure and then to give verbal guidance so that the child can place blocks in the structure.

You may find you have feelings about a child with special needs that you are not "supposed" to have. A friend of ours told us about Kevin, a child with a neurological impairment who drooled continuously. Our friend, an excellent preschool teacher, was surprised to find that she was repulsed by Kevin's drooling. It brought up childhood memories of another youngster who had been teased and tormented by children as the neighborhood "dummy." Our friend took care to spend extra time with Kevin, made an effort to see him as a person, and eventually found that she not only forgot about

Table 12.1 Suggestions for Including a Child with Special Needs

- Learn about the child by talking with his or her family members. They will be your best source of information about the child's strengths and needs. Be sure to listen carefully to family members and others who know the child.

- Consult with the child's doctor, therapists, and former teachers for additional information. Find out whether the child is taking medication and any side effects that might be an issue. Ask what special classes or forms of therapy the child participates in and find out any precautions, limitations or requirements you should know about.

- Maintain regular communication with the family and other specialists who are working with the child.

- Find out what services will be available to support your work with the child.

- Brainstorm with the experts and consultants on how you can best support the development of this child.

- Be careful not to make judgments based on first impressions. Get to know the child and be sure to look for strengths and abilities.

- Ask yourself: "How can I make classroom activities relevant to this child and also meet the needs of the other children?"

- Be patient—some children may need to be told or shown many times.

- Be flexible and open to learning new things about children and about yourself.

his drooling but enjoyed his sense of humor and appreciated his affectionate nature. She also worked hard to help the other children in her class accept Kevin—something you want to do for every child in your group.

If you were Kevin's teacher, you might react negatively to him at first. Yet it is important that teachers be positive and supportive, for we know that children with disabilities often develop low self-esteem, become negative, do poorly in school, and even develop symptoms of emotional disturbance when they are in nonsupportive environments.

Program Modifications

Your knowledge of what is developmentally appropriate for young children in general will guide your planning as you decide what materials, activities, and teaching strategies to use for the child with special needs in your classroom. As in teaching any other child, you will observe this child's strengths, interests, and preferences to help him or her engage productively in learning experiences. Just as you support other children's learning you will model desired behavior, demonstrate sequences in an activity, and play with the child. Remember to let the child take the lead when possible, provide encouragement and contact, and stay near the child so you can offer support when it is needed. As you prepare for a child with special needs, always keep in mind:

> Young children are alike in many ways. They also are different in just as many ways. Too often the ways an exceptional child is like other children are overlooked, never put to good use; the focus is on the remediation of their delays and disabilities. (Allen & Schwartz 1996, 46)

You will make your classroom a good place for a child with special needs if you do some thinking first, and then make some fairly simple modifications in the learning environment and curriculum. Begin by thinking about the goals of your program and experiences you are providing for children. Keep in mind that all children, particularly those with special needs, need to have opportunities to develop confidence; to explore; to plan what they want to do and implement their plans; to practice self control, communication, and cooperation; and to develop relationships.

The next thing you will do is to take a careful look at the learning environment and schedule and see if these need to be modified to accommodate the child with special needs. Reflect on your classroom routines, especially circle time and the transitions as children enter school in the morning, move between activities, and leave at the end of the school day. These are challenging times.

Think too about whether the experiences you are presenting to your group will be interesting and relevant to the child with special needs and whether that child will have access to all of the learning opportunities available in the classroom. A daily program that includes a variety of learning experiences is just as important to a child with special needs as it is to other children. Free play and teacher-directed times, child- and teacher-chosen activities, large as well as small groups—all provide valuable opportunities for learning.

This process of reflection will help you to decide the kinds of modifications you can make in your program to assist the special needs child. Sandall and Schwartz, in their book *Building Blocks for Teaching Preschoolers with Special Needs,* give helpful guidance for this process. They define *curriculum modification* as a change to the ongoing classroom activity or materials in order to facilitate or maximize a child's participation. And they point out that modifications should be easy-to-

> **Reflect on how you might feel as the parent of a child with special needs**
>
> If you were the parent of a child with a disability, what kind of educational program would you want for your child? How would you like your child to be treated? How would you like early childhood professionals to treat you?

implement changes that require some planning, but most do not require additional resources (2002, 45).

Six types of curriculum modifications can help children with special needs to participate in the daily program as fully as possible, according to Sandall and Schwartz. These offer a good framework for thinking about what you can do in your classroom.

Environmental support involves modifying the learning environment, to make it responsive to the needs of children. For example, if a child has trouble with mobility you may need to widen pathways between areas. You can also do things like open a quiet center for a child to go at the end of an activity, and give the child a picture of the activity or area they are to go to next. You can also review your schedule. Many circle times are too long for most young children, let alone those who have additional challenges. Be sure to arrange the learning environment (including materials and activities) in ways that promote the child's interactions with peers.

Materials adaptations are modifications of materials that support the child's participation. An occupational or physical therapist can help you figure out simple adaptations that make a big difference. For example, wrapping tape or yarn around the handles of brushes, sewing handles on stuffed animals, providing short-handled eating utensils, lowering the easel, taping blocks to the pedals of the bike, and using nonslip materials to keep toys from sliding will make it easier for children with motor difficulties to be full participants in the classroom.

Simplify activities for children who are having difficulties with complex tasks. Task analysis is a useful tool. It involves breaking down a complex task into its component parts and teaching them separately as a series of sub-skills. Tasks such as putting on clothes and brushing teeth can be practiced in components for a time as preparation for carrying out the whole task. If you have ever taught a toddler to pull up his or her pants you have some practical experience with task analysis. Reading, a special education class, or workshop can help you learn to do task analysis. You can also do things like give the child materials one at a time, design an activity to have fewer steps, and make photo cards that show the steps in a sequence.

Adaptive devices can be employed to support a child's involvement. Again, an occupational or physical therapist can recommend equipment that will help. For example, you can help a child in a wheelchair or brace get near an activity by providing a special table. Adaptive scissors can assist a child who has fine motor difficulties. A child with large motor difficulties may benefit from using footrests and back props in his or her chair. High-tech resources are also available that can help a child to express ideas and show what they know and can do. Professionals who are experts in the design and provision of assistive technology will help you in identifying what the child needs and how to provide it (Bowe 2000; Mulligan 2003).

Peer support can be very helpful and encouraging. Peers are good models. It may work well to pair the child who has special needs with one who knows the activities and routines and will be supportive. You could suggest that children invite the child with special needs to join them in play or share a discovery.

Invisible support involves sequencing activities to support the child's participation. This might include making sure that the special needs child has a chance to see how other children are doing an activity, letting the child pour last so the pitcher isn't too full, providing more movement activities during circle time so the child is able to attend longer, or having the child with special needs go first to ensure that he or she has enough time to complete an activity.

> **Reflect on your experiences with children with special needs**
>
> Think about the ways that children with disabilities were a part of your early school experiences. How do you think your teachers felt about these children? How did you feel? What implications do your reflections have for your teaching?

The inclusion of children with special needs is supported by NAEYC's position statement on developmentally appropriate practice (DAP), which says that teachers should be prepared to meet the identified special needs of individual children, including those with disabilities (Bredekamp & Copple 1997).

Play is the primary vehicle for learning for all young children. Sometimes teachers of children with special needs become so concerned with remediation that they forget that *all* children need opportunities for play. Play is particularly important for children who have disabilities because it is through play that they experience those feelings of mastery, resourcefulness, and competence that are so crucial for development of a positive self-concept.

To facilitate play you will provide children who have disabilities with support and guidance. Support might include allowing a child with special needs additional time to develop comfort and competence in play situations. You may need to do some direct teaching of play skills and take an active role in helping a child strengthen these developing skills.

Children with special needs, like all children, need opportunities to engage with a variety of both open-ended and specific-purpose materials. Clay, paint, blocks, and dress-up clothes and props stimulate exploration and creative play. More defined activities such as lotto, puzzles, and pegboards provide experiences in developing and strengthening specific skills and problem-solving strategies.

Teaching children with identified disabilities requires individualized teaching and individualized education plans (IEPs). These plans identify the accommodations and adjustments necessary for children with disabilities to participate in the general education curriculum or for preschool children to participate in the appropriate activities provided to nondisabled children.

In the past, IEPs tended to be based on the development of specific skills drawn from developmental inventories or standardized assessments. This very often led to teaching the assessments rather than focusing on the child. It is also possible to base the development of IEPs on the philosophy, goals, and instructional practices of the regular classroom and for them to reflect the philosophy of a constructivist, play-based, early childhood program and current views about the ways that young children learn. IEPs can be written to focus on the whole child, linking evaluations with developmentally appropriate instructional practices (Edmiaston, Dolezal, Doolittle, Erickson, & Merritt 2000; McCormick & Feeney 1995).

Collaboration

When you work with children with special needs you will be called upon to *collaborate* with other professionals. You might collaborate with special education teachers, consultants, and professionals from different disciplines. In the past, specialists worked in isolation; collaboration is advocated today so that teams can address the needs of children and families in a more integrated and systematic way.

Collaboration can often be a challenging component of teaching children with special needs. Working with a team involves crossing discipline boundaries and may require some new behaviors. In order to serve children effectively, team members need to have a commitment to smooth relationships, work on building trusting relationships, respect the contributions of others, and have effective communication skills (Sandall & Schwartz 2002; Turnbull, Turnbull, Shank, & Smith 2004; Wolery & Wilbers 1994). It can also be satisfying and worthwhile as a team of educators, specialists, and families share their resources and strengths to solve problems in creative and responsive ways.

STRATEGIES FOR WORKING WITH YOUNG CHILDREN WITH SPECIAL NEEDS

Since development varies so greatly between individuals, the distinction between a "disabled" and "typically developing" child is often not clear. Moreover, the professionals who deal with exceptional children—doctors, psychologists, educators, and others—tend to define *normalcy* and *exceptionality* somewhat differently. So even though

some agreed-on guidelines about what constitutes a disability have been established, the professionals don't always agree about it. The Individuals with Disabilities Education Act (IDEA) defines more than a dozen categories of disabilities—including mental retardation, hearing impairment, speech or language impairments, visual impairment, serious emotional disturbance, orthopedic impairments, autism, traumatic brain injury, other health impairments, specific learning disability, and developmental delay.

Kostelnik and her colleagues (2002) suggest that there are both positive and negative aspects to identifying and labeling disabilities. On the positive side, a label is necessary in order for a child to get special education services, and it can help adults to know where to look for more information about a child's condition. The negative aspects are that the label focuses on only one dimension rather than giving a full picture of a child. Although it has shortcomings, the practice of identifying children by disability is still in use and is likely to continue until a better system is put in place.

Following is a very brief overview of some of the kinds of disabilities that you may encounter in early childhood settings and some suggestions for how you might work effectively with children who have these disabilities. Keep in mind that a category does not give you a full picture of a child. Characteristics observed in children in one category are often similar to those of children in other categories. Children with a similar diagnosis often differ from each other as much as they differ from children in other categories. And children who have been identified as having different disabilities may behave in similar ways.

Young Children with Orthopedic Impairments

Children who have *orthopedic impairments* have difficulty controlling or easily moving their bodies. Orthopedic impairments may be caused by specific conditions such as missing limbs; disorders of feet, knees, or hips; damage caused by disease such as polio; and neurological disorders such as cerebral palsy.

Some adaptations of your classroom environment will make it easier for a child with an orthopedic impairment to participate as fully as possible in your program. Here are some things you can do:

- Rearrange furniture.
- Adjust table and easel heights.
- Relocate supplies and toys to make them more accessible.
- Adapt standard equipment, like tricycles.
- Let the child discover his or her own abilities and limitations by trying activities.
- Encourage independence by teaching self-help skills, like dressing and eating.

Consult with the family and the physical therapist before you make changes. Talk to the family and therapist to learn about activities the child enjoys that could be used with the whole group. For example, body awareness activities will be helpful in improving all children's appreciation for their bodies. Emphasize activities that give a child with a physical disability the opportunity to play with other children.

Young children are often fascinated by special equipment, like walkers or wheelchairs. Check with the family—they may be willing for the other children to satisfy their curiosity by trying out the equipment. You might also invite an adult with an orthopedic impairment to visit with the children and answer their questions.

Young Children with Sensory Impairments

Vision

A child whose inability to see interferes with easy participation in daily activities is considered *visually impaired*. A child with partial sight may have a visual acuity problem that is correctable with glasses. Few children are completely unable to see. Many can see light and dark areas, broad shapes, but not details, or have peripheral rather than frontal vision.

The development of children whose blindness occurred after birth generally resembles that of other children, but the development of children who were blind at birth tends to be much slower. Not surprisingly, children with visual impairments may be advanced in speech and language and may excel at listening and memory activities. Because they lack visual stimulation, which encourages exploration of the environment, children with visual impairments often lag in physical development. Many large and small muscle activities are learned by imitation. Children watch and then copy movement. Movement may be perceived as dangerous since it could result in getting hurt. Because young children's social play is generally physically active, the fear of movement may affect social development.

You can do many things to help a child with a visual impairment benefit from your program:

- Provide good overall lighting and avoid areas of glare or deep contrasts between light and shade.
- Keep the room arrangement and traffic patterns simple and uncluttered—and when a change is needed, have children participate in making it.
- Use detailed description to accompany your actions when you introduce an activity or game.
- Keep a child with visual impairment close to you for group activities so that you can provide physical cues for participation.
- Provide larger toys and add different textures or sounds to materials when possible.
- Teach the child to look in the direction of the person speaking.
- Because social cues such as facial expressions that convey feelings may not be seen, be sure to add clear verbal directions.

Hearing

Children are considered *hearing impaired* when they have difficulty understanding and responding to speech or sounds. When children cannot hear, even with the use of a hearing aid, they are said to be deaf. Children who are hard of hearing have a permanent but less severe hearing loss in which the use of a hearing aid is helpful. A hearing impairment may involve volume or clarity of sound.

When children cannot hear well, they have difficulty learning to speak. Their spoken words may be unclear and difficult to understand. The rhythm and voice quality of their speech may be unusual. Social interactions are hindered when it is difficult for children to express feelings or needs or to have others understand them. Cognitive skills may be slower to develop if hearing loss has resulted in a language delay.

There are a number of things you can do to help a child with a hearing impairment in your classroom:

- Place yourself facing a light source and at the child's eye level when you establish eye contact in order to attract and hold attention.
- In a group activity, have children sit in a circle, so all faces are visible.
- Address the child by name, speak clearly in a normal voice, and use simple phrasings but whole sentences.
- If the child seems not to understand, rephrase your sentence instead of simply repeating it.
- Use visual clues and gestures to aid understanding and allow the child time to direct attention to an object or gesture and then look back at you.
- Encourage participation in activities like dramatic play and puppets that involve lots of language.

If the child is receiving speech therapy, ask the therapist for ideas for games you can share with the group. If the child uses a hearing aid, ask the family to teach you how it works and how to care for it. Find out what to look for to make sure it is working—you can't tell just by looking whether the hearing aid is actually functioning!

Hearing problems are often first noticed in school. If a child has trouble paying attention, especially in group activities, doesn't answer when called, seems confused by directions or questions, does not understand them at all, or often gives the wrong answer, you should suspect a hearing impairment. Sometimes hearing loss is only temporary, caused by a middle ear infection, but since frequent infections can lead to permanent hearing loss your role in urging families to seek treatment is important.

Young Children with Communication Disorders

It is typical for young children to have problems with communication and language. Lack of fluency is part of normal speech development; so are errors in articulation. There are several kinds of communication disorders that are considered disabilities or are associated with other disabilities.

Children with *receptive language problems* have difficulty understanding the meaning of words or the way words are put together. Children with *auditory processing problems* may be unable to tell the difference between speech sounds (auditory discrimination), may be unable to isolate the sounds from a noisy background, may have trouble remembering what they hear, or may confuse the correct order of a series of sounds. Children with *speech problems* are difficult to understand. When they lack the ability to use language effectively (*expressive language problems*) they have difficulty verbalizing ideas, selecting appropriate words, or using correct grammatical structures. Speech or language impairments may also be associated with hearing impairment, cleft palate, autism, cerebral palsy, attention deficit disorder, an emotional problem, or a learning disability.

When children cannot communicate, they have difficulty learning. Social interactions are hindered when it is difficult for others to understand them. The child with a communication disorder may become aggressive or passive.

The strategies that you use with all young children are effective when you work with a child who has speech or language problems. You can:

- Be careful not to interrupt, rush, or pressure the child.
- Model correct language.
- Use simple constructions and vocabulary.
- Expand the child's own comments.

- Provide many opportunities for all children to enjoy language in activities like learning trips.
- Incorporate songs, rhymes, and chants into daily routines.
- Pay attention to the child's efforts at communication. If he or she has difficulty with expressive language, listen closely to decipher communication. Ask to make sure you have understood what the child meant: "You have a bunny like that at your house?"
- Encourage the child to talk about his or her feelings during times of stress, frustration, or excitement.
- Encourage conversation among all the children.
- Redirect the communication to another child: "Could you tell Willie what you just told me?"

You should be concerned about a child's language development if he or she does not talk by age 2, is not speaking in two- or three-word sentences by age 3, is very difficult to understand after age 3, or uses poor sentence structure or stutters after age 5. Preschool children exhibit many normal articulation errors such as, for example, substituting an *f* sound for *th* (*wif* for *with*). When these articulation differences persist beyond the age of 5, or if unusual pitch, volume, or voice quality characterizes a child's speech, an evaluation by a speech therapist is in order.

Young Children with Cognitive Delays

Cognitive deficits, often called *mental retardation,* can occur before, during, or after birth. Although all children learn at different rates, some learn significantly more slowly than their peers. During the preschool years children with cognitive delays appear much younger than their chronological age and may have difficulty learning skills and developing concepts. They may be unable to remember things, or may be unable to use information to solve problems. They may have trouble developing and using language or may encounter difficulties playing cooperatively, initiating activities or interactions, or learning to function independently.

Children who have mild cognitive delay may seem little different from the youngest children in an age group. Children who have moderate cognitive deficit will have greater difficulties in self-help skills, motor development, social skills, and language development. They may tend to behave like children about half their age. Children with severe cognitive impairment will have trouble functioning in most areas of development.

When you have a child in your group who has a cognitive delay, you will relate as you would to a slightly younger child. You can:

- Break down directions, giving them more slowly.
- Provide many opportunities for the child to successfully practice a new skill.
- Simplify routines, and allow more time for transitions.
- Emphasize self-help skills.

- Use shorter sentences and a simpler vocabulary than you might with the other children.
- Spend more time and use a multisensory approach when you teach a new activity.
- Focus on contrast and give lots of examples when helping the child learn a concept. For example, for the concept of circle, present a variety of shapes so the child can see "circle" versus "not circle," and present many real-life examples throughout the school day.

Because you have no certain way to discover the cognitive competency of a young child, do not assume what a child can do and can't do. Encourage the child to try.

Young Children with Learning Disabilities

The term *learning disabilities* refers to a variety of problems exhibited by children with normal intelligence but below age-level academic functioning. Children with learning disabilities tend to be extremely uneven in their development. For example, a child may have good motor skills but have a considerable delay in language. What identifies this condition is the severity and the extent to which it interferes with the child's ability to function at home or in school.

Learning disabilities in preschool children may not have much impact on daily functioning. In school-age children, however, the inconsistency between ability in one area of development and disability in another often leads to their being blamed for not trying hard enough or of being lazy, uncontrollable, or stubborn.

When you work with a child with learning disabilities be sure to focus on strengths and provide lots of encouragement for successes. There are different kinds of learning disabilities and different strategies for teaching children with learning disabilities. The strategies are largely the same as what you do with other children, but they are more critical. You can:

- Use several sensory modalities so that you help the child learn in the way he or she learns best.
- Allow the child to touch and manipulate materials.
- Be planned and organized and keep activities short.
- Keep transitions and large group times short to avoid situations where the child is waiting with nothing to do.
- Allow adequate time and opportunities for the child to practice new concepts and skills.
- Avoid overstimulation to help the child concentrate.
- Simplify activities so that the child experiences success.
- If needed, add more deliberate attention-getting strategies such as using words like *look, listen,* or *watch me.*

Children with Attention Deficit/Hyperactivity Disorder

When children show impulsive behavior beyond what seems developmentally appropriate and an inability to focus and stay on task, they may have an attention deficit/hyperactivity disorder. In the past it has been called hyperactivity or attention deficit disorder (ADD). The term in use now is *attention deficit/hyperactivity disorder* (ADHD). It usually occurs in conjunction with a learning disability and may not always include hyperactivity.

ADHD occurs more frequently in boys and tends to appear by age 3. Children with ADHD are easily excitable, have trouble waiting for explanations or taking turns, and can seldom pause long enough to relax, watch, or listen. Many cannot tolerate physical restriction and may have trouble getting along with other children. Jeremy, the child in the example earlier in this chapter on page 370, may be suffering from this disorder.

Children with ADHD may have difficulty learning because they have difficulty focusing. They also may develop a negative self-image because they experience few successes in the classroom. If you have a child who is identified as having ADHD in your class, you may find it helpful to:

- Simplify the physical environment and reduce visual stimulation to help the child focus on a task.
- Define the child's work or play area.
- Position yourself nearby so you can offer assistance or encouragement.
- Acknowledge constructive and appropriate behavior.

Not every active young child has an attention deficit/hyperactivity disorder. Children with this problem are identifiable because of the extremes of their behavior. A child must exhibit several characteristics (e.g., impulsiveness, short attention span, distractibility, inability to focus on a task, difficulty organizing and completing work, constant motion, and difficulty following through on directions) to be considered as having ADHD. Children with attention deficit/hyperactivity disorders are sometimes disruptive in the classroom, so you may need a professional evaluation to determine the best course of action.

Some children who have been diagnosed by a pediatrician take prescription drugs such as Ritalin or Dexedrine to control the symptoms of ADHD. These drugs are not always effective and may have negative side effects. In recent years (perhaps because some teachers have unrealistic expectations for children's behavior) ADHD has been overdiagnosed and drugs have been inappropriately prescribed to many children.

Young Children with Emotional or Behavioral Disorders

Children with emotional problems may be more aggressive, unhappy, anxious, or withdrawn than their peers. Children with severe problems are extreme in their reactions and may require specialized care. Withdrawal, anxiety, or aggression may char-

acterize their behavior. They may exhibit unusual behaviors such as self-mutilation, rocking, running with arms flapping, extreme fearfulness, withdrawal, or total loss of self-control.

Frequent and severe emotional difficulties can result from a number of different causes, including inadequate nurture, abuse and neglect, physical injury, or biochemical imbalance. Some stressful life events such as death, divorce, separations, moving, and community violence can provoke emotional distress. Emotional problems interfere with establishing meaningful relationships, with learning, and with the development of a positive sense of self.

If you have a child in your group who seems to require an unusual amount of adult supervision and assistance, or one who is overlooked because he or she so rarely interacts with others, carefully document your observations. The child may exhibit symptoms of emotional disturbance in response to highly stressful situations or as a learned behavior pattern. In any case, the child may benefit from treatment.

A child with emotional problems may be difficult for you to handle, not only because the child is intense but also because even the experts disagree about the causes, classification, and treatment of these conditions. The section on challenging behaviors in Chapter 9 may provide helpful guidance. You may also want to consult with a mental health professional who works in your program or community to help you understand and work with this child.

If you have a child who has emotional difficulties in your class, you may find it helpful to:

- Make sure that daily routines are consistent and predictable.
- Provide soothing activities like water play.
- Make an effort to build a warm, supportive relationship with the child. Start by finding the things you really like about the child and telling them to yourself and to the child.
- Give the child extra support and nurture.
- Be sensitive in comforting the child—one child may love being hugged while another may shrink away from too much physical contact.
- Find an activity or interest that you can talk about with the child. Make an effort to incorporate this into the environment or curriculum.
- Observe the child and talk to the other adults who know the child well to learn what topics, activities, or ways of interacting are distressing to the child. Then try to avoid or limit these.

In today's society, with its lack of adequate of support for families and increased societal violence, more children with behavioral problems are part of early childhood programs. You may need to be persistent in finding appropriate assistance for these children and their families.

Young Children with Autism

Autism is a developmental disability that significantly affects a child's ability to communicate, to understand language, to play, and to relate to others. It is not related to intelligence. At present our best understanding is that autism is a neurological disorder that results from some abnormality in brain development. It may be associated with problems in pregnancy or brain damage at birth. The causes of autism may not be understood, but its prevalence is increasing and more autistic children than ever before are being served in early childhood settings (Bowe 2000; Turnbull et al. 2004).

Autism is typically identified in the first 3 years of life and is four times more common in boys than in girls. The number of children with autism appears to be increasing quite rapidly (some recent figures suggest that 1 child in every 500 shows symptoms of autism). Children who have autism may engage in repetitive activities like rocking or hand flapping, have intense interests and communicate only about a particular topic, be over- or underresponsive to sensory stimuli, look away from the speaker rather than making eye contact, have problems with peer relationships, not engage in pretend play or understand pretend, and be aggressive or injure themselves. Temple Grandin, a writer who has eloquently described her experiences as a child with autism, explains that she was almost unbearably sensitive to things like the rubbing of new clothing on her body and that she was unable to modulate noise. She says that she "had to shut it all out and withdraw or let in all in like a freight train" (Turnbull et al. 2004, 288).

A great deal can be done to help a child with autism learn to be a functional member of society, especially if appropriate intervention begins at an early age. We used to believe that children with autism would not be able to learn language. It now appears that the great majority of them can learn verbal communication if they begin their education before age 5.

There are a number of things you can do in your classroom to assist a child with autism to have a positive school experience. You can:

- Provide consistent and predictable schedules and routines in order not to trigger anxiety.
- Alert the child well in advance if there are going to be changes in the schedule or routines.
- Clearly define behavioral expectations and help the child to learn what is expected.
- Use a variety of strategies in teaching: demonstrate, give visual cues, give clear and consistent directions.
- As appropriate, limit extraneous stimulation by providing the child with earplugs or a quiet and protected place to work.

> **Reflect on working with children with disabilities**
>
> Think about working with children with disabilities. Does the idea make you feel excited and comfortable, or anxious and uncomfortable? Why? What implications does this reflection have for you as a teacher?

OTHER SPECIAL NEEDS

In addition to knowledge about children with disabilities, you will need knowledge and skills to deal with children who have other special needs. They may have been abused or neglected, have chronic health problems, or be gifted and talented.

Children Who Have Been Abused or Neglected

Children who have been abused or neglected have special needs. *Child abuse* is defined as intentional physical and/or emotional maltreatment of a child by an adult, usually a person responsible for the child's welfare. Adults with poor coping skills may maltreat children when confronted with too much stress in their lives. Family conflict, substance abuse, and mental health problems can also lead to abuse. The abusing adult may have been abused as a child and thus learned to use physical, sexual, or verbal violence as a means to control others and to release tensions and frustrations.

The child who has been abused has special needs that can be met by caring adults in a thoughtfully planned program. To rebuild a healthy self-concept and the ability to trust adults, extra time and attention must be devoted to the child. One person in a team should be designated as the child's primary contact, responsible for being physically and emotionally available to meet needs for positive attention, care, comfort, and positive discipline. The consistency of loving firmness can help the child realize that adults can be trustworthy, predictable in their reactions, and in control of themselves and the environment. The child's experience of daily activities and expectations should be carefully structured to promote feelings of mastery, security, and control. A caring adult can participate with the child in sensory activities, such as play dough and water play—first as a way to foster the nurturing relationship, and then as a bridge to encourage normal interest in play activities and socialization with other children and adults.

It is your responsibility as a professional to be aware of the indicators of abuse and neglect (see Table 12.2) and to report suspected cases to the appropriate agency so that the child and family can receive the help they need as soon as possible. As a professional, you also have other legal and ethical responsibilities related to child abuse and neglect. For instance, it is your responsibility as a professional to:

- Be aware of the indicators of abuse and neglect.
- Report suspected cases to the appropriate agency so that the child and family can receive assistance.

Table 12.2 **Warning Signs of Child Abuse or Neglect**

Children who have been abused and neglected may:
- Be overly compliant and passive
- Avoid confrontation with children and adults
- Be extremely demanding or aggressive
- Be extremely dependent
- Be developmentally delayed
- Exhibit infantile behavior
- Show physical injuries such as burns, unusual bruises, or marks at different stages of healing
- Act out the role of a violent adult with another child or a doll as a passive or powerless victim
- Attend school inconsistently
- Appear hungry, underweight, unwell, or dirty
- Be inappropriately dressed for weather conditions
- Demonstrate unusual competence in caring for themselves
- Take on adult responsibilities
- Have difficulty playing cooperatively with other children
- Have difficulty handling changes in the daily routine
- Show precocious sexual awareness in play or talk
- Seem frightened or intimidated when with a particular family member

Abusive families may:
- Withhold emotional support and positive attention
- Make strong verbal attacks—threats of physical harm, name calling, or profanity directed at the child

- Inform families of your reporting obligation as part of their orientation to the program.
- Use the NAEYC Code of Ethical Conduct for guidance.
- Know what is available in your community for educating families about how to interact with their children in constructive ways and about the risks to the child of excessively harsh behaviors.

Every program should have a policy of informing families of their reporting obligation as part of their orientation to the program. Staff should receive written procedures for how to report suspected cases. If your program does not have these policies and procedures, urge the administration to develop some immediately.

Children with Chronic Health Conditions

Children with chronic health conditions also require special consideration. These children may have a wide variety of ailments including respiratory conditions, diabetes, severe allergies, cancer, and many other disorders and conditions.

Health issues may have an impact on the child's ability to function in the school setting. Children who have been ill may lag in the development of motor skills. They may also tire easily and need extra time or support for their participation in class activities. Some may be more dependent on adults. In dealing with a child who has a chronic health problem, as in all of the other situations we discuss in this book, you will need to know the strengths, interests, and needs of the child, to provide support and encouragement that will let the child function as much as possible like others in the classroom or group.

A child's need for support from the teacher or early childhood program will vary with the nature and seriousness of the health condition. A child with a serious allergy, for example, might need only protection from the dangerous allergen and a trained teacher to administer emergency first aid, while a child with chronic asthma might need regular administration of a nebulizer and a carefully modified large motor development curriculum.

The child's pediatrician and the health department in your state will be able to help you plan for inclusion of a child with health issues. When a child with a severe chronic health condition enters your program, you will need to be involved in planning and collaboration with health professionals. A team including school personnel, a nurse from the school or a community agency, the child's family members, and others can be convened to take the responsibility for developing an *individualized health care plan* (IHCP). This plan will address routine health care procedures, who is responsible for addressing needs, and communication networks among the members of the team. Some of the provisions of the plan will be handled by health care specialists. Teachers may be trained to deal with other procedures like giving the child medication (French 2004).

Children with Special Gifts and Talents

Children who have unusual strengths, abilities, or talents are often called *gifted*. No single measure can identify giftedness in children. There may be a single unusual strength or ability, such as a child who has a phenomenal ability to remember, read, or perform music at a very young age. Or a child may have both a "gift" and a disability, as did the son of a friend of ours who had unusual verbal and artistic ability *and* a learning disability.

Children who are gifted may exhibit intense curiosity, ask many questions, conduct investigations into how things work, develop a passionate interest in a particular topic (or topics), demonstrate the capacity for abstract thinking and the use of symbol systems at an early age, be highly independent, be unusually perceptive, have extraordinary memories, show great persistence in self-chosen tasks, or have advanced language ability and the ability to use and appreciate verbal humor.

If you have a child in your program who appears to be unusually advanced in one or more areas of development, you can provide encouragement by offering many opportunities for the child to develop and extend his or her interests. The child will benefit from learning materials that are open-ended, and from self-directed activities that require active involvement and problem solving. Find out what the child really wants to know or do, and then find the materials that will support his or her desire to learn. You may have to find materials designed for children older than the ones with whom you are working. The child who is gifted may have less need for structure than most other children and may work quite independently. Large blocks of time for exploration will give the child the opportunity to concentrate and to work in depth. You support his or her learning by providing a variety of materials and by being available as a resource.

Working with Families of Children with Special Needs

Your relationship with the families of children with special needs will be in most ways like your relationship with families of all the children in your care. The information presented in Chapter 13, "Working with Families," will give you general guidance.

When you have concerns about a child, like Jeremy who we described at the beginning of this chapter, you will schedule a conference with the family after you have collected observational data and researched community resources. Do not approach the family by saying, "I want to talk with you about Jeremy," or "Jeremy has a problem." This kind of statement invariably arouses their anxiety to such a degree that open communication becomes difficult, if not impossible. Instead, make a simple statement about the problem: "Jeremy has some difficulty in getting involved in play activities either alone or with other children. I'd like to talk with you about what we're trying at school and see what works for you at home. Can we get together some afternoon this week to talk about it?"

When you meet with a family to discuss a concern, begin on a positive note. Parents appreciate hearing what you especially enjoy about their child, so begin with positive comments. Tell them what you see as their child's strengths and capabilities. Then share the recorded observations that caused your concern. Work to build an alliance with the family by asking them if they have observed similar behavior and how they handled it. Offer to work with them to clarify the problem and seek assistance for the child. If you think they need some time to think over what you have talked about, you might want to schedule a second meeting to discuss it further.

Often parents have had concerns but have not known where to turn for help. They may be relieved to learn that you are committed to supporting them as you attempt to find answers to your mutual questions. The information and insight you offer may prompt them to arrange a referral for evaluation of the child, or they may ask the school to arrange for the referral. On the other hand, some families may react defensively and reject the possibility that something could be "wrong" with their child. They may prefer to believe it is something the child will outgrow. When this reaction occurs, you can explore other avenues for getting help and support while you continue working with the family. All families need to be reassured that a concern about a child does not mean that you or your program is going to reject the child and family.

The family of a child with special needs faces some difficult challenges: accepting the fact that their child has a disability, finding help for the child, providing special care, and interacting with professionals who are working with them and the child. Like all families, they need your respect and support. Keep in mind that they have their own culture and unique set of strengths, values, skills, expectations, and needs. They need acceptance, open communication, and to be treated as part of a team working on behalf of the child.

The family of a child with disabilities has both the right and the responsibility to play a primary role in determining the nature and extent of services provided for them and their child. They should always be involved in decisions and give their consent to any special services their child receives in addition to those provided for all children in the program. You can help by being a bridge between the family and other professionals, working to ensure that communication is clear among home, school, and professional helpers.

Confidentiality is an important issue. How much is it appropriate to reveal to others about a child's disability? Other families in your program may have questions you must be prepared to answer. They may need to be reassured that the disability itself or the child's behaviors are not "catching." They need to know that children rarely adopt any developmentally inappropriate behavior displayed by a child with a disability. It is important to keep private specific details about the disability or the family. To a pointed question you might reply, "Amy needs extra help in some ways. If you'd like to know more about it, you might want to ask her family." You can offer general reassurance, emphasizing the benefits when children learn to accept differences and to be caring and respectful in relationships with all people. You can encourage families to help the family of the child with a disability feel welcome. Your own attitude will provide a positive model.

FINAL THOUGHTS

We wrote this book to help you learn to care for and educate a broad range of children. What you know about being a caring and competent early childhood educator will help you a great deal in dealing with children who have special needs. We believe that the most important thing you can do is to provide a child who has special needs the opportunity to feel a sense of belonging and to interact with his or her typically abled peers through the process of inclusion. The current commitment to inclusion marks a recognition of the common humanity in all children and is in our view a very positive movement in the early childhood field. Working with a child who has special needs also has the potential to be an unprecedented learning experience in your own development as an educator. You will learn about the child and family, and you will develop skills in collaboration as you help to coordinate the efforts of individuals working with the child. And you will learn more about our shared humanity through the wide spectrum of individual differences.

LEARNING OUTCOMES

When you read this chapter, thoughtfully complete selected assignments from the "To Learn More" section, and prepare items from the "For Your Portfolio" section, you will be demonstrating your progress in meeting the following NAEYC standards for professional development.

Standard 1: Promoting Child Development and Learning

Key elements:

- Knowing and understanding young children's characteristics and needs

- Knowing and understanding the multiple influences on development and learning

- Using developmental knowledge to create healthy, respectful, supportive, and challenging learning environments

Standard 2: Building Family and Community Relationships

Key elements:

- Knowing about and understanding family and community characteristics

- Supporting and empowering families and communities through respectful, reciprocal relationships

- Involving families in their children's development and learning

Standard 3: Observing, Documenting, and Assessing to Support Young Children and Families

Key elements:

- Understanding the goals, benefits, and uses of assessment

- Knowing about and using observation, documentation, and other appropriate assessment tools and approaches

- Understanding and practicing responsible assessment
- Knowing about assessment partnerships with families and other professionals

Standard 4: Teaching and Learning

Key elements:

- Knowing, understanding, and using positive relationships and supportive interactions
- Knowing, understanding, and using effective approaches, strategies, and tools for early education

- Using your own knowledge and other resources to design, implement, and evaluate meaningful, challenging curriculum to promote positive outcomes

Standard 5: Becoming a Professional

Key elements:

- Knowing about and upholding ethical guidelines and other professional standards
- Engaging in continuous, collaborative learning to inform practice

To Learn More

Observe a Program: Observe an early childhood program that includes a child with a disability or other special need. Report on how the staff works to meet the child's needs. How do they appear to feel about the child? Reflect and then comment on the effect that this child has on children and staff in the program. What did you learn from this observation?

Interview a Teacher: Interview a teacher of a child with a disability—a child who was evaluated and placed in a regular early childhood classroom—to find out what procedures were followed in identifying and planning for his or her educational experience. Describe this process and your reactions to it.

Observe a Child I: For at least an hour, observe and "put yourself in the shoes" of a child who has been identified or is suspected of having a disability. Describe what you think the child's experience might be. Based on this experience, discuss how well the program appears to be meeting this child's needs and how it might do so more effectively.

Observe a Child II: Observe a child with a disability who is included in a regular preschool setting. Report on what you would do if you were going to have a conference with the

child's parents. What would you tell them? What questions would you ask? How would you create a climate of safety and trust within the conference?

Research Resources I: Find out what services are offered in your community for disabled children between birth and age 8 (these might be housed in departments of education, health, and/or social services). Write a pamphlet for teachers that explains this information. Include a brief description of the services, who is eligible, phone numbers, and names of contact persons.

Research Resources II: Contact your local school district and see who is eligible for IDEA services. How long does it take for an assessment to be done? What services are available for infants and toddlers? Preschool children? Elementary children?

Research Resources III: Contact the child welfare agency serving your area to find out how child abuse and neglect reports are handled. How is abuse and neglect defined? What kind of help is available to families who are at risk of abuse or have already abused their children?

For Your Portfolio

Write a Community Resources Pamphlet: Research and write a pamphlet on resources for children with special needs and available resources for teachers in your community.

Document Work with a Child: Work with a child who has a special need for a semester and document the things you did to meet the child's needs and what you learned.

13

Working with Families

Just keep in mind though it seems hard I know, most parents once were children long ago—incredible.

Harold Rome

*C*hildren come to school wrapped in the values, attitudes, and behaviors of their families. Although your first and primary role will be working directly with children, you need to be aware that each child is a part of a unique family whose members play a critical role in the child's life and are the child's first and most important teachers. Because of this, your work with families is of the utmost importance.

> *Sasha, a teacher in a typical 3-year-old class, welcomes the children and families as they enter. In the first half-hour she greets Leah and her grandma Carol; Maré, her mother Selina, and baby brother Sol; Tara and her stepdad Will; Emily and her "Nang-nang" (great-grandmother); Emma and her half-brother Suli; Cole and his mom Trudy; and Noah and his mom's boyfriend Sam.*

Families today take a variety of forms that sometimes include adults other than parents (stepparents, siblings, grandparents, and other relatives or friends) who may assume parental roles. To simplify the wording of this chapter, we will most often use the term *family* and in doing so we are speaking of the entire cast of adults who play an intimate and significant role in a child's life. When we speak of *parenting*, we are discussing the nurturing done by all of the important adults who take on a parental role.

You probably chose to become an early childhood educator because of your interest in and commitment to children and may not have realized that working with families would be an important part of your job. Contemporary research suggests that the most effective programs for young children are those that involve two (or more) generations—children and their families. When educators have strong relationships with families and collaboration takes place between home and the early childhood program, children's development and learning are enhanced. Teachers and family members working collaboratively can have positive and long-lasting effects on a child's development and learning.

Relating to children's families has its own unique challenges and rewards. The awareness and sensitivity that you have developed in your work with children are also important to your work with families. Members of a child's family need relationships in which they feel safe and respected, just like their children. Families may differ in their needs, interests, awareness, knowledge, and skill, but many similarities can be found among them. All families are concerned with the welfare of their children. They want the best for them and want to be kept informed of the important events of their lives away from home. The basis for your relationships with families is your commitment to a joint venture of providing support for learning and good experiences for their children.

While you need to create a program that is "family-friendly" (that is, one in which families feel welcome, respected, included, and where their needs are considered), you do not need to become close friends with children's families, nor do you need to be an authority on child rearing. You can offer yourself—a knowledgeable professional who cares about their children and who will make every effort to collaborate with family members and support their children's growth.

As a new teacher you will have had many opportunities to develop skills in working with children but are likely to have less experience and fewer skills in working with adults. Working with families may seem challenging for a number of reasons. You may encounter family members who are not as attentive to the child and the early childhood program as you would like them to be. You might find it difficult to relate to a family whose background, values, and ideas about child rearing are very different from yours. You may find that adults are more inclined to make negative judgments, especially if you are a young teacher with no children of your own. And you might encounter some resentment from a family because they feel in competition with you for the child's affection. If any of these issues arise, try to keep in mind that you and the family need to work together on the child's behalf and that families are often preoccupied with concerns for a number of critical aspects of their lives.

As you begin to work with families, it is helpful to think about differences between the role of a teacher and that of a parent. Although important similarities characterize these roles, we have found the distinctions described by Lilian Katz in "Mothering and Teaching—Some Significant Distinctions" (1980) to be very helpful for beginning teachers. Katz talks about how parents' and teachers' roles are different and how they can complement one another in helping the child grow and learn. Parents and teachers need to be quite different in their attachment to a child. Teachers need to appreciate children realistically. They need to keep enough distance to observe children objectively, balance the requirements of the individual with the welfare of the group, and have goals and plans and the ability to evaluate objectively. Parents need to be their children's most passionate advocates and fans. They care about their children for an infinite amount of time, while educators care about children for the time that they are involved with them. Do not expect families to have an educator's perspective—their job is to be their child's champion. And they need to realize that, though you are committed to their child's learning, your relationship to the child is much different from theirs.

As you come to understand more about families and your relationship with them, you are likely to enjoy working with them. When you demonstrate your understanding and appreciation of a child, most families will be pleased and grateful. Those who recognize the importance of their children's early years will appreciate your effort and skill as few others can. Because they know their child best, family members will be the first to notice when your work has had a positive impact. As you enrich their children's lives and help them with the task of parenting, you can develop warm relationships that may even blossom into friendships. Learning that you have made a difference to a family is among the most rewarding experiences that an early childhood educator can have.

> **Reflect on your feelings about working with families**
>
> When you think about working with families, what interests you? What concerns you? What characteristics and skills do you have that you think will help? What information do you want to have and what skills do you think you will need to develop?

PREPARING TO WORK WITH FAMILIES

The attitudes, knowledge, and skills that you are developing to work with children will serve you well as you begin to interact with families. There are some additional things that you need to learn and think about that will help you to be effective in this important part of the role of the early childhood educator.

Just as you examined your values and attitudes about working with children, you need to look at your values and attitudes regarding families. You will meet families with a variety of approaches to child rearing that reflect differences in values, cultures, and lifestyles. You will encounter family members who have a range of views about education. You will want to be prepared to deal with these differences in constructive ways—without assuming the role of "expert" or assigning blame.

Because of your commitment to children, it may be hard to accept parents whose goals for children are significantly different from yours, who appear uncaring, or who seem to treat a young child in a harsh way. It may sometimes be difficult to decide which behavior simply reflects a difference in values or skill and which constitute abuse for which you have a legal and ethical obligation to intervene. You need to keep in mind that parenting is difficult, that few resources are available, and that the great majority of families *are* doing the best they can given their particular circumstances.

What Parenting Is Like

Your work with families will be enhanced by your awareness of the many aspects of parenting—the joys as well as the struggles. Being sympathetic and supportive is easier when you realize that parenting is not an easy task. It involves a total, day-in, day-out responsibility that is unrelenting and that cannot be ignored or avoided. The stresses can sometimes overshadow the pleasures. By helping parents to understand their child's stage of development and the ways in which he or she is unique, you can help parents renew their pleasure in their child and enjoy the process of parenting.

People enter into child-rearing with many kinds of expectations. The reality is almost certain to be different from what was anticipated. As parents develop, they seem to follow a relatively predictable sequence. Ellen Galinsky (1981) describes the early childhood years as the time in their child's life when parents learn to be nurturers and define themselves as authority figures in the family.

During the last half-century the purpose of the family has enlarged from the performance of specific survival functions such as providing food, shelter, clothing, and supervision to ensure children's physical well-being. It now includes the more abstract tasks of providing psychological security and skills in dealing with an increasingly complex and dangerous world. Society's view of family roles has changed over the last several decades. Today we are aware of the importance of the early years in children's development and learning. Some families feel pressure to hurry their children into activities that are supposed to ensure success—academic tutoring; music, dance, and athletic lessons; team sports; and entrance into the "best" preschool to ensure access to the best primary school, high school, and even college.

Today's world is extremely complex. Because of the great diversity of situations and structures common in any group of families today, the ways in which some of the children in your program are raised will be quite different from what you remember from your childhood. These differences create special responsibilities for you as an early childhood educator.

Your first responsibility is to be aware. While many children live with both their parents with relatives nearby, single parents and stepparents are commonplace. Newly "blended" families that include the children of a parent's new marriage, grandparents, and other related and unrelated adults are also common. Families with same-sex parents are increasingly frequent. Your next responsibility is to be accepting of the wide range of family structures you will encounter.

In every community, families experience stress. Whether you work in a suburban, rural, or inner-city classroom, children's families will be dealing with some kinds of stress. Families of children in your class may be coping with financial need, divorce and family changes, unmet child care needs, stressful work situations, drug and alcohol abuse, parents who are too young for the responsibility of child rearing, child abuse, inadequate health care, family and community violence, or homelessness.

Because of financial need in many families, both parents must work. They must deal with multiple roles of parent, spouse, and employee; and may lack time and energy to nurture their children. Single-parent families (a dramatically increasing number, most frequently mothers) must provide all the care for their children. They have even less time and fewer resources, often living in poverty. Since families move frequently, many lack the community and extended family support that was common in a less mobile society. If they are struggling to survive financially they may be forced to rely on social agencies, including early childhood education and care programs, to perform many of the roles that were once the responsibility of the extended family.

Many young parents, especially those who become parents while they are teenagers, are not prepared for the challenges of child rearing. They may need information and assistance, which needs to be provided with tact and respect. You can help them, along with other parents, to understand that their children need love, protection, health care, good nutrition, and a sense of belonging. Simple strategies for caring for and guiding children can be shared informally in conversation and through modeling.

You cannot, as an early childhood teacher, take on the role of therapist, social worker, or extended family. However, you can support families by doing your job with competence and by understanding their needs. Your program can be a good place to help families learn about children's needs and to provide support for them in the day-to-day tasks of parenting. Your positive relationships with families will help them to feel easier about turning to you for assistance and about sharing some of the responsibility for their child with you.

Reflect on a family you know

Think about a family you know that is facing some challenges. What are the issues that this family is dealing with? How do they cope with the challenges? What services would be helpful to them? What is the impact on the child and the family if these services are not available?

We live in a diverse society. So it is inevitable that the children in your class will come from families whose culture, religion, race, ethnicity, and lifestyle are different from your own. In order to support all children and families it is necessary to respect these differences. Understanding and learning to accept and respect diverse families and their child-rearing practices may be more challenging than you think. Your views of a good family have their origins in your own childhood. They reflect your culture and your experiences. You may not realize the extent to which they are a part of who you are.

It is typical for people to view differences as "wrong" rather than different. By becoming an early childhood educator you are making a commitment to learning about and being open to the range of families and the ways they care for and raise their children. Remember too, that cultural differences are not only reflected in differences in skin color, language, religion, and country of origin. Cultural differences are present between families that are racially similar but from different socioeconomic backgrounds. Differences in culture are found between families with the same ethnic backgrounds whose families emigrated in different generations. Cultural differences exist between families who originate from different parts of the same country, including our own. While many child-rearing practices are cultural in origin, others reflect individual families' preferences and values.

When you support diverse families you do not make assumptions. You do not assume that every family celebrates the same holidays, has a mother and a father, eats the same foods, sees the role of child and parent in the same way, believes in the same (or any) god, has the same ways of caring for a child, or shares the same view of death and what happens after death. To avoid making assumptions, tell families that you respect and honor them for who they are and ask them to help you to support their child by explaining their perspectives and beliefs to you. One way to begin this kind of dialogue is to ask families to tell you about if and how they celebrate holidays and birthdays (see Figure 13.1).

When you work with diverse families you are almost certain to encounter child-rearing practices and ideas about children that are different from your own. These are influenced by values, culture, education, religious views, and even the books that parents have read about parenting.

Four-year-old Kayla comes to school dressed in shiny white shoes, a crisply ironed dress, with her hair elaborately combed, braided, and decorated with barrettes. Her friend Toni arrives in sneakers, old shorts, a clean T-shirt, and disheveled hair. By the end of the day Kayla's shoes are scuffed, her dress is painted, and her barrettes are missing. Her mother scolds her, "You wrecked your new dress! I can't afford to buy you new clothes every week!" Toni's shirt is covered with paint and she has torn her shorts. Her dad says, "Looks like you had fun today!" and gives her a hug.

In the story above, which parent's viewpoint was closest to yours? Did you react strongly to either child's dress or either parent's behavior? When you find that you are reacting strongly to a family it is a sign that you need to look more deeply.

It is beyond the scope of this book to provide you with information on the multitude of ways that culture can influence families and their views of children and education. However it is useful to be aware that when you encounter

> **Reflect on your ideas about child-rearing**
>
> Choose two or three of the areas of child rearing listed on the following pages. Think about how these were handled in your home when you were a child. How have you dealt with these in your experiences with children? Do you find you have some strong views about how these things are supposed to be done? How might your feelings about this impact on your work with families?

Figure 13.1   **Celebration Survey Form**

CELEBRATION SURVEY

Most people have special days that they celebrate, that are part of their cultural and family traditions. We want to be respectful of your family's beliefs and would like to recognize your family's celebrations in our program. In order to be as inclusive as possible we would like to find out about celebrations in your family. Please let us know by completing the following survey. If, for religious or philosophical reasons, you prefer that your children not participate in celebrations or activities we want to know that too. We're beginning with the fall celebrations that are coming up but would like to know about any celebrations or holidays that are important in your family. Thanks for your help.

Family name: _____

Are there any holidays, celebrations, or celebration activities that you prefer we avoid while your child is enrolled? Please describe:

Please tell us about what you celebrate in your family and how you celebrate

Holiday	How you celebrate it in your family	Would you like to share your celebration at school in some way? How?
Birthdays		
Fall		
Halloween		
Day of the Dead		
Rosh Hashanah		
Other fall celebrations		
Winter		
Christmas		
Kwanzaa		
New Year's Day		
Valentine's Day		
Lunar (Chinese) New Year		
Other winter celebrations		
Spring		
Ramadan		
Girl's Day		
St. Patrick's Day		
Mother's Day		
Other spring celebrations		
Summer		
Father's Day		
4th of July		
Other summer celebrations		

differences in various areas of child socialization, what you may be experiencing is a cultural difference. Cultural differences exist in the following areas:

- *Toileting*, including the age that families expect children to be toilet trained, and the process that families use to teach children to use the toilet
- *Food and feeding*, including when different foods are introduced, what foods are considered appropriate and inappropriate to eat, how much food children are expected to eat, where and with whom the child should eat, table manners, and what times children are fed
- *Nursing, bottles, and pacifiers*, including views on whether children should be nursed and if so until what age and in what circumstances, whether infants are fed on demand or on a schedule, at what age bottle-fed babies should be expected to give up the bottle, and whether pacifiers are given
- *Sleeping arrangements* for children, including with whom the child sleeps, when and where the child is put to sleep, and whether the child takes regular naps
- *Bathing and grooming*, including how often the child is bathed and the time and attention given to creating and maintaining neat hair, nails, clean teeth, and the extent to which children are expected/allowed to get messy
- *Ways children demonstrate respect/disrespect* for adults, including whether children are expected to make eye contact or not as a sign of respect, whether children are expected to ask adults questions or make jokes with adults, and the names adults are called by children
- *Role of the child in the family*, including whether children or adults are central in the household and family, the extent to which children's activities and belongings dominate the household, and whether children are included or excluded from important family events such as weddings and funerals
- *Responsibilities of children*, including whether children are expected to perform household tasks, and the age at which serious responsibility such as caring for younger siblings is given to children
- *Relative value placed on play and academics*, including whether play is viewed as an important task or a distraction, and if academics are viewed as the most significant type of learning
- *Definitions of safe and healthy*, including whether children should be protected from health and safety risks like getting cold or climbing high, or if they should be exposed to risks to build strength and skill
- *Appropriate dress* for school and other situations, including whether the child is dressed in specially purchased school clothes that the child is expected to keep clean, or sent to school in play clothes that can get dirty
- *Sex roles*, including whether the child is expected to play and behave in ways designated by sex (e.g., playing with dolls versus roughhousing), and whether adults are expected to adhere to traditional sex roles
- *Modesty*, including what body parts should be covered, what types of clothing and adornment are considered appropriate/inappropriate for young children and adults
- *Appropriate knowledge for children*, including whether and what age children are exposed to such things as the proper names of body parts, sexuality, birth, illness, disability, death, and violence
- *Attitudes toward emerging sexuality*, including whether children are expected to be innocent and ignorant of sexuality and whether adults think that exploration of sexuality is appropriate

> **Reflect on your feelings about differences in families**
>
> How do you feel about families whose lifestyles are different from your own? How do you feel about families who raise their children differently from what you were brought up to think is right? What child-rearing practices have you heard of that feel uncomfortable or strange to you? What might you do to learn more about them?

399

This list is by no means comprehensive. Indeed every aspect of life is in some way influenced by culture. Some of the biggest areas of miscommunication with families concern the things we take for granted because of our cultures. With insight and awareness of these differences you will find yourself more open and more ready to accept and appreciate all families.

Building Relationships

To work effectively with families, you need to focus on building good relationships with them. Although this task need not be difficult or time-consuming, it does require thoughtfulness and attention. Good relationships with families do not develop simply because you have good intentions.

All people are more trusting and open in an atmosphere of concern, respect, acceptance, and individual attention. The things that you do to build such an atmosphere for families in your program are usually small, easy to overlook, and as simple as common courtesy. Good relationships begin when families feel welcome in your program. You convey that welcome when you greet family members by name, invite them in, and have provisions for regular sharing of information.

All relationships are based on sharing and trust. Take time to find out what family members are interested in, what they do, and what they care about. Share information that will help them know about their child in school. Acknowledge events and transitions in the child's life in your program and at home. Recognize and share a family's joys and sorrows. It is also appropriate to let them get to know you as a person with particular enthusiasms and skills (though it is not appropriate to share *your* personal problems). Be scrupulous about maintaining confidentiality. Nothing destroys trust faster than idle gossip and broken confidences.

You will want to convey to families that you are committed to hearing their concerns (at appropriate times) and seeking solutions to problems rather than avoiding issues or insisting on your own methods. Skills in active listening, giving I-messages, and avoiding roadblocks (introduced in Chapter 9) will be helpful. You may sometimes feel that listening to families' concerns is extra work. Remember that the time you spend may ultimately contribute to the quality of the relationship and benefit the child.

Communication Skills

Both families and you possess information that you each need for the child's well-being. Families bring knowledge and experience of their child as a unique human being, and you bring your knowledge of children in general and awareness of current best practices in working with young children. Both types of information are vital if you are to create the best possible experience for each child.

Your knowledge of child development and early childhood education will influence your relationships with children and serves as a basis for the kind of program you plan for them. In order for families to understand your goals and how the program contributes to their child's growth and learning, you need to be able to communicate your knowledge in ways that they can understand. Communicating specialized information means translating professional jargon into language that is clear to families. Saying that you provide opportunities for motor development is not as valuable as letting a family know that swinging, sliding, trike riding, and climbing help their child to develop physical strength, and coordination. And it may not be nearly as meaningful as letting them know that physical skill and confidence contribute to social and academic success.

As family members observe your approach to curriculum and classroom management and learn more about the rationale for what you do, they will be better able to support their child's learning at home. For example, you can tell families that you have chosen not to provide workbooks for their children because young children learn concepts through real experiences. You might then show a sorting activity where children make discriminations similar to a workbook task and share some ways that similar activities (such as sorting clothes and putting away the silverware) might be provided at home. Similarly, you may demonstrate the effectiveness of providing choices to children as a great "trick" for gaining cooperation.

Providing families with information that is meaningful to them is a skill that you will develop with time and experience. Share what you know and be willing to admit what you don't know but are willing to learn more about. Remember that you and the family both have worthwhile ideas and that neither of you is infallible. You *are* the professional in these situations, however, and although you need to be respectful of families, you also need to act on your best professional judgment. If their requests violate what you know to be best for children, you have an ethical responsibility to do what is right for children—but you will need to explain the reasons.

As an available and knowledgeable professional, you may find yourself being asked for advice or may feel a strong desire to offer it when you are not asked. We have found that it works better to offer such advice only when it is asked for and in a tentative fashion. To a parent who has difficulty coping with a whiny child at a late pick-up you might say, "All of the children seem to get cranky when they're hungry and it's close to supper. I have found that it helps when families bring a small, nutritious snack to give to them on the ride home."

How to Support Families in Times of Stress

Even though you are not a counselor, you will need to have information and strategies for supporting families during times of stress. Some kinds of stress are relatively minor, the result of juggling the responsibilities of a busy life; others are more serious such as a change in the family structure. Family members who are experiencing stress will respond best to low-key, sensitive, and respectful ways of interacting with them.

You will help families in times of stress in several ways. The first is by being there and doing your job. Children and families are supported when teachers are present, attentive, and professional. Families often need assistance when the family structure changes, as with a new baby, death, divorce, or remarriage. One of the simplest ways that you can help is by keeping a child's school life as stable as possible during the period of change. When you establish good relationships with families before there is a problem, and honor confidentiality, then they will feel comfortable letting you know when a problem exists.

The second way that you help families in times of stress is by helping them find needed assistance. To do this you need to have knowledge of programs such as child guidance and divorce clinics, mental health services, shelters for victims of family violence, family mediation organizations, and neighborhood resources.

As a person who works closely with a family in today's society, it is almost inevitable that you will find yourself being asked to play a supportive role for one or both parents in divorce or child custody conflicts. Because these conflicts can be traumatic, policies and procedures need to be established prior to a problem occurring. A clear policy statement can help the parents to understand that your primary commitment is to the child's welfare. You can also communicate that such problems are by no means unique or a sign of family failure. When a divorce or custody battle does take place, it can be tempting to express your preference for one parent or the other. Keep in mind that you serve a child better by maintaining neutrality unless the child appears endangered. In cases where family members are in conflict, the NAEYC Code of Ethical Conduct states, in section P-2.10, "We shall work openly, sharing our observations of the child, to help all parties involved make informed decisions. We shall refrain from becoming an advocate for one party" (see Appendix A).

Reflect on your strengths and challenges in supporting families

What do you see as your potential strengths in communicating with families and supporting them when they are dealing with stressful situations? What might be challenging for you? What experiences, understandings, and skills do you have that may help you? What understandings, and skills do you need to work on?

Ethical and Legal Responsibilities

You have many professional responsibilities to the children and families with whom you work. You also have ethical and legal obligations.

Confidentiality is an ethical obligation of every professional and one whose importance we cannot stress strongly enough. One of your first ethical obligations to families is to keep information about them and their children confidential and to share it only when there is legitimate need to do so. A related legal responsibility has to do with the confidentiality of children's records. Generally, the only individuals who have access to a child's file are parents or guardians and those professionals who need to have the information to serve the best interests of the child. The Family Education Rights and Privacy Act (FERPA) grants families the right to examine their child's official records and protects the privacy of the records. In most programs, official files are stored in a locked file cabinet.

As we told you in Chapter 12, early childhood educators are obligated to report suspected cases of child abuse or neglect. Even though you have an obligation to work with families as cooperatively and sensitively as possible, it is also your responsibility to be aware of the indicators of abuse and neglect and to report suspected cases. Every program should have written policies that notify families of their obligation to report child abuse and neglect and of policies designed to protect children. It can help to preserve relationships when families are notified upon entering a program that early childhood educators are "mandated reporters," just like doctors, and that the staff's goal is to work with them to educate and protect their children. Become familiar with the reporting procedures of your program and the resources in your community so that you know what to do when you must meet this responsibility.

When you suspect a potential for child abuse or neglect, you, or a colleague or administrator, need to confer with the family to develop a plan for addressing the situation, provide consultation and parent education as appropriate, and make referrals to agencies that might help the family. If you find yourself in this situation make every effort to maintain positive relationships with the family at this time. Focus on positive aspects of the child in discussion and make an effort to notice and comment on attempts to handle the child's behavior in a constructive way.

If you are convinced that the child is being abused, a report must be made to a child protective services agency. Most schools and child care centers have a person, often the principal or director, who will provide guidance for you in documenting your concerns and who is designated to report cases of abuse. Parents who are under the stress of an investigation of child abuse need extra support from staff, not less. Let the family know that your goal is to support them and help them cope better. Avoid doing anything that might make the parent feel inadequate or incompetent. Neither child nor parent should be labeled as "abused" or "abuser" and confidentiality should be scrupulously kept.

Every state has its own laws and regulations pertaining to early childhood education programs. Compliance is often the obligation of program administrators; however, it is important for you to be aware of your ethical and legal responsibilities. You can learn more about legal mandates from the agency that regulates early childhood programs in your state.

INCLUDING FAMILIES IN THE EARLY CHILDHOOD PROGRAM

Early childhood educators have always realized that including families was an important part of the educational process. This has recently been acknowledged beyond early childhood programs in Goal 8 of the National Education Goals, which states:

> By the year 2000, every school will promote partnerships that will increase parental involvement and participation in promoting the social, emotional, and academic growth of children. (National Education Goals Panel 1997)

Family involvement can run the gamut from early childhood programs that include parents at all levels to those in which parents are contacted only rarely when a problem needs to be addressed. Ideally, you and children's families will work closely in a variety of ways. Family members will participate in classroom activities; plan or attend parent education programs; serve on committees and policy-making groups; and contribute to the program through work on facilities, fund-raising, and lobbying in the community on its behalf.

There are many things you can do to create such an ideal family involvement program. You can begin the minute a family visits your program. You can continue until the day that their child moves on to the next school. In between, you can consistently welcome families to your program, share information, conduct conferences, create ways for family members to be involved, and help provide parent education.

Making Families Welcome

> It is the middle of the morning during the first month of school. Jackie, the 3-year-olds' teacher, is making cinnamon toast with the children. Sienna's mom comes through the door. "Hi Tara!" Jackie says, looking up and smiling. "Would you like to join us?" In the 4-year-old classroom across the hall, Matt's mom, Amanda, enters. Wendy, Matt's teacher, is reading a story. She looks up, her brows knit, and she frowns. Amanda stands by the classroom door for about 15 minutes without acknowledgment. Finally, she signs Matt out and leaves without having talked to a teacher.

The ways that these family members were treated give very different messages about whether the school is a place where they are welcome. Whether it is the first or fortieth time a person enters your classroom, it is important always to make family members feel welcome. What makes a parent feel welcome? It is welcoming when teachers call parents by name. It is welcoming when there is an "open door"—meaning family members can visit at any time. It is welcoming when parents are treated like guests, not problems or intruders.

You can make family members feel welcome every day. If possible, be available to greet them and answer their questions. Work to learn their names. Remember what they tell you about their child and family and ask how they are doing. Invite them to come into the classroom. Give them meaningful ways to help out at school and at home. When you do these simple things you are building relationships that will support the family, the child, and your program.

Sharing Information

You help families to understand and support your program by sharing information with them. When they know what you are doing and why, it helps them to contribute and to be better equipped to work with their children at home in activities that support learning.

Getting Started

The first opportunity to share information with a family may occur when they visit your program to learn about it and to decide whether it is right for them. Though they may not do more than observe in your classroom, you can aid them in their decision-making if they ask questions by providing an understandable explanation of what is done in your classroom and why.

Once a family has chosen your program, other avenues open up for continuing and expanding this new relationship. Whenever a child starts, the family should receive an orientation to the program and your classroom. At the beginning of a year or when a number of new families enter the program, you may have an orientation meeting. Otherwise you may do this for one family at a time.

In most programs you will have an opportunity to ask parents to share information about their child's growth, development, and family situation; their perspective on their child as a person; and their methods of child rearing—and you can ask them to tell you how they would like to be involved in the program. You may want to provide a form similar to the one in Figure 13.2.

The initial visit and orientation meeting are useful in setting the climate for future interactions and family involvement; however, they are only the beginning of an ongoing process of communication. The basis for your relationship with families is your intimate knowledge of and your commitment to their child. Because of previous experiences with schools and teachers, some people do not feel comfortable in their initial contacts with an early childhood program. In the beginning, you will need to take the lead and assume the bulk of the responsibility for building the relationship. You can accomplish this groundwork by frequent and positive sharing of information about the program's activities and your observations of their child. Sharing the small joys and sorrows of the child's life creates a bond between you and the family.

Daily Communication

Good daily communication with families requires flexible and creative planning, and it is important to use all the avenues that are available to you. In most preschools, families enter the program each day to drop off and pick up their children.

When they do, you have an opportunity to share what you have observed about children:

"Sidney worked really hard in the block area today. He was very persistent and figured out how to make his tower as tall as the shelf. His face shone with delight when he finally was able to make his tower strong enough not to topple."

"Courtney had a kind of hard day today. She was unhappy when Shan wouldn't play with her. Then her bunny got buried in the sand and we couldn't find it at nap time and she couldn't sleep for a long time. She finally slept a little and felt better this afternoon, especially after we found bunny."

Every classroom needs a place where families know they can go to get a quick update on what's happening in their child's school. There is usually a sign-in sheet at the entrance to the school or classroom. A message center here, where each family has a mailbox or message pocket, helps to make communication easier. Families can be informed of the activities of the program by reading a week's plans posted near the sign-in area or sent home each week.

Every teacher needs to send home regular written communication (usually a newsletter) to every family, especially if family members do not have the opportunity

Figure 13.2 **Child History and Health Inventory Form**

Child History and Health Inventory

Please help us get to know your child better.

Child's name, birthdate, and place of birth:

Name your child answers to, or preferred name:

Family Information

Parent/guardian's names:

Siblings names and ages:

Family structure: _____ Nuclear _____ Single-parent
_____ Blended _____ Extended

Languages spoken at home:

Does your child live in more than one household (not including child care at another family member's home)?

If yes, what percentage of time does your child spend in each?

Who lives in your child's household(s)?

Name: **Relationship**

Has your child had a pet? _____

Pet's type and name:

Birth and Developmental Milestones

Child's birth weight: _____ Was your child premature? _____

Were there any illnesses or problems during pregnancy/labor/delivery? If so please describe:

When did your child start walking? _____ Talking? _____ Using the toilet? _____

Health and Routines

Does your child nap regularly? _____ At what time(s)? _____ For how long? _____

What time does your child usually go to bed? _____

At what time does s/he usually wake up? _____

Does your child have a comfort object/toy that s/he usually sleeps with? _____

What is it? _____

Does your child sleep alone, or with another person? _____

Describe your child's usual bedtime routine:

Does your child eat big or small meals? _____

When do you usually eat breakfast? _____ Lunch? _____ Snacks? _____

What are your child's food preferences?

Does your child have any known allergies?

Has your child had any serious illnesses or hospitalizations? Please describe:

Is your child able to play outside on a regular basis? _____ How often? _____ Where? _____

Does your child watch TV or view videos on a regular basis? _____ How often? _____

For how long? _____

(continued)

405

Figure 13.2 **Child History and Health Inventory Form** *(Continued)*

Life/Social Experiences

How many different homes has your child lived in? _____

How long has your child lived in your current home? _____

What social/separation experiences has your child had (check all that apply)?

_____ With friends/relatives at their home?

_____ With friends'/relatives' children in their homes?

_____ With family child care provider/baby sitter/nanny?   How often? _____

_____ With playgroup?   How often? _____

_____ Preschool/child care center?   How long did your child attend? _____

Has your child had any intense experiences in the last year (e.g., divorce, separation, remarriage, move, death or illness of a friend, relative, or pet)?

Your Perspective

Describe your child's personality:

Does your child have any strong fears? Please describe (e.g., loud noises, dogs):

How does your child adjust to new situations?

What does your child do especially well?

How do you discipline your child?

Do you have concerns about your child's present behaviors?

Is there anything else the staff should know about your child?

to come into the school. Bulletin boards and newsletters offer opportunities to explain aspects of the program in greater detail, to solicit assistance from families, and to provide information about child development and other topics of interest. These techniques are most successful if they are visible, attractive, short and to the point, and easy to read. If reading them is built into some other routine, such as sign-in, they are more likely to get the attention of family members.

Another way to communicate to families that they are valued parts of the program is to create a family corner. This area might have a comfortable adult chair or a couch, reading material, coffee or tea, pictures of the children at play, or even a slide/tape presentation about the program. Parents may enjoy talking to one another in this area or a child and parent might spend a quiet moment there together.

Keeping in contact with busy working parents involves a special effort. If your program runs for more than 8 hours, responsibility for communicating with family members at beginning or end of the day may need to be assigned to another teacher since you may not get to talk with families during your work hours. We have found it effective to keep a communication log (in a notebook or folder) for each family near the sign-in sheet to serve as a substitute for face-to-face communication. Staff and family members read and write in it frequently to share information about the child.

In most elementary schools and in some preschools family members drop off and pick up their children without coming to the classroom. You may rarely have an opportunity to communicate with them. When this is the case it is important to devise alternative ways to keep in touch with families. A weekly newsletter, a log that goes home with the child and returned each day, or regular phone calls can help you to maintain frequent communication with families.

If some of the families in your program have special communication needs, if they are non-English-speaking, or if literacy is a problem, then you will need to make a special effort to ensure that you communicate with them. Bilingual staff and family members might be designated as translators and others as readers for those who have difficulty reading. Information can be presented graphically as well as in written form to enhance the communication. In order to reach everyone, the guiding principle is to present the same information in many different forms.

Addressing Questions and Concerns

Because families are so deeply concerned about their children, it is inevitable that some questions and concerns will arise regarding things that are happening in your program. It is valuable to remind yourself that not only is it a *right* of parents to ask questions, it is their *responsibility*. Parents who are doing their job want to know what you are doing and why you are doing it. Such questioning can lead to an open exchange of information and ideas that can help you gain greater insight into the family's values and goals for their children.

We have found that there are some predictable areas of concern for families whose children are enrolled in early childhood programs. They are most likely to express concerns about their child's health and safety in the program, about the care of their child's possessions and clothing, and about the purpose of play and their child's academic progress. These issues relate to their expectations about children and school and may relate to their culture.

Despite a good relationship, addressing concerns can be challenging. It is essential that family members feel heard, that their issues are addressed, and that their efforts and judgment are respected. If you consistently display sensitivity in dealing with their concerns, families are more likely to hear yours. To be prepared, you need to be able to respond to questions in ways that keep the lines of communication open and without being defensive.

Questions sometimes arise because of the nature and philosophy of the program. Young children's programs often are quite different from other kinds of schools. The materials and experiences provided may seem to bear little relationship to traditional education. Families may wonder why their children play so much, why they're not learning "academic" skills, why they come home dirty, or why you let them do things that appear risky.

Concerns about play often reflect a lack of understanding of how young children learn. Family members may relax as you help them to understand that children learn in ways that are significantly different from adults, and that the development of motor and perceptual skills form the base of later, more abstract learning. Because the most recent formal educational experiences of most adults have usually been in lecture situations, they may have lost touch with the learning that goes on in active, hands-on experiences. Remind parents of the things that they learned by doing—cooking, driving a car, bathing a baby, using a computer—and that *doing* is an important way of learning. Explain the sequence of development in concrete terms: "Children first have to learn to tell the difference between more obvious things like blue round beads and square purple ones before they can tell the difference between more subtle things like numbers and letters." Specific examples will help adults to see the purpose of the activities that you do with children.

Rose, the mother of 4-year-old Ethan, came into the her son's class one morning and said to Gary, the teacher, "I don't think you're offering Ethan enough challenge. Ethan will write his ABC's when I sit down with him at home. But all he does here is play with blocks and ride trikes. He's going to go to kindergarten in the fall, you know."

What could Gary have said? If he answered defensively—"We told you when Ethan started here at our center that we had a play-based program. Research tells us that children learn through play."—he would not have demonstrated that he had heard or cared about what Rose said. Similarly, if he had not taken responsibility—"Well, a lot of the children are interested in letters but Ethan just doesn't seem to unless we force him"—he would not have addressed the parent's concern.

When families question you about the curriculum, it is essential that you take their concerns seriously and not dismiss them. It is equally important that you speak from your own knowledge and experience of developmentally appropriate practice. We are educators because of our specialized expertise, and it is our responsibility to address families' concerns with sensitivity. Gary, in the previous example, might instead have had a dialogue with Rose that sounded something like this:

> **Gary:** *Thank you for telling me about what you've been doing and what you're worrying about. I've noticed that Ethan can write the alphabet. But it doesn't seem to be what he's most interested in at school. Does he enjoy writing the alphabet at home?*
>
> **Rose:** *Well, not unless I sit him down. But he knows he has to do his work.*
>
> **Gary:** *What I've noticed is that Ethan loves to look at books and listen to stories. That's a really important first step in learning to love reading. Some other things I've noticed about Ethan is that he likes playing with rhyming words. Believe it or not, that's another important part of learning to read.*
>
> **Rose:** *What about teaching letters and words? I bought a workbook at the drugstore last week, and that's his homework—just like his big brother. Why aren't you teaching him anything like that at school?*
>
> **Gary:** *What I've been doing here at school is that I've introduced a word bank for each of the children. Here's Ethan's file of "special words." He has five words—all the members of his family. I've also been introducing more print into the room. You know, back at the beginning of the year I put up some labels on different things in the classroom, like the box of bristle blocks. Ethan's also been enjoying a "hunt the letter" game we've been playing. What seems to work best for Ethan is when I make letter activities personal and active.*
>
> **Rose:** *Yeah, he really does like to move.*
>
> **Gary:** *I want him to keep on liking school, so I want to make learning about reading fun and meaningful. His whole group is going to kindergarten in the fall and we were already planning more letter activities for the rest of the year. I'll be sure to let you know how Ethan responds to them. Does that sound good to you?*
>
> **Rose:** *Oh yes.*

Parents who feel heard are much more likely to be supportive of your program. They are also much more likely to hear your answers and explanations when they have concerns.

The messes inherent in the sensory development, art, and science curricula are also frequent topics of concern. Knowing the purpose of these activities may make them easier for families to appreciate. Discomfort may be eased if the activities are announced in advance, if children are sent to school in play clothes, and if you provide smocks to protect clothing from damage.

Some adults may be astonished and alarmed by the physical challenges that children undertake in the early childhood education and care setting. They may never have allowed children to climb to the top of a climbing structure or to use functional saws, scissors, or knives. They may not understand why you do. They may not be aware of what young children can safely do with close supervision. People vary greatly in their judgment of what is or is not dangerous. We find it helpful to let family members know that we share their concerns and then go on to talk about the value of the activity and the safeguards that we take. You can let families and children know that you won't allow or encourage children to attempt activities that are clearly beyond their capacities, but that your situation safely provides opportunities for exploration that contribute to development.

Conducting Conferences

A conference provides you and family members with time to share information and perceptions. They provide for in-depth and personal exchange of information that is not possible in other ways. A central purpose of a conference is to form an alliance with the family that will support the child's growth and learning. During conferences, you may explore issues relating to the child at home and in the program. At a conference you can provide information as well as help family members express and clarify their feelings and values and develop their skills and resources. It is a time when you may learn about personal or family problems. Regular conferences support your work and build relationships. If conferences are held rarely or only in the event of a problem, they will be more stressful and less productive.

Planning will help you to spend conference time effectively. First you will need to plan for quiet, undisturbed space and sufficient time. Providing these things ensures that the conference will be unpressured and productive. Scheduling 10 conferences for 20 minutes each on one day is neither an effective nor pleasant way to plan for this important task.

You can prepare for the conference by looking over your anecdotal records, assessments, samples of work, and other records on the child. Many teachers prepare a portfolio (as described in Chapter 5), write a summary, or fill out a checklist to use as a conference guideline.

Family members may be apprehensive if they do not understand the purpose of the conference. You will want to begin by explaining that conferences are regularly scheduled times for parents and teachers to share information and get to know one another better. Assure them that you welcome their ideas and questions and that the conference is a joint process. You may use the conference as an opportunity to set common goals for the child. In some elementary schools the child participates in the conference and takes the lead in describing classroom activities and sharing his or her work. Teachers who have done this kind of conference are very pleased with how effectively it involves the family and communicates the child's school experience.

As you share your perceptions of the child in school, try to describe what the child *does* rather than saying what he or she *is*: "Matthew usually watches the others use a new piece of equipment before he tries it. He seems to like to have a quiet space and a long period of time." Do not say, "Matthew is very shy." It is best to discuss the child's areas of strength and look at other areas in terms of areas for future growth.

When it is necessary to discuss a problem—for example when you are working with a parent to find ways to help a child find alternatives to hurting others—assume that solutions can be found. You can use conference time to clarify the issues, agree on goals, develop a plan of action for home and in the program, and decide when you will meet again to evaluate what you have done. We recommend writing down what you agree on with families and providing a copy for each of you (see Figure 13.3).

It is natural and necessary for families to be intense, emotional, and partial to their child. Educators play a different role—they must be less intense and more objective. In approaching conferences, assume that family members have good intentions and that they will share as honestly as you do. You may disagree with one another because of your different experiences in life and with the child, but you are ultimately on the same side—the child's.

Involving Families in the Program

You can play an important role in supporting family participation in your program. Involved family members can work with the children, orient other families to classroom participation, provide input into program policy, and strengthen the relationship of the entire program to the community. When family members participate as volunteers in the classroom, it can enrich your program and enable you to do more. They support children's experience when they work with individuals and small groups in the classroom and accompany you as you take children on trips outside of the program environment.

Figure 13.3 **Example of a Family Conference Form**

Family Conference Form

Child: _____   Date: _____

Family member(s): _____

Teacher(s): _____

Topics to Discuss

Ideas for supporting the child's growth at school:

Ideas for supporting the child's growth at home:

Resources requested by family at the conference:

Questions or concerns raised at the conference:

Follow-up plan:

Family's plan for child's future (next school, etc.):

When family members volunteer in the classroom, everyone can benefit: the families, the staff, and the children. When *family members* participate in the program, they:

- Have an opportunity to learn about new ways of guiding growth and development
- Gain firsthand insight into the meaning of the curriculum that they may be able to apply at home
- Gain a sense of competence and a feeling of being needed as they contribute to the program

When family members participate in the program, the *children*:

- Have a chance to see their family members in a different role
- Become acquainted with adults who have skills, feelings, and ways of relating that are different from their own family members and teachers
- Have more individualized attention available to them
- Experience a richer curriculum

When family members participate in the program, the *teachers*:

- Have a chance to expand their program because of the improved ratio
- Can learn from the knowledge and expertise parents bring and share
- Have an opportunity to observe the relationship between the child and members of the family
- Have a chance to develop a more meaningful relationship with individual family members
- Have more opportunity to interact with individual children

It takes awhile for families to become comfortable with classroom involvement, so begin in simple stages. It is a rare parent who will insist on being involved. Instead, involvement will require that you have available a wide variety of ways that family members can make a genuine contribution to their child's school experience. When a family first enrolls in your program it is a good time to find out how they want to be involved. The family involvement survey that we have included in Figure 13.4 makes some suggestions and is a good place to start.

It is easy to invite family members to visit and observe their child in the classroom. With just a little additional planning, they can be invited to come for special occasions such as a birthday or a special child-prepared luncheon. More thought and preparation are required for other kinds of involvement. You can prepare book, art, or nature packs with activities for families to sign out and do at home with their children. You can also prepare materials for parents to create at home for the class (e.g., all the ingredients or materials needed plus instructions to make play dough, a game, smocks for the class).

A traditional form of family involvement is to provide opportunities for family members to work with you and the children in the classroom. This works well if a family member is not working outside the home. But do not assume that working family members are unable to participate. A parent may have a vacation day when you are open. Firefighters, retail workers, police officers, and many others work on weekends and at night and so have time during the week that they may wish to spend with their child in school.

To ensure successful classroom participation, have family members begin with a simple task such as joining you on a walk, reading a story to two or three children, or assisting you as you set up activities. It is important to allow family members to participate in ways that feel comfortable and natural to them and to offer them support in developing skills. As they become more comfortable, some may take a more active part in the program by planning with you and possibly sharing unique abilities or special knowledge.

You may need to make an effort to ensure that men as well as women participate, because men may feel that the early childhood program is not their natural province and may not be certain that they have anything to contribute. In fact, most men will

Figure 13.4 **Family Involvement Survey Form**

Family Involvement Survey

Family members are important people at our center. We welcome your involvement in the little and big aspects of the program. Participating in your child's early childhood program is a great way to share in your child's experiences. It helps the teachers, shows your child you care about his or her education, and it can be fun too! There are lots of ways for you to participate depending on your time and interests. We know that not everyone will want or be able to do everything. To help us help you get involved, please fill out this survey and return it with your enrollment forms.

Your name: _____ Phone number: _____ E-mail: _____

The Program for Children

_____ I'd like to come and have lunch with the children at school.

_____ I'd like to come on a field trip and assist.

_____ I'd like to help out in the classroom.

_____ I'd like to help plan an event for the children (a trip, a party, etc.).

_____ I'd like to bring in an activity to do with the children such as cook, share a story, work in the garden, teach a song. I'd like to:

Best days and times for me:

The Program for Families

_____ I'd like to attend a parent social event such as a potluck, campout, or a picnic. .

_____ I'd like to meet with other parents for a parent support group.

_____ I'd like to attend a parent education event (about guidance or child development and learning, etc.).

_____ I'd like to Join the *Parents & Friends Club* and participate in their activities.

_____ I'd like to work with other parents on fund-raising or planning events for families and children. Specifically I'd like to help with:

Improving and Maintaining the Environment

_____ I'd like to send in plastic bags or other recyclables that we use (ask first please ☺).

_____ I'd like to help out on a work day, on a weekend, or school break.

_____ I'd like to borrow/return library books, or do shopping.

_____ I'd like to make or mend something for the classroom (we have lots of projects for someone who's handy: make a new batch of play dough, sew or mend dress-up clothes, make pillows, put together a game or scrapbook). Specifically I'd like to:

Managing or Promoting the Program

_____ I'd like to sit on a committee/board to give input into how the school is run.

_____ I'd like to help out in the office.

_____ I'd like to speak as a parent representative to legislators or community groups.

_____ I'd like to organize a display in the community to educate others about the program.

Other ideas that staff haven't thought of:

be perfectly comfortable doing the activities just suggested. They may require a special invitation from you to feel assured that they are welcome. Alternatively, they may feel more at ease if you begin by asking them to lend their expertise in a realm in which they already feel competent, such as painting the classroom.

Remember that when family members participate, you have the additional responsibility of supervising them. An informal orientation to learn routines and procedures will help family members to feel prepared and ensure that they understand program philosophy and policies so that quality is maintained. A satisfying classroom experience is enhanced when you can find time to cooperatively plan activities and meet at the end of the school day to discuss experiences and give each other feedback.

A card file containing information about activities and jobs that need to be done is useful for letting family members know what kind of participation is needed and will be welcomed. Posting written statements in each area of the classroom describing the purpose of the activities and how adults can interact with children is another good technique for supporting participation.

Family members who lack the time or who are uncomfortable participating in the classroom may be involved in a variety of other ways. It is important to be especially aware of including options for single parents who may have more stressful lives and less time (but no less interest) than two-parent or extended families.

Some family members may volunteer to use their skills to create items for the classroom. Others may enjoy making educational materials at home. If people express an interest, help them get started by organizing a workshop on how to create educational materials. Involve them in identifying what specific materials would help round out the curriculum in their child's classroom. This workshop can include ideas for useful junk to save and materials to be purchased.

As families become involved in the program they often become your greatest allies. Some may offer to help in finding resources such as participating in fundraising events or grant-writing projects. Others may be willing to join with the staff to do renovation, repair, or clean-up projects. Many programs periodically hold work days at which families and staff spend a day cleaning or doing repairs. Work days are better attended when families have had some say in what most needs doing and can choose jobs based on their skills and interests. To ensure a successful work day, the staff and families must identify the work to be accomplished, gather the required equipment and materials, arrange for child care and food, and make sure that the jobs can be done in the designated time. If participants can end the work day with a feeling of accomplishment, they are more likely to volunteer for another one.

Family members can also be involved in advisory and policy boards. This form of involvement can help your program more accurately reflect the interests and needs of the families you serve. Family members who participate in policy-making feel that the program truly belongs to them and their children. They are willing to expend more of their energy and resources because of their greater commitment. These parents become valuable advocates for your program.

As the staff member who works directly with children, you are the person most likely to know the special interests, concerns, and talents of the families. Family members, children, and the program benefit when you invite families to participate.

> **Reflect on how your family was involved**
>
> Recall the ways your family participated in your educational experiences. How did the school encourage family participation? What do you remember about the impact of this participation on you and on your family?

Providing Family Education

Traditionally, programs for young children have included family education activities. Family education can help family members to understand the importance of their role in their child's development and education. It can take many forms. You may act as a direct provider of education, or you may help families find other resources. Informally, you may talk with them and model effective strategies for interacting with children in the course of your daily contacts. Such informal education can be powerful. More formal methods such as newsletters, workshops, discussion groups, and child-rearing courses can also be provided. Programs we have worked in have offered many educational services to families—including a weekly newsletter with a "Help Your Child Learn at Home" feature; workshops on making and choosing toys, preparing children for kindergarten, language and reading, and nutrition; courses on parenting skills and child guidance; and parent-coordinated support groups.

Another excellent way to provide family education is to develop a library of books for families to borrow. Such a family education library might include books like these:

Touchpoints: Your Child's Emotional and Behavioral Development, by T. Berry Brazelton

Infants and Mothers, by T. Berry Brazelton

Toddlers and Parents, by T. Berry Brazelton

The Parent's Guide: Systematic Training for Effective Parenting, by Don Dinkmeyer

Raising a Responsible Child, by Don Dinkmeyer

Positive Discipline for Preschoolers, by Jane Nelson

A Good Enough Parent, by Bruno Bettelheim

Mother's Almanac, by Marguerite Kelly

Father's Almanac, by S. Adams Sullivan

I'm Scared, by Elizabeth Crary

Raising Your Spirited Child, by Mary Sheedy Kurcinka

From Neurons to Neighborhoods: The Science of Early Childhood Development, by Jack P. Shonkoff, Deborah Phillips, & The National Research Council

Ages and Stages, by Karen Miller

Learning to Say Goodbye: When a Parent Dies, by Eda Leshan

Who's Calling the Shots? by Nancy Carlsson Paige & Diane Levin

You may fund such a library by asking a local business or foundation to make a contribution or by having a fund-raiser run by parents. An area in the classroom or near the school office can be designated for the library. It is effective to set up a topical display to entice parents to look at and borrow books.

Family education can encompass many topics. When you find that a number of family members share areas of concern, you can structure opportunities to provide them with appropriate information. If a topic is beyond your skills and expertise you can draw on resources in your school and community.

Families and community members who have been involved in your program may have resources for a family education program. For example, we have experienced workshops as diverse as a workshop on allergies conducted by a parent who was a pediatrician and a workshop on scrapbooking presented by a young, creative mom who had scrapbooking skills. Family members who understand the values and goals of the program will often be willing to share their special skills and knowledge and even invite their friends to contribute.

Like other aspects of the early childhood program, a family education program requires planning. It is important to survey the families to learn what they most wish to learn about. It is disconcerting to invite an expert on child development to speak to a group and present your speaker with a nearly empty house—or worse, to have families attend but talk through the presentation. If you uncover the reason, you may discover that the topic was a staff idea and the families would have been interested in another subject. Or you may discover that the interest was there but child care was an issue or the time was inconvenient. It is also important to realize that the success of a meeting is not measured by the number of bodies in the room but by the impact on the individuals who did attend. Assessing the interests and needs of families can be accomplished in a variety of ways. Small groups can get together and brainstorm everything they would like to learn about children and family life. Even if the representation is small, the initial list of topics can be distributed to the rest of the families for additions, comment, and prioritization. After an initial list of topics has been generated, you can distribute the list in subsequent years with space for families to indicate topics they would like to know more about and those in which they have special expertise that they would be willing to share with others. Do leave space for adding new topics.

When you have a list of topics relevant to the families currently enrolled in your program, a good idea of some likely presenters, and/or knowledge of other sources of the desired information (films, videos, printed materials), it is time to attend to the quality of presentation. Printed materials can be made available to families in the special area or room you provide for them in your facility. Films and videos can also be shown in a family lounge or area of the school if you have the appropriate equipment. Workshops, courses, or lectures, like all other family meetings, need to be scheduled at a convenient time for family members. If provisions for child care, a meal, and a comfortable location are offered, good participation is much more likely. Finally, to ensure a well received session, it is essential that someone from the program communicate to presenters about the skill and knowledge level of the families and check that the presentation will be lively and appropriate. The best learning experiences for adults almost always combine the presentation of information with the opportunity for active participation.

Working with Families of Children with Special Needs

Families of children with special needs, just like families of typically developing children, need regular communication and sharing of positive information. Be sure that the family has access to you in several different ways. Conferences should feel "safe" so family members can hear information about their child without feeling it is prejudiced or judgmental. The anecdotal records you keep on the child can serve as the basis for a dialogue between you and family members. Make a special effort to collect data on children with disabilities, because the more data you have, the easier it will be to see progress that you can share with the family. Having a communication log for each child may make it easier for some family members who may be more comfortable sharing a concern in writing rather than speaking to you directly.

If the family has been in your program for awhile before their child is identified as having a disability, you may need to increase the frequency of communication to ensure that the child and family get needed services. Make a special effort to keep the family involved in ordinary events as well. Even if they can't participate much while they are adjusting to this new dimension of their lives, later they will appreciate being kept informed.

Families of children with special needs should be a welcome part of the ongoing life of the program. Be sure they meet other families at program activities or when they drop off or pick up their child. You might say, "Mrs. Brown, I'd like you to meet Mrs. Nishimoto. Her daughter Lisa was Nicole's partner on our field trip today." Don't hesitate to ask the family members of a child with a disability to help at a work day or provide field trip transportation just as you would with any other family.

FINAL THOUGHTS

In the field of early childhood education and care, we generally think of ourselves as providing education and care for children. In fact, in caring for the children we are also caring for their families. As an early childhood educator you will work with both children and their families.

You will play an important role in the lives of many families. You will be part of the network of people who will lend support to the families' efforts to function in a complex society while nurturing their children. Families and early childhood professionals share common goals—to educate and care for children in ways that support optimal development. Childhood needs protection from many of the stresses of contemporary life, and as an early childhood professional you will support families as they provide their children with the protection and nurture they need.

LEARNING OUTCOMES

When you read this chapter, thoughtfully complete selected assignments from the "To Learn More" section, and prepare items from the "For Your Portfolio" section, you will be demonstrating your progress in meeting NAEYC **Standard 2: Building Family and Community Relationships**.

Key elements:

- Knowing about and understanding family and community characteristics
- Supporting and empowering families and communities through respectful, reciprocal relationships
- Involving families in their children's development and learning

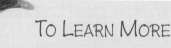

TO LEARN MORE

Interview and Observe in a Program: **Choose an early childhood program. Interview the director or family involvement coordinator to discover the kinds of family involvement available, the program's philosophy regarding family involvement, and the ways the program communicates with families. Ob-**serve the school environment and note any efforts to communicate with families (e.g., parent bulletin boards). Discuss what you learned from your exploration.

Compare Two Programs: **Repeat the preceding activity with a second program and compare and contrast the two.**

Compare Family Materials: Choose two early childhood programs. Collect a sample of the materials that each program gives to families: brochure, application, handbook, newsletter, policy statements, and so forth. Compare and evaluate the materials based on the ideas presented in this chapter and write about how the programs appear to differ in their philosophy and attitudes toward families and what you learned from this experience that may be helpful to you as a teacher.

Interview Family Members: Interview one or two family members of children in early childhood programs. Ask them to talk about the day-to-day experience of parenting a young child. Ask what they expect from their child's program in terms of information and support. Find out how well they think the program is doing in providing these things. Write about what you learned and its implication for you as an early childhood educator.

Interview Your Family: Interview your own parents or guardians. Ask them to recall what it was like to parent you as a young child and what kinds of support they got from your schools. If possible, look at the "artifacts" that they have (report cards, school newsletters, parent handbook). Ask them to describe the ways they were involved in programs you attended as a child. Reflect and write about what you learned and its implication for you as an early childhood educator.

For Your Portfolio

Write a Newsletter for Families: Write a newsletter article to help family members of children in an early childhood program to understand children's development and learning. Select an area of development, write the article, and distribute it to families. Ask families for feedback. Put a copy of the article and a summary of the feedback in your portfolio.

Make a Classroom Family-Friendly: Assess a classroom for young children and find ways to make it more family-friendly. For example, add an adult-sized chair, create a parent area, make a parent bulletin board, or create information for family members and post it in the interest centers. Write about, photograph, and include samples in your portfolio to show how you made the room more family-friendly.

Involve Families in an Early Childhood Program: Help involve families in an early childhood program. Meet with a teacher and one or two family members and create a list of ways for family members to get involved. Include on-site involvement and at-home involvement (like sewing pillows or doing laundry). Share the list with families and invite them to participate. In your portfolio include the list and a description of how families responded to it.

Create a Parent Event: Plan and implement a parent event such as an open house, potluck, or parent workshop. In your portfolio include the poster or newsletter in which the event is announced as well as a description of what happened, photos if you have them, and a reflection on whether it was effective in involving families in the program.

Develop a Resource Directory for Families: Research agencies in your community that provide services to families with young children and community resources and events that might be interesting to families. Give contact information, referral procedures, and a brief description of each one.

14

Making a Commitment to Being an Early Childhood Professional

Those of us who are in this world to educate—to care for—young children have a special calling: a calling that has very little to do with the collection of expensive possessions but has a lot to do with the worth inside of hearts and heads. In fact, that's our domain: the heads and hearts of the next generation, the thoughts and feelings of the future.

Fred Rogers

When you began your journey through this book in Chapter 1 we asked you to reflect on what you saw in your imagination when you thought of an early childhood teacher. Your ideas may have been quite simple—our students often envision a "nice lady" who reads stories, teaches the ABC's, and puts on Band-Aids. As you reach this last chapter, you have realized that teaching young children is a much more complex and demanding task. In fact, as Mister Rogers says in the above quote, it is a calling. More than an occupation, it is an inwardly felt dedication. Do you hear early childhood education and care calling to you? If so, you may be wondering what's next. You may be questioning what a commitment to young children and early childhood education and care entails. And you may be worrying about whether or not a career in early childhood can sustain you.

We write this last chapter to help you think about these things. We want to encourage you to make a commitment to early childhood education and care because young children, families, and society need you.

Now it is time to think about the path you might take to becoming an early childhood professional and if you wish to do so. We will provide a map with some directions for your journey and show you some of the predictable stops you may encounter in your career. We want to prepare you by suggesting some tools you'll need. We also want to forewarn you because there are potholes in the roads along which you will travel and there may be a few wild beasts lurking in the forests along the path. Finally, we want to let you know that the burdens you will carry on your journey will be shared.

MAKE A COMMITMENT TO CHILDREN

What seems to matter most is intent. When your motive is to give the best, you grow into ways of giving it.

Fred Rogers

Your first, most important, and ultimate commitment as a professional is your allegiance to children. When you choose to work with young children you are choosing the most important job in the world. Tomorrow's adults, in their most vulnerable stage of life, will be in your hands. Today's young children need to be protected, so tomorrow's adults will be healthy and strong. They need nurturing, so tomorrow's adults will be sensitive and care about those who are like themselves and those who are different. They need

experiences that will help them to delight in learning, so tomorrow's adults will be knowledgeable, creative thinkers, discoverers, and eager problem-solvers. They will have many problems to solve. They need guidance, so tomorrow's adults will appreciate the fragile world in which we live. Today's young children need to learn to cooperate, so tomorrow's adults will be peacemakers at home and in the world. To adequately meet the needs of the young children you will teach, you need a philosophical base, knowledge and skill, and a commitment to ethical behavior.

Develop a Philosophy

You have come to some conclusions, developed some beliefs, and begun to integrate an image of yourself as a professional with your image of yourself as a person. James Hymes (1981), wrote "I am persuaded that good teachers, first of all, must hold strong commitments and convictions from which their practices flow." When you have strong commitments and convictions you are better able to choose among alternatives by judging which action is most consistent with your values and beliefs. You will be better able to withstand the pressures that will urge you to follow practices that are not in the best interests of children, families, and teachers if you are able to articulate the reasons for your choices when others question or challenge your views.

You come into the field of early care and education with some ideas about children and how they should be taught, and some vision of who you wish to be in their lives. As you begin to work in the field, reflect on your practice, and learn more, these ideas will coalesce into a philosophy. This philosophy is an important part of your identity as an early childhood educator—it will continue to evolve and change throughout your career as you grow and change.

We suggested in Chapter 1 that you start a professional portfolio and write about what you believe and value for young children. Now is a good time to go back to what you wrote and reflect on whether or not this still represents what you believe, who you are, and who you want to be in the lives of children. As you revisit this you can write a statement that can become your "working educational philosophy."

Know About Children and Best Practice

At the center of your knowledge as a professional is your appreciation for, and understanding of, children. Observing and understanding children is the first and usually most lasting challenge for early childhood professionals—and because children are complex and theory is ever-changing, it is something you will continue to learn about throughout your career.

Reflect on who you want to be in the lives of children

Reflect on what you value about young children and childhood. What do you believe young children in early childhood programs need? What do you know about how young children learn and what do you believe that means to you as a teacher? What do you think early childhood programs should be like? What role do you believe an early childhood teacher should play in the life of a child and a family? Who do you want to be in the lives of children?

Use your reflections on these things as the basis of your written educational philosophy.

When you hear new ideas about curriculum, guidance, and children's development, they may sometimes conflict with what you have been taught or what you believe to be true. Keep an open mind when you hear these ideas so that you can make use of the new information. But don't blindly accept everything that "experts" tell you, particularly if they have something to sell. Trust what you know from your own observations. Sometimes a new theory or idea will make you say, "Yes! That makes sense. I can really see that in the children I know." At other times you may find yourself wondering if the writer or researcher ever spent time with real children. Sometimes this dissonance reflects cultural or community differences; at other times it reflects the expectations of the author or researcher. When you observe children objectively it helps you distinguish between what is true and what is just a passing fad.

Remember, only a few years ago some of today's accepted practices (e.g., putting up a poster of the alphabet, cooking in the classroom, allowing mildly ill children to come to school, integrating children with special needs in regular classrooms) were considered poor or unnecessary practice. At the same time, now discredited practices (e.g., lengthy group times for toddlers, time-out, changing diapers without gloves, and providing playground equipment over non-impact-absorbing surfacing) were considered perfectly okay. There is danger both in being blindly accepting of new trends and in being stubbornly attached to old ways.

> **Reflect on a time when you changed**
>
> Think about a time when you learned something that changed the way you did something you had always done (the way you write papers, travel to a destination, do a household routine). Did you make the change all at once, try it and then go back to your old way, or think about it for a long time and then change? Do you enjoy change or resist it? What do you hope to do when you are asked to make a change in your work with children?

Understand and Use the Code of Ethical Conduct[1]

In Chapter 1 we introduced you to the NAEYC Code of Ethical Conduct and core values. We hope that you will use it seriously and find it helpful in guiding you to act on the shared ethical responsibilities that form a part of your professional commitment to children and families. This will not always be comfortable or easy.

Understanding your ethical responsibilities will help you to resist the temptation to do what is easy or what will make you popular, at the expense of doing what is right. When you choose to do something because it is easy or expedient but it violates your ethical responsibilities (e.g., taking personal phone calls while you are on the floor with children), it cannot be morally justified. You have an ethical responsibility to give children and your work your full attention so that you provide care and education that is thoughtful and safe. It is important to remember that personal convenience is not a professional value.

The NAEYC Code delineates your ethical responsibilities and it also gives you guidance when you encounter *ethical dilemmas* (professional predicaments for which there is more than one justifiable solution). In a dilemma, the good of one group

---

[1] Parts of this section were adapted from *Ethics and the Early Childhood Educator,* by Stephanie Feeney and Nancy Freeman.

or individual to whom you owe professional allegiance is in conflict with the good of another group or individual to whom you also have a professional responsibility.

Ethical dilemmas cannot be resolved easily by applying rules and relying on facts. Rules and regulations may even give contradictory directions. You won't find resolutions for many of the dilemmas you face in your early childhood workplace in any book. Consider the following dilemmas:

A mother of a 4-year-old asks you to prevent her child from napping because when he naps he stays up very late and the family's schedule gets disrupted. The boy takes a long nap every day and is grouchy and unhappy if he isn't allowed to nap. Whose needs should you try to meet—the child's or the family's?

A coworker makes an insulting joke about an ethnic group. It makes you feel uncomfortable. You think it shows prejudice. But other staff members laugh. Should you speak your mind and possibly damage your relationships with your coworkers, or remain silent and give tacit approval?

You have a good job teaching first grade. The principal tells you to use a curriculum guaranteed to improve the reading performance of the children. It requires children to be seated for long periods of time and requires you to follow a script. Do you use a curriculum that violates guidelines for developmentally appropriate practice, or do you refuse and jeopardize your job?

Deciding on the right course of action can be difficult because a dilemma puts the interests of one person or group in conflict with those of another. To determine whether you are facing an ethical dilemma, think about the people involved in the situation. What are your obligations to each one? Does the problem involve a conflict between core values? Will you have to choose to meet the interests of one individual or group over the interests of another? If the answer is yes you are dealing with an ethical dilemma and will need to weigh your obligations to the people involved to make a morally justifiable decision.

For example, more than one "right" resolution might be chosen for the situation in which the mother asks you not to let her child nap in school. The core values that guide our work acknowledge the early childhood educator's obligation to respect the parent's wishes *and* the obligation to meet the needs of the child. The decision to honor either one of these values is reasonable and can be justified. Each choice involves advantages and disadvantages.

Addressing an Ethical Dilemma

Ethical behavior is a social process that involves dialogue, so if you are facing a dilemma it is best to discuss it with a colleague (or group of colleagues), director, or mentor. Having a different perspective will help you to see all sides of the situation. A series of steps can help you work through an ethical dilemma:

1. Review the core values and the ideals sections in the appropriate section of the NAEYC Code of Ethical Conduct to identify the conflicting values that have created this dilemma.

2. Think about whether there is anything that you can do to solve the problem without having to make a choice between the conflicting values. The term *ethical finesse* can be used to describe this process of sidestepping hard moral choices by finding a way to resolve a problem that is satisfactory to everyone involved (Kipnis 1987).

3. If ethical finesse is not possible, return to the NAEYC Code to look for guidance on how to prioritize the conflicting values and deal with the problem. Sometimes the code gives clear direction. Sometimes you must work hard to come up with the best alternative. In either case, the code helps you clarify and prioritize values.

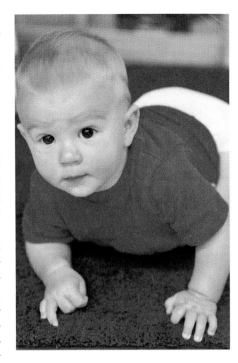

4. Consider whether there is anything more you need to know.

5. Consider all of the possible courses of action. For each alternative ask:
   - Is this the way I think all professionals in our field should act?
   - Could I publicly justify this course of action if I were asked to do so?
   - Is this solution respectful of people and relationships?

6. Decide on a course of action that will work in your situation and that is consistent with the values of the field.

7. After the decision is made, reflect on your rationale for the choice, consider the success of the outcome, and assess any implications for changes in policies or procedures.

Common sense is the key to solving most dilemmas you will face as you work with young children and their families. Your experiences in early childhood settings and your own professional expertise are likely to point you toward a good solution most of the time. If you are faced with a particularly difficult ethical dilemma it helps to talk it over with someone who is experienced and who will give you honest feedback, not just tell you what you want to hear. Such an individual can help you to find the best, most ethical resolution.

Learning to identify and address dilemmas takes practice and skill and will become easier as you gain more experience working with children, families, and colleagues. With experience you will learn to make well reasoned ethical decisions. The NAEYC Code can help you find a resolution, and the book *Ethics and the Early Childhood Educator: Using the NAEYC Code* (Feeney & Freeman 1999) can help you develop skills in systematic, reflective ethical decision-making.

MAKE A COMMITMENT TO YOURSELF

Throughout this book we have emphasized the importance of reflecting on and understanding yourself. We began by asking you to reflect on yourself as a person,

because that is the foundation of who you will be as a teacher. Now we ask you to make a commitment to yourself as a person and a professional.

No book, toy, video, or computer program can substitute for *you,* a human being who knows about, cares for, and is sensitive to young children. *You* are the vital ingredient. And *you* are the only real tool that you have to accomplish the many worthy goals that we have described in this book. What you have to give is yourself—your caring, your energy, your knowledge and skills, and your commitment.

Take Care of Yourself

In order to accomplish the demanding task of providing care and education for young children, you need good physical and emotional health. Take care of your body by paying attention to nutrition, exercise, and relaxation. Nurture your mind, so you stay excited and motivated as a learner. Stay connected to others, so you feel appreciated, meaningfully involved, and intellectually stimulated. Nurture your spirit by taking time for quiet reflection, for enjoying beauty and nature, for creative pursuits.

As a new practitioner it is important that you set realistic goals for yourself, that you find your strengths and build on them, and that you acknowledge your mistakes and learn from them. It is also important not to expect to be able to do everything perfectly, especially in your first year or two of teaching. In order to accomplish the many tasks of being a teacher you need to be satisfied with doing a "good enough" job. Put the children first. You will have many years to develop a more perfect classroom and curriculum.

Connect with Colleagues

Another way to take care of yourself as you begin your career is to build good relationships with colleagues. Your colleagues are more than coworkers. They are the people who share your workplace and your commitments. If you are fortunate they will share your philosophy and your passion, understand your joys and sorrows, and give you a sympathetic ear, a pat on the back, honest feedback, and words of encouragement and advice.

Communication and good working relationships with your coworkers will enhance the program for children and make your work easier and more pleasant. The communication skills you learned in Chapter 9 will help you to develop good working relationships with adults as well as with children. People will regard you as a good colleague if you make every effort to be pleasant and fair and if you make sure that you do your share (and even a little more than your share) of the work. Be sensitive to, and respectful of the cultural expectations, values, and ways of interacting of those you work with. Be sure that you are aware of your ethical responsibilities to your coworkers and employer, which are spelled out in Section III, Parts A and B, of the NAEYC Code (Appendix A).

Feeling happy ultimately comes from being kind, not from all the stuff we collect in life. Everyone is looking for the something that is missing. Pledge to help children and remember what life is all about.

Fred Rogers

You have learned many important things and have begun to develop the skills that you need to be a caring and competent early childhood educator. You know that it is important to know yourself and be able to reflect on your actions. You have some understanding of the past and the current status of the field of early care and education. You have learned about child development from the theories and research of experts and from your own observations of children. You have learned that play is the important "work" of children in the early years. You have developed beginning skill in communicating positively with children and guiding their behavior in respectful ways. You understand the importance of a planned learning environment. You know what goes into the design of a meaningful and appropriate curriculum. And you have begun to realize the importance of building good relationships with families and know some ways to do so.

You have many choices to make as you join the field. They are personal choices, value choices, and career choices. There are some things that you can do and think about that will help you make those career choices.

The first question to ask yourself is: What age of children are you drawn to as a teacher? Each stage in early childhood has its charms and needs teachers who love its particular joys and challenges. Some teachers are drawn to infants or toddlers, some to preschoolers, some to kindergartners, and others to primary grade children. Still others can find joy working with more than one of these ages. Which one are you? You will be happier in your career choice, and children will be better taught, if you select the right age(s). You do no service to yourself or children if you work with one age of children but think that you're "not really teaching" because of their stage of development, or if you try to teach in inappropriate ways because you'd really prefer to work with a different age group.

The next question to consider is: What role do you want to play? Do you want to teach alone most of the time or do you want to be part of a team in which teaching decisions are made by a group? Do you want to be "in charge" or would you prefer to start out assisting someone else who shoulders more of the responsibility? Sometimes, after they have completed a practicum placement and realized the scope of a teacher's work, our students decide that they want to start their careers as assistant teachers.

Another issue to consider is how much independence you desire and whether or not you want to work within the constraints and with the benefits of a large bureaucracy. Everyone wants to make a decent salary and everyone wants to be allowed the freedom to do what they believe is best. There is usually some trade-off, however, between having freedom to teach in ways you feel are best and having the stability and better salary and benefits of a larger system.

No job is perfect. But if you prefer working with younger children, on a team, with fewer dictates about how and what to teach, you probably will be happier working in preschool and infant-toddler programs. If you favor teaching older children, with less teamwork, a better salary, and are comfortable with curriculum specified by the school or district, you will be happier teaching in kindergarten and elementary schools. Knowing this will help you make choices about your educational path.

Should you be in a program that prepares you to work with children younger than 5, one that will enable you to teach in elementary schools, or one that will allow you the flexibility to do either? Make this decision consciously. We have had students who were rudely surprised to discover that with an associate's degree they would need several more years of school and a different degree in order to move into a kindergarten teaching position. And we have colleagues who were shocked to discover that despite a teaching credential and a master's degree, they had to go back to school to get the training required for working with infants and toddlers.

Career decisions are not set in concrete and don't have to last forever. As you grow and change, so do your needs for professional fulfillment. The more experience you have in working with children of different ages in a variety of early childhood settings, the sooner it will become clear whether working with young children is the right choice for you and what kinds of positions will suit you best. Many kinds of work offer opportunities for you to act upon your commitment to children. What is most important is that you learn about yourself and about the field and make a decision that will be good for you and for children and their families.

> **Reflect on your future career**
>
> In what settings and with what children would you like to work as you begin your career? What do you think would be a perfect job for you in early childhood education and care? What would it be like? Why does it appeal to you? What training would you need for this job?

Understand Your Development as a Teacher

Just like the children with whom you will work, you will pass through developmental stages in your career and you will continue to grow and learn. Like the children, you need appropriate stimulation and nurturing to reach your full potential.

As a beginning teacher you will be focused on your direct work with children and the network of relationships that go with it. If you are working in settings for children younger than 5, you are most likely to work under the supervision of another teacher. If you graduate with a four-year degree and begin to teach in a kindergarten or primary grade classroom you will probably have sole responsibility for all aspects of the classroom, with less direct oversight from a grade level supervisor or a principal.

New teachers often describe feeling totally exhausted trying to accomplish many new tasks and trying to live up to unrealistically high expectations they set for themselves. They may be barraged with demands that may or may not be consistent with their philosophy and beliefs.

Katz (1995) calls this stage *Survival* because it is often hard and stressful to apply the knowledge you gained in college in the real world. In your first year of working with young children you are likely to want advice and lots of practical suggestions. You will want someone to appreciate your triumphs and help you to understand your challenges and failures. A more experienced teacher, or a supervisor, can serve as your mentor to help you feel connected to other professionals as you learn to teach in the real world. As college teachers we teach what we believe is best practice, but it is not always what you will find in the "real world" of teaching. We have often served as sounding boards to graduates of our programs who struggled to maintain their confidence and beliefs.

With experience, day-to-day tasks get easier and you will have different needs and seek new challenges. Once you have become adept at basic "survival" in the classroom, you will begin to bring together what you know to create a more personal approach to working with children. Katz calls this stage *Consolidation.* During this time you may be ready to expand your skills with the assistance of consultants and the advice of colleagues.

If one morning, after a few years of teaching, you wake up feeling bored or dissatisfied with your job and feel that there is not enough challenge working with children, you may be in the stage of teacher development that Katz calls *Renewal.* This is a critical time in which you will either renew your commitment to being a practitioner or decide on a change in direction. You can build on your knowledge and skill by doing professional reading, going to conferences or workshops, doing action research, becoming a mentor to a new teacher, becoming active in your professional association, or visiting other schools. Doing so may renew your enthusiasm and give you new ideas as well as a greater sense of belonging and professionalism. This may be the time when you really make a commitment to working in the early childhood field.

After you have been working with children for a number of years and have mastered the practical details of day-to-day life in a classroom you will have reached what Katz calls *Maturity.* At this time you may find yourself interested in consideration of the values, theories, issues, and philosophy that underlie your work. At this stage attending seminars, work on advanced degrees, and more theoretical professional reading may renew a sense of excitement and provide you with new areas of interest and involvement. You may be ready to take on leadership roles and responsibilities. With deeper understanding and expertise you may want to become a trainer or administrator.

There is no prescribed time line for your development as a teacher. Some teachers find themselves in the survival stage for longer than a year, while others slip gracefully into consolidation in a few months. We have known professionals who still loved the day-to-day challenges of life in the classroom in their sixties and others who left the classroom to become trainers, administrators, or researchers in their twenties.

Other Roles

People concerned with the education and welfare of young children and trained in early childhood education can do many different jobs. Each person has to find the career that best reflects his or her interests, talents, and style.

In addition to working directly with young children, training in early childhood education may help to prepare you for positions—such as center director, principal, or curriculum specialist—that involve program support and administration. Specialized training is helpful for positions that provide support for teachers and programs—staff developer, teacher educator, speech-language therapist, curriculum developer, school librarian, and counselor or advocate for young children and their families. Your background in early childhood establishes a good foundation for careers that provide services for families—such as parent educator, child psychologist, pediatrician, nurse, social worker, child care licensing worker, and resource and referral agency worker. Your path in early childhood education and care may lead you to places you don't yet imagine.

MAKE A COMMITMENT TO YOUR PROFESSION

We live in a world in which we need to share responsibility. It is easy to say "It's not my child, not my community, not my world, not my problem." Then there are those who see the need and respond. I consider those people my heroes.

Fred Rogers

Educating and caring for young children is caring for the future. You are caring for the future by making a commitment to your profession. Your initial professional commitments will evolve as you gain experience and mature as a professional. When you join a professional group, help parents understand how children learn, share your knowledge at a workshop or conference, mentor a new teacher, speak to a friend or legislator on behalf of children, or take a stand based on the code of ethics, you are caring for the profession and the future of us all.

Behave Like a "True Professional"

You make a commitment to children, yourself, and your profession when you commit to behaving like a professional. We have all heard someone called a "true professional." That term is generally meant as a high form of praise. Being a "true professional" means that in dealing with children, families, and society you:

- Take pride in the important work you do
- Commit yourself to supporting children's development and families in their task of child rearing
- Are objective in viewing children and families and rational in your dealings with them
- Are honest in dealing with children and families and take care not to exaggerate your knowledge, training, or skills
- Build relationships with families and colleagues based on trust
- Are trustworthy—honest and scrupulous in upholding confidentiality, resisting the urge to gossip though the temptation is strong
- Follow through on commitments and keep your promises, being careful not to promise what you can't deliver
- Commit yourself to being a good colleague and a good employee
- Seek out opportunities to continue to learn and grow as a professional
- Carry yourself with dignity
- Are a good model for children and families
- Advocate for children, families, and program practices that meet their needs

By choosing to behave according to the highest professional standards you fulfill your commitment to children. Behaving according to high ideals of professionalism will make you feel good about yourself; earn you the respect of families, colleagues, and community members; and help the field of early childhood education to achieve professional recognition.

Continue to Learn and Grow

One of the hallmarks of a professional is the desire to learn and grow. Like children, you need resources, time, and encouragement to explore, experiment, and learn. Once you have passed the basic survival stage of teaching you will gain knowledge and inspiration from reading and pursuing topics that interest you. Elizabeth Jones and Gretchen Reynolds suggest that educators can regard their intellectual interests and concerns as a form of play (Jones & Reynolds 1992). You can pursue topics that are interesting and fun and make decisions about what *you* want to learn and do.

Join a Professional Organization

You may wonder why your college instructors, and the authors of this text, are always promoting professional organizations. You have probably been given a brochure or been strongly encouraged to spend a sum of money to become a member of one or another professional groups.

Why is membership in an organization so highly valued? One reason is clear as you browse through the bibliographies at the end of this book. You will notice that professional organizations publish books and journals that further the knowledge base of

the field. Another reason is that professional organizations do important work on behalf of children, practitioners, and the profession. They gather the research, provide information, create position statements, develop standards and uphold beliefs of professionals, advocate for children, and provide a collective voice for the field.

Joining a professional organization gives you the opportunity for growth and participation with the community of your peers. Organizations provide their members with a sense of common purpose and support in the form of publications, conferences, and community events. Find an organization that is active in your area and get involved in it. Not only will you gain valuable information but you will get to spend time with others who do the same work you do, who care about some of the same things, and who may have similar concerns. Sharing with colleagues is one of the great joys of being an early childhood educator.

A professional organization can only represent you if you are a part of it. You do not join a professional organization to get a journal, a membership card, reduced conference fees, or lowered insurance rates. You join a professional organization to declare yourself a member of a profession and to support it. Figure 14.1 provides you with contact information for a number of different early childhood professional organizations. You cannot join them all, but as a good professional you will find one (or more) that best represents you and give it (or them) your support. If you reside in a country outside of the United States, there are other early childhood professional organizations. We have included a few of them in Figure 14.1 as well, and you can find others in your geographic or interest areas by searching the World Wide Web.

Advocate

Another of your professional commitments is *advocacy*. What does advocacy mean? Advocacy means giving public support to a policy or cause that you believe to be right. The idea of advocacy may seem quite alien to you. You have chosen a career that involves very personal relationships and in which you are encouraged to be warm, accepting, nonconfrontational, and nurturing. Advocacy seems to require the opposite traits. Some advocacy for children is very public and involves speaking out in assertive ways to policy makers. But it can also be personal and nonconfrontational. When you make a careful display of children's art that demonstrates your belief in its beauty and worth, you are advocating for children. When you treat children with dignity and respect in your classroom and ask others to do so, you are advocating for children. When, at a staff meeting, you suggest a change in the time snack is served because you have observed that children are hungry, you are advocating for children.

As we grow as a profession, experienced early childhood educators are becoming increasingly committed to advocacy. We are slowly trying to change our image from

Figure 14.1 Professional ECE Organizations

U.S. Early Childhood Professional Organizations

American Montessori Society
281 Park Ave. South, 6th Floor
New York, NY 10010-6102
www.amshq.org

Association for Childhood Education
International (ACEI)
17904 Georgia Ave., Suite 215
Olney, MD 20832
www.udel.edu/bateman/acei

Center for the Child Care Workforce
733 15th St. NW,
Suite 1037
Washington, DC 20005
www.ccw.org

National Association for the Education of
Young Children (NAEYC)
1509 16th St. NW
Washington, DC 20036
www.naeyc.org

Council for Early Childhood Professional
Recognition (a program of NAEYC)
www.cdacouncil.org

Southern Early Childhood
Association (SECA)
P.O. Box 55930
Little Rock, AR 72215-5930
www.southernearlychildhood.org

U.S. Professional Organizations Representing Subsections of Early Childhood Education and Care

Council for Exceptional Children
1920 Association Dr
Reston, VA 22091
www.cec.sped.org

National Association for Family Child Care
525 SW 5th St., Suite A
Des Moines, IA 50309-4501
E-mail: nafcc@nafcc
www.nafcc.org

National Association of Child Care
Resource and Referral Agencies
1319 F Street NW, Suite 500
Washington, DC 20004-1106
www.naccrra.org

National Coalition for Campus Children's
Centers (NCCCC)
122 S. Michigan Ave., Suite 1776
Chicago, IL 60603
E-mail: ncccc@smtp.bmai.com
www.campuschildren.org

ECE Professional Organizations Outside the United States

International ECE Organizations

Association Montessori International
Koninginneweg 161
1075 CN Amsterdam, The Netherlands
E-mail: info@montessori-ami.org
www.montessori-ami.org/ ami.htm

Organization Mondiale pour l'Education
Préscolaire (OMEP)
U.S. National Committee
www.omep-usnc.org/ omep-us.html

The Canadian Child Care Federation
201-383 Parkdale Ave
Ottawa, ON K1Y 4R4
1-800-858-1412 or (613) 729-5289
Fax: (613) 729-3159
E-mail: info@cccf-fcsge.ca
www. cccf-fcsge.ca/home_en.html

The Canadian Association for Young
Children (CAYC)
Membership Service
Ricor Marketing
612 W. 23rd St.
North Vancouver, BC V7M 2C3
E-mail: caycmeb@cayc.ca
www.cayc.ca

Early Childhood Australia Inc.,
formerly the Australian Early
Childhood Association
P.O. Box 105
Watson ACT 2602
Australia ABN 44 950 767 752
Telephone: (02) 6242-1800
Fax: (02) 6242-1818 • 1-800-356-900
E-mail: eca@earlychildhood.org.au
www.aeca.org.au

Te Tari Puna Ora O Aotearoa/New
Zealand Childcare Association
P.O. Box 11-863, Manners St.
Wellington, New Zealand
Telephone: 04-473-4672
Fax: 04-473-7295
0800-CHILDCARE (0800-244-532)
www.nzchildcare.ac.nz

---

one of "nice ladies" to advocates for children. We are becoming more sophisticated about the political process and are forming alliances with others who have similar concerns in order to heighten community awareness and influence public attitudes and legislation on behalf of young children and their families. You are furthering the goals of your profession when you become informed about the political process; when you stay informed about community, state, and national efforts to improve programs and services for children; and when you express your views and share your knowledge with the media, members of your community, and government leaders.

Why should you be an advocate? Though you may not believe it now, you are an influential person. You are influential with your family and friends. They know and trust you and what you tell them about early childhood education and care is more powerful than what they read in the newspaper or see on television. You are influential in your community. The people on your street, in your neighborhood, in your town know you. You are *their* expert on early childhood education and care, the one they trust. You are influential in your local government. You know the friends, families, and associates of the members of your local school board, your municipal council, and your state legislature. You represent the opinions and votes of those who elected them. You are more important than an expert to them. With your vote and your advocacy you influence their lives just as they influence yours and children's.

In a large and diverse country such as ours it is easy to feel hopeless about influencing national policy. You are just one person, probably a young person, and you are not yet an acknowledged expert in your field. But you are a citizen, you are a voter, and you influence other citizens and other voters. Each time you join with other early childhood educators, each time you influence another person, you strengthen the voice of the field. Let your legislators know this, and they will listen to you because your opinions will count.

POTHOLES, WILD BEASTS, AND OTHER PERILS

It is a difficult time to be an early childhood educator. In the previous edition of this book we optimistically wrote that it was the threshold of a new era. There was new recognition of the importance of the early years, new acknowledgment for the critical role of early childhood programs, and a new respect for the important role of well trained early childhood professionals. Today many of these gains have been lost beneath a rising tide of policies that focus on accountability rather than children. Though we are hopeful that by the time this seventh edition is printed, the tide will have turned and public policy will be more child- and family-friendly, we would be remiss if we did not tell you about some of the realities of becoming an early childhood educator at this moment in history, and if we did not provide you with some coping strategies.

You have learned that young children learn best through the natural activities of childhood: play, hands-on exploration, and individualized interaction with a teacher who is knowledgeable and a sensitive observer. You know that we must consider each child in the context of family, culture, and community. Developmentally appropriate practices like this are under assault. What might this mean to you?

- You might be asked to eliminate play, art, nap, recess, or snack to spend more time on academic work.
- You might be asked to teach children content or use methods that are not appropriate to their age and ability.

Historically, we have provided shamefully few resources for our youngest and most vulnerable citizens, and families have borne the financial burden of providing care and education. Today, with the mounting cost of war, the increases in tax cuts, and the lessening of funding to states for social programs of all kinds, the resources available for early childhood education and care have been, and are likely to continue to be, diminished. States have already cut child care assistance, lowered the eligibility for families, increased family copayments for children receiving subsidies, and cut funding to prekindergarten programs (National Association for the Education of Young Children

2003). What does that mean to you as an early childhood teacher and a citizen? It means that:

- If you are a parent, you will have to finance the care and education of your own children and may find the cost unmanageable and the quality inadequate.
- There are few protections in place, and fewer resources available, to ensure that you are able to give children what they need.
- You will make less money and have fewer benefits (like vacation, sick leave, pension, and health insurance) if you choose to work with infants, toddlers, or preschoolers than if you choose to become a teacher of older children.
- You will have lower status and will be accorded less professional respect than if you worked in another field with similar responsibilities and qualifications.

Our job is to be a grain of sand in an oyster.

Fred Rogers

We promised that we would not merely warn you about these threats but that we would help you to deal with them. What can you do? You could bury your head in the sand. You could find another field. You could move to another country. While all three of these options hold some appeal, none is really satisfactory. If you don't want to ignore it or run away, you could do what Mister Rogers suggests: "Be a grain of sand in an oyster."

To be the grain of sand that forms the core of the pearl, you must learn the gentle art of using attacks to your advantage. You can find and acknowledge what little is right in these attacks against children and early childhood programs. That does not mean that you should acquiesce to demands to provide inappropriate curriculum. When pushed to teach young children academic content, you can acknowledge that the early years *are* a critical time for laying academic foundations—in doing so, you may gain allies. But you must insist that because the early years are so critical, it *is* crucial that we provide educational experiences that actually work.

Then you'll have to demonstrate what works. To do so you must understand and be able to articulate how play and other forms of appropriate instruction help children to be academically prepared. You must do more than say "Children learn through play." You must *know* what research tells us about how children learn. You must learn to observe and document children's learning, so that you can make it visible to their parents, to administrators, and to policy makers. You must stay connected to other early childhood educators so that you have colleagues and supporters—you can't do this alone. You must support the champions—the ones who stand up for us all.

And you must choose when to stand firm and when not to. Not every issue is worth fighting; not every battle can be won. As an ethical professional, you may have hard choices to make. We urge you to stand up for children; to say no when asked to do what is wrong; to insist on speaking what you know to be true; to risk making yourself suspect and unpopular; and to give others the courage to do the same. It's a lot to ask. You will get few rewards for doing it. But it's the right thing to do, and children need you to do it.

FINAL THOUGHTS

Who will you be in the lives of children? Who will you be as an early childhood educator? Becoming a professional in early childhood education takes time and experience, caring and commitment, and a willingness to keep on learning. It can be difficult and challenging. But it brings with it the joy and the satisfaction of being with young children and the knowledge that you are helping to shape the future. As your colleagues, we welcome you.

LEARNING OUTCOMES

When you read this chapter, thoughtfully complete selected assignments from the "To Learn More" section, and prepare items from the "For Your Portfolio" section, you will be demonstrating your progress in meeting NAEYC **Standard 5: Becoming a Professional.**
Key elements:
- Identifying and involving oneself with the early childhood field

- Knowing about and upholding ethical guidelines and other professional standards
- Engaging in continuous, collaborative learning to inform practice
- Integrating knowledgeable, reflective, and critical perspectives on early education
- Engaging in informed advocacy for children and the profession

TO LEARN MORE

Join Your Local Professional Association: Find out what professional associations have active chapters in your community. Attend a meeting and join the association. Reflect on what you learn.

Use the Process for Resolving an Ethical Dilemma: With a colleague or mentor, using an ethical dilemma that you have experienced or one of the examples provided, use the process described on pages 422–423 to decide on an ethical course of action. Write about what you did and what you decided and why.

Create a 5-Year Plan: Consider your professional goals and create a 5-year plan for your career. Show it to a friend and a family member and talk to them about your plans. Take it to a college counselor and find out what kind of financial resources might be available to help make your plan a reality. Document what you have done.

Create a Professional Pledge: Read the section in this chapter on becoming a "true professional" and the NAEYC Statement of Commitment at the end of the code of ethics in Appendix A.

Write your own professional pledge. Post it by your mirror or on your bulletin board and put it in your professional portfolio.

Read a Professional Journal: Read one or more of the professional journals listed below.

Child Care Information Exchange • P.O. Box 2890 • Redmond, WA 98073 • www.ccie.com

Childhood Education •
www.udel.edu.bateman/acei/ cehp.htm

Early Childhood Research Quarterly • www.naeyc.org/pubs

Early Childhood Research and Practice •
www.ecrp.uiuc.edu

Exceptional Children • www.dec-sped.org/journals.html

Journal of Research in Childhood Education •
www.udel. edu/bateman.acei.jrcehp.htm

Scholastic Early Childhood Today • Scholastic Inc. •
555 Broadway • New York, NY 10012 •
http://teacher. scholastic.com/products.ect.htm

Young Children • www.journal.naeyc.org

Learn About an Advocacy Organization: Go online and learn about one of the following advocacy organizations for young children.

Canadian Coalition for the Rights of Children • www.rightsofchildren.ca

Center for the Future of Children • www.futureofchildren.org

Child Rights Information Network • www.crin.org

Child Welfare League of America • www.cwla.org

Children's Defense Fund • www.childrensdefense.org

Children Now • www.childrennow.org

The Children's Foundation • www.childrensfoundation.net

National Committee for Prevention of Child Abuse • www.childabuse.org

Save the Children • www.savethechildren.org

FOR YOUR PORTFOLIO

Clarify Your Position: Read and revise your autobiography, personal mission statement, and educational philosophy.

Join Your Local Professional Association: Attend a meeting. Reflect on what you have done and what you learned for the professionalism section of your portfolio.

Document an Act of Advocacy: Write about a visit to a legislator, a public display of children's work, a letter to the editor, or some other advocacy of your choice.

Bibliography

Chapter 1

Barnett, W. S., K. B. Robin, J. T. Hustedt, & K. L. Schulman. 2004. *The State of Preschool: 2003 State Preschool Yearbook*. Rutgers, NJ: National Institute for Early Education Research.

Bowman, B., M. S. Donovan, & M. S. Burns (eds.), & Committee on Early Childhood Pedagogy, National Research Council. 2000. *Eager to Learn: Educating Our Preschoolers*. Washington, DC: National Academy Press.

Bransford, J., A. Brown, & R. R. Cocking (eds.). 2000. Committee on Developments in the Science of Learning, National Research Council. *How People Learn: Brain, Mind, Experience, and School*. Washington, DC: National Academy Press.

Bredekamp, S. 1992a. Composing a Profession. *Young Children* 47(2): 52–54.

Bredekamp, S. 1992b. The Early Childhood Profession Coming Together. *Young Children* 47(6): 36–38.

Burks, J., & M. Rubenstein. 1979. *Temperament Styles in Adult Interaction*. New York: Brunner/Mazel.

Cartwright, S. 1999. What Makes Good Early Childhood Teachers? *Young Children* 54(6): 4–7.

Derman-Sparks, L. 1989. *Anti-Bias Curriculum: Tools for Empowering Young Children*. Washington, DC: NAEYC.

Feeney, S., & R. Chun. 1985. Effective Teachers of Young Children. *Young Children* 41(1): 47–52.

Feeney, S., & N. Freeman. 1999. *Ethics and the Early Childhood Educator: Using the NAEYC Code*. Washington, DC: NAEYC.

Feeney, S., & K. Kipnis. 1989. Professional Ethics in Early Childhood Education. *Young Children* 45(1): 24–29.

Fleet, A., & M. Clyde. 1993. *What's in a Day? Working in Early Childhood*. Wentworth Falls, NSW, Australia: Social Science Press.

Gardner, H. 1983. *Frames of Mind*. New York: Basic Books.

Gonzalez-Mena, J. 1993. *The Child in the Family and the Community*. Upper Saddle River, NJ: Merrill/Prentice Hall.

Grieshaber, S. 2001. Advocacy and Early Childhood Educators: Identity and Cultural Conflicts. In S. Grieshaber & G. S. Cannella (eds.), *Embracing Identities in Early Childhood Education*. New York: Teachers College Press.

Hendrick, J. 1987. *Why Teach?* Washington, DC: NAEYC.

Hyson, M. 2003. Introducing NAEYC's Early Learning Standards: Creating the Conditions for Success. *Young Children* 58(1): 66–68.

Isenberg, J. P., & M. R. Jalongo. 2003. *Major Trends and Issues in Early Childhood Education: Challenges, Controversies, and Insights*. New York: Teachers College Press.

Jalongo, M. R., & J. P. Isenberg. 2004. *Exploring Your Role: A Practitioner's Introduction to Early Childhood Education* (2nd ed.). Upper Saddle River, NJ: Merrill/Prentice Hall.

Jersild, A. 1955. *When Teachers Face Themselves*. New York: Teachers College Press.

Johnson, J., & J. B. McCracken (eds.). 1994. *The Early Childhood Career Lattice: Perspectives on Professional Development*. Washington, DC: NAEYC.

Jones, E., & G. Reynolds. 1992. *The Play's the Thing: Teachers' Roles in Children's Play*. New York: Teachers College Press.

Katz, L. G. 1993, October. Helping Others with Their Teaching. Retrieved May 21, 2004, from the Clearinghouse on Early Education and Parenting (http://ceep.crc.uiuc.edu/eecearchive/books/helpteac.html).

Katz, L., & E. Ward. 1978 (rev. 1993). *Ethical Behavior in Early Childhood Education*. Washington, DC: NAEYC.

Kidder, R. 1995. *How Good People Make Tough Choices*. New York: Simon and Schuster.

Kipnis, K. 1987. How to Discuss Professional Ethics. *Young Children* 42(4): 26–33.

Kohl, H. 1984. *Growing Minds: On Becoming a Teacher*. New York: Harper & Row.

Kontos, S., & A. Wilcox-Herzog. 2001. How Do Education and Experience Affect Teachers of Young Children? *Young Children* 56(4): 85–91.

Moustakas, C. 1982. *The Authentic Teacher*. New York: Irvington.

Myers, I. B., with P. B. Myers. 1995. *Gifts Differing: Understanding Personality Type*. Palo Alto, CA: Davies-Black.

National Association for the Education of Young Children. 1991. Early Childhood Teacher Certification: A Position Statement of the Association of Teacher Educators and the National Association for the Education of Young Children. Adopted July/August 1991. *Young Children* 47(1): 16–21.

National Association for the Education of Young Children. 1998. Code of Ethical Conduct and Statement of Commitment (rev. ed.). Washington, DC: NAEYC.

National Association for the Education of Young Children. 2004. Final Draft, Early Childhood Program Standards and Suggested Accreditation Performance Criteria. Available on the NAEYC Web site (www.naeyc.org/accreditation/naeyc_accred/draft_standards/ter.html).

Rodd, J. 1994. *Leadership in Early Childhood: The Pathway to Professionalism*. New York: Teachers College Press.

Strike, K. A., E. Haller, & J. F. Soltis. 1988. *The Ethics of School Administration*. New York: Teachers College Press.

Thomas, A., & S. Chess. 1977. *Temperament and Development*. New York: Brunner/Mazel.

VanderVen, K. 1994. Professional Development: A Contextual Model. In J. Johnson & J. B. McCracken (eds.), *The Early Childhood Career Lattice*. Washington, DC: NAEYC.

Whitebook, M., C. Howes, & D. Phillips. 1990. *Who Cares? Child Care Teachers and the Quality of Care in America*.

Oakland, CA: Child Care Employee Project.

Willer, B. A. 1994. Conceptual Framework for Early Childhood Professional Development. In J. Johnson & J. B. McCracken (eds.), *The Early Childhood Career Lattice*. Washington, DC: NAEYC.

Chapter 2

Administration for Children, Youth, and Families. 2004. Head Start FACES, chapter 5. Retrieved June 19, 2004, from the Web site of the Administration for Children and Families (www.acf.dhhs.gov/programs.core. pubs.reports/faces.meas.99).

Barnett, W. S. 1995. Long-Term Effects of Early Childhood Programs on Cognitive and School Outcomes. In R. E. Behrman (ed.), Long-Term Outcomes of Early Childhood Programs. *The Future of Children* 5(3). Los Altos, CA: Center for the Future of Children, David and Lucile Packard Foundation.

Barnett, W. S. 2003. Better Teachers, Better Preschools: Student Achievement Linked to Teacher Qualifications. *Preschool Policy Matters* (No. 2). New Brunswick, NJ: National Institute for Early Education Research, Rutgers University.

Boyer, E. L. 1991. *Ready to Learn: A Mandate for the Nation*. Princeton, NJ: Carnegie Foundation for the Advancement of Teaching.

Bredekamp, S, & C. Copple. 1997. *Developmentally Appropriate Practice in Early Childhood Programs* (rev. ed.). Washington, DC: NAEYC.

Bredekamp, S., & B. Willer (eds.). 1996. *NAEYC Accreditation: A Decade of Learning and the Years Ahead*. Washington, DC: NAEYC.

Burts, D. C., C. H. Hart, R. Charlesworth, P. O. Fleege, J. Mosley, & R. H. Thomasson. 1992. Observed Activities and Stress Behaviors of Children in Developmentally Appropriate and Inappropriate Kindergarten Classrooms. *Early Childhood Research Quarterly* 7: 297–318.

Carnegie Corporation. 1994. Starting Points: Executive Summary of the Report of the Carnegie Corporation of New York Task Force on Meeting the Needs of Young Children. *Young Children* 49(5): 58–61.

Center for the Early Childhood Workforce. 2004. *Current Data on the Salaries and Benefits of the U.S. Early Childhood Education Workforce*. Washington, DC: American Federation of Teachers Educational Foundation.

Children's Defense Fund. 1999. *The State of America's Children Yearbook*. Washington, DC: Children's Defense Fund.

Children's Defense Fund. 2002. *The State of Children in America's Union*. Washington, DC: Children's Defense Fund.

Clifford, R. M., M. Cochran, & S. L. Kagan. 2003. Challenges for Early Childhood Education and Care Policy. In D. Cryer and R. M. Clifford (eds.), *Early Childhood Education and Care in the United States* (191–208). Baltimore: Brookes.

Crnic, K., & G. Lamberty. 1994, April. Reconsidering School Readiness: Conceptual and Applied Perspectives. *Early Education and Development* 5(2): 91–105.

Cryer, D. 2003. Defining and Assessing Early Childhood Program Quality. *Annals of the American Academy of Political and Social Science 563*: 39–55.

Department of Defense. Overview of the Military Child Development System. Retrieved June 20, 2004, from the Web site of the Department of Defense (http://mfc-dod.qul.org/MCY/mm_cdc.htm).

Elmore, R. F. The National Education Goals Panel: Purposes, Progress, and Prospects. Paper prepared for the National Education Goals Panel. Retrieved June 19, 2004, from the NEGP Web site (www.negp.gov/reports/elmoref.htm).

Federal Interagency Forum on Child and Family Statistics. 2001. Retrieved June 19, 2004, from the official Web site of the Federal Interagency Forum on Child and Family Statistics (www.childstats.gov/ac2001/edtxt.asp#ed2).

Feeney, S., M. E. Brandt, & D. Grace. 2002. *Ready for Success in Kindergarten: A Comparative Analysis of Community Beliefs: Preschool and Kindergarten Parents, Teachers, and Administrators*. Honolulu: Hawaii Educational Policy Center.

Frank Porter Graham Center. 1999, October. *Early Learning, Later Success: The Abecedarian Study*. Chapel Hill,

NC: Frank Porter Graham Child Development Center, University of North Carolina.

Galinsky, E. 1989. The Staffing Crisis. *Young Children* 44(3): 2–4.

Gomby, D. S., M. B. Larner, C. S. Stevenson, E. M. Lewit, & R. E. Behrman. 1995, Winter. Long-Term Outcomes of Early Childhood Programs: Analysis and Recommendations. In R. E. Behrman (ed.), Long-Term Outcomes of Early Childhood Programs. *The Future of Children* 5(3). Los Altos, CA: Center for the Future of Children, David and Lucile Packard Foundation.

Graves, D. H. 2002. *Testing Is Not Teaching: What Should Count in Education*. Portsmouth, NH: Heinemann.

Haring, N. G., L. McCormick, & T. G. Haring. 1994. *Exceptional Children and Youth: An Introduction to Special Education* (6th ed.). Upper Saddle River, NJ: Merrill/Prentice Hall.

Head Start Bureau. 2004. Head Start Fact Sheet. Retrieved June 19, 2004, from the Web site of the Administration for Children and Families (www.acf.hhs. gov/programs/hsb/research/2004. htm).

Holloway, J. H. 2003, April. When Children Aren't Ready for Kindergarten (Research Link). *Educational Leadership*.

Hyson, M. 2003. Introducing NAEYC's Early Learning Standards: Creating the Conditions for Success. *Young Children* 58(1): 66–68.

Johnson, I., & J. B. McCracken (eds.). 1994. *The Early Childhood Career Lattice: Perspectives on Professional Development*. Washington, DC: NAEYC.

Jorde-Bloom, P. 1997. *A Great Place to Work: Improving Conditions for Staff in Young Children's Programs* (rev. ed.). Washington, DC: NAEYC.

Kagan, S. L., & N. E. Cohen. 1997. *Not By Chance: Creating an Early Care and Education System for America's Children*. Abridged Report: The Quality 2000 Initiative. New Haven, CT: Bush Center for Child Development and Social Policy.

Kagan, S. L., C. Scott-Little, & V. Stebbins Frelow. 2003. Early Learning Standards for Young Children: A Survey of the States. *Young Children* 58(5): 58–64.

Karoly, L. A., P. W. Greenwood, S. S. Everingham, J. Hoube, M. R. Kilburn, C. P. Rydell, M. R. Sanders, & J. R. Chiesa. 1998. *Investing in Our Children: What We Know and Don't Know About the*

Costs and Benefits of Early Childhood Interventions. Santa Monica, CA: Rand Corporation.

Kisker, E. E., & C. M. Ross. 1997, Spring. Arranging Child Care. In R. E. Behrman (ed.), *The Future of Children* 7(1). Los Altos, CA: The Center for the Future of Children, The David and Lucile Packard Foundation.

Kohn, A. 2000. *The Case Against Standardized Tests: Raising the Scores, Ruining the Schools*. Portsmouth, NH: Heinemann.

Larner, M. B., D. L. Terman, & R. E. Behrman. 1997, Spring. Welfare to Work: Analysis and Recommendations. In R. E. Behrman, ed. *The Future of Children* 7(1). Los Altos, CA: Center for the Future of Children, David and Lucile Packard Foundation.

Lazar, I., & R. Darlington. 1983. *As the Twig Is Bent: Lasting Effects of Preschool Programs*. Hillsdale, NJ: Erlbaum.

Lawrence, Charles R., III. 2004, March 18. *Who Is the Child Left Behind? The Racial Meaning of the New School Reform*. Lecture at the William S. Richardson School of Law, Honolulu.

Lewit, E. M., & L. Baker. 1995, Summer-Fall. School Readiness. *The Future of Children* 5(2): 128-139.

McKey, R. H. (ed.). 1985. Project Head Start, a National Evaluation: Summary of the Study. In D. G. Hayes (ed.), *Britannia Review of American Education* (235-243). Chicago: Encyclopedia Britannica.

McLean, M. E., & S. L. Odom. 1993. Practices for Young Children With and Without Disabilities: A Comparison of DEC and NAEYC Identified Practices. *Topics in Early Childhood Special Education* 13(3): 274-292.

Meisels, S. 1999. Assessing Readiness. In R. C. Pianta & M. J. Cox (eds.), *Transition to Kindergarten*. Baltimore: Brookes.

Mitchell, A. 2001. *Prekindergarten Programs in the States: Trends and Issues*. Retrieved June 20, 2004, from the Web site of the National Child Care Information Center (www. nccic.org/pubs/prekinderprogtrends.pdf).

Morgan, G. G. 2003. Regulatory Policy. In D. Cryer & R. M. Clifford (eds.), *Early Childhood Education and Care in the United States* (65-85). Baltimore: Brookes.

National Association for the Education of Young Children. 1991a. *Accreditation Criteria and Procedures of the National Academy of Early Childhood Programs* (rev. ed.). Washington, DC: NAEYC.

National Association for the Education of Young Children. 1991b. Early Childhood Teacher Certification: A Position Statement of the Association of Teacher Educators and the National Association for the Education of Young Children. Adopted July/August 1991. *Young Children* 47(1): 16-21.

National Association for the Education of Young Children. 1993a. Position Statement on School Readiness. Washington, DC: NAEYC.

National Association for the Education of Young Children. 1993b. NAEYC Position Statement on Violence in the Lives of Children. *Young Children* 48(6): 80-84.

National Association for the Education of Young Children. 1994. NAEYC Position Statement: A Conceptual Framework for Early Childhood Professional Development. *Young Children* 49(3): 68-77.

National Association for the Education of Young Children. 1997. NAEYC Position Statement on Licensing and Public Regulation of Early Childhood. *Young Children* 53(1): 43-50.

National Association for the Education of Young Children. 2003. *Early Learning Standards: Creating the Conditions for Success*. Joint position statement of NAEYC and the National Association of Early Childhood Specialists in State Departments of Education. Executive Summary. *Young Children* 58(1): 69-70.

National Association for the Education of Young Children. 2004, April 1. Policy Brief on Head Start Reauthorization. Washington, DC: NAEYC.

National Association of State Boards of Education. 1988. *Right from the Start*. Alexandria, VA: National Association of State Boards of Education.

National Board for Professional Teaching Standards. 1994. *What Teachers Should Know and Be Able to Do*. Detroit, MI, and Washington, DC: National Board for Professional Teaching Standards.

National Center on Children in Poverty. Kith and Kin Committee Report. Retrieved July 19, 2004, from the Alabama Child Care Consortium Web site (www.circ.uab.edu/childcare/kithcom.htm).

National Commission on Excellence in Education. 1983. *Nation at Risk: The Imperative for Educational Reform*. Washington, DC: U.S. Government Printing Office.

National Educational Goals Panel. 1995. *Reconsidering Children's Early Development and Learning: Toward Common Views and Vocabulary*. Washington, DC: National Educational Goals Panel.

National Education Goals Report. 1997. Available on Ready Web (http://readyweb.crc.uiuc.edu/library/1997/goals/info.html), a Web site sponsored by the University of Illinois at Urbana-Champaign.

National Home Education Research Institute Fact Sheet 1. 2004. Retrieved July 20, 2004, from the NHERI Web site (www.nheri.org/index.php).

National Household Education Surveys Program. 2002. *Comparative Indicators of Education in the United States and Other G-8 Countries*. Washington, DC: National Center for Education Statistics. Retrieved June 20, 2004, from the NCES Web site (http://nces.ed.gov/nhes/).

National Institute of Child Health and Human Development, Early Child Care Research Network. 1999. Child Outcomes When Child Care Center Classes Meet Recommended Standards for Quality. *American Journal of Public Health* 89(7): 1072-1077.

Noonan, M. J., & L. McCormick. 1993. *Early Intervention in Natural Environments*. Pacific Grove, CA: Brooks/Cole.

Pregnancy Info. Statistics on Teen Pregnancy. Retrieved June 20, 2004, from the Web site of Pregnancy-Info.net (www. pregnancy-info.net/teen_pregnancy_statistics.html).

Public Law 101-476. 1990, October. Individuals with Disabilities Education Act. Stat. 1103.

Raver, C. C., & E. F. Zigler. 2004. Another Step Back: Assessing Readiness in Head Start. *Young Children* 59(1): 58-63.

Robinson, S. L. 1987. Kindergarten in America. *Phi Delta Kappan* 68(7): 529-530.

Saluja, G., C. Scott-Little, & R. Clifford. 2000. Readiness for School: A Survey of State Policies and Definitions. *Early Childhood Research and Practice* 2(2) (http://ecrp.uiuc.edu/v2n2/saluja.html).

437

Schulman, K. 2000. The High Cost of Child Care Puts Quality Care out of Reach for Many Families. Issue Brief. Washington, DC: Children's Defense Fund.

Schultz, T., & J. Lombardi. 1989. Right from the Start: A Report on the NASBE Task Force on Early Childhood Education. *Young Children* 44(2): 6–10.

Schweinhardt, L. J., & D. P. Weikart. 1997. *Lasting Differences: The High/Scope Preschool Curricululm Comparison Study Through Age 23.* Ypsilanti, MI: High/Scope Press.

Seefeldt, C. 1990. *Continuing Issues in Early Childhood Education.* Upper Saddle River, NJ: Merrill/Prentice Hall.

Smith, M. M. 1989. Confronting Tough Issues. *Young Children* 45(1): 32–37.

Smith, S., M. Fairchild, & S. Groginsky. 1995. *Early Childhood Care and Education: An Investment That Works.* Washington, DC: National Conference of State Legislatures.

Stipek, D. J., R. Feiler, R. Ryan, S. Milburn, & J. M. Salmon. 1998. Good Beginnings: What Difference Does the Program Make in Preparing Young Children for School? *Journal of Applied Developmental Psychology* 19: 41–66.

Turnbull, R., A. Turnbull, M. Shank, & S. J. Smith. 2004 (4th ed.). *Exceptional Lives: Special Education in Today's Schools.* Upper Saddle River, NJ: Merrill/Prentice Hall.

U.S. Department of Education, National Center for Education Statistics. 1998. *Characteristics of Children's Early Care and Education Programs: Data from the 1995 National Household Education Survey.* U.S. Department of Education, Office of Educational Research and Improvement, NCES 98-128.

Van Horn, M. L., & S. L. Ramey. 2003. The Effects of Developmentally Appropriate Practices on Academic Outcomes Among Former Head Start Students and Classmates Grades 1–3. *American Educational Research Journal* 40(4): 961–990.

Wheatley, K. F. 2003. Promoting the Use of Content Standards. *Young Children* 58(2): 96–101.

Whitebook, M. 2003. *Early Education Quality: Higher Teacher Qualifications for Better Learning Environments. A Review of the Literature.* Berkeley: Center for the Study of Child Care Employment, University of California.

Whitebook, M., & A. Eichberg. 2002. Finding a Better Way: Defining Policies to Improve Child Care Workforce Compensation. *Young Children* 57(3): 66–72.

Whitebook, M., C. Howes, & D. Phillips. 1990. *Who Cares? Child Care Teachers and the Quality of Care in America: Executive Summary.* Washington, DC: National Center for the Early Childhood Workforce.

Whitebook, M., C. Howes, & D. Phillips. 1998. *Worthy Works, Unlivable Wages: The National Child Care Staffing Study, 1988–1997.* Washington, DC: Center for the Child Care Workforce.

Willer, B. 1994. A Conceptual Framework for Early Childhood Professional Development (NAEYC Position Statement, Adopted November, 1993). In J. Johnson & J. B. McCracken (eds.), *The Early Childhood Career Lattice: Perspectives on Professional Development.* Washington, DC: NAEYC.

Willer, B., S. L. Hofferth, E. E. Kisker, P. Divine-Hawkins, E. Farquhar, & F. B. Glantz. 1991. *The Demand and Supply of Child Care in 1990.* Washington, DC: NAEYC.

Willer, B. A., & L. D. Johnson. 1989. *The Crisis Is Real: Demographics on the Problem of Recruiting and Retaining Early Childhood Staff.* Washington, DC: NAEYC.

Williams, L. R., & D. P. Fromberg (eds.). 1992. *Encyclopedia of Early Childhood Education.* New York: Garland.

Wirt, J., S. Choy, P. Rooney, S. Provasnik, A. Sen, & R. Tobin. Trends in Full- and Half-Day Kindergarten. *The Condition of Education 2004* (NCES 2004-077). U.S. Department of Education, National Center for Education Statistics. Washington, DC: U.S. Government Printing Office.

Chapter 3

Antler, J. 1987. *Lucy Sprague Mitchell: The Making of a Modern Woman.* New Haven: Yale University Press.

Auleta, M. S. 1969. *Foundations of Early Childhood Education.* New York: Random House.

Beatty, B. 1995. *Preschool Education in America. The Culture of Young Children from the Colonial Era to the Present.* New Haven and London: Yale University Press.

Braun, S. J., & E. P. Edwards. 1972. *History and Theory of Early Childhood Education.* Belmont, CA: Wadsworth.

Brosterman, N. 1997. *Inventing Kindergarten.* New York: Abrams.

Castle, A. L. 1989. Harriet Castle and the Beginnings of Progressive Kindergarten Education in Hawaii 1894–1900. *Hawaiian Journal of History* 23: 119–136.

Clarke-Stewart, A. 1977. *Childcare in the Family: A Review of Research and Some Propositions for Policy.* New York: Academic Press.

Cleverley, J., & D. C. Phillips. 1986. *Visions of Childhood: Influential Models from Locke to Spock* (rev. ed.). New York: Teachers College Press.

Cremin, A. A. 1964. *The Transformation of the School: Progressivism in American Education, 1876–1957.* New York: Vintage Books.

Cuffaro, H. K. 1995. *Experimenting with the World: John Dewey and the Early Childhood Classroom.* New York: Teachers College Press.

Cunningham, H. 1992. *Children of the Poor: Representations of Childhood Since the 17th Century.* Cambridge, MA: Blackwell.

Cunningham, H. 1995. *Children and Childhood in Western Society Since 1500.* London and New York: Longman.

Deasey, D. 1978. *Education Under Six.* New York: St. Martin's Press.

Dewey, J. 1961. *The School and Society.* Chicago: University of Chicago Press. (Original work published 1899; rev. ed. 1943)

Dewey, J. 1972. *Experience and Education.* New York: Collier Books.

Edwards, C. P. 2002, Spring. Three Approaches from Europe: Waldorf, Montessori, and Reggio Emilia. *Early Childhood Research and Practice* 4(1). Available online at the SCRP Web site (http://ecrp.uiuc.edu/v4n1/edwards.html).

Edwards, C., P. Gandini, & G. Forman (eds.). 1998. *The Hundred Languages of Children.* Norwood, NJ: Ablex.

Featherstone, J. 1971. *Schools Where Children Learn.* New York: Liveright.

Gandini, L., & A. Gambetti. 1997. An Inclusive System Based on Cooperation: The Schools for Young Children in Reggio Emilia, Italy. In E. A. Hebert (ed.), *Schools for Everyone: A New Perspective on Inclusion* (63–76). San Francisco: Jossey-Bass.

Goetz, H. W. 1993. *Life in the Middle Ages from the Seventh to the Thirteenth Century*. Notre Dame, IN: University of Notre Dame Press.

Goffin, S. G., & C. Wilson. 2001. *Curriculum Models and Early Childhood Education: Appraising the Relationship* (2nd ed.). Upper Saddle River, NJ: Merrill/Prentice Hall.

Grubb, W. N., & A. M. W. Lazerson. 1988. *Broken Promises: How Americans Fail Their Children* (rev. ed.). Chicago: University of Chicago Press.

Gutek, G. L. 1972. *A History of the Western Educational Experience*. New York: Random House.

Gutek, G. L. 1997. *Historical and Philosophical Foundations of Education: A Biographical Introduction* (2nd ed.). Upper Saddle River, NJ: Merrill/Prentice Hall.

Haas, L. 1998. *The Renaissance Man and His Children: Childhood and Early Childhood in Florence 1300–1600*. New York: St. Martin's Press.

Haring, N. G., L. McCormick, & T. G. Haring. 1994. *Exceptional Children and Youth: An Introduction to Special Education* (6th ed.). Upper Saddle River, NJ: Merrill/Prentice Hall.

Hartley, D. 1993. *Understanding the Nursery School*. London: Cassel.

Hendrick, J. (ed.). 1997. *First Steps Toward Teaching the Reggio Way*. Upper Saddle River, NJ: Merrill/Prentice Hall.

Herlihy, D. 1978. Medieval Children. In B. K. Lackner & K. R. Philip (eds.), *Essays on Medieval Civilization* (109–141). Austin: University of Texas Press.

High/Scope Education Research Foundation. 1989. *The High/ Scope K–3 Curriculum: An Introduction*. Ypsilanti, MI: High/Scope Press.

Hohmann, M., & D. P. Weikart. 2002. *Educating Young Children: Active Learning Practices for Preschool and Child Care Programs* (2nd ed.). Ypsilanti, MI: High/Scope Press.

Hymes, J. L. 1996. Industrial Day Care's Roots in America. In K. M. Paciorek & J. H. Munro (eds.), *Sources: Notable Selections in Early Childhood Education* (2nd ed.). Guilford, CT: Dushkin/McGraw-Hill.

Jones, J. P. 1979. *Thomas More*. Boston: Twayne.

Kramer, R. 1988. *Maria Montessori: A Biography*. Reading, MA: Addison-Wesley.

Lascarides, V. C., & B. F. Hinitz. 2000. *History of Early Childhood Education*. New York and London: Falmer.

McMillan, M. 1919. *The Nursery School*. New York: Dutton.

Michel, S. 1999. *Children's Interest/Mothers' Rights: The Shaping of America's Child Care Policy*. New Haven: Yale University Press.

Mitchell, A., & J. David (eds.). 1992. *Explorations with Young Children: A Curriculum Guide from the Bank Street College of Education*. Mt. Rainier, MD: Gryphon House.

Montessori, M. 1965. *Dr. Montessori's Own Handbook*. New York: Schocken.

Montessori, M. 1967. *The Absorbent Mind*. New York: Holt, Rinehart & Winston.

Murphy, D. 1995. *Comenius: A Critical Reassessment of His Life and Work*. Portland, OR: Irish Academic Press.

Nager, N., & E. Shapiro (eds.). 2000. *Revisiting Progressive Pedagogy: The Developmental Interaction Approach*. Albany, NY: SUNY Press.

Noonan, M. J., & L. McCormick. 1993. *Early Intervention in Natural Environments*. Pacific Grove, CA: Brooks/Cole.

Osborn, D. K. 1991. *Early Childhood Education in Historical Perspective* (3rd ed.). Athens, GA: Education Associates.

Paciorek, K. M., & J. H. Munro (eds.). 1996. *Sources: Notable Selections in Early Childhood Education*. Guilford, CT: Dushkin.

Paciorek, K. M., & J. H. Munro (eds.). 1999. *Sources: Notable Selections in Early Childhood Education* (2nd ed.). Guilford, CT: Dushkin/McGraw-Hill.

Prochner, L. 1998. Missing Pieces: A Review of History Chapters in Introductory Early Childhood Education Textbooks. *Journal of Early Childhood Teacher Education* 19(1): 31–42.

Roopnarine, J. L., & J. E. Johnson (eds.). 2005. *Approaches to Early Childhood Education* (4th ed.). Upper Saddle River, NJ: Merrill/Prentice Hall.

Schultz, J. A. 1995. *The Knowledge of Childhood in the German Middle Ages, 1100–1350*. Philadelphia: University of Pennsylvania Press.

Schwarcz, J. H. 1991. *The Picture Book Comes of Age: Looking at Childhood Through the Art of Illustration*. Chicago: American Library Association.

Schweinhardt, L. J., & D. P. Weikart. 1997. Lasting Differences: The High/Scope Preschool Curriculum Comparison Study Through Age 23. Ypsilanti, MI: High/Scope Press.

Shapiro, M. S. 1983. *Child's Garden: The Kindergarten Movement from Fröebel to Dewey*. University Park: Pennsylvania State University Press.

Silber, K. 1965. *Pestalozzi: The Man and His Work*. New York: Schocken.

Silberman, C. E. 1970. *Crisis in the Classroom*. New York: Random House.

Smith, E. A. 1994. *Educating the Under-Fives*. London: Cassel.

Standing, E. M. 1959. *Maria Montessori: Her Life and Work*. Fresno, CA: Academy Library Guild.

Steiner, G. Y. 1976. *The Children's Cause*. Washington, DC: Brookings Institution.

Steinfels, M. O. 1973. *Who's Minding the Children?* New York: Simon & Schuster.

Weber, E. 1969. *The Kindergarten: Its Encounter with Educational Thought in America*. New York: Teachers College Press.

Weber, E. 1984. *Ideas Influencing Early Childhood Education: A Theoretical Analysis*. New York: Teachers College Press.

Weber, L. 1971. *The English Infant School and Informal Education*. Upper Saddle River, NJ: Merrill/Prentice Hall.

Williams, C. L., & J. E. Johnson. 2005. The Waldorf Approach to Early Childhood Education. In J. L. Roopnarine & J. E. Johnson (eds.), *Approaches to Early Childhood Education* (4th ed.), 336–362 Upper Saddle River, NJ: Merrill/Prentice Hall.

Williams, L. R. 1993. Historical and Philosophical Roots of Early Childhood Practice. *Encyclopedia of Early Childhood Education*. New York: Garland.

Wolfe, J. 2002. *Learning from the Past: Historical Voices in Early Childhood Education* (2nd ed.). Mayerthorpe, Alberta, Canada: Piney Branch Press.

Wortham, S. C. 1992. *Childhood, 1892–1992*. Wheaton, MD: Association for Childhood Education International.

Zigler, E. 1992. *Head Start: The Inside Story of America's Most Successful Educational Experiment*. New York: Basic Books.

Zigler, E., & A. J. Valentine. 1979. *Project Head Start: A Legacy of the War on Poverty*. New York: Free Press.

Chapter 4

Ainsworth, M. 1979. *Patterns of Attachment*. New York: Halsted Press.

Bailey, D. B., Jr., J. T. Bruer, F. J. Symons, & J. W. Lichtman (eds.). 2001. *Critical Thinking About Critical Periods*. Baltimore: Brookes.

Belsky, J. 1988. The Effects of Infant Day Care Reconsidered. *Early Childhood Research Quarterly 3:* 235–272.

Berk, L. E. 1996. *Infants and Children: Prenatal Through Middle Childhood* (2nd ed.). Needham Heights, MA: Allyn & Bacon.

Berk, L. E. 1999. *Infants and Children Prenatal Through Middle Childhood*, 3rd ed., Needham Heights, MA: Allyn & Bacon.

Berk, L. E. 2003. *Child Development* (6th ed.). Needham Heights, MA: Allyn & Bacon.

Berk, L. E., & A. Winsler. 1995. Scaffolding Children's Learning: Vygotsky and Early Childhood Education. Washington, DC: NAEYC.

Black, J., M. Puckett, & M. Bell. 1992. *The Young Child: Development from Prebirth Through Age Eight*. Upper Saddle River, NJ: Merrill/Prentice Hall.

Bloom, B. 1964. *Stability and Change in Human Characteristics*. New York: Wiley.

Bowlby, J. 1951. *Maternal Care and Mental Health*. Geneva: World Health Organization.

Bruer, J. T. 2001. A Critical and Sensitive Period Primer. In D. B. Bailey, Jr., J. T. Bruer, F. J. Symons, & J. W. Lichtman (eds.), *Critical Thinking About Critical Periods*. Baltimore: Brookes.

Bruer, J. T., & W. T. Greenough. 2001. The Subtle Science of How Experience Affects the Brain. In D. B. Bailey, Jr., J. T. Bruer, F. J. Symons, & J. W. Lichtman (eds.), *Critical Thinking About Critical Periods*. Baltimore: Brookes.

Bruner, J. 1983. *Child's Talk: Learning to Use Language*. New York: Norton.

Caine, R. N., & G. Caine. 1994. *Making Connections: Teaching and the Human Brain*. Menlo Park, CA: Addison-Wesley Innovative Learning Publications.

Chess, S., & A. Thomas. 1996. *Temperament: Theory and Practice*. New York: Brunner/Mazel.

Clarke-Stewart, A., M. Perlmutter, & S. Friedman. 1988. *Lifelong Human Development*. New York: Wiley.

Cratty, B. J. 1986. *Perceptual and Motor Development in Infants and Children* (3rd ed.). Upper Saddle River, NJ: Merrill/Prentice Hall.

Damon, W. 1988. *The Moral Child*. New York: Free Press.

Dennis, W. 1973. *Children of the Crech*. New York: Appleton-Century-Crofts.

DeVries, R., & B. Zan. 1994. *Moral Classrooms, Moral Children: Creating a Constructivist Atmosphere in Early Education*. New York: Teachers College Press.

Donaldson, M. C. 1978. *Children's Minds*. New York: Norton.

Edwards, C. P. 1986. *Promoting Social and Moral Development in Young Children*. New York: Teachers College Press.

Eisenberg, N. 1992. *The Caring Child*. Cambridge, MA: Harvard University Press.

Eisenberg, N., & P. Mussen. 1989. *The Roots of Prosocial Behavior in Children*. New York: Cambridge University Press.

Erikson, E. 1963. *Childhood and Society* (rev. ed.). New York: Norton.

Flavell, J. H. 1977. *Cognitive Development*. Upper Saddle River, NJ: Merrill/Prentice Hall.

Flavell, J. H., P. H. Miller, & S. A. Miller. 2002. *Cognitive Development* (4th ed.). Upper Saddle River, NJ: Merrill/Prentice Hall.

Gardner, H. 1983. *Frames of Mind*. New York: Basic Books.

Gardner, H. 1991. *The Unschooled Mind*. New York: Basic Books.

Gesell, A. 1940. *The First Five Years of Life*. New York: Harper & Row.

Gesell, A., & F. L. Ilg. 1974. *The Child from Five to Ten* (rev. ed.). New York: Harper & Row.

Gilligan, C. 1982. *In a Different Voice*. Cambridge, MA: Harvard University Press.

Ginsburg, H., & S. Opper. 1988. *Piaget's Theory of Intellectual Development* (3rd ed.). Upper Saddle River, NJ: Merrill/Prentice Hall.

Gonzalez-Mena, J., & D. W. Eyer. 2004. *Infants, Toddlers, and Caregivers* (6th ed.). New York: McGraw-Hill.

Harris, A. C. 1993. *Child Development* (2nd ed.). Minneapolis/St Paul: West.

Healy, J. M. 1990. *Endangered Minds*. New York: Simon & Schuster.

Honig, A. S., & D. S. Wittmer. 1992. *Prosocial Development in Children*. New York: Garland.

Hunt, J. M. 1961. *Intelligence and Experience*. New York: Ronald Press.

Kagan, J. 1984. *The Nature of the Child*. New York: Basic Books.

Kamii, C., & R. DeVries. 1993. *Physical Knowledge in Preschool Education*. New York: Teachers College Press.

Katz, L. G., & D. McClellan. 1997. *Fostering Children's Social Competence: The Teacher's Role*. Washington, DC: NAEYC.

Kohlberg, L. (ed.). 1981. *The Philosophy of Moral Development: Moral Stages and the Idea of Justice*. San Francisco: Harper & Row.

Kohlberg, L. 1984. *The Psychology of Moral Development: The Nature and Validity of Moral Stages*. New York: Harper & Row.

Kostelnik, M. J., A. Whiren, A. K. Soderman, K. Gregory, & L. C. Stein. 2002. *Guiding Children's Social Development* (3rd ed.). Albany, NY: Delmar.

Kurcinka, M. S. 1991. *Raising Your Spirited Child*. New York: HarperCollins.

Lickona, T., G. Geis, & L. Kolhberg (eds.). 1976. *Moral Development and Behavior: Theory, Research, and Social Issues*. New York: Holt, Rinehart & Winston.

Lin, H. L., F. R. Lawrence, & J. Gorrell. 2003. Kindergarten Teachers' Views of Children's Readiness for School. *Early Childhood Research Quarterly 18*(2): 225–236.

Mahler, M. S. 1975. *The Psychological Birth of the Human Infant: Symbiosis and Individuation*. New York: Basic Books.

Maslow, A. H. 1968. *Toward a Psychology of Being*. Princeton, NJ: Van Nostrand.

Maslow, A. 1970. *Motivation and Personality* (2nd ed.). New York: Harper & Row.

McCall, S. G., & B. Plemons. 2001. The Concept of Critical Periods and Their Implications for Early Childhood Services. In D. B. Bailey, Jr., J. T. Bruer, F. J. Symons, & J. W. Lichtman (eds.), *Critical Thinking About Critical Periods*. Baltimore: Brookes.

McDevitt, T. M., & J. E. Ormrod. 2002. *Child Development and Education*. Upper Saddle River, NJ: Merrill/Prentice Hall.

Miller, K. 1985. Ages and Stages: Developmental Descriptions and Activities Birth Through Eight Years. Chelsea, MA: Telshare.

Moore, S. G., & C. R. Cooper (eds.). 1982. *The Young Child: Reviews of Research*. Washington, DC: NAEYC.

Moskowitz, A. 1979. The Acquisition of Language. *Scientific American* 239(5): 82–89.

National Institute of Child Health and Human Development. The NICHD Study of Early Child Care, On-Line Publication available from: http://secc.rti.org/.

Papalia, D. E., & S. J. Olds. 1993. *A Child's World: Infancy Through Adolescence* (6th ed.). New York: McGraw-Hill.

Piaget, J. 1965. *The Moral Judgment of the Child*. New York: Free Press. (Original work published 1932)

Piaget, J. 1966. *The Origins of Intelligence in Children* (2nd ed.). New York: International Universities Press.

Rothbart, M. K., B. A. Ahadi, & D. E. Evans. 2000. Temperament and Personality: Origins and Outcomes. *Journal of Personality and Social Psychology* 78: 122–135.

Santrock, J. W. 2005. *Child Development* (8th ed.). New York: McGraw-Hill.

Schickedanz, J. A., D. I. Schickedanz, K. Hansen, & P. Forsyth. 1993. *Understanding Children* (2nd ed.). Mountain View, CA: Mayfield.

Schickedanz, J. A., D. I. Schickedanz, K. Hansen, P. Forsyth, & G. A. Forsyth. 2001. *Understanding Children and Adolescents* (4th ed.). Boston: Allyn & Bacon.

Shore, R. 1997. *Rethinking the Brain*. New York: Families and Work Institute.

Skeels, H. M. 1966. Adult Status of Children with Contrasting Early Life Experiences. *Monographs of the Society for Research in Child Development* 31 (Serial No. 105).

Smetana, J. G., M. Killen, & E. Turiel. 1991. Children's Reasoning About Interpersonal and Moral Conflicts. *Child Development* 62: 629–644.

Stern, D. N. 1990. *Diary of a Baby*. New York: Basic Books.

Sylwester, R. 1995. *A Celebration of Neurons: An Educator's Guide to the Human Brain*. Alexandria, VA: Association for Supervision, Curriculum, and Development.

Thelen, E., & L. B. Smith. 1998. Dynamic Systems Theory. In W. Damon (ed.), *Handbook of Child Psychology* (5th ed., vol. 1). New York: Wiley.

Thomas, A., & S. Chess. 1977. *Temperament and Development*. New York: Brunner/Mazel.

Thomas, R. M. 1985. *Comparing Theories of Child Development* (2nd ed.). Belmont, CA: Wadsworth.

Tough, J. 1977. *The Development of Meaning*. Boston: Allen & Unwin.

Vygotsky, L. S. 1962. *Thought and Language*. Cambridge, MA: MIT Press.

Vygotsky, L. S. 1978. *Mind in Society: The Development of Higher Psychological Processes*. Cambridge, MA: Harvard University Press.

Wadsworth, B. J. 1989. *Piaget's Theory of Cognitive and Affective Development* (4th ed.). New York: Longman.

Walker, L. J. 1995. Sexism in Kohlberg's Moral Psychology? In W. M. Kurtines & J. L. Gewirtz (eds.), *Moral Development: An Introduction*. Boston: Allyn & Bacon.

Wells, G. 1981. *Learning Through Interaction: The Study of Language Development*. New York: Cambridge University Press.

Wells, G. 1985. *The Meaning Makers*. Portsmouth, NH: Heinemann.

Werner, E. E., J. M. Bierman, & F. E. French. 1971. *The Children of Kauai: A Longitudinal Study from the Prenatal Period to Age Ten*. Honolulu: University of Hawaii Press.

Werner, E. E., & R. S. Smith. 1992. *Overcoming the Odds: High Risk Children from Birth to Adulthood*. Ithaca, NY: Cornell University Press.

Williams, L. R. 1992. Perspectives on Children. *Encyclopedia of Early Childhood Education*. New York: Garland.

Chapter 5

Almy, M., & C. Genishi. 1979. *Ways of Studying Children* (rev. ed.). New York: Teachers College Press.

Bagnato, S. J., J. T. Neisworth, & S. M. Munson. 1989. *Linking: Developmental Assessment and Early Intervention*. Rockville, MD: Aspen.

Beaty, J. J. 1994. *Observing the Development of the Young Child*. Upper Saddle River, NJ: Merrill/Prentice Hall.

Benjamin, A. C. 1994. Observations in Early Childhood Classrooms: Advice from the Field. *Young Children* 49(6): 14–20.

Bentzen, W. R. 1993. *Seeing Young Children: A Guide to Observing and Recording Behavior*. Albany, NY: Delmar.

Cryan, J. R. 1986. Evaluation: Plague or Promise? *Childhood Education* 62(5): 344–350.

Dodge, D. T., L. J. Colker, & C. Heroman. 2002. *The Creative Curriculum for Preschool* (4th ed.). Washington, DC: Teaching Strategies.

Genishi, C. (ed.). 1992. *Ways of Assessing Children and Curriculum: Stories of Early Childhood Practice*. New York: Teachers College Press.

Graves, D. H. 2002. *Testing Is Not Teaching: What Should Count in Education*. Portsmouth, NH: Heinemann.

Gronlund, G., & B. Engel. 2001. *Focused Portfolios: A Complete Assessment for the Young Child*. St. Paul, MN: Redleaf Press.

Gullo, D. F. 2005. *Understanding Assessment and Evaluation in Early Childhood Education* (2nd ed.). New York: Teachers College Press.

Helm, J., S. Beneke, & K. Steinheimer. 1998. *Windows on Learning: Documenting Young Children's Work*. New York: Teacher's College Press.

Hills, T. W. 1993. Assessment in Context—Teachers and Children at Work. *Young Children* 48(5): 20–28.

Jones, J. 2004. Framing the Assessment Discussion. In D. Koralek (ed.), *Spotlight on Young Children and Assessment*. Washington, DC: NAEYC.

Kamii, C. (ed.). 1990. *Achievement Testing in the Early Grades*. Washington, DC: NAEYC.

Kohn, A. 2000. *The Case Against Standardized Testing: Raising the Scores, Ruining the Schools*. Portsmouth, NH: Heinemann.

Koralek, D. (ed.). 2004. *Spotlight on Young Children and Assessment*. Washington, DC: NAEYC.

Losardo, A. & A. Notari-Syverson. 2001. *Alternative Approaches to Assessing Young Children*. Baltimore: Brookes.

Marion, M. 2004. *Using Observation in Early Childhood Education*. Upper Saddle River, NJ: Merrill/Prentice Hall.

Marsden, D. B., A. L. Dombro, & M. L. Dichtelmiller. 2003. *The Ounce Scale User's Guide*. New York: Pearson Early Learning.

McAfee, O., & D. J. Leong. 1997. *Assessing and Guiding Young Children's Development and Learning* (2nd ed.). Needham Heights, MA: Allyn & Bacon.

McAfee, O., D. Leong, & E. Bodrova. 2004. *Basics of Assessment: A Primer for Early Childhood Educators*. Washington, DC: NAEYC.

Meisels, S. J. 1989. *Developmental Screening in Early Childhood Education* (3rd ed.). Washington, DC: NAEYC.

Meisels, S. J. 1993. Remaking Classroom Assessment with the Work Sampling System. *Young Children* 48(5): 34–40.

Meisels, S. J., J. R. Jablon, D. B. Marsden, M. L. Dichtelmiller, A. B. Dorfman, & D. M. Steele. 1995. *The Work Sampling System: An Overview*. Ann Arbor, MI: Rebus Planning Associates.

National Association for the Education of Young Children. 1988. Position Statement on Standardized Testing of Young Children 3 Through 8 Years of Age. *Young Children* 43(3): 42–47.

National Association for the Education of Young Children. 1991. Guidelines for Appropriate Curriculum Content and Assessment in Programs Serving Children Ages 3 Through 8. *Young Children* 46(3): 21–38.

National Association for the Education of Young Children (NAEYC) & National Association of Early Childhood Specialists in State Departments of Education (NAECS/SDE). 2003. Joint Position Statement. Early Childhood Curriculum, Assessment, and Program Evaluation: Building an Effective, Accountable System in Programs for Children Birth Through Age 8. Available on the NAEYC Web site (www.naeyc.org/about/positions/pdf/CAPExpand.pdf).

Nicolson, S., & S. G. Shipstead. 1994. *Through the Looking Glass: Observation in the Early Childhood Classroom*. Upper Saddle River, NJ: Merrill/Prentice Hall.

Nyberg, D. 1971. *Tough and Tender Learning*. Palo Alto, CA: National Press Books.

Puckett, M. B., & J. K. Black. 2000. *Authentic Assessment of the Young Child: Celebrating Development and Learning* (2nd. ed.). Upper Saddle River, NJ: Merrill/Prentice Hall.

Schweinhart, L. J. 1993. Observing Young Children in Action: The Key to Early Childhood Assessment. *Young Children* 48(5): 29–33.

Seefeldt, C. (ed.). 1990. *Assessing Young Children*. Upper Saddle River, NJ: Merrill/Prentice Hall.

Shepard, L., S. L. Kagan, & E. Wurtz (eds.). 1998. *Principles and Recommendations for Early Childhood Assessments*. Washington, DC: National Education Goals Panel.

Williams, L. R., & D. P. Fromberg (eds.). 1992. *Encyclopedia of Early Childhood Education*. New York: Garland.

Wortham, S. C. 1990. *Tests and Measurements in Early Childhood Education*. Upper Saddle River, NJ: Merrill/Prentice Hall.

Wortham, S. C. 1996. *The Integrated Classroom: The Assessment-Curriculum Link in Early Childhood Education*. Upper Saddle River, NJ: Merrill/Prentice Hall.

Wortham, S. C. 2005. *Assessment in Early Childhood Education* (4th ed.). Upper Saddle River, NJ: Merrill/Prentice Hall.

Chapter 6

Athey, I. 1984. Contributions of Play to Development. *Child's Play: Development and Applied*. Hillside, NJ: Erlbaum.

Bergen, D. (ed.). 1988. *Play as a Medium for Learning and Development: A Handbook of Theory and Practice*. Portsmouth, NH: Heinemann.

Bodrova, E., & D. J. Leong. 2003. Chopsticks and Counting Chips: Do Play and Foundational Skills Need to Compete for the Teacher's Attention in an Early Childhood Classroom? *Young Children* 58(3): 10–17.

Bredekamp, S., & C. Copple. 1997. *Developmentally Appropriate Practice in Early Childhood Programs*. Washington, DC: NAEYC.

Bronson, M. B. 2000. *Self-Regulation in Early Childhood: Nature and Nurture*. New York: Guilford Press.

Bruner, J., S. Jolly, & K. Sylva (eds.). 1976. *Play: Its Role in Development and Evolution*. New York: Basic Books.

Caplan, F., & T. Caplan. 1974. *The Power of Play*. New York: Anchor/Doubleday.

Carlsson-Paige, N., & D. E. Levin. 1987. *The War Play Dilemma: Balancing Needs and Values in the Early Childhood Classroom*. New York: Teachers College Press.

Christie, J. F., & F. Wardle. 1992. How Much Time Is Needed for Play? *Young Children* 47(3): 28–31.

Derman-Sparks, L. 1989. *Anti-Bias Curriculum: Tools for Empowering Young Children*. Washington, DC: NAEYC.

Elkind, D. 1981. *The Hurried Child: Growing Up Too Fast Too Soon*. Menlo Park, CA: Addison-Wesley.

Frost, J. S., S. C. Wortham, & S. Reifel. 2005. *Play and Child Development* (2nd ed.). Upper Saddle River, NJ: Merrill/Prentice Hall.

Gonzalez-Mena, J. 1997. *Multicultural Issues in Child Care* (2nd ed.). Mountain View, CA: Mayfield.

Hughes, F. 1995. *Children, Play, and Development* (2nd ed.). Boston: Allyn & Bacon.

Johnson, J. E., J. F. Christie, & T. D. Yawkey. 1999. *Play and Early Childhood Development* (2nd ed.). Glenview, IL: Scott, Foresman.

Jones, E. 2004. Playing to Get Smart. In D. Koralek (ed.), *Spotlight on Young Children and Play* (24–27). Washington, DC: NAEYC.

Jones, E., & G. Reynolds. 1992. *The Play's the Thing: Teachers' Roles in Children's Play*. New York: Teachers College Press.

Klugman, E. (ed.). 1995. *Play, Policy, and Practice*. St. Paul, MN: Redleaf Press.

Klugman, E., & S. Smilansky (eds.). 1990. *Children's Play and Learning: Perspectives and Policy Implications*. New York: Teachers College Press.

Krogh, S. L. 1994. *Educating Young Children Infancy to Grade Three*. New York: McGraw-Hill.

Levin, D. E. 1998. *Remote Control Childhood: Combating the Hazards of Media Culture*. Washington, DC: NAEYC.

Levin, D. E. 2004. Beyond Banning War and Superhero Play: Meeting Children's Needs in Violent Times. In D. Koralek (ed.), *Spotlight on Young Children and Play* (46–49). Washington, DC: NAEYC.

Levy, J. 1978. *Play Behavior*. New York: Wiley.

McKee, J. S. (ed.). 1986. *Play: Working Partner of Growth*. Wheaton, MD: Association for Childhood Education International.

Monighan-Nourot, P. 1992. The Role of Play in Development. In L. R. Williams & D. P. Fromberg (eds.), *Encyclopedia of Early Childhood Education* (229–231). New York: Garland.

Monighan-Nourot, P., & J. Van Hoorn. 1991. Symbolic Play in Preschool and Primary Settings. *Young Children* 46(6): 40–47.

Monighan-Nourot, P., B. Scales, & J. Van Hoorn. 1987. *Looking at Children's Play: A Bridge Between Theory and Practice*. New York: Teachers College Press.

National Association for the Education of Young Children. 1990. NAEYC Position Statement on Media Violence in Children's Lives. *Young Children* 45(5): 18–21.

National Association for the Education of Young Children. 1991. Early Childhood Teacher Certification: A Position Statement of the Association of Teacher Educators and the National Association for the Education of Young Children. Adopted July/August 1991. *Young Children* 47(1): 16–21.

National Association for the Education of Young Children. 2004. NAEYC Draft, Early Childhood Program Standards and Suggested Accreditation Performance Criteria. Available on the NAEYC Web site (www.naeyc.org/accreditation/naeyc_accred/draft_standards/ter.html).

Parten, M. B. 1932. Social Participation Among Preschool Children. *Journal of Abnormal Psychology* 27(3): 243–269.

Piaget, J. 1962. *Play, Dreams, and Imitation in Childhood*. New York: Norton.

Reynolds, G., & E. Jones. 1997. *Master Players: Learning from Children at Play*. New York: Teachers College Press.

Rogers, C. S., & J. K. Sawyers. 1988. *Play in the Lives of Children*. Washington, DC: NAEYC.

Scales, B., M. Almy, A. Nicolopoulou, & S. Ervin-Tripp (eds.). 1991. *Play and the Social Context of Development in Early Care and Education*. New York: Teachers College Press.

Schickedanz, J. A., D. I. Schickedanz, & P. D. Forsythe. 1993. *Understanding Children*. Mountain View, CA: Mayfield.

Smilansky, S. 1968. *The Effects of Sociodramatic Play on Disadvantaged Pre-School Children*. New York: Wiley.

Smilansky, S., & L. Shefatya. 1990. *Facilitating Play: A Medium for Promoting Cognitive, Socio-Emotional, and Academic Development in Young Children*. Gaithersburg, MD: Psychosocial and Educational Publications.

Trawick-Smith, J. 1994. *Interactions in the Classroom: Facilitating Play in the Early Years*. Upper Saddle River, NJ: Merrill/Prentice Hall.

United Nations General Assembly. 1989. *Convention on the Rights of the Child*. New York: United Nations, November 20.

Van Hoorn, J., B. Scales, P. Nourot, & K. R. Alward (eds.). 2003. *Play at the Center of the Curriculum* (3rd ed.). Upper Saddle River, NJ: Merrill/Prentice Hall.

Ward, C. 1996. Adult Intervention: Appropriate Strategies for Enriching the Quality of Children's Play. *Young Children* 51(3): 20–25.

Chapter 7

American Academy of Pediatrics, American Public Health Association, & National Resource Center for Health and Safety in Child Care. 2002. *Caring for Our Children: National Health and Safety Performance Standard: Guidelines for Out-of-Home Child Care Programs* (2nd ed.). Elk Grove Village, IL: AAP, APHA, & NRC. Available on the Web site of the National Resource Center for Health and Safety in Child Care (http://nrc.uchsc.edu).

American Academy of Pediatrics, American Public Health Association, & National Resource Center for Health and Safety in Child Care. 2003. *Stepping Stones to Using "Caring for Our Children"* (2nd ed.). Elk Grove Village, IL: AAP, APHA, & NRC. Available on the Web site of the National Resource Center for Health and Safety in Child Care (http://nrc.uchsc.edu).

Aronson, S. 2002a. *Model Child Care Health Policies*. Washington, DC: NAEYC.

Aronson, S. (ed.). 2002b. With P. M. Spahr. *Healthy Young Children: A Manual for Programs*. Washington, DC: NAEYC.

Blakely, B., R. Blau, E. Brady, C. Streibert, A. Zavitkovsky, & D. Zavitkovsky. 1989. *Activities for School-Age Child Care*. Washington, DC: NAEYC.

Bredekamp, S., & C. Copple (eds.). 1997. *Developmentally Appropriate Practices in Early Childhood Programs* (rev. ed.). Washington, DC: NAEYC.

Bright Horizons. [n.d.] *Ready to Respond Emergency Preparedness Plan for Early Care and Education Centers*. Available on the Bright Horizons Family Solutions Web site (www.brighthorizons.com/talktochildren).

Christie, J. F., & F. Wardle. 1992. How Much Time Is Needed for Play? *Young Children* 47(3): 28–31.

Chun, R. 1994. *Capturing Childhood's Magic: Creating Outdoor Play Environments for Hawaii's Young Children*. Honolulu: Hawaii Association for the Education of Young Children.

Galinsky, E. 1971a. *School Beginnings: The First Day*. New York: Bank Street College of Education.

Galinsky, E. 1971b. *School Beginnings: The First Weeks*. New York: Bank Street College of Education.

Gonzalez-Mena, J. 1997. *Multicultural Issues in Child Care* (2nd ed.). Mountain View, CA: Mayfield.

Gonzalez-Mena, J., & D. W. Eyer. 2004. *Infants, Toddlers, and Caregivers* (6th ed.). New York: McGraw-Hill.

Harms, T., R. Clifford, & D. Cryer. 1998. *The Early Childhood Environment Rating Scale*. New York: Teachers College Press.

Hirsch, E. [n.d.] *Transition Periods: Stumbling Blocks of Education*. New York: Early Childhood Education Council of New York.

Holland, M. "That Food Makes Me Sick!" Managing Food Allergies and Intolerances in Early Childhood Settings. *Young Children* 47(3): 42–46.

Huettig, C., C. Sanborn, N. DiMarco, A. Popejoy, & S. Rich. 2004. The O Generation: Our Youngest Children Are at Risk for Obesity. *Young Children* 59(2): 50–55.

Jacobs, N. L. 1992. Unhappy Endings. *Young Children* 47(3): 23–27.

Jones, E., & G. Reynolds. 1992. *The Play's the Thing: Teachers' Roles in Children's Play*. New York: Teachers College Press.

Jordan, N. H. 1993. Sexual Abuse Prevention Programs in Early Childhood Education: A Caveat. *Young Children* 48(6): 76–79.

Kaplan, L. J. 1978. *Oneness and Separation: From Infant to Individual*. New York: Simon & Schuster.

Koralek, D. G., L. Colker, & D. T. Dodge. 1993. *The What, Why, and How of High Quality Early Childhood Education: A Guide for On-Site Supervision*. Washington, DC: NAEYC.

Moravcik, E. 1981. *Good Snacks for Hawaii's Young Children*. Honolulu: University of Hawaii.

Mulroy, M., J. Bothell, & M. Gaudio. 1992. First Steps in Preventing Childhood Lead Poisoning: The Role of Child Care Practitioners. *Young Children* 47(3): 20–25.

National Academy of Early Childhood Programs. 1998. *Accreditation Criteria and Procedures of the National Association for the Education of Young Children*. Washington, DC: NAEYC.

National Association for the Education of Young Children. 1993. The Effects of Group Size, Ratios, and Staff Training on Child Care Quality. *Young Children* 48(2): 65–67.

Pianta, R. C., M. J. Cox, D. Early, L. Taylor. 1999. Kindergarten Teachers' Practices Related to the Transition to School: Results of a National Survey.

Elementary School Journal 100(1): 71-86.

Sanders, S. 2002. Active for Life: Developmentally Appropriate Movement Programs for Young Children. Washington, DC: NAEYC.

Stonehouse, A. (ed.). 1990. Trusting Toddlers: Planning for One- to Three-Year-Olds in Child Care Centers. St. Paul, MN: Toys 'n Things Press.

Strickland, J. 1988. Do You Have Swiss Cheese Liability Insurance? *Child Care Information Exchange 62:* 75-77.

U.S. Consumer Products Safety Commission. 1997. *Handbook for Public Playground Safety*. Washington, DC: U.S. Government Printing Office.

U.S. Department of Health and Human Services. 2003. *Easing the Transition from Preschool to Kindergarten: A Guide for Early Childhood Teachers and Administrators*. Available on the Web site of the Administration for Children and Families, Head Start Information and Publication Center (www.headstartinfo.org/recruitment/trans_hs.htm).

Chapter 8

Bredekamp, S., & C. Copple (eds.). 1997. *Developmentally Appropriate Practice in Early Childhood Programs* (rev. ed.). Washington, DC: NAEYC.

Bronson, M. B. 1996. *The Right Stuff for Children Birth to 8: Selecting Play Materials to Support Development*. Washington, DC: NAEYC.

Burns, M. S., L. Goin, & J. T. Donlon. 1990. A Computer in My Room. *Young Children 45*(2): 62-67.

Chandler, P. A. 1994. *A Place for Me: Including Children with Special Needs in Early Care and Education Settings*. Washington, DC: NAEYC.

Christakis, D. A., F. J. Zimmerman, D. L. DiGiuseppe, & C. A. McCarty. 2004. Early Television Exposure and Subsequent Attentional Problems in Children. *Pediatrics 113*(4): 708-713.

Chun, R. 1994. Capturing Childhood's Magic: Creating Outdoor Play Environments for Hawaii's Young Children. Honolulu: Hawaii Association for the Education of Young Children.

Click, P. 1994. *Caring for School-Age Children*. Albany, NY: Delmar.

Crosser, S. 1992. Managing the Early Childhood Classroom. *Young Children 47*(2): 23-29.

Cuffaro, H. K. 1995. *Experimenting with the World: John Dewey and the Early Childhood Classroom*. New York: Teachers College Press.

Curtis, D., & M. Carter. 2003. *Designs for Living and Learning: Transforming Early Childhood Environments*. St. Paul, MN: Redleaf Press.

Dodge, D. T., L. J. Colker, & K. Heroman. 2002. *Creative Curriculum for Preschool* (4th ed.). Washington, DC: Teaching Strategies.

Dombro, A. L., L. J. Colker, & D. T. Dodge. 1997. *Creative Curriculum for Infants and Toddlers*. Washington, DC: Teaching Strategies.

Edwards, C., P. Gandini, & G. Forman (eds.). 1998. *The Hundred Languages of Children*. Norwood, NJ: Ablex.

Elkind, D. 1998. Computers for Infants and Young Children. *Child Care Information Exchange 47*(2): 44-46.

Feeney, S., & E. Moravcik. 1987. A Thing of Beauty: Aesthetic Development and Young Children. *Young Children 42*(6): 7-15.

Frost, J. L. 1992. *Play and Playscapes*. Albany, NY: Delmar.

Frost, J. L., & S. C. Wortham. 1988. The Evolution of American Playgrounds. *Young Children 43*(5): 19-27.

Gandini, L. 1984, Spring. Not Just Anywhere: Making Child Care Centers into "Particular" Places. *Beginnings:* 17-20.

Gareau, M., & C. Kennedy. 1991. Structure, Time and Space to Promote Pursuit of Learning in the Primary Grades. *Young Children 46*(4): 46-50.

Garner, A., P. Skeen, & S. Cartwright. 1984. *Woodworking for Young Children*. Washington, DC: NAEYC

Gonzalez-Mena, J. 1997. *Multicultural Issues in Child Care* (2nd ed.). Mountain View, CA: Mayfield.

Gonzalez-Mena, J., & D. W. Ever. 1997. *Infants, Toddlers, and Caregivers* (4th ed.). Mountain View, CA: Mayfield.

Greenman, J. 1988. *Caring Spaces, Learning Places: Children's Environments That Work*. Redmond, WA: Exchange Press.

Greenman, J. 1998. *Places for Childhoods: Making Quality Happen in the Real World*. Redmond, WA: Exchange Press.

Greenman, J., & A. Stonehouse. 1996. *Prime Times: A Handbook for Excellence in Infant and Toddler Programs*. St. Paul, MN: Redleaf Press.

Gross, D. W. 1972. Equipping a Classroom for Young Children. In K. R. Baker (ed.),

Ideas That Work with Young Children (35-38). Washington, DC: NAEYC.

Harms, T., & R. Clifford. 1980. *Early Childhood Environment Rating Scale*. New York: Teachers College Press.

Haugland, S. W., & D. D. Shade. 1988. Developmentally Appropriate Software for Young Children. *Young Children 43*(4): 37-43.

Henniger, M. L. 1994. Planning for Outdoor Play. *Young Children 49*(4): 10-15.

Hignett, W. F. 1988. Infant/Toddler Day Care: Yes, But We'd Better Make It Good. *Young Children 44*(1): 32-33.

Hill, D. M. 1977. *Mud, Sand, and Water*. Washington, DC: NAEYC.

Hirsch, E. 1984. *The Block Book*. Washington, DC: NAEYC.

Jones. E. 1984. *Dimensions of Teaching-Learning Environments: A Handbook for Teachers in Elementary Schools and Day Care Centers* (2nd ed.). Pasadena, CA: Pacific Oaks College.

Kirkland, L., J. Aldridge, & P. Kuby. 1999, Fall. Isn't That Cute? *Focus on Pre-K and K:* 1-3.

Koralek, D. G., L. J. Colker, & D. T. Dodge. 1993. *The What, Why, and How of High-Quality Early Childhood Education: A Guide for On-Site Supervision*. Washington, DC: NAEYC.

Kritchevsky, S., E. Prescott, & L. Walling. 1969. *Planning Environments for Young Children: Physical Space*. Washington, DC: NAEYC.

Lowman, L., & L. Ruhmann. 1998. Simply Sensational Spaces: A Multi- "S" Approach to Toddler Environments. *Young Children 53*(3): 11-17.

National Academy of Early Childhood Programs. 1998. *Accreditation Criteria and Procedures of the National Association for the Education of Young Children*. Washington, DC: NAEYC.

National Association for the Education of Young Children. 1993. The Effects of Group Size Ratios and Staff Training on Child Care Quality. *Young Children 48*(2): 65-67.

National Association for the Education of Young Children. 1996. NAEYC Position Statement: Technology and Young Children—Ages Three Through Eight. *Young Children 51*(6): 11-16.

Phillips, D. A. 1987. *Quality in Childcare: What Does Research Tell Us?* Washington, DC: NAEYC.

Prescott, E. 1978. Is Day Care as Good as a Good Home? *Young Children 33*(2): 16-23.

Readdick, C. A. 1993. Solitary Pursuits: Supporting Children's Privacy Needs in Group Settings. *Young Children* 49(1): 60–64.

Seefeldt, C. 2002. *Creating Rooms of Wonder*. Beltsville, MD: Gryphon House.

Shade, D. 1996. Software Evaluation. *Young Children* 51(6): 17–21.

Sommer, R. 1969. *Personal Space: The Behavioral Basis for Design*. Upper Saddle River, NJ: Merrill/Prentice Hall.

Stone, J. G. 1970. *Play and Playgrounds*. Washington, DC: NAEYC.

Stonehouse, A. (ed.). 1990. *Trusting Toddlers: Planning for One- to Three-Year-Olds in Child Care Centers*. St. Paul, MN: Toys 'n Things Press.

U.S. Consumer Products Safety Commission. 1997. *Handbook for Public Playground Safety*. Washington, DC: U.S. Government Printing Office.

Chapter 9

Adams, S., & J. Baronberg. 2005. *Promoting Positive Behavior: Guidance Strategies for Early Childhood Settings*. Upper Saddle River, NJ: Merrill/Prentice Hall.

Beaty, J. 1995. *Converting Conflicts in Preschool*. Orlando, FL: Harcourt Brace College Publishers.

Bettelheim, B. 1950. *Love Is Not Enough*. New York: Free Press.

Bowlby, J. 1982. *Attachment and Loss: Vol. 1. Attachment*. London: Hogarth.

Brazelton, T. B., & S. I. Greenspan. 2000. *The Irreducible Needs of Children: What Every Child Must Have to Grow, Learn, and Flourish*. New York: Perseus.

Bredekamp, S., & C. Copple (eds.). 1997. *Developmentally Appropriate Practices in Early Childhood Programs* (rev. ed.). Washington, DC: NAEYC.

Bronson, M. 2000. Recognizing and Supporting the Development of Self-Regulation in Young Children. *Young Children* 55(2): 32–37.

Canter, L. 1988. Assertive Discipline and the Search for the Perfect Classroom. *Young Children* 43(2): 24.

Crosser, S. 1992. Managing the Early Childhood Classroom. *Young Children* 47(2): 23–29.

Dennison, G. 1969. *The Lives of Children*. New York: Vintage Books.

Derman-Sparks, L. 1989. *Anti-Bias Curriculum: Tools for Empowering Young Children*. Washington, DC: NAEYC.

Dillon, J. T. 1971. *Personal Teaching*. Upper Saddle River, NJ: Merrill/Prentice Hall.

Dreikurs, R. 1969. *Psychology in the Classroom*. New York: Harper & Row.

Erikson, E. H. 1963. *Childhood and Society*. New York: Norton.

Essa, E. 1998. *A Practical Guide to Solving Preschool Behavior Problems* (3rd ed.). Albany, NY: Delmar.

Faber, A., & E. Mazlish. 1980. *How to Talk So Kids Will Listen and Listen So Kids Will Talk*. New York: Avon.

Fields, M. V., & C. Boesser. 1998. *Constructive Guidance and Discipline: Preschool and Primary Education*. Upper Saddle River, NJ: Merrill/Prentice Hall.

Gartrell, D. 1987a. Assertive Discipline: Unhealthy for Children and Other Living Things. *Young Children* 42(1): 55–61.

Gartrell, D. 1987b. Punishment or Guidance? *Young Children* 42(2): 55–61.

Gartrell, D. 1994. *A Guidance Approach to Discipline*. Albany, NY: Delmar.

Gartrell, D. 1995. Misbehavior or Mistaken Behavior? *Young Children* 50(5): 27–34.

Gartrell, D. 2001. Replacing Time-Out: Part One—Using Guidance to Build an Encouraging Classroom. *Young Children* 56(6): 8–16.

Gartrell, D. 2002. Replacing Time-Out: Part Two—Using Guidance to Maintain an Encouraging Classroom. *Young Children* 57(2): 36–43.

Gartrell, D. 2004. *The Power of Guidance: Teaching Social-Emotional Skills in Early Childhood Classrooms*. Clifton Park, NY: Delmar; and Washington, DC: NAEYC.

Ginott, H. 1972. *Teacher and Child: A Book for Parents and Teachers*. New York: Macmillan.

Gonzalez-Mena, J. 1997. *Multicultural Issues in Child Care* (2nd ed.). Mountain View, CA: Mayfield.

Gonzalez-Mena, J. 2001. *Foundations: Early Childhood Education in a Diverse Society* (2nd ed.). Mountain View, CA: Mayfield.

Gonzalez-Mena, J., & D.W. Eyer. 2004. *Infants, Toddlers, and Caregivers* (6th ed.). Mountain View, CA: Mayfield.

Gordon, A., & K. W. Browne. 1996. *Guiding Young Children in a Diverse Society*. Needham Heights, MA: Allyn & Bacon.

Gordon, T. 1974. *Teacher Effectiveness Training*. New York: David McKay.

Greenberg, P. 1987. Ideas That Work with Young Children: Child Choice—Another Way to Individualize—Another Form of Preventive Discipline. *Young Children* 43(1): 48–54.

Greenberg, P. 1988. Ideas That Work with Young Children: Avoiding Me Against You Discipline. *Young Children* 44(3): 24–29.

Greenberg, P. 1991a. *Character Development: Encouraging Self-Esteem and Self-Discipline in Infants, Toddlers, and Two-Year-Olds*. Washington, DC: NAEYC.

Greenberg, P. 1991b. Why Not Academic Preschool? Part 2. Autocracy or Democracy in the Classroom? *Young Children* 47(6): 27–81.

Greenberg, P. 1992. How to Institute Some Simple Democratic Practices Pertaining to Respect, Rights, Roots, and Responsibilities in Any Classroom. *Young Children* 48(6): 10–17.

Greenman, J. 2001. *What Happened to the World? Helping Children Cope in Turbulent Times*. New York: Greenman.

Hitz, R. 1998. Assertive Discipline: A Response to Lee Canter. *Young Children* 43(2): 25.

Hitz, R., & A. Driscoll. 1998. Praise or Encouragement: New Insights into Praise. *Young Children* 43(5): 6–13.

Honig, A. S. 1985. Compliance, Control, and Discipline. *Young Children* 40(3): 47–52.

Howes, C., & S. Ritchie. 2002. *A Matter of Trust: Connecting Teachers and Learners in the Early Childhood Classroom*. New York: Teachers College Press.

Hyson, M. 2002. Emotional Development and School Readiness. *Young Children* 57(6): 76–78.

Jones, E., & G. Reynolds. 1992. *The Play's the Thing: Teachers' Roles in Children's Play*. New York: Teachers College Press.

Kaiser, B., & J. S. Rasminsky. 1999. *Meeting the Challenge: Effective Strategies for Challenging Behaviors in Early Childhood Environments*. Ottawa, Ontario, Canada: Canadian Child Care Federation.

Kaiser, B., & J. S. Rasminsky. 2003. *Challenging Behavior in Young Children: Understanding, Preventing, and Responding Effectively*. Ontario, Canada: Pearson Education.

Katz, L. G. 1971, February. Condition with Caution: Think Thrice Before

Conditioning. *Preschool Education Newsletter.*

Katz, L. G. 1984. The Professional Early Childhood Teacher. *Young Children* 39(5): 3–10.

Kohn, A. 2001. Five Reasons to Stop Saying "Good Job!" *Young Children* 56(5): 24–28.

Kostelnik, M., A. Whiren, A. Soderman, L. Stein, & K. Gregory. 2003. *Guiding Children's Social Development* (4th ed.). Albany, NY: Delmar.

Kounin, J. 1970. *Discipline and Group Management in Classrooms.* New York: Holt, Rinehart & Winston.

Malaguzzi, L. 1993. For an Education Based on Relationships. *Young Children* 49(1): 9–12.

Marion, M. 2003. *Guidance of Young Children* (6th ed.). Upper Saddle River, NJ: Merrill/Prentice Hall.

Marshall, H. 2001. Cultural Influences on the Development of Self-Concept: Updating Our Thinking. *Young Children* 56(6):19–25.

Maslow, A. 1968. *Toward a Psychology of Being.* New York: Van Nostrand Reinhold.

Miller, D. F. 2004. *Positive Child Guidance* (4th ed.). Albany, NY: Delmar.

National Association for the Education of Young Children. 1993. *Violence in the Lives of Young Children.* Position Statement. Washington, DC: NAEYC.

Oken-Wright, P. 1992. From Tug-of-War to "Let's Make a Deal": The Teacher's Role. *Young Children* 48(1): 15–20.

Readdick, C. A. 1993. Solitary Pursuits: Supporting Children's Privacy Needs in Early Childhood Settings. *Young Children* 49(1): 60–64.

Reynolds, E. 2001. *Guiding Young Children: A Child-Centered Approach* (3rd ed.). Mountain View, CA: Mayfield.

Riley, S. S. 1984. *How to Generate Values in Young Children: Integrity, Honesty, Self-Confidence, and Wisdom.* Washington, DC: NAEYC.

Rogers, F. 2003. *The World According to Mr. Rogers: Important Things to Remember.* New York: Hyperion.

Stonehouse, A. (ed.). 1990. *Trusting Toddlers.* St. Paul, MN: Toys 'n Things Press.

Vance, E., & P. J. Weaver. 2002. *Class Meetings: Young Children Solving Problems Together.* Washington, DC: NAEYC.

Weber-Schwartz, N. 1987. Patience and Understanding. *Young Children* 42(3): 52–54.

Weichert, S. 1989. *Keeping the Peace.* Philadelphia: New Society.

Wheeler, J. 2004. *Conflict Resolution in Early Childhood: Helping Children Understand and Resolve Conflicts.* Upper Saddle River, NJ: Merrill/Prentice Hall.

Chapter 10

Althouse, R., M. H. Johnson, & S. T. Mitchell. 2003. *The Colors of Learning: Integrating the Visual Arts into the Early Childhood Curriculum.* New York: Teachers College Press.

Armstrong, D. G. 1989. *Developing and Documenting the Curriculum.* Boston: Allyn & Bacon.

Beal, N., with G. B. Miller. 2001. *The Art of Teaching Art to Children: In School and at Home.* New York: Farrar, Straus & Giroux.

Bowman, B. (ed.). 2003. *Love to Read: Essays in Developing and Enhancing Early Literacy Skills of African American Children.* Washington, DC: National Black Child Development Institute.

Bredekamp, S., & T. Rosegrant. 1995. *Reaching Potentials: Transforming Early Childhood Curriculum and Assessment* (vol. 2). Washington, DC: NAEYC.

Buchanan, B. L., & J. M. Rios. 2004. Teaching Science to Kindergartners: How Can Teachers Implement Science Standards? *Young Children* 59(3): 82–87.

Campbell, D. 2000. *The Mozart Effect in Children: Awakening Your Child's Mind, Body, and Creativity with Music.* New York: Avon.

Cazden, C. (ed.). 1981. *Language in Early Childhood Education* (rev. ed.). Washington, DC: NAEYC.

Chaillé, C., & L. Britain. 2003. *The Young Child as Scientist: A Constructivist Approach to Early Childhood Science Education.* Boston: Allyn & Bacon.

Children's Defense Fund. 1999. The State of America's Children Yearbook. Washington, DC: Children's Defense Fund.

Colbert, J. 2003, August–September. Understanding Curriculum: An Umbrella View. *Early Childhood News:* 16–23.

Comenius, J. A. 1967. *Didactica Magna.* Translated and edited by M. W. Keating. New York: Russell & Russell. (Original translation published 1896)

Copley, J. V. 2000. *The Young Child and Mathematics.* Washington, DC: NAEYC.

Derman-Sparks, L., & ABC Task Force. 1989. *Anti-Bias Curriculum: Tools for Empowering Young Children.* Washington, DC: NAEYC.

Dickinson, D., & P. O. Tabors. 2002. Fostering Language and Literacy in Classrooms and Homes. *Young Children* 57(2): 10–18.

Edwards, C., L. Gandini, & G. Forman. 1993. *The Hundred Languages of Children.* Norwood, NJ: Ablex.

Edwards, L. C., K. M. Bayless, & M. E. Ramsey. 2005. *Music: A Way of Life for the Young Child* (5th ed.). Upper Saddle River, NJ: Merrill/Prentice Hall.

Epstein, A. S. 2001. Thinking About Art: Encouraging Art Appreciation in Early Childhood Settings. *Young Children* 56(3): 38–43.

Feeney, S., & E. Moravcik. 1987. A Thing of Beauty: Aesthetic Development in Young Children. *Young Children* 42(6): 7–15.

Feeney, S., & E. Moravcik. 1995. *Discovering Me and My World.* Circle Pines, MN: American Guidance Service.

Fields, M. V. 1989. *Literacy Begins at Birth.* Tucson: Fisher Books.

Fields, M. V., L. A. Groth, & K. L. Spangler. 2004. *Let's Begin Reading Right: A Developmental Approach to Emergent Literacy* (5th ed.). Upper Saddle River, NJ: Merrill/Prentice Hall.

Fröebel, F. 1885. *The Education of Man.* Translated by J. Jarvis. New York: Lovell.

Geist, E. 2001. Children Are Born Mathematicians. *Young Children* 56(4): 12–19.

Geist, E. 2003. Infants and Toddlers Exploring Mathematics. *Young Children* 58(1): 10–12.

Harlan, J. D., & M. S. Rivkin. 2004. *Science Experiences for the Early Childhood Years: An Integrated Affective Approach* (8th ed.). Upper Saddle River, NJ: Merrill/Prentice Hall.

Healy, J. M. 1990. *Endangered Minds.* New York: Simon & Schuster.

Healy, J. M. 1992. *Is Your Bed Still There When You Close the Door and Other Playful Ponderings.* New York: Doubleday.

Hirsch, E. S. (ed.). 1996. *The Block Book* (3rd ed.). Washington, DC: NAEYC.

Holt, B. G., 1989. *Science with Young Children* (rev. ed.). Washington, DC: NAEYC.

Hymes, J. L. 1947. (2001 [1947]). Planning Ahead for Young Children. Speech to the National Association for Nursery Education. Reprinted in *Young Children* 56(4): 62–94.

Jalongo, M. R. 2004. *Young Children and Picture Books: Literature from Infancy to Six*. Washington, DC: NAEYC.

Jones, E., & J. Nimmo. 1994. *Emergent Curriculum*. Washington, DC: NAEYC.

Kagan, S. L., C. Scott-Little, & V. S. Frelow. 2003. Early Learning Standards for Young Children: A Survey of the States. *Young Children* 58(5): 58–64.

Kamii, C., & R. DeVries. 1993. *Physical Knowledge in Preschool Education*. New York: Teachers College Press.

Kostelnik, M. J., A. K. Soderman, & A. P. Whiren. 1999. *Developmentally Appropriate Curriculum* (2nd ed.). Upper Saddle River, NJ: Merrill/Prentice Hall.

Lowenfeld, V., & W. L. Brittain. 1987. *Creative and Mental Growth* (8th ed.). New York: Macmillan.

Marlay, A. 1993. The Importance and Value of the Development of Aesthetic Awareness in the Education of Young Children. *Professional News* 1(2): 19–27.

Mitchell, A., & J. David (eds.). 1992. *Explorations with Young Children*. Mt Rainier, MD: Gryphon House.

Moravcik, E. 2000. Music All the Livelong Day. *Young Children* 55(4): 27–29.

Moskowitz, A. 1979. The Acquisition of Language. *Scientific American* 239(5): 82–89.

National Association for the Education of Young Children & National Association of Early Childhood Specialists in State Departments of Education. 2003. Executive Summary Early Learning Standards: Creating Conditions for Success. *Young Children* 58(1): 69–70.

National Council of Teachers of Mathematics & National Association for the Education of Young Children. 2003. Learning Paths and Teaching Strategies in Early Mathematics. *Young Children* 58(1): 41–42.

National Research Council. 1996. *National Science Education Standards*. Washington, DC: National Academy Press.

Neelly, L. P. 2001. Developmentally Appropriate Music Practice: Children Learn What They Live. *Young Children* 56(3): 32–37.

Neuman, S. B., C. Copple, & S. Bredekamp. 1999. *Learning to Read and Write*. Washington, DC: NAEYC.

Neuman, S. B., & K. A. Roskos. 1993. *Language and Literacy Learning in the Early Years: An Integrated Approach*.

Orlando, FL: Harcourt Brace Jovanovich.

Orlick, T. 1982. *The Second Cooperative Sports and Games Book*. New York: Pantheon.

Palmer, H. 2001. The Music, Movement, and Learning Connection. *Young Children* 56(5): 13–17.

Perry, G., & M. Rivkin. 1992. Teachers and Science. *Young Children* 47(4): 9–16.

Pica, R. 1995. *Experiences in Movement*. Albany, NY: Delmar.

Ramsey, P. G. 1998. *Teaching and Learning in a Diverse World* (2nd ed.). New York: Teacher's College Press.

Roskos, K. A., J. F. Christie, & D. J. Richgels. 2003. The Essentials of Literacy Instruction. *Young Children* 58(2): 52–60.

Ross, M. 1981. *The Aesthetic Imperative: Relevance and Responsibility in Art Education*. Oxford: Pergamon.

Sanders, S. W. 2002. *Active for Life: Developmentally Appropriate Movement Programs for Young Children*. Washington, DC: NAEYC.

Schickedanz, J. 1999. *Much More than the ABC's*. Washington, DC: NAEYC.

School Readiness Task Force, Good Beginnings Alliance. 2003. *Hawaii Preschool Content Standards: Curriculum Guidelines for Programs for Four-Year-Olds*. Honolulu: Good Beginnings Alliance.

Seefeldt, C. 1997. *Social Studies for the Preschool/Primary Child* (5th ed.). Upper Saddle River, NJ: Merrill/Prentice Hall.

Seefeldt, C. (ed.). 2005. *The Early Childhood Curriculum: Current Findings in Theories and Practice* (3rd ed.). New York: Teachers College Press.

Smith, N. R., C. L. Fucigna, M. Kennedy, & L. Lord. 1993. *Experience and Art: Teaching Children to Paint* (2nd ed.). New York: Teachers College Press.

Smith, S. S. 2001. *Early Childhood Mathematics* (2nd ed.). Needham Heights, MA: Allyn & Bacon.

Sobel, J. 1984. Everybody Wins: 393 Noncompetitive Games for Young Children. New York: Walker.

Sutherland, Z. 1997. *Children and Books*. New York: Longman.

Taylor, B. J. 1993. *Science Everywhere: Opportunities for Very Young Children*. Fort Worth, TX: Harcourt Brace Jovanovich.

Teale, W., & E. Sulzby. 1986. *Emergent Literacy: Writing and Reading*. Norwood, NJ: Ablex.

Temple, C., M. Martinez, J. Yokota, & A. Naylor. 1998. *Children's Books in Children's Hands*. Boston: Allyn & Bacon.

Vygotsky, L. S. 1962. *Thought and Learning*. Cambridge, MA: MIT Press.

Vygotsky, L. S. 1978. *Mind in Society: The Development of Higher Psychological Process*. Cambridge, MA: Harvard University Press.

Wasserman, S., & G. W. G. Ivany. 1988. *Teaching Elementary Science: Who's Afraid of Spiders?* New York: Harper & Row.

Wells, G. 1981. *Learning Through Interaction: The Study of Language Development*. New York: Cambridge University Press.

Wells, G. 1985. *The Meaning Makers*. Portsmouth, NH: Heinemann.

Wheatley, K. F. 2003. Promoting the Use of Content Standards: Recommendations for Teacher Educators. *Young Children* 58(2): 96–101.

Wittmer, D. S., & A. Honig. 1994. Encouraging Positive Social Development in Young Children. *Young Children* 49(5): 4–12.

Zimmerman, E., & L. Zimmerman. 2000. Art Education and Early Childhood Education: The Young Child as Creator and Meaning Maker Within a Community Context. *Young Children* 55(6): 87–92.

Chapter 11

Althouse, R., M. H. Johnson, & S. T. Mitchell. 2003. *The Colors of Learning: Integrating the Visual Arts into the Early Childhood Curriculum*. New York: Teachers College Press.

Barclay, K. H., & W. C. Breheny. 1994. Letting the Children Take Over More of Their Own Learning: Collaborative Research in the Kindergarten Classroom. *Young Children* 49(6): 33–39.

Berk, L. E., & A. Winsler. 1995. *Scaffolding Children's Learning*. Washington, DC: NAEYC.

Biber, B. 1969. *Challenges Ahead for Early Childhood Education*. Washington, DC: NAEYC.

Bloom, B. S., B. B. Mesia, & D. Krathwohl. 1964. Taxonomy of Educational Objectives (Two Volumes: The Affective Domain and The Cognitive Domain). New York: David McKay.

Bredekamp, S., & C. Copple. 1997. *Developmentally Appropriate Practice in Early Childhood Programs* (rev. ed.). Washington, DC: NAEYC.

Bredekamp, S., & T. Rosegrant (eds.). 1992. *Reaching Potentials: Appropriate Curriculum and Assessment for Young Children* (vol. 1). Washington, DC: NAEYC.

Bredekamp, S., & T. Rosegrant (eds.). 1995. *Reaching Potentials: Transforming Early Childhood Curriculum & Assessment for Young Children* (vol. 2). Washington, DC: NAEYC.

Carter, M., & D. Curtis. 1996. *Spreading the News: Sharing the Stories of Early Childhood Education*. St. Paul, MN: Redleaf Press.

Chenfeld, M. B. 1994. *Teaching in the Key of Life*. Washington, DC: NAEYC.

Cuffaro, H. K. 1995. *Experimenting with the World*. New York: Teacher's College Press.

Dittmann, L. L. (ed.). 1977. *Curriculum Is What Happens: Planning Is the Key*. Washington, DC: NAEYC.

Edwards, C., L. Gandini, & G. Forman. 1993. *The Hundred Languages of Children*. Norwood, NJ: Ablex.

Feeney, S., & E. Moravcik. 1995. *Discovering Me and My World*. Circle Pines, MN: American Guidance Service.

Goffin, S. G. 1994. *Curriculum Models and Early Childhood Education: Appraising the Relationship*. New York: Macmillan.

Harlan, J. D., & M. S. Rivkin. 2004. *Science Experiences for the Early Childhood Years: An Integrated Affective Approach* (8th ed.). Upper Saddle River, NJ: Merrill/Prentice Hall.

Helm, J., S. Beneke, & K. Steinheimer. 1998. *Windows on Learning: Documenting Young Children's Work*. New York: Teacher's College Press.

Helm, J. H., & L. Katz. 2001. *Young Investigators: The Project Approach in the Early Years*. New York: Teachers College Press.

Hendrick, J. (ed.). 2004. *Next Steps Toward Teaching the Reggio Way* (2nd ed.). Upper Saddle River, NJ: Merrill/Prentice Hall.

Hirsch, R. A. 2004. *Early Childhood Curriculum: Incorporating Multiple Intelligences, Developmentally Appropriate Practice, and Play*. Boston: Allyn & Bacon.

Jones, E., & J. Nimmo. 1994. *Emergent Curriculum*. Washington, DC: NAEYC.

Katz, L. G. 1993. Dispositions as Educational Goals. Urbana, IL: ERIC Clearinghouse on Elementary and Early Childhood Education. ERIC Identifier: ED363454.

Katz, L. G., & S. C. Chard. 1989. *Engaging Children's Minds: The Project Approach*. Norwood, NJ: Ablex.

Katz, L. G., & S. C. Chard. 1996. The Contribution of Documentation to the Quality of Early Childhood Education. ERIC Digest (EDO-PS-96-2). Urbana, IL: ERIC Clearinghouse on Elementary and Early Childhood Education.

Krogh, S. 1990. *The Integrated Early Childhood Curriculum*. New York: McGraw-Hill.

Lawton, J. T. 1988. *Introduction to Child Care and Early Childhood Education*. Glenview, IL: Scott, Foresman.

McCracken, J. B. 1993. *Valuing Diversity: The Primary Years*. Washington, DC: NAEYC.

Mitchell, A., & J. David (eds.). 1992. *Explorations with Young Children*. Mt Rainier, MD: Gryphon House.

Petersen, E. A. 1996. *A Practical Guide to Early Childhood Planning, Methods, and Materials*. Boston: Allyn & Bacon.

Roopnarine, J. L., & J. E. Johnson (eds.). 1993. *Approaches to Early Childhood Education* (2nd ed.). Upper Saddle River, NJ: Merrill/Prentice Hall.

Schickedanz, J., M. L. Pergantis, J. Kanosky, A. Blaney, & J. Ottinger. 1997. *Curriculum in Early Childhood: A Resource Guide for Preschool and Kindergarten Teachers*. Boston: Allyn & Bacon.

Schwartz, S. L., & H. F. Robison. 1982. *Designing Curriculum for Early Childhood*. Boston: Allyn & Bacon.

Seefeldt, C. (ed.). 2005. *The Early Childhood Curriculum: Current Findings in Theories and Practice* (3rd ed.). New York: Teachers College Press.

Spodek, B., & O. Saracho (eds.). 1991. *Yearbook in Early Childhood Education: Vol. 2. Issues in Early Childhood Curriculum*. New York: Teachers College Press.

Wortham, S. 1994. *Early Childhood Curriculum: Developmental Bases for Learning and Teaching*. Upper Saddle River, NJ: Merrill/Prentice Hall.

Chapter 12

Allen, K. E., & I. S. Schwartz. 1996. *The Exceptional Child: Mainstreaming in Early Childhood Education* (3rd ed.). Albany, NY: Delmar.

Allred, K. W., R. Briem, & S. J. Black. 2003. Collaboratively Addressing Needs of Young Children with Disabilities. In C. Copple (ed.), *A World of Difference: Readings on Teaching Young Chil-*

dren in a Diverse Society. Washington, DC: NAEYC.

Aronson, S. S. (ed.). 2002. *Healthy Young Children: A Manual for Programs* (4th ed.). Washington, DC: NAEYC.

Atwater, J. B., J. J. Carta, I. S. Schwartz, & S. R. McConnell. 1994. Blending Developmentally Appropriate Practice and Early Childhood Special Education: Redefining Best Practice. In B. L. Mallory & R. S. New (eds.), *Diversity and Developmentally Appropriate Practices: Challenges for Early Childhood Education*. New York: Teachers College Press.

Bailey, D. B., & M. Wolery. 1992. *Teaching Infants and Preschoolers with Disabilities* (2nd ed.). Upper Saddle River, NJ: Merrill/Prentice Hall.

Bredekamp, S., & C. Copple. 1997. *Developmentally Appropriate Practice in Early Childhood Programs* (rev. ed.). Washington, DC: NAEYC.

Bowe, F. G. 2000. *Birth to Five: Early Childhood Special Education*. Albany, NY: Delmar.

Carta, J. J., I. S. Schwartz, J. B. Atwater, & S. R. McConnell. 1991. Developmentally Appropriate Practice: Appraising Its Usefulness for Young Children with Disabilities. *Topics in Early Childhood Special Education 13*(1): 1-20.

Chandler, P. 1994. *A Place for Me: Including Children with Special Needs in Early Care and Education*. Washington, DC: NAEYC.

Cook, R. E., A. Tessier, & M. D. Klein. 2000. *Adapting Early Childhood Curricula for Children in Inclusive Settings* (5th ed.). Upper Saddle River, NJ: Merrill/Prentice Hall.

Davis, M. D., J. L. Kilgo, & M. Gamel-McCormick. 1998. *Young Children with Special Needs: A Developmentally Appropriate Approach*. Boston: Allyn & Bacon.

Edmiaston, R., V. Dolezal, S. Doolittle, C. Erickson, & S. Merritt. 2000. Developing Individualized Education Programs for Children in Inclusive Settings: A Developmentally Appropriate Framework. *Young Children 55*(4): 36-41.

Featherstone, H. 1980. *A Difference in the Family: Life with a Disabled Child*. New York: Basic Books.

French, K. 2004. Supporting a Child with Special Health Care Needs. *Young Children 59*(2): 62-63.

Galinsky, E. 1988. Parents and Teacher-Caregivers: Sources of Tension,

Sources of Support. *Young Children* 43(3): 4.

Gargiulo, R., & J. L. Kilgo. 2000. *Young Children with Special Needs: An Introduction to Early Childhood Special Education*. Albany, NY: Delmar.

Gold, B. 1996. Who Will Care for Our Children? A Historical Perspective of Services for Young Children with Disabilities. In A. Kuschner, L. Cranor, & L. Brekken (eds.), *Project Exceptional: A Guide for Training and Recruiting Child Care Providers to Serve Young Children with Disabilities*. Sacramento: California Department of Education.

Hull, K., J. Goldhaber, & A. Capone. 2002. *Opening Doors: An Introduction to Inclusive Early Childhood Education*. Boston: Houghton Mifflin.

Kaplan-Sanoff, M., & E. F. Kletter. 1985. The Developmental Needs of Abused Children: Classroom Strategies. *Beginnings* 2(4): 15-19.

Koplow, L. 1985. Premature Competence in Young Children: A False Declaration of Independence. *Beginnings* 2(4): 8-11.

Kostelnik, M., E. Onaga, B. Rohde, & A. Whiren. 2002. *Children with Special Needs: Lessons for Early Childhood Professionals*. New York: Teachers College Press.

Mallory, B. R. 1998. Educating Young Children with Developmental Differences: Principles of Inclusive Practice. In C. Seefeldt & A. Galper (eds.), *Continuing Issues in Early Childhood Education* (2nd ed.). Upper Saddle River, NJ: Merrill/Prentice Hall.

McCormick, L. 1994. Infants and Young Children with Special Needs. In N. Haring, L. McCormick, & T. Haring (eds.), *Exceptional Children and Youth* (6th ed.). Upper Saddle River, NJ: Merrill/Prentice Hall.

McCormick, L., & S. Feeney. 1995. Modifying and Expanding Activities for Children with Disabilities. *Young Children* 50(4): 10-17.

Meisels, S. J., & B. A. Wasik. 1990. Who Should Be Served? Identifying Children in Need of Early Intervention. In S. J. Meisels & J. P. Schonkoff (eds.), *Handbook of Early Childhood Intervention*. New York: Cambridge University Press.

Mulligan, S. A. 2003. Assistance Technology: Supporting the Participation of Children with Disabilities. *Young Children* 58(6): 50-53.

Murray, K. 1985. Reporting Child Abuse: What Are Teachers' Responsibilities? *Beginnings* 2(4): 35-37.

National Association for the Education of Young Children. 1998. Code of Ethical Conduct and Statement of Commitment (rev. ed.). Washington, DC: NAEYC.

Noonan, M. J., & L. McCormick. 2006. *Young Children with Disabilities in Natural Environments: Methods and Procedures*. Baltimore: Brookes.

Sandall, S. R., & I. S. Schwartz. 2002. *Building Blocks for Teaching Preschoolers with Special Needs*. Baltimore: Brookes.

Surr, J. 1992. Early Childhood Programs and the Americans with Disabilities Act. *Young Children* 47(5): 18-21.

Turnbull, A., R. Turnbull, M. Shank, & S. J. Smith. 2004. *Exceptional Lives: Special Education in Today's Schools* (4th ed.). Upper Saddle River, NJ: Merrill/Prentice Hall.

Udell, T., J. Peters, & T. P. Templeman. 1998. From Philosophy to Practice in Inclusive Early Childhood Programs. *Teaching Exceptional Children* 30: 44-49.

Wolery, M., P. S. Strain, & D. B. Bailey. 1992. Reaching Potentials of Children with Special Needs. In S. Bredekamp & T. E. Rosegrantz (eds.), *Reaching Potentials: Appropriate Curriculum and Assessment for Young Children*. Washington, DC: NAEYC.

Wolery, M., & J. S. Wilbers (eds.). 1994. Including Children with Special Needs in Early Childhood Programs. *Research Monographs of the National Association for the Education of Young Children, Vol. 6*. Washington, DC: NAEYC.

Chapter 13

Barbour, C., N. H. Barbour, & P. A. Scully. 2005. *Families, Schools, and Communities: Building Partnerships for Educating Children* (3rd ed.). Upper Saddle River, NJ: Merrill/ Prentice Hall.

Berger, E. H. 2004. *Parents as Partners in Education: The School and Home Working Together* (6th ed.). Upper Saddle River, NJ: Merrill/Prentice Hall.

Brand, S. 1996. Making Parent Involvement a Reality: Helping Teachers Develop Partnerships with Parents. *Young Children* 51(2): 76-81.

Bredekamp, S., & C. Copple. 1997. *Developmentally Appropriate Practice in Early Childhood Programs* (rev. ed.). Washington, DC: NAEYC.

Breslin, D., & E. Marino. 2002. Family Ties: Parents as Partners. *Young Children* 57(1): 95.

Carter, M. 1996. July-August. Communicating with Parents. *Child Care Information Exchange*: 80-83.

Clinton, H. R. 1996. *It Takes a Village and Other Lessons Children Teach Us*. New York: Simon & Schuster.

Copple, C. (ed.). 2003. *A World of Difference: Readings on Teaching Young Children in a Diverse Society*. Washington, DC: NAEYC.

DeJong, L. 2003. Using Erikson to Work More Effectively with Teenage Parents. *Young Children* 58(2): 87-95.

DeSteno, N. 2000. Parent Involvement in the Classroom: The Fine Line. *Young Children* 55(3): 13-17.

Diffily, D., & K. Morrison (eds.). 1996. *Family-Friendly Communication for Early Childhood Programs*. Washington, DC: NAEYC.

Eldridge, D. 2001. Parent Involvement: It's Worth the Effort. *Young Children* 56(4): 65-69.

Elkind, D. 1981. *The Hurried Child: Growing Up Too Fast, Too Soon*. Menlo Park, CA: Addison-Wesley.

File, N. 2001. Family-Professional Partnerships: Practice That Matches Philosophy. *Young Children* 56(4): 70-74.

Galinsky, E. 1981. *Between Generations: The Six Stages of Parenting*. New York: Times Books.

Galinsky, E. 1999. *Ask the Children: What America's Children Really Think About Working Parents*. New York: Morrow.

Gennarelli, C. 2004. Communicating with Families: Children Lead the Way. *Young Children* 59(1): 98-99.

Goldberg, S. 1997. *Parent Involvement Begins at Birth: Collaboration Between Parents and Teachers of Children in the Early Years*. Boston: Allyn & Bacon.

Gonzalez-Mena, J. 2001. *Multicultural Issues in Child Care* (3rd ed.). Mountain View, CA: Mayfield.

Gonzalez-Mena, J. 2002. *The Child in the Family and the Community* (3rd ed.). Upper Saddle River, NJ: Merrill/ Prentice Hall.

Gonzalez-Mena, J. 2005. *Diversity in Early Education Programs: Honoring Differences* (4th ed.). Boston: McGraw-Hill.

Gordon, T. 1974. *Parent Effectiveness Training*. New York: David McKay.

Hannigan, I. 1998. *Off to School: A Parent's-Eye View of the Kindergarten Year*. Washington, DC: NAEYC.

Heath, P. 2005. *Parent-Child Relations: History, Theory, Research, and Context*. Upper Saddle River, NJ: Merrill/Prentice Hall.

Honig, A. 1975. *Parent Involvement in Early Childhood Education*. Washington, DC: NAEYC.

Katz, L. 1980. Mothering and Teaching—Some Significant Distinctions. In L. Katz (ed.), *Current Topics in Early Childhood Education* (vol. 3, 47-63). Norwood, NJ: Ablex.

Kaufman, H. O. 2001. Skills for Working with All Families. *Young Children* 56(4): 81-83.

Kieff, J., & K. Wellhousen. 2000. Planning Family Involvement in Early Childhood Programs. *Young Children* 55(3): 18-25.

Lawrence, G., & M. Hunter. 1978. *Parent-Teacher Conferencing*. El Segundo, CA: Theory into Practice.

Lee, L., & E. Seiderman. 1998. *The Parent Services Project*. Cambridge, MA: Harvard Family Research Project.

Levine, J. A., D. T. Murphy, & S. Wilson. 1993. *Getting Men Involved: Strategies for Early Childhood Programs*. New York: Scholastic.

Lightfoot, S. L. 1978. *Worlds Apart: Relationships Between Families and Schools*. New York: Basic Books.

Lilly, E., & C. Green. 2004. *Developing Partnerships with Families Through Children's Literature*. Upper Saddle River, NJ: Merrill/Prentice Hall.

National Association for the Education of Young Children. 1998. Code of Ethical Conduct and Statement of Commitment (rev. ed.). Washington, DC: NAEYC.

National Education Goals Panel. 1997. *National Education Goals*. Washington, DC: National Education Goals Panel.

Powell, D. R. 1989. Families and Early Childhood Programs. *Research Monographs of the National Association for the Education of Young Children*. Washington, DC: NAEYC.

Rappoport, R., R. Strelitz, & Z. Strelitz. 1980. *Fathers, Mothers, and Society: Perspectives on Parenting*. New York: Vintage Books.

Ricci, I. 1980. *Mom's House/Dad's House*. New York: Collier Books.

Riojas-Cortez, M., B. B. Flores, & E. R. Clark. 2003. Los Ninos Aprenden en Casa: Valuing and Connecting Home Cultural Knowledge with an Early Childhood Program. *Young Children* 58(6): 78-83.

Sammons, W. A. H., & J. M. Lewis. 2000. What Schools Are Doing to Help the Children of Divorce. *Young Children* 55(5): 64-65.

Stevens, J. H., & M. Matthews (eds.). 1979. *Mother/Child, Father/Child Relationships*. Washington, DC: NAEYC.

Stipek, D., L. Rosenblatt, & L. DiRocco. 1994. Making Parents Your Allies. *Young Children* 49(3): 4-9.

Stone, J. G. 1987. *Teacher-Parent Relationships*. Washington, DC: NAEYC.

Stonehouse, A. 1994. *How Does It Feel? Child Care from a Parent's Perspective*. Canberra, Australia: Australian Early Childhood Association.

Taylor, K. 1981. *Parents and Children Learn Together* (3rd ed.). New York: Teachers College Press.

Turbiville, V. P., G. T. Umbarger, & A. C. Guthrie. 2000. Fathers' Involvement in Programs for Young Children. *Young Children* 55(4): 74-79.

Turnbull, A. P., & H. R. Turnbull, III. 2001. *Families, Professionals, and Exceptionality: Collaborating for Empowerment* (4th ed.). Upper Saddle River, NJ: Merrill/Prentice Hall.

Walker-Dalhouse, D., & A. D. Dalhouse. 2001. Parent-School Relations: Communicating More Effectively with African American Parents. *Young Children* 56(4): 75-80.

Chapter 14

DeVault, L. 2003. The Tide Is High, but We Can Hold On: One Teacher's Thoughts on the Rising Tide of Academic Expectations. *Young Children* 58(6): 90.

Feeney, S., & N. Freeman. 1999. *Ethics and the Early Childhood Educator: Using the NAEYC Code*. Washington, DC: NAEYC.

Goffin, S. G., & J. Lombardi. 1988. *Speaking Out: Early Childhood Advocacy*. Washington, DC: NAEYC.

Hymes, J. L., Jr. 1981. *Teaching the Child Under Six* (3rd ed.). Columbus, OH: Merrill.

Isenberg, J. P., & M. R. Jalongo. 2003. *Major Trends and Issues in Early Childhood Education: Challenges, Controversies, and Insights*. New York: Teachers College Press.

Johnson, J., & J. B. McCracken (eds.). 1994. *The Early Childhood Career Lattice: Perspectives on Professional Development*. Washington, DC: NAEYC.

Jones, E., & G. Reynolds. 1992. *The Play's the Thing: Teachers' Roles in Children's Play*. New York: Teachers College Press.

Jorde-Bloom, P. 1988. *A Great Place to Work: Improving Conditions for Staff in Young Children's Programs*. Washington, DC: NAEYC.

Katz, L. G. 1995. The Developmental Stages of Teachers. In L. G. Katz, *Talks with Teachers of Young Children* (203-210). Norwood, NJ: Ablex.

Kidder, R. 1995. *How Good People Make Tough Choices*. New York: Simon & Schuster.

Kipnis, K. 1987. How to Discuss Professional Ethics. *Young Children* 42(4): 26-30.

Kohn, A. 2000. *The Case Against Standardized Testing: Raising the Scores, Ruining the Schools*. Portsmouth, NH: Heinemann.

National Association for the Education of Young Children. 1998. Code of Ethical Conduct and Statement of Commitment (rev. ed.). Washington, DC: NAEYC.

National Association for the Education of Young Children. 2003. Washington Update: Cutting Opportunities for Families and Young Children. *Young Children* 58(2): 63.

Nieto, S. 2003. *What Keeps Teachers Going?* New York: Teachers College Press.

Noddings, N. 1984. *Caring: A Feminine Approach to Ethics and Moral Education*. Berkeley: University of California Press.

Rogers, Fred. 2003. *The World According to Mr. Rogers: Important Things to Remember*. New York: Hyperion.

Stonehouse, A. 1994. *Not Just Nice Ladies*. Castle Hills, NSW, Australia: Pademelon Press.

VanderVen, K. 1991. The Relationship Between Notions of Care Giving Held by Early Childhood Practitioners and Stages of Career Development. In B. P.-K. Chan (ed.), *Early Childhood Toward the 21st Century: A Worldwide Perspective* (245-256). Hong Kong: Yew Chung Educational Publishing.

Whitebook, M. 1980. *Who's Minding the Child Care Workers? A Look at Staff Burnout*. Berkeley, CA: Child Care Staff Education Project.

Appendix A
The NAEYC Code of Ethical Conduct

PREAMBLE

NAEYC recognizes that many daily decisions required of those who work with young children are of a moral and ethical nature. The NAEYC Code of Ethical Conduct offers guidelines for responsible behavior and sets forth a common basis for resolving the principal ethical dilemmas encountered in early childhood care and education. The primary focus is on daily practice with children and their families in programs for children from birth through 8 years of age, such as infant/toddler programs, preschools, child care centers, family child care homes, kindergartens, and primary classrooms. Many of the provisions also apply to specialists who do not work directly with children, including program administrators, parent and vocational educators, college professors, and child care licensing specialists.

CORE VALUES

Standards of ethical behavior in early childhood care and education are based on commitment to core values that are deeply rooted in the history of our field. We have committed ourselves to

- Appreciating childhood as a unique and valuable stage of the human life cycle
- Basing our work with children on knowledge of child development
- Appreciating and supporting the close ties between the child and family
- Recognizing that children are best understood and supported in the context of family, culture, community, and society
- Respecting the dignity, worth, and uniqueness of each individual (child, family member, and colleague)
- Helping children and adults achieve their full potential in the context of relationships that are based on trust, respect, and positive regard

CONCEPTUAL FRAMEWORK

The Code sets forth a conception of our professional responsibilities in four sections, each addressing an arena of professional relationships: (1) children, (2) families, (3) colleagues, and (4) community and society. Each section includes an introduction to the primary responsibilities of the early childhood practitioner in that arena, a set of ideals pointing in the direction of exemplary professional practice, and a set of principles defining practices that are required, prohibited, and permitted.

The ideals reflect the aspirations of practitioners. **The principles** are intended to guide conduct and assist practitioners in resolving ethical dilemmas encountered in the field. There is not necessarily a corresponding principle for each ideal. Both ideals and principles are intended to direct practitioners to those questions which, when responsibly answered, will provide the basis for conscientious decisionmaking. While the Code provides specific direction and suggestions for addressing some ethical dilemmas, many others will require the practitioner to combine the guidance of the Code with sound professional judgment.

The ideals and principles in this Code present a shared conception of professional responsibility that affirms our commitment to the core values of our field. The Code publicly acknowledges the responsibilities that we in the field have assumed and in so doing supports ethical behavior in our work. Practitioners who face ethical dilemmas are urged to seek guidance in the applicable parts of this Code and in the spirit that informs the whole.

Ethical Dilemmas Always Exist

Often, "the right answer" — the best ethical course of action to take? is not obvious. There may be no readily apparent, positive way to handle a situation. One important value may contradict another. When we are caught "on the horns of a dilemma," it is our professional responsibility to consult with all relevant parties in seeking the most ethical course of action to take.

Source: National Association for the Education of Young Children, 1998. *Code of Ethical Conduct and Statement of Commitment* (rev. ed.). Copyright © 1998 NAEYC. All rights reserved. Reprinted with permission.

Section I: Ethical Responsibilities to Children

Childhood is a unique and valuable stage in the life cycle. Our paramount responsibility is to provide safe, healthy, nurturing, and responsive settings for children. We are committed to support children's development, respect individual differences, help children learn to live and work cooperatively, and promote health, self-awareness, competence, self-worth, and resiliency.

Ideals

I-1.1. To be familiar with the knowledge base of early childhood care and education and to keep current through continuing education and in-service training.

I-1.2. To base program practices upon current knowledge in the field of child development and related disciplines and upon particular knowledge of each child.

I-1.3. To recognize and respect the uniqueness and the potential of each child.

I-1.4. To appreciate the special vulnerability of children.

I-1.5. To create and maintain safe and healthy settings that foster children's social, emotional, intellectual, and physical development and that respect their dignity and their contributions.

I-1.6. To support the right of each child to play and learn in inclusive early childhood programs to the fullest extent consistent with the best interests of all involved. As with adults who are disabled in the larger community, children with disabilities are ideally served in the same settings in which they would participate if they did not have a disability.

I-1.7. To ensure that children with disabilities have access to appropriate and convenient support services and to advocate for the resources necessary to provide the most appropriate settings for all children.

Principles

P-1.1. Above all, we shall not harm children. We shall not participate in practices that are disrespectful, degrading, dangerous, exploitative, intimidating, emotionally damaging, or physically harmful to children. This principle has precedence over all others in this Code.

P-1.2. We shall not participate in practices that discriminate against children by denying benefits, giving special advantages, or excluding them from programs or activities on the basis of their race, ethnicity, religion, sex, national origin, language, ability, or the status, behavior, or beliefs of their parents. (This principle does not apply to programs that have a lawful mandate to provide services to a particular population of children.)

P-1.3. We shall involve all of those with relevant knowledge (including staff and parents) in decisions concerning a child.

P-1.4. For every child we shall implement adaptations in teaching strategies, learning environment, and curricula, consult with the family, and seek recommendations from appropriate specialists to maximize the potential of the child to benefit from the program. If, after these efforts have been made to work with a child and family, the child does not appear to be benefiting from a program, or the child is seriously jeopardizing the ability of other children to benefit from the program, we shall communicate with the family and appropriate specialists to determine the child's current needs; identify the setting and services most suited to meeting these needs; and assist the family in placing the child in an appropriate setting.

P-1.5. We shall be familiar with the symptoms of child abuse, including physical, sexual, verbal, and emotional abuse, and neglect. We shall know and follow state laws and community procedures that protect children against abuse and neglect.

P-1.6. When we have reasonable cause to suspect child abuse or neglect, we shall report it to the appropriate community agency and follow up to ensure that appropriate action has been taken. When appropriate, parents or guardians will be informed that the referral has been made.

P-1.7. When another person tells us of a suspicion that a child is being abused or neglected, we shall assist that person in taking appropriate action to protect the child.

P-1.8. When a child protective agency fails to provide adequate protection for abused or neglected children, we acknowledge a collective ethical responsibility to work toward improvement of these services.

P-1.9. When we become aware of a practice or situation that endangers the health or safety of children, but has not been previously known to do so, we have an ethical responsibility to inform those who can remedy the situation and who can protect children from similar danger.

Section II: Ethical Responsibilities to Families

Families are of primary importance in children's development. (The term family may include others, besides parents, who are responsibly involved with the child.) Because the family and the early childhood practitioner have a common interest in the child's welfare, we acknowledge a primary responsibility to bring about collaboration between the home and school in ways that enhance the child's development.

Ideals

I-2.1. To develop relationships of mutual trust with families we serve.

I-2.2. To acknowledge and build upon strengths and competencies as we support families in their task of nurturing children.

I-2.3. To respect the dignity of each family and its culture, language, customs, and beliefs.

I-2.4. To respect families' childrearing values and their right to make decisions for their children.

I-2.5. To interpret each child's progress to parents within the framework of a developmental perspective and to help families understand and appreciate the value of developmentally appropriate early childhood practices.

I-2.6. To help family members improve their understanding of their children and to enhance their skills as parents.

I-2.7. To participate in building support networks for families by providing them with opportunities to interact with program staff, other families, community resources, and professional services.

Principles

P-2.1. We shall not deny family members access to their child's classroom or program setting.

P-2.2. We shall inform families of program philosophy, policies, and personnel qualifications, and explain why we teach as we do, which should be in accordance with our ethical responsibilities to children (see Section I).

P-2.3. We shall inform families of and when appropriate, involve them in policy decisions.

P-2.4. We shall involve families in significant decisions affecting their child.

P-2.5. We shall inform the family of accidents involving their child, of risks such as exposures to contagious disease that may result in infection, and of occurrences that might result in emotional stress.

P-2.6. To improve the quality of early childhood care and education, we shall cooperate with qualified child development researchers. Families shall be fully informed of any proposed research projects involving their children and shall have the opportunity to give or withhold consent without penalty. We shall not permit or participate in research that could in any way hinder the education, development, or well-being of children.

P-2.7. We shall not engage in or support exploitation of families. We shall not use our relationship with a family for private advantage or personal gain, or enter into relationships with family members that might impair our effectiveness in working with children.

P-2.8. We shall develop written policies for the protection of confidentiality and the disclosure of children's records. These policy documents shall be made available to all program personnel and families. Disclosure of children's records beyond family members, program personnel, and consultants having an obligation of confidentiality shall require familial consent (except in cases of abuse or neglect).

P-2.9. We shall maintain confidentiality and shall respect the family's right to privacy, refraining from disclosure of confidential information and intrusion into family life. However, when we have reason to believe that a child's welfare is at risk, it is permissible to share confidential information with agencies and individuals who may be able to intervene in the child's interest.

P-2.10. In cases where family members are in conflict, we shall work openly, sharing our observations of the child, to help all parties involved make informed decisions. We shall refrain from becoming an advocate for one party.

P-2.11. We shall be familiar with and appropriately use community resources and professional services that support families. After a referral has been made, we shall follow up to ensure that services have been appropriately provided.

Section III. Ethical Responsibilities to Colleagues

In a caring, cooperative work place, human dignity is respected, professional satisfaction is promoted, and positive relationships are modeled. Based upon our core values, our primary responsibility in this arena is to establish and maintain settings and relationships that support productive work and meet professional needs. The same ideals that apply to children are inherent in our responsibilities to adults.

A. Responsibilities to Co-workers

Ideals

I-3A.1. To establish and maintain relationships of respect, trust, and cooperation with co-workers.

I-3A.2. To share resources and information with co-workers.

I-3A.3. To support co-workers in meeting their professional needs and in their professional development.

P-3A.4. To accord co-workers due recognition of professional achievement.

Principles

P-3A.1. When we have concern about the professional behavior of a co-worker, we shall first let that person know of our concern, in a way that shows respect for personal dignity and for the diversity to be found among staff members, and then attempt to resolve the matter collegially.

P-3A.2. We shall exercise care in expressing views regarding the personal attributes or professional conduct of co-workers. Statements should be based on firsthand knowledge and relevant to the interests of children and programs.

B. Responsibilities to Employers

Ideals

I-3B.1. To assist the program in providing the highest quality of service.

I-3B.2. To do nothing that diminishes the reputation of the program in which we work unless it is violating laws and regulations designed to protect children or the provisions of this Code.

Principles

P-3B.1. When we do not agree with program policies, we shall first attempt to effect change through constructive action within the organization.

P-3B.2. We shall speak or act on behalf of an organization only when authorized. We shall take care to acknowledge when we are speaking for the organization and when we are expressing a personal judgment.

P-3B.3. We shall not violate laws or regulations designed to protect children and shall take appropriate action consistent with this Code when aware of such violations.

C. Responsibilities to Employees

Ideals
I-3C.1. To promote policies and working conditions that foster mutual respect, competence, well-being, and positive self-esteem in staff members.

I-3C.2. To create a climate of trust and candor that will enable staff to speak and act in the best interests of children, families, and the field of early childhood care and education.

I-3C.3. To strive to secure equitable compensation (salary and benefits) for those who work with or on behalf of young children.

Principles
P-3C.1. In decisions concerning children and programs, we shall appropriately utilize the education, training, experience, and expertise of staff members.

P-3C.2. We shall provide staff members with safe and supportive working conditions that permit them to carry out their responsibilities, timely and nonthreatening evaluation procedures, written grievance procedures, constructive feedback, and opportunities for continuing professional development and advancement.

P-3C.3. We shall develop and maintain comprehensive written personnel policies that define program standards and, when applicable, that specify the extent to which employees are accountable for their conduct outside the work place. These policies shall be given to new staff members and shall be available for review by all staff members.

P-3C.4. Employees who do not meet program standards shall be informed of areas of concern and, when possible, assisted in improving their performance.

P-3C.5. Employees who are dismissed shall be informed of the reasons for their termination. When a dismissal is for cause, justification must be based on evidence of inadequate or inappropriate behavior that is accurately

documented, current, and available for the employee to review.

P-3C.6. In making evaluations and recommendations, judgments shall be based on fact and relevant to the interests of children and programs.

P-3C.7. Hiring and promotion shall be based solely on a person's record of accomplishment and ability to carry out the responsibilities of the position.

P-3C.8. In hiring, promotion, and provision of training, we shall not participate in any form of discrimination based on race, ethnicity, religion, gender, national origin, culture, disability, age, or sexual preference. We shall be familiar with and observe laws and regulations that pertain to employment discrimination.

SECTION IV: ETHICAL RESPONSIBILITIES TO COMMUNITY AND SOCIETY

Early childhood programs operate within a context of an immediate community made up of families and other institutions concerned with children's welfare. Our responsibilities to the community are to provide programs that meet its needs, to cooperate with agencies and professions that share responsibility for children, and to develop needed programs that are not currently available. Because the larger society has a measure of responsibility for the welfare and protection of children, and because of our specialized expertise in child development, we acknowledge an obligation to serve as a voice for children everywhere.

Ideals
I-4.1. To provide the community with high-quality (age and individually appropriate, and culturally and socially sensitive) education/care programs and services.

I-4.2. To promote cooperation among agencies and interdisciplinary collaboration among professions concerned with the welfare of young children, their families, and their teachers.

I-4.3. To work, through education, research, and advocacy, toward an environmentally safe world in which all children receive adequate health care, food, and shelter, are nurtured, and live free from violence.

I-4.4. To work, through education, research, and advocacy, toward a society in which all young children have access to high-quality education/care programs.

I-4.5. To promote knowledge and understanding of young children and their needs. To work toward greater social acknowledgment of children's rights and greater social acceptance of responsibility for their well-being.

I-4.6. To support policies and laws that promote the well-being of children and families, and to oppose those that impair their well-being. To participate in developing policies and laws that are needed, and to cooperate with other individuals and groups in these efforts.

I-4.7. To further the professional development of the field of early childhood care and education and to strengthen its commitment to realizing its core values as reflected in this Code.

Principles

P-4.1. We shall communicate openly and truthfully about the nature and extent of services that we provide.

P-4.2. We shall not accept or continue to work in positions for which we are personally unsuited or professionally unqualified. We shall not offer services that we do not have the competence, qualifications, or resources to provide.

P-4.3. We shall be objective and accurate in reporting the knowledge upon which we base our program practices.

P-4.4. We shall cooperate with other professionals who work with children and their families.

P-4.5. We shall not hire or recommend for employment any person whose competence, qualifications, or character makes him or her unsuited for the position.

P-4.6. We shall report the unethical or incompetent behavior of a colleague to a supervisor when informal resolution is not effective.

P-4.7. We shall be familiar with laws and regulations that serve to protect the children in our programs.

P-4.8. We shall not participate in practices which are in violation of laws and regulations that protect the children in our programs.

P-4.9. When we have evidence that an early childhood program is violating laws or regulations protecting children, we shall report it to persons responsible for the program. If compliance is not accomplished within a reasonable time, we will report the violation to appropriate authorities who can be expected to remedy the situation.

P-4.10. When we have evidence that an agency or a professional charged with providing services to children, families, or teachers is failing to meet its obligations, we acknowledge a collective ethical responsibility to report the problem to appropriate authorities or to the public.

P-4.11. When a program violates or requires its employees to violate this Code, it is permissible, after fair assessment of the evidence, to disclose the identity of that program.

STATEMENT OF COMMITMENT

As an individual who works with young children, I commit myself to furthering the values of early childhood education as they are reflected in the NAEYC Code of Ethical Conduct.

To the best of my ability I will

- Ensure that programs for young children are based on current knowledge of child development and early childhood education.
- Respect and support families in their task of nurturing children.
- Respect colleagues in early childhood education and support them in maintaining the NAEYC Code of Ethical Conduct.
- Serve as an advocate for children, their families, and their teachers in community and society.
- Maintain high standards of professional conduct.
- Recognize how personal values, opinions, and biases can affect professional judgment.
- Be open to new ideas and be willing to learn from the suggestions of others.
- Continue to learn, grow, and contribute as a professional.
- Honor the ideals and principles of the NAEYC Code of Ethical Conduct.

Appendix B

Environment Checklists

SAFETY CHECKLIST

This checklist can be used to evaluate the safety of an existing environment for children or to plan an environment.

Program _____ **Date** _____

Number of staff _____ **Number of children** _____ **Age of children** _____

Use the following code as appropriate: ✓ = yes/adequate ▬ = no/inadequate

General

_____ Program is licensed or meets licensing standards.

_____ Children are appropriately supervised at all times.

_____ Infants and toddlers are never left unattended, are always visible and within easy physical reach.

_____ Preschoolers are never left unattended and supervised by sight and sound.

_____ School age children may work independently for brief periods if supervised by sight or sound.

_____ Building and equipment are structurally sound, free of rust, peeling paint, and splinters.

_____ Bolts and rough edges on equipment and furniture are recessed or covered.

_____ Environment is documented to be free of lead paint and asbestos.

_____ Entrances and yard are secure. Staff monitor anyone entering the facility.

_____ Arrival and departure procedures ensure children are safe from traffic and from leaving with unauthorized persons.

_____ Sign-in/out procedure is followed and well known to staff and families.

_____ Floors where water is used and entrances have nonskid surfaces.

_____ Inside and outside are free of debris and standing water.

_____ Sharp tools, glass items, and bleach spray are out of children's reach.

_____ Stairs, ramps, lofts, decks, and platforms above 20″ have stable guard railings.

_____ Stairs, ramps, lofts, and platforms are kept free of toys and clutter.

_____ Equipment is free of entrapment hazards (openings are less than 3.5″ in width or more than 9″).

_____ Medicines, cleansers, pesticides, aerosol sprays, and other poisonous items are locked out of children's reach.

_____ Equipment and furniture are appropriately sized for the children enrolled.

_____ Pathways between play areas are kept clear of toys and equipment to prevent tripping.

_____ Kitchen, storage closets, gardening sheds, and other areas with hazardous materials are secured from children.

_____ Procedure for regularly surveying and maintaining program safety is in place.

_____ Shooting or projectile toys are not permitted.

_____ Plastic bags and balloons are kept out of children's reach.

Emergency Prevention and Preparation

____ A telephone is accessible with emergency numbers posted nearby.

____ Records for each child include health records, permission for emergency treatment, and permission for pick-up.

____ A medical practitioner and facility are prepared to provide emergency care and advice.

____ At least one supervising adult is trained in first aid and CPR. Certificates are current.

____ There is a procedure for handling first aid emergencies known to staff.

____ A first aid kit is adequately stocked, easily available, and marked for visibility.

____ A first aid kit is carried on trips.

____ A first aid handbook is available.

____ Injury reports are written and an injury log is kept.

____ A plan for handling medical emergencies is in place and is known to all staff.

____ Emergency exits are clearly marked and free of clutter.

____ An emergency evacuation plan is posted. The fire department has evaluated it.

____ Emergency evacuation procedures are practiced monthly.

____ Emergency procedures include a plan for children with special needs.

____ A plan for civil defense emergencies exists and is known to staff.

____ Smoke detectors are installed and functional.

____ A fire extinguisher is available in each room, is annually tested, and staff know how to use it.

____ A plan exists for safe classroom coverage in case a child or teacher must be taken to the hospital.

____ When children are transported by the program they are appropriately, legally, and safely restrained in vehicles.

Inside

____ Environment is arranged so all areas can be easily supervised.

____ Furniture is stable.

____ Heavy AV equipment and equipment carts are secured so that they cannot be tipped over. They are put away when not in use.

____ Equipment is unbroken and in good working order.

____ Low windows, doors, and mirrors have safety glass or Plexiglas.

____ Glass doors and floor level windows have stickers to ensure that people do not walk into them.

____ Heaters, radiators, pipes, and hot water tanks are inaccessible to children.

____ Hot water taps are turned off or are below 120° F so that hot water does not scald.

____ Unused electric outlets are covered in programs for children under the age of 5.

____ Electric cords do not cross pathways or run under rugs.

____ Rugs are secured or backed with nonskid material and edges do not create a tripping hazard.

Outside

____ Outdoor play area is protected by fences and has childproof gates.

____ No poisonous plants grow in the yard.

____ Permanent outdoor equipment is securely anchored and movable equipment is stable.

____ There is manufactured rubberized surfacing in good condition or 8-10″ of noncompacted sand, woodchips, or pea gravel beneath all climbing, swinging, and sliding equipment extending through fall zones.

____ Slides and climbing structures do not exceed safe height limitations (2 × the height of the average child)

____ Swings are attached with closed fasteners, not open S hooks.

____ Swing seats are constructed of soft or lightweight material.

____ Swings are away from pathways and barriers prevent children from walking into the path of a swing.

____ Metal slides are located so that they are shaded or facing away from the mid-day sun to prevent burns.

____ Equipment has no places where pinching or crushing of fingers can occur.

_____ Cribs, gates, and playpens have slats less than $2^3/_8''$ or mesh less than $^1/_4''$ in diameter.

_____ Cribs, childgates, and playpens have locking devices that work.

_____ Furniture that can be climbed is securely anchored.

_____ Furniture has rounded edges or edges are cushioned.

_____ Mattresses fit snugly in cribs.

_____ Dangling strings do not hang from cribs, playpens, curtains, etc.

_____ There are no dangling appliance cords.

_____ Highchairs and walkers are stable and are used in locations away from stairs and doors.

_____ Strollers and carriages are stable and have adequate brakes.

_____ Strollers, highchairs, and walkers have restraining straps.

_____ Toys are at least $1^1/_2''$ diameter.

_____ Swings support children on all sides.

_____ Stairway gates are locked when children are present.

_____ Separate space is set aside for nonmobile infants.

_____ Diaper supplies are kept within reach of the changing table.

_____ Nuts, popcorn, raisins, and hot dogs and other food that might cause choking are not served.

_____ Infants and toddlers are visually supervised by adults when sleeping.

_____ Infants are placed on their backs to sleep.

HEALTH CHECKLIST

This checklist can be used to evaluate the healthfulness of an existing environment for children or to plan an environment.

Program _____ Date _____

Number of staff _____ Number of children _____ Age of children _____

Use the following code as appropriate: ✓ = yes/adequate — = no/inadequate

Policies and Procedures

____ Program is licensed or meets licensing standards.
____ Health records are well-organized and accessible.
____ Families complete a health history prior to enrollment.
____ Health records include contact information for emergencies including the child's health care provider.
____ A basic manual of childhood health and disease is available.

____ Program has written health policies, which are given to staff and parents.
____ A policy and procedure exist for isolating sick children within the setting or for removing them from the setting.

The Environment

____ Clean drinking water is available to children at all times.
____ Toilet facilities are clean and easily accessible to children at all times.
____ Stable, non-skid, stepstools are provided if children must use high toilets, sinks or water fountains.
____ Tissue, soap, paper towels, and toilet paper are available where children can reach.
____ Room temperature is regulated as necessary.
____ Floors are mopped and rugs are vacuumed daily.
____ A sign showing proper hand-washing procedures is posted at every adult sink.

____ Adequate light allows children to see easily as they work without areas of darkness or shadows falling on their work. As much as possible this light is from natural sources with incandescent or full-spectrum fluorescent light used when necessary.
____ Windows and doors are opened regularly to let out pollutants.
____ Air conditioners, air filters, humidifiers, and dehumidifiers are cleaned often to minimize pollutants.
____ Animal cages are cleaned frequently and regularly as needed.

Health Practices

____ Hand-washing procedures are known and practiced by adults and children.
____ Children's clothes are changed as necessary. There are extra clean clothes kept for children.
____ Soiled clothes are stored in closed plastic bags away from children's play areas.
____ Toys are washed and sanitized every time they are soiled or mouthed.
____ Nutritious foods are chosen for meals, snacks, and cooking activities.
____ Food is not withheld as punishment or used as a reward.

____ Children and adults wash their hands after toileting and before handling food.
____ Children are instructed in hand-washing procedures and assisted as necessary.
____ Tables are cleaned and sanitized prior to meals, snack, and food preparation.
____ Children brush their teeth after meals. Toothbrushes are stored hygienically.
____ Clean, individual napping arrangements are available for each child.
____ Trash cans are lined, kept covered, and emptied daily.

_____ Toys are sanitized regularly (e.g. daily or weekly) and when soiled or mouthed.

_____ Healthful diapering procedures are known and practiced.

_____ Changing tables are covered with paper during use and cleaned with disinfecting solution after each use.

_____ Bottles are kept refrigerated.

_____ Pedal-opening trash cans are available for diaper disposal.

_____ Daily records are kept on children's food intake and other health concerns. This information is shared with parents.

_____ Each child has individual sleeping arrangements and bedding, linens are changed at least weekly or when necessary.

_____ No high and unstable shelves are used in rooms with toddlers.

INFANT-TODDLER LEARNING ENVIRONMENT CHECKLIST

This checklist can be used to evaluate the appropriateness of an existing environment for children or to plan an environment. No program will have everything, but the * items are essential and are found in most high quality programs for infants and toddlers.

Program _____   Date _____

Number of staff _____   Number of children _____   Age of children _____

Use the following code as appropriate: ✓ = yes/adequate   ━ = no/inadequate

Overall Atmosphere and Arrangement

Room Arrangement*

_____ 50 square feet per child
_____ Well lit with natural light if possible*
_____ Drinking water, sinks, and toilets accessible*
_____ Sheltered from outside noise and stimulus*
_____ Orderly and attractive*
_____ Ventilated and temperature controlled*
_____ Separation for nonmobile children*

_____ Paths that don't lead through areas
_____ Separate play and rest areas*
_____ Separate storage for staff*
_____ Locked cabinet for hazardous materials*

Activity Areas/Zones*

Areas for infants

_____ Sleeping area is quiet and shielded from stimulus
_____ Eating area is somewhat separate from play areas
_____ Area for immobile babies
_____ Diaper changing and dressing area with sink and hot water close at hand is away from eating and play areas

_____ Flexible play areas with clean, carpeted surfaces for playing and crawling
_____ Different levels on which to crawl and climb
_____ Several play areas for mobile children

Zones for toddlers and twos

_____ Equipment and materials organized into zones
_____ A messy play zone with art and sensory play materials such as sand and water
_____ Zone with tables for books and toys
_____ Sleeping/quiet zone
_____ Active play zone
_____ Safe, enclosed yards scrupulously maintained to minimize hazards
_____ Low portable, stable equipment
_____ Small tubs where an inch or two of water can be safely explored

Outside play environment for infants and toddlers

_____ Outdoor equipment (climbers, water tables, playhouses) scaled to children
_____ Play structures
  • low to the ground, stable and wide
  • wide ramps and entrances and exits to be climbed into and out of
  • without irreversible choices
_____ Stable push vehicles and pull toys without joints that pinch
_____ Low belt swings, and swings with seatbelts.

Organization and Maintenance

_____ Uncluttered shelf tops
_____ Environment cleaned each day
_____ Clean cages or aquariums for pets*

_____ Plants/animals fed, watered, protected*
_____ Equipment/materials complete/working
_____ Equipment washable, can be sanitized

Furniture

____ Low, open shelves for each play area*

____ Equipment for each play area*

____ Comfortable, clean carpets*

____ Child-sized tables and chairs

     ____ stable, comfortable chair or couch

     ____ a special rocker (designed so fingers cannot be pinched)

____ High or closed shelves or closets for staff*

____ Variety of levels for crawling and climbing

____ Locked cabinet for hazardous materials*

Schedule

____ Infants are allowed to regulate their own schedule*

____ Toddlers' schedules are flexible with general times for predictable routines*

Aesthetics

____ Orderly and attractive*

____ Neutral color walls

____ Patterns, colors, and storage coordinate

____ No promotional or media products or characters

____ Items of beauty such as flowers, plants, or sculpture

____ Pictures and displays at infant and toddler eye level*

____ Wall hangings (textured and touchable)

____ Areas decorated with art prints, photographs, children's work, book covers, and displays

____ Many pictures and displays at infant and toddler-carried eye level*

____ Pictures reflect the culture and characteristics of the children and their families

____ Record/tape player and recordings*

____ Appropriate music (e.g., soothing music for nap)*

Routine Areas

Entrance and Departure Area

Location and Space

____ Located where families enter and exit

____ Child-safe gates/doors

____ Bulletin boards and mailboxes for communication between families and staff*

Materials

____ Clock

Furniture

____ Comfortable seating for adults*

____ Cubby shelf for children's things

____ Adult-height counter/table for dressing/ undressing children

Organization and Maintenance

____ Cubbies labeled with names and pictures*

Food Preparation/Eating Area*

Location and Space

____ Located in or near the room

____ Cleanup equipment such as sponges, brooms, mops, etc.*

Furniture and Equipment

_____ Adult-height counter/table for preparing food*
_____ Sink for washing hands and rinsing dishes*
_____ Adult seating for comfortably holding children*

_____ Necessary appliances (refrigerator, stove or microwave, washer/dryer)*
_____ Dishwasher or triple sink if dishes washed*

Organization and Maintenance

_____ Hazardous equipment stored in child-safe cupboards
_____ Shelves and cupboards labeled to facilitate cleanup

_____ Toxic substances stored in locked cupboards*
_____ Equipment and materials stored in an orderly manner*

Materials and Supplies

_____ Clipboard or notebook to record eating
_____ Pots, pans, etc., for cooking and play*

For toddlers

_____ Toddler-sized tables and chairs

Sleeping Area*

Location and Space

_____ Located near the play areas/zones*
_____ Children visible at all times

_____ Protected from activity

Materials

_____ Mirrors, pictures, mobiles, etc., where children can see them*

Furniture

_____ Cribs or other safe, culturally appropriate sleeping arrangements for infants*
_____ Storage for blankets and toys from home

_____ Mats or cots for toddlers*
_____ Storage shelves/bins for bedding*
_____ Rocking chair*

Organization

_____ Equipment and materials stored in an orderly manner
_____ Shelves and cupboards labeled to facilitate cleanup

_____ Clipboard or notebook to record sleeping

Diapering/Changing/Toileting Area*

Location and Space

_____ Located within or next to the play areas/zones*
_____ Low toilets and sinks for toddlers or stepstools to make toilets and sinks accessible*

_____ Adult-height sinks for adults, with warm water for hand washing
_____ A lidded garbage can for soiled diapers*

Organization and Maintenance

_____ A supply of plastic bags for soiled diapers and clothes*
_____ Area clean and pleasant and sanitized daily*
_____ Sanitizing spray and paper for changing surfaces*

_____ A shelf above or beside changing table for easy organization, locked for ointments, etc. *
_____ Clipboard or notebook to record diapering/toileting*

Furniture

_____ Adult-height counter or changing table*

Materials and Supplies

_____ Paper towel dispenser that can be used with one hand

_____ Labeled boxes or bins for each child's diapers and clothes*

Play Areas/Zones

Messy/Sensory Play*

Location and Space

_____ Within classroom close to sinks/washing facilities*

_____ Washable/nonstaining floors*

Furniture

_____ Toddler-sized table and chairs for messy play

_____ Toddler-sized water table

Materials

_____ Mirrors (unbreakable)*

_____ Non-toxic materials such as cornmeal and flour

_____ Sand/water play with lots of containers*

For toddlers and twos

_____ Rhythm instruments

_____ Clay and dough

_____ Paint

_____ Soap and goop

Organization and Maintenance

_____ Materials orderly and attractive

_____ Containers labeled with pictures

Toys and Books

Books and toys can be located throughout this zone for infants and young toddlers. Areas may be divided for twos and older toddlers

Location and Space

_____ Enough space for all the children*

_____ Dumping containers (baskets, buckets)

Furniture

_____ Low, open shelves for storage of materials*

_____ Clean pillows and carpets

_____ Soft, large chairs/couch for adults and children to sit together

Organization and Maintenance

_____ Shelves close to play space*

_____ Materials uncluttered and orderly*

_____ Sets of toys stored separately, not jumbled*

_____ Sets stored separately, not jumbled

_____ Toys and books are in good condition*

_____ Toys and books are neat and orderly*

Toys

____ Nesting containers (plastic bowls, cups)

____ Shape-sorting boxes

____ Large snap beads

____ Stacking toys

____ Boxes with lids

____ Pegboards and pegs (jumbo size)

____ Simple-to-put-together toys

____ Busy boxes

____ Music boxes

For infants and young toddlers

____ Mobiles

____ Jack-in-the-box

____ Squeeze toys

____ Texture balls

____ Toys for sucking and teething

____ "Peek-a-boo" toys

____ Rattles and bells

For toddlers and twos

____ Jumbo wooden beads with strings

____ Pop-up toys

____ Containers and shelves labeled with pictures

____ Complete puzzles with 1–8 pieces*

____ Duplicates of items placed side-by-side

____ 2–3 choices per child

Books

____ Cloth or cardboard picture books*

____ Picture collections (mounted and covered)

____ A variety of styles of illustration*

____ Homemade books with photographs of the children and things they know*

____ New and classic books

For toddlers and twos

____ Low bookshelf that displays covers

____ Simple stories with plots

____ Multiethnic and multiage nonstereotyped characters*

____ Not based on commercial products

____ Nursery rhymes

____ Wordless books and books with text

____ Mood and concept books*

____ Sturdy books that are not board books

Active Play*

Location and Space

____ Within classroom and outside

Materials and Equipment

____ Push and pull toys

____ Small climber with slide

____ Tunnel (purchased or homemade)

____ Large boxes to crawl through

____ Cars and trucks

____ Wagons and buggies to push and pull

____ Soft balls of various sizes

____ Soft pillows to climb on

____ Duplicates of toys and several choices (2–3) per child

Furniture

____ Carpets or mats to cushion falls

____ Steps, stable sofas, cruise bars, platforms, or climbers*

Organization

____ Materials arranged neatly

Outside Environment*

Location and Space

_____ Space to run and play*
_____ Fenced for protection*
_____ Gates with child-safe locks*
_____ Hard surface for vehicles away from other play
_____ Natural features such as boulders, hills, and trees
_____ Access to toilets and sinks*
_____ Shelter from sun, wind, rain*

_____ Sand and dirt for digging*
_____ Located near indoor environment
_____ Levels and textures to touch, crawl, climb on*
_____ Comfortable places to sit and lie*
_____ Access to water for drinking and play*
_____ Separation for nonmobile children*

Materials and Supplies

_____ Clean sand in plentiful supply*
_____ Clean water in plentiful supply*

_____ Toys arranged in an orderly and attractive manner

Equipment

_____ Portable equipment for climbing
_____ Equipment for climbing, sliding, swinging with safe surfacing underneath and to 6' beyond (10" sand, woodchips, etc., or 2" rubber matting)*
_____ Large playground balls that bounce*
_____ Hoops, parachutes, rope, cones

_____ Water play toys (cups/spoons, basters, funnels, pitchers, tubing, water wheels, etc.)
_____ Sand toys (cups/spoons, pots, cars, buckets, trowels, etc.)
_____ Wading pool

For infants

_____ Blankets to lie on

_____ Light catchers and wind chimes hung in trees

For toddlers and twos

_____ Tables for outdoor table activities
_____ Space for art
_____ A line/rack to hang clothes and artwork
_____ A covered sandbox or alternative
_____ Wagons and buggies to push and pull
_____ Toddler-height sand/water table or tub
_____ Shed or other secure storage for outdoor supplies

_____ Natural or manufactured balance beams
_____ Mud toys (shovels, pots, pans, buckets, trowels)
_____ Riding toys to propel by feet
_____ Storage for vehicles
_____ Wheeled pushing, pulling, and child-sized riding vehicles

Organization and Maintenance

_____ Water, sand, mud toys separate from one another
_____ Storage near the sand, water, mud areas for toys*

466

These areas can be separate for older toddlers and twos or may be incorporated into the play zones as for younger toddlers.

Block Area

Location and Space

_____ Space for 2–4 children to work*

_____ Posters or photographs of buildings

Furniture

_____ Low, open shelves where blocks can be stored*

_____ Low-napped carpet or clean floor*

Materials

_____ Unit blocks (100 blocks in 5–10 shapes)

_____ Large figures (animals/people) and vehicles

_____ Table blocks

_____ Large soft blocks

_____ If space allows, 20+ cardboard, plastic, or light wood hollow blocks

Organization

_____ Blocks stored in an orderly fashion*

_____ Shelves labeled with pictures

_____ Blocks clean and unsplintered

Art Area

Location and Space

_____ Located near sink or water source*

_____ Floor is washable/nonstaining

_____ Inside or outside if climate permits daily use

Furniture

_____ Painting surfaces—table, wall, or easel (toddler-sized)

_____ Low tables and chairs*

Materials and Supplies

_____ Non-toxic, washable paints in at least primary colors (red, yellow, blue), black, and white*

_____ Brushes in a variety of sizes: wide and narrow with short handles*

_____ Base or paint for finger painting*

_____ Dough boards and tools*

_____ Large paper for easel painting*

_____ White paper, clean on one side*

_____ Recycled materials (card, Styrofoam, paper, ribbons, fabric, plastic jars and lids)*

_____ Large non-toxic unwrapped crayons and felt pens

_____ Food color

_____ Bowls, spoons, and measuring tools

_____ Wide-weave fabric

_____ Collection of textured materials (fabrics, etc.)

_____ Yarn, string, ribbons

_____ Smocks or old shirts (to protect clothing)*

_____ Clay boards and clay tools*

_____ Special papers (construction, tissue)

_____ Trays and plastic cups or containers*

_____ Potter's clay*

_____ playdough*

_____ White glue and paste*

Organization

____ Storage shelves close to table/easel
____ Brushes clean and stored upright
____ Materials orderly and attractive*

____ Floor and table coverings (plastic or old tablecloths) available

Dramatic Play Center

Location and Space

____ Space for 4 children to work*

Furniture

____ Child-sized table and chairs*
____ Sturdy "bed" or crib mattress for a child and dolls
____ Open shelves for storage*

____ Small open cupboard without doors that pinch fingers
____ Full-length unbreakable mirror

Materials

____ Clothes and props reflect children's families*
____ Uniforms, clothes, and props that reflect a variety of cultures, jobs, and fantasy roles*
____ Two telephones*

____ Pots and pans
____ Unbreakable dishes
____ Large wooden or plastic utensils
____ Pictures depicting family life and other scenes

Organization and Maintenance

____ Clutter minimized*
____ Props and costumes stored in an orderly fashion*

____ Duplicates of items and several choices (2–3) per child
____ Extra props stored and rotated

PRESCHOOL/PRIMARY LEARNING ENVIRONMENT CHECKLIST

This checklist can be used to evaluate the appropriateness of an existing environment for children or to plan an environment. No program will have everything, but the * items are essential and are found in most high quality programs for young children.

Program _____ Date _____

Number of staff _____ Number of children _____ Age of children _____

Use the following code as appropriate: ✓ = yes/adequate   ▬ = no/inadequate

Overall Atmosphere and Arrangement

Room Arrangement

_____ 35 square feet per child*
_____ Arranged in learning centers*
_____ Arranged for easy supervision
_____ Noisy and quiet areas are separate
_____ Paths do not lead through centers*

_____ All areas useful (no "dead" space)*
_____ Sheltered from outside noise and stimulus
_____ Well lit* with natural light if possible
_____ Ventilated* and temperature controlled
_____ Drinking water, sinks, and toilets accessible*

Learning Centers/Areas Include . . .

_____ Unit blocks*
_____ Hollow blocks
_____ Library*
_____ Dramatic play*
_____ Toys and Games*
_____ Art*

_____ Writing
_____ Discovery (science, math, social studies)
_____ Woodworking (may be outdoors)
_____ Private area for children
_____ Outside play environment*

Organization and Maintenance

_____ Each center has equipment/materials complete, working, and in good condition
_____ Space for large group gathering*
_____ Space for messy activities*
_____ Space for active play*
_____ Space for eating snacks/meals (may be in cafeteria for primary children)

_____ Space for resting (* in full-day programs)
_____ Shelf tops uncluttered
_____ Pets have clean cages or aquariums*
_____ Plants and animals are fed, have water, and are protected*
_____ Space for small group gathering

Furniture*

_____ Low, open shelves for each center*
_____ Comfortable, clean carpets
_____ Low tables and child-sized chairs
_____ Adult-sized chair or sofa

_____ Enough chairs and tables for all children in the class
_____ High or closed shelves or closets for staff*
_____ Locked cabinet for hazardous materials*

Aesthetics*

_____ Orderly and attractive*
_____ Neutral wall color
_____ Patterns, colors, and storage coordinates
_____ Areas decorated with art prints, photographs, children's work, book covers, and displays

_____ Provision of appropriate music (e.g., soothing music for naps)
_____ No promotional or media products or characters
_____ Items of beauty such as flowers, plants, or sculpture
_____ Most pictures and displays at child's eye level*

Schedule*

_____ Includes large blocks of time (at least 1 hour in morning and afternoon) for child-selected activity in both learning centers and outside*

Classroom Areas

Unit Block Area*

Location and Space

_____ Enough space for at least 4 children to work*

_____ Posters or photographs of buildings

Furniture

_____ Low, open shelves for storage of blocks*

_____ Low-napped carpet or clean floor*

Organization and Maintenance

_____ Blocks stored so that each type of block has its own individual place*

_____ Blocks clean and unsplintered

_____ Stored so that blocks with similar qualities are near each other.

_____ Placed so that the ways blocks differ is easily seen

_____ Each shelf clearly marked with an outline

Materials

_____ At least 100 hardwood unit blocks* for small areas (1–4 children); 200 or more for larger areas

_____ At least 10 shapes

_____ Figures and vehicles as props*

For primary children

_____ At least 200 blocks, at least 15 shapes

_____ Additional props such as signs and animal figures

_____ Shelves labeled with pictures and words

_____ Paper and pens for writing signs available nearby

Hollow Block Area

Location and Space

_____ Enough space for at least 4 children to work*

_____ Inside, on a covered porch, or outside in a sheltered location

_____ Located near dramatic play area if inside for more diverse and cross-gender play

_____ Posters or photographs

Furniture

_____ Space for all blocks to be stacked easily* on the floor or on shelves

_____ Storage provides protection from the elements if outdoors

_____ Low-napped carpet or soft surfacing to limit noise and prevent damage to the blocks*

Materials

____ At least 15 hollow blocks* and 6 planks

____ At least 3 shapes

____ Hats, sheets, and lengths of fabric as props*

Organization and Maintenance

____ Blocks stored in an orderly fashion*

____ Blocks clean and unsplintered

____ Shelves labeled with pictures and words

Dramatic Play Area*

Location and Space

____ Within classroom and additional center outdoors* if possible

____ Enough space for at least 4 children to work*

____ Located near hollow block area if possible for more diverse and cross-gender play

Furniture

____ Child-sized table and chairs*

____ Low, open shelf to hold props*

____ Small cupboard with doors

____ Pretend stove/sink unit or alternative that can serve different functions

____ Hooks to hang clothes

____ Full-length unbreakable mirror

____ Sturdy "bed" to hold a child and dolls

Materials

____ Clothes and props reflecting children's families*

____ Uniforms, clothes, and props reflecting various cultures, jobs, and fantasy roles*

____ Two telephones*

____ Pots and pans

____ Unbreakable dishes and utensils

____ Props for multiage pretend play

____ Pictures depicting family life and other scenes

Organization and Maintenance

____ Clutter minimized*

____ Extra props stored in kits and rotated with children's interests and topics of study

For primary children

____ Prop boxes accessible to children

____ Props and costumes stored in an orderly fashion*

____ Shelves and racks labeled with pictures and words

____ Boxes, platforms, etc., for children to create stage sets

Toys and Games Area*

Location and Space

____ Within classroom

____ Space for at least 2 children*

____ If possible separate space for building toys and table games

Furniture

____ Low, open shelves for storage of materials*

____ Comfortable carpet or low tables and chairs*

Materials

_____ Variety of materials requiring different skills*
_____ Building toys, such as Legos
_____ Complete puzzles with 8–25 pieces*
_____ Collections of materials such as buttons or caps
_____ Concept games/workjobs that are manufactured or teacher-made
_____ Several choices for every child the area accommodates (2–3 per child)*

For primary children

_____ Puzzles with 25–100 pieces
_____ Large sets with wheels, gears, etc.
_____ Directions and patterns to use with toys
_____ Board games

Organization and Maintenance

_____ Shelves located close to work space*
_____ Multipiece sets stored separately, not jumbled*
_____ All toys/games complete without obviously missing pieces
_____ Trays, mats, or designated table space for work

_____ Containers and shelves labeled with words and pictures
_____ Materials uncluttered, orderly*
_____ Trays or space where children can save and display completed work

Sensory Play Area*

Location and Space

_____ Within classroom or outside when weather permits
_____ Space for at least 4 children*
_____ Located near sink

_____ Near door or porch
_____ Outlet for light table

Furniture

_____ Low, open shelves for storage of materials*
_____ Sand/water table

_____ Table and chairs for dough/clay work
_____ Light table

Materials and Supplies

_____ Basins or tubs
_____ Bowls, cups, and buckets
_____ Ladles, measuring cups, and pitchers
_____ Funnels, basters, whisks, and egg-beaters
_____ Eye droppers and translucent ice-cube trays for light table
_____ Aprons
_____ Plastic tablecloths or shower curtains
_____ Water
_____ Natural materials: sand, dirt, mud

_____ Modeling materials: dough, clay (may be in art area)
_____ Dry materials: sawdust, and aquarium gravel if appropriate; rice, beans, macaroni, oatmeal
_____ Mixtures: cornstarch and water, and "super-sand" and "flubber"
_____ Food color
_____ Dishwashing liquid
_____ Clear colored toys for light table
_____ Tablemats or trays for modeling work

For primary children

_____ Measuring tools
_____ Waterwheels

_____ Tubing/pipes

Organization and Maintenance

_____ Shelves located close to work space*
_____ Containers and shelves labeled with words and pictures

_____ Materials uncluttered, orderly*

Art Center*

Location and Space

_____ Located near sink or water source*
_____ Floor washable/nonstaining

_____ Inside or outside if climate permits daily use

Furniture

_____ Closed or covered storage for materials available to adults
_____ Shelves for materials available to children

_____ An easel adjusted so the smallest child can reach the top of one side*
_____ Low tables and chairs* that may be dirtied or are easily cleaned

Materials and Supplies

_____ Different kinds of paint including: easel paints in at least primary colors, black, and white,* liquid and cake watercolors, fingerpaint
_____ Brushes in a variety of sizes*
_____ Wide-weave fabric
_____ Clay boards and clay tools
_____ For drawing: non-toxic felt pens,* unwrapped non-toxic crayons,* chalk
_____ Playdough
_____ Large paper for easel painting*
_____ Scissors that can be easily used by children in either hand
_____ Dough boards and tools
_____ Recycled materials (cardboard, Styrofoam, wrapping paper, fabric, plastic jars and lids)*

_____ Collection of textured materials and fabric
_____ Yarn, string, ribbons
_____ Smocks or old shirts (to protect clothing)
_____ Base or paint for finger painting*
_____ Food color
_____ Potter's clay*
_____ White glue and paste*
_____ White paper, clean on one side*
_____ Trays and plastic cups or containers*
_____ Bowls, spoons, and measuring tools
_____ Special papers (construction, tissue)
_____ Items of beauty to inspire

Organization and Maintenance

_____ Floor/table coverings available
_____ Materials orderly and attractive*

_____ Storage shelves close to tables/easels*
_____ Storage labelled for adults and children

For primary children

_____ Pencil crayons
_____ Brushes clean and stored upright

_____ Containers and shelves labeled
_____ Oil-base modeling clay

Woodworking Area

Location and Space

_____ Located so it can be supervised*
_____ Located where it is nondisruptive*

_____ Indoors or outdoors if climate permits

Furniture

_____ a good workbench (includes vise) and a platform for different size children to stand on
_____ a sawing table that children can kneel on

_____ Storage rack for tools close to table*

Materials and Supplies

_____ C Clamps or small bar clamp
_____ Teacher's safety glasses (not goggles)
_____ 2 additional pairs of protective safety glasses (not goggles) for children (attach with an adjustable non-elastic glasses strap to make them fit snugly)
_____ 2 lightweight hammers
_____ A regular adult hammer
_____ Hacksaw and extra blades
_____ A small crosscut saw
_____ 2 bit braces for drilling and screwing in screws and drill bits, auger bits and Phillips bits

_____ A good flat head screwdriver
_____ 2 Phillips screwdrivers
_____ A rasp and file
_____ 25″ tape measure
_____ A speed square (to make lines on wood)
_____ Assorted screws, nails, and glue
_____ Sandpaper
_____ Pencils
_____ Soft untreated wood such as pine or fir (never particle board because of hazardous chemicals)

Organization and Maintenance

_____ Tools arranged in an orderly manner (e.g., a storage rack labeled with pictures and words)*

_____ Storage boxes for wood pieces*

Library*

Location and Space

_____ Even lighting so no shadows fall on pages*

_____ Decorated with book jackets/posters and reading-related art prints

Furniture

_____ Low bookshelf that displays covers*
_____ Comfortable, clean pillows and carpets or chairs where children can sit and read*

_____ Big, comfortable chair or couch where an adult can sit with a child and read

Organization and Maintenance

_____ Books in good condition* or repaired

_____ Books uncluttered and orderly*

Books

_____ Appropriate for developmental stage*
_____ A variety of styles of illustration*
_____ Multiethnic and multiage characters in nonstereotyped roles*
_____ Females and males in various roles*
_____ Not based on commercial products
_____ Fiction: realistic and fantasy*

_____ Informational books*
_____ Mood and concept books*
_____ Poetry*
_____ New and classic books*
_____ Child-authored books
_____ Listening center with book-tape sets
_____ Big books and a big-book shelf

Writing

Location and Space

_____ Even lighting so shadows do not fall on work*

_____ Decorated with writing samples, posters, etc.

Furniture

_____ Low tables and chairs*

_____ Storage shelves close to table*

Materials and Supplies

____ Peeled crayons*

____ Non-toxic felt marking pens*

____ Hole punch

____ Rulers, protractors

____ Sharpened primary pencils*

____ Paper cut in uniform sizes*

____ Yarn

____ Recycled envelopes

Organization and Maintenance

____ Baskets, jars, or cans for pens, crayons, etc. *

____ Containers and shelves labeled

____ Materials stored in an orderly manner*

For primary children

____ Pencils and thin wax crayons

____ Dictionary or word file

____ Lined paper

____ Staplers

____ If computer is present it includes simple word processing program

Discovery Area*

Location and Space

____ Located near electric outlets*

____ Located near window*

____ Located near sink

Furniture

____ Low table or counter*

____ Tables and chairs

____ Water/sand table* (may be found outside or in messy play area—tubs/basins may be used instead)

Materials and Supplies

____ Sorting trays*

____ Plastic tubs and pitchers*

____ Measuring cups/spoons

____ Balance and scale

____ Photographs and posters to illustrate concepts

____ Trays*

____ Information books* (may be found in library)

____ Sorting collections (buttons, rocks, etc.)

____ Materials with sequence and proportion

____ Attribute beads or blocks

____ Concept games

____ Colored cubes

____ Globes and maps

____ Social studies games and puzzles

____ Magnifying glass*

____ Machinery to investigate and disassemble

____ Aquariums and animal cages

____ Airtight containers for storage

____ Probes

____ Photographs and posters that illustrate concepts

For primary children

____ Tools like knives and scissors

____ Bulletin-board displays

____ Artifact collections

Outside Zones*

General Requirements of Outside Environment

_____ Large enough space for group to run and play*
_____ Fenced for protection* with gates with child-safe locks*
_____ Located near the classroom

_____ Access to water for drinking and play
_____ Access to toilets and sinks
_____ Shelter from sun, wind, rain
_____ Shed or other secure storage for outdoor supplies*

Transition Zone

_____ Children can see what is available and make choices.
_____ Parking area for trikes, scooters and wagons; vehicles near the entrance to the riding area

_____ Storage for trikes and wagons*
_____ Space for children to wait or gather on benches, tires, steps, or the edge of a wall

Manipulative-Creative Zone

_____ Tables and chairs for outdoor table activities*
_____ Easels

_____ Woodworking table
_____ A line/rack to hang clothes and artwork

Physical Zone

_____ Large grassy areas for running
_____ Comfortable places to sit and lie
_____ Climbing or "super-structure" for climbing, sliding
_____ Play structures for climbing, sliding, swinging*
_____ Surfacing underneath and to 6' beyond structures (10" sand, woodchips, etc., or 2" rubber matting) *
_____ Swings
_____ Portable equipment for building and climbing

_____ Natural or manufactured balance beams*
_____ Materials to encourage active play: hoops, parachutes, rope
_____ Trikes and wagons sized for the children*
_____ Varied sizes of balls that bounce*
_____ Baskets and bags for ball storage
_____ Toys stored in an orderly manner

For primary children

_____ Cargo nets and ropes
_____ Bikes and scooters

_____ Equipment for organized games
_____ Hard surfaces for hopscotch, jump rope, etc.

Natural Elements Zone

_____ Plants, grass*
_____ Natural features such as logs, smooth boulders, hills, and trees
_____ A covered sandbox or appropriate alternative*
_____ Sand/water table or large tub*
_____ Clean sand in plentiful supply*
_____ Clean water in plentiful supply*
_____ Dirt for digging*
_____ Mud
_____ A place to garden
_____ A bird feeder, or house

_____ Pets—if weather permits
_____ Sand toys (cups/spoons, pots, cars, buckets, trowels, etc.)
_____ Water play toys (cups/spoons, basters, funnels, pitchers, tubing, water wheels, etc.)
_____ Mud toys (shovels, pots and pans, buckets, trowels)
_____ Water, sand, mud toys kept separate from one another
_____ Hoses and big buckets*
_____ Kits for bubble play

Social-Dramatic Zone

_____ Space for dramatic play
_____ Playhouse or alternative
_____ Dress-up clothes and props

_____ "Loose parts" (hollow blocks, sheets, small tires, planks, and other movable items)
_____ A vehicle path

Name Index

Administration for Children, Youth, and Families, 37
Ahadi, B. A., 100
Ainsworth, M., 102
Allen, K. E., 372, 375
Almy, M., 136
American Academy of Pediatrics, 191, 195, 200
American Public Health Association, 191, 200
Ames, L., 106
Armstrong, D. G., 296
Aronson, S., 193, 200, 210, 215
Association of Waldorf Schools of North America, 76
Athey, I., 170

Baker, L., 50
Barnett, W. S., 32, 33, 39
Beatty, B., 65, 67, 72
Behrman, R. E., 32
Belsky, J., 102
Bergen, D., 169
Berk, L. E., 99–100, 102, 118, 126, 339
Bettelheim, B., 414
Biber, B., 8, 334
Bierman, J. M., 103
Bloom, B. S., 346
Bodrova, E., 132, 170, 178
Bowe, F. G., 376, 384
Bowlby, J., 101, 271
Bowman, B., 318
Braun, S. J., 61
Brazelton, T. B., 289, 414
Bredekamp, S., 41, 43, 51, 318, 335, 336, 341, 377
Bronson, M., 260, 261
Bronson, M. B., 170, 178
Bruer, J. T., 104
Bruner, J., 112
Burks, J., 8–9
Burts, D. C., 37

Cadwell, L. B., 80
Campbell, D., 311
Capone, A., 369–370, 371, 372
Carlsson-Paige, N., 187
Cartwright, S., 8, 244
Center for the Early Childhood Workforce, 34
Chess, S., 99, 100
Chiesa, J. R., 32
Children's Defense Fund, 31, 34, 36, 317
Choy, S., 42
Christakis, D. A., 250
Christie, J. F., 169, 175, 176, 182, 183, 185
Clarke-Stewart, A., 101–102
Cleverley, J., 60
Clifford, R. M., 47
Cochran, M., 47
Colbert, J., 295
Colker, L. J., 155
Copple, C., 43, 318, 335, 336, 341, 377
Cox, M. J., 218
Crary, E., 414
Cryan, J. R., 159
Cryer, D., 33
Cuffaro, H. K., 72, 73, 224

Damon, W., 123
Darlington, R., 36
David, J., 73
Deasey, D., 59, 69
Dennis, W., 98
Department of Defense, 35, 40
Derman-Sparks, L., 11
Dichtelmiller, M. L., 155, 156
DiGuiseppe, D. L., 250
Dinkmeyer, D., 414
Dodge, D. T., 155
Dolezal, V., 377
Dombro, A. L., 156
Doolittle, S., 377

Dorfman, A. B., 155
Dreikurs, R., 286
Driscoll, A., 267

Early, D., 218
Edmiaston, R., 377
Edwards, C., 81, 122, 123, 224
Edwards, E. P., 61
Eisenberg, N., 123
Elkind, D., 186
Erickson, C., 377
Erikson, E., 126, 127
Evans, D. E., 100
Everingham, S. S., 32
Eyer, D. W., 103

Federal Interagency Forum on Child and Family Statistics, 31
Feeney, S., 161, 377, 421, 423
Feiler, R., 37
Flavell, J. H., 113
Forman, G., 81, 224
Forsyth, G. A., 98
Forsyth, P., 98
Forsythe, P. D., 176
Frank Porter Graham Center, 37
Freeman, N., 421, 423
French, F. E., 103
French, K., 387
Friedman, S., 101–102
Fromberg, D. P., 30
Frost, J. S., 187

Galinsky, E., 395
Gandini, L., 81, 224
Gardner, H., 119
Garelick, M., 356
Garner, A., 244
Gartrell, D., 275, 285, 287
Geis, G., 123
Genishi, C., 136
Gesell, A., 106
Gilligan, C., 123

Ginsburg, H., 113
Goffin, S. G., 71
Goldhaber, J., 369–370, 371, 372
Gomby, D. S., 32
Gonzalez-Mena, J., 103, 277
Good Beginnings Alliance, 326, 328
Gordon, T., 265–266, 270, 271
Gorrell, J., 124
Graves, D. H., 49, 159
Greenman, J., 237, 290
Greenough, W. T., 104
Greenspan, S. I., 289
Greenwood, P. W., 32
Gregory, K., 266
Gutek, G. L., 59

Haller, E., 11
Hansen, K., 98
Hawaii Audubon Society, 356
Head Start Bureau, 36, 37, 38
Healy, J. M., 117
Hendrick, J., 81
Heroman, C., 155
Hitz, R., 267, 287
Hohmann, M., 69
Honig, A. S., 259
Hoube, J., 32
Howes, C., 34, 271
Hughes, F., 170
Hull, K., 369–370, 371
Hunt, J. M., 93, 102
Hymes, J. L., 85, 420
Hyson, M., 15, 48, 260

Ilg, F., 106

Jablon, J. R., 155
Jersild, A., 13–14
Johnson, J. E., 76, 169, 175, 176, 182, 183, 185
Jones, E., 179, 182, 251–252, 428
Jones, J., 131, 132

Kagan, J., 103
Kagan, S. L., 47, 48
Kaiser, B., 288
Kamii, C., 159
Karoly, L. A., 32
Katz, L. G., 8, 23, 286, 355, 394, 426–427
Kelly, M., 414

Kidder, R., 11
Kilburn, M. R., 32
Killen, M., 123
Kipnis, K., 11, 161, 423
Kohlberg, L., 123, 124
Kohn, A., 49, 159, 267
Kontos, S., 15
Kostelnik, M., 266, 373, 378
Kounin, J., 279
Krathwohl, D., 346
Kurcinka, M. S., 414

Larner, M. B., 32
Lawrence, C. R., 49
Lawrence, F. R., 124
Lawton, J. T., 346
Lazar, I., 36
Leong, D. J., 132, 170, 178
Leshan, E., 414
Levin, D. E., 187, 414
Levy, J., 169
Lewit, E. M., 32, 50
Lickona, T., 123
Lillard, P. P., 78
Lin, H. L., 124
Lowman, L., 249

McAfee, O., 132, 149, 151
McCall, S. G., 103
McCarty, C. A., 250
McCormick, L., 88, 368, 377
McDevitt, T. M., 102
McKey, R. H., 36
McMillan, M., 66
Marsden, D. B., 155, 156
Marshall, H., 263
Maslow, A., 98
Meisels, S. J., 155
Merritt, S., 377
Mesia, B. B., 346
Michel, S., 84
Milburn, S., 37
Miller, K., 414
Miller, P. H., 113
Miller, S. A., 113
Mitchell, A., 46, 73
Monighan-Nourot, P., 170
Montessori, M., 78
Morgan, G. G., 40
Mulligan, S. A., 376
Munro, J. H., 67

Nager, N., 73
National Academy of Early Childhood Programs, 193
National Association for the Education of Young Children, 37, 40, 50–51, 132, 160, 289, 290, 431–432
National Audubon Society, 356
National Board of Professional Teaching Standards, 45
National Center for Children in Poverty, 35
National Commission on Excellence in Education, 47
National Education Goals Panel, 47–48, 49, 403
National Home Education Research Institute, 43–44
National Institute of Child Health and Human Development, 32–33
The National Research Council, 325, 414
National Resource Center for Health and Safety in Child Care, 191, 200
Nelson, J., 414
Neuman, S. B., 318
Noonan, M. J., 88
Nyberg, D., 135

Oldfield, L., 76
Onaga, E., 373, 378
Opper, S., 113
Orlick, T., 304
Ormrod, J. E., 102

Paciorek, K. M., 67
Paige, N. C., 414
Perlmutter, M., 101–102
Phillips, D., 34, 414
Phillips, D. C., 60
Piaget, J., 113, 123, 173
Planta, R. C., 218
Plemons, B., 103
Pregnancy Info, 39
Prescott, E., 251–252
Provasnik, S., 42

Ramey, S. L., 37
Rasminsky, J. S., 288

Raver, C. C., 37
Reifel, S., 187
Reynolds, G., 179, 182, 428
Ritchie, S., 271
Rogers, F., 266
Rohde, B., 373, 378
Rooney, P., 42
Ross, M., 314
Rothbart, M. K., 100
Rubenstein, M., 8–9
Ruhmann, L., 249
Ryan, R., 37
Rydell, C. P., 32

Salmon, J. M., 37
Sandall, S. R., 375, 377
Sanders, M. R., 32
Santrock, J. W., 97, 99–100
Schank, M., 377
Schickendanz, D. I., 98, 176
Schickendanz, J. A., 98, 176
Schulman, K., 34
Schwartz, I. S., 372, 375, 377
Schweinhardt, L. J., 36
Scott-Little, C., 48
Sen, A., 42
Shank, M., 38, 384
Shapiro, E., 73
Shefatya, L., 171, 174, 177, 179,
      183, 184
Shonkoff, J. P., 414
Shore, R., 102, 104
Skeels, H. M., 98
Skeen, P., 244
Smetana, J. G., 123

Smilansky, S., 171, 174, 177, 179,
      183, 184, 186
Smith, L. B., 108
Smith, R. S., 103
Smith, S. J., 38, 377, 384
Sobel, J., 304
Soderman, A., 266
Soltis, J. F., 11
Sommer, R., 250, 251
State of Children in America's
      Union, 36
Stebbins Frelow, V., 48
Stein, L., 266
Steiner, R., 76
Stevenson, C. S., 32
Stipek, D. J., 37
Strickland, J., 187
Strike, K. A., 11
Sullivan, S. A., 414
Sulzby, E., 317

Taylor, L., 218
Teale, W., 317
Thelen, E., 108
Thomas, A., 99, 100
Tobin, R., 42
Trawick-Smith, J., 175
Trostli, R., 76
Turiel, E., 123
Turnbull, A., 38, 377, 384
Turnbull, R., 38, 377, 384

U.S. Consumer Products Safety
      Commission, 193
U.S. Department of Education, 31, 46

U.S. Department of Education,
      National Center for Education
      Statistics, 35

Vance, E., 275
Van Horn, M. L., 37
Vygotsky, L., 118

Walker, L. J., 123
Weaver, P. J., 275
Weber, E., 65
Weber, L., 60
Weikart, D. P., 36, 69
Wells, G., 112
Werner, E. E., 103
Whiren, A., 266, 373, 378
Whitebook, M., 34
Wilbers, J. S., 377
Wilcox-Herzog, A., 15
Willer, B., 41
Williams, C. L., 76
Williams, L. R., 30, 65, 66, 69, 118
Wilson, C., 71
Winsler, A., 339
Wirt, J. S., 42
Wolery, M., 377
Wortham, S. C., 132, 159, 187

Yawkey, T. D., 169, 175, 176, 182,
      183, 185

Zigler, E. F., 37
Zimmerman, F. J., 250

Subject Index

Abductions, 196

Abecedarian Study, 36–37

Abstract concepts, 111

Abstract thinking, 120

Abuse

child. *See* Child abuse

substance, 30, 396

Academic achievement, play and, 177

Accidents

prevention of. *See* Safety

toileting, 214

Accommodation, development and, 114

Accountability, educational, 131, 133, 159, 296

Accreditation, 16, 40–41, 252

Accreditation Criteria and Procedures of the National Association for the Education of Young Children (National Academy of Early Childhood Programs), 193

ACEI (Association for Childhood Education International), 65

Achievement tests, 156, 158–159

Active listening, 265–266, 272

Active play zones, 248

Activities

about, 208

by age group

infants, 249, 282

kindergarteners, 64, 209, 243, 340, 341

preschoolers, 209, 243, 283, 340, 341

school-age children, 209, 243, 283, 340, 341

toddlers, 209, 243, 282, 340

art, 243

cleanup, 215

closure of, 347

group, 275, 282, 283, 340–341, 376

guided, 339–340

introducing, 347

mobility, 251

outdoor, 186–187, 193–194, 235, 249

planning. *See* Activity plans

quiet, 227

selecting, 341

special needs, for children with, 376

teacher-child, 339–340

transitioning between, 208, 215–216

Activity plans

about, 341, 343, 344

assessment of learning, 347–348

benefits, 344, 345

documenting results, 349

evaluating, 350

example, 342, 348–349

frequency of use, 350

implementing, 349

objectives, 345–346

preparation, 344, 347

teaching procedures, 347

ADA (Americans with Disabilities Act), 38, 369

Adaptation, development and, 114

Adaptive devices, 376

ADHD (attention deficit/hyperactivity disorder), 288, 382–383

Adjustment to school, play and, 177

Adler, Alfred, 286

Administration for Children, Youth, and Families, 86

Adults

infants, play with, 178, 234

influences on children, 259

learning environment needs, 234, 250

working with, 4–6, 16, 20, 23, 393–394. *See also* Families

Advice, offering, 401

Advocacy, 5, 134, 429–431

Aesthetics

in curriculum, 314, 315

in learning environments, 235–236

Affordability, child care, 34

Age-appropriate teaching techniques, 338–341

Agility, physical, 302–303

AIDS, 200

Alcohol

abuse, 30, 396

child development and, 30, 104

Alexander the Great, 57

Allergies, 204, 386–387

Alone time, 228, 229, 251–252

Alphabetic knowledge, 318

Alternative assessment, 132, 150. *See also* Observation

American Fröebel Union, 65

American Montessori Society (AMS), 78

Americans with Disabilities Act (ADA), 38, 369

AMI (Association Montessori Internationale), 78

Anecdotal records, 141–143, 144, 148, 149, 150, 409

Anger, 272

Animals, safety and, 459

Annotated photographs, 149

Anthropology, study of, 91

Anthroposophy, 75, 76

Appropriate education, 369

Areas, classroom. *See* Environments, learning

Aristotle, 57, 63

Arrival, daily program, 212

Art curriculum, 242–243, 308–311, 315, 467–468, 473

The Art of Block Building (Johnson), 72

Artistic development, culture and, 310

Assertive discipline, 287
Assessment
about, 131, 132
achievement tests, 156, 158–159
activity plans, 347–348
conferences and, 409
confidentiality, 161–162
core items, 152
criterion-referenced, 159
culture and, 157, 160, 161
developmental, 157–158
diagnostic tests, 158
documentation, 149
focus on, 296
formal, 132, 156–160
goals of, 160–161
high-stakes, 49–50
language, 161
norm-referenced, 159
observation. *See* Observation
performance-based, 132, 150
personality, 10
portfolios, children's, 151–154
principles of, 161
purposes of, 132–133
readiness tests, 49–51, 108,
116–117, 158–159, 260
special needs, identifying
children with, 156–158,
369–371, 378
standardized, 159–160
standards, 16
summary reports, 155
summary statements, 153
validity, 159
work samples, 150, 153, 409
Assimilation, development and, 114
Assistant caregivers, 18. *See also*
Teachers
Assistant teachers, 18. *See also*
Teachers
Assisted discovery, 118
Association for Childhood
Education International
(ACEI), 65
Association for Children and
Adults with Learning
Disabilities, 371
Association Montessori
Internationale (AMI), 78
Associative play (Parten), 172
Asthma, 386–387

At-risk children, 35–38
Atalier, 79
Atelierista, 79–80
Attachment, 102, 271
Attention deficit/hyperactivity
disorder (ADHD), 288,
382–383
Audio/video recording, 149–150
Auditory processing
problems, 380
Australian Early Childhood
Association, 26
Authentic assessment, 132, 150.
See also Observation
Authority, teacher, 275, 276–277
Autism, children with, 384–385
Autonomy stage (Piaget), 123
Autonomy stage, shame and doubt
vs. (Erikson), 127, 172

Background information, getting
children's, 405–406
Backmapping, 48
Bank Street Children's School and
College, 71
Bathing, attitudes toward, 399
Bayley Scales of Infant
Development, 157
Beginnings, easing, 205–208
Behavior problems
about, 284
assertive discipline, 287
"button pushers," 284
calming approach, 287
challenging behaviors,
288–289
conferences and, 409–410
consequences, logical, 286
corporal punishment. *See*
Corporal punishment
differentiating child from
behavior, 284
"mistaken behavior"
approach, 285
preventing, 277–280, 281–282
reinforcement techniques, 287
time-out approach, 286
Behavioral disorders, children with,
383–384
Behavioral objectives, 346
Behaviorism, 287
Beliefs, influences of, 334–335

Bias
modeling lack of, 327
standardized testing and, 160
teacher, 11–12, 269
Biber, Barbara, 71
Big ideas, 356–357
Biology, study of, 91
Blindness, 156–157, 379
Blocks, 72, 227, 237–239, 467,
470–471
Bodily kinesthetic intelligence,
10, 119
Body awareness, 199
Body language, 263, 265, 316
Boehm Test of Basic
Concepts, 159
Book knowledge, 318
Books in the classroom, 244,
319–320
Boston Infant School, 84
Brain development, 103–105
British infant schools, 71
Brown v. Board of Education,
87–88
*Building Blocks for Teaching
Preschoolers with Special
Needs* (Sandall & Schwartz),
375–376
Building toys, 240
Burn hazards, 194, 197
"Button pushers," 284

California Children's Centers, 85
Calling, early childhood education
as, 419
Calming, areas for, 287
Canadian Child Care Federation, 26
Caregivers, 18. *See also* Teachers
Caring for Our Children
(American Academy of
Pediatrics et al.), 191, 200
Casa dei Bambini, 76
Catholic church, 58, 59. *See also*
Religion
Cause and effect, understanding,
120
CDAs (Child Development
Associates), 17, 18, 41. *See
also* Teachers
CDF (Children's Defense Fund),
51–52
Celebrations, 398

Centers, classroom. *See* Environments, learning
Cephalocaudal pattern, 95
Certification, educator, 15, 41, 44-45
Challenges, providing, 228-229
Challenging behaviors, 288-289. *See also* Behavior problems
Change, helping children with, 205-208, 215-218, 281-282
Checklists
  diapering/toileting practices, 463
  health, 459-460
  learning environments, 461-466, 467-468, 469-476
  observation, 147-148, 150
  safety, 456-458
  sociodramatic play, 184
Chess, Stella, 8-9
Child abuse
  defined, 385-386
  development and, 104
  families and, 396
  identifying, 386, 395
  preventing, 30, 45, 86, 198, 199
  reporting, 16-17, 386, 402-403
  sexual, 22
  special needs, children with, 385-386
Child care. *See* Programs, early childhood
Child-centered art, 309
Child development
  about, 91-95
  assimilation, 114
  biological basis, 97-101
  child care and, 101-102
  cognitive development. *See* Cognitive development
  domains of, 105-106
  emotional. *See* Emotional development
  expectations based on, 96
  experiences and, 102-103, 104
  individuality of, 105
  influences on, 30, 95, 98, 101-104, 106
  inheritance, 97-98, 100, 106
  integrating, 179-180
  learning and, 104
  norms, 108

patterns of, 93
physical. *See* Physical development
physiological needs, 98, 104
play and, 170
psychological needs, 98-99
race and, 99-100
rates of, 93-94, 106
sensitive periods, 102-103
social development. *See* Social development
socioemotional, 105
temperament, 100-101
theories of
  about, 91-92
  Comenius, John Amos, 59
  Erikson, Erik, 172
  Locke, John, 60
  Parten, M. B., 171, 172
  Pestalozzi, Johann, 61
  Piaget, Jean, 114, 116, 172
  psychosocial, 105, 126-128
  Rousseau, Jean Jacques, 60-61
Child Development Associates (CDAs), 17, 18, 41. *See also* Teachers
Child development centers, 31-32, 46, 66-69, 85. *See also* Programs, early childhood
Child Health Alert, 195
Child Observation Record (COR), High/Scope, 155
Child psychology, study of, 91
Child rearing, 256-258. *See also* Parents
Child-sense, 135
Childfind programs, 157
Childhood and Society (Erikson), 126, 127
Children
  historical views on, 56
  learning about, 420-421
  understanding, 134
Children with Special Needs: Lessons for Early Childhood Professionals (Kostelnik), 373
Children's Bureau, 86
Children's Defense Fund (CDF), 51-52
Children's House (*Casa dei Bambini*), 76

Childwatching, 135-136
Choices, providing, 401
Choking, 192, 194
Chronic health conditions, 386-387
Circle times, 376
City and Country School, 67
Class, education and social, 56, 58-59, 61, 62, 65
Class meetings, 275
Classifying process, 322
Classroom assessment, 132, 150. *See also* Observation
Classroom block sets, 238
Classroom management
  authority, 275, 276-277
  expectations, setting, 277-278
  groups, 280, 282-283
  preventing problems, 277-280, 281-282
Classroom visits, 206
Classrooms. *See* Environments, learning
Clay, play with, 242
Cleaning classroom environment, 201
Cleanup activities, 215
Closed environments, 251
Closed questions, 322
Closure of activities, 347
Clothing, attitudes toward, 399
Clutter, avoiding, 234
Co-ops, parent, 31-32
Code of Ethical Conduct and Statement of Commitment (NAEYC), 19, 20, 23-24, 402, 421-422, 451-455
Cognitive complexity, 120
Cognitive delays, children with, 381-382
Cognitive development
  about, 92-93, 109
  concept development, 109, 110-112
  foundation for, 260
  language development, 112-113
  physical development and, 106
  play and, 179, 180
  theories of
    constructivist, 113-117
    limitations, 113
    multiple intelligences, 9-10, 118-120, 338

Cognitive development, *(continued)*
    Piaget, Jean, 115, 116
    sociocultural, 117–118
Cognitive Skills Assessment
    Battery, 159
Colds, 199
Collaboration, 377
Collage and construction, 309
Colleagues, working with, 424
Collections of materials, 240–241
Colors in learning
    environments, 235
Comenius, John Amos, 59, 63,
    223, 297
Comfort objects, 215
Commercial curriculum, 295–296
Communicable illnesses, 199–200
Communication
    attitude, 263–264
    barriers, 269–271
    cultural differences, 269
    disorders, 380–381
    importance, 263
    with infants/toddlers, 269
    listening, 264–266, 272, 340
    reflective/responsive statements,
        266–267, 272
    strategies, 263–264
    teaching. *See* Communication
        curriculum
Communication curriculum
    goals of, 314–315
    language, 314, 316–317, 321
    literacy, 314–315, 317–319, 321
    literature, 315, 319–320, 321
    resources, 321
Communication logs, 406
Community, education and, 16, 336
Comparing/contrasting
    process, 322
Compensation, child care, 14,
    32–34
Competition, influence on
    children, 261
Complex materials, 251
Composing music, 312
Comprehensive programs, 36
Computer areas, 245–246
Concept books, 319–320
Concept development, 109,
    110–112
Concept games, 241

Concrete concepts, 111
Concrete operations stage (Piaget),
    115, 116, 172
Concrete thinking, 120
Conferences, 409–410
Confidentiality, 23, 161–162,
    388–389, 400–402
Conflict, 196, 272–274, 275
Consequences, 146, 286
Conservation, 114, 116
Consolidation stage of career, 426
Constructive play (Smilansky), 172,
    173, 179
Constructivist theory, 113–117,
    122–124
Content standards, 48, 298,
    325–326, 328, 337
Contrasting/comparing
    process, 322
Control, building inner, 268
Conventional morality, 123, 124
Conversations, language and, 316
Cooking, 204. *See also* Food
Cooperative games, 303, 304
Cooperative learning, 118
Cooperative play (Parten), 171, 172
Cooperatives, parent, 31–32
Coordination, physical, 177–178,
    302–303
COR (High/Scope Child
    Observation Record), 155
Core items, assessment based
    on, 152
Corporal punishment
    family attitudes, 257
    historical views, 57, 58, 60
    results, 255, 259–260, 287
Corridors, 228
Cortisol, child development
    and, 102
Council for Professional
    Recognition, 41
Counter-Reformation, 59
CPR training, 192, 196
Creative arts curriculum
    aesthetics, 314, 315
    art, 242–243, 308–311, 315,
        467–468, 473
    creative movement, 312–314, 315
    goals of, 306
    music, 311–312, 315
    resources, 315, 321

Creative Curriculum
    Developmental Continuum,
    155–156
The Creative Curriculum (Dodge,
    et al.), 155–156, 295
Creative movement curriculum,
    312–314, 315
Criterion-referenced tests, 159
Critical periods, child development
    and, 102–103
Cultural development
    (Vygotsky), 118
Culture
    assessment and, 157, 160, 161
    communication and, 269
    family diversity, 397, 399–400
    feelings and, 273
    food issues, 214
    influence on child development,
        95, 113, 127–128, 310
    influence on curriculum,
        335, 336
    multiple intelligences and, 119
    play and, 175
    progressive education and, 70
    segregation and, 368
Curriculum
    about, 295–296
    by age group, 43, 336, 337, 338
    assessing learning, 334. *See also*
        Assessment
    commercial, 295–296
    delivering, 334, 338–341
    developmentally appropriate,
        59–60, 92, 296
    emergent, 337
    goals, 333–334
    historical, 296
    influences on, 296, 334–337, 355
    integrated. *See* Integrated
        curriculum
    learner-centered, 337
    organizing, 337–338
    packaged, 295
    planned, 296
    play and, 180
    resources, 300
    Second Step, 295
    sensory development, 301–302
    sources of, 296–297
    special needs, for children with,
        375–376

standards for, 298
subject areas
  communication. *See*
    Communication curriculum
  creative arts. *See* Creative arts
    curriculum
  generally, 299, 338
  inquiry. *See* Inquiry curriculum
  language, 314, 316–317, 321
  literacy, 314–315, 317–319, 321
  literature, 315, 319–320, 321
  math, 323–324, 329
  music, 311–312, 315
  science, 325–327, 328, 329
  social studies, 327–329
  umbrella, 295
Curriculum maps, 357–358
Custody conflicts, 401–402
Cuteness in learning
  environments, 237

"Dame schools," 83
DAP (developmentally appropriate
  practice), 5, 37, 43, 335, 377
Day care, 31. *See also* Programs,
  early childhood
Day nurseries, focus of, 85–86
DBAE (discipline-based art
  education), 309
Deafness, 156–157, 379–380
Decision-making skills,
  learning, 340
Decoration in learning
  environments, 236
Democratic approach to
  guidance, 286
Dental care, 201, 202
Department of Defense, 32
Department of Health and Human
  Services, 86
Department of Health, Education
  and Welfare (HEW), 86
Deprivation and childhood
  development, 98, 103
Development. *See* Child
  development
Developmental assessments,
  157–158
Developmental descriptions, 153
Developmental Indicators for
  Assessment of Learning
  (DIAL), 157

Developmental Interaction
  Approach (DIA), 62, 71,
  72–73
Developmental norms, 108
Developmentally appropriate
  education, 59–60, 92, 296
Developmentally appropriate
  practice (DAP), 5, 37, 43,
  335, 377
*Developmentally Appropriate
  Practice in Early Childhood
  Programs* (Bredekamp &
  Copple), 43, 335
Dewey, John, 57, 62, 69–70,
  73–74, 308
Dexedrine, 383
DIA (Developmental Interaction
  Approach), 62, 71, 72–73
Diagnostic tests, 158
DIAL (Developmental Indicators
  for Assessment of
  Learning), 157
Diapering practices
  checklist, 463
  environmental
    considerations, 226
  guidelines, 212–213, 269
  health concerns, 199–200, 201
Digestion, problems with, 204
Dilemmas, ethical, 421–423
*Dimensions of Teaching-Learning
  Environments* (Jones &
  Prescott), 251
Directors, 18. *See also* Teachers
Dirtiness, concerns about, 408
Disabilities, children with. *See*
  Special needs, children with
Disasters, preparing for, 192, 195,
  196, 197, 457
Discipline. *See* Behavior problems
Discipline-based art education
  (DBAE), 309
Discovery centers, 246–247, 475
Disease. *See* Illness
Distraction, 279
Diversity
  educator attitudes toward, 11–12
  family, 84, 174–176, 397, 399–400
  in learning environments,
    236–237
Divorce, families and, 396, 401–402
Documentation, 149

Domestic violence, 30
Dramatic play
  areas, 227, 239–240, 248, 468, 471
  benefits, 178, 179
  materials, 241
  socioeconomic level and, 186
  storage, 239
Dramatic play stage (Smilansky),
  172, 173, 174
Dreikurs, Rudolf, 286
Dress-Up Corner. *See* Dramatic play
Drugs
  abuse of, 30, 396
  ADHD and, 383
  child development and, 104
Dynamic systems theory, 108–109

Early childhood, defined, 4
*Early Childhood Education and
  Care in the United States*
  (Clifford, et al.), 46
Early childhood educators. *See*
  Teachers
Early childhood programs. *See*
  Programs, early childhood
Early Head Start, 36
Early Learning Accomplishment
  Profile, 157
Early Screening Inventory, 157
Eating. *See* Food
Edelman, Marian Wright, 51–52
Education for All Handicapped
  Children Act, 38, 88, 368
Education level, family, 38
Education philosophy, shifts in, 296
Education, responsibility for, 45–46
Educational accountability, 131,
  133, 159, 296
Educational assistants, 19. *See also*
  Teachers
Educators. *See* Teachers
Egocentrism in children, 114, 120
Electrical hazards, 192, 194
Electronic observation techniques,
  137, 148–150
Electronic portfolios,
  children's, 151
Elementary schools, 30
Eliot, Abigail, 67
Emergencies, preparing for, 192,
  195, 196, 197, 457
Emergency Nursery Schools, 84–85

Emergent curriculum, 337
Emergent literacy, 317
Emile (Rousseau), 60
Emotional development
    defined, 93
    milestones, 125
    physiology and, 104–105
    play and, 178–179, 180
    relationships and, 101
    theories of, 126–128
Emotional disorders, children with, 383–384
Empathy, gaining, 134
Employer-sponsored child care, 84–85
Encouragement, 267–269
Ending classes, 216–217
Enlightenment, early childhood education in, 60–61, 63
Environment, natural
    access to, 229
    child development and, 101–102, 106
    influence on program, 236
    learning about, 187
    safety, 193–194
Environments, learning
    adult needs, 250
    aesthetics, 235–236
    cuteness, 237
    designing, 250–252
    diversity, 236–237
    floor plans, example, 230–232
    goals for, 223–224
    indoor, 194, 227–228
    interest areas
        age groups and, 237
        arts, 242–243
        computers, 245–246
        discovery centers, 246–247, 475
        dramatic play, 227, 239–240, 248, 468, 471
        library, 244–245, 474
        sensory play, 241–242, 472
        woodworking, 243–244, 473–474
        writing, 245, 474–475
    limitations, 225
    open-design, 225–226
    organization, 227
    outdoor. *See* Outdoor learning environments

safety. *See* Safety
    schedules and, 209–210
    self-contained, 225–226
    special needs, for children with, 225, 249, 376
    storage. *See* Storage
    television/video, 250
    use of, 134
    weather conditions and, 227
Equipment, defined, 233
Erasmus, Desiderius, 58
Erikson, Erik, 71, 126, 127, 170, 172
Ethical dilemmas, 421–423
Ethical finesse, 423
Ethics
    assessment, 161
    confidentiality, 23, 161–162, 388–389, 400–402
    educator, 10–11, 19–24, 402–403, 421–423, 432. *See also Code of Ethical Conduct and Statement of Commitment* (NAEYC)
Ethics and the Early Childhood Educator: Using the NAEYC Code (Feeney & Freeman), 421, 423
Ethnicity, 84, 397, 399–400
European educational methods
    influence on early childhood education, 55, 74–75
    Montessori method, 76–78, 81, 82
    Reggio Emilia approach, 78–81, 83, 224, 242, 310
    Waldorf education, 75, 76, 81, 82
Even Start Family Literacy Program, 39
Event samples, 146–147, 150
Evidence-based programs, 49–50
Exceptional children. *See* Special needs, children with
Exceptionality, 378
Exercise, physical, 202–203, 204, 302–303
Expectations
    of children, 49–50
    development-based, 96
    setting, 277–278
Experience, defined, 94
Experiences, child development and, 104
Exploration, 169, 322

Expressive language problems, 380
External speech (Vygotsky), 118

FACES (Family and Child Experiences Survey), 37
Facilities, safety of, 192
Fairness, teaching, 274–275
Falls, injuries from, 193
Families
    about, 393–394, 395, 396
    addressing concerns, 407–409
    advising, 401
    communicating with, 216, 400–401, 404–410
    diversity in, 38, 84, 174–176, 397, 399–400
    educating, 413–415
    ethics, 401
    influence of, 261–262, 336
    involving in program, 105, 403, 410–413
    orientations for, 206, 412, 412–413
    pressures on, 396
    relationships with, 393–394, 400, 403–404
    resources for, 401, 414
    separation from, 5
    special needs, and children with, 388–389, 415–416
    stress and, 401–402
    supporting, 396, 400, 401–403
    values/attitudes of, 212–214, 257–258, 395
    welcoming, 403–404
    working with, 4–6, 16, 20, 23, 393–394
Family and Child Experiences Survey (FACES), 37
Family child care providers, 17. *See also* Teachers
Family corner, 406
Family Education Rights and Privacy Act (FERPA), 402
Feelings, 199, 273, 273
Fiction, 319
Figure-ground relationships, 182
Financial pressures, families and, 396
Finesse, ethical, 423
Fire safety, 194, 196, 197
First aid training, 192, 196

Fit-together toys, 240
Flooring, classroom, 194, 227, 238, 249, 251
Flow, 279
Flu, 199
"Flubber," 241
Follow Through study, 68
Food
  attitudes toward, 399
  cooking, 204
  culture and, 214
  guidelines, 214
  health practices, 459
  preparation/storage, 201–202
  resistance to, 214
  scheduling, 210, 214
  as sensory exploration material, 301–302
  teaching children about, 203–204
Force, appropriate use of physical, 198
Formal assessment, 132, 156–160
Formal operations period (Piaget), 116
Frank Porter Graham Child Development Center, 36
Freud, Anna, 71, 170
Freud, Sigmund, 67, 170, 178
Fröebel, Friedrich Wilhelm, 57, 62–63, 73, 223, 297
Full-day programs, 31, 210–211
Full inclusion, 43. *See also* Inclusion
Functional play (Smilansky), 172, 173, 179
Funding of early childhood programs, 30, 32, 84–85
Furniture
  adults, 234
  dramatic play, 239, 240
  infants, 233–234, 248–249
  library area, 244
  safety, 234, 456, 457, 458
  selecting, 233–234, 235–236
  toddlers, 234, 249
  woodworking, 243
  writing area, 245

Games, 241, 303, 304, 471–472. *See also* Toys
Games with rules (Piaget), 172, 173
Gardner, Howard, 9, 119

Gender differences
  historical views on, 56, 57, 58
  moral development, 123
  play and, 175, 176, 188
  social development and, 121, 122
  stereotypes, 188, 399
Generalizing process, 322
Genetic inheritance, 97–98, 100, 106
Gesell Developmental Assessment, 159
Gifted children, 387
Gifts (Fröebel), 64
Goodness of fit, 100
Government involvement in child care, 84–88
Grade school students. *See* School-age children
Grandin, Temple, 384
Greece, early childhood education in, 56–57, 63
Grooming, attitudes toward personal, 399
Groos, Karl, 169
Group activities, 275, 282, 283, 340–341, 376
Group focus, 279
Group management. *See* Classroom management
Group size, 211, 212
Guidance
  about, 259
  goals for, 256, 259–260
  strategies for, 256–258, 271–272, 275, 286
Guided activities, 339–340
Guidelines
  accreditation, 16, 40–41, 252
  classroom, 277–278
  diapering practices, 212–213, 269
  nutrition, 214
  training, 15
Guilt stage, initiative vs. (Erikson), 127, 172

Hall, G. S., 169
Hand washing, 200, 202
Handbook for Public Playground Safety (U.S. Consumer Products Safety Commission), 193
Handicapped Children's Early Education Assistance Act, 88

Handicaps, children with. *See* Special needs, children with
Harlow, Harry, 98
Harlow, Margaret, 98
Harms-Clifford Early Childhood Environmental Rating Scale, 252
Hawaii State Preschool Content Standards, 326, 328
Head Start
  federal support of, 86
  history, 36, 37–38
  legislation, 37
  salaries, educator, 14
  special needs, children with, 38, 88, 372
  teacher requirements, 15, 40
Head Start Act, 37
Head teachers, 18. *See also* Teachers
Headmasters, 19. *See also* Teachers
Health
  attitudes toward, 399
  checklists, 459–460
  chronic conditions, 386–387
  educator training, 202
  environmental considerations, 200–202, 209–210, 226
  information on children, gathering, 405–406
  NAEYC standard, 191
  promoting, 86, 198–200, 302
  providers, 202
  psychological
    developmental stage and, 208–209
    importance, 204–205
    promoting, 205–208, 210–216. *See also* Transitions
  teaching, 202–204
Healthy Young Children (Aronson), 191
Hearing impairments, children with, 156–157, 379–380
Hearing, supporting development of, 301
Hepatitis, 200
Heteronomy, 123
HEW (Department of Health, Education and Welfare), 86
Hiding places, creating, 228
High mobility activities, 251

High/Scope Child Observation Record (COR), 155
High/Scope model, 62, 68–69
High-stakes accountability, 133. *See also* Educational accountability
High-stakes testing, 49–50
Hill, Patty Smith, 67, 68
History, getting child's, 405–406
History of early childhood education
about, 55
curriculum, influences on, 296
Enlightenment, 60–61, 63
European influences, 55
Greece, 56–57, 63
humanistic traditions, 56
medieval, 57–58
19th century, 61–62, 63
nursery schools, 31–32, 46, 66–69, 85
Reformation, 58–59, 63
Renaissance, 58–59
Rome, 57, 63
special needs education, 368
United States, 81, 83–86
HIV/AIDS, 200
Holidays
celebrations of, 398
as topics for study, 355
Hollow blocks, 237, 238–239
Home Centers. *See* Dramatic play
Home visitors, 17. *See also* Teachers
Home visits, 205–206
Homelessness, 30, 396
Homeschooling, 41, 42, 43
Ho'oponopono, 275
Housekeeping areas. *See* Dramatic play
Humanistic approach to education, 56
Humiliation, results of, 255
"The Hundred Languages of Children," 79
Hunt, J. McVicker, 86
Hymes, James L., Jr., 85, 297
Hyperactivity disorder, children with, 288, 382–383
Hypothesizing process, 322

I-messages, 271–272
IDEA (Individuals with Disabilities Education Act), 38, 368–369, 372, 378

Identifying process, 322
IEPs (individualized education plans), 38, 369, 377
IFSPs (individualized family services plans), 38, 369
IHCPs (individualized health care plans), 386
IKU (International Kindergarten Union), 65
Illness. *See also* Health
child development and, 103, 106
childhood education and, 31, 199–200
communicable, 199–200
programs for children with, 31
Immunization, 200
Impact materials, 193
Improvising music, 312
Inclusion, 43, 369, 371–375, 389
Inclusion principle, 369
Indentured servitude, 83
Indigenous language revitalization, 30
Individual profiles, 153
Individualized education plans (IEPs), 38, 369, 377
Individualized family services plans (IFSPs), 38, 369
Individualized health care plans (IHCPs), 386
Individuals with Disabilities Education Act (IDEA), 38, 368–369, 372, 378
Indoor environments, safety of, 194
Industry-sponsored child care, 84–85
Industry vs. inferiority stage (Erikson), 127, 172
Infant School Society (ISS), 62, 84
Infant schools, 62, 84
Infants
active listening with, 266
activities, 249, 282
age of, 105
art supplies, 243
books and, 244
child care, 31
cognitive development, 110, 114
communication about, 216
communication with, 269
curriculum for, 336, 337

diapering practices. *See* Diapering practices
emotional development, 101, 125, 127
environmental considerations, 226, 248, 249, 461–466
equipment, 248–249
furniture, 233–234, 248–249
health and, 199, 202, 460. *See also* Health
learning techniques, 338
physical development, 107
play and, 172, 178, 181, 234
program floor plans, example, 230
rest time, 215
safety, 192, 240, 249, 458. *See also* Safety
schedules, 209
self-concept, 262
self-control, 261
social development, 101, 114, 121
starting school, 206
stopping actions, 272
teaching techniques, 341
television use, 250
Infectious diseases, 199–200
Inference from observations, 137
Inferiority stage, industry vs. (Erikson), 127, 172
Informational books, 319
Inherited characteristics, 97–98, 100, 106
Initiative vs. guilt stage (Erikson), 127, 172
Inner control, building, 268
Inquiry curriculum
goals of, 321–322
math, 323–324, 329
resources, 329
science, 325–327, 328, 329
social studies, 327–329
Inquiry processes, 322
Instinct theory of play, 169
Instruments, musical, 311
Integrated curriculum
about, 338
ending, 361, 363
evaluating, 363
example, 352
goals of, 355
implementing, 359–360
materials for, 358

planning, 343, 350-351, 353, 356-359, 362
selecting, 353-355
Integration, 372
Intelligence and Experience (Hunt), 102
Intelligence tests, 156, 158
Intelligence, types of, 9-10, 118-120, 338
Intensive waiting, 135
International Kindergarten Union (IKU), 65
Internet resources
development interaction approach, 73
disaster planning, 196
High/Scope model, 69
international associations, 26
Montessori method, 78
personality assessment, 10
Reggio Emilia approach, 80-81
safety, 191
Waldorf education, 76
Interpersonal intelligence, 10, 119
Interpretation, subjective, 138-140
Interpreting behavior, 137-140, 143-144
Interviews, 148, 150
Intrapersonal intelligence, 10, 119
Introducing activities, 347
Intrusion, 251-252
Invisible support, 376
ISS (Infant School Society), 62, 84
Itard (French physician), 76-77

Johnson, Harriet, 67, 72, 73-74
Johnson, Lyndon, 87
Jottings, 143
Journal of Pediatrics, 250

Kaiser centers, 85
Kaufman Assessment Battery for Children (KABC-II), 158
Kid watching, 135-136
Kidnappings, 196
Kindergarten
assessment, 49-50
availability, 30
history, 62, 64-66, 73, 86
primary schools vs., 66
progressive approach, 65-66
purpose, 41-43

Kindergarteners
activities, 64, 209, 243, 340, 341
curriculum for, 337, 338
development, 105, 107, 110-111, 121-122, 125
environmental considerations, 226
interest areas, 237, 245
play and, 172
program floor plan, example, 231
rest time, 215
safety, 192-193
schedules, 209
starting school, 206
television use, 250
toys for, 237, 238
transitions, 218
Kinesthetic intelligence, 10, 119
Kinesthetic sense, supporting development of, 301
"Kith and kin" care, 30, 34-35
Knives, 192, 197

LADs (language acquisition devices), 112
Language
assessment, 161
conversations and, 316
curriculum, 314, 316-317, 321
development of, 93, 112-113, 118, 316, 380-381
historical, 58
impairments, 380
influence on thinking, 115-116
non-English speakers, 43
revitalization of indigenous, 30
scaffolds, 112, 118
Language acquisition devices (LADs), 112
Lanham Act, 85
LAP (Learning Accomplishment Profile), 158
Lead poisoning, 194
Lead teachers, 18. *See also* Teachers
Leadership skills, learning, 340
Learner-centered curriculum, 337
Learning
child development and, 104
cooperative, 118
windows of opportunity for, 103, 104
Learning Accomplishment Profile (LAP), 158
Learning disabilities, 157, 382

Learning environments. *See* Environments, learning
Least restrictive environment principle, 369
"Leave No Child Behind," 51-52
Legal issues, 16-17, 23, 42, 195, 368-369, 402-403
Lesson plans. *See* Activity plans
Liability, legal, 195
Library areas, 244-245, 474
Licensure
educator, 44-45
program, 40
Lifestyle, family diversity, 397, 399-400
Light tables, 242
Limits, setting, 277-278
Linguistic intelligence, 10, 119
Listening, 264-266, 272, 340
Literacy centers, 244-245
Literacy curriculum, 314-315, 317-319, 321
Literature curriculum, 315, 319-320, 321
Locke, John, 60, 63
Logical consequences, 286
Logical-mathematical intelligence, 10, 119
Logico-mathematical knowledge (constructivist theory), 114
Logs, communication, 406
Long-term planning, 343
Low-income children. *See* Poverty
Low mobility activities, 251
Luther, Martin, 58-59, 63

Mainstreaming, 369, 372
Major understandings, 356-357
Make believe, 173-175, 177-179, 184, 186
Malaguzzi, Loris, 79, 83
Mandatory schooling, 42
Manipulative-creative zones, 248
Manipulative toys, 241
Maps, curriculum, 357-358
Maslow, Abraham, 98
Master teachers, 18. *See also* Teachers
Materials
about, 233
attitudes toward, 234-235
cleaning, 201
collections of, 240-241

Materials, *(continued)*
  physical development, 302, 305
  safety, 192, 196, 233, 242
  selecting, 234
  special needs, children with, 376–377
  storage, 242
  types, 251
Maternal depression, 104
Maternal deprivation, 98
Maternal schools, 59
Math areas, 247
Math curriculum, 323–324, 329
Mathematical intelligence, 10, 119
Maturation, defined, 94
Maturational theory, 106, 108
Maturity stage of career, 427
MBTI (Myers-Briggs Type Indicators), 10
McMillan, Margaret, 62, 66, 74, 224
McMillan, Rachel, 62, 66, 74, 224
Mealtimes. *See* Food
Media
  child development and, 105
  violence in, 187, 188, 261, 288, 289
Mediator role, 184–185
Medical problems, identifying children with, 156–157
Medieval era, early childhood education in, 57–58
Meetings, class, 275
Men in child care, 34
Mental retardation, 381–382
Merrill-Palmer Institute, 67
Messiness, concerns about, 408
Military children, 35, 40
Mind-mapping, 357–358
Mistaken behavior, 285
Mister Rogers, 419, 432
Mistrust stage, trust vs. (Erikson), 127, 172
Mitchell, Lucy Sprague, 72, 73–74
Model Child Care Health Policies (Aronson), 200
Modeling, 309
Modesty, attitudes toward, 399
Momentum, 279
Montessori, Dr. Maria, 76–77, 78, 82, 223
Montessori method, 76–78, 81, 82
Mood books, 319–320

The Moral Judgment of the Child (Piaget), 123
Morality
  development of, 123, 124
  educator, 10–11
  gender differences, 123
  learning, 120
  Piaget on, 123
  types of, 123, 124
More, Sir Thomas, 58
"Mothering and Teaching—Some Significant Distinctions" (Katz), 394
Mothers, 83, 98, 104. *See also* Parents
Motor skills development, 95, 108
Moving groups of children, 216
Mud, play with, 242
Multidomain developmental screening tests, 157
Multiple intelligences, 9–10, 118–120, 338
Muscle control, 95, 108
Muscle development, 302–303, 305
Music curriculum, 311–312, 315
Musical intelligence, 10, 119
Myers-Briggs Type Indicators (MBTI), 10

NACW (National Association of Colored Women), 84
NAEYC. *See* National Association for the Education of Young Children
NANE (National Association for Nursery Education), 68
Nannies, 17, 35. *See also* Teachers
Naps, 209, 215, 399
Narcissism, 262
Narrative observation, 137, 138–140. *See also* Observation
Narrative summaries, 162
Nation at Risk (National Commission on Excellence in Education), 47
National Academy of Early Childhood Programs, 41
National Association for Family Day Care, 17, 41
National Association for Nursery Education (NANE), 68

National Association for the Education of Young Children (NAEYC)
  accreditation guidelines, 16, 40–41, 252
  adult/child ratio standards, 211, 212
  Code of Ethical Conduct, 19, 20, 23–24, 402, 421–422, 451–455
  health standards, 191
  history, 68
  learning standards, 48
  membership in, 47
  position on DAP, 377
  position on standardized testing, 160
  salaries and, 34
  training guidelines, 15
National Association of Colored Women (NACW), 84
National Board for Professional Teaching Standards (NBPTS), 45
National Child Care Staffing Study, 34
National Committee on Science Education, 326
National Council for Accreditation of Teacher Education (NCATE), 45
National Council for Teachers of Mathematics, 48
National Council for the Social Studies, 48
National Council of Primary Education, 65
National Early Childhood Program Accreditation Commission, 41
National Education Goals, 49, 403
National Educational Goals Panel (NEGP), 47, 50
National Institute for Early Childhood Professional Development, 47
National Institute of Child Health and Human Development (NICHD), 33, 102
National Kindergarten Association (NKA), 65
National Reading Association, 48

National School Age Care
  Alliance, 41
National Science Education
  Standards, 325
    natural consequences, 286
    natural development
      (Vygotsky), 118
    natural elements zones, 248
    natural world, learning about, 187
    naturalist intelligence, 10, 119
    nature vs. nurture debate, 60,
      96–97, 104
NBPTS (National Board for
  Professional Teaching
  Standards), 45
NCATE (National Council for
  Accreditation of Teacher
  Education), 45
NCLB (No Child Left Behind),
  48–49
Neglect
  child development and, 104
  helping children suffering from,
    385–386
  reporting, 16–17, 386, 402–403
  warning signs of, 386
NEGP (National Educational Goals
  Panel), 47, 50
New Harmony, 62
The New York Longitudinal Study
  (Thomas & Chess), 99–100
New Zealand Teachers Council, 26
Newsletters, 414
NICHD (National Institute of Child
  Health and Human
  Development), 33, 102
19th century, early childhood
  education in, 61–62, 63
NKA (National Kindergarten
  Association), 65
No Child Left Behind (NCLB),
  48–49
Nonverbal messages, 263, 265, 316
Norm-referenced tests, 159
Normalcy, 378
Nursery for the Children of Poor
  Women, 84
Nursery school blocks, 238
Nursery school movement, 74
Nursery schools, 31–32, 46,
  66–69, 85
Nursing, attitudes toward, 399

Nurture vs. nature debate, 60,
  96–97, 104
Nutrition. See also Food
  guidelines for, 214
  programs for, 86
  study of, 91
  teaching children about,
    203–204

Obesity in children, 204
Object permanence, 94, 116
Objective description, 138–140
Objectives, 334
Observation
  about, 133, 135
  benefits, 134, 135
  commercial systems, 154–155
  information gained from, 134
  interpreting, 137–140, 143–144
  process, 135–136, 137
  recording, 135
  techniques
    anecdotal records, 141–143,
      144, 148, 149, 150, 409
    checklists, 147–148, 150
    electronic, 148–150
    event samples, 146–147, 150
    interviews, 148, 150
    narrative, 137, 138–140,
      144–145
    photographic, 149, 150
    rating scales, 147–148, 150
    running records, 140–141, 150
    selecting, 150
    structured, 137, 145–148
    time samples, 145–146, 150
    video/audio recording,
      149–150
Observer role, 182–183
Occupations (Fröebel), 64
Office of Child Development, 86
Office of Economic
  Opportunity, 87
Online resources. See Internet
  resources
Onlooker stage of play, 171
Open-Air Nursery School and
  Training Centre, 66
Open-design classrooms,
  225–226
Open-ended questions, 322, 322
Open environments, 251

Optimal match between
  understanding and skill, 93
Orbus Pictus (Comenius), 59
Orientations, family, 206,
  412–413
Orthopedic impairments, children
  with, 378–379
Ounce Scale, 156
Outdoor activities, 186–187,
  193–194, 235, 249
Outdoor learning environments
  for infants/toddlers, 249
  playground design, 225, 227–229,
    235–236, 247–248, 466, 476
  safety, 228, 248, 457
Overextensions, 112–113
Overgeneralizations, 113
Overlappingness, 279
Overprotecting children, 374
Overscheduled children, play
  and, 186
Owen, Robert, 57, 61–62, 63, 84

Packaged curriculum, 295
Painting, 309. See also Art
  curriculum
Parallel play (Parten), 172
Parent cooperatives, 31–32
Parenting, attitudes about, 256–258
Parents. See also Families
  education programs for, 39
  furniture for, 234
  roles of, 393–396
  teenage, 39, 396
Parten, M. B., 171, 172
Participant role, 185–186
Patrick, G. T. W., 169
Peabody Developmental Motor
  Scales, 157
Peabody, Elizabeth, 65
Peabody Individual Achievement
  Test, 159
Peabody Picture Vocabulary Test
  (PPVT-III), 158
Pedagogistas, 79
Pedagogy, defined, 295
PEEK kit, 295
Peers
  influences on children, 261–262
  support from educator's, 376
Perceptual-motor coordination,
  177–178, 302–303

Performance-based assessment, 132, 150. *See also* Observation
Personal information, confidentiality of, 23, 161–162, 388–389, 400–402
Personal items, safety and, 201
Personality assessment, 10
Personality Pathways, 10
Pestalozzi, Johann, 61, 63
Phonological awareness, 318
Phonology, 112
Photographic observation, 149, 150
Physical contact, children's need for, 98
Physical development
  about, 92
  brain, 103–105
  coordination, 177–178, 302–303
  milestones, 107
  motor skills, 95, 108
  muscle development, 302–303, 305
  physiology, 95
  play and, 177–178, 179–180, 303
  prenatal, 96–97, 103
  requirements for, 101
  resources for, 300, 306
  sensory development, 301–302
  theories of, 106, 108–109
Physical force, appropriate use of, 198
Physical knowledge (constructivist theory), 113
Physical punishment. *See* Corporal punishment
Piaget, Jean
  cognitive change model, 115, 116
  influence on High/Scope model, 68
  views on child development, 71, 86–87, 113–117
  views on moral development, 123
  views on play, 170, 171, 172, 173
Piazza, 79
Placement decisions, making, 133
"Plan-do-review" process, 69
Planned curriculum, 296
Planned Variation/Follow Through research, 71
Planned Variation study, 68
Planning activities. *See* Activity plans

Plato, 56–57, 63
Play
  about, 167–170
  attitudes toward, 180–181, 399
  benefits, 176–180
  curriculum and, 180
  diversity and, 174–176, 186, 188
  gender differences, 175, 176, 188
  historical views on, 57
  overscheduled children and, 186
  planning for, 339
  role in learning, 88
  skill training for, 174
  social-cognitive play scale, 183
  special needs, children with, 377
  stages of, 170–174
  supporting, 180–186
  theories of, 169
  types
    associative, 172
    constructive, 172, 173, 179
    cooperative, 171, 172
    dramatic. *See* Dramatic play
    outdoor, 186–187, 193–194, 235, 249
    parallel, 172
    practice (Piaget), 172, 173
    sociodramatic, 173–175, 177–179, 184, 186
    spontaneous, 339
    violent, 186, 187–188
Play and Early Childhood Development (Johnson et al.), 182, 183
Playgrounds
  aesthetics of, 235
  safety of, 193, 196, 457
  structures, 235
  supervising, 194
Poetry, 320
Poisoning, 192, 193–194, 197
Poor children. *See* Poverty
Portage Guide to Early Education, 158
Portfolios
  children's, 143, 145, 151–155, 162, 409
  educator's, 15, 20–21
Postconventional morality, 123, 124
Poverty
  behavior problems and, 288
  child care and, 31, 38

early childhood education and, 66
families and, 396
programs for children in, 35–38, 68, 83, 86, 87
segregation and, 368
PPVT-III (Peabody Picture Vocabulary Test), 158
Practice play (Piaget), 172, 173
Practice theory of play, 169
Practitioners. *See* Teachers
Pragmatics, 112
Praise, 267–269
Pratt, Caroline, 67, 72, 73–74, 224
Preconventional morality, 123, 124
Prejudice. *See* Bias
Preoperational stage of development (Piaget), 114, 116, 172
Preschool Content Standards for Social Studies, 328
Preschool programs, 31–32, 46, 66–69, 85
Preschoolers
  activities, 209, 243–244, 282, 283, 340, 341
  behavior problems, managing, 278, 286
  curriculum for, 336, 337, 338
  development, 105, 107, 110–111, 121–122, 125, 127
  environmental considerations, 226, 469–476
  interest areas, 237, 244, 245
  play and, 172, 181
  program floor plan, example, 231
  rest time, 215
  safety, 192–193
  schedules, 209
  self-concept, 262
  self-control, 261
  starting school, 206, 207–208
  teaching techniques, 341
  toys for, 237, 238
  transitions, 281
Pretend areas. *See* Dramatic play
Pretend play. *See* Dramatic play
Pretend writing, 319
Primary children. *See* School-age children
Primary schools, 66
Principals, 19. *See also* Teachers

Print, concepts of, 318
Print-making, 309
Privacy
    of information, 23, 161–162,
        388–389, 400–402
    learning environments, 227, 228,
        248, 249, 251–252
Private schools, 30
Problem behaviors. *See* Behavior
    problems
Problem-solving skills, learning, 340
Profession, defined, 14
Professional organizations,
    428–429, 430
Professionalism, educator, 14, 47–48
Programs, early childhood
    affordability, 32–34
    child development and, 101–102
    developmental stage and,
        208–209
    evaluation, tools for, 133
    evidence-based, 49–50
    expectations of, 191–192
    full-day, 31, 210–211
    funding, 30, 32, 84–85
    government involvement in child
        care, 84–88
    historical view, 51
    incorporating play, 211
    for infants/toddlers/preschoolers
        about, 30–31
        center-based, 31–34
        developmentally
            appropriate, 37
        home-based, 34–35
        low-income children, 35–38
        parent education, 39
        regulation of, 39–41
        special needs, 38–39
        teacher education, 41
    for kindergarteners/school-age
        children, 41–44
    need for, 46
    part-day, 31–32, 211
    purposes of, 30
    quality, 32–33
    scheduling, 210–212, 215–216
    school-age, 43–44
    for sick children, 31
    special needs, children with,
        38–39, 43
    statistics, 31
    trends, 51–52, 421

trilemma, 32–34
    types, 31
Progress reports, 162
Progressive education, 62,
    69–74
Project Approach, 71, 338. *See also*
    Integrated curriculum
Prosocial behavior, 120
Protector role, 184–185
Protestant Reformation, early
    childhood education in,
    58–59, 63
Providers. *See* Teachers
Provocation, 80
Proximodistal pattern, 95
Psychosocial development, 105
Psychosocial theory, 126–128
Punishment, defined, 259. *See also*
    Corporal punishment
Puzzles, 240, 241

QCA (Quality, Compensation, and
    Affordability), 32–34
Quakers, 83
Quality, Compensation, and
    Affordability (QCA), 32–34
Quality of child care, 32–33
Questions, use of, 322, 322
Quiet activities, 227
Quiet, need for, 248, 249
Quintilian, 57

Race
    child development and, 99–100
    education and, 38, 87–88
    families and, 397, 399–400
    history of early childhood
        education and, 84
    progressive education and, 70
    segregation and, 368
Racetracks, 228
Rating scales, 147–148, 150
Ratios, staff/child, 211, 212
Readiness, 49–51, 108, 116–117,
    158–159, 260
Reading, 43, 314–315, 317–320, 321
Recapitulation theory of
    play, 169
Receptive language problems, 380
Recording observations, 135
Recordkeeping, 4
Recreation theory of play, 169
Red-shirting, 50

Redirection, 279
Reflection, educator, 12–13
Reflective statements, 266–267, 272
Reformation, early childhood
    education in, 58–59, 63
Reggio Emilia approach, 78–81, 83,
    224, 242, 310
Reinforcement techniques, 287
Relationships with children. *See
    also* Communication
    barriers to, 269–271
    building, 264
    characteristics of, 255–256
    child development and,
        101–102, 271
Relaxation theory of play, 169
Reliability, test, 159
Religion
    family diversity, 397, 399–400
    history of early childhood
        education and, 58, 59, 60
    influence on curriculum,
        335, 355
    influence on education, 59
    Waldorf education and, 76
Relocating groups of
    children, 216
Renaissance, early childhood
    education in, 58–59
Renewal stage of career, 426–427
Report cards, 162
The Republic (Plato), 56
Resource teachers, 19. *See also*
    Teachers
Resources
    curriculum, 300, 315, 321, 329
    development interaction
        approach, 73
    disaster planning, 196
    High/Scope model, 69
    international associations, 26
    Montessori method, 78
    personality assessment, 10
    physical development,
        300, 306
    Reggio Emilia approach, 80–81
    safety, 191
    Waldorf education, 76
Respect
    differing expectations, 399
    teaching, 274–275
    treating children with, 269
Responsive statements, 266–267, 272

Rest time, 209, 215, 399
Rethinking the Brain (Shore), 104
Rhymes, 320
Risk, concerns about, 408–409
Ritalin, 383
Rogers, Fred, 419, 432
Romantic movement, 61
Rome, early childhood education in, 57, 63
Rousseau, Jean Jacques, 57, 60–61, 63
Routines, 208, 210–216, 213, 339
Ruggles Street Nursery School and Training Center, 67
Rules, classroom, 277–278
Running records, 140–141, 150

Safety. *See also* Health
  about, 191, 192
  abuse, 198, 199
  animals and, 459
  art supplies and, 242
  attitudes toward, 399
  checklist, 456–458
  concerns about, 408–409
  creative movement and, 313
  developmental differences, 192–193
  ensuring, 195–196
  expectations, 191–192
  fire, 194, 196, 197
  first aid/CPR training, 192, 196
  furniture, 234, 456, 457, 458
  indoor, 194, 226
  infants, 192, 240, 249, 458. *See also* Safety
  kindergarteners, 192–193
  materials, 192, 196, 233, 242
  outdoor, 193, 196, 226, 228, 248, 457
  personal items and, 201
  physical development and, 303
  preschoolers, 192–193
  resources, Internet, 191
  school-age children, 192–193
  special needs, children with, 193
  supervision and, 195–196
  teaching children about, 196–198, 199
  toddlers, 192, 240, 249, 458
  toys, 195, 196, 240
  vehicle, 195, 197

  water, 198
  woodworking, 243, 244
Salaries, educator, 14, 32–34
Sand, play with, 242
Sanitizing classroom materials, 201
SAT test, 159
Scaffolds, language, 112, 118
Schedules
  adapting for children with special needs, 376
  for age groups, 209
  example, 210
  physical setting, affect on, 209–210
  programs, early childhood, 210–212, 215–216
Schemata, development and, 114
School-age children
  activities, 209, 243–244, 282, 283, 340, 341
  behavior problems, managing, 278, 286
  curriculum for, 336–338
  development, 105, 107, 111, 122, 125, 127
  environmental considerations, 226, 469–476
  interest areas, 237, 244, 245
  play and, 172, 181
  program floor plan, example, 232
  rest time, 215
  safety, 192–193
  schedules, 209
  self-concept, 262
  self-control, 261
  starting school, 206
  television use, 250
  toys for, 237
  transitions, 218, 281
School-age program leaders, 18. *See also* Teachers
"School of the mother's knee," 59
Schurz, Margarethe Meyer, 65
Science areas, 247
Science curriculum, 325–327, 328, 329
Scissors, 192, 197
Screening instruments, 156–157, 369–371
Scribble writing, 319
Sculpting, 309

Seclusion of classroom areas, 227, 228, 248, 249, 251–252
Second Step curriculum, 295
Secrets vs. surprises, 199
Security, need for, 98
Segregation, 368
Seguin (French physician), 76–77
Self-actualization, need for, 98
Self-care, educator, 424
Self-concepts, 260–263
Self-contained classrooms, 225–226
Self-control, learning, 260, 261
Self-direction, building, 268
Self-discipline, learning, 260
Self-esteem, building, 199, 262–263, 268
Self-knowledge, educator, 12–14, 423–424
Semantics, 112
Sensitive periods, child development and, 102–103
Sensorimotor development, 114, 116
Sensorimotor stage of development (Piaget), 172, 173
Sensory development curriculum, 301–302
Sensory materials, 302
Sensory play, 241–242, 472
Separation process, 5, 205–206
Setting, affect on schedule, 209–210
Sex roles, attitudes toward, 188, 399
Sexuality, attitudes toward, 399
Shame and doubt stage, autonomy vs. (Erikson), 127, 172
Sharp implements, 192, 197
Shaw, Pauline Agassiz, 84
Sick children, programs for, 31
Sight, supporting development of, 301
Signs, classroom, 318
Simple materials, 251
Singing, 311
Skill, matching to understanding, 93
Skinner, B. F., 287
Slavery, 84
Sleeping, 209, 215, 399
Smell, supporting development of, 301
Smilansky, Sara, 171, 173
Snack times. *See* Food
Social class, play and, 175

Social-cognitive play scale, 183
Social development
    about, 93
    communication disorders
        and, 380
    milestones, 120, 121–122
    play and, 178–179, 180
    relationships and, 101, 124,
        134, 256
    teaching, 275
    theories of, 122–123, 124
Social-dramatic zones, 248
Social knowledge (constructivist
    theory), 114
Social studies areas, 247
Social studies curriculum,
    327–329
Society for the Relief and
    Employment of the Poor, 83
Sociocultural theory, 117–118
Sociodramatic play (Smilansky),
    173–175, 177–179, 184, 186
Socioeconomic level, play
    and, 186
Socioemotional development, 105
Sociology, study of, 91
Solitary play (Parten), 172
Spanking. See Corporal
    punishment
Spatial intelligence, 10, 119
Special education, 87–88, 368
Special needs, children with
    acceptance of, 373
    behavioral objectives, 346
    challenging behavior and, 288
    collaboration in teaching, 377
    environments, learning, 225,
        249, 376
    families of, 388–389, 415–416
    history of educating, 368
    identifying, 156–158, 369–371, 378
    IEPs, 377
    inclusion, 43, 369, 371–375, 389
    legal issues, 368–369
    materials adapted for, 376–377
    play and, 377
    programs for, 38–39, 43, 87–88,
        375–376
    risk factors for, 38–39
    safety, 193
    specific conditions
        abuse. See Child abuse

attention deficit/hyperactivity
    disorder (ADHD), 288,
    382–383
autism, 384–385
cognitive delays, 381–382
communication disorders,
    380–381
emotional/behavioral
    disorders, 383–384
gifted/talented, 387
health conditions, chronic,
    386–387
hearing impairments, 156–157,
    379–380
learning disabilities, 157, 382
mental retardation, 381–382
neglect. See Neglect
orthopedic impairments,
    378–379
visual impairments,
    156–157, 379
strategies for working with
    generally, 378
teaching skills for, 368, 372, 373
technology and, 246
terminology for, 367–368
toileting practices, 214
Specialist teachers, 19. See also
    Teachers
Specimen records, 140–141, 150
Speech, learning, 380
Spencer, Herbert, 169
Spontaneous play, 339
Staff-child ratio, 211, 212
Staff, furniture for, 234
Staff turnover, 33–34
Stage manager role, 181–182
Standardized testing, 159–160
Standards
    content, 48, 298, 325–326,
        328, 337
    educator, 15
Standards for Professional
    Preparation (NAEYC), 45
Stanford-Binet Intelligence
    Scale, 158
Starting school, easing, 205–208
Steiner, Rudolf, 75, 82, 224
Stereotypes
    defined, 11
    gender, 188, 399
Stolz, Dr. Lois Meek, 85

Storage
    art supplies, 242
    design of, 229, 233, 234, 236
    discovery center, 247
    dramatic play, 239
    food, 201–202
    materials, 242
    toys, 238, 241
    writing center, 245
Stress
    child development and, 102,
        103, 104
    families and, 396, 401–402
    starting school and, 206–207
Structured observation techniques,
    137, 145–148
Studio art, 309
Subject area curriculum, 299, 338
Subject area knowledge, 299, 300
Subject-matter-centered art, 309
Subjective interpretation, 138–140
Substance abuse, 30, 396
Suffocation, 194
Summary reports, 155
Summary statements, 153
Sun exposure, dangers of, 194
"Super sand," 241
Supervision, safety and, 195–196
Supplies, 233, 242–243, 245
Surfaces, safe outdoor, 228
Surplus energy theory of play, 169
Surprises vs. secrets, 199
Survival stage of career, 426
Symbolic play (Piaget), 172, 173
Synapse development, 104
Syntax, 112

Tabula rasa, view of mind as, 60
Talented children, 387
Talking skills, learning group, 340
Talking with children. See
    Communication
Taste, supporting development
    of, 301
Tax credits, 86
Teacher aids, 18. See also Teachers
Teacher-child activities, 339–340
Teacher Effectiveness Training
    (Gordon), 266
Teachers
    attitudes, 256, 307
    backgrounds, 6–7, 12–13

Teachers, *(continued)*
  behavior, 14, 16
  career planning, 425–427
  challenges for, 29, 431
  changing, 216–217
  characteristics, 3–4, 7–10, 12–14,
    91, 262, 423–424
  colleagues and, 424
  diversity and, 11–12
  knowledge needed by, 15, 298,
    299, 300
  legal issues, 16–17, 23, 42, 195,
    368–369, 402–403
  licensure/certification, 15, 41,
    44–45
  male, 34
  philosophies of, 420
  portfolios, 15, 20–21
  professionalism, 14, 47–48
  race of, 38, 87–88
  responsibilities, 4–6, 15–17,
    17–19, 396, 419–420,
    427–431
  salaries, 14, 32–34
  self-care, 424
  skill development, 295
  standards, 15
  training, 15, 17–19, 20, 41, 47,
    91, 202
  types of, 17–19
  values/ethics, 10–11, 19–24
  view of education as calling, 419
Teaching assistants, 18. *See also*
    Teachers
Teaching techniques, age-
    appropriate, 338–341
"Teaching to the test," 160
Teamwork, educator, 6
Technology
  special needs, and children
    with, 376
  as teaching tool, 350
Technology areas, 245–246
Teenage parents, 39, 396
Teeth brushing, 201, 202
Television
  affect on children, 250
  child development and, 105
  violence, 187, 188, 261, 288, 289
Temperament
  child's, 100–101
  educator, 8–9

Teratogens, child development
    and, 103
Testing. *See* Assessment
Thematic planning, 338. *See also*
    Integrated curriculum
Themes, 351
Theory, defined, 91
Thomas, Alexander, 8–9
Thought and Language
    (Vygotsky), 118
"Three bears" principle, 353
"Three R's," 83
Time-outs, 286
Time samples, 145–146, 150
Toddlers
  active listening with, 266
  activities, 209, 243, 249, 282, 340
  age of, 105
  art work and, 308
  child care for, 31
  cognitive development, 110
  communication about, 216
  communication with, 197, 269
  curriculum for, 336–338
  diapering/toileting practices. *See*
    Diapering practices
  dramatic play, 240
  emotional development,
    125, 127
  environmental considerations,
    226, 249, 461–468
  equipment, 249
  furniture, 234, 249
  health, 199, 460. *See also* Health
  interest areas, 237
  learning techniques, 338
  physical development, 107
  play and, 172, 181
  program floor plan, example, 230
  rest time, 215
  safety, 192, 240, 249, 458. *See also*
    Safety
  schedules, 209
  self-concept, 262
  self-control, 261
  social development, 121
  starting school, 206, 207–208
  stopping actions, 272
  teaching healthy behaviors, 202
  teaching techniques, 341
  television use, 250
  toys for, 237, 238

Toileting practices
  about, 212–214
  attitudes toward, 399
  checklists, 463
  environmental considerations, 226
  facilities for, 225
  health considerations, 201
Touch
  children's need for physical, 98
  supporting development of, 301
Toy and games areas, 471–472
Toys
  about, 240–241
  for age groups, 237, 238
  blocks, 72, 227, 237–239, 467,
    470–471
  building, 240
  fit-together, 240
  games, 241, 303, 304, 471–472
  manipulative, 241
  puzzles, 240, 241
  safety, 195, 196, 240
  storage, 238, 241
Training
  CPR/first aid, 192, 196
  educator, 15, 17–19, 20, 41, 47, 91
  health, 202
  play skills, 174
Transition zones, 247–248
Transitional objects, 208
Transitions, 208, 215–218, 281–282,
Trauma, child development
    and, 104
Trilemma of child care, 32–34
Trip safety, 195, 197
Trust, building, 271
Trust vs. mistrust stage (Erikson),
    127, 172
Turnover, staff, 33–34
Tutor role, 186

Umbrella curriculum, 295
Understanding, matching to skill, 93
Unemployment, child care
    programs and, 30
Unit blocks, 72, 237–238
Unit planning, 338. *See also*
    Integrated curriculum
United Nations Convention on the
    Rights of the Child, 52
United States
  educational system of, 45–46

history of early childhood education, 81, 83–86
Units, 351
Unoccupied behavior stage of play, 171
U.S. Office of Education, 49

Vaccinations, 200
Validity, test, 159
Values
    educator, 10–11, 19–24
    families', 212–214, 257–258, 395
    influence on curriculum, 334–335
    learning, 120
    respect for differing, 257–258
Vehicle safety, 195, 197
Video/audio recording, 149–150
Vineland Adaptive Behavior Scales, 158
Violence
    behavior problems and, 288
    children coping with, 289–290
    domestic, 30
    families and, 396
    in media, 187, 188, 261, 288, 289
    modeling behavior without, 246
    play and, 186, 187–188
Vision, supporting development of, 301
Visits, classroom/home, 205–206
Visual boundaries between play areas, 229

Visual impairments, children with, 156–157, 379
Volunteers, program, 410–413
Vygotsky, Lev Semenovich, 117–118, 170, 340

Waiting
    children's tolerance for, 281
    intensive, 135
Waldorf education method, 75, 76, 81, 82
Walking trips, 195
"War on Poverty," 87
Water
    drinking, 225, 226
    play with, 242
    safety, 198
Weather conditions, learning environments and, 227
Web resources. *See* Internet resources
Webs, 357–358
Weekly plans, 343
Weikart, David, 68
Welcoming families, 403–404
"Wendy Corners." *See* Dramatic play
White, Edna Noble, 67
Whole child concept
    defined, 5
    development, 92–93, 177
    play and, 179
    progressive education, 70, 71
    Waldorf education, 75

Willard, Frances, 84
Windows of opportunity for learning, 103, 104
With-it-ness, 279
Woodworking, 243–244, 473–474
Woodworking for Young Children (Garner et al.), 244
Work, difference from play, 168–169
Work samples, assessment based on, 150, 153, 409
Work Sampling System, 155
Workjobs, 241, 340
Writing, 314–315, 317–319, 321
Writing areas, 245, 474–475

You-messages, 272
Young Geographers (Mitchell), 72

Zone of proximal development (ZPD), 118, 170, 340
Zones, classroom
    about, 227–228
    active play, 248
    manipulative-creative, 248
    natural elements, 248
    outdoor. *See* Outdoor learning environments
    social-dramatic, 248
    transition, 247–248
ZPD (zone of proximal development), 118, 170, 340